A FRAMEWORK FOR MARKETING MANAGEMENT
Third Edition

Philip Kotler
Northwestern University

Kevin Lane Keller
Dartmouth College

PEARSON

Prentice
Hall

Upper Saddle River, New Jersey 07458

Library of Congress Cataloging-in-Publication Data

Kotler, Philip.
   A framework for marketing management / Philip Kotler.—3rd ed.
     p. cm.
   Includes bibliographical references and index.
   ISBN 0-13-145258-4
    1. Marketing—Management. I. Title.
HF5415.13.K636 2006

Senior Acquisitions Editor: Katie Stevens
VP/Editorial Director: Jeff Shelstad
Product Development Manager: Ashley Santora
Project Manager: Melissa Pellerano
Editorial Assistant: Christine Ietto
Media Project Manager: Peter Snell
Marketing Manager: Ashaki Charles
Marketing Assistant: Joanna Sabella
Associate Director of Production Editorial: Judy Leale
Production Manager: Renata Butera
Production Editor: Theresa Festa
Permissions Supervisor: Charles Morris
Production Manager: Arnold Vila
Manufacturing Buyer: Diane Pierano
Manager, Multimedia Production-Print: Christy Mahon
Designer: Steve Frim
Interior Design: Janet Slowik / Blair Brown
Cover Design: Steve Frim
Composition/Full-Service Project Management: Laserwords Private Limited / Preparé
Printer/Binder: VonHoffman/Lehigh
Typeface: 10/12 Janson Text

Credits and acknowledgments borrowed from other sources and reproduced, with permission, in this textbook appear on appropriate page within text.

Pearson Education LTD.
Pearson Education Singapore, Pte. Ltd
Pearson Education, Canada, Ltd
Pearson Education–Japan
Pearson Education Australia PTY, Limited

Pearson Education North Asia Ltd
Pearson Educación de Mexico, S.A. de C.V.
Pearson Education Malaysia, Pte. Ltd
Pearson Education Upper Saddle River, New Jersey

10 9 8 7 6 5 4 3 2 1
0-13-145258-4

Brief Contents

Preface   xv

Part I   UNDERSTANDING MARKETING MANAGEMENT   1

1.   Defining Marketing for the Twenty-First Century   1
2.   Developing and Implementing Marketing Strategies and Plans   21
3.   Understanding Markets, Market Demand, and the Marketing Environment   40

Part II   CONNECTING WITH CUSTOMERS   63

4.   Creating Customer Value, Satisfaction, and Loyalty   63
5.   Analyzing Consumer Markets   83
6.   Analyzing Business Markets   101
7.   Identifying Market Segments and Targets   116

Part III   BUILDING STRONG BRANDS   135

8.   Creating Brand Equity   135
9.   Creating Positioning and Dealing with Competition   154

Part IV   SHAPING THE MARKET OFFERINGS   177

10.   Setting Product Strategy and Marketing Through the Life Cycle   177
11.   Designing and Managing Services   200
12.   Designing Pricing Strategies and Programs   217

Part V   DELIVERING VALUE   239

13.   Designing and Managing Value Networks and Channels   239
14.   Managing Retailing, Wholesaling, and Logistics   259

Part VI   COMMUNICATING VALUE   278

15.   Designing and Managing Integrated Marketing Communications   278
16.   Managing Mass Communications   294
17.   Managing Personal Communications   313

Part VII   CREATING SUCCESSFUL LONG-TERM GROWTH   331

18.   Managing Marketing in the Global Economy   331

Glossary   347

Index   353

Contents

Preface   xv

Part I   UNDERSTANDING MARKETING MANAGEMENT   1

1.   Defining Marketing for the Twenty-First Century   1

The Importance of Marketing   2

The Scope of Marketing   2

What Is Marketing?   3

Exchange and Transactions   3

What Is Marketed?   4

Marketers and Markets   5

Company Orientations Toward the Marketplace   6

The Production Concept   6

The Product Concept   7

The Selling Concept   7

The Marketing Concept   7

The Holistic Marketing Concept   8

Fundamental Marketing Concepts, Trends, and Tasks   12

Core Concepts   12

Marketing Management Tasks   15

Executive Summary   **17**

Notes   **18**

2.   Developing and Implementing Marketing Strategies and Plans   21

Marketing and Customer Value   22

The Value Delivery Process   22

The Value Chain   23

Core Competencies   24

A Holistic Marketing Orientation and Customer Value   25

Corporate and Division Strategic Planning   26

Defining the Corporate Mission   26

Establishing Strategic Business Units (SBUs)   27

Assessing Growth Opportunities   28

Organization and Organizational Culture   29

Business Unit Strategic Planning   29

Business Mission   30

SWOT Analysis   30

Goal Formulation   31

Strategy Formulation   31

Program Formulation and Implementation   32

Feedback and Control   33

The Nature and Contents of a Marketing Plan   33

Measuring Marketing Performance   34

Using Marketing Metrics   34

Measuring Marketing Plan Performance   35

Using Profitability Analysis   36

Executive Summary   37

Notes   38

3. **Understanding Markets, Market Demand, and the Marketing Environment**   **40**

Supporting Marketing Decisions With Information, Intelligence, and Research   41

Internal Records   41

Marketing Intelligence System   42

Marketing Research System   42

Forecasting and Demand Measurement   48

Which Market to Measure?   48

Demand Measurement   49

Company Demand and Sales Forecast   50

Estimating Current Demand   50

Estimating Future Demand   51

Macroenvironmental Trends and Forces   52

Demographic Environment   53

Economic Environment   55

Social-Cultural Environment   56

Natural Environment   58

Technological Environment   58

Political-Legal Environment   59

Executive Summary   60

Notes   61

Part II   CONNECTING WITH CUSTOMERS   63

4.   Creating Customer Value, Satisfaction, and Loyalty   63

Defining Customer Value and Satisfaction   64

Customer Perceived Value   64

Total Customer Satisfaction   66

Measuring Satisfaction   66

Product and Service Quality   68

Maximizing Customer Lifetime Value   68

Customer Profitability and Competitive Advantage   69

Measuring Customer Lifetime Value   70

Customer Equity   71

Cultivating Customer Relationships   72

Attracting, Retaining, and Growing Customers   72

Building Loyalty   75

Reducing Customer Defection   75

Forming Strong Customer Bonds   76

Customer Databases and Database Marketing   77

Executive Summary   79

Notes   80

5.   Analyzing Consumer Markets   83

What Influences Consumer Behavior?   84

Cultural Factors   84

Social Factors   85

Personal Factors   87

Key Psychological Processes   88

The Buying Decision Process: The Five-Stage Model   91

Problem Recognition   92

Information Search   92

Evaluation of Alternatives   93

Purchase Decisions   94

Postpurchase Behavior   95

Executive Summary   97

Notes   98

6.   Analyzing Business Markets   101

What Is Organizational Buying?   102

The Business Market Versus the Consumer Market   102

Institutional and Organizational Markets   102

Buying Situations   104

Systems Buying and Selling   105

Participants In the Business Buying Process   106
  The Buying Center   106
  Buying Center Influences   106
  Buying Center Targeting   108
Stages In the Business Buying Process   109
  Problem Recognition   109
  General Need Description and Product
    Specification   109
  Supplier Search   110
  Proposal Solicitation   110
  Supplier Selection   111
  Order-Routine Specification   111
  Performance Review   112
  Business Relationships: Risks and Opportunism   112
Executive Summary   113
Notes   114

7.   **Identifying Market Segments and Targets   116**
Levels of Market Segmentation   117
  Segment Marketing   117
  Niche Marketing   117
  Local Marketing   118
  Customerization   118
  Patterns of Market Segmentation   119
Segmenting Consumer and Business Markets   120
  Bases for Segmenting Consumer Markets   120
  Bases for Segmenting Business Markets   125
Market Targeting   127
  Effective Segmentation Criteria   127
  Evaluating and Selecting Market Segments   128
  Additional Considerations   131
Executive Summary   132
Notes   132

Part III   **BUILDING STRONG BRANDS   135**
8.   **Creating Brand Equity   135**
What Is Brand Equity?   136
  The Role of Brands   136
  The Scope of Branding   136
  Defining Brand Equity   137
  Brand Equity as a Bridge   138

Building Brand Equity   138
    Choosing Brand Elements   139
    Designing Holistic Marketing Activities   140
    Leveraging Secondary Associations   142
Measuring Brand Equity   143
    Brand Audits   143
    Brand Tracking   143
    Brand Valuation   144
Managing Brand Equity   144
    Brand Reinforcement   144
    Brand Revitalization   144
    Brand Crisis   145
Developing A Brand Strategy   146
    The Branding Decision: To Brand or Not to Brand?   146
    Brand Extensions   148
    Brand Portfolios   149
Executive Summary   150
Notes   151

9.   **Creating Positioning and Dealing with Competition   154**
Developing and Communicating a Positioning Strategy   155
    Competitive Frame of Reference   156
    Points-of-Parity and Points-of-Difference   156
    Establishing Category Membership   157
    Choosing POPs and PODs   157
    Creating POPs and PODs   158
Differentiation Strategies   159
    Product Differentiation   159
    Services Differentiation   160
    Personnel Differentiation   161
    Channel Differentiation   161
    Image Differentiation   161
Competitive Forces and Competitors   161
    Identifying Competitors   162
    Industry Concept of Competition   163
    Market Concept of Competition   164
Analyzing Competitors   165
    Strategies   166
    Objectives   166
    Strengths and Weaknesses   166
    Selecting Competitors   167

Competitive Strategies   167
    Market-Leader Strategies   167
    Other Competitive Strategies   170
    Market-Follower Strategies   172
    Market-Nicher Strategies   172
    Balancing Customer and Competitor
      Orientations   172
Executive Summary   173
Notes   174

Part IV   **SHAPING THE MARKET OFFERINGS   177**
  10. **Setting Product Strategy and Marketing Through the Life Cycle   177**
Product Characteristics and Classifications   178
    Product Levels   178
    Product Classifications   179
Product Relationships   180
    Product-Line Analysis   180
    Product-Line Length   181
    Line Modernization, Featuring, and Pruning   181
Packaging, Labeling, Warranties, and Guarantees   182
    Packaging   182
    Labeling   183
    Warranties and Guarantees   183
Managing New Products   183
    Why New Products Fail—and Succeed   184
    New Product Development   185
The Consumer Adoption Process   190
    Stages in the Adoption Process   191
    Factors Influencing the Adoption Process   191
Marketing Through the Product Life Cycle   192
    Product Life Cycles   192
    Marketing Strategies: Introduction Stage and the Pioneer Advantage   193
    Marketing Strategies: Growth Stage   193
    Marketing Strategies: Maturity Stage   194
    Marketing Strategies: Decline Stage   194
    Critique of the Product Life-Cycle Concept   196
Executive Summary   196
Notes   197

11.   Designing and Managing Services   200

The Nature of Services   201
     Categories of Service Mix   201
     Distinctive Characteristics of Services   202
Marketing Strategies for Service Firms   204
     A Shifting Customer Relationship   204
     Holistic Marketing for Services   205
     Differentiating Services   206
     Developing Brand Strategies for Services   207
Managing Service Quality   208
     Customer Expectations   208
     Best Practices of Service-Quality Management   209
Managing Product Support Services   212
     Identifying and Satisfying Customer Needs   212
     Post-Sale Service Strategy   213
Executive Summary   213
Notes   214

12.   Developing Pricing Strategies and Programs   217

Understanding Pricing   218
     How Companies Price   218
     Consumer Psychology and Pricing   218
Setting the Price   219
     Step 1: Selecting the Pricing Objective   220
     Step 2: Determining Demand   220
     Step 3: Estimating Costs   222
     Step 4: Analyzing Competitors' Costs, Prices, and Offers   223
     Step 5: Selecting a Pricing Method   224
     Step 6: Selecting the Final Price   229
Adapting the Price   230
     Geographical Pricing   230
     Price Discounts and Allowances   230
     Promotional Pricing   231
     Differentiated Pricing   232
     Product-Mix Pricing   232
Initiating and Responding to Price Changes   233
     Initiating Price Cuts   233
     Initiating Price Increases   233
     Reactions to Price Changes   234
     Responding to Competitors' Price Changes   234

Executive Summary   236
Notes   236

Part V   DELIVERING VALUE   239

13.   **Designing and Managing Value Networks and Channels   239**
Marketing Channels and Value Networks   240
The Importance of Channels   240
Value Networks   241
The Role of Marketing Channels   241
Channel Functions and Flows   242
Channel Levels   244
Service Sector Channels   245
Channel-Design Decisions   245
Analyzing Customers' Desired Service Output Levels   245
Establishing Objectives and Constraints   245
Identifying Major Channel Alternatives   246
Evaluating the Major Alternatives   247
Channel-Management Decisions   248
Selecting Channel Members   248
Training Channel Members   248
Motivating Channel Members   249
Evaluating Channel Members   249
Modifying Channel Arrangements   249
Channel Dynamics   251
Vertical Marketing Systems   251
Horizontal Marketing Systems   252
Multichannel Marketing Systems   252
Conflict, Cooperation, and Competition   252
Legal and Ethical Issues in Channel Relations   254
E-Commerce Marketing Practices   254
Pure-Click Companies   255
Brick-and-Click Companies   255
Executive Summary   256
Notes   256

14.   **Managing Retailing, Wholesaling, and Logistics   259**
Retailing   260
Types of Retailers   260
Retailer Marketing Decisions   262
Trends in Retailing   265

Private Labels   266
  House Brands   266
  The Private Label Threat   267
Wholesaling   267
  The Growth and Types of Wholesaling   268
  Wholesaler Marketing Decisions   269
  Trends in Wholesaling   270
Market Logistics   270
  Integrated Logistics Systems   270
  Market-Logistics Objectives   272
  Market-Logistics Decisions   273
  Market Logistics Lessons   275
Executive Summary   275
Notes   276

Part VI   COMMUNICATING VALUE   278
  15.   Designing and Managing Integrated Marketing
           Communications   278
The Role of Marketing Communications   279
  Marketing Communications and Brand
    Equity   279
  Communications Process Models   280
Developing Effective Communications   282
  Identify the Target Audience   283
  Determine the Communications Objectives   283
  Design the Communications   283
  Select the Communications Channels   285
  Establish the Total Marketing Communications
    Budget   287
Deciding on the Marketing Communications Mix   288
  Characteristics of the Marketing Communications
    Mix   288
  Factors in Setting the Marketing Communications
    Mix   289
  Measuring Communication Results   290
Managing the Integrated Marketing Communications
Process   290
  Coordinating Media   290
  Implementing IMC   291
Executive Summary   291
Notes   292

16.   Managing Mass Communications   294

Developing and Managing an Advertising Program   295

Setting the Objectives   295

Deciding on the Advertising Budget   296

Developing the Advertising Campaign   296

Deciding on Media and Measuring Effectiveness   297

Sales Promotion   302

Purpose of Sales Promotion   302

Major Decisions   303

Events and Experiences   306

Events Objectives   306

Major Decisions   307

Public Relations   308

Marketing Public Relations   308

Major Decisions in Marketing PR   308

Executive Summary   309

Notes   310

17.   Managing Personal Communications   313

Direct Marketing   314

The Benefits of Direct Marketing   314

Direct Mail   314

Catalog Marketing   315

Telemarketing   316

Other Media for Direct-Response Marketing   316

Interactive Marketing   317

The Benefits of Interactive Marketing   317

Designing an Attractive Web Site   317

Placing Ads and Promotion Online   318

E-Marketing Guidelines   319

Designing the Sales Force   319

Sales Force Objectives and Strategy   320

Sales Force Structure   321

Sales Force Size   321

Sales Force Compensation   322

Managing the Sales Force   323

Recruiting and Selecting Sales Representatives   323

Training and Supervising Sales Representatives   324

Sales Rep Productivity   324

Motivating Sales Representatives   325

Evaluating Sales Representatives   326

Principles of Personal Selling   326
    Negotiation   326
    Relationship Marketing   327
Executive Summary   327
Notes   328

Part VII   **CREATING SUCCESSFUL LONG-TERM GROWTH   331**
18.   **Managing Marketing in the Global Economy   331**
Managing Global Marketing   332
    Deciding Whether to Go Abroad   332
    Deciding Which Markets to Enter   333
    Deciding How to Enter the Market   334
    Deciding on the Marketing Program   335
Internal Marketing   337
    Organizing the Marketing Department   337
    Relations with Other Departments   340
Managing the Marketing Process   340
    Evaluation and Control   341
    Efficiency Control   342
    Strategic Control   342
Executive Summary   344
Notes   344

Glossary   347

Index   353

Preface

A *Framework for Marketing Management* is a concise paperback adapted from Philip Kotler and Kevin Lane Keller's number-one text, *Marketing Management, Twelfth Edition.* Its streamlined approach will appeal to those professors who want an authoritative account of current marketing management practices and theory plus a text that is short enough to allow the incorporation of outside cases, simulations, and projects. Like previous editions, *A Framework for Marketing Management, Third Edition* is dedicated to helping companies, groups, and individuals adapt their marketing strategies and management to the marketplace of the twenty-first century.

FEATURES OF THE THIRD EDITION

New Themes: Holistic Marketing

One major new theme in this edition is holistic marketing. *Holistic marketing* can be seen as the development, design, and implementation of marketing programs, processes, and activities that recognize the breadth and interdependencies involved in today's marketing environment. Holistic marketing recognizes that "everything matters" with marketing and that a broad, integrated perspective is often necessary. Holistic marketing has four key dimensions:

- *Internal marketing.* Ensuring everyone in the organization embraces appropriate marketing principles, especially senior management.
- *Integrated marketing.* Ensuring that multiple means of creating, delivering, and communicating value are employed and combined in an optimal manner.
- *Relationship marketing.* Having rich, multi-faceted relationships with customers, channel members, and other marketing partners.
- *Socially responsible marketing.* Understanding the ethical, environmental, legal, and social effects of marketing.

These four dimensions are woven throughout the book and at times are spelled out explicitly.

Two additional themes of this text are *marketing personalization* and *marketing accountability.* The former reflects all the attempts to make marketing more individually relevant; the latter reflects the need to understand and justify the return on marketing investments within organizations.

New Organization

For this edition of *Framework,* we move away from a four-part organization and introduce a seven-part organization. The new modular structure will allow for greater flexibility in the classroom.

- Part I Understanding Marketing Management
- Part II Connecting with Customers
- Part III Building Strong Brands
- Part IV Shaping the Market Offerings
- Part V Delivering Value
- Part VI Communicating Value
- Part VII Creating Successful Long-Term Growth

THE TEACHING AND LEARNING PACKAGE
Marketing Management Cases

Through Prentice Hall Custom Business instructors can create Custom Coursepacks or CustomCaseBooks for each course. Resources include top-tier cases from Darden, Harvard, Ivey, NACRA, and Thunderbird, plus full access to a database of articles. For details on how to order these value-priced packages, contact your local rep or visit the Prentice Hall Custom Business Web site at **www.prenhall.com/custombusiness**. To aid in your case selection, we have provided the following list of cases from our custom business web site:

9-583-151	National Chemical Corp.: Tiger-Tread	Richard N. Cardozo	General Marketing	Harvard Business School Publishing
9-396-264	Virtual Vineyards	Jeffrey F. Rayport, Alvin J. Silk, Thomas A. Gerace, Lisa R. Klein	Marketing Strategy	Harvard Business School Publishing
9-593-064	Colgate-Palmolive Co.: The Precision Toothbrush	John A. Quelch, Nathalie Laidler	Marketing Strategy	Harvard Business School Publishing
9-504-009	XM Satellite Radio (A)	David B. Godes, Elie Ofek	Marketing Strategy	Harvard Business School Publishing
9-501-021	Freeport Studio	Rajiv Lal, James B. Weber	Market Research	Harvard Business School Publishing
9-501-002	Omnitel Pronto Italia	Rajiv Lal, Carin-Isabel Knoop, Suma Raju	Market Research	Harvard Business School Publishing
9-593-082	Bayerische Motoren Werke AG (BMW)	Robert J. Dolan	Market Research	Harvard Business School Publishing
9-703-516	Ice-Fili	Michael G. Rukstad, Sasha Mattu, Asya Petinova	Market Research	Harvard Business School Publishing
9-599-113	The Coop: Market Research	Ruth Bolton, Youngme Moon	Market Research	Harvard Business School Publishing
9-500-024	The Brita Products Co	John Deighton	Customer Retention	Harvard Business School Publishing
9-501-050	Customer Value Measurement at Nortel Networks—Optical Networks Division	Das Narayandas	Customer Retention	Harvard Business School Publishing
9-582-026	CIBA-GEIGY Agricultural Division	Benson P. Shapiro, Anne T. Pigneri, Roy H. Schoeman	Consumer Marketing	Harvard Business School Publishing
9-595-035	Nestle Refrigerated Foods: Contadina Pasta & Pizza (A)	V. Kasturi Rangan, Marie Bell	Consumer Marketing	Harvard Business School Publishing
9-500-052	Webvan: Groceries on the Internet	John Deighton, Kayla Bakshi	Consumer Marketing	Harvard Business School Publishing
9A99A009	Augat Electronics, Inc.	Adrian Ryans	Business-to-Business Marketing	Ivey
9-500-041	VerticalNet (www.verticalnet.com)	Das Narayandas	Business-to-Business Marketing	Harvard Business School Publishing
9-598-056	L'Oreal of Paris: Bringing "Class to Mass" with Plenitude	Robert J. Dolan	Market Segmentation	Harvard Business School Publishing

9-594-001	American Airlines' Value Pricing (A)	Alvin J. Silk, Steven C. Michael	Market Segmentation	Harvard Business School Publishing
9-596-036	Land Rover North America, Inc.	Susan Fournier	Brands	Harvard Business School Publishing
9-591-133	Barco Projection Systems (A): Worldwide Niche Marketing	Rowland T. Moriarty Jr., Krista McQuade	Product Lines	Harvard Business School Publishing
9-594-074	Planet Reebok (A)	John A. Quelch, Jamie Harper	Advertising	Harvard Business School Publishing
9-500-024	The Brita Products Co.	John Deighton	Marketing Strategy	Harvard Business School Publishing
9-582-103	Sealed Air Corp.	Robert J. Dolan	Market Positioning	Harvard Business School Publishing
9-594-023	Mary Kay Cosmetics: Asian Market Entry	John A. Quelch, Nathalie Laidler	Market Positioning	Harvard Business School Publishing
9-596-076	Dewar's (A): Brand Repositioning in the 1990s	Alvin J. Silk, Lisa R. Klein	Brands	Harvard Business School Publishing
UVA-M-0246	Ogilvy & Mather: (A Light Beer from Pabst)	Gary Shaw, Lawrence J. Ring	Market Positioning	Darden
9-593-064	Colgate-Palmolive Co.: The Precision Toothbrush	John A. Quelch, Nathalie Laidler	Product Positioning	Harvard Business School Publishing
9-500-070	Priceline.com: Name Your Own Price	Robert J. Dolan	Marketing Strategy	Harvard Business School Publishing
SAW007	TiVo: Changing the Face of Television	Mohanbir Sawhney	Product Positioning	Kellogg
9-592-035	Calyx and Corolla	Walter J. Salmon, David Wylie	Services Management	Harvard Business School Publishing
9-388-064	ServiceMaster Industries, Inc.	James L. Heskett	Services Management	Harvard Business School Publishing
9-597-063	Computron, Inc. – 1996	John A. Quelch	Pricing Strategy	Harvard Business School Publishing
M284A	Value Pricing at Procter & Gamble	Rajiv Lal, Mitchell Kristofferson	Pricing Strategy	Harvard Business School Publishing
9-598-109	FreeMarkets Online	V. Kasturi Rangan	Pricing Strategy	Harvard Business School Publishing
9-575-060	Southwest Airlines (A)	Christopher H. Lovelock	Pricing Strategy	Harvard Business School Publishing
9-595-001	RCI Master Distributor: The Evolution of Supplier Relationships	V. Kasturi Rangan	Distribution Channels	Harvard Business School Publishing
9-500-015	Autobytel.com	Youngme Moon	Distribution Channels	Harvard Business School Publishing
9-800-305	Staples.com	Joanna Jacobson, Thomas Eisenmann, Gillian Morris	Distribution Channels	Harvard Business School Publishing
9-799-158	Matching Dell	Jan W. Rivkin, Michael E. Porter	Strategic Planning	Harvard Business School Publishing
9-593-094	MathSoft, Inc. (A)	V. Kasturi Rangan, Gordon Swartz	Strategic Planning	Harvard Business School Publishing
9-585-019	Suave (C)	Mark S. Albion	Marketing Communications	Harvard Business School Publishing
9-594-051	Northern Telecom (A): Greenwich Investment Proposal (Condensed)	Robert J. Dolan	Marketing Strategy	Harvard Business School Publishing
9-593-104	Northern Telecom (B): The Norstar Launch	Robert J. Dolan	Marketing Strategy	Harvard Business School Publishing
UVA-M-0340	Reagan-Bush '84 (A)	John Norton	Marketing Strategy	Darden
9-584-012	Milford Industries (A)	Benson P. Shapiro, Robert J. Dolan	Marketing Communications	Harvard Business School Publishing
9-584-013	Milford Industries (B)	Benson P. Shapiro, Robert J. Dolan	Marketing Communications	Harvard Business School Publishing
9-504-009	XM Satellite Radio (A)	David B. Godes, Elie Ofek	International Markets	Harvard Business School Publishing
9-598-150	Biopure Corp.	John T. Gourville	International Markets	Harvard Business School Publishing
9-595-026	Citibank: Launching the Credit Card in Asia-Pacific (A)	V. Kasturi Rangan	International Markets	Harvard Business School Publishing
9A99A016	Rougemont Fruit Nectar: Distributing in China	Tom Gleave, Paul Beamish	International Markets	Ivey

Instructor's Manual

This component contains chapter overviews and teaching objectives, plus suggested lecture outlines—providing structure for class discussions around key issues. A listing of key contemporary articles is included, along with synopses and ideas for class/course utilization of the materials. Harvard case analyses are also provided, integrating the current topic areas.

Test Item File

The Test Item File includes more than 70 questions per chapter, consisting of multiple-choice, true/false, essay, and mini-cases. Page references and suggested answers are provided for each question. Prentice-Hall's TestGen test-generating software is newly available for this edition and is easily customizable for individual needs.

PowerPoint Basic

This simple presentation consists of basic outlines and key points from each chapter. No animation or forms of rich media are integrated, which makes the total file size manageable and easier to share online or via email.

PowerPoint Media Rich

This presentation includes basic outlines and key points from each chapter, plus art from the text, images from outside the text, discussion questions, and Web links.

Marketing Management Video Gallery

Make your classroom "newsworthy." Using today's popular newsmagazine format, students are taken on location and behind closed doors. Each news story profiles a well-known company leading the way in its industry. Highlighting 18 companies, including American Express, the NFL, Eaton, and Wild Planet, the issue-focused footage includes interviews with top executives and objective reporting by real news anchors, industry research analysts, and marketing and advertising experts. A video guide, including synopses and discussion questions, is available. The video library is offered on both DVD and VHS, and instructors can choose to have it shrink-wrapped with this text.

Companion Web Site

The companion Web site, **www.prenhall.com/kotler**, offers students valuable resources, including two quizzes per chapter. The Concept Check Quiz is to be administered prior to reviewing the chapter, in order to assess students' initial understanding. The Concept Challenge Quiz is to be administered after studying the chapter, allowing students to determine the areas they need to review further. Also featured is the text glossary, as well as a link to Case Pilot. Case Pilot is a one-of-a-kind interactive tool that helps students develop the fundamentals of case study analysis. Three sample cases from the high-technology, service, and consumer-product sectors enable students to write problem statements, identify key marketing issues, perform SWOT analysis, and develop solutions.

Instructor's Resource Center (IRC)

The IRC is available online at **www.prenhall.com/kotler**, where instructors can access an array of teaching materials, consisting of the Instructor's Manual, Test Item File, TestGen, Video Guide, and Basic PowerPoint slides. These materials are also available on CD-ROM, where the Media Rich PowerPoint slides and an Image Library can be found as well.

The Marketing Plan Handbook, 2nd edition with Marketing Plan Pro

Marketing PlanPro

Marketing PlanPro is a highly rated commercial software program that guides students through the entire marketing plan process. The software is totally interactive and features ten sample marketing plans, step-by-step guides, and customizable charts. Customize your marketing plan to fit your marketing needs by following easy-to-use plan wizards. Follow the clearly outlined steps from strategy to implementation. Click to print, and your text, spreadsheet, and charts come together to create a powerful marketing plan. The new *The Marketing Plan Handbook*, by Marian Burk Wood, supplements the in-text marketing plan material with an in-depth guide to what student marketers really need to know. A structured learning process leads to a complete and actionable marketing plan. Also included are timely, real-world examples that illustrate key points, sample marketing plans, and Internet resources. The Handbook and Marketing PlanPro software are available as value-pack items. Contact your local Prentice Hall representative for more information.

We've partnered
for you.

Texts from Prentice Hall.
Simulations from Interpretive.
Value for your students.

NEW! When you adopt a Prentice Hall textbook packaged *with* an Interpretive simulation, each new textbook purchased will contain a **coupon (ISBN: 0131875787)** that can be used when purchasing a simulation online from Interpretive.

To ensure your students receive textbooks that contain discount coupons, make sure your bookstore orders the appropriate value-package ISBN. Your local Prentice Hall representative will be happy to assist.

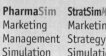

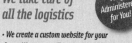

PharmaSim

Predominantly used in: Marketing Management, Brand Management, and Marketing Strategy,

Take the role of a Brand Manager in the over-the-counter cold medicine market.

This leading marketing management online simulation drives home the Four P's of Marketing: Pricing, Promotion, Product and Place (distribution), while introducing students to the concepts of brand equity and marketing planning for multiple product lines.

In PharmaSim, students take the role of a Brand Manager in the over-the-counter pharmaceutical industry and manage 'Allround,' the leading multi-symptom cold medicine. Over the course of up to 10 simulated periods, students may reformulate their brand, introduce a line extension, and launch a new product. PharmaSim is modeled from a brand management perspective, but the issues raised apply to marketers in any industry.

StratSim

Predominantly used in: Marketing strategy, marketing management and other advanced marketing courses.

Use a market-oriented strategy to navigate the fast-paced automobile industry.

This competitive marketing strategy simulation allows teams to target consumer segments and B2B opportunities based on market attractiveness and core competencies. Students have the opportunity to utilize advanced marketing research techniques such as conjoint analysis, perceptual mapping, and concept testing to enhance their understanding of the environment and consumers.

StratSim*Marketing* also highlights the importance of integrated decision-making by demonstrating the impact of marketing decisions on other functional areas of the business such as operations and finance.

ACKNOWLEDGMENTS

This edition of *A Framework for Marketing Management* bears the imprint of many people who have contributed to the previous edition of this text and to *Marketing Management, Twelfth Edition*. We are sincerely grateful to Marian Burk Wood for her development and editorial work. Many thanks also to the professional editorial and production teams at Prentice Hall. We gratefully acknowledge the many reviewers who helped shape this new edition.

John H. Antil, University of Delaware
Bill Archer, Northern Arizona University
Timothy W. Aurand, Northern Illinois University
Ruth Clottey, Barry University
Jeff Conant, Texas A&M University
Mike Dailey, University of Texas, Arlington
Brian Engelland, Mississippi State University
Brian Gibbs, Vanderbilt University
Thomas Gruca, University of Iowa
Mark Houston, University of Missouri, Columbia
Nicole Howatt, University of Central Florida
Gopal Iyer, Florida Atlantic University
Jack Kasulis, University of Oklahoma
Susan Keaveney, University of Colorado, Denver

Bob Kent, University of Delaware
Robert Kuchta, Lehigh University
Jack K. H. Lee, City University of New York Baruch College
Ning Li, University of Delaware
Steven Lysonski, Marquette University
Naomi Mandel, Arizona State University
Ajay K. Manrai, University of Delaware
Denny McCorkle, Southwest Missouri State University
James McCullough, Washington State University
Ron Michaels, University of Central Florida
George R. Milne, University of Massachusetts, Amherst
Marian Chapman Moore, Duke University
Steve Nowlis, Arizona State University

Louis Nzegwu, University of Wisconsin, Platteville
K. Padmanabhan, University of Michigan, Dearborn
Mary Anne Raymond, Clemson University
William Robinson, Purdue University
Carol A. Scott, University of California at Los Angeles

Stanley F. Slater, Colorado State University
Robert Spekman, University of Virginia
Edwin Stafford, Utah State University
Vernon Stauble, California State Polytechnic
Mike Swenson, Brigham Young University
Kimberly A. Taylor, Florida International University
Bronis J. Verhage, Georgia State University

Philip Kotler
S. C. Johnson & Son Distinguished Professor of International Marketing
Kellogg School of Management
Northwestern University
Evanston, Illinois

Kevin Lane Keller
E.B. Osborn Professor of Marketing
Tuck School of Business
Dartmouth College
Hanover, New Hampshire

CHAPTER 1

Defining Marketing for the Twenty-First Century

In this chapter, we will address the following questions:

1. Why is marketing important?
2. What is the scope of marketing?
3. What are some fundamental marketing concepts?
4. What are the tasks necessary for successful marketing management?

MARKETING MANAGEMENT AT APPLE COMPUTER

When Apple Computer launched its iPod digital music player, CEO Steve Jobs called it "the twenty-first-century Walkman," a reference to the Sony product that, starting in 1979, revolutionized the way consumers listen to music on the go. The stylish iPod has more than fulfilled that prophecy. Despite intense competition from Sony, Samsung, and other rivals, the iPod product line has captured more than 60 percent of the U.S. market for digital music players. Just as important, the now iconic iPod plays a strategic role as the cornerstone of Apple's ambitious marketing drive to bring its brand to a broader customer base and boost long-term profits.

Apple's marketers know that customers associate the brand with user-friendly functionality, innovative technology, and sleek design. Therefore, every Apple product—iPod players, Macintosh desktop and laptop computers, even the online iTunes Music Store and Tiger software—is consistent with this image and delivers the kind of experience that customers expect from the brand. The iPod's runaway success has brought new attention to the rest of Apple's offerings and, as more customers try other Apple products, is helping reverse the

Macintosh's steep decline in market share. However, market share is only one measure of marketing accomplishment, as the CEO well knows. Can Apple's marketing managers keep up the momentum in building relationships with customers and profits for shareholders?[1]

Good marketing is no accident, but a result of careful planning and execution, as the Apple Computer example shows. In virtually all industries, marketing practices are continually being refined and reformed to increase the chances of success. Yet marketing excellence is rare and difficult to achieve. Marketing is both an "art" and a "science"—there is constant tension between the formulated side and the creative side. It is easier to learn the formulated side, which will occupy most of our attention in this book, but we will also describe how real creativity and passion operate in many organizations. This book will help to improve your understanding of marketing and your ability to make the right marketing decisions. In this chapter, we lay the foundation for our study by reviewing a number of important marketing concepts, tools, frameworks, and issues.

THE IMPORTANCE OF MARKETING

Financial success often depends on marketing ability. Finance, operations, accounting, and other business functions will not really matter if there is not sufficient demand for goods and services so the company can make a profit. There must be a top line for there to be a bottom line. Many companies have now created a Chief Marketing Officer (CMO) position to put marketing on a more equal footing with other C-level executives such as the Chief Executive Officer (CEO) and Chief Financial Officer (CFO).

Marketing is tricky, however, and it has been the Achilles' heel of many formerly prosperous companies. Large, well-known businesses such as Sears, Levi's, General Motors, Kodak, and Xerox have confronted newly empowered customers and new competitors, and have had to rethink their business models. Even market leaders such as Microsoft, Wal-Mart, Intel, and Nike recognize that they cannot afford to relax. The companies at greatest risk are those that fail to carefully monitor their customers and competitors and to continuously improve their value offerings. They take a short-term, sales-driven view of their business and, ultimately, they fail to satisfy their stockholders, their employees, their suppliers, and their channel partners.

Skillful marketing is a never-ending pursuit and can take many forms. Jim Koch, founder of Boston Beer Company, started out carrying bottles of Samuel Adams from bar to bar to persuade bartenders to carry it. For 10 years, he sold his beer through direct selling and grassroots public relations. Today the company leads the U.S. craft beer market, and its marketing professionals continue the drive to delight its customers by offering more variety than any other craft brewer, including Chocolate Bock and Black Lager. "At Samuel Adams, we are constantly innovating and creating new ideas that will push the envelope and revolutionize beer drinkers' expectations for beer," the founder notes.[2]

THE SCOPE OF MARKETING

To prepare to be a marketer, you need to understand what marketing is, how it works, what is marketed, and who does the marketing.

What Is Marketing?

Marketing deals with identifying and meeting human and social needs. One of the shortest definitions of marketing is "meeting needs profitably." EBay recognized that people were unable to locate some of the items they desired most and created an online auction clearinghouse; IKEA noticed that people wanted good furniture at a substantially lower price and created knock-down furniture. Both of these companies demonstrated marketing savvy and turned a private or social need into a profitable business opportunity.

The American Marketing Association offers the following definition. Marketing is: *an organizational function and a set of processes for creating, communicating, and delivering value to customers and for managing customer relationships in ways that benefit the organization and its stake holders.*[3] We see **marketing management** as *the art and science of choosing target markets and getting, keeping, and growing customers through creating, delivering, and communicating superior customer value.*

exchange marketing

Marketing has often been described as "the art of selling products," but the most important part of marketing is not selling. In fact, Peter Drucker, a leading management theorist, says that "the aim of marketing is to make selling superfluous. The aim of marketing is to know and understand the customer so well that the product or service fits him and sells itself. Ideally, marketing should result in a customer who is ready to buy. All that should be needed then is to make the product or service available."[4] When Apple launched its iPod digital music player and when Toyota introduced its Lexus automobile, these companies were swamped with orders because they had designed the "right" product based on careful marketing homework.

Exchange and Transactions

Exchange, the core concept of marketing, is the process of obtaining a desired product from someone by offering something in return. For exchange potential to exist, five conditions must be satisfied:

1. There are at least two parties.
2. Each party has something that might be of value to the other party.
3. Each party is capable of communication and delivery.
4. Each party is free to accept or reject the exchange offer.
5. Each party believes it is appropriate or desirable to deal with the other party.

Exchange is a value-creating process because it normally leaves both parties better off. Two parties are engaged in exchange if they are negotiating—trying to arrive at mutually agreeable terms. When an agreement is reached, a transaction has taken place. A **transaction** is a trade of values between two or more parties, involving at least two things of value, agreed-upon conditions, a time of agreement, and a place of agreement. For example, Dell may sell customer X a television set; in return, customer X pays $400 to Dell. A legal system is in place to support and enforce compliance on the part of the transactors.

Note that a transaction differs from a transfer. In a **transfer**, party A gives something to party B but does not receive anything tangible in return. Gifts, subsidies, and charitable contributions are all transfers. Transfer behavior can also be understood through the concept of exchange. Typically, the transferer expects to receive something in exchange for his or her gift—for example, gratitude or seeing changed behavior in the recipient. Professional fund-raisers provide benefits to donors, such as thank-you notes, donor magazines, and invitations to events. Marketers have broadened the concept of marketing to include the study of transfer behavior as well as transaction behavior.

In the most generic sense, marketers seek to elicit a behavioral response from another party. A business wants a purchase, a political candidate wants a vote, a church wants an active member, and a social-action group wants the passionate adoption of some cause. Marketing consists of actions undertaken to elicit desired responses from a target audience.

To make successful exchanges, marketers analyze what each party expects from the transaction. Simple exchange situations can be mapped by showing the two actors and the wants and offerings flowing between them. Suppose John Deere, a worldwide leader in agricultural equipment, researches the benefits that a typical large-scale farm enterprise wants when it buys tractors, combines, planters, and sprayers. These benefits include high-quality equipment, a fair price, on-time delivery, good financing terms, and good parts and service. The items on this want list are not equally important and may vary from buyer to buyer. One of John Deere's tasks is to discover the relative importance of these different wants to the buyer.

John Deere also has a want list. It wants a good price for the equipment, on-time payment, and good word of mouth. If there is a sufficient match or overlap in the want lists, a basis for a transaction exists. John Deere's task is to formulate an offer that motivates the farm enterprise to buy John Deere equipment. The farm enterprise might in turn make a counteroffer. This process of negotiation leads to mutually acceptable terms or a decision not to transact.

What Is Marketed?

Marketing people are involved in marketing 10 types of entities: goods, services, experiences, events, persons, places, properties, organizations, information, and ideas.

- *Goods.* Physical goods constitute the bulk of most countries' production and marketing effort. For example, U.S. companies alone market billions of fresh, canned, bagged, and frozen food products and other tangible items. Thanks in part to the Internet, even individuals can effectively market goods.

- *Services.* As economies advance, a growing proportion of their activities is focused on the production of services. The U.S. economy today consists of a 70–30 servicesto-goods mix. Services include the work of airlines, hotels, car rental firms, barbers and beauticians, maintenance and repair people, as well as professionals working within or for companies, such as accountants and programmers. Many market offerings consist of a variable mix of goods and services, as when a restaurant offers both food and service.

- *Events.* Marketers promote time-based events, such as major trade shows, artistic performances, and company anniversaries. Global sporting events such as the Olympics or World Cup are promoted aggressively to both companies and fans.

- *Experiences.* By orchestrating several services and goods, a firm can create, stage, and market experiences. Walt Disney World's Magic Kingdom represents experiential marketing: Customers visit a fairy kingdom, a pirate ship, or a haunted house. There is also a market for customized experiences, such as spending a few days at a baseball camp playing with retired baseball greats.[5]

- *Persons.* Celebrity marketing is a major business. Artists, musicians, CEOs, physicians, high-profile lawyers and financiers, chefs, and other professionals draw help from celebrity marketers.[6]

- *Places.* Cities, states, regions, and whole nations compete to attract tourists, factories, company headquarters, and new residents.[7] Las Vegas, Nevada, spends millions of dollars annually marketing itself as a tourist destination and a business convention city. Its "What happens in Vegas, stays in Vegas" advertising campaign has helped the city attract 37 million visitors every year.[8] Place marketers include economic development specialists, real estate agents, commercial banks, local business associations, and advertising and public relations agencies.

- *Properties.* Properties are intangible rights of ownership of either real property (real estate) or financial property (stocks and bonds). Individuals and organizations buy and sell properties through the marketing efforts of real estate agents, investment companies, and banks.

- *Organizations.* Organizations actively work to build a strong, favorable, and unique image in the minds of their target publics. Tesco's "Every Little Bit Helps" marketing program has vaulted it to the top of the supermarket chains in the United Kingdom. Universities, museums, performing arts organizations, and nonprofits use marketing to boost their public images and to compete for audiences and funds.

- *Information.* Schools and universities essentially produce and distribute information at a price to parents, students, and communities. Encyclopedias and nonfiction books market information, as do magazines and newspapers. The production, packaging, and distribution of information is one of our society's major industries.[9] Even companies that sell physical products add value through the use of information. The CEO of Siemens Medical Systems, for instance, says the company's product "is not necessarily an X-ray or an MRI, but information. Our business is really health-care information, and our end product is really an electronic patient record: information on lab tests, pathology, and drugs as well as voice dictation."[10]

- *Ideas.* Every market offering includes a basic idea. For instance, social marketers are busy promoting such ideas as "Friends Don't Let Friends Drive Drunk"[11] and "A Mind Is a Terrible Thing to Waste."

Marketers and Markets

A **marketer** is someone who seeks a response (attention, a purchase, a vote, a donation) from another party, called the **prospect**. If two parties are seeking to sell something to each other, we call them both marketers.

Traditionally, a "market" was a physical place where buyers and sellers gathered to buy and sell goods. Economists describe a market as a collection of buyers and sellers who transact over a particular product or product class (e.g., the housing market or grain market). On the other hand, marketers often use the term *market* to cover various groupings of customers and view the sellers as constituting the industry. They talk about need markets (the diet-seeking market), product markets (the shoe market), demographic markets (the youth market), and geographic markets (the French market); or other types of markets, such as voter markets, labor markets, and donor markets.

As Figure 1.1 shows, sellers send goods, services, and communications (ads, direct mail) to the market; in return they receive money and information (attitudes, sales data). The inner loop shows an exchange of money for goods and services; the

FIGURE 1.1   A Simple Marketing System

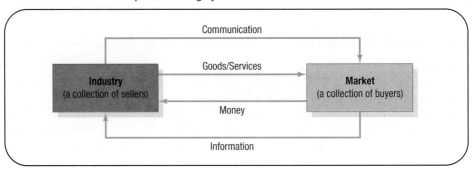

outer loop shows an exchange of information. In general, marketers may serve consumer markets, business markets, global markets, nonprofit markets, government markets, or some combination of these.

Today we can distinguish between a *marketplace* and *marketspace*. The marketplace is physical, as when you shop in a store; marketspace is digital, as when you shop on the Internet.[12] Mohan Sawhney has proposed the concept of a *metamarket* to describe a cluster of complementary products and services that are closely related in the minds of consumers but are spread across a diverse set of industries.

The automobile metamarket consists of automobile manufacturers, new car and used car dealers, financing companies, insurance companies, mechanics, spare parts dealers, service shops, auto magazines, classified auto ads in newspapers, and auto sites on the Internet. Car buyers can get involved in many parts of this metamarket. This has created an opportunity for metamediaries to assist buyers to move seamlessly through these groups, although they are disconnected in physical space. One example is Edmund's (**www.edmunds.com**), where buyers can find the features and prices of different vehicles and search for the lowest-price dealer, for financing, for car accessories, and for used cars at bargain prices. Metamediaries can also serve other metamarkets, such as the home ownership market and the wedding market.[13]

COMPANY ORIENTATIONS TOWARD THE MARKETPLACE

What philosophy should guide a company's marketing efforts? What relative weights should be given to the interests of the organization, the customers, and society? Very often these interests conflict. The competing concepts under which organizations have conducted marketing activities include the production concept, product concept, selling concept, marketing concept, and holistic marketing concept.

The Production Concept

The production concept is one of the oldest concepts in business. It holds that consumers will prefer products that are widely available and inexpensive. Managers of production-oriented businesses concentrate on achieving high production efficiency, low costs, and mass distribution. This orientation makes sense in developing countries such as China, where the largest PC manufacturer, Lenovo, takes advantage of the huge inexpensive labor pool to keep costs and prices low, thereby dominating the market. This orientation is also used when a company wants to expand the market.[14]

The Product Concept

The product concept holds that consumers will favor those products that offer the most quality, performance, or innovative features. Managers in these organizations focus on making superior products and improving them over time. However, these managers are sometimes caught up in a love affair with their products. They might commit the "better-mousetrap" fallacy, believing that a better mousetrap will lead people to beat a path to their door. A new or improved product will not necessarily be successful unless the product is priced, distributed, advertised, and sold properly.

The Selling Concept

The selling concept holds that consumers and businesses, if left alone, will ordinarily not buy enough of the organization's products. The organization must, therefore, undertake an aggressive selling and promotion effort. The selling concept is epitomized in the thinking of Sergio Zyman, Coca-Cola's former vice president of marketing: The purpose of marketing is to sell more stuff to more people more often for more money in order to make more profit.[15]

The selling concept is practiced most aggressively with unsought goods, goods that buyers normally do not think of buying, such as insurance, encyclopedias, and funeral plots. Most firms practice the selling concept when they have overcapacity. Their aim is to sell what they make rather than make what the market wants. However, marketing based on hard selling carries high risks. It assumes that customers who are coaxed into buying a product will like it; and that if they do not, they will not return it or bad-mouth it or complain to consumer organizations, or they might even buy it again.

The Marketing Concept

The marketing concept emerged in the mid-1950s.[16] Instead of a product-centered, "make-and-sell" philosophy, business shifted to a customer-centered, "sense-and-respond" philosophy. Here, the job is not to find the right customers for your products, but the right products for your customers. The marketing concept holds that the key to achieving organizational goals consists of the company being more effective than competitors in creating, delivering, and communicating superior customer value to its chosen target markets.

Theodore Levitt of Harvard drew a perceptive contrast between the selling and marketing concepts: Selling focuses on the needs of the seller; marketing on the needs of the buyer. Selling is preoccupied with the seller's need to convert his product into cash; marketing with the idea of satisfying the needs of the customer by means of the product and the whole cluster of things associated with creating, delivering and finally consuming it.[17]

Several scholars have found that companies who embrace the marketing concept achieve superior performance.[18] This was first demonstrated by companies practicing a *reactive market orientation*—understanding and meeting customers' expressed needs. Some critics say this means companies develop only low-level innovations. Narver and his colleagues argue that high-level innovation is possible if the focus is on customers' latent needs. He calls this a *proactive marketing orientation*.[19] Companies such as 3M,

Hewlett-Packard, and Motorola have made a practice of researching or imagining latent needs through a "probe-and-learn" process. Companies that practice both a reactive and proactive marketing orientation are implementing a *total market orientation* and are likely to be the most successful.

The Holistic Marketing Concept

A whole set of forces that appeared in the last decade call for new marketing and business practices. Companies have new capabilities that can transform the way they have been doing marketing; they also need a more complete, cohesive approach that goes beyond traditional applications of the marketing concept.

The **holistic marketing** concept is based on the development, design, and implementation of marketing programs, processes, and activities that recognize their breadth and interdependencies. Holistic marketing recognizes that "everything matters" with marketing—and that a broad, integrated perspective is often necessary. Four components of holistic marketing are relationship marketing, integrated marketing, internal marketing, and social responsibility marketing (see Figure 1.2). Holistic marketing is thus an approach to marketing that attempts to recognize and reconcile the scope and complexities of marketing activities.

Relationship Marketing   **Relationship marketing** has the aim of building mutually satisfying long-term relationships with key parties—customers, suppliers, distributors, and other marketing partners—in order to earn and retain their business.[20] Relationship marketing builds strong economic, technical, and social ties among the parties. This involves cultivating the right kind of relationships with the right constituent groups. For marketing, key constituents are customers, employees, marketing partners (channels, suppliers, distributors, dealers, agencies), and members of the financial community (shareholders, investors, analysts).

FIGURE 1.2   Holistic Marketing Dimensions

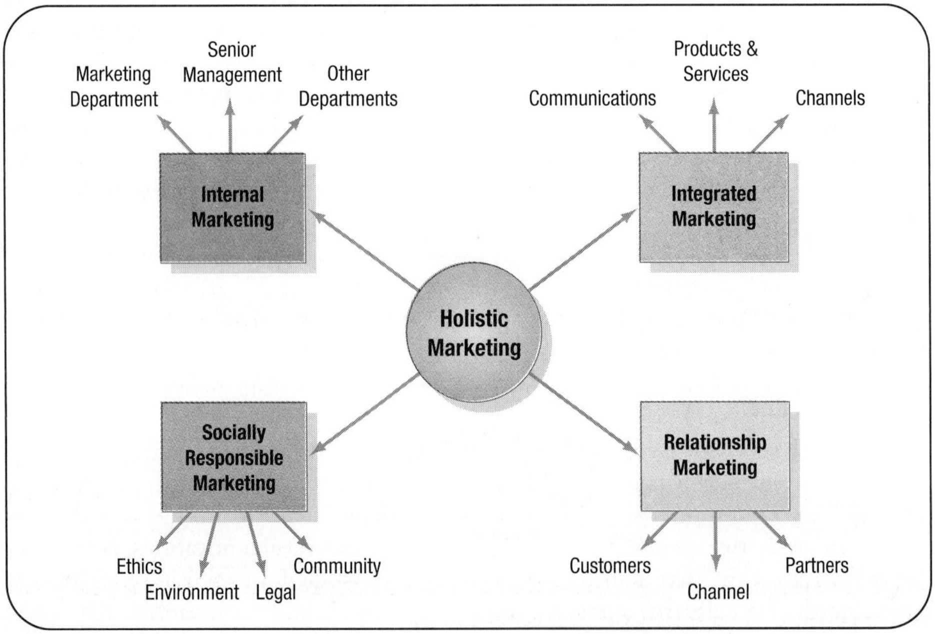

The ultimate outcome of relationship marketing is the building of a unique company asset called a marketing network. A **marketing network** consists of the company and its supporting stakeholders (customers, employees, suppliers, distributors, retailers, ad agencies, university scientists, and others) with whom it has built mutually profitable business relationships. Increasingly, competition is not between companies but between marketing networks, with the prize going to the company that has built the better network. The operating principle is simple: Build an effective network of relationships with key stakeholders, and profits will follow.[21]

The development of strong relationships requires an understanding of the capabilities and resources of different groups, as well as their needs, goals, and desires. A growing number of today's companies are now shaping separate offers, services, and messages to individual customers. These companies collect information on each customer's past transactions, demographics, psychographics, and media and distribution preferences. They hope to achieve profitable growth through capturing a larger share of each customer's expenditures by building high loyalty and customer lifetime value. Now that BMW, for example, allows buyers to design their own vehicles from 350 variations, 500 options, 90 exterior colors, and 170 trims, up to 30 percent of its U.S. customers and up to 80 percent of its European customers are doing so.[22] Such rich, multifaceted relationships with key constituents create the foundation for a mutually beneficial arrangement for both parties.

Integrated Marketing   With **integrated marketing**, the marketer's task is to devise marketing activities and assemble marketing programs that maximize the ability to create, communicate, and deliver value for consumers. Marketing activities come in all forms. One traditional depiction of marketing activities is in terms of the marketing mix, which has been defined as the set of marketing tools the firm uses to pursue its marketing objectives.[23] McCarthy classified these tools into four broad groups, which he called *the four Ps* of marketing: product, price, place, and promotion (see Figure 1.3).[24]

Marketing-mix decisions must be made for influencing the trade channels as well as the final consumers. Figure 1.4 shows the company preparing an offering mix of products, services, and prices, and utilizing a communications mix of advertising, sales promotion, events and experiences, public relations, direct marketing, and personal selling to reach the trade channels and the target customers. The firm can change its price, sales force size, and advertising expenditures in the short run. However, it can develop new products and modify its distribution channels only in the long run. Thus the firm typically makes fewer period-to-period marketing-mix changes in the short run than the number of marketing-mix decision variables might suggest.

The four Ps represent the sellers' view of the marketing tools available for influencing buyers. From a buyer's point of view, each marketing tool is designed to deliver a customer benefit. Robert Lauterborn suggested that the sellers' four Ps correspond to the customers' four Cs.[25]

Four Ps	Four Cs
Product	Customer solution
Price	Customer cost
Place	Convenience
Promotion	Communication

Winning companies will be those that can meet customer needs economically and conveniently and with effective communication.

FIGURE 1.3 The Four P Components of the Marketing Mix

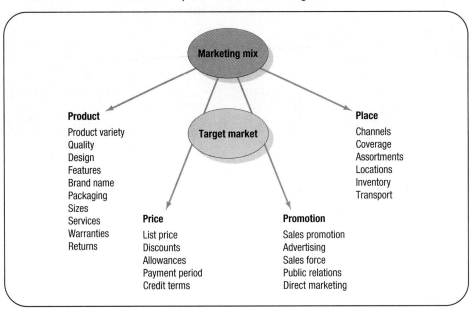

Two key themes of integrated marketing are that (1) many different marketing activities are employed to communicate and deliver value and (2) all marketing activities are coordinated to maximize their joint effects. In other words, the design and implementation of any one marketing activity is done with all other activities in mind. Businesses must integrate their systems for demand management, resource management, and network management.

FIGURE 1.4 Marketing-Mix Strategy

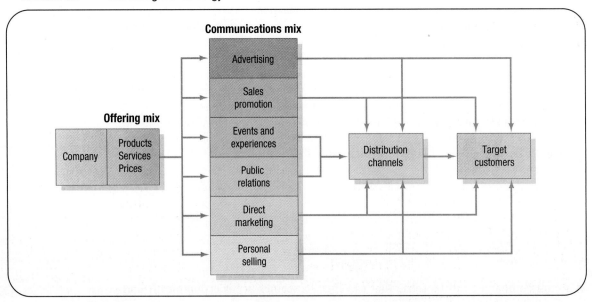

Internal Marketing   Holistic marketing incorporates *internal marketing*, ensuring that everyone in the organization embraces appropriate marketing principles, especially senior management. Internal marketing is the task of hiring, training, and motivating able employees who want to serve customers well. Smart marketers recognize that marketing activities within the company can be as important as, or even more so than, marketing activities directed outside the company. It makes no sense to promise excellent service before the company's staff is ready to provide it (see "Marketing Skills: Internal Marketing").

Internal marketing must take place on two levels. At one level, the various marketing functions—sales force, advertising, customer service, product management, marketing research—must work together and be coordinated from the customer's point of view. At another level, marketing must be embraced by the other departments, who must also "think customer." In fact, marketing thinking must be pervasive throughout the company. Xerox goes so far as to include in every job description an explanation of how that job affects the customer. Xerox factory managers know that visits to the factory can help sell a potential customer if the factory is clean and efficient. Xerox accountants know that customer attitudes are affected by Xerox's billing accuracy and promptness in returning calls.

MARKETING SKILLS: INTERNAL MARKETING

One of the most valuable skills marketers can have is the ability to select, educate, and rally people inside the organization so all employees enthusiastically help to build satisfying and profitable long-term relationships with customers. Internal marketing starts with the selection of managers and employees who have a positive attitude toward the company, its products, and its customers. The next step is to train, motivate, and empower the entire staff so they have the knowledge, tools, and authority to play their roles in delivering value to the customer base. After establishing standards for employee performance, the final step is to monitor employee actions and reward good performance—then continue the cycle of internal marketing through ongoing communication, motivation, and feedback.

Developing internal marketing skills takes planning, time, and perseverance. Not every communication or motivation attempt will successfully influence every employee, just as not every advertisement or sales call will successfully influence every customer. Nor is internal marketing going to be effective if it is treated as a slogan or passing fad. When internal marketing really works, however, it can help propel a company to the top of its industry.

For example, internal marketing is a key strength at Southwest Airlines, where top management pays close attention to recruitment and training, internal communication, and workforce motivation. The CEO and president constantly visit different Southwest facilities, thank employees for their efforts, send birthday cards to employees, and share customer comments with employees. Southwest's employees deliver superior service with a smile, and they are so dedicated that some have worked without pay to keep the airline's costs down during difficult periods. Clearly, Southwest's managers are good role models for learning to apply the critical skill of internal marketing.[26]

Institutional Advertising

Social Responsibility Marketing   Holistic marketing incorporates *social responsibility marketing* and understanding broader concerns and the ethical, environmental, legal, and social context of marketing activities and programs. The causes and effects of marketing clearly extend beyond the company and the consumer to society as a whole. Social responsibility also requires that marketers carefully consider the role that they are playing and could play in terms of social welfare.

Are companies that do an excellent job of satisfying consumer wants necessarily acting in the best long-run interests of consumers and society? Fast-food chains, for instance, have been criticized for offering tasty but unhealthy meals. Recognizing these criticisms, companies like McDonald's have added healthier items, such as salads, to their menus and have introduced environmental initiatives, replacing polystyrene foam sandwich clamshells with paper wraps and recycled materials. McDonald's has even ordered its meat suppliers to eliminate the use of antibiotics that are also given to humans, specifically when those drugs are used to make animals grow faster. "We saw lots of evidence that showed the declining rate of effectiveness of antibiotics in human medicine," says McDonald's senior director of social responsibility. "We started to look at what we could do."[27]

Situations like this one call for a new term that enlarges the marketing concept. We propose calling it the *societal marketing concept*, which holds that the organization's task is to determine the needs, wants, and interests of target markets and to deliver the desired satisfactions more effectively and efficiently than competitors in a way that preserves or enhances the well-being of both consumer and society. The societal marketing concept calls upon marketers to build social and ethical considerations into their marketing practices. They must balance and juggle the often conflicting criteria of company profits, consumer want satisfaction, and public interest.

Yet a number of companies, including Ben & Jerry's, have achieved notable sales and profit gains by adopting and practicing a form of the societal marketing concept called *cause-related marketing*. Pringle and Thompson define this as activity by which a company with an image, product, or service to market builds a relationship or partnership with a "cause," or a number of "causes," for mutual benefit."[28] Companies see cause-related marketing as an opportunity to enhance their corporate reputation, raise brand awareness, increase customer loyalty, build sales, and increase media coverage. They believe that customers will increasingly look for signs of good corporate citizenship that go beyond supplying rational and emotional benefits. Avon, for instance, is the largest corporate supporter of the drive to find a cure for breast cancer, having generated more than $350 million since its first program in 1992.

FUNDAMENTAL MARKETING CONCEPTS, TRENDS, AND TASKS

To understand the marketing function, we need to understand certain fundamental concepts and tasks, as well as current trends.

Core Concepts

A core set of concepts creates a foundation for marketing management and a holistic marketing orientation.

Needs, Wants, and Demands   The marketer must try to understand the target market's needs, wants, and demands. *Needs* are the basic human requirements. People need food, air, water, clothing, and shelter to survive. People also have strong needs for recreation, education, and entertainment. These needs become *wants* when they are directed to specific objects that might satisfy the need. An American needs food but may want a hamburger, French fries, and a soft drink. A person in Mauritius needs food but may want a mango, rice, lentils, and beans. Wants are shaped by one's society. *Demands* are wants for specific products backed by an ability to pay. Many people want a Mercedes; only a few are willing and able to buy one. Companies must measure not only how many people want their product but also how many would actually be willing and able to buy it.

These distinctions shed light on the frequent criticism that "marketers create needs" or "marketers get people to buy things they don't want." Marketers do not create needs: Needs preexist marketers. Marketers, along with other societal factors, influence wants. Marketers might promote the idea that a Mercedes would satisfy a person's need for social status. They do not, however, create the need for social status.

Understanding customer needs and wants is not always simple. Some customers have needs of which they are not fully conscious, or they cannot articulate these needs, or they use words that require some interpretation. Consider the customer who says he wants "an inexpensive car." A marketer may distinguish among five types of needs in this case:

1. Stated needs: The customer wants an inexpensive car.
2. Real needs: The customer wants a car with a low operating cost, not a low initial price.
3. Unstated needs: The customer expects good service from the dealer.
4. Delight needs: The customer would like the dealer to include an onboard navigation system.
5. Secret needs: The customer wants to be seen by friends as a savvy consumer.

Responding only to the stated need may shortchange the customer. As stated by Carpenter, "Simply giving customers what they want isn't enough any more—to gain an edge, companies must help customers learn what they want."[29] In the past, "responding to customer needs" meant studying customer needs and making a product that fit these needs on the average. Today, companies are instead responding to each customer's individual needs, the way Dell provides product platforms on which each buyer customizes the features desired in the computer. This is a change from a "make-and-sell" philosophy to a philosophy of "sense and respond."

Target Markets, Positioning, and Segmentation   A marketer can rarely satisfy everyone in a market. Not everyone likes the same cereal, hotel room, automobile, college, or movie. Therefore, marketers identify and profile distinct groups of buyers who might prefer or require varying product and service mixes by examining demographic, psychographic, and behavioral differences among buyers. The marketer then decides which segments present the greatest opportunity—which are its *target markets*. For each chosen target market, the firm develops a *market offering*. The offering is *positioned* in the minds of the target buyers as delivering some central benefit(s). For example, Volvo develops its cars for buyers who hold automobile safety as a major concern. Volvo, therefore, positions its car as the safest a customer can buy. Companies do best when they choose their target market(s) carefully and prepare tailored marketing programs.

Offerings and Brands Companies address needs by offering a value proposition, a set of intended benefits to satisfy their customers' needs. The intangible value proposition is made physical by an *offering*, which can be a combination of products, services, information, and experiences. A *brand* is an offering from a known source. The associations that customers have with a brand name such as McDonald's, including hamburgers, fun, children, fast food, convenience, and golden arches, make up the brand image. All companies strive to build brand strength—that is, a strong, favorable, and unique brand image.

Value and Satisfaction The offering will be successful if it delivers value and satisfaction to the target buyer. The buyer chooses between different offerings on the basis of which is perceived to deliver the most value. *Value* reflects the perceived tangible and intangible benefits and costs to customers. Value can be seen as primarily a combination of quality, service, and price, called the "customer value triad." Value increases with quality and service and decreases with price, although other factors can also play an important role.

Value is a central marketing concept. Marketing can be seen as the identification, creation, communication, delivery, and monitoring of customer value. *Satisfaction* reflects a person's comparative judgments resulting from a product's perceived performance or outcome in relation to his or her expectations. If the performance falls short of expectations, the customer is dissatisfied and disappointed. If the performance matches the expectations, the customer is satisfied. If the performance exceeds expectations, the customer is highly satisfied or delighted.

Marketing Channels To reach a target market, the marketer uses three kinds of marketing channels. *Communication channels* deliver and receive messages from target buyers, and include newspapers, magazines, radio, television, mail, telephone, billboards, posters, fliers, CDs, audiotapes, and the Internet. Beyond these, communications are conveyed by facial expressions and clothing, the look of retail stores, and many other media. Marketers are increasingly adding dialogue channels, including e-mail and toll-free numbers, to counterbalance the more normal monologue channels, such as ads.

The marketer uses *distribution channels* to display, sell, or deliver the physical product or service(s) to the buyer or user. These include distributors, wholesalers, retailers, and agents. The marketer also uses *service channels* to carry out transactions with potential buyers. Service channels that facilitate transactions include warehouses, transportation companies, banks, and insurance companies. Marketers clearly face a design problem in choosing the best mix of communication, distribution, and service channels for their offerings.

Supply Chain Whereas marketing channels connect the marketer to the target buyers, the supply chain describes a longer channel stretching from raw materials to components to final products that are carried to final buyers. The supply chain for women's purses starts with hides, and moves through tanning operations, cutting operations, manufacturing, and the marketing channels bringing products to customers. The supply chain represents a value delivery system. Each company captures only a certain percentage of the total value generated by the supply chain. When a company acquires competitors or moves upstream or downstream, its aim is to capture a higher percentage of supply chain value.

Competition Competition includes all the actual and potential rival offerings and substitutes that a buyer might consider. Suppose an automobile company is planning to buy steel for its cars. There are several possible levels of competitors facing steel suppliers. The car manufacturer can buy steel from integrated steel mills in the United States, such from U.S. Steel, or from mills abroad, such as Angang New Steel in China; or it can buy steel from a mini-mill, Nucor. Other alternatives are to buy aluminum for certain parts to lighten the car's weight from a company such as Alcoa, or to buy engineered plastics for bumpers instead of steel from GE Plastics. Clearly, U.S. Steel would be thinking too narrowly of competition if it thought only of other integrated steel companies. In fact, U.S. Steel is more likely to be hurt in the long run by substitute products than by its immediate steel company rivals. It must also consider whether to make substitute materials or stick only to those applications where steel offers superior performance.

Marketing Environment Competition represents only one force in the environment in which the marketer operates. The marketing environment consists of the task environment and the broad environment.

The *task environment* includes the immediate actors involved in producing, distributing, and promoting the offering, such as the company, suppliers, distributors, dealers, and the target customers. Included in the supplier group are material suppliers and service suppliers such as marketing research agencies, advertising agencies, banks and insurance companies, transportation companies, and telecommunications companies. Included with distributors and dealers are agents, brokers, manufacturer representatives, and others who facilitate finding and selling to customers.

The *broad environment* consists of six components: demographic environment, economic environment, physical environment, technological environment, political-legal environment, and social-cultural environment. These environments contain forces that can have a major impact on the actors in the task environment. Market actors must pay close attention to the trends and developments in these environments and make timely adjustments to their marketing strategies.

Marketing Planning The marketing planning process consists of analyzing marketing opportunities; selecting target markets; designing marketing strategies; developing marketing programs; and managing the marketing effort. Figure 1.5 presents a grand summary of the marketing process and the forces shaping an organization's marketing strategy.

Marketing Management Tasks

Marketing management is changing as marketers fundamentally rethink their philosophies, concepts, and tools (see Table 1.1). In today's highly competitive environment, the most successful organizations will be those that are able to change their marketing as their marketplaces and marketspaces shift.

In the context of these important shifts, marketing managers must accomplish the following tasks:

- *Develop marketing strategies and plans.* The first task is to identify the organization's potential long-run opportunities, given its market experience and core competencies. Chapter 2 discusses this process in detail.

- *Capture marketing insights.* Understand what is happening inside and outside the organization by monitoring the marketing environment and conducting marketing

FIGURE 1.5   Factors Influencing Company Marketing Strategy

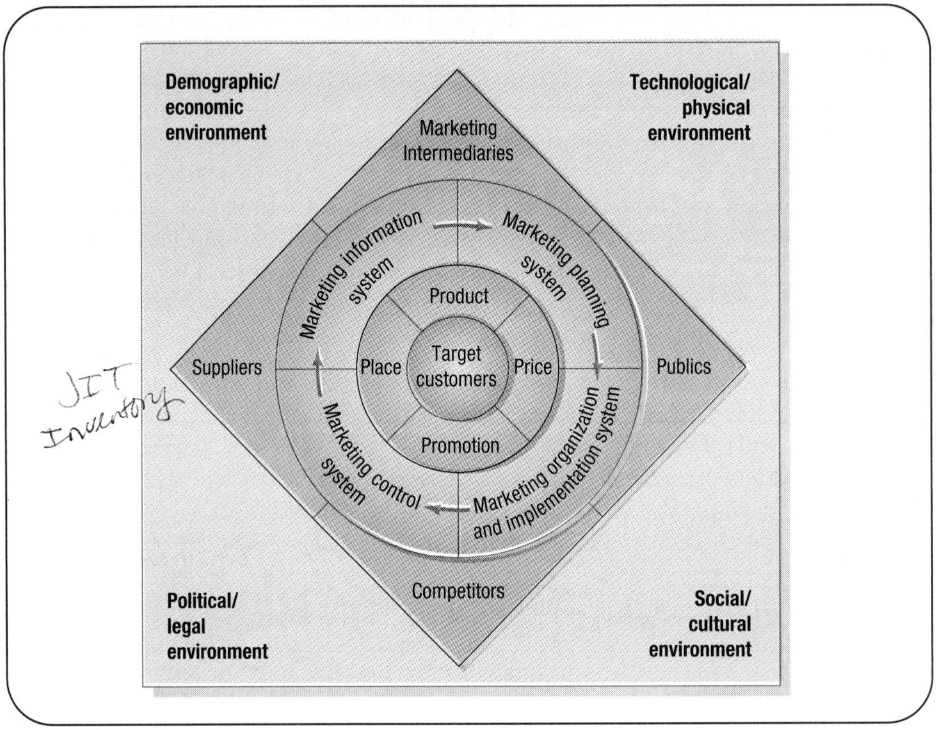

research to assess buyer needs and behavior, as well as actual and potential market size. Chapter 3 looks at markets, market demand, and the marketing environment; Chapters 5 and 6 explore the analysis of consumer and business markets.

■ *Connect with customers.* Determine how to best create value for the chosen target markets and develop strong, profitable, long-term relationships with consumers and business customers, as discussed in Chapter 4. Then identify major market segments, evaluate each, and target those that the organization can serve most effectively. Chapter 7 examines both segmentation and targeting.

■ *Build strong brands.* Understand the brand's strengths and weaknesses, what customers associate with the brand, and how to measure and manage brand equity—the subject of Chapter 8. Because brands never exist in a vacuum, marketers must not only deal with the competitive situation, they must both develop and communicate an appropriate positioning. Chapter 9 explains how to do this.

■ *Shape market offerings.* The product at the heart of the marketing program involves decisions about product quality, design, features, and packaging. See Chapter 10 for a discussion of product strategy. As outlined in Chapter 11, marketers may also design services as part of the marketing offering; in addition, pricing is a key element, as shown in Chapter 12.

■ *Delivering value.* Determine how to deliver the offering's value to the target market by identifying, recruiting, and linking with marketing facilitators such as retailers, wholesalers, and physical-distribution firms. Value networks and channels are examined in Chapter 13; retailing, wholesaling, and logistics are examined in Chapter 14.

TABLE 1.1   Shifts in Marketing Management

From	To
The marketing department is responsible for marketing	Every employee has an impact on the customer and sees customers as the source of the organization's prosperity
Organizing by product units	Organizing by customer segments
Making everything internally	Retaining core activities while outsourcing activities that others can do cheaply and better
Using many suppliers	Partnering with fewer suppliers to deliver value
Relying on old market positions	Moving ahead to uncover new marketing advantages
Emphasizing tangible assets	Recognizing the value of brands, the customer base, employees, distributor and supplier relations, and intellectual capital
Building brands through advertising	Building brands through performance and integrated communications
Attracting customers through stores and salespeople	Making products available online
Selling to everyone	Working to be the best company serving well-defined target markets
Focusing on profitable transactions	Focusing on customer lifetime value
Seeking to gain market share	Seeking to build customer share
Being local	Being both global and local
Focusing on the financial scorecard	Focusing on the marketing scorecard
Focusing on shareholders	Focusing on stakeholders

- *Communicating value.* Convey the value embodied by the offering to the target market through marketing communications activities that inform, persuade, and remind consumers about the company's brand(s). Chapter 15 discusses the design and management of integrated marketing communications; Chapter 16 explores mass communications such as advertising and sales promotion, while Chapter 17 looks at personal communications such as direct marketing and personal selling.

- *Creating long-term growth.* Take a long-term view of products, brands, and how profits should be increased. The company's marketing strategy must take into account changing global opportunities and challenges. Moreover, the company must put in place a marketing organization capable of implementing the marketing plan. See Chapter 18 for more detail.

EXECUTIVE SUMMARY

A company's long-term prosperity often depends on its marketing ability. Marketing deals with identifying and meeting human and social needs in ways that provide value for customers and the organization's stakeholders. Marketing management is the art and science of choosing target markets and getting, keeping, and growing customers through creating, delivering, and communicating superior customer value.

Every marketing exchange requires at least two parties—both with something valued by the other party, both capable of communication and delivery, both free to accept or reject the offer, and both finding it appropriate or desirable to deal with the other. An agreement to exchange constitutes a transaction, whereas a transfer occurs when one party does not receive anything tangible in return. Marketers are involved in marketing 10 types of entities: goods, services, events, experiences, persons, places, properties, organizations, information, and ideas. They operate in four different marketplaces: consumer, business, global, and nonprofit.

Organizations can choose to conduct their business under one of five competing concepts: the production concept, product concept, selling concept, marketing concept, and holistic marketing concept. The holistic marketing concept is based on the development, design, and implementation of marketing programs, processes, and activities that recognize their breadth and interdependencies. Holistic marketing recognizes that "everything matters" with marketing and that a broad, integrated perspective is often necessary. Four components of holistic marketing are relationship marketing, integrated marketing, internal marketing, and socially responsible marketing.

Marketing management has experienced a number of shifts in recent years as companies seek marketing excellence. Successful marketing managers must accomplish these tasks: develop marketing strategies and plans, connect with customers, build strong brands, shape the market offerings, deliver and communicate value, capture marketing insights and performance, and create successful long-term growth.

NOTES

1. Jim Dalrymple, "Apple's Uphill Climb," *MacWorld*, June 2005, pp. 16+; Nick Wingfield, "But Will Apple See a Boost?" *Wall Street Journal*, April 28, 2005, pp. B1+; Randall Stross, "How the iPod Ran Circles Around the Walkman," *New York Times*, March 13, 2005, sec. 3, p. 5.

2. "The Boston Beer Company," *Beverage Industry*, January 2005, p. 19; Sam Hill and Glenn Rifkin, *Radical Marketing* (New York: HarperBusiness, 1999); Gerry Khermouch, "Keeping the Froth on Sam Adams," *BusinessWeek*, September 1, 2003, pp. 54–56.

3. American Marketing Association, 2004.

4. Peter Drucker, *Management: Tasks, Responsibilities, Practices* (New York: Harper and Row, 1973), pp. 64–65.

5. Philip Kotler, "Dream Vacations: The Booming Market for Designed Experiences," *The Futurist* (October 1984): 7–13; B. Joseph Pine II and James Gilmore, *The Experience Economy* (Boston: Harvard Business School Press, 1999); Bernd Schmitt, *Experience Marketing* (New York: Free Press, 1999); Mark Hyman, "The Family That Fields Together," *Business Week*, February 9, 2004, p. 92.

6. Irving J. Rein, Philip Kotler, and Martin Stoller, *High Visibility* (Chicago: NTC Publishers, 1998); H. Lee Murphy, "New Salton Recipe: Celeb Chefs," *Crain's Chicago Business*, April 4, 2005, p. 4.

7. Philip Kotler, Irving J. Rein, and Donald Haider, *Marketing Places: Attracting Investment, Industry, and Tourism to Cities, States, and Nations* (New York: Free Press, 1993); and Philip Kotler, Christer Asplund, Irving Rein, and Donald H. Haider, *Marketing Places in Europe: Attracting Investment, Industry and Tourism to Cities, States and Nations* (London: Financial Times Prentice-Hall, 1999); *Marketing Places Europe* (London: Financial Times Prentice-Hall, 1999).

8. Connie Lewis, "Bullish Figures Not All Fun, Games for Hoteliers," *San Diego Business Journal*, January 24, 2005, pp. 3+.

9. Carl Shapiro and Hal R. Varian, "Versioning: The Smart Way to Sell Information," *Harvard Business Review* (November–December 1998): 106–114.

10. John R. Brandt, "Dare to Be Different," *Chief Executive*, May 2003, pp. 34–38.

11. Paige Albiniak, "A Sober Success Story," *Broadcasting & Cable*, March 28, 2005, p. 60.

12. Jeffrey Rayport and John Sviokla, "Managing in the Marketspace," *Harvard Business Review* (November–December 1994): 141–150. Also see their "Exploring the Virtual Value Chain," *Harvard Business Review* (November–December 1995): 75–85.

13. Mohan Sawhney, *Seven Steps to Nirvana* (New York: McGraw-Hill, 2001).

14. Gerry Khermouch, "Breaking into the Name Game," *BusinessWeek*, April 7, 2003, p. 54; "China's Challenge," *Marketing Week*, October 2, 2003, pp. 22–24.

15. Bruce I. Newman, ed., *Handbook of Political Marketing* (Thousand Oaks, CA: Sage Publications, 1999); and Bruce I. Newman, *The Mass Marketing of Politics* (Thousand Oaks, CA: Sage Publications, 1999).

16. John B. McKitterick, "What Is the Marketing Management Concept?" in Frank M. Bass ed. *The Frontiers of Marketing Thought and Action* (Chicago: American Marketing Association, 1957), pp. 71–82; Fred J. Borch, "The Marketing Philosophy as a Way of Business Life," *The Marketing Concept: Its Meaning to Management* (Marketing series, no. 99) (New York: American Management Association, 1957), pp. 3–5; Robert J. Keith, "The Marketing Revolution," *Journal of Marketing* (January 1960): 35–38.

17. Theodore Levitt, "Marketing Myopia," *Harvard Business Review* (July–August 1960) 50.

18. Ajay K. Kohli and Bernard J. Jaworski, "Market Orientation: The Construct, Research Propositions, and Managerial Implications," *Journal of Marketing* (April 1990): 1–18; John C. Narver and Stanley F. Slater, "The Effect of a Market Orientation on Business Profitability," *Journal of Marketing* (October 1990): 20–35; Stanley F. Slater and John C. Narver, "Market Orientation, Customer Value, and Superior Performance," *Business Horizons* (March–April 1994), 22–28; A. Pelham and D. Wilson, "A Longitudinal Study of the Impact of Market Structure, Firm Structure, Strategy and Market Orientation Culture on Dimensions of Business Performance," *Journal of the Academy of Marketing Science* 24, no. 1 (1996): 27–43; Rohit Deshpande and John U. Farley, "Measuring Market Orientation: Generalization and Synthesis," *Journal of Market-Focused Management* 2 (1998): 213–232.

19. John C. Narver, Stanley F. Slater, and Douglas L. MacLachlan, "Total Market Orientation, Business Performance, and Innovation," Working Paper Series, Journal of Marketing Science Institute, Report No. 00-116, 2000, pp. 1–20. See also Ken Matsuno and John T. Mentzer, "The Effects of Strategy Type on the Market Orientation–Performance Relationship," *Journal on Marketing* (October 2000): 1–16.

20. Evert Gummesson, *Total Relationship Marketing* (Boston: Butterworth-Heinemann, 1999); Regis McKenna, *Relationship Marketing* (Reading, MA: Addison-Wesley, 1991); Martin Christopher, Adrian Payne, and David Ballantyne, *Relationship Marketing: Bringing Quality, Customer Service, and Marketing Together* (Oxford, U.K.: Butterworth-Heinemann, 1991).

21. James C. Anderson, Hakan Hakansson, and Jan Johanson, "Dyadic Business Relationships within a Business Network Context," *Journal of Marketing* (October 15, 1994): 1–15.

22. Laura Mazur, "Personal Touch Is Now Crucial to Growing Profits," *Marketing*, November 27, 2003, p. 18.

23. Neil H. Borden, "The Concept of the Marketing Mix," *Journal of Advertising Research* 4 (June): 2–7. For another framework, see George S. Day, "The Capabilities of Market-Driven Organizations," *Journal of Marketing* 58, no. 4 (October 1994): 37–52.

24. E. Jerome McCarthy, *Basic Marketing: A Managerial Approach*, 12th ed. (Homewood, IL: Irwin, 1996). Two alternative classifications are worth noting. Frey proposed that all marketing decision variables could be categorized into two factors: the offering (product,

packaging, brand, price, and service) and methods and tools (distribution channels, personal selling, advertising, sales promotion, and publicity). See Albert W. Frey, *Advertising*, 3rd ed. (New York: Ronald Press, 1961), p. 30. Lazer and Kelly proposed a three-factor classification: goods and services mix, distribution mix, and communications mix. See William Lazer and Eugene J. Kelly, *Managerial Marketing: Perspectives and Viewpoints*, rev. ed. (Homewood, IL: Irwin, 1962), p. 413.

25. Robert Lauterborn, "New Marketing Litany: 4P's Passé; C-Words Take Over," *Advertising Age*, October 1, 1990, p. 26.

26. Barney Gimbel, "Southwest's New Flight Plan," *Fortune*, May 16, 2005, pp. 93+; Jane Lewis, "The Leaders Who Changed HR," *Personnel Today*, January 22, 2002, pp. 2+; Kim Clark, "Nothing But the Plane Truth," *U.S. News & World Report*, December 31, 2001, p. 58.

27. "McDonald's Corp.'s Poultry Suppliers in the United States and Europe Have Ceased Using Human Antibiotics as Growth Promoters in Chickens, the Company Said," *Nation's Restaurant News Daily NewsFax*, January 14, 2005, p. 1; William Greider, "Victory at McDonald's," *The Nation*, August 18, 2003.

28. Hamish Pringle and Marjorie Thompson, *Brand Soul: How Cause-Related Marketing Builds Brands* (New York: John Wiley & Sons, 1999); Richard Earle, *The Art of Cause Marketing* (Lincolnwood, IL: NTC, 2000).

29. Private conversation with Carpenter.

CHAPTER 2

Developing and Implementing Marketing Strategies and Plans

In this chapter, we will address the following questions:

1. How does marketing affect customer value?
2. How is strategic planning carried out at different levels of the organization?
3. What does a marketing plan include?
4. How can management assess marketing performance?

MARKETING MANAGEMENT AT STARBUCKS

When Howard Schultz visited Italy in the early 1980s, he was so impressed by the espresso bars that he returned to Seattle with a marketing idea that ultimately transformed Starbucks into a $5 billion business. Schultz—currently Starbucks' chairman—spotted an opportunity to bring "coffeehouse culture" to the U.S. market by serving brewed-to-order gourmet coffees in a relaxed café atmosphere. Coffee-lovers responded so enthusiastically that within 20 years, Starbucks was able to expand from a single location to nearly 9,000 stores in 35 nations.

Over the years, Starbucks has introduced a variety of new products and services to create and deliver value for customers, sometimes partnering with other firms that have special expertise. For instance, the sweet and icy Frappuccino was such a big hit in Starbucks' cafés that the company formed a partnership with Pepsi-Cola to bottle the beverage and get it on supermarket shelves. Starbucks also joined with Jim Beam to develop and market Starbucks coffee liqueur. With customer convenience in mind, marketers came up with the Starbucks Card to make paying for a latte or espresso quicker and easier. And Starbucks acquired Tazo Tea to offer its customers yet more beverage choices. Today, customers can go into a local Starbucks to buy music CDs, surf the Web, or apply for a Starbucks Duetto Visa card. Social responsibility issues such as helping small coffee growers in developing countries are a high priority as well. As one Starbucks executive notes, "Corporate social responsibility adds value to a company"—a message that customers, suppliers, and other stakeholders want to hear.[1]

Starbucks executives know that a key ingredient of the marketing management process is the formulation of insightful, creative strategies and plans to guide marketing activities effectively. Developing the right marketing strategy over time requires a blend of discipline and flexibility: Firms must stick to a strategy but must also find new ways to constantly improve it, as Starbucks has done.[2] This chapter begins by examining in more detail how marketing affects customer value. Next is a discussion of strategic planning on the corporate and division levels, followed by a discussion of strategic planning on the business unit level. After outlining the information that should be included in a marketing plan, the chapter looks at how managers can measure marketing performance.

MARKETING AND CUSTOMER VALUE

Marketing involves satisfying customers' needs and wants; the task of any business is to deliver customer value at a profit. In a hypercompetitive economy where buyers are faced with abundant choices, a company can win only by fine-tuning the value delivery process and choosing, providing, and communicating superior value.

The Value Delivery Process

The traditional view of marketing is that the firm makes something and then sells it (Figure 2.1a). In this view, marketing takes place in the second half of the process. The company knows what to make and the market will buy enough units to produce profits. Companies that subscribe to this view have the best chance of succeeding in economies marked by goods shortages where consumers are not fussy about quality, features, or style—for example, with basic staple goods in developing markets.

In economies where people face abundant choices, however, the "mass market" is actually splintering into numerous micromarkets, each with its own wants, perceptions, preferences, and buying criteria. The smart competitor must design and deliver offerings for well-defined target markets. This belief is at the core of the new view of business processes, which places marketing at the beginning of planning. Instead of emphasizing making and selling, these companies see themselves as part of a value delivery process.

Figure 2.1b illustrates the value creation and delivery sequence. The first phase, *choosing the value*, represents the "homework" marketing must do before any product exists. The marketing staff must segment the market, select the appropriate market target, and develop the offering's value positioning. The formula "segmentation, targeting, positioning" (STP) is the essence of strategic marketing. Once the business unit has chosen the value, the second phase is *providing the value*. Marketing must determine specific product features, prices, and distribution. The task in the third

FIGURE 2.1   Two Views of the Value Delivery Process

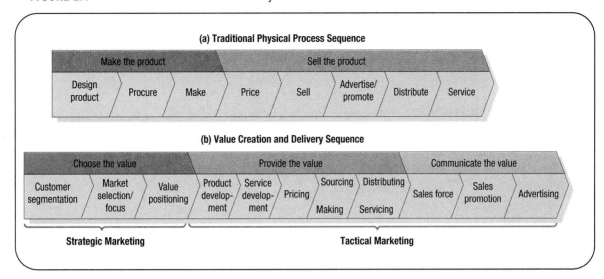

Source: Michael J. Lanning and Edward G. Michaels, "A Business Is a Value Delivery System," McKinsey Staff Paper no. 41, June 1988. Copyright © McKinsey & Co., Inc.

phase is *communicating the value* by utilizing the sales force, sales promotion, advertising, and other communication tools to announce and promote the product. Each of these value phases has cost implications.

The Value Chain

Michael Porter of Harvard has proposed the **value chain** as a tool for identifying ways to create more customer value.[3] According to this model, every firm is a synthesis of activities performed to design, produce, market, deliver, and support its product. The value chain identifies nine strategically relevant activities that create value and cost in a specific business. These consist of five primary activities and four support activities, as shown in Figure 2.2.

The firm's task is to examine its costs and performance in each value-creating activity and look for ways to improve. In addition to estimating its competitors' costs and performances as *benchmarks* against which to compare its own costs and performances, the firm should also study the "best of class" practices of the world's best companies.[4] Ultimately, success depends on how well each department performs its work as well as how well the various departmental activities are coordinated. To more smoothly manage delivery of quality customer service, companies need to manage these five *core business processes:*[5]

- *The market sensing process.* All the activities involved in gathering market intelligence, disseminating it within the firm, and acting on it.
- *The new offering realization process.* All the activities involved in researching, developing, and launching new, high-quality offerings quickly and within budget.
- *The customer acquisition process.* All the activities involved in defining target markets and prospecting for new customers.

FIGURE 2.2 The Generic Value Chain

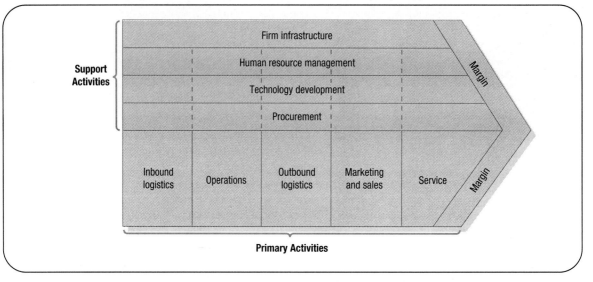

Source: Reprinted with the permission of The Free Press, an imprint of Simon & Schuster, from Michael E. Porter, *Competitive Advantage: Creating and Sustaining Superior Performance.* Copyright 1985 by Michael E. Porter.

■ *The customer relationship management process.* All the activities involved in building deeper understanding of, relationships with, and offerings to individual customers.

■ *The fulfillment management process.* All the activities involved in receiving and approving orders, shipping the goods on time, and collecting payment.

A firm successful firm looks for competitive advantage beyond its own operations, into the value chains of suppliers, distributors, and customers. In fact, many companies today partner with specific suppliers and distributors to create a superior **value delivery network** (also called a **supply chain**).[6]

Core Competencies

To carry out its core business processes, a company needs resources—labor power, materials, machines, information, and energy. Traditionally, companies owned and controlled most of the resources that entered their businesses, but this situation is changing. Many companies today outsource less critical resources if they can be obtained at better quality or lower cost. Frequently, outsourced resources include cleaning services, landscaping, auto fleet management, even information technology management.

The key, then, is to own and nurture the resources and competencies that make up the essence of the business. Nike, for example, does not manufacture its own shoes, because certain Asian manufacturers are more competent in this task; Nike nurtures its superiority in shoe design and shoe merchandising, its two core competencies. We can say that a **core competency** has three characteristics: (1) It is a source of competitive advantage in that it makes a significant contribution to perceived customer benefits, (2) it has applications in a wide variety of markets, and (3) it is difficult for competitors to imitate.[7]

Competitive advantage also accrues to companies that possess distinctive capabilities. Whereas core competencies tend to refer to areas of special technical and production expertise, *distinctive capabilities* tend to describe excellence in broader business processes. Competitive advantage ultimately derives from how well the company has fitted its core competencies and distinctive capabilities into tightly interlocking "activity systems." Competitors find it hard to imitate companies such as Southwest Airlines, Dell, or IKEA because they are unable to copy their activity systems.

A Holistic Marketing Orientation and Customer Value

(Relationship Marketing)

A holistic marketing orientation can provide insight into the process of capturing customer value. One conception of holistic marketing views it as "integrating the value exploration, value creation, and value delivery activities with the purpose of building long-term, mutually satisfying relationships and co-prosperity among key stakeholders."[8] According to this view, holistic marketers succeed by managing a superior value chain that delivers a high level of product quality, service, and speed. Figure 2.3, a holistic marketing framework, shows how the interaction between relevant actors (customers, company, and collaborators) and value-based activities (value exploration, value creation, and value delivery) helps to create, maintain, and renew customer value.

The holistic marketing framework addresses three key management questions:

1. *Value exploration: How can a company identify new value opportunities?* This requires an understanding of the customer's *cognitive space*, existing and latent needs and dimensions such as the need for participation, stability, freedom, and change. The company's *competency space* can be described in terms of breadth and depth. The collaborator's

FIGURE 2.3   A Holistic Marketing Framework

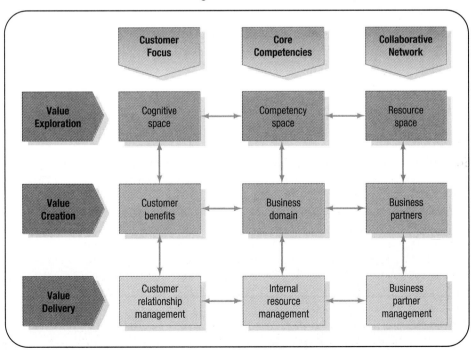

Source: P. Kotler, D. C. Jain, and S. Maesincee, "Formulating a Market Renewal Strategy," in *Marketing Moves* (Part 1), Fig. 1-1 (Boston: Harvard Business School Press, 2002), p. 29.

resource space involves partnerships the company forges to exploit market opportunities and serve value creation.

2. *Value creation: How can a company efficiently create more promising new value offerings?* Here, marketers must identify new customer benefits from the customer's view, apply core competencies, and partner effectively with collaborators.

3. *Value delivery: How can a company use its capabilities and infrastructure to deliver the new value offerings more efficiently?* The company must become proficient at customer relationship management by understanding its customers and responding accordingly. Effective response depends on internal resource management and business partnership management.

CORPORATE AND DIVISION STRATEGIC PLANNING

How companies choose, create, deliver, and communicate value to customers depends on strategic planning at four levels: the corporate level, division level, business unit level, and product level. Corporate headquarters is responsible for designing a corporate strategic plan to guide the whole enterprise; it makes decisions on the amount of resources to allocate to each division, as well as on which businesses to start or eliminate. Each division establishes a plan covering the allocation of funds to each business unit within the division. Each business unit develops a strategic plan to carry that business unit into a profitable future. Moreover, each product level (product line, brand) within a business unit develops a marketing plan for achieving its objectives in its market. Once these plans are implemented at all levels, management monitors the results and takes corrective action when necessary. The complete strategic planning, implementation, and control cycle is shown in Figure 2.4.

All corporate headquarters undertake four planning activities: defining the corporate mission; establishing strategic business units (SBUs); assigning resources to each SBU; and assessing growth opportunities.

Defining the Corporate Mission

An organization exists to accomplish something: to make cars, lend money, provide a night's lodging, and so on. Its specific mission or purpose is usually clear when the

FIGURE 2.4   The Strategic Planning, Implementation, and Control Processes

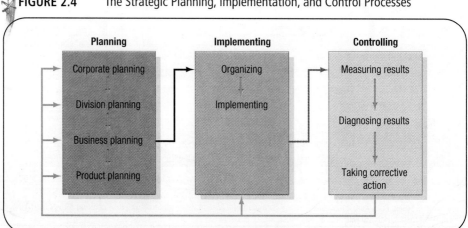

business starts. Over time, the mission may change, to take advantage of new opportunities or respond to new market conditions. Amazon.com changed its mission from being the world's largest online bookstore to becoming the world's largest online store.

To define its mission, the company should address Peter Drucker's classic questions:[9] What is our business? Who is the customer? What is of value to the customer? What will our business be? What should our business be? Successful companies continuously raise these questions and answer them thoughtfully and thoroughly.

An organization develops a **mission statement** to share with managers, employees, and—in many cases—customers. A clear, thoughtful mission statement provides employees with a shared sense of purpose, direction, and opportunity and guides geographically dispersed employees to work independently and collectively toward realizing the organization's goals. The Internet search technology firm Google, for instance, says its mission "is to organize the world's information and make it universally accessible and useful."

Good mission statements focus on a limited number of goals, stress the company's major policies and values, and define the company's major competitive spheres. These include:

- *Industry.* The range of industries in which a company will operate. For example, DuPont prefers to operate in the industrial market; Dow operates in the industrial and consumer markets; and 3M will go into almost any industry where it can make money.

- *Products and applications.* The range of products and applications that a company will supply. St. Jude Medical aims to "serve physicians worldwide with high-quality products for cardiovascular care."

- *Competence.* The range of technological and other core competencies that a company will master and leverage. Japan's NEC has built its core competencies in computing, communications, and components to support production of laptop computers, television receivers, and handheld telephones.

- *Market-segment.* The type of market or customers a company will serve. For example, Porsche makes only expensive cars; Gerber serves primarily the baby market.

- *Vertical.* The number of channel levels from raw material to final product and distribution in which a company will participate. At one extreme are companies with a large vertical scope; at the other extreme are firms with low or no vertical integration that outsource functions such as design, manufacture, marketing, and distribution.[10]

- *Geographical.* The range of regions or countries in which a company operates. Some companies operate in a specific city or state. At the other extreme are multinationals such as Unilever and Caterpillar, which operate in almost every country in the world.

Mission statements should not be revised in response to every new economic development. However, a company must make changes if its mission has lost credibility or no longer defines an optimal course.[11]

Establishing Strategic Business Units (SBUs)

A business can be defined in terms of three dimensions: customer groups, customer needs, and technology.[12] For example, a company that defines its business as designing incandescent lighting systems for television studios would have television studios as its customer group; lighting as its customer need; and incandescent lighting as its technology. In line with Levitt's argument that market definitions of a business are superior to product definitions,[13] these three dimensions describe the business in terms of a customer-satisfying process, not a goods-producing process. Products are transient, but basic needs and customer groups endure forever. Transportation is a need; the horse and carriage, the automobile, the railroad, the airline, and the truck are products that meet that need.

Large companies normally manage quite different businesses, each requiring its own strategy. A **strategic business unit (SBU)** has three characteristics: (1) It is a single business or collection of related businesses that can be planned separately from the rest of the company; (2) it has its own set of competitors; and (3) it has a manager responsible for strategic planning and profit performance who controls most of the factors affecting profit.

The purpose of identifying the company's strategic business units is to develop separate strategies and assign appropriate funding to the entire business portfolio. Senior management knows that its portfolio of businesses usually includes a number of "yesterday's has-beens" as well as "tomorrow's breadwinners." Yet it cannot rely on impressions; it needs analytical tools to classify its businesses by profit potential.[14]

Assessing Growth Opportunities

Assessing growth opportunities involves planning new businesses, downsizing, or terminating older businesses.

For higher sales and profits, a company's options include intensive growth, integrative growth, and diversification growth.

- *Intensive growth*. Ansoff has proposed the product–market expansion grid as a framework for detecting new intensive growth opportunities.[15] In this grid, the company first considers whether it could gain market share with its current products in current markets (market-penetration strategy) by encouraging current customers to buy more, attracting competitors' customers, or convincing nonusers to start buying its products. Next it considers whether it can find or develop new markets for its current products (market-development strategy). Then it considers whether it can develop new products for its current markets (product-development strategy). Later it will also review opportunities to develop new products for new markets (diversification strategy).

- *Integrative growth*. Often growth can be achieved through backward integration (acquiring a supplier), forward integration (acquiring a distributor), or horizontal integration (acquiring a competitor). If these sources do not deliver the desired results, the company should consider diversification.

- *Diversification growth*. This makes sense when good opportunities exist outside the present businesses. Three types of diversification are possible. The company could seek new products that have technological or marketing synergies with existing product lines, even though the new products themselves may appeal to a different group of customers (concentric diversification strategy). Second, the company might search for new products that appeal to its current customers but are technologically unrelated to the current product line (horizontal diversification strategy). Finally, the company might seek new businesses that have no relationship to the company's current technology, products, or markets (conglomerate diversification strategy).

Of course, companies must not only develop new businesses but also carefully prune, harvest, or divest tired, old businesses in order to release needed resources and reduce costs. Weak businesses require a disproportionate amount of managerial attention; managers should therefore focus on growth opportunities rather than wasting energy and resources trying to save hemorrhaging businesses.

Organization and Organizational Culture

Strategic planning is done within the context of the organization. A company's **organization** consists of its structures, policies, and corporate culture, all of which can become dysfunctional in a rapidly changing business environment. **Corporate culture** has been defined as "the shared experiences, stories, beliefs, and norms that characterize an organization." Sometimes corporate culture develops organically and is transmitted directly from the CEO's personality and habits to employees. Such is the case with computer giant Microsoft. Even as a multi-billion-dollar company, Microsoft hasn't lost the hard-driving culture perpetuated by founder Bill Gates. This ultracompetitive culture may be the biggest key to Microsoft's success and to its much-criticized dominance in the industry.[16]

History

Successful companies may need to adopt a new view of how to craft their strategies. The traditional view is that senior management hammers out the strategy and hands it down. Gary Hamel offers the contrasting view that imaginative ideas on strategy exist in many places within a company.[17] Senior management should encourage fresh ideas from three groups who tend to be underrepresented in strategy making: employees with youthful perspectives; employees who are far removed from company headquarters; and employees who are new to the industry.

Moreover, management should develop strategy by identifying and selecting among different views of the future. The Royal Dutch/Shell Group has pioneered **scenario analysis,** developing plausible representations of a firm's possible future that make different assumptions about forces driving the market and include different uncertainties. Managers think through each scenario with the question: "What will we do if it happens?" They then adopt one scenario as the most probable and watch for signs that might confirm or disconfirm that scenario.[18]

BUSINESS UNIT STRATEGIC PLANNING

The business unit strategic-planning process consists of the eight steps shown in Figure 2.5. We examine each step in the sections that follow.

FIGURE 2.5   The Business Unit Strategic-Planning Process

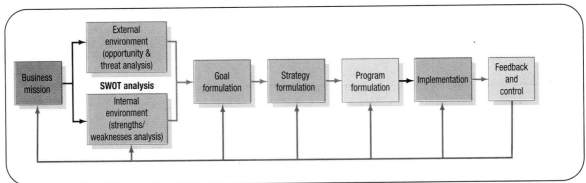

Business Mission

Each business unit needs to define its specific mission within the broader company mission. Thus, a television studio-lighting-equipment company might define its mission as "The company aims to target major television studios and become their vendor of choice for lighting technologies that represent the most advanced and reliable studio lighting arrangements."

SWOT Analysis

The overall evaluation of a business's strengths, weaknesses, opportunities, and threats is called *SWOT analysis*. It consists of an analysis of the external and internal environments.

External Environment (Opportunity and Threat) Analysis   A business unit has to monitor key *macroenvironment forces* (demographic-economic, technological, political-legal, and social-cultural) and *microenvironment actors* (customers, competitors, distributors, and suppliers) that affect its ability to earn profits. Then, for each trend or development, management needs to identify the associated marketing opportunities and threats.

A **marketing opportunity** is an area of buyer need and interest in which there is a high probability that the company can profitably satisfy that need. There are three main sources of market opportunities.[19] The first source is to supply something that is in short supply. The second is to supply an existing product or service in a new or superior way by asking consumers for their suggestions (*problem detection method*); asking consumers to imagine an ideal version of the offering (*ideal method*); and by asking consumers to chart their steps in acquiring, using, and disposing of a product (*consumption chain method*). The third source often leads to a totally new product or service.

Next the company applies **market opportunity analysis (MOA)** to determine the attractiveness and success probability of each opportunity by asking five questions:

1. Can the benefits involved in the opportunity be articulated to a defined target market?
2. Can the target market(s) be located and reached with cost-effective media and trade channels?
3. Does the company have access to the capabilities and resources needed to deliver the customer benefits?
4. Can the company deliver the benefits better than any actual or potential competitors?
5. Will the financial rate of return meet or exceed the company's threshold for investment?

An **environmental threat** is a challenge posed by an unfavorable external trend or development that would lead, in the absence of defensive marketing action, to lower sales or profit. Threats should be classified according to seriousness and probability of occurrence. Minor threats can be ignored; somewhat more serious threats must be carefully monitored; and major threats require the development of contingency plans that spell out changes the company can make if necessary.

Internal Environment (Strengths and Weaknesses) Analysis   It is one thing to discern attractive opportunities and another to be able to take advantage of these opportunities. Each business needs to evaluate its internal strengths and weaknesses in marketing, finance, manufacturing, and organizational capabilities. Clearly, the business does not have to correct all its weaknesses, nor should it gloat about all its strengths. The big question is whether the business should limit itself to those opportunities in which it possesses the required strengths or consider opportunities that might mean acquiring or developing certain strengths.

Sometimes a business does poorly because its departments do not work together well as a team. It is therefore critically important to assess interdepartmental working relationships as part of the internal environmental audit. Each year, for example, Honeywell asks each department to rate its own strengths and weaknesses and those of the other departments with which it interacts. The notion is that each department is a supplier to some departments and a customer of other departments. If one department has weaknesses that hurt its "internal customers," Honeywell wants to correct them.

Goal Formulation

Once the company has performed a SWOT analysis, it can develop specific goals for the planning period in a process called **goal formulation**. Managers use the term *goals* to describe objectives that are specific with respect to magnitude and time. To be effective, goals must (1) be arranged hierarchically (from most to least important) to guide the businesses in moving from broad to specific objectives for departments and individuals; (2) be stated quantitatively whenever possible; (3) be realistic; and (4) be consistent. Other important trade-offs include: short-term profit versus long-term growth; deep penetration of existing markets with development of new markets; profit goals versus nonprofit goals; and high growth versus low risk. Each choice in this set of goal trade-offs calls for a different marketing strategy.

Strategy Formulation

Goals indicate what a business unit wants to achieve; **strategy** describes the game plan for achieving those goals. Every business strategy consists of a *marketing strategy* plus a compatible *technology strategy* and *sourcing strategy*. Porter has proposed three generic strategies that form a good starting point for strategic thinking: overall cost leadership, differentiation, and focus.[20]

- *Overall cost leadership.* The business works to achieve the lowest production and distribution costs so that it can price lower than competitors and win a large market share. Firms pursuing this strategy must be good at engineering, purchasing, manufacturing, and physical distribution; they need less skill in marketing. The problem is that rivals will usually compete with still lower costs and hurt the firm that rested its whole future on cost leadership.

- *Differentiation.* The business concentrates on achieving superior performance in an important customer benefit area valued by a large part of the market and cultivates strengths that will contribute to this differentiation.

- *Focus.* The business focuses on one or more narrow market segments, getting to know these segments intimately and pursuing either cost leadership or differentiation within the target segment.

Firms pursuing the same strategy directed to the same target market constitute a **strategic group**. The firm that carries off that strategy best will make the most profits. Firms that do not pursue a clear strategy and try to be good on all strategic dimensions do the worst. Porter draws a distinction between operational effectiveness and strategy.[21]

Companies are also discovering that they need strategic partners if they hope to be effective. Even giant companies such as IBM, Philips, and Siemens often cannot achieve leadership, either nationally or globally, without forming alliances with domestic or multinational companies that complement or leverage their capabilities and resources. Marketing alliances may involve products or services (licensing or jointly marketing a product); promotions (promoting a complementary offering); logistics (delivering or distributing a complementary product); or pricing (bundling offers for price discounts). Corporations have begun developing organizational structures to support these alliances and have come to view the ability to form and manage partnerships as a core skill (called **Partner Relationship Management, PRM**).[22]

Program Formulation and Implementation

Once the business unit has developed its principal strategies, it must work out detailed supporting programs. If the business wants to attain technological leadership, it must strengthen its R&D department, gather technological intelligence, develop leading-edge products, train the technical sales force, and communicate its technological leadership to the target market.

Next, the marketing people must estimate their costs for each program. Questions arise: Is participating in a particular trade show worth it? Will a specific sales contest pay for itself? Will hiring another salesperson contribute to the bottom line? Activity-based cost (ABC) accounting should be applied to each marketing program to determine whether it is likely to produce sufficient results to justify the cost.[23]

A great marketing strategy can be sabotaged by poor implementation. Indeed, strategy is only one of seven "S" elements, according to McKinsey & Company, that the best-managed companies exhibit.[24] Strategy, structure, and systems are considered the "hardware" of success; style (how employees think and behave), skills (to carry out the strategy), staff (able people who are properly trained and assigned), and shared values (values that guide employees' actions) are the "software." When these software elements are present, companies are usually more successful at implementing strategy (see "Marketing Skills: Managing Implementation" for more about how marketing managers can prepare to handle this vital process).[25]

Feedback and Control

As it implements its strategy, the firm needs to track the results and monitor new developments. Some environments are fairly stable from year to year. Other environments evolve slowly, in a fairly predictable way. Still other environments change rapidly in major and unpredictable ways. Nonetheless, a company can count on one thing: The marketplace will change; and when it does, the company will need to review and revise its implementation, programs, strategies, or even objectives.

A company's strategic fit with the environment will inevitably erode because the market environment changes faster than the company's 7 Ss. Thus, a company might remain efficient while it loses effectiveness. Peter Drucker pointed out that it is more important to "do the right thing" (effectiveness) than "to do things right" (efficiency). The most successful companies excel at both. Note that once an organization fails to respond to a changed environment, it becomes increasingly hard to recapture its lost position. Consider what happened to Lotus Development Corporation. Its Lotus 1-2-3 software was once the world's leading software program, and now its market share in desktop software has slipped so low that analysts do not even bother to track it.

MARKETING SKILLS: MANAGING IMPLEMENTATION

Creative implementation can translate a good marketing strategy into great profits. Implementation management involves careful attention to detail, excellent people skills, flexibility, and a sense of urgency. First, marketers have to learn to break every program down into its component activities, identify the needed resources and their associated costs, estimate how long each activity should last and who should be responsible for it, and set up measures to monitor progress toward program objectives. Second, during the planning process, marketers must find ways of enlisting the support and enthusiasm of managers and employees in other departments that are involved, even peripherally, in implementation. This not only gets more people looking for potential implementation problems and opportunities, but it also injects more creativity and spreads the word about important programs.

Third, marketing managers have to become flexible enough to find workable options when dealing with unexpected twists such as late delivery of materials. Finally, marketers need to instill a sense of urgency about every phase of every program, day in and day out. Using words and actions, they should communicate that implementation is critical and deserves immediate attention if the company is to achieve its objectives. One study found that grocery retailers can significantly increase sales and profits by speeding up the movement of new products to store shelves—meaning faster implementation of buying decisions.

Consider what managers at 20th Century Fox Home Entertainment do to ensure successful implementation of the company's strategy for marketing movies released on DVD. In advance of every release, they determine exactly which marketing activities are most appropriate for that DVD and develop a detailed schedule for promotions such as advertising, online games, and giveaways. The release date itself is chosen to coincide with seasonal buying patterns and to avoid conflicts with other high-profile DVD releases taking place during the same period. Managers also work closely with retailers to have new releases displayed in prominent locations during the all-important first days of sale. When 20th Century Fox releases a DVD, its executives visit major stores to check on displays, identify problems, and make changes quickly to keep sales on track. Thanks to the company's skill at managing implementation, it sold 35 percent of its *Fat Albert* DVDs on the first day of release—almost twice as fast as the usual sales rate.[26]

THE NATURE AND CONTENTS OF A MARKETING PLAN

Working within the plans set by the levels above them, product managers come up with a marketing plan for individual products, lines, brands, channels, or customer groups. Each product level (product line, brand) must develop a marketing plan for achieving its goals. A **marketing plan** is a written document that summarizes what the marketer has learned about the marketplace and how the firm plans to reach its marketing objectives.[27] It operates at two levels: strategic (laying out the target markets and the value proposition to be offered) and tactical (specifying the marketing programs and the financial allocations to be implemented over the planning period).[28] A typical marketing plan includes these basic sections:

Mission Statement →

- *Executive summary and table of contents.* The plan should open with a brief summary of the main goals and recommendations, followed by a table of contents.
- *Situation analysis.* This section presents relevant background data on sales, costs, profits, the market, competitors, and the macroenvironment. How is the market defined, how big is it, how fast is it growing? What are the critical issues facing the company? All this information is used to carry out a SWOT analysis.
- *Marketing strategy and programs.* Here the product manager defines the mission and the marketing and financial objectives to be achieved. The product manager also defines the target market and the needs that the offerings are intended to satisfy, establishes the product line's competitive positioning, and explains the programs that are planned. This is all done with inputs from other organizational areas to ensure proper support for effective implementation.
- *Financial projections.* In this section, management includes a sales forecast (by month and product), an expense forecast (marketing costs broken down into finer categories), and a break-even analysis (showing how many units must be sold to offset fixed costs and average per-unit variable costs).
- *Implementation controls.* The plan's final section outlines the controls for monitoring and adjusting implementation of the plan. Typically, the goals and budget are spelled out for each month or quarter so management can review each period's results and take corrective action as needed. Sometimes contingency plans for handling specific environmental developments (such as price wars) are included.

No two companies handle marketing planning and marketing plan content exactly the same way. Most marketing plans cover one year and vary in length; some firms take their plans very seriously, while others use them as only a rough guide to action. The most frequently cited shortcomings of marketing plans, according to marketing executives, are lack of realism, insufficient competitive analysis, and a short-run focus.

MEASURING MARKETING PERFORMANCE

How do companies know whether their marketing plans are achieving the marketing and financial objectives that have been set? More than ever, senior managers are holding marketers accountable for marketing investments and asking that marketing expenditures be justified.[29] In a recent Accenture survey, 70 percent of marketing executives stated that they did not have a handle on the return on their marketing investments.[30] Another study revealed that 63 percent of senior managers were dissatisfied with their firm's marketing performance measurement system and wanted marketing to supply prior and posterior estimates of the impact of marketing programs.[31] Therefore, as discussed in the sections that follow, a growing number of managers are measuring marketing performance using marketing metrics, analyses of marketing plan performance, and profitability analysis.

Using Marketing Metrics

Marketing metrics are the set of measures a company uses to quantify, compare, and interpret marketing performance. Brand managers can apply marketing metrics to design marketing programs; senior management can use marketing metrics to decide on financial allocations. When marketers can estimate the dollar contribution of marketing activities, they are better able to justify the value of marketing investments to senior management.[32]

Many marketing metrics relate to customer-level concerns such as their attitudes and behavior; others relate to brand-level concerns such as market share, relative price premium, or profitability.[33] Management can also monitor metrics internal to the company. As one example, the online retailer Amazon.com checks average customer contacts per order, average time per contact, the breakdown of e-mail versus telephone contacts, and the total cost to the company of each contact. In all, the manager of Amazon's customer service and distribution operations looks at about 300 charts a week for his division.[34]

A summary set of relevant internal and external measures can be assembled in a *marketing dashboard* for synthesis and interpretation. As input to the marketing dashboard, companies can prepare two market-based scorecards that reflect performance and provide possible early warning signals. A **customer performance scorecard** records how well the company is doing year after year on such customer-based measures as the percentage of new customers to average number of customers and the percentage of target market customers who have brand awareness or recall. The second measure is called a **stakeholder-performance scorecard**. Companies need to track the satisfaction of various constituencies who have a critical interest in and impact on the company's performance: employees, suppliers, banks, distributors, retailers, stockholders. Norms should be set for each measure and management should take action when actual results get out of bounds or one or more stakeholder groups register increased levels of dissatisfaction.[35]

Measuring Marketing Plan Performance

Four ways to measure key aspects of the marketing plan's performance are sales analysis, market share analysis, marketing expense-to-sales analysis, and financial analysis. **Sales analysis** consists of measuring and evaluating actual sales in relation to goals. With **sales-variance analysis**, management measures the relative contribution of different factors to a gap in sales performance. With **microsales analysis,** management looks at specific products, territories, and other factors that failed to produce the expected sales levels.

However, sales analyses do not reveal how well the company is performing relative to competitors. For this purpose, management needs to track its market share, which can be measured in three ways. **Overall market share** is the company's sales expressed as a percentage of total market sales. **Served market share** is its sales expressed as a percentage of the total sales to its served market. Its **served market** is all the buyers who are able and willing to buy its product. Note that served market share is always larger than overall market share. A company could capture 100 percent of its served market and yet have a relatively small share of the total market. **Relative market share** can be expressed as market share in relation to its largest competitor. A relative market share over 100 percent indicates a market leader; a relative market share of exactly 100 percent means that the company is tied for the lead. A rise in relative market share means a company is gaining on its leading competitor.

Managers can check whether the company is overspending to achieve sales goals by examining the *marketing expense-to-sales* ratio. In one company, this ratio was

30 percent and consisted of five component expense-to-sales ratios: sales force-to-sales (15 percent); advertising-to-sales (5 percent); sales promotion-to-sales (6 percent); marketing research-to-sales (1 percent); and sales administration-to-sales (3 percent). The company should investigate fluctuations outside the normal range of such ratios and examine the behavior of successive observations within even the upper and lower control limits to catch potential problems early.

The expense-to-sales ratios should be analyzed in an overall financial framework to determine how and where the company is making its profits. For instance, companies use financial analysis to identify the factors that affect the company's *rate of return on net worth*.[36] As shown in Figure 2.6, this ratio is the product of the company's *return on assets* and its *financial leverage*. To improve return on net worth, the company must increase its ratio of net profits to assets or increase the ratio of its assets to net worth. Also, the company should analyze the composition of its assets (i.e., cash, accounts receivable, inventory, and plant and equipment) to see if it can improve its asset management. The return on assets is the product of two ratios, the *profit margin* and the *asset turnover*. Companies can improve performance in return on assets in two ways: (1) increase the profit margin by increasing sales or cutting costs; and (2) boost the asset turnover by increasing sales or reducing assets (e.g., inventory, receivables) that are held against a given level of sales.[37]

Using Profitability Analysis

By measuring the profitability of their products, territories, customer groups, segments, trade channels, and order sizes, companies can determine whether any should be expanded, reduced, or eliminated. Managers first identify the expenses for each marketing function (such as advertising and delivery) and assign these functional expenses to marketing entities (such as each type of channel or each product). Next,

FIGURE 2.6   Financial Model of Return on Net Worth

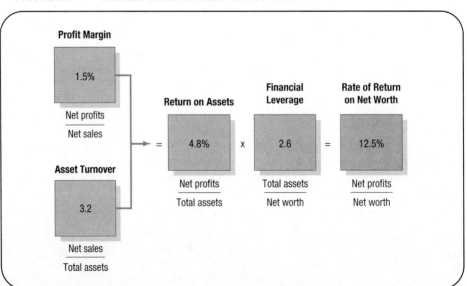

they prepare a profit-and-loss statement for each marketing entity. In the final step, they determine whether corrective action is needed to improve the relative profitability of different marketing entities.

Companies are showing a growing interest in using marketing-profitability analysis or its broader version, activity-based cost accounting (ABC), to quantify the true profitability of different activities.[38] To improve profitability, managers can then examine ways to reduce the resources required to perform various activities, or make the resources more productive or acquire them at lower cost. Alternatively, management may raise prices on products that consume heavy amounts of support resources. The contribution of ABC is to refocus management's attention away from using only labor or material standard costs to allocate full cost, and toward capturing the actual costs of supporting individual products, customers, and other entities.

Marketing accountability also means that marketers can more precisely estimate the effects of different marketing investments. *Marketing-mix models* analyze data from a variety of sources, such as retailer scanner data, company shipment data, pricing, media, and promotion spending data, to understand more precisely the effects of specific marketing activities. To deepen understanding, multivariate analyses are conducted to sort through how each marketing element influences marketing outcomes of interest such as brand sales or market share.[39]

EXECUTIVE SUMMARY

Companies can profit by putting marketing at the beginning of a three-part sequence in which they (1) choose the value by segmenting the market, selecting the appropriate market target, and developing the offering's value positioning; (2) provide the value by determining product features, prices, and distribution; and (3) communicate the value using the sales force, advertising, and other tools. The value chain identifies nine strategically relevant activities that create value and cost in a business. Among them are five core business processes: market sensing, new offering realization, customer acquisition, customer relationship management, and fulfillment management. In carrying out these core processes, companies nurture their core competencies, which lead to distinctive capabilities that build competitive advantage.

The holistic marketing framework shows how the interaction between relevant actors (customers, company, and collaborators) and value-based activities (value exploration, value creation, and value delivery) enables companies to create, maintain, and renew customer value. Strategic planning occurs at four levels: the corporate level, division level, business unit level, and product level. At the corporate level, planning includes defining the mission; establishing SBUs; assigning resources to each SBU; and assessing growth opportunities. The company's structures, policies, and corporate culture can all affect strategic planning and implementation.

At the business unit level, strategic planning covers the business mission; SWOT analysis; goal, strategy, and program formulation; implementation; and feedback and control. Each product or brand needs a marketing plan—a written document summarizing what is known about the marketplace and how the marketing objectives will be achieved. The sections of a typical marketing plan include: executive summary and table of contents; situation analysis; marketing strategy and programs; financial projections; and implementation controls. Because companies want to determine whether their marketing plans are accomplishing the objectives that have been set, many managers now assess performance by using marketing metrics, measuring marketing plan performance, and applying profitability analysis.

NOTES

1. Stanley C. Plog, "Starbucks: More Than a Cup of Coffee," *Cornell Hotel & Restaurant Administration Quarterly*, May 2005, pp. 284+; Bruce Finley, "Starbucks Executive Reflects on Corporate Social Responsibility," *Denver Post*, April 12, 2002, (*www.denverpost.com);* Howard Schultz, *Pour Your Heart Into It* (New York: Hyperion, 1997).
2. H. Hammonds, "Michael Porter's Big Ideas," *Fast Company*, March 2001, pp. 150–154.
3. Michael E. Porter, *Competitive Advantage: Creating and Sustaining Superior Performance* (New York: Free Press, 1985).
4. See Robert Hiebeler, Thomas B. Kelly, and Charles Ketteman, *Best Practices: Building Your Business with Customer-Focused Solutions* (New York: Simon and Schuster, 1998).
5. See Michael Hammer and James Champy, *Reengineering the Corporation* (New York: Harper Business, 1993).
6. Myron Magnet, "The New Golden Rule of Business," *Fortune*, November 28, 1994, pp. 60–64.
7. C. K. Prahalad and Gary Hamel, "The Core Competence of the Corporation," *Harvard Business Review* (May–June 1990): 79–91.
8. *Pew Internet and American Life Project Survey*, November–December 2000.
9. See Peter Drucker, *Management: Tasks, Responsibilities and Practices* (New York: Harper & Row, 1973), ch. 7.
10. See "The Hollow Corporation," *BusinessWeek*, March 3, 1986, pp. 57–59. Also see William H. Davidow and Michael S. Malone, *The Virtual Corporation* (New York: HarperBusiness, 1992).
11. For more discussion, see Laura Nash, "Mission Statements—Mirrors and Windows," *Harvard Business Review* (March–April 1988), pp. 155–156.
12. Derek Abell, *Defining the Business: The Starting Point of Strategic Planning* (Upper Saddle River, NJ: Prentice Hall, 1980), ch. 3.
13. Theodore Levitt, "Marketing Myopia," *Harvard Business Review* (July–August 1960): 45–56.
14. Tilman Kemmler, Monika Kubicová, Robert Musslewhite, and Rodney Prezeau, "E-Performance II—The Good, the Bad, and the Merely Average," an exclusive to *mckinseyquarterly.com*, 2001.
15. The same matrix can be expanded into nine cells by adding modified products and modified markets. See S. J. Johnson and Conrad Jones, "How to Organize for New Products," *Harvard Business Review* (May–June 1957): 49–62.
16. "Business: Microsoft's Contradiction," *The Economist*, January 31, 1998, pp. 65–67; Andrew J. Glass, "Microsoft Pushes Forward, Playing to Win the Market," *Atlanta Constitution*, June 24, 1998, p. D12; Ron Chernow, "The Burden of Being a Misunderstood Monopolist," *BusinessWeek*, November 22, 1999, p. 42.
17. E. Jerome McCarthy, *Basic Marketing: A Managerial Approach*, 12th ed. (Homewood, IL: Irwin, 1996).
18. Paul J. H. Shoemaker, "Scenario Planning: A Tool for Strategic Thinking," *Sloan Management Review* (Winter 1995): 25–40.
19. Philip Kotler, *Kotler on Marketing* (New York: Free Press, 1999).
20. See Michael E. Porter, *Competitive Strategy: Techniques for Analyzing Industries and Competitors* (New York: Free Press, 1980), ch. 2.

21. Michael E. Porter, "What Is Strategy?" *Harvard Business Review* (November–December 1996), pp. 61–78.

22. For some readings on strategic alliances, see Peter Lorange and Johan Roos, *Strategic Alliances: Formation, Implementation and Evolution* (Cambridge, MA: Blackwell, 1992); Jordan D. Lewis, *Partnerships for Profit: Structuring and Managing Strategic Alliances* (New York: The Free Press, 1990); John R. Harbison and Peter Pekar Jr., *Smart Alliances: A Practical Guide to Repeatable Success* (San Francisco: Jossey-Bass, 1998); *Harvard Business Review on Strategic Alliances* (Cambridge, MA: Harvard Business School Press, 2002).

23. See Robin Cooper and Robert S. Kaplan, "Profit Priorities from Activity-Based Costing," *Harvard Business Review* (May–June 1991): 130–35.

24. See Thomas J. Peters and Robert H. Waterman, Jr., *In Search of Excellence: Lessons from America's Best-Run Companies* (New York: Harper & Row, 1982) pp. 9–12. The same framework is used in Richard Tanner Pascale and Anthony G. Athos, *The Art of Japanese Management: Applications for American Executives* (New York: Simon & Schuster, 1981).

25. See Terrence E. Deal and Allan A. Kennedy, *Corporate Cultures: The Rites and Rituals of Corporate Life* (Reading, MA: Addison-Wesley, 1982); "Corporate Culture," *BusinessWeek*, October 27, 1980, pp. 148–60; Stanley M. Davis, *Managing Corporate Culture* (Cambridge, MA: Ballinger, 1984); and John P. Kotter and James L. Heskett, *Corporate Culture and Performance* (New York: Free Press, 1992).

26. Miles Hanson, "Fresh Ideas Are Nothing Without Implementation," *Marketing*, March 21, 2002, p. 1; "In-Store Implementation Key," *Frozen Food Age*, October 2000, p. 22; Elaine Dutka, "Coming Soon to a Store Near You: Fox Executives," *Los Angeles Times*, April 19, 2005, p. E1.

27. Marian Burk Wood, *The Marketing Plan Handbook*, 2d ed. (Upper Saddle River, NJ: Prentice Hall, 2005).

28. Donald R. Lehmann and Russell S. Winer, *Product Management*, 3d ed. (Boston: McGraw-Hill/Irwin, 2001).

29. John McManus, "Stumbling into Intelligence," *American Demographics* (April 2004): 22–25.

30. John Gaffney, "The Buzz Must Go On," *Business 2.0*, February 2002, pp. 49–50.

31. Tim Ambler, *Marketing and the Bottom Line: The New Metrics of Corporate Wealth* (London: FT Prentice Hall, 2000).

32. Bob Donath, "Employ Marketing Metrics with a Track Record," *Marketing News*, September 15, 2003, p. 12.

33. Kusum L. Ailawadi, Donald R. Lehmann, and Scott A. Neslin, "Revenue Premium as an Outcome Measure of Brand Equity," *Journal of Marketing* 67 (October 2003): 1–17.

34. Fred Vogelstein, "Mighty Amazon," *Fortune*, May 26, 2003, pp. 60–74.

35. Robert S. Kaplan and David P. Norton, *The Balanced Scorecard* (Boston: Harvard Business School Press, 1996).

36. Alternatively, companies need to focus on factors affecting shareholder value. The goal of marketing planning is to increase shareholder value, which is the present value of the future income stream created by the company's present actions. Rate-of-return analysis usually focuses on only one year's results. See Alfred Rappaport, *Creating Shareholder Value*, rev. ed. (New York: The Free Press, 1997).

37. For additional reading on financial analysis, see Peter L. Mullins, *Measuring Customer and Product Line Profitability* (Washington, DC: Distribution Research and Education Foundation, 1984).

38. Robin Cooper and Robert S. Kaplan, "Profit Priorities from Activity-Based Costing," *Harvard Business Review* (May–June 1991): 130–135.

39. Jack Neff, "P&G, Clorox Rediscover Modeling," *Advertising Age*, March 29, 2004, p. 10.

CHAPTER 3

Understanding Markets, Market Demand, and the Marketing Environment

In this chapter, we will address the following questions:

1. What are the components of a modern marketing information system?
2. How can marketers improve marketing decisions through intelligence systems and marketing research?
3. How can demand be more accurately measured and forecasted?
4. What are some of the key macroenvironmental developments that marketers must understand?

MARKETING MANAGEMENT AT SONY

Before Sony launches a new product like the PlayStation Portable (PSP)—before its engineers and designers even build a prototype—its marketing managers examine marketplace opportunities and threats very carefully. When developing the PSP game device, Sony's marketers knew that boys and young men, who grew up with video games and often have considerable disposable income, were the prime target for competitor Nintendo's Game Boy and DS products.

They also knew that the size of the U.S. market for video-game consoles was estimated at $1 billion. Sony already dominated the global market for game consoles, with more than 82 million PlayStations sold. Through research, the marketers realized that a new portable game device would have to satisfy multiple consumer needs to ride the new wave of technological convergence and "break free of the hand-held gaming ghetto." Therefore, they decided the PSP should be able to store and display digital photos, download and play music, and play movies as well as videogames.

The U.S. launch of the PSP was backed by a promotional budget of nearly $100 million. With demand primed by television ads, bus and subway posters, and other ads, 500,000 units were sold in the first two days alone. Sales and brand awareness are only two of the factors that Sony's marketers look at when gauging the effectiveness of the PSP campaign. Sony has been running 30-second commercials as part of the previews on 8,000 movie screens because research shows they work, year in and year out. However, today's top products can easily lose favor, which is why Sony's marketers are always scanning the marketing environment for clues to the next big opportunity.[1]

The major responsibility for identifying and interpreting marketplace changes falls to marketers. More than any other group in the company, they must be trend trackers and opportunity seekers, being as alert to new product possibilities and new markets as Sony's marketers. This chapter begins by considering processes and systems for gathering information, identifying trends, and conducting research to support more informed marketing decisions. The chapter then examines a number of important macroenvironmental forces that can affect the company, its markets, and its competitors.

SUPPORTING MARKETING DECISIONS WITH INFORMATION, INTELLIGENCE, AND RESEARCH

Marketing managers need a continuous flow of information if they are to understand and track changes in customer needs, wants, preferences, and consumption patterns. A **marketing information system (MIS)** consists of people, equipment, and procedures to gather, sort, analyze, evaluate, and distribute needed, timely, and accurate information to marketing decision makers. Such a system is developed from internal company records, marketing intelligence activities, and marketing research.

Internal Records

Marketing managers rely on data from internal reports about orders, sales, prices, costs, inventory levels, receivables, payables, and so on. By analyzing this information, they can spot important opportunities and problems.

The heart of the internal records system is the order-to-payment cycle. Sales representatives, dealers, and customers dispatch orders to the firm. The sales department prepares invoices and transmits copies to various departments. Out-of-stock items are back ordered. Shipped items are accompanied by shipping and billing documents that are sent to various departments. Companies need to perform these steps quickly and accurately, because customers favor firms that can promise timely delivery.

Not only is technology helping improve the speed, accuracy, and efficiency of the order-to-payment cycle for many companies, it is providing marketing managers with timely and accurate reports on current sales. Wal-Mart, for example, knows which items have been delivered to each of its 5,100 stores, where each item is shelved within each store, and how many of each product has been sold in each store every day. The retailer shares its sales data with larger suppliers such as Procter & Gamble so these companies can react quickly in shipping replacement stock to stores as needed.[2]

Today companies organize information in databases—customer databases, product databases, salesperson databases—and then combine data from the different databases. For example, the customer database will contain every customer's name, address, past transactions, and even demographics and psychographics (activities, interests, and opinions) in some instances. Companies warehouse these data and make them easily accessible to decision makers to better plan, target, and track marketing programs. Furthermore, analysts skilled in statistical methods can "mine" the data and garner fresh insights into neglected customer segments, recent customer trends, and other useful information. As an example, Wells Fargo can track and analyze every bank transaction made by its 10 million retail customers. Combining such data with personal information provided by customers, Wells Fargo can come up with offerings targeted to life-changing events of individual customers. As a result, compared with the industry average of 2.2 products per customer, Wells Fargo sells 4.[3]

Marketing Intelligence System

The internal records system supplies *results* data, but the marketing intelligence system supplies *happenings* data. A **marketing intelligence system** is a set of procedures and sources used by managers to obtain everyday information about developments in the marketing environment. Marketing managers collect marketing intelligence by reading books, newspapers, and trade publications; talking to customers, suppliers, and distributors; checking Internet sources; and meeting with other company managers. A company can take six steps to improve the quality of its marketing intelligence (see Table 3.1).

In some companies, staff members collect marketing intelligence, summarizing relevant developments and distributing the information through internal news bulletins, intranet postings, and other methods. This enables marketing managers to stay in touch with the latest market happenings and assess the effect on marketing decisions and programs.

Marketing Research System

Marketing managers often commission formal marketing studies of specific problems and opportunities, such as a market survey, a product-preference test, a sales forecast by region, or an advertising evaluation. We define **marketing research** as the systematic design, collection, analysis, and reporting of data and findings relevant to a specific marketing situation facing the company.

A company can obtain marketing research in a number of ways. Most large companies have their own marketing research departments. Procter & Gamble's large market research function is called Consumer & Market Knowledge (CMK). CMK professionals leverage traditional research basics, such as brand tracking, and leading-edge research approaches such as experiential consumer contacts and knowledge synthesis events. They then connect market insights from all these sources to help shape P&G's long-term plans, such as acquisitions to round out the product portfolio, and operational choices, such as which product formulations are launched.

TABLE 3.1   Improving the Quality of Marketing Intelligence

Action	Example
Train and motivate the sales force to spot and report new developments that may be missed by other means.	Have sales representatives observe how customers use the company's products in innovative ways, which can lead to new-product ideas.
Motivate distributors, retailers, and other intermediaries to pass along important intelligence.	Use mystery shoppers to identify service problems that can be addressed by revamping processes and retraining employees.
Network internally to collect data in ethical, legal ways.	Offer prizes to employees who submit new information about what competitors are doing.
Establish a customer advisory panel.	Invite the largest or the most representative, outspoken, or sophisticated customers to provide feedback on products.
Take advantage of government data resources.	Check U.S. Census data to learn more about demographic groups, population swings, regional migrations, and changing family structure.
Buy information from outside suppliers at a lower cost than gathering it directly.	Obtain supermarket scanner data from Information Resources, Inc.; obtain data on television audiences from Nielsen; obtain consumer-panel data from MRCA Information Services.
Collect competitive intelligence from online customer feedback systems.	Check consumer ratings on Web sites such as Epinions.com to learn more about competitors' product strengths and weaknesses.

Typically, companies budget marketing research at 1 to 2 percent of company sales. Much of this budget is spent with outside research firms, which fall into three categories. Syndicated-service research firms such as Nielsen Media Research gather consumer and trade information, which they sell for a fee. Custom marketing research firms design studies, carry them out, and report the findings. Specialty-line marketing research firms provide specialized services such as field interviewing.

Smaller companies can hire the services of a marketing research firm or conduct research in creative and affordable ways. They can engage students or professors to design and carry out projects; they can use the Internet; and they can visit their competitors. Karmaloop, which calls itself an online urban boutique, has recruited 3,000 street team members to ferret out new trends and promote company brands.[4]

Effective marketing research involves the six steps shown in Figure 3.1. We illustrate these steps with the following situation: Assume that American Airlines is reviewing new ideas for serving its customers. In particular, it wants to develop services for its first-class passengers, many of whom are businesspeople whose high-priced tickets pay most of the freight. Among these ideas are (1) to supply an Internet connection with limited access to Web pages and e-mail; (2) to offer 24 channels of satellite cable TV; and (3) to offer a 50-CD audio system that lets each passenger create a customized play list of in-flight music and movies. The marketing research manager is assigned to find out how first-class passengers would rate these services—particularly the Internet connection—and the price they would pay for each. According to one estimate, airlines might realize revenues of $70 billion over the next decade from in-flight Internet access if enough first-class passengers were willing to pay $25 for this service. Making the connection available would cost AA $90,000 per plane.[5]

FIGURE 3.1   Marketing Research Process

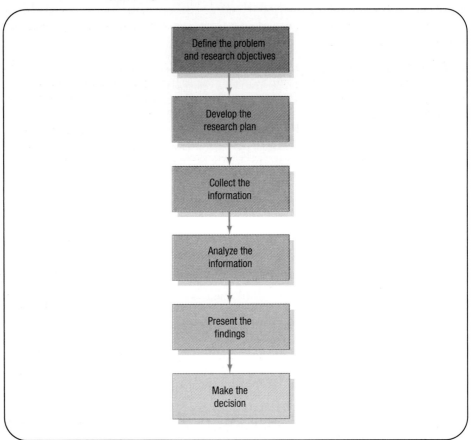

Step 1: Define the Problem, Decision Alternatives, and Research Objectives
Marketing management must be careful not to define the problem too broadly or narrowly for the researcher. American's marketing manager and marketing researcher defined the problem this way: "Will offering an in-flight Internet service create enough incremental preference and profit for American Airlines to justify its cost against other possible investments American might make?" They agreed on these specific research objectives: (1) What types of first-class passengers would respond best to an in-flight Internet service? (2) How many first-class passengers are likely to use the Internet service at different price levels? (3) How many extra first-class passengers might choose American because of this new service? (4) How much long-term goodwill will this service add to American Airlines' image? (5) How important is Internet service to first-class passengers relative to providing other services such as enhanced entertainment?

   Not all research projects are this specific. Some research is exploratory, to shed light on the real nature of the problem and to suggest possible solutions or new ideas. Some research is descriptive, to ascertain certain magnitudes, such as how many first-class passengers would buy Internet access at $25. Some research is causal, to test a cause-and-effect relationship.

Step 2: Develop the Research Plan   The second step calls for designing an efficient, affordable research plan for gathering the needed information. This entails decisions about data sources, research approaches, research instruments, sampling plan, and contact methods.

DATA SOURCES   The researcher can gather secondary data, primary data, or both. *Secondary data* are data that were collected for another purpose and that already exist somewhere. *Primary data* are freshly gathered for a specific purpose or a specific research project.

Researchers usually start by examining secondary data to see whether the problem can be partly or wholly solved without collecting costlier primary data. Secondary data provide a starting point for research and offer the advantages of low cost and ready availability. When the needed data do not exist or are dated, inaccurate, incomplete, or unreliable, the researcher will have to collect primary data.

RESEARCH APPROACHES   Researchers can collect primary data for marketing research in five ways: observation, focus groups, surveys, behavioral data, and experiments.

Combine observation w/ experiment

- *Observational research.* Fresh data can be gathered by observing the relevant actors and settings. The American Airlines researchers might meander around first-class lounges in airports to hear travelers talk about different carriers, or they can fly on competitors' planes to observe in-flight service.

- *Focus-group research.* A **focus group** is a gathering of six to ten people who are carefully selected based on certain demographic, psychographic, or other considerations and brought together to discuss at length various topics of interest, assisted by a professional research moderator. In the American Airlines research, the moderator might ask with a broad question such as "How do you feel about first-class air travel?" and then move to discussions of different airlines and proposed services such as Internet access.

- *Survey research.* Using surveys, companies can learn about people's knowledge, beliefs, preferences, and satisfaction, and can measure these magnitudes in the general population. American Airlines researchers might prepare their own questions, add questions to a larger survey, survey an ongoing consumer panel, or survey people in a shopping mall.

- *Behavioral data.* Customers leave traces of their purchasing behavior in store scanning data, catalog and Internet purchase records, and customer databases. Much can be learned by analyzing such data. Customers' purchases reflect their preferences and often are more reliable than their statements to researchers. People often report preferences for popular brands, yet they actually buy other brands. American Airlines can analyze ticket purchase records to obtain useful information about passengers.

- *Experimental research.* The most scientifically valid research is experimental research. Its purpose is to capture cause-and-effect relationships by eliminating competing explanations of the observed findings. American Airlines might experiment by introducing Internet access on one of its regular international flights at a price of $25 one week and only $15 the next week. If the plane carried the same number of first-class passengers each week, and particular weeks made no difference, any significant difference in the number of people using the service could be related to price.

RESEARCH INSTRUMENTS Marketing researchers have a choice of three main research instruments in collecting primary data: questionnaires, qualitative measures, and mechanical devices. A questionnaire consists of a set of questions presented to respondents. Because of its flexibility, the questionnaire is by far the most common instrument used to collect primary data. Questionnaires need to be carefully developed, tested, and debugged before they are administered on a large scale. Questionnaires can contain closed-end and open-end questions. Closed-end questions specify all of the possible answers, so they are easy to interpret and tabulate. Open-end questions allow respondents to answer in their own words. They are especially useful in exploratory research, where the researcher is looking for insight into how people think rather than measuring how many people think a certain way.

Some marketers prefer more qualitative methods for gauging consumer opinion because consumer actions do not always match their answers to survey questions. *Qualitative research techniques* are relatively unstructured measurement approaches that permit a range of possible responses, and they are a creative means of ascertaining consumer perceptions that may otherwise be difficult to uncover. For example, the design firm IDEO uses a variety of techniques to understand the customer experience. One technique is shadowing, observing people using products or shopping. Another is behavior mapping, photographing people within a space, such as a hospital waiting room, over two or three days. A third technique is camera journals, asking consumers to keep visual diaries of their activities and impressions relating to a product.[6]

Mechanical devices are occasionally used in marketing research. Galvanometers measure the interest or emotions aroused by exposure to a specific ad or picture. Eye cameras study respondents' eye movements to see where their eyes land first, how long they linger on a given item, and so on.[7]

SAMPLING PLAN After deciding on the research approach and instruments, the marketing researcher must design a sampling plan, based on three decisions:

1. *Sampling unit: Who is to be surveyed?* The researcher must define the target population to be sampled. In the American Airlines survey, should the sampling unit be only first-class business travelers, first-class vacation travelers, or both? Once the sampling unit is determined, a sampling frame must be developed so that everyone in the target population has an equal or known chance of being sampled.

2. *Sample size: How many people should be surveyed?* Large samples give more reliable results than small samples. However, samples of less than 1 percent of a population can be reliable with a credible sampling procedure.

3. *Sampling procedure: How should the respondents be chosen?* To obtain a representative sample, a probability sample of the population should be drawn. Probability sampling allows the calculation of confidence limits for sampling error. When the cost or time involved in probability sampling is too high, marketing researchers use nonprobability sampling, even though these do not allow sampling error to be measured.

CONTACT METHODS Once the sampling plan has been determined, the marketing researcher must decide how to contact subjects. Choices include mail, telephone, personal, and online interviews. The advantages and disadvantages of these methods are summarized in Table 3.2.

TABLE 3.2 Marketing Research Contact Methods

Contact Method	Advantages	Disadvantages
Mail questionnaire	Ability to reach people who would not give personal interviews or whose responses might be biased or distorted by the interviewers.	Response rate is usually low or slow.
Telephone interview	Ability to gather information quickly and clarify questions respondents do not understand; higher response rate than mail questionnaires.	Interviews must be short and not too personal; contact getting more difficult because of consumers' growing antipathy toward being called at home and the federal "Do Not Call" registry.
Personal interview	Ability to ask more questions and record additional observations about respondents, such as dress and body language.	Most expensive contact method; requires more planning and supervision; is subject to interviewer bias or distortion.
Online interview	Ability to post questions on the Web; place a banner, sponsor a chat room, or use other techniques to quickly, easily recruit and survey participants. Inexpensive and versatile; respondents tend to be more honest online.	Samples can be small and skewed. Also, online research is prone to technological problems and inconsistencies.

Step 3: Collect the Information   The data collection phase of marketing research is generally the most expensive and the most prone to error. In the case of surveys, four major problems arise. Respondents who are not at home must be recontacted or replaced. Other respondents will not cooperate. Still others will give biased or dishonest answers. Finally, some interviewers will be biased or dishonest. Getting the right respondents is critical.

Mediamark Research, for instance, interviews 26,000 Americans at home to determine the kinds of media they use, the brands and products they use, and their attitudes toward topics such as sports and politics. Until recently, the company had tended to exclude non-English-speaking Hispanics from the research. Now Mediamark has a bilingual traveling task force so that respondents in Hispanic households can answer the survey in English or Spanish. Its researchers are creating a more seamless interviewing database by asking the same questions of all people, no matter what language they speak and what level of acculturation they have.[8]

Step 4: Analyze the Information   The next step in the marketing research process is to extract findings from the collected data. The researcher tabulates the data and develops frequency distributions. Averages and measures of dispersion are computed for the major variables. The researcher will also apply some advanced statistical techniques and decision models in the hope of discovering additional findings.

Step 5: Present the Findings   In this step, the researcher presents the major findings that are relevant to the key marketing decisions facing management. The main survey findings for the American Airlines case, for example, show that the chief reasons for using in-flight Internet service are to pass the time Web surfing and to exchange e-mail messages. Passengers would put the charge on a credit card and be repaid by their companies. About 5 first-class passengers out of every 10 would use the service at $25; about 6 would use it at $15. Thus, a charge of $15 would produce less revenue ($90 = 6 × $15) than $25 ($125 = 5 × $25). By charging $25, AA would collect $125 a flight. Assuming that the same flight takes place 365 days a year, AA would annually collect $45,625 ($125 × 365). Since the investment is $90,000, AA would break even in about two years. Also, in-flight Internet service would boost AA's image as an innovative airline, bring in new passengers, and build goodwill with customers.

Step 6: Make the Decision   The managers who commission the research need to weigh the evidence. If American Airlines' managers have little confidence in the findings, they may decide against introducing the in-flight Internet service. If they are predisposed to launching the service, the findings support their inclination. They may even decide to do more research. The decision is theirs, but the research will have provided some insight into the problem.[9]

FORECASTING AND DEMAND MEASUREMENT

One major reason for using marketing research is to identify market opportunities. Once the research is complete, marketers must measure and forecast the size, growth, and profit potential of each market opportunity. Sales forecasts, based on demand estimates, are used by finance departments to plan for the needed cash for investment and operations; by manufacturing to establish capacity and output levels; by purchasing to acquire the right amount of supplies; and by human resources to hire the needed number of workers. The first step is to determine which market to measure.

Which Market to Measure?

The size of a market hinges on the number of buyers who might exist for a particular market offer. Although the **potential market** is the set of consumers who have a sufficient level of interest in a market offer, interest is not enough to define a market. Potential consumers must have enough income and have access to the product offer. The **available market** is thus the set of consumers who have interest, income, and access to a particular offer. The **target market** is the part of the *qualified available market* (those with the interest, income, access, and qualifications for a particular offer) that the company decides to pursue. Finally, the **penetrated market** is the set of consumers who are buying the company's product.

These market definitions are useful tools for market planning. If the company is not satisfied with its current sales, it can try to attract more buyers from its target market; lower the qualifications of potential buyers; expand its available market by adding distribution or lowering price; or reposition itself in the minds of customers. When discounter Target Stores faced stiff competition from Wal-Mart and Kmart, it began running an unusual advertising campaign in the Sunday magazines of top metropolitan newspapers. With the look of department store ads, these hip spots featuring models wearing and using products with Target's trademark red-and-white bull's eye gained the chain a reputation as the "upstairs" mass retailer and fueled rapid expansion by attracting more affluent consumers.[10]

Demand Measurement

Once the company has defined its market, the next step is to estimate market demand. **Market demand** for a product is the total volume that would be bought by a defined customer group in a defined geographical area in a defined time period in a defined marketing environment under a defined marketing program. Market demand is not a fixed number but rather a function of the stated conditions. For this reason, it can be called the *market demand function*.

The dependence of total market demand on underlying conditions is illustrated in Figure 3.2a. The horizontal axis shows different possible levels of industry marketing expenditure in a given time period. The vertical axis shows the resulting demand level. The curve represents the estimated market demand associated with varying levels of industry marketing expenditure. Some base sales (called the *market minimum*, labeled Q_1 in the figure) would take place without any such expenditures. Higher levels of industry marketing expenditures would yield higher levels of demand, first at an increasing rate, then at a decreasing rate. Marketing expenditures beyond a certain level would not stimulate much further demand, suggesting an upper limit called the *market potential* (labeled Q_2).

The total size of an *expansible market* is much affected by the level of industry marketing spending. In Figure 3.2a, the distance between Q_1 and Q_2 is relatively large. However, in a *nonexpansible market*—one not much affected by the level of marketing expenditures—the distance between Q_1 and Q_2 would be relatively small. Organizations that sell in a nonexpansible market must accept the market's size (the level of *primary demand* for the product class) and try to win a larger **market share** (the level of selective demand for the company's product).

The market demand curve shows alternative current forecasts of market demand associated with alternative possible levels of industry marketing effort in the current period. Only one level of industry marketing expenditure will actually occur; the market demand at this level is the **market forecast**. This forecast shows expected market demand, not maximum market demand.

FIGURE 3.2   Market Demand Functions

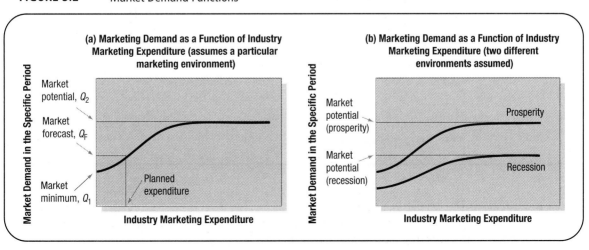

(a) Marketing Demand as a Function of Industry Marketing Expenditure (assumes a particular marketing environment)

(b) Marketing Demand as a Function of Industry Marketing Expenditure (two different environments assumed)

Market potential is the limit approached by market demand as industry marketing expenditures approach infinity for a given marketing environment. The phrase "for a given marketing environment" is crucial. The market potential for many products is higher during prosperity than during recession, as illustrated in Figure 3.2b. Companies cannot do anything about the position of the market demand function, which is determined by the marketing environment, but their marketing spending can influence their location on the function.

Company Demand and Sales Forecast

Company demand is the company's estimated share of market demand at alternative levels of company marketing effort in a given time period. The company's share of market demand depends on how its products, services, prices, communications, and so on are perceived relative to the competitors'. If other things were equal, the company's market share would depend on the size and effectiveness of its market expenditures relative to competitors. Marketing model builders have developed sales-response functions to measure how a company's sales are affected by its marketing expenditures, marketing mix, and marketing effectiveness.[11]

Once marketers have estimated company demand, they next choose a level of marketing effort to produce an expected level of sales. The **company sales forecast** is the expected level of company sales based on a chosen marketing plan and an assumed marketing environment. The company sales forecast is graphed with company sales on the vertical axis and company marketing effort on the horizontal axis, as in Figure 3.2. Note that the sales forecast is the result of an assumed marketing expenditure plan.

A **sales quota** is the sales goal set for a product line, company division, or sales representative. It is primarily a managerial device for defining and stimulating sales effort. Generally, sales quotas are set slightly higher than estimated sales to stretch the sales force's effort. A **sales budget** is a conservative estimate of the expected sales volume and is used primarily for making current purchasing, production, and cash flow decisions. The sales budget is based on the sales forecast and avoidance of excessive risk, so it is generally set slightly lower than the sales forecast.

Company sales potential is the sales limit approached by company demand as company marketing effort increases relative to competitors. The absolute limit of company demand is, of course, the market potential. In most cases, company sales potential is less than market potential, even when company marketing expenditures increase considerably, because each competitor has a core of loyal buyers who are not very responsive to other companies' efforts to woo them.

Estimating Current Demand

In estimating current market demand, marketing executives want to examine total market potential, area market potential, total industry sales, and market shares.

Total Market Potential   **Total market potential** is the maximum number of sales that might be available to all of the firms in an industry during a given period, under a given level of industry marketing effort and environmental conditions. A common way to estimate total market potential is to estimate the potential number of buyers times the average quantity purchased by a buyer times the price. Assume that 100 million people buy books each year, the average customer buys three books a year, and the average price of a book is $20. In this case, the total market potential for books will be $6 billion (100 million × 3 × $20).

The most difficult component to estimate is the number of buyers for the specific product or market. Companies can start with a total population, eliminate groups that obviously would not buy the product, and do research to eliminate groups without interest or money to buy. This leaves a prospect pool of potential buyers that companies can include in the calculation of total market potential.

Area Market Potential   Companies face the problem of selecting the best territories and allocating their marketing budget optimally among these territories. Therefore, they need to estimate the market potential of different cities, states, and nations. Business marketers primarily use the market-buildup method, whereas consumer marketers primarily use the multiple-factor index method.

The **market-buildup method** calls for identifying all of the potential buyers in an area and estimating their potential purchases. This works well if firms have a list of all potential buyers and a good estimate of what each will buy—data that can be difficult to gather. An efficient method makes use of the *North American Industry Classification System (NAICS)*, a six-digit code of classifying industry sectors that provides statistics comparable across the United States, Canada, and Mexico.[12] To use the NAICS, a lathe manufacturer would first determine the six-digit NAICS codes that represent products whose manufacturers are likely to require lathe machines. Then the manufacturer determines an appropriate base for estimating the number of lathes that will be used, such as customer industry sales. Once the company estimates the rate of lathe ownership relative to the customer industry's sales, it can compute the market potential.

Consumer companies also estimate area market potentials, but because their customers are too numerous to be listed, they often use the index method. A drug marketer, for example, might assume that the market potential for drugs is directly related to population size. If Virginia has 2.28 percent of the U.S. population, the company might assume that state will account for 2.28 percent of all drugs sold. In reality, drug sales are also influenced by other factors. Thus, it makes sense to develop a multiple-factor index with each factor assigned a specific weight. For example, if Virginia has 2.00 percent of the U.S. disposable personal income, 1.96 percent of U.S. retail sales, and 2.28 percent of U.S. population, with respective weights of 0.5, 0.3, and 0.2, the buying-power index for drugs in Virginia would be:

$$0.5 (2.00) + 0.3 (1.96) + 0.2 (2.28) = 2.04$$

In addition to estimating total market potential and area potential, a company needs to know the actual industry sales in its market. This means identifying its competitors and estimating their sales. Some information may be available from trade associations and marketing research firms, although not for individual competitors. Business marketers typically have a harder time estimating industry sales and market shares than consumer-goods manufacturers do.

Estimating Future Demand

Forecasting is the art of anticipating what buyers are likely to do under a given set of conditions. Very few products or services lend themselves to easy forecasting of future demand. Those that do generally involve a product whose absolute level or trend is

TABLE 3.3   Sales Forecast Methods

Forecast Method	Description	Use
Survey of buyers' intentions	Survey consumers or businesses about purchase probability, future finances, and expectations about the economy.	To estimate demand for industrial products, consumer durables, purchases requiring advance planning, and new products.
Composite of sales force opinions	Have sales representatives estimate how many current and prospective customers will buy the company's products.	To gather detailed forecast estimates broken down by product, territory, customer, and sales rep.
Expert opinion	Obtain forecasts from experts such as dealers, distributors, suppliers, consultants, and trade associations; can be purchased from economic-forecasting firms.	To gather estimates from knowledgeable specialists who may offer good insights.
Past-sales analysis	Use time-series analysis, exponential smoothing, statistical demand analysis, or econometric analysis to analyze past sales.	To project future demand on the basis of an analysis of past demand.
Market-test method	Conduct a direct market test to understand customer response and estimate future sales.	To better forecast sales of new products or sales in a new area.

fairly constant and for which competition is nonexistent (public utilities) or stable (pure oligopolies). In most markets, total demand and company demand are not stable. Good forecasting becomes a key factor in company success. The more unstable the demand, the more critical is forecast accuracy, and the more elaborate is forecasting procedure.

Companies commonly use a three-stage procedure to prepare a sales forecast: They prepare a macroeconomic forecast first, then an industry forecast, then a company sales forecast. The macroeconomic forecast projects inflation, unemployment, interest rates, consumer spending, business investment, government spending, net exports, and other variables. The result is a forecast of gross domestic product, which is used, along with other indicators, to forecast industry sales. Finally, the company derives its sales forecast by assuming that it will win a certain market share. Methods for sales forecasting are shown in Table 3.3.

MACROENVIRONMENTAL TRENDS AND FORCES

Marketers find many opportunities by identifying trends in the macroenvironment. A **trend** is a direction or sequence of events that has some momentum and durability. In contrast, a **fad** is "unpredictable, short-lived, and without social, economic, and political significance."[13] A new product or marketing program is likely to be more successful if it is in line with strong trends rather than opposed to them. This is why marketers have to develop their trendspotting skills (see "Marketing Skills: Spotting Trends"). Still, detecting a new market opportunity does not guarantee its success, even if it is technically feasible.

Companies and their suppliers, marketing intermediaries, customers, and competitors all operate in a macroenvironment of forces and trends that shape opportunities and pose threats. Within the rapidly changing global picture, six major forces represent

MARKETING SKILLS: SPOTTING TRENDS

Futurists stress that much of our world remains the same for long periods; when this continuity is interrupted, the emerging change may endure for some time. Marketers, therefore, need to develop the skill of spotting trends so they can take action in time to turn a change into a profitable opportunity rather than a dangerous threat. First they must develop their "splatter vision," the ability to look at the entire environment without becoming too focused on one particular factor. Marketers who routinely concentrate on certain competitors or customers will probably miss signs of competition from an entirely new industry or signs of new customer needs. Marketers should also use their mental models of future expectations—based on sales or industry forecasts—to scan for and explain deviations. This means not only identifying anomalies, but also analyzing their causes and effects to fuel timely marketing decisions.

In the ever-changing technology industry, experts develop a more accurate picture of the future using a combination of five approaches: seeing the future as an extension of the past; searching for cycles and patterns; analyzing the actions of customers and other stakeholders; monitoring technical and social events as they unfold; and discerning potential trends from the interaction of these four approaches. The final challenge for any marketer is to understand the true nature of the trend and determine how it is likely to influence the macroenvironment and microenvironment—in particular, customers, industry players, the company, and its offerings.

For example, Herman Miller, which manufactures office furniture, has one employee surfing the Web full-time to collect breaking information about the business world, design, retailing, and other issues,and then summarize the results in a daily e-mail to management. In addition, the president—who travels between headquarters in Michigan and a New York City office—carries a digital camera to photograph images that may prove helpful in identifying new design trends. Thanks to the firm's trend-spotting ability, it was an early mover in the market for small business and home-office furniture. It has also identified opportunities for expanding into new product categories, such as creating partitions and display units that retailers and museums can move quickly and easily to reallocate floor space when needs change.[14]

"noncontrollables" which the company must monitor and to which it must respond: demographic, economic, social-cultural, natural, technological, and political-legal. Although these forces will be described separately, marketers must pay attention to their interactions, because these set the stage for new opportunities as well as threats. For example, population growth (demographic) leads to resource depletion and pollution (natural environment), which leads consumers to call for more laws (political-legal). The restrictions stimulate new technological solutions and products (technology). If the solutions and products are affordable (economic environment), they may actually change attitudes and behavior (social-cultural).

Demographic Environment

Marketers monitor *population* trends because people make up markets. Marketers are keenly interested in the size and growth rate of the population in different cities, regions, and nations; age distribution and ethnic mix; educational levels; household patterns; and regional characteristics and movements.

Worldwide Population Growth   The world population stands at over 6.3 billion and is expected to exceed 7.9 billion by 2025.[15] Population growth is a source of concern for two reasons. First, certain resources that are needed to support this much human life (fuel, food, and minerals) are limited and may run out at some point. Second, population growth is highest in areas that can least afford it. The less-developed regions of the world currently account for 76 percent of the world population and are growing at 2 percent per year, whereas the population in the more developed countries is growing at only 0.6 percent per year. Feeding, clothing, and educating children, while also providing a rising standard of living, is nearly impossible in the less-developed areas.

Worldwide population growth has major implications for business. A growing population does not mean growing markets unless these markets have sufficient purchasing power. Nonetheless, companies that carefully analyze their markets can find major opportunities. For example, the Chinese government limits families to one child per family. Toy marketers, in particular, see that parents, grandparents, great-grandparents, aunts, and uncles pamper these "little emperors." This trend has helped U.S.-based Mattel and Hasbro profit from marketing in China, despite competition from Denmark's Lego, Italy's Chicco, and thousands of local toy manufacturers.[16]

Population Age Mix   National populations vary in their age mix, although there is a global trend toward an aging population.[17] A population can be subdivided into six age groups: preschool, school-age children, teens, young adults age 25 to 40, middle-aged adults age 40 to 65, and older adults age 65 and up. The most populous age groups shape the marketing environment. In the United States, the 78 million "baby boomers" born between 1946 and 1964 are a powerful force shaping the marketplace. Baby boomers grew up with television ads, so they are an easier market to reach than Generation X, the 45 million people born between 1965 and 1976. Gen Xers are typically cynical about hard-sell marketing pitches that promise more than they can deliver.[18] The next demographic group is Generation Y, the 72 million people born between 1977 and 1994, a group that is highly fluent and comfortable with computer and Internet technology. Mountain Dew's promotional connections to extreme sports that attract Gen Xers and Gen Yers have helped boost the brand's share to fourth place in the soft drink category.[19]

Ethnic Markets   Countries also vary in ethnic and racial makeup. The United States was originally called a "melting pot," but people now call it a "salad bowl" society, with ethnic groups maintaining their ethnic differences, neighborhoods, and cultures. Major groups within the U.S. population include whites, African Americans, Latinos (with major subgroups of Mexican, Puerto Rican, and Cuban descent), and Asian Americans (with subgroups of Chinese, Filipino, Japanese, Asian Indian, and Korean descent). Moreover, nearly 25 million people living in the United States—more than 9 percent of the population—were born in another country.

Each group has certain specific needs, wants, and buying habits that marketers need to understand. After PacifiCare Health Systems learned that 20 percent of its 3 million insurance customers are Hispanic, it set up a new unit, Latino Health Solutions, to market its products in Spanish and refer customers to Spanish-speaking doctors.[20] Yet marketers must be careful not to overgeneralize about ethnic groups. Within each ethnic group are consumers who are quite different from each other.

Educational Groups   The population in any society falls into five educational groups: illiterates, high school dropouts, high school degrees, college degrees, and professional degrees. In Japan, 99 percent of the population is literate, whereas in the United States up to 15 percent of the population may be functionally illiterate. However, around 36 percent of the U.S. population is college educated, one of the world's highest percentages; this education level fuels demand for quality books, magazines, and travel.

Household Patterns   One out of eight U.S. households is "diverse" or "nontraditional," and includes single live-alones, adult live-togethers of one or both sexes, single-parent families, childless married couples, and empty nesters. More people are divorcing or separating, not marrying, marrying later, or marrying without the intention to have children. Each group has a distinctive set of needs and buying habits. For example, single, separated, widowed, or divorced people need smaller apartments, smaller appliances and furniture, and food packaged in smaller sizes.

   Marketers must increasingly consider the special needs of nontraditional households, because they are now growing more rapidly than traditional households. Compared to the average American, respondents who classify themselves as gay are more than 10 times as likely to be in professional jobs, almost twice as likely to own a vacation home, eight times more likely to own a notebook computer, and twice as likely to own individual stocks.[21] Companies such as Absolut, American Express, IKEA, Procter & Gamble, and Subaru have recognized the potential of this market and the nontraditional household market as a whole.

Geographical Shifts in Population   This is a period of great migratory movements between and within countries. Within countries, population movement also occurs as people migrate from rural to urban areas, and then to suburban areas. Although the United States experienced a rural rebound in the 1990s as nonmetropolitan counties attracted large numbers of urban refugees, urban markets now are growing more rapidly due to a higher birth rate, a lower death rate, and foreign immigration to U.S. cities.[22]

   Location makes a difference in goods and service preferences. As an example, almost one in two people over the age of five (120 million) moved at least once between 1995 and 2000—with many moving to the Sunbelt states and away from the Midwest and Northeast.[23] As a result, demand for warm clothing and home heating equipment is decreasing while demand for air conditioning is increasing. In addition, suburban growth and a disdain for commuting has helped those businesses that cater to the growing small office-home office segment. Nearly 40 million Americans work out of their homes with the help of electronic conveniences like computers, cell phones, Internet access, and fax machines. Kinko's and its parent, FedEx, are only two of the many businesses that are profiting from this trend.

Economic Environment

Markets require purchasing power as well as people. The available purchasing power in an economy depends on current income, savings, debt, and credit availability. Marketers must pay careful attention to trends affecting purchasing power because these can have a strong impact on business, especially for companies offering products geared to high-income and price-sensitive consumers.

Income Distribution   Nations vary greatly in level and distribution of income and industrial structure. The four types of industrial structures are: *subsistence economies*, which offer few marketing opportunities; *raw-material-exporting economies* like Zaire (copper) and Saudi Arabia (oil), good markets for equipment, tools, and luxury goods for the rich; *industrializing economies* like India and the Philippines, where a new rich class and a growing middle class demand new types of goods; and *industrial economies*, which are rich markets for all sorts of goods.

Marketers often distinguish countries with five different income-distribution patterns: (1) very low incomes; (2) mostly low incomes; (3) very low, very high incomes; (4) low, medium, high incomes; and (5) mostly medium incomes. From 1973 to 1999, the income of the wealthiest 5 percent of the U.S. population grew by 65 percent, while the income for the middle fifth households grew only 11 percent. This is leading to a two-tier U.S. market, with affluent people buying expensive goods and working-class people spending more carefully by shopping at discount stores and selecting less expensive store brands. Conventional retailers who offer medium-price goods are the most vulnerable to these changes. Companies can prosper if they respond to this trend by tailoring their products and pitches to these two very different Americas.[24] Gap, for example, has profited by positioning Banana Republic for higher-income shoppers, Gap for the mid-market, and Old Navy for the budget conscious.[25]

Savings, Debt, and Credit Availability   Consumer savings, debt, and credit availability affect consumer expenditures. U.S. consumers have a high debt-to-income ratio, which may slow down further expenditures on housing and large-ticket items. Credit is very available in the United States, but lower-income borrowers pay fairly high interest rates. Here the Internet is offering a helping hand, with many financial services firms vying for the business of consumers who apply for credit on sites such as **www.lendingtree.com**.[26]

Outsourcing and Free Trade   An economic issue of increasing importance is the migration of manufacturers and service jobs off shore. Many firms see outsourcing as a competitive necessity, but many domestic workers see it as a cause of unemployment. The savings are dramatic, with companies cutting 20 to 70 percent of their labor costs, assuming the work is of comparable quality. However, beyond the short-term gain for employers and pain for displaced U.S. employees is the scarier long-term prospect. The exodus of programming work, in particular, throws the future of America's tech dominance into doubt. Bombay, for example, has high-speed Internet access, a world-class university, and a venture capital industry—all the ingredients needed to spawn the next earthshaking technology innovation.[27]

Social-Cultural Environment

Society shapes our beliefs, values, and norms. People absorb, almost unconsciously, a worldview that defines their relationship to themselves, others, organizations, society, nature, and the universe. Other cultural characteristics of interest to marketers include the persistence of core cultural values, the existence of subcultures, and shifts of values through time.

- *Views of themselves.* People vary in their relative emphasis on self-gratification. Today, some U.S. consumers are more conservative in their behaviors and ambitions. Currently, the most popular leisure activities include walking for exercise, gardening, swimming, photography, and bicycling.[28]

- *Views of others.* People are concerned about the homeless, crime, and other social problems. At the same time, they hunger for long-lasting relationships with others. These trends portend a growing market for offerings that promote direct relations among human beings (such as health clubs) and for offerings that allow people who are alone to feel that they are not (such as home video games).

- *Views of organizations.* People vary in their attitudes toward corporations, government agencies, trade unions, and other organizations. There has been an overall decline in organizational loyalty due to downsizings and scandals such as those at Enron and WorldCom.[29] As a result, companies need to find new ways to win back consumer and employee confidence through honesty and good corporate citizenship.

- *Views of society.* People have varying attitudes toward society. Some defend it, some run it, some take what they can from it, some want to change it, some look for something deeper, and some want to leave it.[30] Consumption patterns often reflect social attitude; those who want to change it, for example, may drive more fuel-efficient cars and live more frugally.

- *Views of nature.* People vary in their attitude toward nature. A long-term trend has been humankind's growing mastery of nature through technology. Recently, however, people have awakened to nature's fragility and finite resources. Businesses are responding to increased consumer interest in hiking, camping, boating, and other outdoor activities with appropriate goods and services, such as tenting equipment and wilderness tours.

- *Views of the universe.* People vary in their beliefs about the origin of the universe and their place in it. Most Americans are monotheistic, although religious conviction and practice have varied through the years.

High Persistence of Core Values   The people living in a particular society hold many *core beliefs* and values that tend to persist. Core beliefs and values are passed on from parents to children and are reinforced by major social institutions—schools, churches, business, and government. *Secondary beliefs* and values are more open to change. Marketers may change secondary values but have little chance of changing core values. For instance, the nonprofit organization Mothers Against Drunk Drivers (MADD) does not try to stop the sale of alcohol, but it does promote the idea of appointing a designated driver who will not drink; it also lobbies to raise the legal drinking age.

Existence of Subcultures   Each society contains **subcultures**, groups with shared values emerging from their special life experiences or circumstances. Members share common beliefs, preferences, and behaviors. To the extent that subcultural groups exhibit different wants and consumption behavior, marketers can target particular subcultures. For instance, marketers love teenagers because they are trendsetters in fashion, music, entertainment, and attitudes. Marketers know that if they attract someone as a teen, they will probably keep that customer for years. Frito-Lay, which draws 15 percent of its sales from teens, has seen more chip-snacking by grown-ups. "We think it's because we brought them in as teenagers," says a Frito-Lay marketing director.[31]

Shifts of Secondary Cultural Values Through Time   Although core values are fairly persistent, cultural swings do take place, bringing new marketing opportunities or threats. Just as rock music and musicians had a major impact on young people's hairstyles and clothing in the 1960s, today's young people are influenced by new heroes and new activities: U2's Bono, baseball star LeBron James, and skateboarder Tony Hawk are just three examples.

Natural Environment

The deterioration of the natural environment is a major global concern. In many world cities, air and water pollution have reached dangerous levels. In Western Europe, "green" parties have pressed for public action to reduce industrial pollution. However, new regulations protecting the natural environment have hit certain industries very hard. Steel companies have had to invest in expensive pollution-control equipment and earth-friendly fuels, while automakers have had to install expensive emission controls in their vehicles. In general, marketers need to be aware of threats and opportunities related to four trends: the shortage of raw materials, the increased cost of energy, increased pollution levels, and the changing role of governments.

Shortage of Raw Materials   The earth's raw materials consist of the infinite, the finite renewable, and the finite nonrenewable. *Infinite resources,* such as air and water, are becoming a problem. *Finite renewable resources,* such as forests and food, must be used wisely. Forestry companies are required to reforest timberlands, for example. *Finite nonrenewable resources* such as oil will pose a serious problem as the point of depletion approaches. Firms making products that require these resources face substantial cost increases; meanwhile, firms engaged in research and development have excellent opportunities to create substitute materials.

Increased Energy Costs   One finite nonrenewable resource, oil, has created serious problems for the world economy as oil prices have gyrated, setting off a search for alternative energy forms such as solar, nuclear, and wind. Firms are also developing more energy-efficient products, such as the Toyota Prius, a car with an electric motor boosting the gasoline engine for better fuel efficiency.

Anti-Pollution Pressures   Some industrial activity will inevitably damage the natural environment. Consider the dangerous mercury levels in the ocean and the littering of the landscape with bottles and other packaging materials. A large market has been created for pollution-control solutions, opening the way for alternative production and packaging methods. For example, 3M's Pollution Prevention Pays program has reduced pollution and costs; Dow's ethylene plant in Alberta uses 40 percent less energy and releases 97 percent less wastewater.[32]

Changing Role of Governments   Governments vary in their concern and efforts to promote a clean environment. The German government is vigorous in its pursuit of environmental quality, partly because of the strong green movement in Germany and partly because of the ecological devastation in the former East Germany. Many poor nations are doing little about pollution because they lack the funds or the political will. It is in the richer nations' interest to help the poorer nations control their pollution, but even the richer nations today lack the necessary funds.

Technological Environment

One of the most dramatic forces shaping people's lives is technology. New technology can lead to product breakthroughs, yet it is also a force for "creative destruction." Autos hurt the railroads, and television hurt the newspapers. Instead of moving into the new technologies, many old industries fought or ignored them, and their businesses declined. Also, technological progress can be sporadic; for example, railroads sparked investment, and then investment petered out until the auto industry emerged. In the time between major innovations, an economy can stagnate, despite minor innovations that fill the gap. Marketers must monitor these trends in technology: the pace of change, the opportunities for innovation, varying R&D budgets, and increased regulation.

Accelerating Pace of Technological Change   Many common products, such as video recorders, were not available decades ago. The lag between new ideas and their successful implementation is all but disappearing, as is the time between introduction and peak production. These technological changes are changing markets and needs. For example, technology enabling people to *telecommute*—work at home instead of traveling to an office—may reduce auto pollution, bring families closer, and create home-centered shopping and entertainment opportunities.

Unlimited Opportunities for Innovation   Scientists today are working on a startling range of new technologies (such as biotechnology and robotics) that will revolutionize products and production processes. The challenge in innovation is not only technical but also commercial—to develop affordable new versions of products. Companies are already harnessing the power of *virtual reality*, the combination of technologies that allows users to experience three-dimensional, computer-generated environments through sound, sight, and touch. Virtual reality has helped firms to gather consumer reactions to new car designs, kitchen layouts, and other potential offerings.

Varying R&D Budgets   Although the United States leads the world in R&D expenditures, a growing portion is going into the development side in America, raising concerns about whether the country can maintain its lead in basic science. Many firms are content to put their money into copying competitors' products and making minor feature and style improvements. Even basic research companies such as DuPont and Pfizer are proceeding cautiously. Increasingly, research directed toward major breakthroughs is conducted by consortiums of companies rather than by single companies.

Increased Regulation of Technological Change   As products become more complex, the public needs to be assured of its safety. Consequently, government agencies' powers to investigate and ban potentially unsafe products have been expanded. In the United States, the Federal Food and Drug Administration must approve all drugs before they can be sold. Safety and health regulations have also increased in the areas of food, automobiles, clothing, electrical appliances, and construction. Marketers must be aware of these regulations when proposing, developing, and launching new products.

Political-Legal Environment

Marketing decisions are strongly affected by developments in the political and legal environment, which is composed of laws, government agencies, and pressure groups that influence and limit organizations and individuals. Sometimes these laws also create new opportunities for business. Mandatory recycling laws, for example, have spurred companies to make new products from recycled materials. Two major trends deal with business legislation and special interest groups.

Increase in Business Legislation Business legislation has three main purposes: to protect firms from unfair competition, to protect consumers from unfair business practices, and to protect society from unbridled business behavior. Over the years, legislation affecting business has steadily increased. The European Community has enacted laws that cover competitive behavior, product standards, product liability, and commercial transactions. The United States has laws covering issues such as competition, product safety and liability, fair trade, and packaging and labeling.[33]

At what point do the costs of regulation exceed the benefits? Although each new law may have a legitimate rationale, it may have the unintended effect of sapping initiative and retarding economic growth. Companies need a good working knowledge of business legislation, with legal review procedures and ethical standards to guide marketing managers.

Growth of Special-Interest Groups The number and power of special-interest groups have increased over the past decades. Political-action committees (PACs) lobby government officials and pressure businesses to pay more attention to consumer rights, women's rights, senior citizens' rights, minority rights, and gay rights. Many companies have public-affairs and consumer-affairs departments to deal with these groups and issues. An important force affecting business is the **consumerist movement**—an organized movement of citizens and government to strengthen the rights and powers of buyers in relation to sellers. Consumerists have won many rights, including the right to know the true interest cost of a loan and the true benefits of a product. Yet new laws and growing pressure from special-interest groups continue to add more restraints, moving many private marketing transactions into the public domain.

EXECUTIVE SUMMARY

A marketing information system (MIS) consists of people, equipment, and procedures to gather, sort, analyze, evaluate, and distribute needed, timely, and accurate information to marketing decision makers. This system covers internal records with data about the order-to-payment cycle and sales; a marketing intelligence system to obtain everyday information about developments in the marketing environment; and marketing research for the systematic design, collection, analysis, and reporting of data and findings relevant to a particular marketing situation.

Companies can conduct their own marketing research or hire other firms to do it for them. The marketing research process consists of: defining the problem, alternatives, and objectives; developing the research plan; collecting the information; analyzing the information; presenting the findings to management; and making the decision. In conducting research, firms must decide whether to collect primary data, secondary data, or both. They must also decide which research approach (observation, focus groups, surveys, behavioral data, or experiments) and which research instrument (questionnaire, qualitative measure, or mechanical device) to use. In addition, they have to decide on a sampling plan and contact methods.

One purpose of marketing research is to discover market opportunities that are then evaluated on the basis of sales forecasts of market and company demand. Companies start by defining the market based on the potential, available, target, and penetrated markets. Next, they estimate the market potential and prepare company demand estimates and sales forecasts.

Marketers are responsible for identifying significant macroenvironmental changes, especially opportunities and threats posed by trends in six environmental forces. In the demographic environment, they must look at population growth; changes in age, ethnic composition, and educational levels; household patterns; and geographic population shifts. Within the economic environment, marketers should focus on income distribution and savings; debt, and credit availability; outsourcing and free trade. Within the social-cultural environment, they must understand people's views of themselves, others, organizations, society, nature, and the universe; the persistence of core values and shifts of secondary values over time; and the existence of subcultures. Within the natural environment, they need to watch raw-materials shortages, higher energy costs, anti-pollution pressures, and the changing role of governments in environmental protection. In the technological environment, they should note the faster pace of technological change, opportunities for innovation, varying R&D budgets, and increased governmental regulation. Within the political-legal environment, marketers must be aware of more business legislation and of the growth of special-interest groups.

NOTES

1. "Sony Says PSP Sells More Than a Half Million Units in Its First 2 Days," *Wireless News*, April 10, 2005, www.10meters.com; Nick Wingfield, "Games for Grown-Ups," *Wall Street Journal*, March 17, 2005, pp. B1+; John Teresko, "ASIA: Yesterday's Fast Followers Today's Global Leaders," *Industry Week*, February 2004, pp. 22–28; Gregory Solman, "Sony's Got Game on Movie, TV Screens," *Adweek*, November 26, 2003, p. NA.
2. "Real-World RFID," *InformationWeek*, May 25, 2005, www.informationweek.com.
3. Mara Der Hovanesian, "Wells Fargo," *BusinessWeek*, November 24, 2004, p. 96.
4. Emily Sweeney, "Karmaloop Shapes Urban Fashion by Spotting Trends Where They Start," *Boston Globe*, July 8, 2004, p. D3.
5. For background information on in-flight Internet service, see "In-Flight Dogfight," *Business 2.0*, January 9, 2001, pp. 84–91; John Blau, "In-Flight Internet Service Ready for Takeoff," *IDG News Service*, June 14, 2002; "Boeing In-Flight Internet Plan Goes Airborne," *Associated Press*, April 18, 2004.
6. Bruce Nussbaum, "The Power of Design," *BusinessWeek*, May 17, 2004, pp. 86–94.
7. Elizabeth Roger D. Blackwell, James S. Hensel, Michael B. Phillips, and Brian Sternthal, *Laboratory Equipment for Marketing Research* (Dubuque, IA: Kendall/Hunt, 1970); and Wally Wood, "The Race to Replace Memory," *Marketing and Media Decisions*, July 1986, pp. 166–67. See also Gerald Zaltman, "Rethinking Market Research: Putting People Back In," *Journal of Marketing Research* 34, no. 4 (November 1997): 424–37; Andy Raskin, "A Face Any Business Can Trust," *Business 2.0* (December 2003): pp. 58–60; and Louise Witt, "Inside Intent," *American Demographics* (March 2004): 34–39.
8. Witt, "Inside Intent," pp. 34–39.
9. See Kevin J. Clancy and Peter C. Krieg, *Counterintuitive Marketing: How Great Results Come from Uncommon Sense* (New York: The Free Press, 2000).
10. Barbara Thau, "Target Has Home, Expansion in Its Sights," *HFN*, May 23, 2005, p. 4; Janet Moore and Ann Merrill, "Target Market," *Minneapolis-St. Paul Star Tribune*, July 27, 2001; "Hitting the Bulls-Eye: Target Sets Its Sights on East Coast Expansion," *Newsweek*, October 11, 1999.
11. For further discussion, see Gary L. Lilien, Philip Kotler, and K. Sridhar Moorthy, *Marketing Models* (Upper Saddle River, NJ: Prentice Hall, 1992).
12. See www.naics.com and www.census.gov/epcd/naics02.

13. Gerald Celente, *Trend Tracking* (New York: Warner Books, 1991).
14. "Herman Miller Sees Growth in Technology," *Associated Press*, June 7, 2005, www.forbes.com; Riza Cruz, "This Design Exec Manages 31 People Spread Over Two States," *Business 2.0*, April 2002, p. 115; Cynthia G. Wagner, "Top 10 Reasons to Watch Trends," *The Futurist*, March–April 2002, pp. 68+; Wayne Burkan, "Developing Your Wide-Angle Vision," *The Futurist*, March 1998, pp. 35+; Edward Cornish, "How We Can Anticipate Future Events," *The Futurist*, July 2001, pp. 26+; "Techniques for Forecasting," *The Futurist*, March 2001, p. 56.
15. Donald G. McNeil Jr., "Demographic 'Bomb' May Only Go 'Pop!" *New York Times*, August 29, 2004, sec. 4, p. 1; "World Population Profile: 1998—Highlights," *U.S. Census Bureau*, March 18, 1999, *www.census.gov/ipc/www/wp98001.html*.
16. Kathy Chen, "China Sees Growth in Toy Market," *Wall Street Journal*, December 2, 2003, p. B4; Sally D. Goll, "Marketing: China's (Only) Children Get the Royal Treatment," *Wall Street Journal*, February 8, 1995, p. B1.
17. Sebastian Moffett, "Senior Moment: Fast-Aging Japan Keeps Its Elders on the Job Longer," *Wall Street Journal*, June 15, 2005, pp. A1+.
18. "Further Along the X-Axis," *American Demographics*, May 2004, pp. 21–24.
19. John Rodwan Jr., "Seeking Growth: Convenience Store Volume Increases to 12 Percent," *National Petroleum News*, May 2005, p. 19; "Top-10 U.S. Soft Drink Companies and Brands for 2000," *Beverage Digest*, February 15, 2001.
20. Brian Grow, "Hispanic Nation," *BusinessWeek*, March 15, 2004, pp. 58–70.
21. Laura Koss-Feder, "Out and About," *Marketing News*, May 25, 1998, pp. 1, 20.
22. "Rural Population and Migration: Overview," Economic Research Service, U.S. Department of Agriculture.
23. Christopher Reynolds, "Magnetic South," *Forecast*, September 2003, p. 6.
24. David Leonhardt, "Two-Tier Marketing," *BusinessWeek*, March 17, 1997, pp. 82–90; Robert H. Franc, "Yes, the Rich Get Richer, but There's More to the Story," *Columbia Journalism Review*, November 1, 2000.
25. Louise Lee, "The Gap Has Reason to Dance Again," *BusinessWeek*, April 19, 2004, p. 42.
26. Anthony Garritano, "Eyeing LendingTree Deal's Implications," *Origination News*, October 2004, p. 50.
27. Stephen Baker and Manjeet Kripalani, "Software: Will Outsourcing Hurt America's Supremacy?" *BusinessWeek*, March 1, 2004, pp. 84–94; Jennifer Reingold, "Into Thin Air," *Fast Company*, April 2004, pp. 76–82.
28. "Where Does the Time Go?" *American Demographics*, April 2002, p. 56.
29. Pamela Paul, "Corporate Responsibility," *American Demographics*, May 2002, pp. 24–25.
30. Arnold Mitchell of the Stanford Research Institute, private publication.
31. Laura Zinn, "Teens: Here Comes the Biggest Wave Yet," *BusinessWeek*, April 11, 1994, pp. 76–86.
32. Francoise L. Simon, "Marketing Green Products in the Triad," *The Columbia Journal of World Business* (Fall and Winter 1992): 268–285; Jacquelyn A. Ottman, *Green Marketing: Responding to Environmental Consumer Demands* (Lincolnwood, IL: NTC Business Books, 1993); Ajay Menon and Anil Menon, "Enviropreneurial Marketing Strategy: The Emergence of Corporate Environmentalism as Market Strategy," *Journal of Marketing* (January 1997): 51–67; Michael Rothschild, "Carrots, Sticks, and Promises: A Conceptual Framework for the Management of Public Health and Social Issue Behaviors," *Journal of Marketing* (October 1999): 29–37.
33. See Dorothy Cohen, *Legal Issues on Marketing Decision Making* (Cincinnati: South-Western, 1995).

CHAPTER 4

Creating Customer Value, Satisfaction, and Loyalty

In this chapter, we will address the following questions:

1. How can companies deliver customer value, satisfaction, and loyalty?
2. What is the lifetime value of a customer?
3. How can companies cultivate strong customer relationships?
4. What is database marketing, and why is it important?

MARKETING MANAGEMENT AT CATERPILLAR

One of the world's largest manufacturers is also one of the most customer-centered companies around. Caterpillar, with more than $30 billion in annual sales, has a long history of listening to customers. From equipment for infrastructure work such as highway construction to agricultural machinery, Caterpillar offers a range of products and services for business and government buyers on every continent. The company has built a satisfied, loyal customer base by creating and delivering value that, in turn, helps customers meet their objectives.

When Caterpillar was developing a new tractor line not long ago, it surveyed hundreds of growers to identify needs, buying criteria, and desirable benefits. It also gathered feedback from customers and from grower and dealer advisory panels. The company field-tested prototypes and studied how the features helped customers achieve their goals of higher productivity. When advertising this line, Caterpillar's marketers communicated the value of "farmer-driven design." Looking ahead, the company is equipping more of its products with global positioning systems, energy-efficient engine batteries, and other advanced features that customers want. Finally, its Value Chain Accelerator Program coordinates the flow of materials and parts from suppliers to factories so Caterpillar can meet its customers' expectations for timely and cost-effective offerings.[1]

Today, companies face their toughest competition ever. Moving from a product-and-sales philosophy to a marketing philosophy, however, gives a company a better chance of outperforming competition, and the cornerstone of a well-conceived marketing orientation is strong customer relationships. A successful marketer such as Caterpillar truly connects with customers, informing, engaging, and even energizing them in the process. In this chapter, we discuss how companies can win customers and beat competitors. The answers lie largely in doing a better job of meeting or exceeding customer expectations over the long term, in a profitable manner.

DEFINING CUSTOMER VALUE AND SATISFACTION

Consumers are more educated and informed than ever, and they have the tools to verify companies' claims and seek out superior alternatives.[2] How then do they ultimately make choices? Customers tend to be value-maximizers. Within the bounds of search costs and limited knowledge, mobility, and income, they estimate which offer will deliver the most perceived value and act on it. Whether or not the offer lives up to expectation affects customer satisfaction and the probability that the customer will purchase the product again.

Customer Perceived Value

Customer perceived value (CPV) is the difference between the prospective customer's evaluation of all the benefits and costs of an offering and the perceived alternatives (see Figure 4.1). **Total customer value** is the perceived monetary value of the bundle of economic, functional, and psychological benefits customers expect from a given market offering. **Total customer cost** is the bundle of costs that customers expect to incur in evaluating, obtaining, using, and disposing of the given market offering.

FIGURE 4.1   Determinants of Customer-Delivered Value

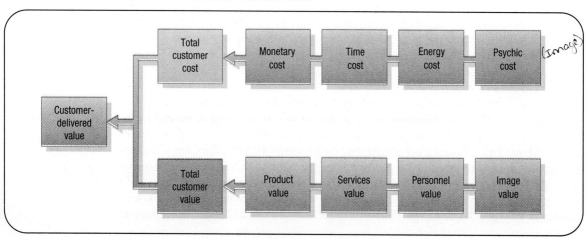

As an example, suppose the buyer for a residential construction company wants to buy a tractor from either Caterpillar or Komatsu. After evaluating the two tractors, he decides that Caterpillar has a higher product value, based on perceived reliability, durability, performance, and resale value. He also decides that Caterpillar's personnel are more knowledgeable and perceives that the company will provide better services, such as maintenance. Finally, he places higher value on Caterpillar's corporate image. He adds up all of the values from these four sources—product, services, personnel, and image—and perceives Caterpillar as delivering greater customer value.

The buyer also examines his total cost of transacting with Caterpillar versus Komatsu. In addition to the monetary cost, the total customer cost includes the buyer's time, energy, and psychic costs. Then the buyer compares Caterpillar's total customer cost to its total customer value and compares Komatsu's total customer cost to its total customer value. In the end, the buyer will buy from the company that he perceives as offering the highest delivered value.

According to this theory of buyer decision making, Caterpillar can succeed in selling to this buyer by improving its offer in three ways. First, it can increase total customer value by improving product, services, personnel, and/or image benefits. Second, it can reduce the buyer's nonmonetary costs by lessening the time, energy, and psychic costs. Third, it can reduce its product's monetary cost to the buyer. If Caterpillar wants to win the sale, it must offer more delivered value than Komatsu does.[3]

Some marketers might argue that this process is too rational, because buyers do not always choose the offer with the highest delivered value. Suppose the customer chose the Komatsu tractor. How can we explain this choice? Three possibilities are:

1. *The buyer might be under orders to buy at the lowest price, regardless of delivered value.* To win this sale, Caterpillar must convince the buyer's manager that buying only on price will result in lower long-term profits.
2. *The buyer will retire before the company realizes that the Komatsu tractor is more expensive to operate than the Caterpillar tractor.* To win this sale, Caterpillar must convince other people in the buyer's company that its delivers greater long-term value.
3. *The buyer enjoys a long-term friendship with the Komatsu salesperson.* Here, Caterpillar must show the buyer that the Komatsu tractor will draw complaints from the tractor operators when they discover its high fuel cost and need for frequent repairs.

Customer perceived value is a useful framework that applies to many situations and yields rich insights. Here are its implications: First, the seller must assess the total customer value and total customer cost associated with each competitor's offer to know how the offer rates in the buyer's mind. Second, the seller who is at a disadvantage as far as customer perceived value can try to increase total customer value or try to decrease total customer cost.[4]

Consumers have varying degrees of loyalty to specific brands, stores, and companies. Oliver defines **loyalty** as "A deeply held commitment to re-buy or re-patronize a preferred product or service in the future despite situational influences and marketing efforts having the potential to cause switching behavior."[5] The key to high customer loyalty is to deliver high customer value. Michael Lanning says that a company must design a competitively superior value proposition aimed at a specific market segment, backed by a superior value-delivery system.[6] The **value-delivery system** includes all the experiences the customer will have on the way to obtaining and using the offering.

The **value proposition** consists of the whole cluster of benefits the company promises to deliver; it is more than the core positioning of the offering. For example, Volvo's core positioning has been "safety," but the buyer is promised more than just a safe car; other benefits include a long-lasting car, good service, and a long warranty period. Basically, the value proposition is a statement about the resulting experience customers will gain from the company's market offering and from their relationship with the supplier. The brand must represent a promise about the total experience customers can expect. Whether the promise is kept depends on the company's ability to manage its value-delivery system.

Total Customer Satisfaction

Whether the buyer is satisfied after making a purchase depends on the offer's performance in relation to the buyer's expectations. Recall from Chapter 1 that **satisfaction** is a person's feelings of pleasure or disappointment resulting from comparing a product's perceived performance (or outcome) in relation to his or her expectations. If the performance falls short of expectations, the customer is dissatisfied. If performance matches expectations, the customer is satisfied; if it exceeds expectations, the customer is highly satisfied or delighted.[7]

Buyers form their expectations from past buying experience, friends' and associates' advice, and marketers' and competitors' information and promises. If marketers raise expectations too high, the buyer is likely to be disappointed. However, if the company sets expectations too low, it won't attract enough buyers (although it will satisfy those who do buy). Some of today's most successful companies are raising expectations and delivering performance to match. JetBlue Airways, for example, raised customers' expectations of low-fare carriers. With its new Airbus jets, comfy leather seats, seat-back satellite TV, and free wireless Internet access, the airline has attracted plenty of passengers, built profits, and inspired many low-fare/high-service copycats.[8]

Although the customer-centered firm seeks to create high customer satisfaction, that is not its ultimate goal. If the company increases customer satisfaction by lowering its price or increasing its services, the result may be lower profits. The company might be able to increase its profitability by means other than increased satisfaction (for example, by improving manufacturing processes). Also, the company has many stakeholders, including employees, dealers, suppliers, and stockholders. Spending more to increase customer satisfaction might divert funds from increasing the satisfaction of other "partners." Ultimately, the company must try to deliver a high level of customer satisfaction subject to delivering acceptable levels of satisfaction to the other stakeholders, given its total resources.

Measuring Satisfaction

Companies should measure customer satisfaction regularly because a highly satisfied customer generally stays loyal longer, buys more as the company introduces new products and upgrades existing products, talks favorably about the company and its products, pays less attention to competing brands and is less sensitive to price, offers product or service ideas to the company, and costs less to serve than new customers because transactions are routine. The link between satisfaction and loyalty, however, is not proportional.

Suppose customer satisfaction is rated on a scale from one to five. At a very low level of customer satisfaction (level one), customers are likely to abandon the company and even bad-mouth it. At levels two to four, customers are fairly satisfied but still find it easy to switch when a better offer comes along. At level five, the customer is very likely to repurchase and even spread good word of mouth about the company. High satisfaction or delight creates an emotional bond with the brand or company, not just a rational preference. Xerox's senior management found out that its "completely satisfied" customers were six times more likely to repurchase Xerox products over the following 18 months than its "very satisfied" customers.[9]

When customers rate their satisfaction with an element of the company's performance—say, delivery—the company needs to recognize that customers vary in how they define good delivery. It could mean early delivery, on-time delivery, and so on. The company must also realize that two customers can report being "highly satisfied" for different reasons. One may be easily satisfied most of the time and the other might be hard to please but was pleased on this occasion[10] (measuring satisfaction is the focus of "Marketing Skills: Gauging Customer Satisfaction").

MARKETING SKILLS: GAUGING CUSTOMER SATISFACTION

Over and over, research has shown that satisfying customers pays off in repeat purchasing, forming a solid foundation for profitability. This is why marketers need the vital skill of gauging customer satisfaction. This skill requires a working knowledge of marketing research coupled with a sensitivity for customer concerns. Start by defining the goal as it relates specifically to customer satisfaction: Is the purpose to pinpoint problems? To identify elements of the offering that are particularly strong contributors to satisfaction? To tease out concerns of loyal customers? This helps focus the research design on the critical data to be gathered.

Now marketers build on their knowledge of customer behavior and attitudes to encourage participation. The key is understanding not only what will entice customers to participate but also what discourages participation. Volvo of North America, for example, heard from its dealers that car buyers felt "surveyed to death." So the company trimmed its customer satisfaction survey from 33 questions to 20 and invited customers to respond on the Internet, by phone, or by mail. Marketers should communicate research findings internally to highlight good news, act on bad news, and plan new ways of satisfying customers. Finally, continuously surveying customers or repeating research at regular intervals allows marketers to follow satisfaction trends and determine the effect of changes.

McAlister's Deli, a 178-unit restaurant chain based in Mississippi, prints a satisfaction survey invitation on every receipt. Customers who call in and respond to a five-minute automated telephone survey receive a $3 discount on their next purchase. For its part, McAlister's Deli receives timely, specific customer feedback about the service, food quality, and ambiance in each store. CEO Phil Friedman says that making changes based on this research has definitely made a difference in the chain's financial results: "Satisfaction equals loyalty equals increased checks."[11]

Product and Service Quality

Satisfaction will also depend on product and service quality. What exactly is quality? Various experts have defined it as "fitness for use," "conformance to requirements," and "freedom from variation."[12] We will use the American Society for Quality Control's customer-centered definition: **Quality** (or grade) is the totality of features and characteristics of a product or service that bear on its ability to satisfy stated or implied needs.[13] We can say that the seller has delivered quality whenever the product or service meets or exceeds the customers' expectations. It is important to distinguish between *conformance* quality and *performance* quality. A Lexus provides higher performance quality than a Hyundai: The Lexus rides smoother, goes faster, and lasts longer. Yet both a Lexus and a Hyundai can be said to deliver the same conformance quality if all the units deliver their respective promised quality.

Total quality is the key to value creation and customer satisfaction. Total quality is everyone's job, just as marketing is everyone's job. Marketing managers have two responsibilities in a quality-centered company. First, they must participate in formulating strategies and policies to help the company win through total quality excellence. Second, they must deliver marketing quality alongside production quality. Each marketing activity—marketing research, sales training, advertising, customer service, and so on—must be performed to high standards.

In the quest to maximize customer satisfaction, some firms have adopted total quality management principles. **Total quality management (TQM)** is an organization-wide approach to continuously improving the quality of all the organization's processes, products, and services. Product and service quality, customer satisfaction, and company profitability are intimately connected. Higher levels of quality result in higher levels of customer satisfaction, which support higher prices and (often) lower costs. Studies have shown a high correlation between relative product quality and company profitability.[14]

Marketers play six roles in helping their companies define and deliver high-quality goods and services to target customers. First, they bear the major responsibility for correctly identifying the customers' needs and requirements. Second, they must communicate customer expectations properly to product designers. Third, they must make sure that customers' orders are filled correctly and on time. Fourth, they must check that customers have received proper instructions, training, and technical assistance in the use of the product. Fifth, they must stay in touch with customers after the sale to ensure that they are satisfied and remain satisfied. Sixth, they must gather customer ideas for product and service improvements and convey them to the appropriate departments. When marketers do all this, they are making substantial contributions to total quality management and customer satisfaction, as well as to customer and company profitability.

MAXIMIZING CUSTOMER LIFETIME VALUE

Ultimately, marketing is the art of attracting and keeping profitable customers. According to an American Express executive, the best customers outspend others by ratios of 16 to 1 in retailing, 13 to 1 in the restaurant business, 12 to 1 in the airline business, and 5 to 1 in the hotel and motel industry.[15] Yet every firm loses money on some of its customers. The well-known 20–80 rule says that the top 20 percent of the customers may generate as much as 80 percent of the profits. Sherden suggested amending the rule to read 20–80–30, to reflect the idea that the top 20 percent of customers generate 80 percent of the profits, half of which is lost serving the bottom 30 percent of unprofitable customers. The implication is that a firm could improve its profits by "firing" its worst customers.[16]

Furthermore, it is not necessarily the company's largest customers who yield the most profit. The largest customers demand considerable service and receive the deepest discounts. The smallest customers pay full price and receive minimal service, but transaction costs reduce small customers' profitability. The midsize customers receive good service, pay nearly full price, and are often the most profitable. This is why many large firms are now invading the middle market. Major air express carriers, for instance, are finding that it does not pay to ignore the small and midsize international shippers. Programs geared toward smaller customers provide a network of drop boxes, which allow for substantial discounts over letters and packages picked up at the shipper's place of business. In addition to putting more drop boxes in place, United Parcel Service (UPS) conducts seminars to instruct exporters in the finer points of shipping overseas.[17]

Customer Profitability and Competitive Advantage

What makes a customer profitable? A **profitable customer** is a person, household, or company that over time yields a revenue stream that exceeds by an acceptable amount the company's cost stream of attracting, selling, and servicing that customer. Note that the emphasis is on the lifetime stream of revenue and cost, not on one transaction's profitability.

Although many firms measure customer satisfaction, most fail to measure individual customer profitability. Banks say this is because a customer uses different banking services and the transactions are logged in different departments. However, banks that have succeeded in linking customer transactions find the number of unprofitable customers in their customer base appalling. Some banks report losing money on over 45 percent of their customers. There are only two solutions to unprofitable customers: raise fees or reduce service support.[18]

Figure 4.2 shows a useful type of profitability analysis.[19] Customers are arrayed along the columns and products are arrayed along the rows. Each cell contains a symbol standing for the profitability of selling that product to that customer. Customer 1 is very profitable, buying three profitable products. Customer 2 represents mixed profitability, buying one profitable and one unprofitable product. Customer 3 is a losing customer, buying one profitable and two unprofitable products. What can the company do about customers 2 and 3? It can either (1) raise the price of its less profitable products or eliminate them, or (2) try to sell profitable products to the unprofitable customers. In fact, this company would benefit by encouraging unprofitable customers to switch to competitors.

Customer profitability analysis (CPA) is best conducted with the tools of an accounting technique called Activity-Based Costing (ABC). The company estimates all revenue coming from the customer, less all costs (including production and distribution costs, customer-contact costs, and the costs of all company resources that went into serving that customer). This helps the company classify customers into different profit tiers: platinum customers (most profitable), gold customers (profitable), iron customers (low profitability but desirable), and lead customers (unprofitable and

FIGURE 4.2   Customer-Product Profitability Analysis

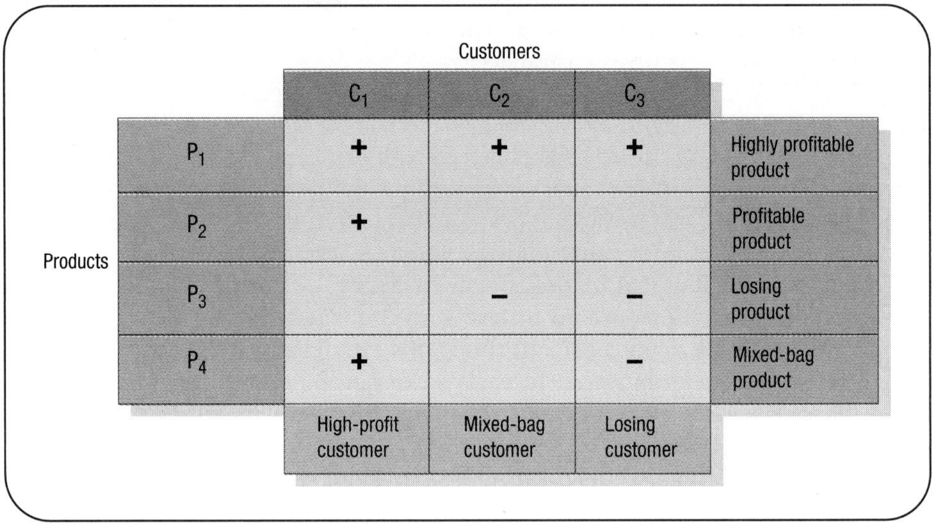

		Customers		
		C_1	C_2	C_3	
Products	P_1	+	+	+	Highly profitable product
	P_2	+			Profitable product
	P_3		−	−	Losing product
	P_4	+		−	Mixed-bag product
		High-profit customer	Mixed-bag customer	Losing customer	

undesirable). The company then uses marketing to move iron and gold customers into higher tiers while dropping the lead customers or making them profitable by raising their prices or lowering the cost of serving them.

Companies must be able to create not only high absolute value, but also high value relative to competitors at a sufficiently low cost. **Competitive advantage** is a company's ability to perform in one or more ways that competitors cannot or will not match. Michael Porter urged companies to build a sustainable competitive advantage.[20] A company that hopes to endure must continuously invent new competitive advantages. Moreover, any competitive advantage must be seen by customers as a *customer advantage*. For example, if a company delivers faster than its competitors, this will not be a customer advantage if customers do not value speed.

Measuring Customer Lifetime Value

The case for maximizing long-term customer profitability is captured in the concept of customer lifetime value. **Customer lifetime value (CLV)** describes the net present value of the stream of future profits expected over the customer's lifetime purchases. The company must subtract from the expected revenues the expected costs of attracting, selling, and servicing that customer, applying the appropriate discount rate (e.g., 10 to 20 percent, depending on cost of capital and risk attitudes). Various CLV estimates have been made for different products and services. General Motors, for instance, estimates its lifetime customers to be worth $276,000 on average—a vivid illustration of the importance of keeping a customer satisfied to better the chances of a repeat purchase.[21]

To see how CLV can be estimated, assume a company analyzes its new-customer acquisition cost:

- Cost of average sales call (including salary, commission, benefits, and expenses): $300
- Average number of sales calls to convert an average prospect into a customer: 4
- Cost of attracting a new customer: $1,200

This is an underestimate because no promotion costs are included (and only a fraction of all pursued prospects become customers). Now suppose this company estimates average customer lifetime value as follows:

- Annual customer revenue: $500
- Average number of loyal years: 20
- Company profit margin: 10 percent
- Customer lifetime value: $1,000

Clearly, the company is spending more to attract new customers than they are worth. Unless it can sign up customers with fewer sales calls, spend less per call, stimulate higher new-customer spending, retain customers longer, or sell them higher-profit products, it is headed for bankruptcy. Of course, in addition to an average customer estimate, a company needs a way of estimating CLV for each individual customer to decide how much to invest in each customer.

Customer Equity

The aim of customer relationship management (CRM) is to produce high customer equity. **Customer equity** is the total of the discounted lifetime values of all of the firm's customers.[22] Clearly, the more loyal the customers, the higher the customer equity. Rust, Zeithaml, and Lemon distinguish three drivers of customer equity: value equity, brand equity, and relationship equity.[23] This formulation integrates *value management*, *brand management*, and *relationship management* within a customer-centered focus.

- *Value equity* is the customer's objective assessment of the utility of an offering based on perceptions of its benefits relative to its costs. The subdrivers of value equity are quality, price, and convenience. Each industry has to define the specific factors underlying each subdriver in order to find programs to improve value equity. An airline passenger might define quality as seat width; a hotel guest might define quality as room size. Value equity makes the biggest contribution to customer equity when products are differentiated and when they are more complex and need to be evaluated. Value equity especially drives customer equity in business markets.

- *Brand equity* is the customer's subjective and intangible assessment of the brand, above and beyond its objectively perceived value. The subdrivers of brand equity are customer brand awareness, customer attitude toward the brand, and customer perception of brand ethics. Companies use advertising, public relations, and other communication tools to affect these subdrivers. Brand equity is more important than the other drivers of customer equity where products are less differentiated and have more emotional impact. We consider brand equity in detail in Chapter 8.

- *Relationship equity* is the customer's tendency to stick with the brand, above and beyond objective and subjective assessments of its worth. Subdrivers of relationship equity include loyalty programs, special recognition and treatment programs, community-building programs, and knowledge-building programs. Relationship equity is especially important where personal relationships count for a lot and where customers tend to continue with suppliers out of habit or inertia.

An alternative formulation to customer equity is provided by Blattberg, Getz, and Thomas. They view customer equity as driven by three components: acquisition, retention, and add-on selling.[24] Acquisition is affected by the number of prospects, the acquisition probability of a prospect, and acquisition spending per prospect. Retention is influenced by the retention rate and retention spending level. Add-on spending is a function of the efficiency of add-on selling, the number of add-on selling offers given to existing customers, and the response rate to new offers. Marketing activities can then be judged by how they affect these three components.

CULTIVATING CUSTOMER RELATIONSHIPS

Many companies are intent on developing stronger customer bonds through **customer relationship management (CRM)**. This is the process of managing detailed information about individual customers and carefully managing all customer "touch points" to maximize customer loyalty. A *customer touch point* is any occasion on which a customer encounters the brand and product—from actual experience to personal or mass communications to casual observation. The touch points for a hotel include reservations, check-in and check-out, frequent-stay programs, room service, business services, exercise facilities, and restaurants. For instance, the Four Seasons relies on personal touches, such as having employees address guests by name and be attentive to the needs of sophisticated business travelers. Each of its hotels also features at least one best-in-region facility, such as a premier restaurant or spa.[25]

Customer relationship management enables companies to provide excellent real-time customer service through the effective use of individual account information. Based on what they know about each valued customer, companies can customize market offerings, services, programs, messages, and media. CRM is important because a major driver of company profitability is the aggregate value of the company's customer base.[26]

Peppers and Rogers outline a four-step framework for one-to-one marketing that can be adapted to CRM marketing as follows:[27]

- *Identify your prospects and customers.* Do not go after everyone. Build, maintain, and mine a rich customer database with information derived from all the channels and customer touch points.
- *Differentiate customers in terms of (1) their needs and (2) their value to your company.* Spend proportionately more effort on the most valuable customers. Calculate customer lifetime value and estimate net present value of all future profits coming from purchases, margin levels, and referrals, less customer-specific servicing costs.
- *Interact with individual customers to improve your knowledge about their individual needs and to build stronger relationships.* Facilitate customer/company interaction through the company contact center and Web site.
- *Customize products, services, and messages to each customer.* Formulate customized offerings that are communicated in a personalized way.

Table 4.1 shows some strategies that a firm can implement to improve the value of its customer base.

Attracting, Retaining, and Growing Customers

Customers today are smarter, more price conscious, more demanding, less forgiving, and approached by many more competitors with equal or better offers. The challenge,

TABLE 4.1   Improving the Value of the Company's Customer Base

Strategy	Example
1. Reduce the rate of customer defection.	PrimeTrust Bank in Tennessee uses customer profitability analysis to identify its best customers, and then delivers very personalized service so these customers want to stay with PrimeTrust.[i]
2. Increase the longevity of the customer relationship.	The more involved customers are with a company, the more likely they are to continue the relationship. Instant Web Companies, a direct-mail firm, profiles the objectives and programs of a business customer every month. This helps employees better understand what customers are doing and leads to new ideas for creating value and strengthening customer relationships.[ii]
3. Enhance the growth potential of each customer.	Use cross-selling, up-selling, and share-of-wallet.[iii] Harley-Davidson's main focus is on motorcycles, but its brand also adorns clothing, cell phones, cologne, and many other products. Harley rings up more than $200 million in annual sales from such branded merchandise.
4. Make low-profit customers more profitable or terminate them.	Encourage less profitable customers to buy more, forgo certain features or services, or pay more. When Fidelity Investments' more profitable mutual fund customers call for service, they get through more quickly than unprofitable customers, who either wait in a longer phone queue or—for faster service—check Fidelity's Web site, which delivers service at a much lower cost.[iv]

[i]Janet Bigham Bernstal, "Riding Herd on Attrition," *ABA Bank Marketing,* May 2005, pp. 12+.
[ii]Katherine O'Brien, "Differentiation Begins with Customer Knowledge," *American Printer,* July 2003, p. 8.
[iii]Alan W. H. Grant and Leonard A. Schlesinger, "Realize Your Customer's Full Profit Potential," *Harvard Business Review* (September–October 1995): 59–72.
[iv]Larry Selden and Geoffrey Colvin, "Turn Unprofitable Customers into Profitable—or Former," *American Banker,* July 18, 2003, p. 7.

according to Jeffrey Gitomer, is not to produce satisfied customers, but to produce delighted and loyal customers.[28]

Companies seeking to expand their profits and sales have to spend considerable time and resources searching for new customers. To generate leads, the company uses advertising, direct mail, telemarketing, trade shows, and other methods to reach possible new prospects. All this activity produces a list of suspects. *Suspects* are people or organizations who might conceivably have an interest in buying the company's product or service, but who may not have the means or real intention to buy. The next task is to identify which suspects are really good *prospects*—customers with the motivation, ability, and opportunity to make a purchase—by interviewing them, checking on their financial standing, and so on. Then it is time to send out the salespeople.

Too many companies suffer from high **customer churn**—high customer defection. Many cellular carriers, for example, lose 25 percent of their subscribers each year at an estimated cost of $2 billion to $4 billion. Although customer acquisition is vital, companies also need to focus marketing attention on retaining and cultivating existing customer relationships. There are two main ways to strengthen customer retention. One is to erect high switching barriers. Customers are less inclined to switch when this would involve high capital costs, high search costs, or the loss of loyal-customer discounts. The better approach is to deliver high customer satisfaction, making it harder for competitors to offer lower prices or inducements to switch.

Some companies think they are getting a sense of customer satisfaction by tallying complaints, but 96 percent of dissatisfied customers don't complain; they just stop buying.[29] The best thing a company can do is to make it easy for the customer to complain. Suggestion forms, toll-free numbers, Web sites, and e-mail addresses allow for quick, two-way communication. The 3M Company says that over two-thirds of its product improvement ideas come from listening to customer complaints.

In addition to listening, the company must respond quickly and constructively to complaints. As Albrecht and Zemke observe: "Of the customers who register a complaint, between 54 and 70 percent will buy again if their complaint is resolved. The figure goes up to a staggering 95 percent if the customer feels the complaint was resolved quickly. Customers whose complaints were satisfactorily resolved tell an average of five people about the good treatment they received."[30]

More companies are recognizing the benefits of satisfying and retaining current customers. Remember, acquiring new customers can cost five times more than the cost of satisfying and retaining current customers. On average, companies lose 10 percent of their customers each year. Yet by reducing the customer defection rate by 5 percent, companies can increase profits by 25 percent to 85 percent, depending on the industry. Also, the customer profit rate tends to increase over the life of the retained customer.[31]

Figure 4.3 shows the customer-development process. The starting point is everyone who might conceivably buy the product or service (*suspects*). From these the company determines the most likely prospects, who it hopes to convert into *first-time customers*, then into *repeat customers*, and then into *clients*, whom the company treats as special. The next challenge is to turn clients into *members* by starting a program that offers benefits to customers who join and then into *advocates* who recommend the company and its offerings to others. The ultimate challenge is to turn advocates into *partners*.

FIGURE 4.3   The Customer-Development Process

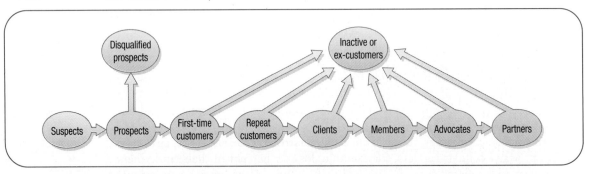

Source: See Jill Griffin, *Customer Loyalty: How to Earn It, How to Keep It* (New York: Lexington Books, 1995), p. 36. Also see Murray Raphel and Neil Raphel, *Up the Loyalty Ladder: Turning Sometime Customers into Full-Time Advocates of Your Business* (New York: HarperBusiness, 1995).

Building Loyalty

How much should a company invest in building loyalty so that the costs do not exceed the gains? We can distinguish five levels of investment in customer relationship building:

1. *Basic marketing.* Simply selling the product.
2. *Reactive marketing.* Selling the product and encouraging customers to offer questions, comments, or complaints.
3. *Accountable marketing.* Following up after the sale to see whether the product meets expectations and to ask for improvement suggestions and any specific disappointments.
4. *Proactive marketing.* Contacting customers periodically with suggestions about new product uses or new products.
5. *Partnership marketing.* Working continuously with customers to find ways to perform better.

Most companies practice only basic marketing when their markets contain many customers and their unit profit margins are small. Whirlpool is not going to phone each washing machine buyer to express appreciation. At best, it may set up a customer hot line or e-mail process. At the other extreme, marketers with few customers and high profit margins can move toward partnership marketing. Boeing, for example, works closely with American Airlines to design airplanes that fully satisfy American's requirements. As Figure 4.4 shows, the likely level of relationship marketing depends on the number of customers and the profit margin level.

Reducing Customer Defection

Companies can take five main steps to reduce defection. First, the firm must define and measure its retention rate. For a magazine, the renewal rate is a good retention measure. For a college, it could be the first- to second-year retention rate or the class graduation rate. Second, the company must distinguish the causes of customer attrition and identify those that can be managed better. The Forum Corporation analyzed the customers lost by 14 major companies for reasons other than leaving the area or going out of business: 15 percent switched to a better product; 15 percent found a cheaper product; and 70 percent left because of poor or little attention from the

FIGURE 4.4   Levels of Relationship Marketing

	High Margin	Medium Margin	Low Margin
Many customers/ distributors	Accountable	Reactive	Basic or reactive
Medium number of customers/ distributors	Proactive	Accountable	Reactive
Few customers/ distributors	Partnership	Proactive	Accountable

supplier. Clearly, firms can take steps to retain customers who leave because of poor service, shoddy products, or high prices.[32]

Third, the company needs to estimate how much profit it loses when it loses customers. For one customer, the lost profit is equal to the **customer lifetime value**—the present value of the profit stream that the company would have realized if the customer had not defected prematurely—through some of the preceding calculations. Fourth, the company needs to figure out how much it would cost to reduce the defection rate. As long as the cost is less than the lost profit, the company should spend the money. Finally, nothing beats plain old listening to customers. Deere & Company, which makes John Deere tractors, has retired employees interviewing defectors and customers. Listening helps Deere retain nearly 98 percent of its customers in some product areas.[33]

Forming Strong Customer Bonds

Companies that want to develop strong customer bonds can follow three value-building approaches, say Berry and Parasuraman: adding financial benefits, adding social benefits, and adding structural ties.[34]

Adding Financial Benefits Two financial benefits that help companies bond customers more closely are frequency programs and club marketing programs. **Frequency programs (FPs)** reward customers who buy frequently and/or in substantial amounts.[35] Frequency marketing acknowledges that 20 percent of a company's customers might account for 80 percent of its business.

American Airlines was a frequency program pioneer when it began offering free mileage credit to its customers in the early 1980s. Hotels next adopted FPs, with frequent guests receiving room upgrades or free rooms after earning so many points. Car rental firms soon started FPs, then credit-card companies began to offer points and rebates for card usage. Today most supermarket chains offer price club cards, which provide member customers with discounts on particular items.[36] Typically, the first company to introduce an FP gains the most benefit. After competitors respond, FPs can become a financial burden to all of the offering companies.

Many companies have created club membership programs. Club membership can be open to everyone who purchases a product or service, or it can be limited to an affinity group or to those willing to pay a small fee. Although open clubs are good for building a database or snagging customers from competitors, limited membership clubs are more powerful long-term loyalty builders. Fees and membership conditions prevent those with only a fleeting interest in a company's products from joining. Limited membership clubs attract and keep those customers who are responsible for the largest portion of business.

Adding Social Benefits Company personnel work on increasing social bonds with customers by individualizing and personalizing customer relationships. In essence, thoughtful companies turn their customers into clients. Donnelly, Berry, and Thompson draw this distinction: "Customers may be nameless to the institution; clients cannot be nameless. Customers are served as part of the mass or as part of larger segments; clients are served on an individual basis. Customers are served by anyone who happens to be available; clients are served by the professional assigned to them."[37]

Adding Structural Ties The company may supply special equipment or computer linkages to help customers manage their orders, payroll, inventory, and so on. A good example is McKesson Corporation, a leading pharmaceutical wholesaler, which invested millions of dollars in electronic capabilities to help independent pharmacies manage inventory, order entry processes, and shelf space. The marketer's goal should be to increase the consumer's *proclivity to repurchase* the company's brand. Wunderman suggests creating structural ties with the customer by:[38]

1. *Creating long-term contracts.* A newspaper subscription replaces the need to buy a newspaper each day; a twenty-year mortgage replaces the need to reborrow money each year.
2. *Charging less for ongoing purchases.* Offer lower prices to people who agree to be supplied regularly with a certain brand of toothpaste, detergent, or beer.
3. *Turning the product into a long-term service.* DaimlerChrysler could sell "miles of reliable transportation" instead of cars, with the consumer able to lease different cars at different times or for different occasions, such as a station wagon for shopping and a convertible for the weekend.

Customer Databases and Database Marketing

Marketers must know their customers, and in order to know its customers, the company must collect information, store it in a database, and do database marketing. A **customer database** is an organized collection of comprehensive information about individual customers or prospects that is current, accessible, and actionable for such marketing purposes as lead generation, lead qualification, sale of a product or service, or maintenance of customer relationships. **Database marketing** is the process of building, maintaining, and using customer databases and other databases (products, suppliers, resellers) to make contact, facilitate transactions, and build customer relationships.

A customer database contains much more information than a *customer mailing list*, which is simply a set of names, addresses, and telephone numbers. Ideally, a customer database would contain the consumer's past purchases, demographics (age, income, family members, birthdays), psychographics (activities, interests, and opinions), mediagraphics (preferred media), and other useful information. A **business database** should contain past purchases of business customers; past volumes, prices, and profits; buyer team member names (and their ages, birthdays, hobbies, and favorite foods); status of current contracts; an estimate of the supplier's share of the customer's business; competitive suppliers; assessment of competitive strengths and weaknesses in selling and servicing the account; and buying practices, patterns, and policies.

Figure 4.5 shows a method for selectively gaining greater share of a customer's business, based on the presumption that the firm has a deep understanding of the customer.

Data Warehouses and Data Mining Savvy companies capture information every time a customer comes into contact with any of its departments by making a purchase, requesting a service call, sending an online query or returning a mail-in rebate card. They store this information in a **data warehouse** and analyze it to draw inferences about each individual customer's needs and responses. This allows the company's

FIGURE 4.5   Increasing Customer Share of Requirements

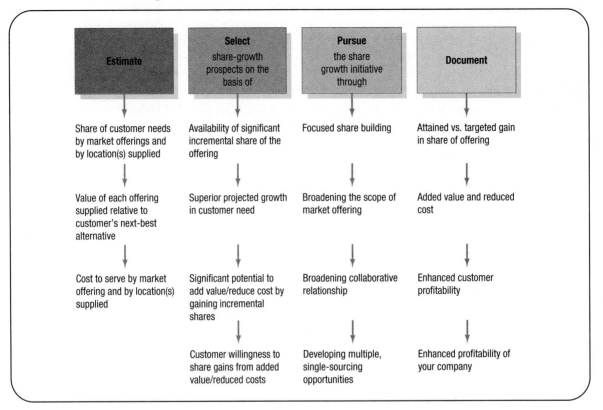

customer service reps or telemarketers to respond knowledgeably to customer inquiries based on a total picture of the customer relationship. Through **data mining**,[39] marketing statisticians can extract useful information about individuals, trends, and segments from a massive data warehouse. Datamining involves the use of sophisticated statistical and mathematical techniques such as cluster analysis, automatic interaction detection, predictive modeling, and neural networking.[40]

In general, companies can use their databases to (1) identify the best prospects by sorting through a mass of responses; (2) match a specific offer with a specific customer as a way to sell, cross-sell, and up-sell; (3) deepen customer loyalty by remembering customer preferences and offering relevant incentives and information; (4) reactivate customer purchasing through reminders or timely promotions; and (5) avoid serious mistakes such as sending a customer two offers for the same product but at different prices.

The Downside of Database Marketing and CRM Four problems can deter a firm from effectively using database marketing for CRM. The first is the large investment in computer hardware, database software, analytical programs, communication links, and skilled personnel as well as the difficulty in collecting the right data on all the occasions of company interaction with individual customers. Thus, building a customer database would not be worthwhile where the product is a once-in-a-lifetime purchase (e.g., a grand piano); where customers show little brand loyalty; where the unit sale is very small (e.g., a candy bar); and where the cost of gathering data is extremely high.

The second problem is the difficulty of getting everyone in the company to be customer oriented and to use the available information for CRM rather than carrying on traditional transaction marketing. The third problem is that not all customers want an ongoing relationship with a company and may resent having their personal data collected and stored. Marketers must be concerned about customer attitudes toward privacy and security. For example, America Online, under fire from privacy advocates, junked a plan to sell subscribers' telephone numbers. Online companies would be smart to explain their privacy policies and allow consumers to avoid having their information stored in a database.

A fourth problem is that the assumptions behind CRM may not always hold true.[41] For example, it may not always cost less to serve more loyal customers. High-volume customers often know their value and can extract premium service and/or price discounts; loyal customers may expect and demand more from the firm and resent the company charging full or higher prices. One consulting firm reported that 70 percent of companies found little or no improvement from implementing a CRM system. The companies' reasons were that the system was poorly designed, it became too expensive, employees didn't make much use of it or report much benefit, and so on. Thus, each company must determine how much to invest in building and using database marketing to manage its customer relationships.

EXECUTIVE SUMMARY

Customers are value maximizers. They form an expectation of value and act on it. Buyers will buy from the firm that they perceive to offer the highest customer-delivered value, defined as the difference between total customer value and total customer cost. Satisfaction is a function of the product's perceived performance and the customer's expectations. Recognizing that high satisfaction leads to high customer loyalty, many companies today are aiming for total customer satisfaction. For such companies, customer satisfaction is both a goal and a marketing tool. Satisfaction also depends on quality, the totality of features and characteristics of a product or service that bear on its ability to satisfy stated or implied needs.

Companies need to understand which customers are profitable and calculate the customer lifetime value, which is the net present value of the stream of future profits expected over the customer's lifetime purchases. Losing profitable customers, especially through high customer churn, can dramatically affect a firm's profits. The cost of attracting a new customer is estimated to be five times the cost of keeping a current customer happy. The key to retention is customer relationship marketing, the process of managing detailed information about individual customers and managing all customer touch points to maximize loyalty. Three ways to develop strong customer bonds are to add financial benefits, add social benefits, and add structural ties.

To get to know its customers, the company must collect information, store it in a customer database, and do database marketing. This means building, maintaining, and using customer databases and other databases for the purpose of contacting, transacting, and building customer relationships. Data stored in a data warehouse are analyzed through data mining to extract useful information about customer needs, segments, and trends. In this way, marketers can identify the best prospects, match a specific offer with a specific customer, offer relevant incentives, reactivate customer purchasing, and avoid serious marketing mistakes.

NOTES

1. Mike Gatz, "Giving Brains to Off-Highway Brawn," *Machine Design*, March 3, 2005, pp. 69+; Frank Byrt, "Caterpillar's Earnings Rose 38% in Quarter on Strong Revenue," *Wall Street Journal*, April 21, 2005, p. A9; Hubble Smith, "Caterpillar's Diversity Helps Company During Economic Slumps, Executive Says," *Las Vegas Review-Journal*, March 21, 2002 (*www.lvrj.com*); Jill Jusko, "Caterpillar Program Aims to Drive Down Costs, Improve Collaboration," *Industry Week*, September 24, 2001 (*www.industryweek.com*); Dave Mowitz, "Niche Marketing to Large Farms Helps Small Operations as Well," *Successful Farming*, December 15, 2001, p. 29; Barb Baylor Anderson, "Caterpillar Relies on Customer Input for Tractor Launch," *Agri Marketing*, November–December 2001, pp. 40+.
2. Glen L. Urban, "The Emerging Era of Customer Advocacy," *MIT Sloan Management Review*, Winter 2004, pp. 77–82.
3. See Irwin P. Levin and Richard D. Johnson, "Estimating Price-Quality Tradeoffs Using Comparative Judgments," *Journal of Consumer Research* (June 11, 1984): 593–600. Customer perceived value can be measured as a difference or as a ratio. If total customer value is $20,000 and total customer cost is $16,000, then the customer perceived value is $4,000 (measured as a difference) or 1.25 (measured as a ratio). Ratios that are used to compare offers are often called *value-price ratios*.
4. For more on customer perceived value, see David C. Swaddling and Charles Miller, *Customer Power* (Dublin, Ohio: The Wellington Press, 2001).
5. Gary Hamel, "Strategy as Revolution," *Harvard Business Review* (July–August 1996): 69–82.
6. Michael J. Lanning, *Delivering Profitable Value* (Oxford, U.K.: Capstone, 1998).
7. For some provocative analysis, see Susan Fournier and David Glenmick, "Rediscovering Satisfaction," *Journal of Marketing* (October 1999): 5–23.
8. Sally B. Donnelly, "Friendlier Skies," *Time*, January 26, 2004, pp. 39–40; Arlyn Tobias Gahilan, "The Amazing JetBlue," *FSB: Fortune Small Business*, May 2003, pp. 50–60.
9. Thomas O. Jones and W. Earl Sasser Jr., "Why Satisfied Customers Defect," *Harvard Business Review* (November–December 1995): 88–99.
10. Note that managers and salespeople can manipulate customer satisfaction ratings: They can be especially nice to customers just before the survey; they can also try to exclude unhappy customers. Another danger is that if customers know the company will go out of its way to please them, some may express high dissatisfaction in order to receive more concessions.
11. Christine Zimmerman, "Consumer Reports: Web-Based Results from Customer Surveys Give McAlister's Solutions for Satisfaction," *Chain Leader*, April 2005, pp. 48+; Jack Hayes, "Industry Execs: Best Customer Feedback Info Is 'Real' Thing," *Nation's Restaurant News*, March 18, 2002, pp. 4+; Leslie Wood and Michael Kirsch, "Performing Your Own Satisfaction Survey," *Agency Sales Magazine*, February 2002, pp. 26; Arlena Sawyers, "Volvo Trims Fat from Buyer Survey," *Automotive News*, February 4, 2002, p. 50.
12. "The Gurus of Quality: American Companies Are Heeding the Quality Gospel Preached by Deming, Juran, Crosby, and Taguchi," *Traffic Management* (July 1990): 35–39.
13. Cyndee Miller, "U.S. Firms Lag in Meeting Global Quality Standards," *Marketing News*, February 15, 1993.

14. Robert D. Buzzell and Bradley T. Gale, *The PIMS Principles: Linking Strategy to Performance* (New York: The Free Press, 1987), ch. 6.

15. Quoted in Don Peppers and Martha Rogers, *The One to One Future: Building Relationships One Customer at a Time* (New York: Currency Doubleday, 1993), p. 108.

16. William A. Sherden, *Market Ownership: The Art & Science of Becoming #1* (New York: Amacom, 1994), p. 77.

17. Robert J. Bowman, "Good Things, Smaller Packages," *World Trade* 6, no. 9 (October 1993): pp. 106–110.

18. Rakesh Niraj, Mahendra Gupta, and Chakravarthi Narasimhan, "Customer Profitability in a Supply Chain," *Journal of Marketing* (July 2001): 1–16.

19. See Thomas M. Petro, "Profitability: The Fifth P of Marketing," *Bank Marketing*, September 1990, pp. 48–52; and Petro, "Who Are Your Best Customers?" *Bank Marketing*, October 1990, pp. 48–52.

20. Michael E. Porter, *Competitive Strategy: Techniques for Analyzing Industries and Competitors* (New York: Free Press, 1980).

21. Greg Farrel, "Marketers Put a Price on Your Life," *USA Today*, July 7, 1999, p.3B.

22. Robert C. Blattberg and John Deighton, "Manage Marketing by the Customer Equity Test," *Harvard Business Review* (July to August 1996): 136–144.

23. Roland T. Rust, Valerie A. Zeithaml, and Katherine A. Lemon, *Driving Customer Equity* (New York: Free Press, 2000).

24. Robert C. Blattberg, Gary Getz, and Jacquelyn S. Thomas, *Customer Equity: Building and Managing Relationships as Valuable Assets* (Boston: Harvard Business School Press, 2001); Robert C. Blattberg and Jacquelyn S. Thomas, "Valuing, Analyzing, and Managing the Marketing Function Using Customer Equity Principles," in *Kellogg on Marketing*, edited by Dawn Iacobucci (New York: John Wiley & Sons, 2002).

25. Nora A. Aufreiter, David Elzinga, and Jonathan W. Gordon, "Better Branding," *The McKinsey Quarterly*, no. 4 (2003): 29–39.

26. Lanning, *Delivering Profitable Value*.

27. Don Peppers and Martha Rogers, *The One-to-One Future: Building Relationships One Customer at a Time;* Don Peppers and Martha Rogers, *Enterprise One to One: Tools for Competing in the Interactive Age* (New York: Currency, 1997); Don Peppers and Martha Rogers, *The One-to-One Manager: Real-World Lessons in Customer Relationship Management* (New York: Doubleday, 1999); Don Peppers, Martha Rogers, and Bob Dorf, *The One-to-One Fieldbook: The Complete Toolkit for Implementing a One-to-One Marketing Program* (New York: Bantam, 1999); Don Peppers and Martha Rogers, *One-to-One B2B: Customer Development Strategies for the Business-To-Business World* (New York: Doubleday, 2001).

28. See Jeffrey Gitomer, *Customer Satisfaction Is Worthless: Customer Loyalty Is Priceless: How to Make Customers Love You, Keep Them Coming Back, and Tell Everyone They Know* (Austin, TX: Bard Press, 1998).

29. Technical Assistance Research Programs (TARP), *U.S. Office of Consumer Affairs Study on Complaint Handling in America*, 1986.

30. Karl Albrecht and Ron Zemke, *Service America!* (Homewood, IL: Dow Jones-Irwin, 1985), pp. 6–7.

31. See Frederick F. Reichheld, *The Loyalty Effect* (Boston: Harvard Business School Press, 1996).

32. See Frederick F. Reichheld, "Learning from Customer Defections," *Harvard Business Review* (March–April 1996): 56–69.

33. Reichheld, "Learning from Customer Defections."

34. Leonard L. Berry and A. Parasuraman, *Marketing Services: Competing Through Quality* (New York: Free Press, 1991), pp. 136–42. See also Richard Cross and Janet Smith, *Customer Bonding: Pathways to Lasting Customer Loyalty* (Lincolnwood, IL: NTC Business Books, 1995).

35. For a review, see Grahame R. Dowling and Mark Uncles, "Do Customer Loyalty Programs Really Work?" *Sloan Management Review* 38, no. 4 (1997): 71–82.

36. Thomas Lee, "Retailers Look for a Hook," *St. Louis Post-Dispatch*, December 4, 2004, p. A1.

37. James H. Donnelly Jr., Leonard L. Berry, and Thomas W. Thompson, *Marketing Financial Services—A Strategic Vision* (Homewood, IL: Dow Jones-Irwin, 1985), p. 113.

38. From a privately circulated paper, Lester Wunderman, "The Most Elusive Word in Marketing," June 2000. Also see Lester Wunderman, *Being Direct* (New York: Random House, 1996).

39. Peter R. Peacock, "Data Mining in Marketing: Part 1," *Marketing Management* (Winter 1998): 9–18, and "Data Mining in Marketing: Part 2," *Marketing Management* (Spring 1998): 15–25; Ginger Conlon, "What the !@#!*?!! Is a Data Warehouse?" *Sales & Marketing Management* (April 1997): 41–48; Skip Press, "Fool's Gold? As Companies Rush to Mine Data, They May Dig Up Real Gems—Or False Trends," *Sales & Marketing Management* (April 1997): 58, 60, 62; John Verity, "A Trillion-Byte Weapon," *BusinessWeek*, July 31, 1995, pp. 80–81.

40. James Lattin, Doug Carroll, and Paul Green, *Analyzing Multivariate Data* (Florence, KY: Thomson Brooks/Cole, 2003); Simon Haykin, *Neural Networks: A Comprehensive Foundation*, 2d ed. (Upper Saddle River, NJ: Prentice Hall, 1998); Michael J. A. Berry and Gordon Linoff, *Data Mining Techniques: For Marketing, Sales, and Customer Support* (New York: John Wiley & Sons, 1997).

41. Werner Reinartz and V. Kumar, "The Mismanagement of Customer Loyalty," *Harvard Business Review* (July 2002): 86–94; Susan M. Fournier, Susan Dobscha, and David Glen Mick, "Preventing the Premature Death of Relationship Marketing," *Harvard Business Review* (January–February 1998): 42–51.

CHAPTER 5

Analyzing Consumer Markets

In this chapter, we will address the following questions:

1. How do cultural, social, and personal factors influence consumer buying behavior?
2. What major psychological processes influence consumer behavior to marketing stimuli?
3. How do consumers make purchasing decisions?

MARKETING MANAGEMENT AT NIKE

More than forty years after Nike hit the ground running with high-performance footwear for serious athletes, it remains the dominant force in that industry. Nike's marketing has always featured winning athletes, a decision to take advantage of what the company calls the "pyramid of influence," in which product and brand choices are influenced by the preferences and behavior of a small percentage of top athletes. One of its most successful campaigns, titled "Just Do It," challenged athletic enthusiasts to chase their goal—a natural manifestation of Nike's attitude of self-empowerment through sports.

As the company began expanding into Europe, however, it found that its American-style ads were seen as too aggressive and its brand image was perceived as too fashion-oriented. Nike realized it had to "authenticate" its brand overseas the way it had in America by associating its shoes with well-known area athletes. The big break came in 1994, when the Brazilian team (at the time, the only national team for which Nike had any real sponsorships) won the World Cup. The victory led Nike to sign other winning teams, and by 2003 overseas revenues surpassed U.S. revenues for the first time. Today Nike continues to connect with consumers in innovative ways. Recently, it put up an electronic billboard in New York City's Times Square to promote NikeID personalized shoes. Thousands of consumers called in and created unique shoe designs using the telephone keypad to make color choices. The giant billboard flashed each personalized design for 60 seconds, and then stored the image on a Web site for the creator to download and—of course—order a pair, or even two.[1]

The aim of marketing is to meet and satisfy target customers' needs and wants better than competitors. **Consumer behavior** is the study of how individuals, groups, and organizations select, buy, use, and dispose of goods, services, ideas, or experiences to satisfy their needs and desires. Applying the holistic marketing orientation, marketers that gain an in-depth understanding of consumers can more effectively market the right products to the right consumers in the right way. Knowing this, Nike researches what consumers want and need, uses marketing to reinforce brand associations with top athletes, and allows consumers to express themselves through personalized shoe designs. This chapter explores individual consumer buyer dynamics; the next chapter explores the buying dynamics of businesses.

WHAT INFLUENCES CONSUMER BEHAVIOR?

The starting point for understanding consumer buying behavior is the stimulus-response model shown in Figure 5.1. Both marketing and environmental stimuli enter the buyer's consciousness. In turn, the combination of consumer characteristics and psychological processes results in decision processes and a purchase. The marketer's task is to understand what happens in the consumer's consciousness between the arrival of outside stimuli and the ultimate purchase decision.

As Figure 5.1 shows, a consumer's buying behavior is influenced by cultural, social, and personal factors. Cultural factors exert the broadest and deepest influence.

Cultural Factors

Culture, subculture, and social class are particularly important influences on consumer buying behavior. **Culture** is the most fundamental determinant of a person's wants and

FIGURE 5.1   Model of Consumer Behavior

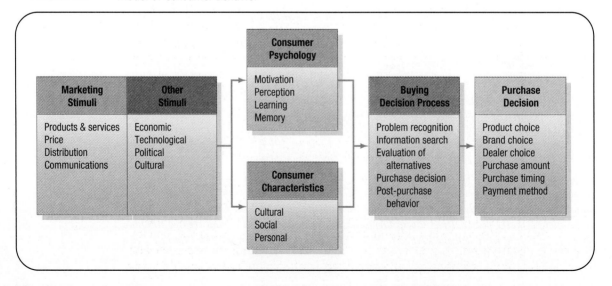

behavior. A child growing up in the United States is exposed to these broad cultural values: achievement and success, activity, efficiency and practicality, progress, material comfort, individualism, freedom, external comfort, humanitarianism, and youthfulness.[2]

Each culture consists of smaller subcultures that provide more specific identification and socialization for their members. Subcultures include nationalities, religions, racial groups, and geographic regions. When subcultures grow large and affluent enough, companies often design specialized marketing programs to serve them. *Multicultural marketing* grew out of careful marketing research showing that ethnic and demographic niches did not always respond favorably to mass-market advertising. For instance, the 40 million Hispanic Americans are attractive to bank and life insurance marketers because, despite rising income levels, they are not yet big consumers of financial services.

Social classes are relatively homogeneous and enduring divisions in a society. They are hierarchically ordered and their members share similar values, interests, and behavior. One classic depiction of social classes in the United States defined seven ascending levels, as follows: (1) lower lowers, (2) upper lowers, (3) working class, (4) middle class, (5) upper middles, (6) lower uppers, and (7) upper uppers.[3]

Those within each class tend to behave more alike than do persons from different social classes. Social classes differ in dress, speech patterns, recreational preferences, and many other characteristics. In addition, persons are perceived as occupying inferior or superior positions according to social class. Note that social class is indicated by a cluster of variables—such as occupation, income, and education—rather than by any single variable. Finally, individuals can move up or down the social-class ladder during their lifetime. Marketers need to be aware that social classes show distinct product and brand differences in many areas; because of language differences, they also must use advertising copy and dialogue that ring true to the targeted class.

Social Factors

In addition to cultural factors, a consumer's behavior is influenced by such social factors as reference groups, family, and social roles and statuses.

Reference Groups   **Reference groups** consist of all of the groups that have a direct (face-to-face) or indirect influence on a person's attitudes or behavior. Groups having a direct influence on a person are called **membership groups**. Some *primary groups* are family, friends, neighbors, and co-workers, with whom individuals interact fairly continuously and informally. *Secondary groups*, such as professional and trade-union groups, tend to be more formal and require less continuous interaction. Reference groups expose people to new behaviors and lifestyles, influence attitudes and self-concept, and create pressures for conformity that may affect product and brand choices. People are also influenced by groups to which they do not belong. **Aspirational groups** are those that the person hopes to join; **dissociative groups** are those whose values or behavior an individual rejects.

Manufacturers of products and brands where group influence is strong must reach and influence the opinion leaders in these reference groups. An **opinion leader** is the person in informal, product-related communications who offers advice or information about a specific product or product category.[4] Marketers try to reach opinion leaders by identifying demographic and psychographic characteristics associated with opinion leadership, identifying the preferred media of opinion leaders, and directing messages at opinion leaders. In Japan, high school girls have often been credited with creating the buzz that makes products such as Shiseido's Neuve nail polish a big hit.[5] In the United States, the hottest trends in teenage music, language, and fashion often start in the inner cities. Therefore, clothing companies like Hot Topic carefully monitor urban opinion leaders' style and behavior.

Family The family is the most important consumer buying organization in society, and family members are the most influential primary reference group.[6] The **family of orientation** consists of parents and siblings. From parents, a person acquires an orientation toward religion, politics, and economics, as well as a sense of personal ambition, self-worth, and love.[7] A more direct influence on the everyday buying behavior of adults is the **family of procreation**—namely, one's spouse and children.

The makeup of the American family has been changing.[8] The U.S. Census Bureau's newest numbers show that married-couple households—the dominant cohort since the country's founding—have slipped from nearly 80 percent in the 1950s to roughly 50 percent today. That means that the United States' 86 million single adults could soon define the new majority. Already, unmarrieds make up 42 percent of the workforce, 40 percent of homebuyers, 35 percent of voters, and one of the most powerful consumer groups. Marketers will have to pay attention not only to the buying habits of "singletons" who have delayed marriage, but also to cohabiting partners, divorced parents who share custody, single parents by choice, and same-sex couples who may or may not have children.

Marketers are interested in the roles and relative influence of family members in the purchase of a large variety of offerings. For example, companies are realizing that men aren't the main buyers of high-tech gizmos and gadgets these days. Women actually buy more technology than men do, which is why some savvy electronics stores are heeding women's complaints of being ignored, patronized, or offended by salespeople. The RadioShack chain began actively recruiting female store managers; now a woman manages about one out of every seven stores.[9]

Nevertheless, men and women may respond differently to marketing messages.[10] One study showed that women valued relationships with family and friends and placed a high priority on people, whereas men related more to competition and placed a high priority on action. Aware of these differences, Gillette Co. researched psychological issues specific to women and then designed its Venus razor to fit a woman's hand.

Another shift in buying patterns is an increase in the amount of money spent and influence wielded by children and teens.[11] Children age 4 to 12 directly or indirectly influence an estimated $500 billion in annual household purchases.[12] Indirect influence means that parents know the brands, product choices, and preferences of their children without hints or outright requests; direct influence refers to children's hints, requests, and demands. By the time children are around 2 years old, they can often recognize characters, logos, and specific brands. Marketers are tapping into that audience with product tie-ins, placed at a child's eye level, on just about everything—from Scooby Doo vitamins to Elmo juice and cookies.[13]

Roles and Statuses A person participates in many groups, such as family, clubs, or organizations. The person's position in each group can be defined in terms of role and status. A **role** consists of the activities a person is expected to perform. Each role carries a **status**. A Supreme Court justice has more status than a sales manager, and a sales manager has more status than an office clerk. People choose products that communicate their role and status in society. Company presidents often drive Mercedes, wear expensive suits, and drink expensive wines. Savvy marketers are aware of the status symbol potential of their products and brands.

Personal Factors

Consumer buying decisions are also influenced by personal characteristics, including the buyer's age; stage in the life cycle; occupation; economic circumstances; personality and self-concept; and lifestyle and values.

Age and Stage in the Life Cycle   People buy different goods and services over a lifetime. They eat baby food in the early years, most foods in the growing and mature years, and special diets in the later years. Taste in clothes, furniture, and recreation is also age related, which is why smart marketers are attentive to the influence of age. Consumption is also shaped by the *family life cycle* and the number, age, and gender of people in the household at any point in time. In addition, research has identified *psychological* life-cycle stages, indicating that adults experience certain "passages" or "transformations" in life.[14] Marketers should consider *critical life events or transitions—* marriage, childbirth, illness, divorce, widowhood—as giving rise to new needs that influence consumption behavior.

Occupation and Economic Circumstances   Occupation is another influence on consumption patterns. A blue-collar worker will buy work clothes, while a company president will buy dress suits and a country club membership. Marketers try to identify the occupational groups that have above-average interest in their offerings and sometimes tailor their products for certain occupations. Software manufacturers, for example, design special programs for engineers, lawyers, physicians, and other occupational groups.

Product choice is greatly affected by a consumer's economic circumstances: spendable income (level, stability, and time pattern), savings and assets (including the percentage that is liquid), debts, borrowing power, and attitude toward spending and saving. Luxury-goods makers such as Gucci and Prada can be vulnerable to an economic downturn. If a recession is likely, marketers can redesign, reposition, and reprice their products to offer more value to target customers.

Personality and Self-Concept   Each person has personality characteristics that influence buying behavior. **Personality** refers to the distinguishing psychological traits that lead to relatively consistent and enduring responses to environmental stimuli. Personality is often described in terms of such traits as self-confidence, dominance, autonomy, deference, sociability, defensiveness, and adaptability.[15] Personality can be useful in analyzing consumer behavior. The idea is that brands also have personalities and that consumers are likely to choose brands whose personalities match their own. **Brand personality** is the specific mix of human traits that may be attributed to a particular brand. Jennifer Aaker's research has identified five brand personality traits: sincerity, excitement, competence, sophistication, and ruggedness.[16]

Marketers often try to develop brand personalities that will attract consumers with the same *self-concept*. Yet it is possible that a person's *actual self-concept* (how she views herself) differs from her *ideal self-concept* (how she would like to view herself) and from her *others'-self-concept* (how she thinks others see her). These effects may be more pronounced for publicly consumed products as compared to privately consumed goods.[17] On the other hand, consumers who are sensitive to how others see them are more likely to choose brands whose personalities fit the consumption situation.[18]

Lifestyle and Values   People from the same subculture, social class, and occupation may actually lead quite different lifestyles. A **lifestyle** is a person's pattern of living as expressed in activities, interests, and opinions. Lifestyle portrays the "whole person" interacting with his or her environment. Marketers search for relationships between their products and lifestyle groups. For example, a computer manufacturer might find that most computer buyers are achievement oriented. The marketer may then aim its brand more clearly at the achiever lifestyle. Lifestyles are shaped partly by whether consumers are *money constrained* or *time constrained*. Companies aiming to serve money-constrained consumers will create lower-cost offerings; those aiming to serve time-constrained consumers will create convenient offerings.

Consumer decisions are also influenced by **core values**, the belief systems that underlie consumer attitudes and behaviors. Core values go much deeper than behavior or attitude and determine, at a basic level, people's choices and desires over the long term. Marketers who target consumers on the basis of their values believe that by appealing to people's inner selves, it is possible to influence their outer selves—their purchase behavior.

Key Psychological Processes

Four key psychological processes—motivation, perception, learning, and memory—fundamentally influence consumer responses to marketing stimuli.

Motivation   A person has many needs at any given time. Some needs are *biogenic*; they arise from physiological states of tension such as hunger, thirst, and discomfort. Other needs are *psychogenic*; they arise from psychological states of tension such as the need for recognition, esteem, or belonging. A need becomes a motive when it is aroused to a sufficient level of intensity. A **motive** is a need that is sufficiently pressing to drive the person to act. Three of the best known theories of human motivation—those of Sigmund Freud, Abraham Maslow, and Frederick Herzberg—carry quite different implications for consumer analysis and marketing strategy.

Sigmund Freud assumed that the psychological forces shaping people's behavior are largely at the subconscious level and that people cannot fully understand their own motivations. In line with Freud's theory, consumers react not only to the stated capabilities of specific brands, but also to other less-conscious cues. Shape, size, weight, material, color, and brand name can all trigger certain associations and emotions. A technique called *laddering* can be used to trace a person's motivations from the stated instrumental ones to the more terminal ones. Then the marketer can decide at what level to develop the message and appeal.[19]

Abraham Maslow sought to explain why people are driven by particular needs at particular times.[20] His theory is that human needs are arranged in a hierarchy, from the most to the least pressing. In order of importance, these are physiological, safety, social, esteem, and self-actualization needs. A consumer will try to satisfy the most important need first; when that need is satisfied, the person will try to satisfy the next most pressing need. Maslow's theory helps marketers understand how various products fit into the plans, goals, and lives of consumers.

Frederick Herzberg developed a two-factor theory that distinguishes *dissatisfiers* (factors that cause dissatisfaction) from *satisfiers* (factors that cause satisfaction).[21] The absence of dissatisfiers is not enough; satisfiers must be present to motivate a purchase. For example, a computer that comes without a warranty would be a dissatisfier.

Yet the presence of a product warranty would not act as a satisfier or motivator of a purchase, because it is not a source of intrinsic satisfaction with the computer. Ease of use would, however, be a satisfier. In line with this theory, marketers should avoid dissatisfiers that might unsell their products. They should also identify and supply the major satisfiers or motivators of purchase because these satisfiers determine which brand consumers will buy.

Perception   A motivated person is ready to act, yet how that person actually acts is influenced by his or her perception of the situation. **Perception** is the process by which an individual selects, organizes, and interprets information inputs to create a meaningful picture of the world.[22] Perception depends not only on physical stimuli but also on the stimuli's relation to the surrounding field and on conditions within the individual. The key point is that perceptions can vary widely among individuals exposed to the same reality because of three perceptual processes: selective attention, selective distortion, and selective retention.

People are exposed to many daily stimuli such as ads; most of these stimuli are screened out—a process called *selective attention.* The result is that marketers must work hard to attract consumers' attention. Through research, marketers have learned that people are more likely to notice stimuli that relate to a current need; this is why car shoppers notice car ads but not appliance ads. Furthermore, people are more likely to notice stimuli that they anticipate, such as computers on display in an electronics store. People are also more likely to notice stimuli whose deviations are large in relation to the normal size of the stimuli, such as an ad offering a $100 discount (not just $5).

Even noticed stimuli do not always come across the way that marketers intend. *Selective distortion* is the tendency to twist information into personal meanings and interpret information in a way that fits our preconceptions. Consumers will often distort information to be consistent with prior product and brand beliefs.[23] Selective distortion can work to the advantage of marketers with strong brands when consumers distort neutral or ambiguous brand information to make it more positive. In other words, beer may seem to taste better, or a car may seem to drive more smoothly, depending on the particular brands involved.

People forget much information to which they are exposed but will tend to retain information that supports their attitudes and beliefs. Because of *selective retention*, we are likely to remember good points mentioned about a product we like and forget good points about competing products. Selective retention again works to the advantage of strong brands; it also explains why marketers repeat messages to ensure that the information is not overlooked.

Learning   When people act, they learn. **Learning** involves changes in an individual's behavior that arise from experience. Most human behavior is learned. Theorists believe that learning is produced through the interplay of drives, stimuli, cues, responses, and reinforcement. A **drive** is a strong internal stimulus that impels action. **Cues** are minor stimuli that determine when, where, and how a person responds.

Suppose you buy a Dell computer. If your experience is rewarding, your response to computers and Dell will be positively reinforced. Later, when you want to buy a printer, you may assume that because Dell makes good computers, it also makes good printers. You have now generalized your response to similar stimuli. A counter-tendency to generalization is *discrimination*, in which the person learns to recognize differences in sets of similar stimuli and adjust responses accordingly. Applying learning theory, marketers can build up demand for a product by associating it with strong drives, using motivating cues, and providing positive reinforcement.

Memory   All the information and experiences individuals encounter as they go through life can end up in their long-term memory. Cognitive psychologists distinguish between *short-term memory (STM)*—a temporary repository of information—and *long-term memory (LTM)*—a more permanent repository.

Most widely accepted views of long-term memory structure involve some kind of associative model formulation.[24] For example, the **associative network memory model** views LTM as consisting of a set of nodes and links. *Nodes* are stored information connected by *links* that vary in strength. Any type of information can be stored in the memory network, including information that is verbal, visual, abstract, or contextual. A spreading activation process from node to node determines the extent of retrieval and what information can actually be recalled in any given situation. When a node becomes activated because external information is being encoded (e.g., when a person reads or hears a word or phrase) or internal information is retrieved from LTM (e.g., when a person thinks about some concept), other nodes are also activated if they are sufficiently strongly associated with that node.

Following this model, consumer brand knowledge in memory can be conceptualized as consisting of a brand node in memory with a variety of linked associations. The strength and organization of these associations will be important determinants of the information that can be recalled about the brand. **Brand associations** consist of all brand-related thoughts, feelings, perceptions, images, experiences, beliefs, attitudes, and so on, that become linked to the brand node. Some companies create mental maps that depict consumers' knowledge of a particular brand in terms of the key associations that are likely to be triggered by marketing and their relative strength, favorability, and uniqueness to consumers. Figure 5.2 displays a simple mental map highlighting brand beliefs for a hypothetical consumer of the Dole brand.

ENCODING   *Memory encoding* refers to how and where information gets into memory. Memory encoding can be characterized according to the amount or quantity of processing that information receives at encoding (i.e., how much a person thinks about it) and the nature or quality of processing that information receives at encoding (i.e., the manner in which a person thinks about it). The quantity and quality of processing will be an important determinant of the strength of an association. In general, the more attention placed on the meaning of information during encoding, the stronger the resulting associations in memory will be.[25] Also, the ease with which new information can be integrated into established knowledge structures depends on the nature of that information, in terms of characteristics such as simplicity, vividness, and concreteness. Repeated exposures provide greater opportunity for processing and the potential for stronger associations. However, high levels of repetition for an uninvolving, unpersuasive ad are unlikely to have as much sales impact as lower levels of repetition for an involving, persuasive ad.

RETRIEVAL   *Memory retrieval* refers to how information gets out of memory. According to the associative network memory model, the strength of a brand association increases both the likelihood that that information will be accessible and the ease with which it can be recalled by "spreading activation." Successful recall of brand information by consumers depends on more than the initial strength of that

FIGURE 5.2   Hypothetical Dole Mental Map

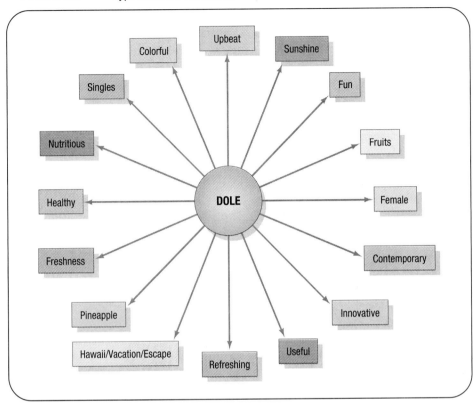

information in memory. Three factors are particularly important. First, *other* product information in memory can produce interference effects, causing one brand's information to be overlooked or confused. Second, the time since exposure to information at encoding affects the strength of a new association; the longer the time delay, the weaker the association.

Finally, information may be "available" in memory (i.e., potentially recallable) but may not be "accessible" (i.e., able to be recalled) without the proper retrieval cues or reminders. The particular associations for a brand that "come to mind" depend on the context in which the brand is considered. The more cues linked to a piece of information, however, the greater the likelihood that the information can be recalled. Thus, in-store marketing not only conveys information at that moment, but also reminds consumers of information conveyed outside the store.

THE BUYING DECISION PROCESS: THE FIVE-STAGE MODEL

Marketers must understand every facet of the consumer buying decision process, from learning about a product to making a brand choice, using the product, and even disposing of it.[26] Figure 5.3 shows a five-stage model of this process. Starting

FIGURE 5.3 Five-Stage Model of the Consumer Buying Process

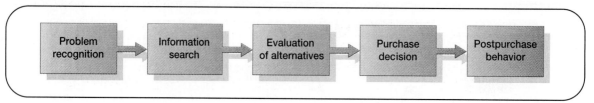

with problem recognition, the consumer passes through the stages of information search, evaluation of alternatives, purchase decision, and postpurchase behavior. Clearly, the buying process starts long before the actual purchase and has consequences long afterward.[27] Although the model implies that consumers pass sequentially through all five stages in buying a product, consumers sometimes skip or reverse some stages. The model provides a good frame of reference, however, because it captures the full range of considerations that arise when a consumer faces a highly involving new purchase.[28]

Problem Recognition

The buying process starts when the buyer recognizes a problem or need, triggered by internal stimuli (such as feeling hunger or thirst) or external stimuli (such as seeing an ad), that then becomes a drive. By gathering information from a number of consumers, marketers can identify the circumstances that trigger a particular need. They can then develop marketing strategies that trigger consumer interest and lead to the second stage in the buying process.

Information Search

An aroused consumer will be inclined to search for more information. We can distinguish between two levels of arousal. At the milder search state of *heightened attention*, a person simply becomes more receptive to information about a product. At the *active information search* level, a person talks with friends, searches online, and visits stores to learn about the product. Information sources fall into four groups: personal sources (family, friends, neighbors, acquaintances), commercial sources (advertising, Web sites, salespersons, dealers, packaging, displays), public sources (mass media, consumer-rating organizations), and experiential sources (handling, examining, using the product). The consumer usually receives the most information from commercial sources, although the most influential information comes from personal sources or public sources that are independent authorities.

Through gathering information, the consumer learns about competing brands and their features. The first box in Figure 5.4 shows the *total set* of brands available to the consumer. The individual consumer will come to know only a subset of these brands (*awareness set*). Some brands will meet initial buying criteria (*consideration set*). As the consumer gathers more information, only a few brands will remain as strong contenders (*choice set*). The consumer makes a final choice from this set.[29]

Figure 5.4 makes it clear that a company must strategize to get its brand into the awareness set, consideration set, and choice set. The company must also identify the

FIGURE 5.4   Successive Sets Involved in Consumer Decision Making

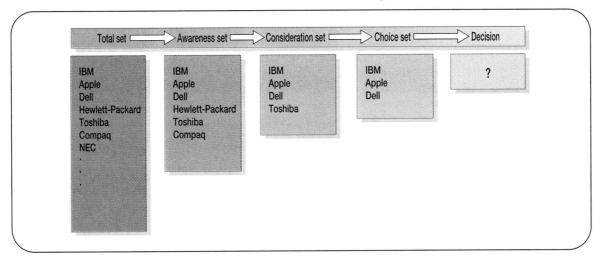

other brands in the consumer's choice set so it can plan appropriate competitive appeals. In addition, the company should identify the consumer's information sources and evaluate their relative importance so it can prepare effective communications for the target market.

Evaluation of Alternatives

How does the consumer process competitive brand information and make a final judgment? There are several evaluation processes; the most current models view the process as being cognitively oriented, meaning that consumers form judgments largely on a conscious and rational basis.

Some basic concepts underlie consumer evaluation processes. First, the consumer is trying to satisfy a need. Second, the consumer is looking for certain benefits from the product solution. Third, each product is viewed as a bundle of attributes with varying abilities for delivering the benefits to satisfy this need. However, the attributes of interest to buyers vary by product. For example, the attributes sought in a camera might be picture sharpness, camera size, and price. In addition, consumers vary as to which product attributes they see as most relevant and the importance they attach to each attribute. Knowing that consumers pay the most attention to attributes that deliver the benefits they seek, marketers can segment their markets according to the attributes that are most important to different consumer groups.

Evaluations often reflect beliefs and attitudes that consumers acquire through experience and learning. These in turn influence buying behavior. A **belief** is a descriptive thought that a person holds about something. Just as important as beliefs are attitudes. An **attitude** is a person's enduring favorable or unfavorable evaluation, emotional feeling, and action tendencies toward some object or idea. People have attitudes toward almost everything: religion, politics, clothes, music, food. Because attitudes economize on energy and thought, they can be very difficult to change. A company is well advised to fit its product into existing attitudes rather than to try to change attitudes.

The consumer arrives at attitudes (judgments, preferences) toward various brands through an attribute evaluation procedure.[30] He or she develops a set of beliefs about where each brand stands on each attribute. The *expectancy-value model* of attitude formation posits that consumers evaluate products and services by combining their brand beliefs—the positives and negatives—according to importance. This model assumes high **consumer involvement**, the level of engagement and active processing a consumer undertakes in response to a marketing stimulus.

Suppose, for example, that Linda Brown has researched laptop computers and narrowed her choice set to four (A, B, C, D) on the basis of memory capacity, graphics capability, size and weight, and price. If one computer laptop dominated the others on all of the criteria, we could predict that Linda would choose it. However, her choice set consists of laptops that vary in their appeal: She sees that A has the best memory capacity, B has the best graphics capability, C has the best size and weight, and D has the best price.

If we knew the weights that Linda attaches to these attributes, we could more reliably predict her choice. Suppose she assigns 40 percent of the importance to memory capacity, 30 percent to graphics capability, 20 percent to size and weight, and 10 percent to price. To find Linda's perceived value for each computer, we multiply her weights by her beliefs about each computer's attributes. So for computer A, if she assigns a score of 8 for memory capacity, 9 for graphics capability, 6 for size and weight, and 9 for price, the overall score would be:

$$0.4 (8) + 0.3 (9) + 0.2 (6) + 0.1 (9) = 8.0$$

Calculating the scores for all of the other computers that Linda is evaluating would show which one has the highest perceived value.[31] Thus, a computer manufacturer who knows how buyers form preferences might take several steps to influence consumer decisions: redesign the computer (real repositioning); alter consumer beliefs about the brand (psychological repositioning); alter consumer beliefs about competitors' brands (competitive depositioning); alter the importance weights (to persuade buyers to attach more importance to attributes in which the brand excels); call attention to neglected attributes (such as styling); or shift the buyer's ideals (to persuade buyers to change ideal levels on one or more attributes).[32]

Purchase Decisions

In the fourth stage, the consumer forms preferences among brands in the choice set and may also form an intention to buy the most preferred brand. Two factors can intervene between the purchase intention and decision.[33] The first is the *attitudes of others*. The extent to which another person's attitude reduces one's preferred alternative depends on two things: (1) the intensity of the other person's negative attitude toward the consumer's preferred alternative, and (2) the consumer's motivation to comply with the other person's wishes.[34] The more intense the other person's negativism and the closer the other person is to the consumer, the more the consumer will adjust his or her purchase intention; conversely, a buyer's preference for a brand will increase if someone respected favors that brand strongly.

The second factor is *unanticipated situational factors* that may erupt to change the purchase intention. A consumer could lose his job, some other purchase might become more urgent, or a store salesperson may offend him, which is why preferences and purchase intentions are not completely reliable predictors of purchase behavior. A consumer's decision to modify, postpone, or avoid a purchase decision is heavily influenced by *perceived risk*.[35] The amount of perceived risk varies with the amounts of money at stake; attribute uncertainty; and consumer self-confidence. Consumers develop routines for reducing risk, such as decision avoidance, information gathering from friends, and preference for national brand names and warranties. Marketers must understand the factors that provoke a feeling of risk in consumers and then provide information and support to reduce the perceived risk.

Postpurchase Behavior   *cognative dissurance, buyer's remorse*

After the purchase, the consumer might experience dissonance stemming from noticing certain disquieting features or hearing favorable things about other brands—and will be alert to information that supports his or her decision. Thus, the marketer's job does not end when the product is bought. Marketers must monitor postpurchase satisfaction, postpurchase actions, and postpurchase product uses.

The buyer's satisfaction with a purchase is a function of the closeness between the buyer's expectations and the product's perceived performance.[36] If performance falls short of expectations, the customer is *disappointed*; if it meets expectations, the customer is *satisfied*; if it exceeds expectations, the customer is *delighted*. These feelings influence whether the customer buys the product again and talks favorably about it to others. The importance of postpurchase satisfaction suggests that product claims must truthfully represent the product's likely performance. Some sellers might even understate performance levels so consumers experience higher-than-expected satisfaction.

Satisfaction or dissatisfaction with the product will influence subsequent behavior. Satisfied consumers will be more likely to buy the product again. For instance, data on car brand choices show a high correlation between high satisfaction with the last brand bought and intention to rebuy that brand. One survey found that 75 percent of Toyota buyers were highly satisfied and about 75 percent intended to buy a Toyota again; 35 percent of Chevrolet buyers were highly satisfied and about 35 percent intended to buy a Chevrolet again. Satisfied customers also tend to say good things about the brand, which is why many marketers say, "Our best advertisement is a satisfied customer."[37]

Dissatisfied consumers may abandon or return the product; take public action by complaining to the company, going to a lawyer, or complaining to government agencies and other groups; or take private actions such as not buying the product or warning friends.[38] In these cases, the seller has done a poor job of satisfying the customer (see "Marketing Skills: Winning Back Lost Customers" for ideas on how to reverse this situation).[39]

Marketers can use postpurchase communications to reduce product returns and order cancellations.[40] Computer companies, for example, might send messages to new buyers congratulating them on having selected a fine computer, place ads

MARKETING SKILLS: WINNING BACK LOST CUSTOMERS

Customers may defect because they are dissatisfied, have new needs, or simply lose interest in certain offerings. However, marketers can hone their skills to win back lost customers. Former customers know the company and its offerings—and the company knows something about these customers—which means it can cost less to win back a lost customer than to attract a new customer. If marketers carefully analyze each lost customer's profitability, they can invest in winning back customers with good profit potential, which will enhance the bottom line.

Win-back starts with recognizing when, why, and how good customers make the decision to leave. Companies that bill monthly learn quickly when a customer leaves, as do companies that receive complaints or cancellation notices. Businesses with unscheduled or less frequent customer contacts—such as stores and Web sites—may not notice for some time. Marketers can also use informal contacts (such as a phone call from the sales rep) or formal marketing research (such as an exit interview) to uncover the reasons why good customers defect. Analyzing data with an open mind will reveal patterns of dissatisfaction or internal problems. Finally, marketers can apologize where warranted and offer to promptly address concerns. Although price adjustments are sometimes appropriate, there are other ways to reestablish the relationship. For instance, customers appreciate personal contact and having many alternatives. If the first approach fails, the company can try communicating a different offer at a later date.

Consider how Cellular One, which, with its owner Alltel Corp., has 6 percent of the U.S. market for cell phone service, handles defections. Its marketers know that contacting customers right after they switch to another cell phone service may annoy them. Therefore, Cellular One waits one or two months before calling—enough time for customers to have a clearer assessment of why they left and of how their new service relationship is going. When Cellular One calls, some former customers come back because their new provider is not living up to their expectations. At the very least, the company gets more honest and objective feedback about why customers left and what it would take to bring them back—important information in the highly competitive cell phone service market.[41]

showing satisfied brand owners, solicit suggestions for improvements, and provide channels for speedy resolution of customer complaints.

Also, marketers should monitor how buyers use and dispose of the product after purchase (see Figure 5.5). A key driver of sales frequency is product consumption rate—the more quickly a product is consumed, the sooner the buyer may be ready to repurchase it. One potential opportunity for this is when consumers' perceptions of product usage differ from actual product usage. Consumers may fail to replace products with relatively short life spans in a timely manner because of a tendency to underestimate product life.[42] Here, marketers can speed up replacement by linking repurchasing to a certain holiday, event, or time of year.

If consumers throw the product away, the marketer needs to know how they dispose of it, especially if it can hurt the environment. Increased public awareness of recycling and ecological concerns, as well as consumer complaints about having to

FIGURE 5.5   How Consumers Use or Dispose of Products

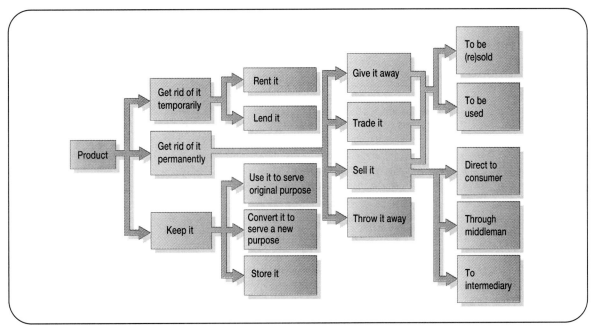

Source: From Jacob Jacoby, Carol K. Berning, and Thomas F. Dietvorst, "What about Disposition?" *Journal of Marketing* (July 1977): 23. Reprinted with permission of the American Marketing Association.

throw away beautiful bottles, led French perfume-maker Rochas to think about introducing a refillable fragrance line.

EXECUTIVE SUMMARY

Consumer behavior is influenced by three factors: cultural (culture, subculture, and social class), social (reference groups, family, and social roles and statuses), personal (age and stage in the life cycle; occupation and economic circumstances; personality and self-concept; and lifestyle and values). The four psychological processes of motivation, perception, learning, and memory also influence consumer responses to marketing stimuli. Research into all of these factors provides clues as to how marketers can reach and satisfy consumers more effectively.

The five-stage model of the consumer buying process consists of problem recognition, information search, evaluation of alternatives, purchase decision, and postpurchase behavior. The marketer's job is to understand the buyer's behavior at each stage—from before to after the purchase—and what influences are operating. Consumers' evaluations of a product, based on attitudes and beliefs acquired through learning and experience, will affect their purchase decisions. The attitudes of others, unanticipated situational factors, and perceived risk also may affect the buying decision, as will consumers' postpurchase satisfaction, the company's postpurchase actions, and consumers' postpurchase use and disposal of the product. Satisfied customers will continue to purchase; dissatisfied customers will stop purchasing the product and may make unfavorable remarks about it to others.

NOTES

1. Mary Cassidy, "Many Paths to Cool, But Big Gains for All," *Brandweek*, June 20, 2005, p. S53; Catherine P. Taylor, "Nike Billboard: A Sign of the Future," *Adweek*, May 30, 2005, p. 26; Justin Ewers and Tim Smart, "A Designer Swooshes In," *U.S. News & World Report*, January 26, 2004, p. 12; "Corporate Media Executive of the Year," *Delaney Report*, January 12, 2004, p. 1; "10 Top Nontraditional Campaigns," *Advertising Age*, December 22, 2003, p. 24; Chris Zook and James Allen, "Growth Outside the Core," *Harvard Business Review* (December 2003): 66+.

2. See Leon G. Schiffman and Leslie Lazar Kanuk, *Consumer Behavior*, 7th ed. (Upper Saddle River, NJ: Prentice Hall, 2000).

3. Richard P. Coleman, "The Continuing Significance of Social Class to Marketing," *Journal of Consumer Research* (December 1983): 265–280; Richard P. Coleman and Lee P. Rainwater, *Social Standing in America: New Dimension of Class* (New York: Basic Books, 1978).

4. Schiffman and Kanuk, *Consumer Behavior*.

5. Norihiko Shirouzu, "Japan's High School Girls Excel in Art of Setting Trends," *Wall Street Journal*, April 27, 1998, pp. B1–B6.

6. Rosann L. Spiro, "Persuasion in Family Decision Making," *Journal of Consumer Research* (March 1983): 393–402; Lawrence H. Wortzel, "Marital Roles and Typologies as Predictors of Purchase Decision Making for Everyday Household Products: Suggestions for Research," in *Advances in Consumer Research*, vol. 7, ed. Jerry C. Olson (Chicago: American Marketing Association, 1989) pp. 212–15; David J. Burns, "Husband–Wife Innovative Consumer Decision Making: Exploring the Effect of Family Power," *Psychology & Marketing*, May–June 1992, pp. 175–89; Robert Boutilier, "Pulling the Family's Strings," *American Demographics*, August 1993, pp. 44–48. For cross-cultural comparisons of husband–wife buying roles, see John B. Ford, Michael S. LaTour, and Tony L. Henthorne, "Perception of Marital Roles in Purchase-Decision Processes: A Cross-Cultural Study," *Journal of the Academy of Marketing Science* (Spring 1995): 120–131.

7. George Moschis, "The Role of Family Communication in Consumer Socialization of Children and Adolescents," *Journal of Consumer Research* (March 1985): 898–913.

8. Michelle Conlin, "Unmarried America," *BusinessWeek*, October 20, 2003, pp. 106–116.

9. Anonymous, "Retailers Learn That Electronics Shopping Isn't Just a Guy Thing," *Wall Street Journal*, January 15, 2004, p. D3.

10. Hillary Chura, "Failing to Connect: Marketing Messages for Women Fall Short," *Advertising Age*, September 23, 2002, pp. 13–14.

11. James U. McNeal, "Tapping the Three Kids' Markets," *American Demographics*, April 1998, pp. 37–41.

12. Carol Angrisani, "Kids Rock!" *Brand Marketing*, February 2001, pp. 26–28.

13. Courtney Kane, "TV and Movie Characters Sell Children's Snacks," *New York Times*, December 8, 2003, p. C7.

14. See Lawrence Lepisto, "A Life Span Perspective of Consumer Behavior," in *Advances in Consumer Research*, vol. 12, ed. Elizabeth Hirshman and Morris Holbrook (Provo, UT: Association for Consumer Research, 1985), p. 47. Also see Gail Sheehy, *New Passages: Mapping Your Life Across Time* (New York: Random House, 1995).

15. See Harold H. Kassarjian and Mary Jane Sheffet, "Personality and Consumer Behavior: An Update," in *Perspectives in Consumer Behavior*, eds. Harold H. Kassarjian and Thomas S. Robertson (Glenview, IL: Scott Foresman, 1981), pp. 160–180.

16. Jennifer Aaker, "Dimensions of Measuring Brand Personality," *Journal of Marketing Research* 34 (August 1997): 347–356.

17. Timothy R. Graeff, "Consumption Situations and the Effects of Brand Image on Consumers' Brand Evaluations," *Psychology & Marketing* 14, no. 1 (1997): 49–70; Timothy

R. Graeff, "Image Congruence Effects on Product Evaluations: The Role of Self-Monitoring and Public/Private Consumption," *Psychology & Marketing* 13, no. 5 (1996): 481–499.

18. Jennifer L. Aaker, "The Malleable Self: The Role of Self-Expression in Persuasion," *Journal of Marketing Research* 36, no. 2 (1999): 45–57.

19. See Thomas J. Reynolds and Jonathan Gutman, "Laddering Theory, Method, Analysis, and Interpretation," *Journal of Advertising Research* (February–March 1988): 11–34.

20. Abraham Maslow, *Motivation and Personality* (New York: Harper & Row, 1954) pp. 80–106.

21. See Frederick Herzberg, *Work and the Nature of Man* (Cleveland, OH: William Collins, 1966); and Henk Thierry and Agnes M. Koopman-Iwerna, "Motivation and Satisfaction," in *Handbook of Work and Organizational Psychology*, ed. P. J. Drenth (New York: John Wiley, 1984), pp. 141–142.

22. Bernard Berelson and Gary A. Steiner, *Human Behavior: An Inventory of Scientific Findings* (New York: Harcourt Brace Jovanovich, 1964), p. 88.

23. J. Edward Russo, Margaret G. Meloy, and T. J. Wilks, "The Distortion of Product Information During Brand Choice," *Journal of Marketing Research* 35 (1998): 438–452.

24. John R. Anderson, *The Architecture of Cognition* (Cambridge, MA: Harvard University Press, 1983); Robert S. Wyer Jr. and Thomas K. Srull, "Person Memory and Judgment," *Psychological Review* 96, no. 1 (1989): 58–83.

25. Fergus I. M. Craik and Robert S. Lockhart, "Levels of Processing: A Framework for Memory Research," *Journal of Verbal Learning and Verbal Behavior* 11 (1972): 671–684; Fergus I. M. Craik and Endel Tulving, "Depth of Processing and the Retention of Words in Episodic Memory," *Journal of Experimental Psychology* 104, no. 3 (1975): 268–294; Robert S. Lockhart, Fergus I. M. Craik, and Larry Jacoby, "Depth of Processing, Recognition, and Recall," in *Recall and Recognition*, ed. John Brown (New York: John Wiley & Sons, 1976).

26. Benson Shapiro, V. Kasturi Rangan, and John Sviokla, "Staple Yourself to an Order," *Harvard Business Review* (July–August 1992): 113–122. See also Carrie M. Heilman, Douglas Bowman, and Gordon P. Wright, "The Evolution of Brand Preferences and Choice Behaviors of Consumers New to a Market," *Journal of Marketing Research* (May 2000): 139–155.

27. Marketing scholars have developed several models of the consumer buying process. See John A. Howard and Jagdish N. Sheth, *The Theory of Buyer Behavior* (New York: Wiley, 1969); James F. Engel, Roger D. Blackwell, and Paul W. Miniard, *Consumer Behavior*, 8th ed. (Fort Worth, TX: Dryden, 1994); Mary Frances Luce, James R. Bettman, and John W. Payne, *Emotional Decisions: Tradeoff Difficulty and Coping in Consumer Choice* (Chicago: University of Chicago Press, 2001).

28. See William P. Putsis, Jr. and Narasimhan Srinivasan, "Buying or Just Browsing? The Duration of Purchase Deliberation," *Journal of Marketing Research* (August 1994): 393–402.

29. See Chem L. Narayana and Rom J. Markin, "Consumer Behavior and Product Performance: An Alternative Conceptualization," *Journal of Marketing*, (October 1975): 1–6. See also Wayne S. DeSarbo and Kamel Jedidi, "The Spatial Representation of Heterogeneous Consideration Sets," *Marketing Science* 14, no. 3, pt. 2 (1995), 326–342; and Lee G. Cooper and Akihiro Inoue, "Building Market Structures from Consumer Preferences," *Journal of Marketing Research* 33, no. 3 (August 1996): 293–306.

30. See Paul E. Green and Yoram Wind, *Multiattribute Decisions in Marketing: A Measurement Approach* (Hinsdale, IL: Dryden, 1973), ch. 2; Leigh McAlister, "Choosing Multiple Items from a Product Class," *Journal of Consumer Research* (December 1979): 213–224; Richard J. Lutz, "The Role of Attitude Theory in Marketing," in eds. Kassarjian and Robertson, *Perspectives in Consumer Behavior*, pp. 317–339.

31. This perceived-value model was developed by Martin Fishbein, "Attitudes and Prediction of Behavior," in *Readings in Attitude Theory and Measurement*, ed. Martin Fishbein (New York: John Wiley, 1967), pp. 477–92. For a critical review, see Paul W. Miniard and Joel B. Cohen, "An Examination of the Fishbein-Ajzen Behavioral-Intentions Model's Concepts and Measures," *Journal of Experimental Social Psychology* (May 1981): 309–339.

32. See Harper W. Boyd Jr., Michael L. Ray, and Edward C. Strong, "An Attitudinal Framework for Advertising Strategy," *Journal of Marketing* (April 1972): 27–33.

33. See Jagdish N. Sheth, "An Investigation of Relationships Among Evaluative Beliefs, Affect, Behavioral Intention, and Behavior," in *Consumer Behavior: Theory and Application*, ed. John U. Farley, John A. Howard, and L. Winston Ring (Boston: Allyn & Bacon, 1974), pp. 89–114.

34. See Fishbein, "Attitudes and Prediction of Behavior."

35. See Raymond A. Bauer, "Consumer Behavior as Risk Taking," in *Risk Taking and Information Handling in Consumer Behavior*, ed. Donald F. Cox (Boston: Division of Research, Harvard Business School, 1967); and James W. Taylor, "The Role of Risk in Consumer Behavior," *Journal of Marketing* (April 1974): 54–60.

36. See Priscilla A. La Barbera and David Mazursky, "A Longitudinal Assessment of Consumer Satisfaction/Dissatisfaction: The Dynamic Aspect of the Cognitive Process," *Journal of Marketing Research* (November 1983): 393–404.

37. See Barry L. Bayus, "Word of Mouth: The Indirect Effects of Marketing Efforts," *Journal of Advertising Research* (June–July 1985): 31–39.

38. See Albert O. Hirschman, *Exit, Voice, and Loyalty* (Cambridge, MA: Harvard University Press, 1970).

39. See Mary C. Gilly and Richard W. Hansen, "Consumer Complaint Handling as a Strategic Marketing Tool," *Journal of Consumer Marketing* (Fall 1985): 5–16.

40. See James H. Donnelly Jr. and John M. Ivancevich, "Post-Purchase Reinforcement and Back-Out Behavior," *Journal of Marketing Research* (August 1970): 399–400.

41. "Alltel Plans to Buy Western Wireless," *Los Angeles Times*, January 11, 2005, p. C6; Jay Kassing, "Increasing Customer Retention: Profitability Isn't a Spectator Sport," *Financial Services Marketing*, March–April 2002, pp. 32+; Jill Griffin and Michael W. Lowenstein, "Winning Back a Lost Customer," *Direct Marketing*, July 2001, pp. 49+; John D. Cimperman, "Win-Back Starts Before Customer Is Lost," *Multichannel News*, February 19, 2001, pp. 53+.

42. John D. Cripps, "Heuristics and Biases in Timing the Replacement of Durable Products," *Journal of Consumer Research* 21 (September 1994): 304–318.

CHAPTER 6

Analyzing Business Markets

In this chapter, we will address the following questions:

1. What is the business market, and how does it differ from the consumer market?
2. What buying situations do organizational buyers face?
3. Who participates in the business-to-business buying process, and how are buying decisions made?
4. How can marketers build strong relationships with business customers?

MARKETING MANAGEMENT AT SAP

German software company SAP has become a leading seller to the business market by specializing in applications to automate business functions such as finance and factory management. SAP has grown annual sales revenue past $10 billion by focusing carefully on what its customers—more than 25,000 businesses worldwide—really value. Moreover, its marketers show customers and prospects how the features of SAP's applications deliver important benefits. "Ten years ago, software customers wanted stability and reliability, and we gave them that," explains CEO Henning Kagermann. "Now they want competitive advantage, differentiation, and most of all, speed."

Partly through acquisitions, SAP is able to offer customers one-stop technology solutions to standardizing a range of business processes. For instance, the company invites customers to mix and match the exact software features they need for solving problems such as how to share information quickly and easily across different communication networks, computer systems, and locations. In fact, SAP's flexible solutions even allow customers to use parts of competing applications if they choose. Also, SAP is targeting the thousands of software developers who customize systems for corporate customers, offering online technical support and assistance. By helping business decision makers and influencers use technology

*in innovative ways to increase both efficiency and effectiveness, SAP is adding to its bottom
line year after year.*[1]

Business organizations do not only sell; they also buy vast quantities of raw materials, manufactured components, plants and equipment, supplies, and business services. SAP buys computer equipment, cleaning services, and other offerings; it also
sells software to thousands of businesses around the world. There are over 13 million
buying organizations in the United States alone. To create and capture value, sellers
such as SAP need to understand these organizations' needs, resources, policies, and
buying procedures—the subject of this chapter.

WHAT IS ORGANIZATIONAL BUYING?

Webster and Wind define **organizational buying** as the decision-making process by
which formal organizations establish the need for purchased products and services and
identify, evaluate, and choose among alternative brands and suppliers.[2] Organizational
buying occurs within the business market, which differs from the consumer market in
a number of significant ways.

The Business Market Versus the Consumer Market

The **business market** consists of all the organizations that acquire goods and services
used in the production of other products or services that are sold, rented, or supplied to
other customers. The major industries making up the business market are agriculture,
forestry, and fisheries; mining; manufacturing; construction; transportation; communication; public utilities; banking, finance, and insurance; distribution; and services.
     More dollars and items are involved in sales to business buyers than to con-
sumers. Consider the process of producing and selling a pair of shoes. Hide dealers
must sell hides to tanners, who sell leather to shoe manufacturers, who sell shoes to
wholesalers, who sell shoes to retailers, who finally sell them to consumers. In turn,
each party in the supply chain also has to buy many other goods and services.
     From the number and size of buyers to geographical location, demand, and buy-
ing behaviors, business markets have a number of characteristics that contrast sharply
with those of consumer markets. These characteristics are described in Table 6.1.

Institutional and Organizational Markets

The overall business market includes institutional and government organizations in
addition to profit-seeking companies. However, the buying goals, needs, and methods
of these two organizational markets generally differ from those of businesses, something firms must keep in mind when planning their business marketing strategies.

The Institutional Market   The **institutional market** consists of schools, hospitals,
nursing homes, prisons, and other institutions that provide goods and services to people
in their care. Many of these organizations have low budgets and captive clienteles. For
example, hospitals have to decide what quality of food to buy for their patients. The buying objective here is not profit, because the food is provided to the patients as part of the
total service package. Nor is cost minimization the sole objective, because poor food will
cause patients to complain and hurt the hospital's reputation. The hospital purchasing

TABLE 6.1   Characteristics of Business Markets

Characteristic	Description	Example
Fewer, larger buyers	Business marketers normally deal with far fewer, much larger buyers than do consumer marketers.	Goodyear Tire Company markets to a few major automakers.
Close supplier–customer relationship	With the smaller customer base and the importance and power of the larger customers, suppliers often must customize offerings to individual business customer needs.	Microsoft depends on 24,000 independent computer consulting firms (value-added resellers) to call on midsize businesses, learn their needs, and provide appropriate software and hardware.
Professional purchasing	Trained purchasing agents follow formal policies, requirements, and constraints when buying. Many of the buying instruments—such as proposals and purchase contracts—are not typical of consumer buying.	Some hospitals buy through group purchasing organizations that negotiate purchase contracts with suppliers and arrange deliveries for individual medical centers.
Multiple buying influences	More people influence business buying decisions; buying committees are common in major purchases. Firms must send knowledgeable salespeople to deal with well-trained buyers.	Salespeople for SecureWorks, a network security firm, talk with key decision makers and invite influencers to participate in Web-based presentations and ask questions.
Multiple sales calls	With more people involved in the process, it takes multiple sales calls to win most business orders, and the sales cycle can take years.	Businesses making major capital equipment purchases may need multiple attempts to fund a project, and the sales cycle—between quoting a job and delivering the product—is often measured in years.
Derived demand	Demand for business goods is ultimately derived from demand for consumer goods, so business marketers must monitor the buying patterns of ultimate consumers.	The Big Three U.S. automakers are seeing higher demand for steel-bar products, mostly derived from consumers' demand for light trucks and similar vehicles, which consume far more steel than cars.
Inelastic demand	Total demand for many business goods and services is inelastic and not much affected by price changes, especially in the short run, because producers cannot make quick production changes.	Shoe manufacturers will not buy much more leather if the price of leather falls. Nor will they buy much less leather if the price rises, unless they can find satisfactory substitutes.
Fluctuating demand	Demand for business products tends to be more volatile than demand for consumer products. An increase in consumer demand can lead to a much larger increase in demand for plant and equipment needed to produce the additional output.	An increase of only 10% in consumer demand might result in a 200% increase in business demand for products and services in the next period; 10% drop in consumer demand might cause a complete collapse in business demand.
Geographically concentrated buyers	More than half of the U.S. business buyers are concentrated in seven states—New York, California, Pennsylvania, Illinois, Ohio, New Jersey, and Michigan—which helps to reduce selling costs.	Because the Big Three U.S. automakers have their U.S. headquarters in the Detroit area, suppliers head there on sales calls.
Direct purchasing	Business buyers often buy directly from manufacturers rather than through intermediaries, especially items that are technically complex or expensive.	Southwest Airlines and other airlines around the world buy airplanes directly from Boeing.

Sources for examples: Jay Greene, "Small Biz: Microsoft's Next Big Thing?" *BusinessWeek*, April 21, 2003, pp. 72–73; "Seeing Double: How Four Companies Overhauled Their Sales Strategies to Spur Growth," *Sales and Marketing Management*, September 2004, pp. 28+; Michael Collins, "Breaking into the Big Leagues," *American Demographics*, January 1996, p. 24; Paula DeJohn, "Central Warehouses Offer Savings, Security," *Hospital Materials Management*, November 2003, pp. 1+.

agent has to search for institutional food vendors whose quality meets or exceeds a certain minimum standard and whose prices are low. Knowing this, many food vendors set up a separate division to respond to the special needs of institutional buyers. Thus, Heinz will produce, package, and price its ketchup differently to meet the different requirements of hospitals, colleges, and prisons.

Being a supplier of choice for the nation's schools or hospitals means big business for marketers such as Cardinal Health. This firm has become the largest U.S. supplier of medical, surgical, and laboratory products. Through its stockless inventory program, Cardinal delivers ordered products to more than 150 hospitals when and where staff members need them. Under the old system, the most-needed items were inevitably in short supply, while the rarely used items were available in great number. Cardinal estimates that stockless inventory saves hospitals an average of $500,000 or more each year.[3]

The Government Market In most countries, government organizations are a major buyer of goods and services. The U.S. government, for example, buys goods and services valued at $200 billion, making it the largest customer in the world. The number of individual purchases is equally staggering: Over 20 million individual contract actions are processed every year. Although the cost of most items purchased is between $2,500 and $25,000, the government also makes purchases in the billions of dollars, often for technology.

Government organizations typically require suppliers to submit bids, and they normally award the contract to the lowest bidder. In some cases, they take into account a supplier's superior quality or reputation for on-time performance. Because their spending decisions are subject to public review, government organizations require considerable documentation from suppliers, who often complain about excessive paperwork, bureaucracy, regulations, decision-making delays, and shifts in procurement personnel. Fortunately for business marketers, the U.S. government has been working to simplify the contracting procedure and make bidding more attractive as well as more efficient.

Buying Situations

Business buyers face many decisions in making a purchase. The number of decisions depends on the buying situation: complexity of the problem being solved, newness of the buying requirement, number of people involved, and time required. Patrick Robinson and others distinguish three types of buying situations: the straight rebuy, the modified rebuy, and the new task.[4]

- *Straight rebuy.* The purchasing department reorders on a routine basis (e.g., office supplies, bulk chemicals). The buyer chooses from suppliers on an "approved list." These suppliers make an effort to maintain product and service quality and often propose automatic reordering systems to save time. "Out-suppliers" attempt to offer something new or to exploit dissatisfaction with a current supplier. Out-suppliers try to get a small order and then enlarge their purchase share over time.
- *Modified rebuy.* The buyer wants to modify product specifications, prices, delivery requirements, or other terms. The modified rebuy usually involves additional

decision participants on both sides. The in-suppliers become nervous and have to protect the account; the out-suppliers see an opportunity to gain some business.

- *New task*. A purchaser buys a product or service for the first time (e.g., office building, new security system). The greater the cost or risk, the larger the number of decision participants and the greater their information gathering—and, therefore, the longer the time to decision completion.[5]

New-task buying passes through several stages: awareness, interest, evaluation, trial, and adoption.[6] Communication tools' effectiveness varies at each stage. Mass media are most important during the initial awareness stage, salespeople have their greatest impact at the interest stage, and technical sources are most important during the evaluation stage.

The business buyer makes the fewest decisions in the straight-rebuy situation and the most in the new-task situation. In the new-task situation, the buyer has to determine product specifications, price limits, delivery terms and times, service terms, payment terms, order quantities, acceptable suppliers, and the selected supplier. Different participants influence each decision and the order in which they make these decisions can vary. The new-task situation is, therefore, the business marketer's greatest opportunity and challenge. For this reason, marketers should try to reach as many key buying influencers as possible and provide helpful information and assistance. Because of the complicated selling involved in new-task situations, many companies use a *missionary sales force* consisting of their best salespeople.

Systems Buying and Selling

Many business buyers prefer to buy a total solution to their problem from one seller. This practice, called *systems buying*, originated with government purchases of major weapons and communication systems. The government solicited bids from *prime contractors*, who would assemble the package or system. The winning contractor then bid out and assembled the system from subcomponents purchased from other contractors. Thus, the prime contractor was providing a *turnkey solution*, so-called because the buyer simply turns one key to get the job done.

Sellers have increasingly recognized that buyers like to purchase in this way, and many have adopted systems selling as a marketing tool. One variant of systems selling is *systems contracting*, where a single supplier provides the buyer with all required MRO supplies (maintenance, repair, and operating supplies). This lowers the buyer's costs because the seller manages the inventory, less time is spent on supplier selection, and provides the buyer with all required MRO (maintenance, repair, and operating) supplies. The seller benefits from lower operating costs because of steady demand and reduced paperwork.

Systems selling is a key industrial marketing strategy in bidding to build large-scale industrial projects such as dams, steel factories, and pipelines. Project engineering firms must compete on price, quality, reliability, and other attributes to win these contracts. For example, when the Indonesian government requested bids to build a cement factory near Jakarta, a U.S. firm made a proposal that included choosing the site, designing the cement factory, hiring the construction crews, assembling the materials and equipment, and turning over the finished factory to the Indonesian government. The Japanese bidder's proposal included all of these services, plus hiring and training the factory workers, exporting the cement, and using the cement to build roads and office buildings in Jakarta. Although the Japanese proposal was more costly, it won. This is true system selling: The firm took the broadest view of its customer's needs.

PARTICIPANTS IN THE BUSINESS BUYING PROCESS

Who buys the trillions of dollars' worth of goods and services needed by business organizations? Purchasing agents are influential in straight-rebuy and modified-rebuy situations, whereas other department personnel are more influential in new-buy situations. Engineering personnel carry the most influence in selecting product components, and purchasing agents dominate in selecting suppliers.[7]

The Buying Center

Webster and Wind call the decision-making unit of a buying organization the **buying center**. The buying center is composed of "all those individuals and groups who participate in the purchasing decision-making process, who share some common goals and the risks arising from the decisions."[8] The buying center includes organizational members who play any of seven roles in the purchase decision process:[9]

1. *Initiators.* People who request that something be purchased, including users or others.
2. *Users.* Those who will use the product or service; often, users initiate the buying proposal and help define product requirements.
3. *Influencers.* People who influence the buying decision, including technical personnel. They often help define specifications and provide information for evaluating alternatives.
4. *Deciders.* Those who decide on product requirements or on suppliers.
5. *Approvers.* People who authorize the proposed actions of deciders or buyers.
6. *Buyers.* People who have formal authority to select the supplier and arrange the purchase terms, including high-level managers. Buyers may help shape product specifications, but their major role is selecting vendors and negotiating.
7. *Gatekeepers.* People who have the power to prevent sellers or information from reaching members of the buying center; examples are purchasing agents, receptionists, and telephone operators.

Several individuals can occupy a given role (e.g., there may be many users or influencers), and the individual may occupy multiple roles.[10] A purchasing manager, for example, often simultaneously occupies the roles of buyer, influencer, and gatekeeper: he or she can determine which sales reps can call on other people in the organization; what budget and other constraints to place on the purchase; and which firm will actually get the business, even though others (deciders) might select two or more potential vendors who can meet the company's requirements. The typical buying center has a minimum of five or six members and often has dozens, including people outside the organization, such as government officials, technical advisors, and members of the marketing channel.

Buying Center Influences

Buying centers usually include several participants with differing interests, authority, status, and persuasiveness. Each participant is likely to give priority to different decision criteria. For example, engineering personnel may be concerned primarily with maximizing product performance; production personnel may be concerned mainly with ease of use and reliability of supply; financial personnel may focus on the purchase's economics; purchasing may be concerned with operating and replacement costs; and so on.

Business buyers also respond to many influences when they make their decisions. Each buyer has personal motivations, perceptions, and preferences, which are influenced by the buyer's age, income, education, job position, personality, attitudes toward risk, and culture (for more about dealing with cultural influences in international business marketing, see "Marketing Skills: Marketing Across Cultures"). Buyers definitely exhibit different buying styles. Some buyers prefer to conduct rigorous analyses of competitive proposals before choosing a supplier; others are "toughies" from the old school and pit competing sellers against one another.

Webster cautions that ultimately, individuals, not organizations, make purchasing decisions.[11] Individuals are motivated by their own needs and perceptions in attempting to maximize organizational rewards (pay, advancement, recognition, and feelings of achievement). Personal needs "motivate" the behavior of individuals but organizational needs "legitimize" the buying decision process and its outcomes. People are buying solutions to two problems: the organization's economic and strategic problem and their own personal "problem" of obtaining individual achievement and reward. In this sense, industrial buying decisions are both "rational" and "emotional," as they serve both the organization's and the individual's needs.[12]

MARKETING SKILLS: MARKETING ACROSS CULTURES

All people are *not* basically alike. This is just one premise to keep in mind when developing the skill of marketing across cultural boundaries—a vital skill in today's global marketplace. Language differences aside, marketers must assume that people from other cultures have different customs, beliefs, preferences, and values, at least until they can confirm similarities with their own cultures. Marketers should research the other culture to learn what to say and do in both business and social settings, because many cultures value a good buyer–seller relationship more than they value price or other aspects of the offer. Just as important, marketers should find out (and emulate) how people in the other culture communicate respect and avoid making judgments based on cultural differences.

In addition, marketers need to understand how businesspeople in other cultures prefer to communicate (are phone calls more acceptable than e-mails?), how they perceive time (are schedules only approximate?), how they make decisions (is consensus a requirement?), and other differences that can affect the buying center. Above all, marketers must be flexible enough to adapt their behavior and attitudes to accommodate cultural differences.

Consider the skills needed by marketers and managers at Digital River, a Minnesota-based company that operates online stores for software companies. When Digital River decided to expand into Japan, it studied business needs and buying influences for more than a year before partnering with a local firm to facilitate its market entrance. The partner helps with Digital River's B2B Web site, a key marketing tool that must be relevant and appealing to decision makers and influencers in Japanese businesses. Using Japanese translators and graphic designers, Digital River's CEO says, ensures "not only that they get the words right, but that they get the culture right."[13]

Buying Center Targeting

To target their efforts properly, business marketers have to figure out the answers to these questions: Who are the major decision participants? What decisions do they influence? What is their level of influence? What evaluation criteria do they use? The marketer is unlikely to know exactly what kind of group dynamics take place during the decision process, although information about personalities and interpersonal factors can be useful. Small sellers concentrate on reaching the *key buying influencers.* Larger sellers go for *multilevel in-depth selling* to reach as many participants as possible. Their salespeople virtually "live" with high-volume customers. Companies will have to rely more heavily on their communications programs to reach hidden buying influences and keep current customers informed.[14]

In defining target segments, four types of business customers can often be identified, with corresponding marketing implications (see Table 6.2). Some companies are willing to handle price-oriented buyers by setting a lower price but establishing restrictive conditions: (1) limiting the quantity that can be purchased; (2) no refunds; (3) no adjustments; and (4) no services.[15] For example, General Electric has installed diagnostic sensors in its airline engines and is now compensated for hours of flight.

Risk-and-gain sharing can be used to offset requested price reductions from customers. For example, suppose Medline, a hospital supplier, signs an agreement with Highland Park Hospital promising $350,000 in savings over the first 18 months in exchange for a tenfold increase in the hospitals' share of supplies. If Medline achieves less than this promised savings, it will make up the difference. If Medline achieves substantially more than this promise, it participates in the extra savings. To make such arrangements work, the supplier must be willing to help the customer to build a historical database, reach an agreement for measuring benefits and costs, and devise a dispute resolution mechanism.

Solution selling can also alleviate price pressure and comes in different forms. Here are three examples.[16]

- *Solutions to Enhance Customer Revenues.* Hendrix Voeders used its sales consultants to help farmers deliver an incremental animal weight gain of 5 to 10 percent over competitors.
- *Solutions to Decrease Customer Risks.* ICI Explosives formulated a safer way to ship explosives for quarries.
- *Solutions to Reduce Customer Costs.* W.W. Grainger employees work at large customer facilities to reduce materials-management costs.

TABLE 6.2   Types of Business Customers

Customer Segment	Characteristics	Selling Approach
Price-oriented	Price is everything.	Transactional selling
Solution-oriented	Want low prices but will respond to arguments about lower cost or more dependable supply/service.	Consultative selling
Gold-standard	Want the best performance in terms of quality, assistance, reliable delivery, etc.	Quality selling
Strategic-value	Want a fairly permanent sole-supplier relationship with the supplier.	Enterprise selling

STAGES IN THE BUSINESS BUYING PROCESS

Business buying passes through eight stages called *buyphases*, as identified by Robinson and associates in the *buygrid* framework shown in Table 6.3.[17] In modified-rebuy or straight-rebuy situations, some of these stages are compressed or bypassed. For example, in a straight-rebuy situation, the buyer normally has a favorite supplier or a ranked list of suppliers, so the supplier search and proposal solicitation stages are skipped. The sections that follow examine each of the eight stages for a typical new-task buying situation.

Problem Recognition

The buying process begins when someone in the company recognizes a problem or need that can be met by acquiring a good or service. The recognition can be triggered by internal or external stimuli. Internally, problem recognition commonly occurs when a firm decides to develop a new product and needs new equipment and materials, when a machine breaks down and requires new parts, when purchased material turns out to be unsatisfactory, or when a purchasing manager senses an opportunity to obtain lower prices or better quality. Externally, problem recognition can occur when a buyer gets new ideas at a trade show, sees an ad, or is contacted by a sales representative offering a better product or a lower price. Business marketers can stimulate problem recognition by direct mail, telemarketing, Internet communications, and calling on prospects.

General Need Description and Product Specification

Next, the buyer has to determine the needed item's general characteristics and required quantity. For standard items, this is simple. For complex items, the buyer will work with others—engineers, users—to define characteristics like reliability, durability, or price. In this stage, marketers can help by describing how their products meet or even exceed the buyer's needs. Hewlett-Packard, for example, has worked hard to become a "trusted advisor" to its customers, selling specific solutions to their unique problems. HP has discovered that some companies want a partner and others simply

TABLE 6.3   Buygrid Framework: Major Stages (Buyphases) of the Industrial Buying Process in Relation to Major Buying Situations (Buyclasses)

		Buyclasses		
		New Task	Modified Rebuy	Straight Rebuy
	1. Problem recognition	Yes	Maybe	No
	2. General need description	Yes	Maybe	No
	3. Product specification	Yes	Yes	Yes
Buyphases	4. Supplier search	Yes	Maybe	No
	5. Proposal solicitation	Yes	Maybe	No
	6. Supplier selection	Yes	Maybe	No
	7. Order-routine specification	Yes	Maybe	No
	8. Performance review	Yes	Yes	Yes

Source: Adapted from Patrick J. Johnson, Charles W. Faris, and Yoram Wind, *Industrial Buying and Creative Marketing* (Boston: Allyn & Bacon, 1967), p. 14.

want a product that works. The company assumes an advisory role when it sells complex products like a network computer system. It estimates that the trusted-advisor approach has contributed to 60 percent growth of its high-end computer business.[18]

The buying organization now develops the item's technical specifications. Often, the company will use *product value analysis*, a cost-reduction approach in which components are studied to determine if they can be redesigned, standardized, or made by cheaper production methods. The PVA team will examine the high-cost components in a given product and identify overdesigned product components that last longer than the product itself. Tightly written specifications will allow the buyer to refuse components that are too expensive or fail to meet the specified standards. Suppliers can also use product value analysis as a tool for positioning themselves to win an account.

Supplier Search

The buyer now tries to identify the most appropriate suppliers through trade directories, contacts with other companies, trade advertisements, and trade shows. Business marketers also put products, prices, and other data on the Internet. *Vertical hubs* focus on industries (plastics, steel, chemicals, paper), and *functional hubs* focus on specific functions (logistics, media buying, advertising, energy management). Companies also manage e-procurement through direct extranet links to major suppliers, buying alliances with other industry members, and company buying sites.

The supplier's task is to get listed in major online catalogs or services, communicate with buyers, and build a good reputation in the marketplace. Suppliers who lack capacity or have a poor reputation will be rejected, while those who qualify may be visited by buyer's agents, who will examine their facilities and meet their personnel. After evaluating each company, the buyer will end up with a short list of qualified suppliers. Many suppliers have changed their marketing to increase the likelihood of making the list. For example, Pittsburgh-based Cutler-Hammer supplies circuit breakers and other electrical equipment to industrial manufacturers such as Ford Motor Company. In response to the growing complexity and proliferation of its products, C-H developed "pods" of salespeople focused on a particular region, industry, or marketplace. Each person brings a degree of expertise about a product or service. Now the salespeople can leverage the knowledge of co-workers to sell to increasingly sophisticated buying teams.[19]

Proposal Solicitation

In this stage, the buyer invites qualified suppliers to submit proposals. When the item is complex or expensive, the buyer will require a detailed written proposal from each qualified supplier. After evaluating the proposals, the buyer will invite a few suppliers to make formal presentations. Business marketers must be skilled in researching, writing, and presenting proposals. Their written proposals should be marketing documents that describe value and benefits in customer terms. Oral presentations should inspire confidence, positioning the company's capabilities and resources so that it stand out from the competition.

A supplier must become qualified or, in some cases, become certified, so it will be invited to submit proposals. Consider the hurdles that Xerox has set up for suppliers. Only suppliers that meet stringent international quality standards qualify for certification. Suppliers must also complete the Xerox Multinational Supplier Quality Survey, participate in Xerox's Continuous Supplier Involvement process, and undergo rigorous quality training and evaluation based on the Malcolm Baldrige National Quality Award criteria. Not surprisingly, only 176 companies worldwide have qualified.[20]

Supplier Selection

Before selecting a supplier, the buying center will specify desired supplier attributes (such as product reliability and service reliability) and indicate their relative importance. It will then rate each supplier on these attributes to identify the most attractive one. Business marketers need to do a better job of understanding how business buyers arrive at their valuations.[21] Anderson, Jain, and Chintagunta conducted a study of the main methods business marketers use to assess customer value and found eight different *customer value assessment (CVA)* methods. Companies tended to use the simpler methods, although the more sophisticated ones promise to produce a more accurate picture of customer perceived value.

The choice and importance of different attributes varies with the type of buying situation.[22] Delivery reliability, price, and supplier reputation are important for routine-order products. For procedural-problem products, such as a copying machine, the three most important attributes are technical service, supplier flexibility, and product reliability. For political-problem products that stir rivalries in the organization (such as the choice of a computer system), the most important attributes are price, supplier reputation, product reliability, service reliability, and supplier flexibility.

The buyer may attempt to negotiate with preferred suppliers for better prices and terms before making the final selection. Despite moves toward strategic sourcing, partnering, and participation in cross-functional teams, buyers still spend a lot of time haggling over price, which remains a key criterion for supplier selection.[23] Marketers can counter a buyer's request for a lower price in several ways. They may be able to show that the "life-cycle cost" of using their product is lower than that of competitors' products. They can also cite the value of the services the buyer now receives, especially where those services are superior to those offered by competitors.

As part of the supplier selection process, buying centers must decide how many suppliers to use. In the past, many companies preferred a large supplier base to ensure adequate supplies and to obtain price concessions. Out-suppliers would try to get in the door by offering an especially low price. Increasingly, however, companies are reducing the number of suppliers. Companies such as Ford, Motorola, and AlliedSignal have cut the number of suppliers by anywhere from 20 percent to 80 percent. The suppliers who remain are responsible for larger component systems, for achieving continuous quality and performance improvements, and for lowering prices annually by a given percentage. There is even a trend toward single sourcing.

Order-Routine Specification

After selecting suppliers, the buyer negotiates the final order, listing the technical specifications, the quantity needed, the delivery schedule, and so on. In the case of MRO items, buyers are moving toward blanket contracts rather than periodic purchase orders. A *blanket contract* establishes a long-term relationship in which the supplier promises to resupply the buyer as needed at agreed-upon prices over a specified period. Because the seller holds the stock, blanket contracts are sometimes called *stockless purchase plans*.

The buyer's computer automatically sends an order to the seller when stock is needed. Blanket contracting leads to more single-source buying and ordering of more items from that single source; out-suppliers have difficulty breaking in unless the buyer becomes dissatisfied with the in-supplier's prices, quality, or service.

Companies that fear a shortage of key materials are willing to buy and hold large inventories. They will sign long-term contracts with suppliers to ensure a steady flow of materials. DuPont, Ford, and several other major companies regard long-term supply planning as a major responsibility of their purchasing managers. For example, General Motors wants to buy from fewer suppliers who are willing to locate close to its plants and produce high-quality components. In addition, marketers are setting up extranets with important customers to facilitate transactions and lower costs. The customers enter orders directly on the computer, and these orders are automatically transmitted to the supplier. Some companies even shift ordering responsibility to their suppliers, in systems called *vendor-managed inventory*. These suppliers are privy to the customer's inventory levels and take responsibility to replenish it automatically through *continuous replenishment programs*.

Performance Review

In the final stage of the buying process, the buyer periodically reviews the performance of the chosen supplier(s) using one of three methods. The buyer may contact the end users and ask for their evaluations; the buyer may rate the supplier on several criteria using a weighted score method; or the buyer might aggregate the cost of poor supplier performance to come up with adjusted costs of purchase, including price. The performance review may lead the buyer to continue, modify, or end the relationship with the supplier. To stay in the running for future purchases, suppliers should monitor the same variables that are monitored by the product's buyers and end users.

Business Relationships: Risks and Opportunism

Building strong business relationships depends on how the buyer perceives the supplier's credibility. *Corporate credibility* refers to the extent to which customers believe that a firm can design and deliver offerings that satisfy their needs and wants. Corporate credibility relates to the reputation that a firm has achieved in the marketplace and is the foundation for a strong business relationship. It is difficult for a firm to develop strong ties with another firm unless it is seen as highly credible, based on these three factors:[24]

- *Corporate expertise.* The extent to which a company is seen as able to make and sell products or conduct services.
- *Corporate trustworthiness.* The extent to which a company is seen as motivated to be honest, dependable, and sensitive to customer needs.
- *Corporate likability.* The extent to which a company is seen as likable, attractive, prestigious, dynamic, and so on.

Buvik and John note that in establishing a customer–supplier relationship, there is tension between safeguarding and adaptation.[25] Vertical coordination between customers and suppliers can facilitate stronger ties but may also increase the risk to the customer's and supplier's specific investments. *Specific investments* are those expenditures tailored to a particular company and value-chain partner (e.g., investments in company-specific training, equipment, and operations).[26] Specific investments help firms grow profits and achieve their positioning.[27] Yet they also entail considerable risk to both customer and supplier. Transaction theory from economics maintains that because these investments are partially sunk, they lock in the firms to a particular relationship. Sensitive cost and process information may need to be exchanged. A buyer may be vulnerable to holdup because of switching costs; a supplier may be more vulnerable to holdup in future contracts because of dedicated assets and/or expropriation of technology/knowledge.[28]

When buyers cannot easily monitor supplier performance, the supplier might not deliver the expected value. *Opportunism* can be thought of as "some form of cheating or undersupply relative to an implicit or explicit contract."[29] It may involve blatant self-interest and deliberate misrepresentation that violates contractual agreements. In creating the 1996 version of the Ford Taurus, Ford Corporation outsourced the whole process to one supplier, Lear Corporation. Lear committed to a contract that, for various reasons, it knew it was unable to fulfill. According to Ford, Lear missed deadlines, failed to meet weight and price objectives, and furnished parts that did not work.[30] A more passive form of opportunism might involve a refusal or unwillingness to adapt to changing circumstances.

Opportunism is a concern because firms must devote resources to control and monitoring that otherwise could be allocated to more productive purposes. Contracts may become inadequate to govern transactions when supplier opportunism becomes difficult to detect; as firms make specific investments in assets that cannot be used elsewhere; and as contingencies are harder to anticipate. A joint venture (versus a simple contract) is more likely when the supplier's degree of asset specificity is high, monitoring the supplier's behavior is difficult, and the supplier has a poor reputation.[31] A supplier with a good reputation will try to avoid opportunism to protect this valuable asset.

EXECUTIVE SUMMARY

The business market consists of all the organizations that acquire goods and services used in the production of other products or services that are sold, rented, or supplied to others. The institutional market consists of schools, hospitals, and other institutions that provide goods and services to people in their care. Government organizations also are a major buyer of goods and services. Compared to consumer markets, business markets have fewer and larger buyers, a closer customer–supplier relationship, and more geographically concentrated buyers. Demand in the business market is derived from demand in the consumer market and fluctuates with the business cycle. Organizations face three types of buying situations: the straight rebuy, the modified rebuy, and the new task.

Organizational buying is the decision-making process by which formal organizations establish the need for purchased products and services, then identify, evaluate, and choose among alternative brands and suppliers. The buying center is the decision-making unit of a buying organization. It consists of initiators, users, influencers, deciders, approvers, buyers, and gatekeepers. To influence these parties, marketers must be aware of environmental, organizational, interpersonal, and individual factors.

The buying process consists of eight stages called buyphases: (1) problem recognition, (2) general need description, (3) product specification, (4) supplier search, (5) proposal solicitation, (6) supplier selection, (7) order-routine specification, and (8) performance review. Business marketers must form strong relationships with their customers, maintain corporate credibility, and deliver the value that organizational buyers expect.

NOTES

1. Andy Reinhardt, "SAP: A Sea Change in Software," *BusinessWeek*, July 11, 2005, pp. 46–47; Janet Guyon, "The Man Who Mooned Larry Ellison," *Fortune*, July 7, 2003, pp. 71–74.
2. Frederick E. Webster Jr. and Yoram Wind, *Organizational Buying Behavior* (Upper Saddle River, NJ: Prentice Hall, 1972), p. 2.
3. Robert Hiebeler, Thomas B. Kelly, and Charles Ketteman, *Best Practices: Building Your Business with Customer-Focused Solutions* (New York: Arthur Andersen/Simon & Schuster, 1998), pp. 124–126.
4. Patrick J. Robinson, Charles W. Faris, and Yoram Wind, *Industrial Buying and Creative Marketing* (Boston: Allyn & Bacon, 1967).
5. See Daniel H. McQuiston, "Novelty, Complexity, and Importance as Causal Determinants of Industrial Buyer Behavior," *Journal of Marketing* (April 1989): 66–79; and Peter Doyle, Arch G. Woodside, and Paul Mitchell, "Organizational Buying in New Task and Rebuy Situations," *Industrial Marketing Management*, February 1979, pp. 7–11.
6. Urban B. Ozanne and Gilbert A. Churchill, Jr., "Five Dimensions of the Industrial Adoption Process," *Journal of Marketing Research* (August 1971): 322–328.
7. See Donald W. Jackson Jr., Janet E. Keith, and Richard K. Burdick, "Purchasing Agents' Perceptions of Industrial Buying Center Influence: A Situational Approach," *Journal of Marketing* (Fall 1984): 75–83.
8. Webster and Wind, *Organizational Buying Behavior*, p. 6.
9. Ibid., pp. 78–80.
10. Frederick E. Webster Jr. and Yoram Wind, "A General Model for Understanding Organizational Buying Behavior," *Journal of Marketing* 36 (April 1972): 12–19; Webster and Wind, *Organizational Buying Behavior*.
11. Frederick E. Webster Jr. and Kevin Lane Keller, "A Roadmap for Branding in Industrial Markets," *Journal of Brand Management* 11 (May 2004): 388–402.
12. Scott Ward and Frederick E. Webster Jr., "Organizational Buying Behavior" in *Handbook of Consumer Behavior*, edited by Tom Robertson and Hal Kassarjian (Upper Saddle River, NJ: Prentice Hall, 1991), ch. 12, pp. 419–458.
13. Beckey Bright, "How Do You Say 'Web'?" *Wall Street Journal*, May 23, 2005, p. R11; Betsy Cummings, "Selling Around the World," *Sales & Marketing Management*, May 2001, p. 70; Rhonda Coast, "Understanding Cultural Differences Is a Priority," *Pittsburgh Business Times*, February 11, 2000, p. 13; John V. Thill and Courtland L. Bovée, *Excellence in Business Communication*, 5th ed. (Upper Saddle River, NJ: Prentice Hall, 2002), ch. 3.
14. Webster and Wind, *Organizational Buying Behavior*, p. 6.
15. Nirmalya Kumar, *Marketing As Strategy: Understanding the CEO's Agenda for Driving Growth and Innovation* (Boston: Harvard Business School Press, 2004).
16. Kumar, *Marketing As Strategy*.
17. Robinson, Faris, and Wind, *Industrial Buying and Creative Marketing*.
18. Rick Mullin, "Taking Customer Relations to the Next Level," *The Journal of Business Strategy* (January–February 1997): 22–26.
19. Robert Hiebeler, Thomas B. Kelly, and Charles Ketteman, *Best Practices: Building Your Business with Customer-Focused Solutions* (New York: Arthur Andersen/Simon & Schuster, 1998) pp. 122–124.

20. See "Xerox Multinational Supplier Quality Survey," *Purchasing*, January 12, 1995, p. 112.

21. Daniel J. Flint, Robert B. Woodruff, and Sarah Fisher Gardial, "Exploring the Phenomenon of Customers' Desired Value Change in a Business-to-Business Context," *Journal of Marketing* 66 (October 2002): 102–117.

22. Donald R. Lehmann and John O'Shaughnessy, "Differences in Attribute Importance for Different Industrial Products," *Journal of Marketing* (April 1974): 36–42.

23. Tim Minahan, "OEM Buying Survey–Part 2: Buyers Get New Roles But Keep Old Tasks," *Purchasing*, July 16, 1998, pp. 208–209. To see how the Internet is affecting supplier selection, see Kevin Ferguson, "Purchasing in Packs," *BusinessWeek*, November 1, 1999, pp. EB32–38.

24. See Robert M. Morgan and Shelby D. Hunt, "The Commitment–Trust Theory of Relationship Marketing," *Journal of Marketing* 58, no. 3 (1994): 20–38; Christine Moorman, Rohit Deshpande, and Gerald Zaltman, "Factors Affecting Trust in Market Research Relationships," *Journal of Marketing* 57 (January 1993): 81–101; Kevin Lane Keller and David A. Aaker, "Corporate-Level Marketing: The Impact of Credibility on a Company's Brand Extensions," *Corporate Reputation Review* 1 (August 1998): 356–378; Bob Violino, "Building B2B Trust," *Computerworld*, June 17, 2002, p. 32.

25. Arnt Buvik and George John, "When Does Vertical Coordination Improve Industrial Purchasing Relationships?" *Journal of Marketing* 64 (October 2000): 52–64.

26. Akesel I. Rokkan, Jan B. Heide, and Kenneth H. Wathne, "Specific Investment in Marketing Relationships: Expropriation and Bonding Effects," *Journal of Marketing Research* 40 (May 2003): 210–224.

27. Mrinal Ghosh and George John, "Governance Value Analysis and Marketing Strategy," *Journal of Marketing* 63 (Special Issue, 1999): 131–145.

28. Buvik and John, "When Does Vertical Coordination Improve Industrial Purchasing Relationships?"

29. Kenneth H. Wathne and Jan B. Heide, "Opportunism in Interfirm Relationships: Forms, Outcomes, and Solutions," *Journal of Marketing* 64 (October 2000): 36–51.

30. Mary Walton, "When Your Partner Fails You," *Fortune*, May 26, 1997, pp. 87–89.

31. Mark B. Houston and Shane A. Johnson, "Buyer–Supplier Contracts Versus Joint Ventures: Determinants and Consequences of Transaction Structure," *Journal of Marketing Research* 37 (February 2000): 1–15.

CHAPTER 7

Identifying Market Segments and Targets

In this chapter, we will address the following questions:

1. How can a company identify the segments that make up a market?
2. What criteria can a company use in selecting attractive segments to enter through market targeting?

MARKETING MANAGEMENT AT HALLMARK

Hallmark has a card for every person and every occasion. The dominant firm in the U.S. greeting-card market, Hallmark carefully studies consumers to identify profitable segments and niches for new products. Its marketers segment by race, religion, occasion, age, national origin, price-sensitivity, and other variables. For example, the Sinceramente Hallmark line covers more than 2,500 cards designed for Hispanic Americans. "Hallmark conducts research to develop a real understanding of who is purchasing each type of card," explains Julio Blanco, marketing manager for this product line. "We want to connect with the heart of each Hispanic consumer through these cards."

Hallmark's Mahogany brand targets African American buyers; the Tree of Life brand targets Jewish Americans; the Fresh Ink brand targets 18-to-39-year-old women; and the Warm Wishes brand—priced at 99 cents—targets cost-conscious buyers. Segmenting the market by occasion, Hallmark has put its brand on cards for a huge variety of special days, including Veterans Day and Eid al-Fitr, marking the end of the Muslim holy month of Ramadan. Over time, the company has tightened its focus by creating products for attractive subsegments. For instance, the Mahogany line covers not only a line of Kwanzaa holiday cards, but also a Legacy of Greatness line recognizing African Americans for their contributions to society. The Veterans Day line includes more than two dozen patriotic cards suitable for Army, Navy, Marine Corps, Air Force, and Coast Guard veterans. Building on this segmentation strategy, Hallmark plans to boost revenues beyond $10 billion by 2010.[1]

To compete more effectively, companies such as Hallmark are embracing target marketing. Instead of scattering their marketing efforts (a "shotgun" approach), they focus on those buyers they have the greatest chance of satisfying (a "rifle" approach). Target marketing requires that marketers (1) identify and profile distinct groups of buyers who differ in their needs and preferences (market segmentation); (2) select one or more segments to enter (market targeting); and (3) establish and communicate the offering's distinctive benefit(s) to the target segment (market positioning). This chapter focuses on the first two steps; Chapter 9 will discuss positioning.

LEVELS OF MARKET SEGMENTATION

Sellers that use **mass marketing** engage in the mass production, distribution, and promotion of one product for all buyers. Henry Ford epitomized this strategy when he offered the Model T Ford "in any color, as long as it is black." Coca-Cola also used mass marketing when it sold only one kind of Coke in a 6.5-ounce bottle.

The argument for mass marketing is that it creates the largest potential market, which leads to the lowest costs, which in turn can lead to lower prices or higher margins. However, critics point to increased splintering of the market, which makes mass marketing more difficult. This proliferation of media and distribution channels is making it increasingly difficult to reach a mass audience. Some claim that mass marketing is dying. Not surprisingly, many companies are turning to *micromarketing* at one of four levels: segments, niches, local areas, and individuals.

Segment Marketing

A market segment consists of a group of customers who share a similar set of wants, such as car buyers who want low-cost transportation and car buyers who want a luxurious driving experience. However, a *segment* is not a *sector*. "Young, middle-income car buyers" is a sector, not a segment, because these buyers will differ in what they want in a car. Marketers do not create the segments; their task is to identify the segments and decide which to target.

Because the wants of segment members are similar but not identical, Anderson and Narus urge marketers to present flexible market offerings instead of one standard offering to all of a segment's members.[2] A **flexible market offering** consists of the product and service elements that all segment members value, plus *discretionary options* (perhaps for an additional charge) that some members value. For example, American Airlines offers economy passengers a seat and soft drinks, but it charges extra for alcoholic beverages.

Niche Marketing

A *niche* is a more narrowly defined customer group seeking a distinctive mix of benefits. Marketers usually identify niches by dividing a segment into subsegments. For example, Progressive, an auto insurer, sells "nonstandard" insurance to drivers with a record of auto accidents, charges a high price for coverage, and builds profits. In an attractive niche, customers have a distinct set of needs, they will pay a premium to the firm that best satisfies their needs, the niche is not likely to attract other competitors, the nicher gains certain economies through specialization, and the niche has size, profit, and growth potential.

Whereas segments are fairly large and attract several competitors, niches are fairly small and may attract one or two rivals. Still, giants such as IBM can and do lose pieces of their market to nichers: Dalgic and Leeuw labeled this confrontation "guerrillas against gorillas."[3] Hallmark and many other giants have, therefore, turned to niche marketing. Niche marketers presumably understand their customers' needs so well that the customers willingly pay a premium. Tom's of Maine, which sells all-natural personal care products, sometimes commands a 30-percent premium on its toothpaste because its unique, environmentally friendly products and charitable donation programs appeal to consumers who have been turned off by big businesses.[4] As marketing efficiency increases, niches that were seemingly too small may become more profitable.[5]

The low cost of Internet marketing has led to many small start-ups aimed at niches. The recipe for Internet niching success: Choose a hard-to-find product that customers don't need to see and touch. Consider Steve Warrington's successful online venture selling ostriches, eggshells, steaks, and 15,000 related products (**www.ostrichesonline.com**). Launched for next to nothing on the Web, the business now serves more than 30,000 customers in 125 countries.[6]

Local Marketing

Target marketing is leading to marketing programs tailored to the needs and wants of local customer groups (trading areas, neighborhoods, even individual stores). Citibank, for instance, adjusts its banking services in each branch depending on neighborhood demographics; Kraft helps supermarket chains identify the cheese assortment and shelf positioning that will optimize cheese sales in different stores and neighborhoods.

Local marketing reflects a growing trend toward grassroots marketing, concentrating on getting as close and personally relevant to individual customers as possible. Much of Nike's initial success has been attributed to the ability to engage target consumers through grassroots marketing such as sponsorship of local school teams and expert-conducted clinics. A large part of grassroots marketing is *experiential marketing*, which promotes an offering by connecting it with unique and interesting experiences. One marketing commentator describes experiential marketing this way: "The idea is not to sell something, but to demonstrate how a brand can enrich a customer's life."[7]

Proponents of local marketing see national advertising as wasteful because it fails to address local needs. Opponents argue that local marketing drives up manufacturing and marketing costs by reducing economies of scale. Logistical problems become magnified when companies try to meet varying local requirements, and a brand's overall image might be diluted if the product and message vary in different localities.

Customerization

The ultimate level of segmentation leads to "segments of one," "customized marketing," or "one-to-one marketing."[8] Today customers are taking more individual initiative in determining what and how to buy. They surf the Web; look up information and evaluations of offers; contact suppliers, users, and product critics; and in many cases, design the product they want. More online companies today are offering a Choiceboard, an interactive online system that allows individual customers to design their own products and services by choosing from a menu of attributes, components, prices, and delivery options. The customer's selections send signals to the supplier's manufacturing system that set in motion the wheels of procurement, assembly, and delivery.[9]

Wind and Rangaswamy see the Choiceboard as a movement toward "customerizing" the firm.[10] **Customerization** combines operationally driven mass customization with customized marketing in a way that empowers consumers to design the product and service offering of their choice. The firm no longer requires prior information about the customer, nor does the firm need to own manufacturing. The firm provides a platform and tools and "rents" out to customers the means to design their own products. A company is customerized when it is able to respond to individual customers by customizing its products, services, and messages on a one-to-one basis.[11]

This level of segmentation may be difficult to implement for complex products such as automobiles, and it can raise the cost of goods to more than the customer is willing to pay. Moreover, some customers do not know what they want until they see actual products, yet they cannot cancel the order after the company has started to work on the product. Despite these difficulties, some companies have been successful with customerization. For example, Andersen Windows, a $1-billion Minnesota-based manufacturer of residential windows, has developed an interactive computer version of its catalog for distributors and retailers. Now in 650 showrooms, the system is linked directly to the factory so salespeople can help customers customize each window, check the design for structural soundness, and generate a price quote. Andersen also developed a "batch of one" manufacturing process in which everything is made to order, reducing its finished parts inventory, a major cost to the company.[12]

Patterns of Market Segmentation

Market segments can be built up in many ways. One common method is to identify *preference segments.* Suppose ice cream buyers are asked how much they value sweetness and creaminess as two product attributes. Three different patterns can emerge:

- *Homogeneous preferences.* Figure 7.1a shows a market where all the consumers have roughly the same preferences, so there are no natural segments. We predict that existing brands would be similar and cluster around the middle of the scale in both sweetness and creaminess.

FIGURE 7.1   Basic Market-Preference Patterns

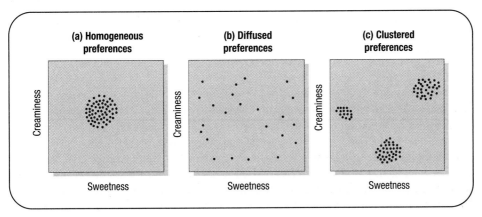

- *Diffused preferences.* At the other extreme, consumer preferences may be scattered throughout the space (Figure 7.1b), indicating great variance in consumer preferences. One brand might position in the center to appeal to most people; if several brands are in the market, they are likely to position throughout the space and show real differences to reflect consumer-preference differences.

- *Clustered preferences.* The market might reveal distinct preference clusters, called *natural market segments* (Figure 7.1c). The first firm in this market might position in the center to appeal to all groups, choose the largest market segment (*concentrated marketing*), or develop several brands for different segments. If the first firm has only one brand, competitors would enter and introduce brands in the other segments.

SEGMENTING CONSUMER AND BUSINESS MARKETS

Because of the inherent differences between consumer and business markets, marketers cannot use exactly the same variables to segment both. Instead, they use one broad group of variables as the basis for consumer segmentation and another broad group for business segmentation.

Bases for Segmenting Consumer Markets

Two broad groups of variables are used to segment consumer markets. Some researchers try to form segments by looking at descriptive characteristics: geographic, demographic, and psychographic. Then they examine whether these customer segments exhibit different needs or product responses. Other researchers try to form segments by looking at "behavioral" considerations, such as responses to benefits, use occasions, or brands. With the segments formed, the researcher sees whether different characteristics are associated with each consumer-response segment.

Regardless of which segmentation scheme is employed, the key is that the marketing program can be profitably adjusted to recognize customer differences. The major segmentation variables—geographic, demographic, psychographic, and behavioral segmentation—are summarized in Table 7.1.

Geographic Segmentation   Geographic segmentation calls for dividing the market into different geographical units such as nations, states, regions, counties, cities, or neighborhoods. The company can operate in one or a few geographic areas or operate in all but pay attention to local variations. For example, Hilton Hotels customizes rooms and lobbies according to location: Northeastern hotels are sleek and cosmopolitan; Southwestern hotels are more rustic. Major retailers such as Wal-Mart and Sears, Roebuck, and Co. allow local managers to stock products that suit the local community.[13]

More and more, regional marketing means marketing right down to a specific zip code.[14] Some approaches combine geographic data with demographic data to yield even richer descriptions of consumers and neighborhoods. Claritas, Inc., has developed a geoclustering approach called PRIZM (Potential Rating Index by Zip Markets) that classifies over half a million U.S. residential neighborhoods into 15 distinct groups and 66 distinct lifestyle segments called PRIZM Clusters.[15] The groupings take into consideration 39 factors in 5 broad categories: (1) education and affluence, (2) family life cycle, (3) urbanization, (4) race and ethnicity, and (5) mobility. The clusters have descriptive titles such as *Blue Blood Estates, Winner's Circle, Hometown Retired, Latino*

TABLE 7.1   Major Segmentation Variables for Consumer Markets

Geographic

Region	Pacific, Mountain, West North Central, West South Central, East North Central, East South Central, South Atlantic, Middle Atlantic, New England
City or metro size	Under 5,000; 5,000–20,000; 20,000–50,000; 50,000–100,000; 100,000–250,000; 250,000–500,000; 500,000–1,000,000; 1,000,000–4,000,000; 4,000,000 or over
Density	Urban, suburban, rural
Climate	Northern, southern

Demographic (vital statistics)

Age	Under 6, 6–11, 12–19, 20–34, 35–49, 50–64, 65+
Family size	1–2, 3–4, 5+
Family life cycle	Young, single; young, married, no children; young, married, youngest child under 6; young, married, youngest child 6 or over; older, married, with children; older, married, no children under 18; older, single; other
Gender	Male, female
Income	Under $10,000; $10,000–$15,000; $15,000–$20,000; $20,000–$30,000; $30,000–$50,000; $50,000–$100,000; $100,000 and over
Occupation	Professional and technical; managers, officials, and proprietors; clerical sales; craftspeople; forepersons; operatives; farmers; retired; students; homemakers; unemployed
Education	Grade school or less; some high school; high school graduate; some college; college graduate
Religion	Catholic, Protestant, Jewish, Muslim, Hindu, other
Race	White, Black, Asian, Hispanic
Generation	Baby boomers, Generation Xers
Nationality	North American, South American, British, French, German, Italian, Japanese
Social class	Lower lowers, upper lowers, working class, middle class, upper middles, lower uppers, upper uppers

Psychographic

Lifestyle	Culture-oriented, sports-oriented, outdoor-oriented
Personality	Compulsive, gregarious, authoritarian, ambitious

Behavioral

Occasions	Regular occasion, special occasion (tradition)
Benefits	Quality, service, economy, speed
User status	Nonuser, ex-user, potential user, first-time user, regular user
Usage rate	Light user, medium user, heavy user
Loyalty status	None, medium, strong, absolute
Readiness stage	Unaware, aware, informed, interested, desirous, intending to buy
Attitude toward product	Enthusiastic, positive, indifferent, negative, hostile

America, Shotguns and Pickups, and *Back Country Folks*. The inhabitants in a cluster tend to lead similar lives, drive similar cars, have similar jobs, and read similar magazines.

Demographic Segmentation In demographic segmentation, the market is divided into groups on the basis of age and the other variables. One reason this is the most popular segmentation method is that consumer wants, preferences, and usage rates are often associated with demographic variables. Another reason is that demographic variables are easier to measure. Even when the target market is described in nondemographic terms, such as a personality type, the link back to demographic characteristics is needed to estimate the size of the target market and the media that can be used to reach it.

Here is how demographic variables can be used to segment consumer markets:

- *Age and life-cycle stage.* Consumer wants and abilities change with age. Toothpaste brands such as Crest and Colgate offer three main lines of products to target kids, adults, and older consumers. Age segmentation can be even more refined. Pampers divides its market into prenatal, newborn (0 to 1 month), infant (2 to 5 months), cruiser (6 to 12 months), toddler (13 to18 months), explorer (19 to 23 months), and preschooler (24 months plus). However, age and life cycle can be tricky segmentation variables.[16]

- *Life stage.* Persons in the same part of the life cycle may differ in their life stage. **Life stage** defines a person's major concern, such as going through a divorce, going into a second marriage, taking care of an older parent, deciding to cohabit with another person, deciding to buy a new home, and so on. These life stages present opportunities for marketers who can help people cope with their major concerns. For instance, JC Penney has identified "Starting Outs" as one of its two major customer groups.[17]

- *Gender.* Men and women tend to have different attitudinal and behavioral orientations, based partly on genetic makeup and partly on socialization. As an example, research shows that men often need to be invited to touch a product, while women are likely to pick it up without prompting.[18] Gender segmentation has long been applied in clothing, cosmetics, and magazines, although some traditionally more male-oriented markets are being segmented by gender today. Finding that women initiate 80 percent of home improvement projects, Lowe's designed its stores with wider aisles and stocked more big-ticket appliances and high-margin home furnishings. Half of its clientele is now female.[19]

- *Income.* Income segmentation is a long-standing practice in such categories as automobiles, boats, clothing, cosmetics, and travel. However, income does not always predict the best customers for a given product. Increasingly, companies are finding that their markets are "hourglass-shaped" as middle-market Americans migrate toward more premium products.[20]

- *Generation.* Each generation is profoundly influenced by the times in which it grows up—the music, movies, politics, and events of that period. Demographers call these groups *cohorts*. Because cohort members share the same experiences and have similar outlooks and values, effective marketing appeals use the icons and images that are prominent in the targeted cohort's experience. Figure 7.2 depicts six well-established cohort groups.

- *Social class.* Social class strongly influences preference in cars, clothing, home furnishings, leisure activities, reading habits, and retailers, which is why many firms design products for specific social classes. However, the tastes of social classes can

FIGURE 7.2   Profiling American Generations

GI generation (16 million people)
   Born 1901–1924
   Shaped by hard times and the Great Depression, financial security is one of their core values. Conservative
   spenders and civic-minded, they are team-oriented and patriotic.
Silent Generation (35 million people)
   Born 1925–1945
   Trusting conformists who value stability, they are now involved in civic life and extended families.
Baby Boomers (78 million people)
   Born 1946–1964
   Great acquisitors, they are value- and cause-driven, despite indulgences and hedonism.
Generation X (57 million people)
   Born 1965–1977
   Cynical and media-savvy, they are more alienated and individualistic.
Generation Y (60 million people)
   Born 1978–1994
   Edgy, focused on urban style, they are more idealistic than Generation X.
Millennials (42 million people)
   Born 1995–2002
   Multicultural, they will be tech-savvy, educated, grow up in affluent society, and have big spending power.

Source: Bonnie Tsui, "Generation Next," *Advertising Age,* January 15, 2001, pp. 14–16.

change over time. The 1990s were about ostentation for the upper classes; affluent tastes now run more conservatively, although Tiffany and other luxury goods makers still successfully sell to those seeking the good life.[21]

Psychographic Segmentation   **Psychographics** is the science of using psychology and demographics to better understand consumers. In *psychographic segmentation,* buyers are divided into different groups on the basis of psychological/personality traits, lifestyle, or values. People within the same demographic group can exhibit very different psychographic profiles.

One of the most popular commercially available classification systems based on psychographic measurements is SRI Consulting Business Intelligence's VALS™ framework. VALS classifies U.S. adults into eight primary groups based on personality traits and key demographics. The segmentation system is based on responses to a questionnaire featuring 4 demographic and 35 attitudinal questions. The VALS system is continually updated with new data from more than 80,000 surveys per year (see Figure 7.3).[22] VALS products include U.S. VALS, Japan VALS™, U.K. VALS and Geo VALS™, estimating the proportion at U.S. VALS types by zip code or block group.

Behavioral Segmentation   In behavioral segmentation, consumers are divided into groups on the basis of their knowledge of, attitude toward, use of, or response to a product. Decision roles are one such variable. People play five roles in a buying decision: *Initiator, Influencer, Decider, Buyer,* and *User.* For example, assume a wife initiates a purchase by requesting a new treadmill for her birthday. The husband may then seek information from many sources, including a friend who has a treadmill and is a key influencer in what models to consider. After presenting the alternative choices to his wife, he then purchases her preferred model, which, as it turns out, ends up being used

FIGURE 7.3   The VALS Segmentation System: An Eight-Part Typology

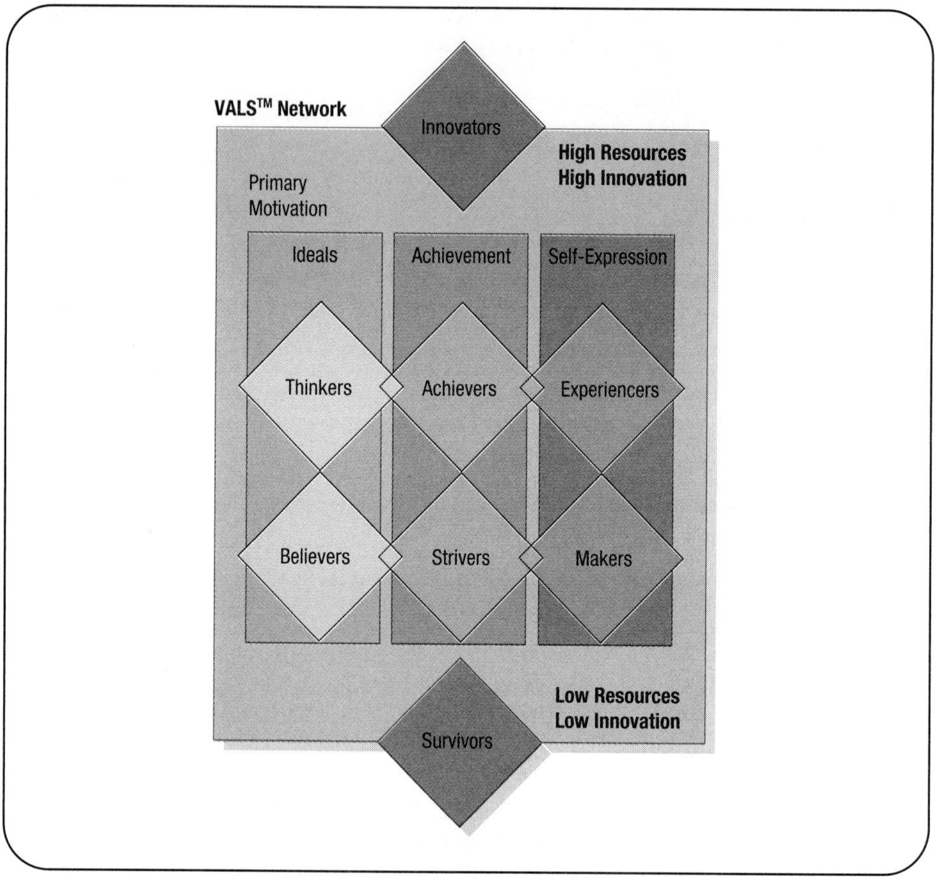

VALS™ Network

Innovators

High Resources
High Innovation

Primary
Motivation

| Ideals | Achievement | Self-Expression |

Thinkers   Achievers   Experiencers

Believers   Strivers   Makers

Low Resources
Low Innovation

Survivors

Source: © 2006 by SRI Consulting Business Intelligence (SRIC-BI), www.sric-bi.com/VALS/.

by the entire family. Different people are playing different roles, but all are crucial in the decision process and ultimate consumer satisfaction.

Many marketers believe that behavioral variables—occasions, benefits, user status, usage rate, loyalty status, buyer-readiness stage, and attitude—are the best starting points for segmentation.

- *Occasions.* Buyers can be distinguished according to the occasions when they develop a need and purchase or use a product. For example, air travel is triggered by business, vacation, or family occasions. Marketers also can try to extend activities associated with certain holidays to other times of the year. Thus, while Christmas, Mother's Day, and Valentine's Day are the three major gift-giving holidays, other occasion-driven gift-giving opportunities are birthdays, weddings, anniversaries, housewarming, and new babies.[23]

- *Benefits.* Buyers can be classified according to the benefits they seek. Mobil did this when it identified five distinct benefit segments: Road Warriors (interested in premium products and services); Generation F (fast fuel/service/food); True Blues (brand-loyal); Home Bodies (convenience); and Price Shoppers (low price). Mobil decided to focus on the less price-sensitive segments and rolled out *Friendly Serve:* cleaner property, bathrooms, better lighting, well-stocked stores, and friendlier personnel. Although Mobil charged 2 cents per gallon more than its competitors, sales increased by 20 to 25 percent.[24]

- *User status.* Markets can be segmented into nonusers, ex-users, potential users, first-time users, and regular users of a product. The company's market position also influences its focus. Market leaders focus on attracting potential users, whereas smaller firms try to lure users away from the leader.

- *Usage rate.* Markets can be segmented into light, medium, and heavy product users. Heavy users are often a small percentage of the market but account for a high percentage of total consumption. Marketers usually prefer to attract one heavy user rather than several light users. A potential problem is that heavy users either are extremely loyal to one brand or are always looking for the lowest price and never stay loyal to a brand.

- *Buyer-readiness stage.* A market consists of people in different stages of readiness to buy a product: Some are unaware of the product, some are aware, some are informed, some interested, some desire the product, and some intend to buy. The relative numbers make a big difference in planning marketing activities.

- *Loyalty status.* Buyers can be divided into four groups according to brand loyalty status: hard-core loyals (always buy one brand), split loyals (loyal to two or three brands), shifting loyals (shift from one brand to another), and switchers (no loyalty to any brand).[25] By studying its hard-core loyals, a company can identify its products' strengths; by studying its split loyals, the company can see which brands are most competitive with its own. By looking at customers shifting away from its brand, the company can learn about its marketing weaknesses and attempt to correct them. One caution: What appears to be brand loyalty may actually reflect habit, indifference, a low price, a high switching cost, or the nonavailability of other brands.

- *Attitude.* Five attitude groups can be found in a market: enthusiastic, positive, indifferent, negative, and hostile. So, for example, workers in a political campaign use the voter's attitude to determine how much time to spend with that voter. They may thank enthusiastic voters and remind them to vote, reinforce those who are positively disposed, try to win the votes of indifferent voters, and spend no time trying to change the attitudes of negative and hostile voters.

The Conversion Model has been developed to measure the strength of the consumer's psychological commitment to brands and their openness to change.[26] To determine how easily a consumer can be converted to another choice, the model assesses commitment based on factors such as consumer attitudes toward and satisfaction with current brand choices in a category and the importance of the brand-selection decision in the category.[27]

Bases for Segmenting Business Markets

Business markets can be segmented with some variables that are employed in consumer market segmentation, such as geography, benefits sought, and usage rate. Yet business marketers can also use several other variables. Bonoma and Shapiro proposed segmenting the business market with the variables in Table 7.2. The demographic variables are the most important, followed by the operating variables—down to the personal characteristics of the buyer. A company should first decide which industries it

TABLE 7.2 Major Segmentation Variables for Business Markets

Demographic

1. *Industry:* Which industries should we serve?

2. *Company Size:* What size companies should we serve?

3. *Location:* What geographical areas should we serve?

Operating Variables

4. *Technology:* What customer technologies should we focus on?

5. *User or nonuser status:* Should we serve heavy users, medium users, light users, or nonusers?

6. *Customer capabilities:* Should we serve customers needing many or few services?

Purchasing Approaches

7. *Purchasing-function organization:* Should we serve companies with highly centralized or decentralized purchasing organizations?

8. *Power structure:* Should we serve companies that are engineering dominated, financially dominated, and so on?

9. *Nature of existing relationships:* Should we serve companies with which we have strong relationships or simply go after the most desirable companies?

10. *General purchase policies:* Should we serve companies that prefer leasing? Service contracts? Systems purchases? Sealed bidding?

11. *Purchasing criteria:* Should we serve companies that are seeking quality? Service? Price?

Situational Factors

12. *Urgency:* Should we serve companies that need quick and sudden delivery or service?

13. *Specific application:* Should we focus on certain applications of our product rather than all applications?

14. *Size of order:* Should we focus on large or small orders?

Personal Characteristics

15. *Buyer–seller similarity:* Should we serve companies whose people and values are similar to ours?

16. *Attitudes toward risk:* Should we serve risk-taking or risk-avoiding customers?

17. *Loyalty:* Should we serve companies that show high loyalty to their suppliers?

Source: Adapted from Thomas V. Bonoma and Benson P. Shapiro, *Segmenting the Industrial Market* (Lexington, MA: Lexington Books, 1983).

wants to serve. Then, within a chosen industry, the company can further segment by company size, possibly setting up separate operations for selling to large and small customers.

Marketing to Small Businesses Small businesses, in particular, have become a Holy Grail for business marketers.[28] Small businesses are responsible for 50 percent of the U.S. gross domestic product, according to the Small Business Administration—and this segment is growing faster than the large company segment. To illustrate, North Carolina-based BB&T Corporation is pursuing the small-business segment by positioning itself as a powerful local bank with a down-home approach. It launched a business-to-business (B2B) advertising campaign featuring Carolina businesses and their owners, each a BB&T customer. These ads serve to reinforce the bank's commitment to small business and show that the bank understands what is important to this segment.[29]

Sequential Segmentation Business marketers generally identify segments through a sequential process. Consider an aluminum company: The company first undertook macrosegmentation. It looked at which end-use market to serve: automobile, residential, or beverage containers. It chose the residential market, and needed to determine the most attractive product application: semifinished material, building components, or aluminum mobile homes. Deciding to focus on building components, it considered the best customer size and chose large customers. The second stage consisted of microsegmentation. The company distinguished among customers buying on price, service, or quality. Because the aluminum company had a high-service profile, it decided to concentrate on the service-motivated segment of the market.

Business buyers seek different benefit bundles based on their stage in the purchase decision process:[30]

- *First-time prospects.* Customers who have not yet purchased but want to buy from a vendor who understands their business, who explains things well, and whom they can trust.
- *Novices.* Customers who are starting their purchasing relationship want easy-to-read manuals, hotlines, a high level of training, and knowledgeable sales reps.
- *Sophisticates.* Established customers want speed in maintenance and repair, product customization, and high technical support.

These segments may also have different channel preferences. First-time prospects would prefer to deal with a company salesperson instead of a catalog or direct-mail channel, because the latter provides too little information. Sophisticates, on the other hand, may want to conduct more of their buying over electronic channels. By addressing these differences, marketers can successfully start or continue relationships with business customers.

MARKET TARGETING

Once the firm has identified its market-segment opportunities, it has to decide how many and which ones to target. Marketers are increasingly combining several variables in an effort to identify smaller, better-defined target groups. Thus, a bank may not only identify a group of wealthy retired adults, but also within that group distinguish several segments depending on current income, assets, savings, and risk preferences. This has led some experts to advocate a *needs-based market segmentation approach*. Roger Best proposed the seven-step approach shown in Table 7.3.

Effective Segmentation Criteria

Not all segmentation schemes are useful. For example, table salt buyers could be divided into blond and brunette customers, but hair color is undoubtedly irrelevant to the purchase of salt. Furthermore, if all salt buyers buy the same amount of salt each month, believe all salt is the same, and would pay only one price for salt, this market would be minimally segmentable from a marketing point of view.

To be useful, market segments must rate favorably on five key criteria:

1. *Measurable.* The size, purchasing power, and characteristics of the segments can be measured.
2. *Substantial.* The segments are large and profitable enough to serve; each should be the largest possible homogeneous group worth going after with a tailored marketing program.
3. *Accessible.* The segments can be effectively reached and served.

TABLE 7.3   Steps in the Segmentation Process

	Description
1. Needs-Based Segmentation	Group customers into segments based on similar needs and benefits sought by customer in solving particular consumption problem.
2. Segment Identification	For each needs-based segment, determine which demographics, lifestyles, and usage behaviors make the segment distinct and identifiable (actionable).
3. Segment Attractiveness	Using predetermined segment attractiveness criteria (such as market growth, competitive intensity, and market access), determine the overall attractiveness of each segment.
4. Segment Profitability	Determine segment profitability.
5. Segment Positioning	For each segment, create a "value proposition" and product-price positioning strategy based on that segment's unique customer needs and characteristics.
6. Segment "Acid Test"	Create "segment storyboards" to test the attractiveness of each segment's positioning strategy.
7. Marketing-Mix Strategy	Expand segment positioning strategy to include all aspects of the marketing mix: product, price, promotion, and place.

Source: Adapted from Robert J. Best, *Market-Based Management* (Upper Saddle River, NJ: Prentice Hall, 2000).

4. *Differentiable.* The segments are conceptually distinguishable and respond differently to different marketing-mix elements and programs. If two segments respond identically to an offer, they are not separate segments.

5. *Actionable.* Effective programs can be formulated for attracting and serving the segments.

Evaluating and Selecting Market Segments

In evaluating different market segments, the firm must look at two factors; the segment's overall attractiveness and the company's objectives and resources. How well does a potential segment score on the five criteria? Does a potential segment have characteristics that make it generally attractive, such as size, growth, profitability, scale economies, and low risk? Does investing in the segment make sense given the firm's objectives, competencies, and resources? Some attractive segments may not mesh with the company's long-run objectives, or the company may lack one or more necessary competencies to offer superior value (see "Marketing Skills: Evaluating Segments").

Having evaluated different segments, the company can consider five patterns of target market selection, as shown in Figure 7.4.

Single-Segment Concentration   Volkswagen concentrates on the small-car market, while Porsche concentrates on the sports car market. Through concentrated marketing, these firms gain a thorough understanding of the chosen segment's needs and achieve a strong market presence. Furthermore, each firm enjoys operating economies by specializing in its production, distribution, and promotion; if it gains leadership, it

MARKETING SKILLS: EVALUATING SEGMENTS

Determining which of the identified segments a company should enter is a high-stakes activity, because choosing the wrong segment(s) can waste money and divert attention from more profitable segments. Therefore, marketers need to develop the vital skill of evaluating segments. To start, they must establish criteria to use in weighing a segment's attractiveness. These may be market growth measures such as size and growth potential; competitive intensity measures such as number of competitors and ease of market entry; and market access measures such as channel access and fit with company resources. This analysis shows which segments are more attractive on each measure.

Now the marketer establishes criteria for screening out unsuitable segments, such as segments that would be illegal or controversial for the company to target. Some marketers use the potential for significant risks—such as imminent political unrest—to eliminate particular segments. The next step is to estimate the likely sales and profits from the remaining segments and use these figures, along with the attractiveness criteria, to rank the segments. Some marketers determine the order of entry by calculating a total score for each segment, giving priority to segments with the highest scores (unless the company's strategy or mission requires another ranking method).

Delta Education, based in New Hampshire, has used segmentation to fuel annual sales growth past $70 million. The company sells science and math products on the Web, through stores, and through catalogs. Among the criteria it uses to evaluate segments are average sales and profits, frequency of purchasing, and recency of purchase. Applying these criteria, Delta ranked multiple-purchase segments ahead of single-purchase segments and more-recent-purchase segments ahead of less-recent-purchase segments. "The faster [customers] get from that first order to that second order," says Delta's head of sales and marketing, "the better their lifetime value and retention."[31]

FIGURE 7.4   Five Patterns of Target Market Selection

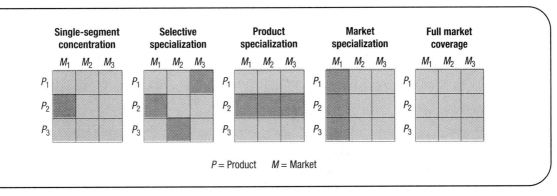

Source: Adapted from Derek F. Abell, *Defining the Business: The Starting Point of Strategic Planning* (Upper Saddle River, NJ: Prentice Hall, 1980), ch. 8, pp. 192–196.

can earn a high return on investment. However, concentrated marketing involves risks: The segment may turn sour because of changes in buying patterns or new competition. For these reasons, many companies prefer to operate in more than one segment.

Companies can try to operate in supersegments rather than in isolated segments. A **supersegment** is a set of segments sharing some exploitable similarity. For example, many symphony orchestras target people who have broad cultural interests, rather than only those who regularly attend concerts.

Selective Specialization   Here the firm selects a number of segments, each objectively attractive and appropriate. There may be little or no synergy among the segments, but each segment promises to be a moneymaker. This strategy has the advantage of diversifying the firm's risk. When Procter & Gamble launched Crest Whitestrips, initial target segments included newly engaged women, brides-to-be, and gay males.

Product Specialization   Another approach is to specialize in making a certain product for several segments. An example would be a microscope manufacturer that sells microscopes to university laboratories, government laboratories, and commercial laboratories. The firm makes different microscopes for different customer groups and builds a strong reputation in the specific product area. The downside risk is that the product may be supplanted by an entirely new technology.

Market Specialization   The firm concentrates on serving many needs of a particular customer group. An example would be a firm that sells an assortment of products only to university laboratories. The firm gains a strong reputation in serving this customer group and becomes a channel for further products that the customer group can use. The downside risk is that the customer group may suffer budget cuts or shrink in size.

Full Market Coverage   The firm attempts to serve all customer groups with all the products they might need. Only very large firms such as IBM (computer market) and General Motors (vehicle market) can undertake a full market coverage strategy. Large firms can cover a whole market through undifferentiated marketing or differentiated marketing.

In *undifferentiated marketing*, the firm ignores segment differences and goes after the whole market with one market offer. It designs a product and a marketing program that will appeal to the broadest number of buyers then uses mass distribution backed by mass advertising to create a superior product image. The narrow product line keeps down costs of research and development, production, inventory, transportation, marketing research, advertising, and product management; the undifferentiated advertising program keeps down advertising costs. Presumably, the company can turn its lower costs into lower prices to win over price-sensitive customers.

In *differentiated marketing*, the firm operates in several market segments and designs different programs for each segment. Cosmetics firm Estée Lauder markets brands that appeal to women (and men) of different tastes: The flagship brand, the original Estée Lauder, appeals to older consumers; Clinique caters to middle-aged women; M.A.C. to youthful hipsters; Aveda to aromatherapy enthusiasts; and Origins to ecoconscious consumers who prefer natural ingredients.[32] Differentiated marketing typically creates more total sales than undifferentiated marketing, but it also increases costs for product modification, manufacturing, administration, inventory, and promotion.

Because differentiated marketing leads to both higher sales and higher costs, we cannot generalize regarding this strategy's profitability. Still, companies should be cautious about oversegmenting their markets. If this happens, they may want to use *countersegmentation* to broaden their customer base. As an example, Smith Kline Beecham introduced Aquafresh toothpaste to attract three benefit segments simultaneously: those seeking fresh breath, whiter teeth, and cavity protection.

Managing Multiple Segments   The best way to manage multiple segments is to appoint segment managers with sufficient authority and responsibility for building the segment's business. At the same time, segment managers should not be so focused as to resist cooperating with other groups in the company. Consider Baxter, which operates several divisions offering different goods and services to hospitals. At one time, each division sent out its own invoices. After hospitals complained about receiving as many as seven different Baxter invoices each month, the company arranged for divisions to send invoices to headquarters so they could be consolidated into a single invoice for each customer.

Additional Considerations

Three other considerations must be taken into account in evaluating and selecting segments: segment-by-segment invasions, updating segmentation schemes, and ethical choice of market targets.

Segment-by-Segment Invasions   A company should enter one segment at a time and avoid letting rivals know what segment(s) will be next. Unfortunately, many companies fail to develop a long-term invasion plan. PepsiCo is an exception, attacking Coca-Cola first in the grocery market, then in the vending-machine market and other markets. A company facing blocked markets can apply **megamarketing**, the strategic coordination of economic, psychological, political, and public relations skills, to gain the cooperation of a number of parties in order to enter or operate in a given market. Pepsi did this to enter India after Coca-Cola left. First, Pepsi worked with a local business group to gain government approval for its entry over the objections of domestic competitors and anti-multinational legislators. Management also offered to help India export agricultural products to cover the cost of importing soft-drink concentrate and promised economic development for some rural areas. Pepsi's bundle of benefits won the support of the key groups, enabling the company to start operating in India.

Updating Segmentation Schemes   Market segmentation analysis must be done periodically because segments change. At one time the personal computer industry segmented its products purely on speed and power. Later, PC marketers recognized an emerging "Soho" market, named for "small office and home office." Mail-order companies such as Dell appealed to this market's requirement for high performance coupled with low price and user friendliness. Shortly thereafter, PC makers began to see Soho as comprised of smaller segments. "Small-office needs might be very different from home-office needs," a Dell executive notes. Today Dell's monthly marketing activities include direct contact with 10 million small, home-office, and mid-sized businesses.[33]

One way to discover new segments is to investigate the hierarchy of attributes consumers examine in choosing a brand if they use phased decision strategies, a process called **market partitioning**. Years ago, most car buyers first decided on the manufacturer and then on one of its divisions (*brand-dominant hierarchy*). A buyer might favor General Motors cars and, within this set, Pontiac. Today, some buyers decide first on the nation from which they want to buy a car (*nation-dominant hierarchy*), then choose the manufacturer and the model. Companies must monitor potential shifts in consumers' hierarchy of attributes and adjust to changing priorities, because segments may have distinct demographics, psychographics, and mediagraphics.[34]

Ethical Choice of Market Targets   Market targeting sometimes generates public controversy.[35] Consumers become concerned when marketers take unfair advantage of vulnerable groups (such as children) or disadvantaged groups (such as poor people), or promote potentially harmful products. For example, the cereal industry has been criticized for marketing to children. Critics worry that high-powered appeals presented through the mouths of animated characters will lead children to eat too much sugared cereal or poorly balanced breakfasts. Not all attempts to target children, minorities, or other segments draw criticism. Colgate-Palmolive's Colgate Junior toothpaste has special features designed to get children to brush longer and more often. Thus the issue is not who is targeted, but rather how and for what purpose. Socially responsible marketing calls for targeting and positioning that serve not only the company's interests but also the interests of the targeted segments.

EXECUTIVE SUMMARY

Target marketing involves three activities: market segmentation, market targeting, and market positioning. Markets can be targeted at four levels: segments, niches, local areas, and individuals. Market segments are large, identifiable groups within a market. A niche is a more narrowly defined group. Many marketers localize their marketing programs for certain trading areas, neighborhoods, and even individual stores. More marketers now practice individual marketing and mass customization.

Consumer characteristics and consumer responses are two bases for segmenting consumer markets. The major segmentation variables for consumer markets are geographic, demographic, psychographic, and behavioral, used singly or in combination. Business marketers can use all of these variables along with operating variables, purchasing approaches, and situational factors. To be useful, market segments must be measurable, substantial, accessible, differentiable, and actionable.

Once a firm has identified its market-segment opportunities, it evaluates the various segments and decides how many and which ones to target: a single segment, several segments, a specific product, a specific market, or the full market. In targeting the full market, it can use either differentiated or undifferentiated marketing. In addition to updating their segmentation analyses periodically and making segment-by-segment invasion plans, marketers should choose target markets in a socially responsible manner.

NOTES

1. Julie Carter, "Hallmark Salutes Veterans with Cards," *VFW Magazine*, November 2003, pp. 16+; Dennis Coday, "Hallmark to Sell Edi al-Fitr Cards," *National Catholic Reporter*, October 3, 2003, p. 7; "Mostly Spanish, Sometimes English," *MMR*, February 24, 2003, p. 26; "AG, Hallmark Build on Ethnic Diversity," *MMR*, October 15, 2001, pp. 37+;

"New Arrangements at Hallmark," *Promo*, May 1, 2001, pp. 77+; Beth Whitehouse, "Season's Greetings," *Newsday*, December 11, 2000, p. B6.

2. See James C. Anderson and James A. Narus, "Capturing the Value of Supplementary Services," *Harvard Business Review* (January–February 1995): 75–83.

3. See Tevfik Dalgic and Maarten Leeuw, "Niche Marketing Revisited: Concept, Applications, and Some European Cases," *European Journal of Marketing* 28, no. 4 (1994): 39–55.

4. Ian Zack, "Out of the Tube," *Forbes*, November 26, 2001, p. 200.

5. Robert Blattberg and John Deighton, "Interactive Marketing: Exploiting the Age of Addressability," *Sloan Management Review* 33, no. 1 (1991): 5–14.

6. Kris Maher, "Career Journal—Help Wanted: Marketing Director with Golden Touch," *Wall Street Journal*, June 11, 2002, p. B10; Paul Davidson, "Entrepreneurs Reap Riches from Net Niches," *USA Today*, April 20, 1998, p. B3 *(www.ostrichesonline.com)*.

7. Peter Post, "Beyond Brand—The Power of Experience Branding," *ANA/The Advertiser* (October/November 2000).

8. See Don Peppers and Martha Rogers, *The One to One Future: Building Relationships One Customer at a Time* (New York: Currency/Doubleday, 1993).

9. Adrian J. Slywotzky and David J. Morrison, *How Digital Is Your Business?* (New York: Crown Business, 2000), p. 39.

10. Jerry Wind and A. Rangaswamy, "Customerization: The Second Revolution in Mass Customization," Wharton School Working Paper, June 1999.

11. Anderson and Narus, "Capturing the Value of Supplementary Services," pp. 75–83.

12. "Creating Greater Customer Value May Require a Lot of Changes," *Organizational Dynamics*, Summer 1998, p. 26.

13. Joann Muller, "Kmart con Salsa: Will It Be Enough?" *BusinessWeek*, September 9, 2002.

14. Kate Kane, "It's a Small World," *Working Woman*, October 1997, p. 22.

15. Another leading supplier of geodemographic data is ClusterPlus (Strategic Mapping).

16. Michael J. Weiss, "To Be About to Be," *American Demographics* (September 2003): 29–36.

17. Sarah Allison and Carlos Tejada, "Mr., Mrs., Meet Mr. Clean," *Wall Street Journal*, January 30, 2003, pp. B1, B3.

18. Jim Rendon, "Rear Window," *Business 2.0*, August 2003, p. 72.

19. Aixa Pascual, "Lowe's Is Sprucing Up Its House," *BusinessWeek*, June 3, 2002, pp. 56–57; Pamela Sebastian Ridge, "Tool Sellers Tap Their Feminine Side," *Wall Street Journal*, June 16, 2002, p. B1.

20. Gregory L. White and Shirley Leung, "Middle Market Shrinks as Americans Migrate toward the Higher End," *Wall Street Journal*, March 29, 2002, pp. A1, A8.

21. Andrew E. Serwer, "42,496 Secrets Bared," *Fortune*, January 24, 1994, pp. 13–14; Kenneth Labich, "Class in America," *Fortune*, February 7, 1994, pp. 114–126.

22. Leah Rickard, "Gerber Trots Out New Ads Backing Toddler Food Line," *Advertising Age*, April 11, 1994, pp. 1, 48.

23. Pam Danziger, "Getting More for V-Day," *Brandweek*, February 9, 2004, p. 19.

24. Allana Sullivan, "Mobil Bets Drivers Pick Cappuccino over Parties," *Wall Street Journal*, January 30, 1995.

25. This classification was adapted from George H. Brown, "Brand Loyalty—Fact or Fiction?" *Advertising Age*, June 1952–January 1953, a series. See also Peter E. Rossi, R. McCulloch, and G. Allenby, "The Value of Purchase History Data in Target Marketing," *Marketing Science* 15, no. 4 (1996): 321–340.

26. Chip Walker, "How Strong Is Your Brand?" *Marketing Tools*, January/February 1995, pp. 46–53.

27. See www.conversionmodel.com.

28. Jesse Berst, "Why Small Business Is Suddenly Big Business," *ZDNet AnchorDesk*, November 29, 1999 *(www.anchordesk.com)*.

29. "BB&T: Picture Perfect," *Financial Services Marketing*, January-February 2001, p. 17.

30. Thomas S. Robertson and Howard Barich, "A Successful Approach to Segmenting Industrial Markets," *Planning Forum* (November–December 1992): 5–11.

31. "Delta Education Boosts Science Offerings in Neo Sci Acquisition," *Educational Marketer*, July 5, 2004, n.p.; Roger J. Best, *Market-Based Management*, 2d ed (Upper Saddle River, NJ: Prentice Hall, 2000), pp. 111–114; Marian Burk Wood, *The Marketing Plan Handbook* (Upper Saddle River, NJ: Prentice Hall, 2005), pp. 63–65; Patricia Odell, "A-Plus," *Direct*, September 15, 2000, p. E7.

32. www.esteelauder.com.

33. "Dell Targets SMBs with Tailored Products," *InformationWeek*, April 28, 2005, n.p.; Catherine Arns, "PC Makers Head for 'SoHo'," *BusinessWeek*, September 28, 1992, pp. 125–126; Gerry Khermouch, "The Marketers Take Over," *Brandweek*, September 27, 1993, pp. 29–35.

34. For a market-structure study of the hierarchy of attributes in the coffee market, see Dipak Jain, Frank M. Bass, and Yu-Min Chen, "Estimation of Latent Class Models with Heterogeneous Choice Probabilities: An Application to Market Structuring," *Journal of Marketing Research* (February 1990): 94–101. For an application of means-end chain analysis to global markets, see Freakel Ter Hofstede, Jan-Benedict E. M. Steenkamp, and Michel Wedel, "International Market Segmentation Based on Consumer–Product Relations," *Journal of Marketing Research* (February 1999): 1–17.

35. See Bart Macchiette and Roy Abhijit, "Sensitive Groups and Social Issues," *Journal of Consumer Marketing* 11, no. 4 (1994): 55–64.

CHAPTER 8

Creating Brand Equity

In this chapter, we will address the following questions:

1. What is a brand, and how does branding work?
2. What is brand equity, and how is it built, measured, and managed?
3. What are the important decisions in developing a branding strategy?

MARKETING MANAGEMENT AT GOOGLE

Founded in 1998 by two Stanford University Ph.D. students, search engine Google's name is a play on the word googol—the number represented by a 1 followed by 100 zeroes—a reference to the huge amount of data online. With 200 million search requests daily, the company has turned a profit by keeping users and advertisers happy. Users like the site's sophisticated search algorithms, which deliver relevant results quickly. Advertisers like being able to target their messages so certain ads are displayed when consumers type in specific search terms.

In what may be the ultimate sign of success, the brand is often used as a verb—"to google" is to search online. Small wonder that branding remains a top priority for Google's co-founders, Sergey Brin and Larry Page, who say, "We believe that the brand identity that we have developed has significantly contributed to the success of our business. We also believe that maintaining and enhancing the Google brand is critical to expanding our base of users, advertisers, and Google Network members." Because people know the brand and what it stands for, Google can accomplish a lot on a relatively small marketing budget: it spends only 10 percent of its net revenue on marketing, compared to the 25 percent that Yahoo! spends. Although Google's market share is higher than Yahoo! and MSN combined, its challenge now is to maintain the long-term loyalty of both consumers and advertisers.[1]

Perhaps the most distinctive skill of professional marketers is their ability to create, maintain, enhance, and protect brands. *Strategic brand management* covers the design and implementation of marketing activities and programs to build, measure, and manage brands to maximize their value. This process involves (1) identifying and establishing brand positioning; (2) planning and implementing brand marketing; (3) measuring and interpreting brand performance; and (4) growing and sustaining brand value. Chapter 9 deals with brand positioning and competition. The remaining topics are discussed in this chapter.

WHAT IS BRAND EQUITY?

The American Marketing Association defines a **brand** as "a name, term, sign, symbol, or design, or a combination of them, intended to identify the goods or services of one seller or group of sellers and to differentiate them from those of competitors." A brand adds dimensions that differentiate the offering in some way from other offerings designed to satisfy the same need. These differences may be functional, rational, or tangible—related to the brand's product performance. They may also be more symbolic, emotional or intangible—related to what the brand represents.

The Role of Brands

Brands identify the source or maker of a product and allow consumers—either individuals or organizations—to assign responsibility to a particular manufacturer or distributor. Consumers may evaluate the identical product differently depending on how it is branded. Consumers learn about brands through past experiences with the product and its marketing program. They find out which brands satisfy their needs and which ones do not. As consumers' lives become more complicated, rushed, and time-starved, the ability of a brand to simplify decision making and reduce risk is invaluable.[2]

Brands also perform valuable functions for firms.[3] Not only do they simplify product handling or tracing, they also help organize inventory and accounting records and offer the firm legal protection for unique product features or elements.[4] The brand name can be protected through registered trademarks; manufacturing processes can be protected through patents; and packaging can be protected through copyrights and designs. Intellectual property rights ensure that the firm can safely invest in the brand and reap the benefits of a valuable asset, as Google has done.

Brands can signal a certain level of quality so that satisfied buyers can easily choose the product again.[5] Brand loyalty provides predictability and security of demand for the firm and creates barriers to entry that make it difficult for other firms to enter the market. Loyalty also can translate into a willingness to pay a higher price—often 20 to 25 percent more.[6] Although competitors may easily duplicate manufacturing processes and product designs, they cannot easily match lasting impressions in the minds of individuals and organizations from years of marketing activity and product experience. In this sense, branding can be seen as a powerful means to secure a competitive advantage.[7]

The Scope of Branding

Branding is endowing products and services with the power of a brand. Branding is all about creating differences. To brand a product, it is necessary to teach consumers "who" the product is—by giving it a name and using other brand elements to help identify it—as well as "what" the product does and "why" consumers should care. Branding involves creating mental structures and helping consumers organize their knowledge about products and services in a way that clarifies their decision making and, in the process, provides value to the firm.

For branding strategies to be successful and brand value to be created, consumers must be convinced that there are meaningful differences among brands in the product or service category. The key to branding is that consumers must not think that all brands in the category are the same. It is possible to brand a physical good (Campbell's soup), a service (Singapore Airlines), a store (Foot Locker specialty stores), a person (Andre Agassi), a place (the city of Sydney), an organization (American Automobile Association), or an idea (free trade).

Defining Brand Equity

Brand equity is the added value endowed to products and services, reflected in how consumers think, feel, and act with respect to the brand, as well as the prices, market share, and profitability that the brand commands for the firm. Brand equity is an important intangible asset that has psychological and financial value to the firm.

Various perspectives are used to study brand equity.[8] **Customer-based brand equity** can be defined as the differential effect that brand knowledge has on consumer response to the marketing of that brand.[9] A brand is said to have positive customer-based brand equity when consumers react more favorably to a product and the way it is marketed when the brand is identified as compared to when it is not. A brand is said to have negative customer-based brand equity if consumers react less favorably to marketing activity for the brand under the same circumstances.

This definition has three key ingredients. First, brand equity arises from differences in consumer response. With no differences, the brand name product essentially would be classified as a commodity or generic version of the product, and competition would probably be based on price. Second, these differences in response are a result of consumer's **brand knowledge**, all the thoughts, feelings, images, experiences, beliefs, and so on that become associated with the brand. Brands must create strong, favorable, and unique brand associations with customers, as has been the case with Volvo (*safety*) and Hallmark (*caring*). Third, the differential response by consumers that makes up the brand equity is reflected in perceptions, preferences, and behavior related to all aspects of the marketing of a brand. Table 8.1 summarizes some of these key benefits of brand equity.

TABLE 8.1   Marketing Advantages of Strong Brands

Improved Perceptions of Product Performance
Greater Loyalty
Less Vulnerability to Competitive Marketing Actions
Less Vulnerability to Marketing Crises
Larger Margins
More Inelastic Consumer Response to Price Increases
More Elastic Consumer Response to Price Decreases
Greater Trade Cooperation and Support
Increased Marketing Communications Effectiveness
Possible Licensing Opportunities
Additional Brand Extension Opportunities

Consumer knowledge is what drives the differences that manifest themselves in brand equity. In an abstract sense, brand equity can be seen as providing marketers with a vital strategic "bridge" from their past to their future.

Brand Equity as a Bridge

From the perspective of brand equity, all the marketing dollars spent each year on offerings are actually investments in consumer brand knowledge. The *quality* of the investment in brand building is the critical factor, not necessarily the *quantity*, beyond some minimal threshold amount. Many brands have amassed considerable brand equity through spending on marketing activities that create valuable, enduring memory traces in the consumers' minds. Despite being outspent by such beverage brand giants as Coca-Cola, Pepsi, and Budweiser, the California Milk Processor Board was able to reverse a decades-long decline in consumption of milk in California partly through its well-designed and executed "Got Milk?" campaign.

At the same time, the brand knowledge created by these marketing investments dictates appropriate future directions for the brand. Consumers will decide, based on what they think and feel about the brand, where and how they believe the brand should go and grant or deny permission to any marketing action or program.

A brand is essentially a marketer's promise to deliver predictable product or service performance. A **brand promise** is the marketer's vision of what the brand must be and do for consumers. Yet a brand's true value and future prospects rest with consumers, their knowledge about the brand, and their likely response to marketing activity as a result of this knowledge. Understanding consumer brand knowledge—all the different things that become linked to the brand in the minds of consumers—is thus of paramount importance because it is the foundation of brand equity.

BUILDING BRAND EQUITY

Marketers build brand equity by creating the right brand knowledge structures with the right consumers. This process depends on *all* brand-related contacts—whether marketer initiated or not. From a marketing management perspective, there are three main sets of *brand equity drivers:*

1. *The initial choices for the brand elements or identities making up the brand (e.g., brand names, URLs, logos, symbols, characters, spokespeople, slogans, jingles, packages, and signage).* To reinforce its nautical theme, Old Spice uses bright-red packaging and its familiar ocean schooner; however, it is also launching deodorant and antiperspirant extensions, adding the High Endurance and Red Zone brand names.[10]

2. *The product and service and all accompanying marketing activities and supporting marketing programs.* Joe Boxer made its name selling colorful underwear with its signature yellow smiley face, Mr. Licky, in a hip, fun way through clever stunts and events that garnered publicity and word of mouth.[11]

3. *Other associations indirectly transferred to the brand by linking it to some other entity (a person, place, or thing).* Subaru used the rugged Australian Outback and actor Paul Hogan of *Crocodile Dundee* movie fame in ads to help craft the brand image of the Subaru Outback line of sports utility wagons.

Choosing Brand Elements

Brand elements are those trademarkable devices that serve to identify and differentiate the brand. Nike has the distinctive "swoosh" logo, the empowering "Just Do It" slogan, and the mythological "Nike" name based on the winged goddess of victory. The test of the brand-building ability of these elements is what consumers would think or feel about the product *if* they only knew about the brand element. A brand element that provides a positive contribution to brand equity, for example, would be one where consumers assumed or inferred certain valued associations or responses. Based on its name alone, a consumer might expect ColorStay lipsticks to be long lasting.

Brand Element Choice Criteria   There are six criteria in choosing brand elements (as well as more specific choice considerations in each case). As shown in Table 8.2, the first three (memorable, meaningful, and likeable) can be characterized as "brand building" in terms of how brand equity can be built through the judicious choice of a brand element. The latter three (protectible, adaptable, and transferable) are more "defensive," concerned with how the brand equity contained in a brand element can be leveraged and preserved in the face of different opportunities and constraints.

Developing Brand Elements   In creating a brand, marketers have many choices of brand elements to identify their products. Often, companies hire a marketing research firm to brainstorm and test names, using vast computer databases to catalog names by association, sounds, and other qualities. Name-research procedures include *association tests* (What images come to mind?), *learning tests* (How easily is the name pronounced?), *memory tests* (How well is the name remembered?), and *preference tests* (Which names are preferred?). Of course, the firm must also be sure that the chosen name has not already been registered.

Brand elements can play a number of brand-building roles. If consumers do not examine much information in making their product decisions, memorable or meaningful brand elements can reduce the burden on marketing communications to build awareness and link brand associations. The different associations that arise from the

TABLE 8.2   Criteria for Choosing Brand Elements

For Building the Brand	For Defending the Brand
Memorable: Is the element easily recalled and recognized at both purchase and consumption? Example: Tide	*Transferable*: Can the element introduce new products in the same or different categories? Can it add to brand equity across geographic boundaries and segments? Example: Nestlé bird nest
Meaningful: Is the element credible and suggestive of the corresponding category? Does it suggest something about an ingredient or a brand user? Example: Lean Cuisine	*Adaptable*: Can the element be adapted and updated? Example: Betty Crocker image
Likeable: Is the element aesthetically appealing and inherently likeable visually, verbally, and in other ways? Example: Firebird	*Protectible*: Is the element legally and competitively protectible and not easily copied? Can the firm retain trademark rights? Example: Yahoo!

likeability and appeal of brand elements may also play a critical role in brand equity. The Keebler elves reinforce home-style baking quality and a sense of magic and fun for their line of cookies.

Brand names are not the only important brand element. Often, the less concrete brand benefits are, the more important it is that brand elements capture the brand's intangible characteristics. Many insurance firms use symbols of strength (the Rock of Gibraltar for Prudential and the stag for Hartford). Slogans also are an efficient means to build brand equity, functioning as "hooks" or "handles" to help consumers grasp what the brand is and what makes it special. Think of the inherent brand meaning in a slogan such as: "Like a Good Neighbor, State Farm is There."

Designing Holistic Marketing Activities

Although the judicious choice of brand elements and secondary associations can make important contributions to building brand equity, the primary input comes from the product or service and supporting marketing activities. Customers come to know a brand through a range of contacts and touch points: personal observation and use, word of mouth, interactions with company personnel, online or telephone experiences, and payment transactions. A **brand contact** can be defined as any information-bearing experience a customer or prospect has with the brand, the product category, or the market that relates to the marketer's product or service.[12] Any of these experiences can be positive or negative. The company must put as much effort into managing these experiences as it does in producing its ads.[13]

Holistic marketers emphasize three key themes in designing brand-building marketing programs: personalization, integration, and internalization.

Personalization *Personalizing marketing* is about making sure that the brand and its marketing are as relevant as possible to as many customers as possible—a challenge, given that no two customers are identical. The Internet is not the only way to personalize marketing. Marketers have embraced concepts such as experiential marketing, one-to-one marketing, and permission marketing to create an intense, active relationship with consumers. Brands such as Harley-Davidson have been able to attain cult status because their marketers closely manage all brand contacts and emphasize personalization, as discussed in "Marketing Skills: Building a Cult Brand."

Integration *Integrating marketing* is about mixing and matching marketing activities to maximize their individual and collective effects.[14] Although firms can use a variety of different marketing activities to reinforce the brand promise, integration is especially critical with marketing communications (as discussed in more detail in Chapter 15). As much as possible, there should be a match among certain communication options so that the effects of any one option are enhanced by the presence of another, making the whole greater than the sum of the parts.

Marketers should judge how effectively and efficiently each communication option influences brand awareness and creates, maintains, or strengthens brand image. **Brand awareness** is consumers' ability to identify the brand under different conditions, as reflected by their brand recognition or recall performance. **Brand image** is the perceptions and beliefs held by consumers, as reflected in the associations held in consumer memory. It is important to employ a mix of communication options, each playing a specific role in building or maintaining brand equity.

Internalization   Marketers must adopt an *internal* perspective to ensure that employees and marketing partners appreciate and understand basic branding notions and know how they can help—or hurt—brand equity.[15] **Internal branding** refers to activities and processes that inform and inspire employees.[16] It is critical for service companies and retailers that all employees have an up-to-date, deep understanding of the brand and its promise. *Brand bonding* occurs when customers experience the company as delivering on its brand promise. All of the customers' contacts with company employees and company communications must be positive. *The brand promise will not be delivered unless everyone in the company lives the brand.*

One of the most potent influences on brand perception is the experience customers have with company personnel. Disney is so successful at internal branding and having employees support its brand that it holds seminars on the "Disney Style" for employees from other companies. Holistic marketers must go even further, training and encouraging distributors and dealers to serve their customers well, which in turn helps strengthen brand image.

MARKETING SKILLS: BUILDING A CULT BRAND

Some brands provoke such strong customer loyalty that they attain cult status—Harley-Davidson motorcycles, for instance. Building a cult brand can significantly increase sales and profits without expensive promotions and without appealing to a mass market, making this skill particularly important for marketers launching unconventional or niche products. Several competencies contribute to this skill. First is the ability to create a "buzz" by stirring excitement among opinion leaders in the targeted segment and personalizing the brand experience. Imagination is the key—widespread, ordinary advertising would dilute the effect. Jones Soda, for instance, sends its Jones RV with a crew to U.S. and Canadian cities to give away samples, talk with people on the street, and bring new customers into the fold.

Next, marketers need to enhance the product's appeal through supply and distribution. A new product that is readily available everywhere will seem less special. This is why Acid cigars are sold through only 500 U.S. retailers plus the company's Web site and why Screaming Eagle vineyards produces just 500 cases of wine per year. Marketers can also provide a framework for brand-based communities like the Harley Owners Group; bringing enthusiasts together for special events makes the brand experience more personal and relevant.

Entrepreneur Peter van Stolk has honed his skills in making Jones Soda a cult hit. After struggling to obtain shelf space in food stores, van Stolk decided to place his products in untraditional outlets that attract the Generation Y target segment, such as surfboard stores and record stores. Customers who tried the colorful soft drinks began asking for it in other stores, paving the way for distribution in convenience stores. The entrepreneur forges an emotional connection by inviting fans to submit their personal photos for possible use on bottle labels. Although only 40 or so are chosen each year from tens of thousands of entries, van Stolk's approach to personalization has built Jones Soda into a cult brand with annual sales of $35 million.[17]

Leveraging Secondary Associations

The third way to build brand equity is, in effect, to "borrow" it by linking brand associations to other entities that have their own associations, thereby creating "secondary" brand associations. In this way, brand equity is created by linking the brand to other information in memory that conveys meaning to consumers (see Figure 8.1).

The brand may be linked to source factors such as the company (through branding strategies), countries or other geographical regions (through identification of product origin), and channels of distribution (through channel strategy). Also, it may be linked to other brands (through co-branding or ingredient branding), characters (through licensing), spokespeople (through endorsements), sporting or cultural events (through sponsorship), or some other third-party sources (through awards or reviews). The Industrial and Commercial Bank of China did this when it arranged to co-brand its new Peony credit card with the American Express logo. This co-branding arrangement allows the Chinese bank to link its national card brand with one of the best-known international card brands.[18]

FIGURE 8.1 Secondary Sources of Brand Knowledge

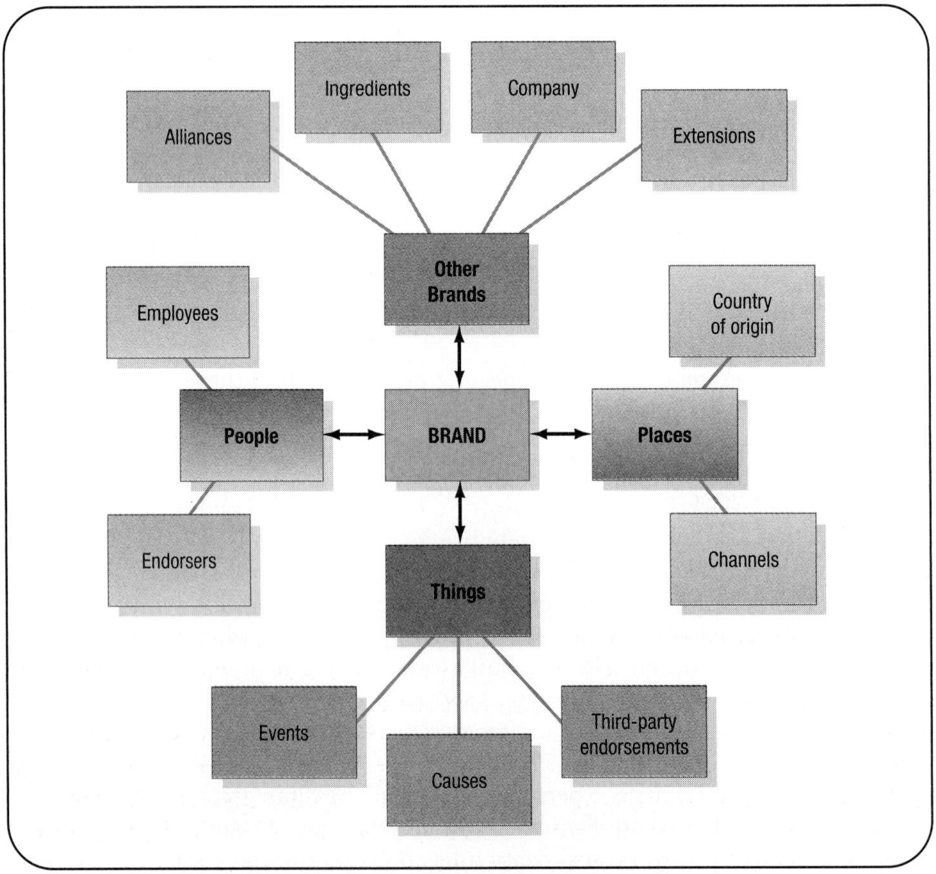

MEASURING BRAND EQUITY

Given that the power of a brand resides in the minds of consumers and how it changes their response to marketing, brand equity must be carefully measured. There are two basic approaches to measuring brand equity. An *indirect* approach assesses potential sources of brand equity by identifying and tracking consumer brand knowledge structures. A *direct* approach assesses the actual impact of brand knowledge on consumer response to different aspects of the marketing. For brand equity to perform a useful strategic function and guide marketing decisions, marketers should fully understand (1) the sources of brand equity and how they affect outcomes of interest, as well as (2) how these sources and outcomes change, if at all, over time. Brand audits are important for the former; brand tracking is important for the latter.

Brand Audits

A **brand audit** is a consumer-focused exercise that involves a series of procedures to assess the health of the brand, uncover its sources of brand equity, and suggest ways to improve and leverage its equity. The brand audit can be used to set strategic direction for the brand. Are the current sources of brand equity satisfactory? Do certain brand associations need to be strengthened? Does the brand lack uniqueness? What brand opportunities exist and what potential challenges exist for brand equity? As a result of this strategic analysis, the marketer can develop a marketing program to maximize long-term brand equity.

In a brand audit, marketers study the sources of brand equity from both the firm's and the consumer's perspectives.[19] From the perspective of the firm, it is necessary to understand exactly what products and services are currently being offered to consumers and how they are being marketed and branded. From the perspective of the consumer, it is necessary to uncover the true meaning of brands and products to the consumer.

Brand audits consist of two steps: the brand inventory and the brand exploratory. The *brand inventory* is a current, comprehensive profile of how all of a company's offerings are marketed and branded, including all associated brand elements and supporting marketing programs. It is also advisable to profile the branding and marketing efforts of competitive brands in as much detail as possible. The *brand exploratory* is research activity conducted to understand what consumers think and feel about the brand and its corresponding product category to identify sources of brand equity. Additional research may be required to better understand how customers shop for and use the offerings and what they think of various brands.

Brand Tracking

Tracking studies collect information from consumers on a routine basis over time. Tracking studies typically employ quantitative measures to provide marketers with current information as to how their brands and marketing programs are performing on the basis of a number of key dimensions. Tracking studies are a means of understanding where, how much, and in what ways brand value is being created. These studies provide valuable diagnostic insights into the collective effects of a host of marketing activities. It is important for marketers to monitor the health of the brand and its equity over time so that proper adjustments can be made as needed.

Brand Valuation

Brand equity needs to be distinguished from *brand valuation*, which is the job of estimating the total financial value of the brand. Certain companies base their growth on acquiring and building rich brand portfolios. Switzerland-based Nestlé has acquired such established brands as Rowntree (U.K.), Carnation (U.S.), Stouffer (U.S.), Buitoni-Perugina (Italy), and Perrier (France), making it the world's largest food company. With well-known companies, brand value is typically over one-half of the total company market capitalization.[20] U.S. companies do not list brand equity on their balance sheets because of the arbitrariness of the estimate. However, brand equity is given a value by some companies in the United Kingdom, Hong Kong, and Australia.

MANAGING BRAND EQUITY

Effective brand management requires a long-term view of marketing decisions. Because responses to marketing activity depend on what consumers know and remember about a brand, short-term marketing actions—which change brand knowledge—necessarily increase or decrease future marketing success. Additionally, marketers who take a long-term view can proactively maintain and enhance customer-based brand equity over time in the face of external changes in the environment and internal changes in the firm's marketing goals and programs.

Brand Reinforcement

Brand equity is reinforced by marketing actions that consistently convey the meaning of the brand to consumers in terms of (1) what products the brand represents; what core benefits it supplies; and what needs it satisfies; as well as (2) how the brand makes those products superior and which strong, favorable, and unique brand associations should exist in the minds of consumers. Nivea, one of Europe's strongest brands, has expanded its scope from a skin-cream brand to a skin-care and personal-care brand through carefully designed and implemented brand extensions reinforcing the Nivea brand promise of "mild," "gentle," and "caring" in a broader arena.

Reinforcing brand equity requires innovation and relevance throughout the marketing program. Marketers must introduce new products and conduct new marketing activities that truly satisfy their target markets. The brand must be moving forward, but always in the right direction, supported by compelling new offerings and new marketing. Brands that fail to do so—such as Oldsmobile—find that their market leadership dwindles or even disappears.

An important consideration in reinforcing brands is the consistency of the type and amount of marketing support the brand receives. Many tactical changes may be necessary to maintain the strategic thrust and direction of the brand. Unless there is some environmental change, however, there is little need to deviate from a successful positioning. In such cases, sources of brand equity should be vigorously preserved and defended.

Brand Revitalization

Changes in consumer tastes and preferences, the emergence of new competitors or new technology, or any new development in the marketing environment could potentially affect the fortunes of a brand. In virtually every product category, there are examples of once prominent and admired brands—such as Smith Corona, Zenith, and TWA—that have fallen on hard times or even disappeared.[21] Nevertheless, some of these brands have made comebacks recently; for instance, Breck and Dr. Scholl's have successfully turned their brand fortunes around to varying degrees.

Reversing a fading brand's fortunes requires either that it "returns to its roots" and restore lost sources of brand equity or that it establish new sources of brand equity are established. Often, the first step in a turnaround is to understand the original sources of brand equity. Are positive associations losing their strength or uniqueness? Have negative associations become linked to the brand? The firm then decides whether to retain the same positioning or create a new positioning, and, if so, which positioning to adopt. Sometimes the positioning is still appropriate; it is the actual marketing program that is failing to deliver on the brand promise. In other cases, the old positioning is not viable, and a "reinvention" strategy is necessary. Mountain Dew completely overhauled its brand image to become a soft-drink powerhouse by appealing to young men. With an action-oriented slogan ("Do the Dew") and ads emphasizing associations to extreme sports, Mountain Dew became the number-three selling soft drink in terms of market share.[22]

To refresh old sources of brand equity or create new sources, two main approaches are possible. First, expand the depth and/or breadth of brand awareness by improving consumer recall and recognition of the brand during purchase or consumption settings. Second, improve the strength, favorability, and uniqueness of brand associations making up the brand image; this approach may involve programs directed at existing or new brand associations.

Brand Crisis

Diverse brands such as Jack in the Box restaurants, Firestone tires, Exxon oil, Suzuki Samurai sport-utility vehicles, and Martha Stewart have all experienced a serious, potentially crippling brand crisis. The stronger the brand equity and corporate image—especially with respect to corporate credibility and trustworthiness—the more likely it is that the firm can weather the storm. Careful preparation and a well-managed crisis management program, however, are also critical. As Johnson & Johnson's nearly flawless handling of the Tylenol product-tampering incident suggests, the key to managing a crisis is that consumers see the response by the firm as both *swift* and *sincere*.

If a firm is slow to respond to a marketing crisis, consumers may form negative impressions as a result of unfavorable media coverage or word of mouth. Perhaps even worse, consumers may find out that they do not really like the brand much after all and permanently switch to alternative brands or products. The firm's response must also be sincere, publicly acknowledging the severity of the impact on consumers and being willing to take whatever steps are necessary and feasible to solve the crisis. Otherwise, consumers may form negative attributions.

For example, when consumers reported finding shards of glass in some jars of its baby food, Gerber tried to reassure the public that there were no problems in its manufacturing plants. However, the company refused to have its baby food withdrawn from food stores. Some consumers clearly found this response unsatisfactory: Gerber's market share slumped from 66 percent to 52 percent within a couple of months. One company official admitted, "Not pulling our baby food off the shelf gave the appearance that we aren't a caring company."[23]

DEVELOPING A BRAND STRATEGY

The **branding strategy** reflects the number and nature of common and distinctive brand elements applied to the different products sold by the firm. In other words, devising a branding strategy involves deciding the nature of new and existing brand elements to be applied to new and existing products. The decision about how to brand new products is especially critical. A company has a number of options that can be categorized into three main choices: (1) It can develop new brand elements for the new product; (2) it can apply some of its existing brand elements; (3) it can use a combination of new and existing brand elements (see Table 8.3).

The Branding Decision: To Brand or Not to Brand?

The branding decision is whether to develop a brand name for a product. Today, branding is such a strong force that hardly anything goes unbranded. So-called commodities do not have to remain commodities. A *commodity* is a product presumably so basic that it cannot be physically differentiated in the minds of consumers. A number of products that once were seen as commodities have become highly differentiated, as strong brands have emerged in the category.[24] Some notable examples (with brand pioneers in parentheses) are: coffee (Maxwell House), flour (Gold Medal), beer (Budweiser), bananas (Chiquita), pineapples (Dole), and even salt (Morton).

General Brand Strategies   A firm that decides to brand its offerings must choose which brand names to use. Four general strategies are:

■ *Individual names.* General Mills uses this strategy (Gold Medal flour, Nature Valley granola bars, and Old El Paso Mexican foods). A major advantage is that the company's reputation is not tied to the product's. If the product fails or appears to have low quality, the company is not hurt. Companies often use different brands

TABLE 8.3   Branding New Products

Concept	Definition
Brand extension	Using an established brand to launch a new product
Sub-brand	Combining a new brand with an existing brand
Parent brand	An existing brand that gives birth to a brand extension
Family brand	A parent brand that is associated with multiple brand extensions
Line extension	Using a parent brand to brand a new product targeting a new market segment within a category served by the parent (i.e. new flavors)
Category extension	Using a parent brand to enter a different product category from that currently served by the parent
Brand line	All products sold under a particular brand
Brand mix	The set of all brand lines that a firm offers to buyers (also known as brand assortment)
Branded variants	Specific brand lines supplied to particular retailers or channels
Licensed product	Using the brand name licensed from one firm on a product made by another firm

for different quality lines within the same product class, the way Delta branded its low-fare air carrier Song in part to protect the equity of its Delta Airlines brand.[25]

- *Blanket family names.* Heinz and General Electric use this strategy. A blanket family name also has advantages. Development cost is less because there is no need for "name" research or expensive advertising to create brand-name recognition. Furthermore, new-product sales are likely to be strong if the manufacturer's name is good; this means instant recognition for a new product.

- *Separate family names for all products.* Sears uses this strategy (Kenmore for appliances, Craftsman for tools). If a company produces quite different products, it is not desirable to use one blanket family name. Swift and Company developed separate family names for its hams (Premium) and fertilizers (Vigoro).

- *Corporate name combined with individual product names.* Kellogg uses this sub-branding strategy (Kellogg's Rice Krispies, Kellogg's Raisin Bran, and Kellogg's Corn Flakes). The company name legitimizes, and the individual name individualizes, the product.

Co-Branding and Ingredient Branding   Sometimes products feature more than one brand. A good example is the emergence of **co-branding**—also called dual branding or brand bundling—in which two or more well-known existing brands are combined into a joint product and/or marketed together in some fashion.[26] Co-branding can take the form of *same-company co-branding*, as when General Mills advertises Trix and Yoplait yogurt. Another form is *joint-venture co-branding*, as in the case of the Citibank AAdvantage credit card, which bears the brands of Citibank and American Airlines. Two more forms are *retail co-branding*, in which two retail establishments, such as fast-food restaurants, use the same location to optimize both space and profits, and *multiple-sponsor co-branding.*[27]

Co-branding's main advantage is that a product may be convincingly positioned by virtue of the multiple brands involved, generating greater sales from the existing target market and opening more opportunities with new consumers and channels. Co-branding also can reduce the cost of product introduction because two well-known images are combined, accelerating potential adoption. Finally, co-branding may help marketers learn more about consumers and how other companies approach them.

Co-branding must be carefully managed to minimize the risks and lack of control from aligning with another brand. First, unsatisfactory performance could hurt both of the brands. Second, if one brand participates in a number of co-branding arrangements, overexposure might dilute the transfer of any association. Third, a company with several co-branding arrangements may focus less on its existing brands.

Ingredient branding is a special case of co-branding that involves creating brand equity for materials, components, or parts that are necessarily contained within other branded products. Some successful ingredient brands include Dolby noise reduction and Gore-Tex water-resistant fibers. Some popular ingredient-branded products are Betty Crocker baking mixes with Hershey's chocolate syrup and Lunchables with Taco Bell tacos. Many manufacturers make components—motors or computer chips—that enter into final branded products, and the components' individual identity normally gets lost. These manufacturers hope their brand will be featured as part of the final product. Intel's consumer-directed brand campaign convinced many people to buy only PCs with "Intel Inside." As a result, many PC manufacturers pay a premium price for Intel's chips rather than buying equivalent chips from an unknown supplier.

Brand Extensions

When a firm uses an established brand to introduce a new product, it is called a **brand extension**. Recognizing that one of their most valuable assets is their brands, many firms leverage that asset by introducing new products under some of their strongest brand names. Most new products are in fact line extensions—typically 80 to 90 percent in any one year. Moreover, many of the most successful new products, as rated by various sources, are extensions (e.g., Microsoft Xbox video game system, Apple iPod digital music player).

Brand extensions can be broadly classified into two general categories.[28] In a **line extension**, the parent brand is used on a new product targeting a new market segment within a category currently served by the parent, such as through new flavors, forms, colors, and package sizes. Dannon has introduced several Dannon yogurt line extensions through the years, including Fruit on the Bottom and Whipped. In a **category extension**, the parent brand is used to enter a different category from that currently served by the parent brand, such as Swiss Army watches.

Advantages of Brand Extensions   One advantage of brand extensions is that they improve the odds of new-product success. With a brand extension, consumers can make inferences and form expectations as to the likely composition and performance of a new product based on what they already know about the parent brand itself and the extent to which they feel this information is relevant to the new product.[29] By setting up positive expectations, extensions reduce risk.[30]

Because of the potentially increased consumer demand resulting from introducing a new product as an extension, it also may be easier to convince retailers to stock and promote a brand extension. From a marketing communications perspective, an introductory campaign for an extension does not have to create awareness of both the brand and the new product but instead can concentrate on the new product itself.[31]

Extensions thus can reduce the cost of the launch campaign, which is important given that establishing a new brand name in the U.S. marketplace for a mass-consumer-packaged good can cost $100 million! They also can avoid the difficulty—and expense—of coming up with a new name. In addition, they allow for packaging and labeling efficiencies and, if coordinated properly, more prominence in the retail store by creating a "billboard" effect. By offering consumers a portfolio of brand variants within a product category, consumers who need a change can switch to a different product type without leaving the brand family.

A second advantage is that brand extensions can provide feedback benefits.[32] Extensions can help to clarify a brand's meaning and its core values or improve consumer perceptions of the credibility of the company behind the extension. Thus, through brand extensions, Crayola means "colorful crafts for kids" and Weight Watchers means "weight loss and maintenance." Line extensions can renew interest and liking for the brand and benefit the parent brand by expanding market coverage. A successful extension may also serve as the basis for subsequent extensions.

Disadvantages of Brand Extensions   On the downside, line extensions may cause the brand name to not be as strongly identified with any one product.[33] Ries and Trout call this the "line-extension trap."[34] By linking its brand to mainstream food products such as mashed potatoes, powdered milk, soups, and beverages, Cadbury ran the risk of losing its more specific meaning as a chocolates and candy brand.[35] **Brand**

dilution occurs when consumers no longer associate a brand with a specific product or highly similar products and start thinking less of the brand.

If a firm launches extensions consumers deem inappropriate, they may question the brand's integrity and competence. Different varieties of line extensions may confuse and perhaps even frustrate consumers: Which version is the "right one" for them? As a result, they may reject new extensions for "tried-and-true" favorites or all-purpose versions. Retailers have to reject many new products and brands because they lack the shelf or display space for them.

The worst possible scenario is that not only does the extension fail, but it also harms the parent brand image in the process. Fortunately, such events are rare. "Marketing failures," where insufficient consumers were attracted to a brand, are typically much less damaging than "product failures," where the brand fundamentally fails to live up to its promise. Even then, failures dilute brand equity only when the extension is seen as very similar to the parent brand.

Even if sales of a brand extension are high and meet targets, it is possible that this revenue may have resulted from consumers switching to the extension from existing product offerings of the parent brand, *cannibalizing* the parent brand. Intrabrand shifts in sales may not necessarily be so undesirable, as they can be thought of as a form of *preemptive cannibalization*. Consumers who might have switched to a competing brand instead choose the line extension. To illustrate, Tide laundry detergent enjoys the same market share now as it did 50 years ago because of the sales contributions of its line extensions (scented and unscented powder, tablet, liquid, and other forms). Finally, by introducing a brand extension, the firm forgoes the chance to create a new brand with its own unique image and equity. Consider the advantages to Disney of having introduced more adult-oriented Touchstone films, for example.

Success Characteristics   A potential new-product extension for a brand must be judged by how effectively it leverages existing brand equity from the parent brand to the new product, as well as how effectively the extension, in turn, contributes to the equity of the parent brand.[36] Crest White Strips leveraged the strong reputation of Crest and dental care to provide reassurance in the teeth-whitening arena while also reinforcing its dental authority image. The most important consideration with extensions is the "fit" in the mind of the consumer. Consumers may see a basis of fit for an extension in many ways—common physical attributes, usage situations, or user types.

One major mistake in evaluating extension opportunities is failing to take *all* of consumers' brand knowledge structures into account. Often marketers mistakenly focus on one or perhaps a few brand associations as a potential basis of fit and ignore other, possibly more important, associations in the process.

Brand Portfolios

All brands have boundaries—a brand can only be stretched so far. Multiple brands are often necessary to pursue multiple market segments. Any one brand is not viewed equally favorably by all the different market segments that the firm would like to target. Other reasons for introducing multiple brands in a category include:[37]

1. To increase shelf presence and retailer dependence in the store;
2. To attract consumers seeking variety who may otherwise have switched to another brand;
3. To increase internal competition within the firm; and

4. To yield economies of scale in advertising, sales, merchandising, and physical distribution.

The **brand portfolio** is the set of all brands and brand lines a particular firm offers for sale to buyers in a particular category. Different brands may be designed and marketed to appeal to different market segments. In the optimal brand portfolio, each brand maximizes equity in combination with all other brands in the portfolio. If profits can be increased by dropping brands, a portfolio is too big; if profits can be increased by adding brands, a portfolio is not big enough. In general, the basic principle is to *maximize market coverage*, so that no potential customers are being ignored, but to *minimize brand overlap*, so brands are not competing to gain customer approval. Each brand should be clearly differentiated and appealing to a sizable enough segment to justify its costs.[38]

Besides these considerations, brands can play a number of specific roles within a brand portfolio:

- *Flankers.* Flanker or "fighter" brands are positioned with respect to competitors' brands so that more important (and more profitable) *flagship brands* retain their desired positioning. As an example, Procter & Gamble markets Luvs diapers as a flanker to the premium-positioned Pampers. Fighter brands must not be so attractive that they take sales away from their higher-priced comparison brands or referents. Yet if a fighter brand is seen as connected to other brands in the portfolio in any way (e.g., by virtue of a common branding strategy), then it must not be designed so cheaply that it reflects poorly on the other brands.

- *Cash cows.* Some brands may be retained despite dwindling sales because they still appeal to a sufficient number of customers and remain profitable with virtually no marketing support. Firms can "milk" these "cash cow" brands by capitalizing on the existing brand equity. For example, even though technological advances have moved much of its market to the newer Mach III brand of razors, Gillette still sells the older Trac II, Atra, and Sensor brands. Because withdrawing these brands may not necessarily result in customers switching to another Gillette brand, it may be more profitable for Gillette to keep them in the portfolio.

- *Low-end entry level.* The role of a relatively low-priced brand in the portfolio may be to attract customers to the brand franchise. Retailers feature these "traffic builders" because they can "trade up" customers to a higher-priced brand. For example, BMW introduced certain models into its 3-series automobiles in part as a way to bring new customers into the brand franchise with the hope of "moving them up" to higher-priced models later, when they trade in their cars.

- *High-end prestige.* A relatively high-priced brand is often used to add prestige and credibility to the entire portfolio. For example, one analyst argued that the real value of Chevrolet's Corvette high performance sports car was "its ability to lure curious customers into showrooms and at the same time help improve the image of other Chevrolet cars. It does not mean a hell of a lot for GM profitability, but there is no question that it is a traffic builder."[39] The Corvette brand was meant to cast a halo over the entire Chevrolet line.

EXECUTIVE SUMMARY

A brand is a name, term, sign, symbol, or design, or some combination of these elements, intended to identify the offerings of one seller or group of sellers and to differentiate these offerings from those of competitors. The different components of a brand—brand names, logos, symbols, package designs, and so on—are brand elements. Brands offer a number of benefits to customers and firms and, as valuable intangible assets, must be managed carefully. The key to branding is that consumers perceive differences among brands in a product category.

Brand equity relates to the fact that different outcomes result in the marketing of a product or service because of its brand, as compared to the results if that same product or service was not identified by that brand. Building brand equity depends on three main factors: (1) the initial choices for the brand elements or identities making up the brand; (2) the way the brand is integrated into the supporting marketing program; and (3) the associations indirectly transferred to the brand through a link to another entity. Brand elements are trademarkable devices that identify and differentiate the brand. Holistic marketers carefully manage all brand contacts and build brands through marketing programs that emphasize personalization, integration, and internalization.

Brand equity needs to be measured in order to be managed well. Brand audits are in-depth examinations of the health of a brand and can be used to set the brand's strategic direction. Tracking studies gather information from consumers on a routine basis over time to evaluate short-term marketing effectiveness. In managing brand equity, marketers plan for brand reinforcement, revitalization, and crisis. A branding strategy identifies which brand elements a firm chooses to apply across its various products. Marketers decide whether to brand and whether to use a brand extension, putting an established brand name on a new product. Brands can play a number of different roles within the brand portfolio; the main purpose is to maximize market coverage without pitting the firm's brands against each other. Brands may play a competitive role as flankers; be cash cows that earn profits at minimal cost; act as low-end entry points for customers new to the brand franchise; or add high-end prestige to the portfolio.

NOTES

1. Ben Elgin, "Google's Leap May Slow Rivals' Growth," *BusinessWeek*, July 18, 2005, p. 45; Saul Hansell, "Google Revenue Nearly Doubles in Quarter," *New York Times*, April 22, 2005, p. C3; Carol Krol, "Google Sees Brand as Key to Expansion," *B to B*, October 25, 2004, p. 22; "How Good Is Google?" *The Economist*, November 21, 2003, pp. 57–58; Fred Vogelstein, "Can Google Grow UP?" *Fortune*, December 8, 2003, pp. 102–111.
2. Jacob Jacoby, Jerry C. Olson, and Rafael Haddock, "Price, Brand Name, and Product Composition Characteristics as Determinants of Perceived Quality," *Journal of Consumer Research* 3, no. 4 (1971): 209–216; Jacob Jacoby, George Syzbillo, and Jacqueline Busato-Sehach, "Information Acquisition Behavior in Brand Choice Situations," *Journal of Marketing Research* (1977): 63–69.
3. Leslie de Chernatony and Gil McWilliam, "The Varying Nature of Brands as Assets," *International Journal of Advertising* 8, no. 4 (1989): 339–349.
4. Constance E. Bagley, *Managers and the Legal Environment: Strategies for the 21st Century*, 2d ed. (Cincinnati, OH: West Publishing, 1995).
5. Tulin Erdem, "Brand Equity as a Signaling Phenomenon," *Journal of Consumer Psychology* 7, no. 2 (1998): 131–157.
6. Scott Davis, *Brand Asset Management: Driving Profitable Growth Through Your Brands*, (San Francisco: Jossey-Bass, 2000); D. C. Bello and M. B. Holbrook, "Does an Absence of Brand Equity Generalize Across Product Classes?" *Journal of Business Research* 34 (1996): 125–131; Mary W. Sullivan, "How Brand Names Affect the Demand for Twin

Automobiles," *Journal of Marketing Research* 35 (1998): 154–165; Adrian J. Slywotzky and Benson P. Shapiro, "Leveraging to Beat the Odds: The New Marketing Mindset," *Harvard Business Review* (September–October 1993): 97–107.

7. The power of branding is not without its critics, however, some of whom reject the commercialism associated with branding activities. See Naomi Klein, *No Logo: Taking Aim at the Brand Bullies* (New York, NY: Picador, 2000).

8. Other approaches are based on economic principles of signaling (e.g., Tulin Erdem, "Brand Equity as a Signaling Phenomenon," *Journal of Consumer Psychology* 7, no. 2 (1998): 131–157); or more of a sociological, anthropological, or biological perspective (e.g., Grant McCracken, "Culture and Consumption: A Theoretical Account of the Structure and Movement of the Cultural Meaning of Consumer Goods," *Journal of Consumer Research* 13 (1986): 71–83; or Susan Fournier, "Consumers and Their Brands: Developing Relationship Theory in Consumer Research," *Journal of Consumer Research* 24, no. 3 (1998): 343–373).

9. London, UK Keller, *Strategic Brand Management.*

10. Christine Bittar, "Old Spice Does New Tricks," *Brandweek*, June 2, 2003, pp. 17–18.

11. Paul Keegan, "The Rise and Fall (and Rise Again) of Joe Boxer, *Business 2.0*, December 2002/January 2003, pp. 76–82.

12. Don E. Schultz, Stanley I. Tannenbaum, and Robert F. Lauterborn, *Integrated Marketing Communications* (Lincolnwood IL: NTC Business Books, 1993).

13. Mohanbir Sawhney, "Don't Harmonize, Synchronize," *Harvard Business Review*, July–August 2001, pp. 101–108.

14. Dawn Iacobucci and Bobby Calder, eds., *Kellogg on Integrated Marketing* (New York: John Wiley & Sons, 2003).

15. Scott Davis and Michael Dunn, *Building the Brand-Driven Business* (New York: John Wiley & Sons, 2002); Colin Mitchell, "Selling the Brand Inside," *Harvard Business Review* (January 2002): 99–105.

16. Stan Maklan and Simon Knox, *Competing on Value* (Upper Saddle River, NJ: Financial Times, Prentice Hall, 2000).

17. Gene G. Marcial, "Inside Wall Street: Sip a Bohemian Raspberry from Jones Soda," *BusinessWeek Online*, July 4, 2005, www.businessweek.com; Bruce Horovitz, "Gen Y: A Tough Crowd to Sell," *USA Today*, April 22, 2002, p. B1; Melanie Wells, "Cult Brands," *Forbes*, April 16, 2001, pp. 150+.

18. "Credit-Card Deal Boosts China's Efforts Toward a National System," *InformationWeek*, March 31, 2004, n.p.

19. Keller, *Strategic Brand Management;* Todd Wasserman, "Sharpening the Focus," *Brandweek*, November 3, 2003, pp. 28–32.

20. To see a ranking of 100 best global brands using Interbrand's valuation method, see Diane Brady, Robert D. Hof, Andy Reinhardt, Moon Ihlwan, Stanley Holmes, and Kerry Capell, "Cult Brands: The BusinessWeek/Interbrand Annual Ranking of the World's Most Valuable Brands Shows the Power of Passionate Consumers," *BusinessWeek*, August 9, 2004, pp. 58+. Also see "Marked by the Market," *The Economist*, December 1, 2001, pp. 59–60 for an illustration of Stern Stewart's Wealth Added Index.

21. Mark Speece, "Marketer's Malady: Fear of Change," *Brandweek*, August 19, 2002, p. 34.

22. Kenneth Hein, "Dew Sports Street Smarts, Woos Urban Influences," *Brandweek*, June 6, 2005, p. 18.

23. Ronald Alsop, "Enduring Brands Hold Their Allure by Sticking Close to Their Roots," *Wall Street Journal Centennial Edition*, 1989.

24. Theodore Levitt, "Marketing Success Through Differentiation—of Anything," *Harvard Business Review* (January–February 1980): 83–91.

25. Dan Reed, "Low-Fare Rivals Keep a Close Eye on Song," *USA Today*, November 25, 2003, p. 6B.

26. Akshay R. Rao and Robert W. Ruekert, "Brand Alliances as Signals of Product Quality," *Sloan Management Review* (Fall 1994): 87–97; Akshay R. Rao, Lu Qu, and Robert W.

Ruekert, "Signaling Unobservable Quality Through a Brand Ally," *Journal of Marketing Research* 36, no. 2 (1999): 258–268.

27. Bernard L. Simonin and Julie A. Ruth, "Is a Company Known by the Company It Keeps? Assessing the Spillover Effects of Brand Alliances on Consumer Brand Attitudes," *Journal of Marketing Research* (February 1998): 30–42; see also C. W. Park, S. Y. Jun, and A. D. Shocker, "Composite Branding Alliances: An Investigation of Extension and Feedback Effects," *Journal of Marketing Research* 33 (1996): 453–466.

28. Peter Farquhar, "Managing Brand Equity," *Marketing Research* 1 (September 1989): 24–33.

29. Byung-Do Kim and Mary W. Sullivan, "The Effect of Parent Brand Experience on Line Extension Trial and Repeat Purchase," *Marketing Letters* 9 (April 1998): 181–193.

30. Kevin Lane Keller and David A. Aaker, "The Effects of Sequential Introduction of Brand Extensions," *Journal of Marketing Research* 29 (February 1992): 35–50; John Milewicz and Paul Herbig, "Evaluating the Brand Extension Decision Using a Model of Reputation Building," *Journal of Product & Brand Management* 3, no. 1 (1994): 39–47.

31. Mary W. Sullivan, "Brand Extensions: When to Use Them," *Management Science* 38, no. 6 (June 1992): 793–806; Daniel C. Smith, "Brand Extension and Advertising Efficiency: What Can and Cannot Be Expected," *Journal of Advertising Research* (November/ December 1992): 11–20. See also Daniel C. Smith and C. Whan Park, "The Effects of Brand Extensions on Market Share and Advertising Efficiency," *Journal of Marketing Research* 29 (August 1992): 296–313.

32. Subramanian Balachander and Sanjoy Ghose, "Reciprocal Spillover Effects: A Strategic Benefit of Brand Extensions," *Journal of Marketing* 67, no. 1 (January 2003): 4–13.

33. John A. Quelch and David Kenny, "Extend Profits, Not Product Lines," *Harvard Business Review* (September–October 1994): 153–160; Perspectives from the Editors, "The Logic of Product-Line Extensions," *Harvard Business Review* (November–December 1994): 53–62; J. Andrews and G. S. Low, "New But Not Improved: Factors That Affect the Development of Meaningful Line Extensions," Working Paper Report No. 98–124 (Cambridge, MA: Marketing Science Institute, November 1998); Maureen Morrin, "The Impact of Brand Extensions on Parent Brand Memory Structures and Retrieval Processes," *Journal of Marketing Research* 36, no. 4 (1999): 517–525.

34. Al Ries and Jack Trout, *Positioning: The Battle for Your Mind* (New York: McGraw-Hill, 1981).

35. David A. Aaker, *Brand Portfolio Strategy: Creating Relevance, Differentiation, Energy, Leverage, and Clarity* (New York: Free Press, 2004).

36. Barbara Loken and Deborah Roedder John, "Diluting Brand Beliefs: When Do Brand Extensions Have a Negative Impact?" *Journal of Marketing* (July 1993): 71–84; Deborah Roedder John, Barbara Loken, and Christopher Joiner, "The Negative Impact of Extensions: Can Flagship Products Be Diluted?" *Journal of Marketing* (January 1998): 19–32; Susan M. Broniarcyzk and Joseph W. Alba, "The Importance of the Brand in Brand Extension," *Journal of Marketing Research* (May 1994): 214–228 (this entire issue of *JMR* is devoted to brands and brand equity). See also R. Ahluwalia and Z. Gürhan-Canli, "The Effects of Extensions on the Family Brand Name: An Accessibility-Diagnosticity Perspective," *Journal of Consumer Research* 27 (December 2000): 371–381; Z. Gürhan-Canli and M. Durairaj, "The Effects of Extensions on Brand Name Dilution and Enhancement," *Journal of Marketing Research* 35 (1998): 464–473; S. J. Milberg, C. W. Park, and M. S. McCarthy, "Managing Negative Feedback Effects Associated with Brand Extensions: The Impact of Alternative Branding Strategies," *Journal of Consumer Psychology* 6 (1997): 119–140.

37. Philip Kotler, *Marketing Management*, 11th ed. (Upper Saddle River, NJ: Prentice Hall, 2003); Patrick Barwise and Thomas Robertson, "Brand Portfolios," *European Management Journal* 10, no. 3 (September 1992): 277–285.

38. Jack Trout, *Differentiate or Die: Survival in Our Era of Killer Competition* (New York: John Wiley, 2000).

39. Paul W. Farris, "The Chevrolet Corvette," Case UVA-M-320, The Darden Graduate Business School Foundation, University of Virginia, Charlottesville, Virginia.

CHAPTER 9

Creating Positioning and Dealing with Competition

In this chapter, we will address the following questions:

1. How can a firm choose and communicate an effective positioning?
2. How are brands differentiated?
3. How do marketers identify primary competitors and analyze their strategies, objectives, strengths, and weaknesses?
4. Should a company compete as a market leader, challenger, follower, or nicher?

MARKETING MANAGEMENT AT PROCTER & GAMBLE

Procter & Gamble (P&G) is one of the world's most skillful marketers of consumer packaged goods. It is known for multi-billion-dollar global brands such as Pampers and Tide—products that lead their category or segment. P&G achieved its success by expanding the total market, defending against rivals, and building market-share profitability. With a research budget of $100 million, P&G is always studying its customers and its competitors. "The consumer is boss," says CEO A. G. Lafley, who often visits consumers at home to find out what they need and how they actually use various products. Design is an important differentiator for P&G, not just in product innovation but also in packaging, communications, the purchase experience, and the user experience. With the acquisition of Gillette, P&G has reinforced its competitive position and its ability to serve more consumers in more markets.

Management takes a long-term approach to capitalizing on opportunities and will invest considerable time and money to succeed in its target markets. In defending its market share,

P&G has been known to spend heavily to outpromote new competitive brands and prevent them from gaining a foothold. Its hefty ad budget is among the largest in the industry, and its creative use of online promotions and product placements has been effective in launching new products and growing existing brands. For instance, after adding its Febreze fabric odor freshener to its Tide detergent, Downy fabric softener, and Bounce antistatic dryer sheets, P&G used advertising to encourage customers who use one brand to buy the others. Through its sales force, the company also maintains close ties with Wal-Mart and other channel members. Thus, P&G's success is based on the effective orchestration of myriad factors that contribute to market leadership.[1]

No company can succeed if its products and offerings resemble every other product and offering. Market-leading firms such as Procter & Gamble gain and keep market share through careful positioning and differentiation, ensuring that each offering represents a distinctive big idea in the mind of the target market. In addition, to effectively devise and implement the best brand positioning strategies, companies must pay keen attention to their competitors.[2] Markets have become too competitive to focus on the customer alone. This chapter explores how companies can effectively position and differentiate their offerings for competitive advantage. It also examines the role of competition and the strategies marketers can use to manage their brands, depending on their market position.

DEVELOPING AND COMMUNICATING A POSITIONING STRATEGY

When a company such as P&G discovers different needs and groups in the marketplace, it starts by targeting the needs and groups that it can satisfy in a superior way. Next, it positions its offering so that the target market recognizes the company's distinctive offering and image. If a company does an excellent job of positioning, then it can work out the rest of its marketing planning and differentiation from its positioning strategy.

Positioning is the act of designing the company's offering and image to occupy a distinctive place in the mind of the target market. The goal is to locate the brand in the minds of consumers to maximize the potential benefit to the firm. A good brand positioning helps guide marketing strategy by clarifying the brand's essence, what goals it helps the consumer achieve, and how it does so in a unique way. The result of positioning is the successful creation of a *customer-focused value proposition*, a cogent reason why the target market should buy the product. Table 9.1 shows how three

TABLE 9.1   Examples of Value Propositions for Target Segments

Company and Product	Target Customers	Benefits	Price	Value Proposition
Perdue (chicken)	Quality-conscious consumers of chicken	Tenderness	10% premium	More tender, golden chicken at a moderate, premium price
Volvo (station wagon)	Safety-conscious "upscale" families	Durability and safety	20% premium	The safest, most durable wagon in which your family can ride
Domino's (pizza)	Convenience-minded pizza lovers	Delivery speed and good quality	15% premium	A good, hot pizza, delivered to your door within 30 minutes of ordering, at a moderate price

companies—Perdue, Volvo, and Domino's—define their value proposition, given their target customers, benefits, and prices.

Competitive Frame of Reference

A starting point in defining a competitive frame of reference for a brand positioning is to determine **category membership**—the products or sets of products with which a brand competes and which function as close substitutes. As discussed later in this chapter, competitive analysis considers a whole host of factors—including the resources, capabilities, and likely intentions of various other firms—in choosing those markets where consumers can be profitably served.

Target market decisions are often a key determinant of the competitive frame of reference. Deciding to target a certain type of consumer can define the nature of competition because certain firms have decided to target that segment in the past (or plan to do so in the future), or consumers in that segment already may look to certain brands in their purchase decisions. Determining the proper competitive frame of reference requires understanding consumer behavior and the consideration sets consumers use in making brand choices. In the United Kingdom, for example, the Automobile Association has positioned itself as the fourth "emergency service"—along with police, fire, and ambulance—to convey greater credibility and urgency.

Points-of-Parity and Points-of-Difference

Once the competitive frame of reference for positioning has been fixed by defining the customer target market and nature of competition, marketers can define the appropriate points-of-difference and points-of-parity associations.[3] *Points-of-difference (PODs)* are attributes or benefits consumers strongly associate with a brand, positively evaluate, and believe that they could not find to the same extent with a competitive brand. Strong, favorable, and unique brand associations that make up points-of-difference may be based on virtually any type of attribute or benefit. Examples are FedEx (*guaranteed overnight delivery*) and Nike (*performance*).

Points-of-parity (POPs), on the other hand, are associations that are not necessarily unique to the brand but may in fact be shared with other brands. Two basic forms are category and competitive points-of-parity. Category points-of-parity are associations consumers view as necessary to be a legitimate and credible offering within a certain category, although perhaps not sufficient for brand choice. Consumers might not consider a travel agency truly a travel agency unless it can make air and hotel reservations, provide advice about leisure packages, and offer various payment options. Category points-of-parity may change over time due to technological advances, legal developments, or consumer trends.

Competitive points-of-parity are associations designed to negate competitors' points-of-difference. If a brand can "break even" in those areas where the competitors are trying to find an advantage and can achieve advantages in other areas, the brand should be in a strong—and perhaps unbeatable—competitive position. To achieve a point-of-parity (POP) on a particular attribute or benefit, a sufficient number of consumers must believe that the brand is "good enough" on that dimension. Often, the key to positioning is not so much in achieving a point-of-difference (POD) as in achieving points-of-parity.

Establishing Category Membership

Target customers are aware that Maybelline is a leading brand of cosmetics, Accenture is a leading consulting firm, and so on. Often, however, marketers must inform consumers of a brand's category membership, especially when the category membership is not apparent (as when a new product is introduced). This uncertainty can be a special problem for high-tech products. There are also situations where consumers know a brand's category membership but may not be convinced that the brand is a valid member of the category. For example, consumers may know that Hewlett-Packard makes digital cameras, but they may not be certain whether Hewlett-Packard cameras are in the same class as Sony, Olympus, and Kodak. Thus, HP might find it useful to reinforce category membership.

Brands are sometimes affiliated with categories in which they do not hold membership. This is one way to highlight a brand's point-of-difference, providing that consumers know the brand's actual membership. However, it is important that consumers understand what the brand stands for, and not just what it is *not*. Brands should not be trapped between categories. The preferred positioning approach is to inform consumers of a brand's membership before stating its point-of-difference. Presumably, consumers need to know what a product is and what function it serves before deciding whether it dominates the brands against which it competes.

There are three main ways to convey a brand's category membership:

1. *Announcing category benefits.* To reassure consumers that a brand will deliver on the fundamental reason for using a category, benefits are frequently used to announce category membership. Thus, a brownie mix might attain membership in the baked desserts category by claiming the benefit of great taste and support this benefit claim by possessing high-quality ingredients (performance).

2. *Comparing to exemplars.* Well-known, noteworthy brands can also be used to specify category membership. When Tommy Hilfiger was an unknown, advertising announced his membership as a great American designer by associating him with recognized category members such as Geoffrey Beene and Calvin Klein.

3. *Relying on the product descriptor.* The product descriptor that follows the brand name is often a concise means of conveying category origin. Consider XM Satellite Radio, which signals consumers that the offering consists of radio delivered via satellite. When the medium was still in its infancy, this descriptor helped consumers grasp the context in which XM should be considered.

Choosing POPs and PODs

Points-of-parity are driven by the needs of category membership (to create category POPs) and the necessity of negating competitors' PODs (to create competitive POPs). In choosing points-of-difference, two important considerations are that consumers find the POD desirable and that the firm has the capabilities to deliver on the POD. Table 9.2 shows three consumer desirability criteria and three key deliverability criteria for PODs.

Research has shown, however, that brands can sometimes be successfully differentiated on seemingly irrelevant attributes *if* consumers infer the proper benefit.[4] Procter & Gamble differentiates its Folger's instant coffee by its "flaked coffee crystals," created through a "unique patented process." In reality, the shape of the coffee particles is irrelevant because the crystals immediately dissolve in the hot water.

TABLE 9.2   Key Criteria for Points-of-Difference

Consumer Desirability Criteria	Deliverability Criteria
■ *Relevance*. The POD must be personally relevant and important to target consumers.	■ *Feasibility*. The firm must be able to actually create the POD.
■ *Distinctiveness*. Target consumers must find the POD both distinctive and superior.	■ *Communicability*. The brand must substantiate that that it can deliver the desired benefit.
■ *Believability*. Target consumers must find the POD believable and credible.	■ *Sustainability*. The positioning must be preemptive, defensible, and difficult to attack.

Creating POPs and PODs

One common difficulty in creating a strong, competitive positioning is that many of the attributes or benefits that make up the points-of-parity and points-of-difference are negatively correlated. If consumers rate the brand highly on one particular attribute or benefit, they also rate it poorly on another important attribute. For example, it might be difficult to position a brand as "inexpensive" and at the same time assert that it is "of the highest quality." Similarly, a food is not easily positioned as both "good tasting" and "low calorie." Moreover, individual attributes and benefits often have positive *and* negative aspects.

A long-lived brand seen as having a great deal of heritage might be associated with experience, wisdom, and expertise. On the other hand, it could also easily be seen as a negative: It might imply being old-fashioned and not up-to-date. For example, Brooks Brothers tried to downplay its heritage during the 1990s by stocking trendier clothing, alienating loyal customers without attracting new ones. After Claudio Del Vecchio bought the company, he used the Brooks Brothers heritage as a positive point-of-difference associated with sophistication, quality, and higher prices. Opening stores in fashionable areas of Italy has only reinforced this positioning.[5]

An expensive but sometimes effective approach to addressing negatively correlated attributes and benefits is to launch two different marketing campaigns, each one devoted to a different brand attribute or benefit. These campaigns may run together at one point in time or sequentially over time. Head & Shoulders shampoo met success in Europe by running one campaign emphasizing how well it removes dandruff and another emphasizing how beautiful it makes hair look. This approach might cause consumers to be less critical when judging the POP and POD benefits in isolation.

Brands can potentially be linked to any entity that possesses the right kind of equity as a means to establish an attribute or benefit as a POP or POD. Branded ingredients may also lend credibility to a questionable attribute in consumers' minds. Borrowing equity, however, is not riskless. Personal computer manufacturers found that the Intel Inside co-op advertising program, which gave Intel exposure in the PC makers' ad, led consumers to seek Intel-based computers. Finally, a potentially powerful but difficult way to address the negative relationship between attributes and benefits is to make the case that the relationship is positive by providing consumers with a different perspective and suggesting that they may be overlooking or ignoring certain considerations.

DIFFERENTIATION STRATEGIES

To be branded, products must be differentiated. The obvious means of differentiation, and often the most compelling ones to consumers, relate to aspects of the product and service. For instance, Method built a $10 million business in a year by creating a unique line of nontoxic household cleaning products with bright colors and sleek designs.[6] A company can also differentiate its market offering through personnel, channel, and image (see Table 9.3).

Product Differentiation

Physical products vary in their potential for differentiation. At one extreme are products that allow little variation: chicken, steel, aspirin. Yet even here, some differentiation is possible: Procter & Gamble offers several laundry detergent brands, each with its own identity. At the other extreme are products that can be highly differentiated, such as cars and furniture. Products can be differentiated through:[7]

- *Form*. **Form** refers to the product's size, shape, or physical structure. For example, aspirin can be differentiated by dosage size, shape, coating, and action time.
- *Features*. The characteristics that supplement the product's basic function are its **features**. Marketers can identify and select new features by researching needs and calculating *customer value* versus *company cost* for each potential feature. They should also think about how many customers want each feature, how long they need to introduce each, and how easily rivals can copy each.
- *Performance quality*. **Performance quality** is the level at which the product's primary characteristics operate. Firms should design a performance level appropriate to the target market and competitors' performance levels, while managing performance quality through time.
- *Conformance quality*. Buyers expect products to have a high **conformance quality**, the degree to which all of the produced units are identical and meet the promised specifications. If a product has low conformance quality, the product will disappoint some buyers.

TABLE 9.3   Differentiation Variables

Product	Services	Personnel	Channel	Image
Form	Ordering ease	Competence	Coverage	Symbols, colors, slogans
Features	Delivery	Courtesy	Expertise	Atmosphere
Conformance	Installation	Credibility	Performance	Events
Durability	Customer training	Reliability		Brand contacts
Reliability	Customer consulting	Responsiveness		
Repairability	Maintenance and repair	Communication		
Style				
Design				
Quality				

- *Durability.* **Durability**, a measure of the product's expected operating life under natural or stressful conditions, is important for products such as vehicles and appliances. However, the extra price must not be excessive, and the product must not be subject to rapid technological obsolescence.

- *Reliability.* Buyers normally will pay a premium for high **reliability**, a measure of the probability that a product will not malfunction or fail within a specified period. Maytag, for instance, has an outstanding reputation for reliable home appliances.

- *Repairability.* **Repairability** measures the ease of fixing a product when it malfunctions or fails. An automobile made with standard parts that are easily replaced has high repairability. Ideal repairability would exist if users could fix the product themselves with little cost in money or time.

- *Style.* **Style** describes the product's look and feel to the buyer. Buyers are normally willing to pay a premium for stylish products. Aesthetics have played a key role in such brands as Apple computers.[8] Style can create distinctiveness that is difficult to copy; however, strong style does not always mean high performance.

- *Design.* As competition intensifies, design offers a potent way to differentiate and position a company's products and services.[9] *Design* integrates all of the qualities just discussed; this means the designer has to figure out how much to invest in form, feature development, performance, conformance, durability, reliability, repairability, and style. To the firm, a well-designed product is one that is easy to manufacture and distribute. To the customer, a well-designed product is one that is pleasant to look at and easy to open, install, use, repair, and dispose of.

Services Differentiation

When the physical product cannot be differentiated easily, the key to competitive success may lie in adding valued services and improving their quality. The main service differentiators are:

- *Ordering ease.* How easy is it for the customer to place an order with the company? Baxter Healthcare eased the ordering process by supplying hospitals with computers through which they send orders to Baxter for delivery directly to individual departments and wards.[10]

- *Delivery.* How well is the offering delivered to the customer? This covers speed, accuracy, and customer care. Mexico's Cemex promises to deliver concrete faster than pizza. Using trucks equipped with a global positioning system (GPS), Cemex can track every load and promise that if delivery is more than 10 minutes late, the customer gets a 20 percent discount.[11]

- *Installation.* This refers to the work done to make a product operational in its planned location. Buyers of heavy equipment expect good installation service. Differentiation by installation is particularly important for companies that offer complex products.

- *Customer training.* Training the customer's employees to use products properly and efficiently is a key differentiator. General Electric not only sells and installs X-ray equipment in hospitals, but also trains users.

- *Customer consulting.* Here, the seller is offering data, information systems, and advising services that meet buyers' needs. For example, the furniture company Herman Miller works with Future Industrial Technologies to show business customers how to get the full ergonomic benefit from office furnishings.[12]

■ *Maintenance and repair.* What is the service program for helping customers keep products in good working order? This is an important consideration for computers and many other products.

Personnel Differentiation

Companies can gain a strong advantage through having better-trained people. Singapore Airlines enjoys an excellent reputation in large part because of its flight attendants. The sales forces of such companies as General Electric and Frito-Lay enjoy an excellent reputation.[13] Well-trained personnel exhibit *competence* (skill and knowledge), *courtesy* (respect and consideration), *credibility* (trustworthiness), *reliability* (consistent and accurate performance), *responsiveness* (quick action), and *communication* (desire to understand customers and communicate clearly).[14]

Channel Differentiation

Companies can achieve competitive advantage through the way they design their distribution channels' *coverage*, *expertise*, and *performance*. Caterpillar's success in the construction-equipment industry is based partly on superior channel development: Its dealers are found in more locations than competitors' dealers, and they are typically better trained and perform more reliably. Dell Computers has also distinguished itself by developing and managing high-quality direct-marketing channels.

Image Differentiation

Buyers respond differently to company and brand images. *Identity* is the way a company aims to identify or position itself or its product, whereas *image* is the way the public perceives the company or its products. An effective identity establishes the offering's character and value proposition, conveys the character in a distinctive way, and delivers emotional power beyond a mental image. The identity must be conveyed through every communication vehicle and brand contact, including symbols, colors, slogans, atmosphere, media, and special events.

COMPETITIVE FORCES AND COMPETITORS

Michael Porter has identified five forces that determine the intrinsic, long-run profit attractiveness of a market or market segment: industry competitors, potential entrants, substitutes, buyers, and suppliers (see Figure 9.1). The threats these forces pose are:

1. *Threat of intense segment rivalry.* A segment is unattractive if it already contains numerous, strong, or aggressive competitors. It is even more unattractive if the segment is stable or declining, if considerable plant capacity is being added, if fixed costs are high, if exit barriers are high, or if competitors have high stakes in staying in the segment. These conditions will lead to frequent price wars, advertising battles, and new-product introductions—making competition more expensive.

2. *Threat of new entrants.* A segment's attractiveness varies with the height of its entry and exit barriers.[15] The most attractive segment has high entry barriers and low exit barriers, so few new firms can enter, while poor-performing firms can exit easily. Profit potential is high when both entry and exit barriers are high, but firms face

FIGURE 9.1   Five Forces That Determine Market Attractiveness

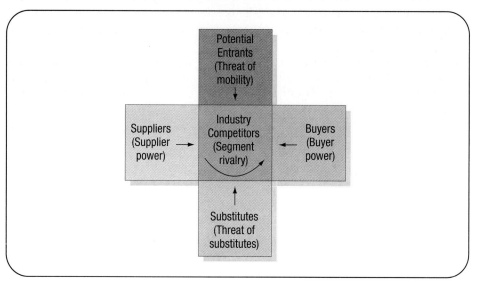

Source: Reprinted with the permission of the Free Press, an imprint of Simon & Schuster, from Michael E. Porter, *Competitive Advantage: Creating and Sustaining Superior Performance.* Copyright © 1985 by Michael E. Porter.

more risk because poorer-performing firms stay in and fight it out. When entry and exit barriers are both low, firms enter and leave the industry easily, and the returns are stable and low. The worst case is when entry barriers are low and exit barriers are high: Firms can enter during good times but find it hard to leave during bad times. The result is chronic overcapacity and depressed earnings for all.

3. *Threat of substitute products.* A segment is unattractive when there are actual or potential substitutes for the product. Substitutes place a limit on prices and on the profits that a segment can earn. The company has to monitor the price trends in substitutes closely. If technology advances or competition increases in these substitute industries, prices and profits in the segment are likely to fall.

4. *Threat of buyers' growing bargaining power.* A segment is unattractive if the buyers possess strong or growing bargaining power. Buyers' bargaining power grows when they become more concentrated or organized, when the product represents a significant fraction of the buyers' costs, when the product is undifferentiated, when the buyers' switching costs are low, when buyers are price sensitive, or when buyers can integrate upstream. To compete, sellers might select buyers with less power to negotiate, switch suppliers, or develop superior offers that strong buyers cannot refuse.

5. *Threat of suppliers' growing bargaining power.* A segment is unattractive if the company's suppliers are able to raise prices or reduce quantity supplied. Suppliers tend to be powerful when they are concentrated or organized, when there are few substitutes, when the supplied product is an important input, when the costs of switching suppliers are high, and when suppliers can integrate downstream. The best defenses are to build win–win relations with suppliers or use multiple supply sources.

Identifying Competitors

It would seem a simple task for a company to identify its competitors. PepsiCo knows that Coca-Cola's Dasani is a major bottled water competitor for its Aquafina Brand;

Sony knows that Microsoft's Xbox competes with the Sony PlayStation. However, the range of a company's actual and potential competitors is actually much broader. A company is more likely to be hurt by emerging competitors or new technologies than by current competitors.

Many businesses failed to look to the Internet for their most formidable competitors. The Barnes & Noble and Borders bookstore chains used to compete to see who could build the most megastores. Meanwhile, Amazon.com opened an online store with a huge selection of books. Now Barnes & Noble is playing catch-up online, the Borders Web site is operated by Amazon, and Amazon itself has grown beyond $7 billion in annual sales.[16]

"Competitor myopia"—a focus on current competitors rather than latent ones—can render a business extinct.[17] Encyclopaedia Britannica, for example, was invited but refused to provide content for Microsoft's Encarta CD-ROM-based encyclopedia. When Encarta was introduced, it was priced at $50, making Encyclopaedia Britannica's $1,250 set of 32 volumes look less appealing to parents. This situation forced Encyclopaedia Britannica to change its business model. Today the company still offers its encyclopedia in print but also offers reference books on CD-ROM, DVD, and through subscription-based Internet access.[18]

Industry Concept of Competition

An **industry** is a group of firms that offers a product or class of products that are close substitutes for each other. Industries are classified according to number of sellers; degree of product differentiation; presence or absence of entry, mobility, and exit barriers; cost structure; degree of vertical integration; and degree of globalization.

Number of Sellers and Degree of Differentiation   The starting point for describing an industry is to specify the number of sellers and determine whether the product is homogeneous or highly differentiated. These characteristics give rise to four industry structure types. In a *pure monopoly*, only one firm provides a certain offering in a specific area (such as a local gas company). An unregulated monopolist might charge a high price, do little or no advertising, and offer minimal service. If partial substitutes are available and there is some danger of competition, the monopolist might invest in more service and technology. A regulated monopolist is required to charge a lower price and provide more service as a matter of public interest.

In an *oligopoly*, a small number of (usually) large firms produce products that range from highly differentiated to standardized. In *pure oligopoly*, a few companies produce essentially the same commodity (such as oil), so all have difficulty charging more than the going price. If competitors match services, the only way to gain a competitive advantage is through lower costs. In *differentiated oligopoly*, a few companies offer products (such as autos) partially differentiated by quality, features, styling, or services. Each competitor may seek leadership in one attribute, attract customers seeking that attribute, and charge a premium for that attribute.

Monopolistic competition means that many competitors are able to differentiate their offers in whole or part (restaurants are a good example). Competitors focus on market segments where they can better meet customer needs and charge more. In *pure competition*, many competitors offer the same product and service, so, without differentiation, all prices will be the same. No competitor will advertise unless advertising can create psychological differentiation (such as cigarettes), in which case the industry is actually monopolistically competitive.

An industry's competitive structure can change over time. For example, the media industry has been steadily consolidating, turning from monopolistic to a differentiated oligopoly. Four media empires can now vertically integrate content with distribution: News Corp., Time Warner, Viacom, and NBC (the smallest). Combining the studios that produce programming with cable and broadcasting units that distribute content saves money and benefits shareholders. However, with fewer people deciding on programming, quality and variety could suffer, and less competition may mean higher prices for cable and satellite subscribers. Also, most importantly, if a few media giants control content and distribution, smaller, more innovative programs could be squeezed out.[19]

Entry, Mobility, and Exit Barriers   Industries differ greatly in ease of entry. It is easy to open a new restaurant but difficult to enter the aircraft industry. Major *entry barriers* include high capital requirements; economies of scale; patents and licensing requirements; scarce locations, raw materials, or distributors; and reputation requirements. Even entering an industry, a firm may face *mobility barriers* as it enters more attractive market segments. Firms often face *exit barriers* such as legal or moral obligations to customers, creditors, and employees; government restrictions; low asset salvage value; lack of alternative opportunities; high vertical integration; and emotional barriers.[20] Many firms stay in an industry as long as they cover their variable costs and some or all of their fixed costs, although this dampens profits for everyone.

Cost Structure   Each industry has a certain cost burden that shapes much of its strategic conduct. For example, steelmaking involves heavy manufacturing and raw-material costs; toy manufacturing involves heavy distribution and marketing costs. Firms strive to reduce their main costs. The integrated steel firm with the most cost-efficient plant will have a great advantage over other steel integrated companies, although its costs may still be higher than those of mini-mills.

Degree of Vertical Integration   Many companies benefit from **vertical integration**, or integrating backward or forward. For example, major oil producers carry on oil exploration and drilling, oil refining, chemical manufacture, and service-station operation. Vertical integration often lowers costs, and the firm gains a larger share of the value-added stream. Also, a vertically integrated firm can manage prices and costs in different parts of the value chain to earn profits where taxes are lowest. On the other hand, vertical integration may raise costs in certain parts of the value chain and restrict a firm's strategic flexibility, which is why firms outsource activities that specialists can handle better and more cheaply.

Degree of Globalization   Some industries are highly local (such as lawn care); others are global (such as oil, aircraft engines, and cameras). Companies in global industries need to compete on a global basis if they are to achieve economies of scale and keep up with the latest advances in technology.[21]

Market Concept of Competition

Using the market approach, competitors are companies that satisfy the same customer need. For example, a customer who buys word processing software really

FIGURE 9.2   Competitor Map—Eastman Kodak

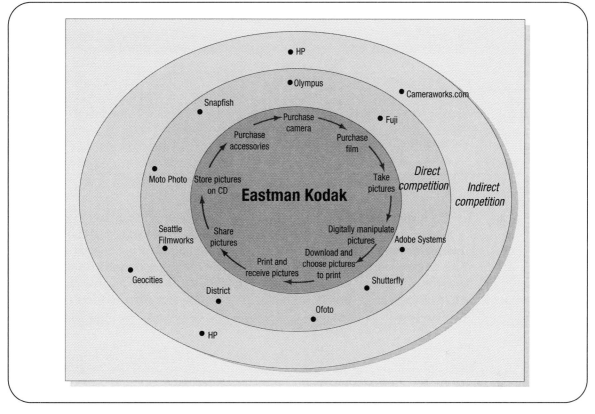

Source: Jeffrey F. Rayport and Bernard J. Jaworski, *E-Commerce* (New York: McGraw-Hill, 2001), p. 53.

wants "writing ability"—a need that can be satisfied by pencils, pens, or typewriters. The market concept of competition reveals a broader set of actual and potential competitors.

Rayport and Jaworski suggest profiling a company's direct and indirect competitors by mapping the buyer's steps in obtaining and using the product. Figure 9.2 illustrates their *competitor map* of Eastman Kodak in the film business. The center shows consumer activities such as buying a camera and sharing pictures. The first outer ring lists Kodak's main competitors with respect to each consumer activity, such as Snapfish for sharing pictures. The second outer ring lists indirect competitors, such as Hewlett-Packard, who may become direct competitors. This analysis highlights a company's opportunities and challenges.[22]

ANALYZING COMPETITORS

Once a company identifies its main competitors, it must ascertain their strategies, objectives, strengths, and weaknesses.

FIGURE 9.3   Strategic Groups in the Major Appliance Industry

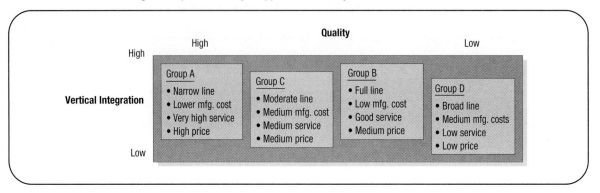

Strategies

A group of firms following the same strategy in a given target market is called a **strategic group**.[23] Suppose a company wants to enter the major appliance industry. What is its strategic group? It develops the chart shown in Figure 9.3 and discovers four strategic groups based on product quality and level of vertical integration. Group A has one competitor (Maytag); group B has three (General Electric, Whirlpool, and Sears); group C has four; and group D has two. Important insights emerge from this exercise. First, the height of the entry barriers differs for each group. Second, if the company successfully enters a group, the members of that group become its key competitors.

Objectives

Once a company has identified its main competitors and their strategies, it must ask: What is each competitor seeking in the marketplace? What drives each competitor's behavior? Many factors shape a competitor's objectives, including size, history, current management, and financial situation. If the competitor is a division of a larger company, it is important to know whether the parent company is running it for growth, profits, or milking it.[24]

   Note that companies differ in the emphasis they put on short- versus long-term profits. Many U.S. firms have been criticized for operating on a short-run model, largely because current performance is judged by stockholders who might lose confidence, sell their stock, and cause the company's cost of capital to rise. Japanese firms operate largely on a market-share-maximization model. They receive much of their funds from banks at a lower interest rate and in the past have readily accepted lower profits. An alternative assumption is that each competitor pursues some mix of objectives: current profitability, market share growth, cash flow, technological leadership, or service leadership. Finally, a company must monitor competitors' expansion plans.

Strengths and Weaknesses

A company should monitor three variables when analyzing the strengths and weaknesses of competitors:

   1. *Share of market.* The competitor's share of the target market.

2. *Share of mind.* The percentage of customers who named the competitor in responding to the statement, "Name the first company that comes to mind in this industry."

3. *Share of heart.* The percentage of customers who named the competitor in responding to the statement, "Name the company from which you would prefer to buy the product."

In general, companies that make steady gains in mind share and heart share will inevitably make gains in market share and profitability. To improve market share, many companies benchmark their most successful competitors, as well as world-class performers.

Selecting Competitors

After the company has conducted customer value analysis and examined competitors carefully, it can focus its attack on one of the following classes of competitors: strong versus weak, close versus distant, and "good" versus "bad."

- *Strong versus weak.* Most companies aim at weak competitors, because this requires fewer resources per share point gained. However, the firm should also compete with strong competitors to keep up with the best. Even strong competitors have some weaknesses.

- *Close versus distant.* Most companies compete with rivals who resemble them the most, yet it is important to also recognize distant competitors. Coca-Cola states that its top competitor is tap water, not Pepsi.

- *"Good" versus "bad".* Every industry contains "good" and "bad" competitors.[25] A firm should support good competitors and attack bad competitors. Good competitors play by the industry's rules; they make realistic assumptions about the industry's growth potential; they set prices in reasonable relation to costs; they favor a healthy industry; they limit themselves to a portion or segment of the industry; they motivate others to lower costs or improve differentiation; and they accept the general level of their share and profits. Bad competitors try to buy share; take large risks; invest in overcapacity; and upset industrial equilibrium.

COMPETITIVE STRATEGIES

A company can gain further insight into its competitive position by classifying its competitors and itself according to the role each plays as market leader, market challenger, market follower, or market nicher. On the basis of this classification, the company can take specific actions in line with its current and desired roles.

Market-Leader Strategies

Many industries contain one firm that is the acknowledged market leader, such as Microsoft (computer software) and McDonald's (fast food). This firm has the largest share of the relevant product market and usually leads the others in price changes, new-product introductions, distribution coverage, and promotional intensity. Unless the leader enjoys a legal monopoly, it must avoid missing key developments. A product innovation may hurt the leader, the way Motorola's analog cell phones suffered when

Nokia's and Ericsson's digital models took over. The leader might continue to spend conservatively while a challenger spends liberally; it might experience higher costs cutting into profits; or it might misjudge its competition and get left behind. Another risk is that the dominant firm might look old-fashioned against newer, peppier rivals.

Remaining number one calls for action on three fronts. First, the firm must find ways to expand total market demand. Second, the firm must protect its current market share through good defensive and offensive actions. Third, the firm can try to increase its market share, even if market size remains constant.

Expanding the Total Market   If Americans increase their consumption of ketchup, Heinz stands to gain the most because it sells almost two-thirds of the country's ketchup. If Heinz can convince more Americans to use ketchup, or use ketchup with more meals, or use more ketchup on each occasion, Heinz will benefit. In general, the market leader should look for new customers or more usage from existing customers. It can try to attract buyers who are unaware of the product or who are resisting it because of price or lack of certain features. A firm can search for new users among buyers who might use the product but do not (*market-penetration strategy*), those who have never used it (*new-market segment strategy*), or those who live elsewhere (*geographical-expansion strategy*).

To increase usage, marketers can boost the *level* or *quantity* of consumption or increase the *frequency* of consumption. Consumption can sometimes be increased through packaging or product design; frequency of use involves identifying additional opportunities to use the brand. Product development can spur new uses. Chewing gum manufacturers are exploring how to use their products as a cheap, effective delivery mechanism for medicine. Some chewing gums sold by Adams (number two in the world) claim health benefits.[26]

Defending Market Share   While trying to expand total market size, the dominant firm must also defend its current business against domestic and foreign rivals. The leader is like a large elephant being attacked by a swarm of bees. Silk organic soymilk must be on constant guard against Stonyfield Farms; Heinz ketchup against Hunt's; and so on.[27] The most constructive response to defending market share is *continuous innovation*. The leader leads the industry in new offerings, distribution effectiveness, and cost cutting. It keeps increasing its competitive strength and value to customers.

Even when it does not launch offensives, the market leader must leave no major flanks exposed. It must keep its costs down, and its prices must reflect the value that customers see in the brand. In addition, the leader must consider what segments to defend (even at a loss) and what segments to surrender. The aim of defensive strategy is to reduce the probability of attack, divert attacks to less threatening areas, and lessen their intensity. A dominant firm can use six defense strategies, as shown in Figure 9.4.[28]

1. *Position defense*. This involves building superior brand power, making the brand almost impregnable. For instance, Heinz let Hunt's mount a costly attack in the ketchup market without striking back. Hunt's expensive strategy failed. Heinz still enjoys over 50 percent U.S. market share, whereas Hunt has 17 percent share.[29]
2. *Flank defense*. The market leader should also erect outposts to protect a weak front or possibly serve as an invasion base for counterattack. Smirnoff, which had 23 percent of the U.S. vodka market, was attacked by the Wolfschmidt brand, priced at $1

FIGURE 9.4 Six Types of Defense Strategies

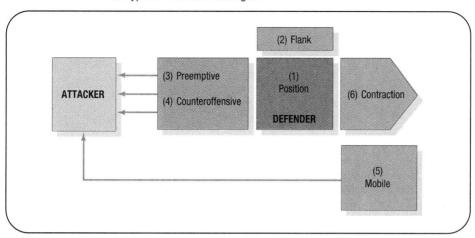

less per bottle. Smirnoff raised its price by $1 and increased advertising; it also launched another brand to compete with Wolfschmidt and a brand to sell for less than Wolfschmidt, thus protecting its flanks.

3. *Preemptive defense.* A more aggressive maneuver is to attack before a rival starts its offense. A company can hit one competitor here and another there, keeping everyone off balance, or it can try to achieve a grand market envelopment. Bank of America's 13,000 ATMs and 4,500 branches nationwide now provide steep competition to local and regional banks. Another approach is to send out market signals and dissuade competitors from attacking.[30] A firm can also introduce a stream of new products supported by *preannouncements*—deliberate communications regarding future actions.[31]

4. *Counteroffensive defense.* When attacked, most leaders will counterattack. One effective counterattack is to invade the attacker's main market so it will have to defend the territory. Another is to use economic or political clout. For example, the leader may subsidize lower prices for a vulnerable product with revenue from more profitable products or lobby legislators to take political action that would inhibit the competition.

5. *Mobile defense.* Here, the leader stretches its domain over new territories that can serve as future centers for defense and offense, using market broadening and market diversification. With *market broadening*, the company focuses on the underlying generic need, not the current product, and gets involved in R&D across the whole range of technology associated with that need. This is how "petroleum" companies recast themselves as "energy" companies to enter oil, nuclear, hydroelectric, and other industries. *Market diversification* into unrelated industries is another approach; U.S. tobacco companies have chosen this approach by moving into unrelated industries such as beer and foods.

6. *Contraction defense.* Large companies sometimes recognize that they can no longer defend all of their territory. The best course of action then appears to be *planned contraction* (also called *strategic withdrawal*), giving up weaker territories and reassigning resources to stronger territories. This consolidates competitive strength in the market and concentrates mass at pivotal positions. Diageo acquired most of Seagram's brands and spun off Pillsbury and Burger King so it could concentrate on major brands such as Smirnoff vodka.[32]

Expanding Market Share   Market leaders can improve profitability by increasing market share. A one-share-point gain in coffee is worth $48 million, and in soft drinks, $120 million! No wonder competition has turned into marketing warfare. Because the cost of buying market share may far exceed its revenue value, a company should first consider three factors. The first is the possibility of provoking antitrust action: Jealous competitors may cry "monopoly" if a dominant firm makes further inroads. The second is economic cost. Profitability may fall, not rise, with further market-share gains after a certain level. "Holdout" customers may dislike the company, be loyal to competitive suppliers, have unique needs, or prefer dealing with smaller suppliers. Also, the cost of legal work, public relations, and lobbying rises with market share. Pushing for higher market share is less justified when there are few scale or experience economies, unattractive market segments exist, buyers want multiple supply sources, and exit barriers are high. Some leaders have even increased profitability by selectively decreasing market share in weaker areas.[33]

The third factor is pursuing the wrong marketing-mix strategy. Companies successfully gaining share typically outperform competitors in three areas: new-product activity, relative product quality, and marketing expenditures.[34] Companies that cut prices more deeply than competitors typically do not achieve significant gains, as enough rivals meet the price cuts and others offer other values so that buyers do not switch. The final factor is the effect of increased market share on actual and perceived quality.[35]

Other Competitive Strategies

Firms that are not market leaders in an industry are often called runner-up, or trailing, firms. Some, such as Ford and Avis, are quite large in their own right. These firms can either attack the leader and other competitors in an aggressive bid for further market share (market challengers), or they can not "rock the boat" (market followers).

Market-Challenger Strategies   A market challenger must first define its strategic objective; most challengers aim to increase market share. Then the challenger must decide whom to attack. Attacking the leader is a high-risk but potentially high-payoff strategy if the leader is not serving the market well. The challenger also can attack firms of its own size that are underperforming and underfinanced, have aging products, charge excessive prices, or are not satisfying customers in other ways. A third choice is to attack small local and regional firms, the way some big banks have gobbled up smaller banks.

Given clear opponents and objectives, five general market-challenger attack options are:

1. *Frontal attack.* Match the opponent's product, advertising, price, and distribution. The side with the greater resources will win in a pure frontal attack. If the competitor can convince the market that its product is equal to the leader's—and if the leader doesn't retaliate—a modified frontal attack can be effective.

2. *Flank attack.* In a geographical attack, the challenger spots areas where a rival is underperforming. Another flanking strategy is to serve uncovered market needs, as Japanese automakers did by developing more fuel-efficient cars. A flanking strategy is another name for identifying shifts in market segments that cause gaps to develop, then filling the gaps and developing them into strong segments. Flank attacks are particularly attractive to a challenger with fewer resources and are more likely to succeed than frontal attacks.

3. *Encirclement attack*. The encirclement maneuver is used to capture a wide slice of the enemy's territory through a "blitz"—launching a grand offensive on several fronts. Encirclement makes sense when the challenger commands superior resources and believes a swift encirclement will break the opponent's will.

4. *Bypass attack*. The most indirect strategy, this involves bypassing the enemy and attacking easier markets to broaden one's resource base. Three lines of approach are diversifying into unrelated products, diversifying into new geographical markets, and leapfrogging into new technologies to supplant existing products. For example, PepsiCo used a bypass when it bought Tropicana and then Quaker Oats (owner of Gatorade) as weapons against Coca-Cola. *Technological leapfrogging* is often used in high-tech industries.

5. *Guerilla warfare*. This consists of small, intermittent attacks to harass and demoralize the opponent and eventually secure permanent footholds. The guerrilla challenger uses both conventional and unconventional means of attack, such as selective price cuts and intense promotional campaigns. Normally, guerrilla warfare is practiced by a smaller firm against a larger one; it can be costly, although less expensive than a frontal, an encirclement, or a flank attack (see "Marketing Skills: Guerrilla Marketing"). Still, guerrilla warfare must be backed by a stronger attack if the challenger hopes to beat the opponent.

Now the challenger must develop more specific strategies, such as price discounts; lower-price goods; value-priced offerings; prestige offerings; product proliferation; product innovation; improved services; distribution innovation; manufacturing-cost reduction; or intensive advertising promotion.

MARKETING SKILLS: GUERRILLA MARKETING

Who needs guerrilla marketing skills? Any marketer who wants to attack and grab share from the leader without risking the higher cost and provocation of a frontal attack. Guerrilla marketing became popular in the 1980s after Jay Conrad Levinson published his first of many books on the subject. To start, guerrilla marketers must think creatively about how to attract maximum customer attention and achieve marketing goals with minimal investment; then test the idea internally and/or locally to spot potential problems and areas for improvement before going national.

During planning, guerilla marketers must anticipate stakeholders' reactions to controversial techniques or messages and be sensitive to legal and ethical concerns. "Guerrilla marketing does not mean being socially irresponsible or taking liberties with the law and ethics of doing business," stresses Levinson. They must plan for how results will be measured and then closely monitor progress during the program. Finally, they must be prepared to move quickly by either modifying or dropping a non-performing guerrilla campaign in favor of a new idea.

As an example, to introduce its Orange brand of online banking services, ING Direct treated morning commuters in Boston, San Francisco, and Washington, D.C., to a morning of free subway or bus rides. ING staffers dressed in orange clothes distributed Orange leaflets to commuters entering transit stations; the fare boxes were orange and the stations, trains, and buses were adorned with Orange posters. This unusual promotion attracted media attention, helped ING stand out, and boosted brand awareness in each metropolitan market.[36]

Market-Follower Strategies

Theodore Levitt has argued that a strategy of *product imitation* might be as profitable as a strategy of *product innovation*.[37] The innovator bears the expense of developing the new product, getting it into distribution, and educating the market. The reward for all this work and risk is normally market leadership—even though another firm can then copy or improve on the new product. Although it probably will not overtake the leader, the follower can achieve high profits because it did not bear any of the innovation expense.

Many companies prefer to follow rather than challenge the leader. This pattern is common in industries such as steel and chemicals, where few opportunities exist for product and image differentiation, service quality is often comparable, and price sensitivity is high. Short-run grabs for market share provoke retaliation, so most firms present similar offers to buyers, usually by copying the leader; this keeps market shares highly stable.

One broad strategy for followers is to be a *counterfeiter*, duplicating the leader's product and package and selling it on the black market or through disreputable dealers. Counterfeiters have plagued both Apple Computer and Rolex, especially in Asia. A second strategy is to be a *cloner*, emulating the leader's products, name, and packaging with slight variations. For example, Ralcorp Holding sells imitations of name-brand cereals in lookalike boxes at lower prices. A third is to be an *imitator*, copying some things from the leader but maintaining differentiation of packaging, advertising, pricing, and so on. The leader does not respond as long as the imitator does not attack aggressively. A fourth strategy is to be an *adapter*, adapting or improving the leader's products, perhaps for different markets. S&S Cycle, for example, supplies engines to firms that build Harley-like cruiser bikes. It buys a new Harley-Davidson bike every year and takes the engine apart to see what it can improve upon.[38]

Normally, a follower earns less than the leader. For example, a study of food processing companies found that only the top two firms were profitable. Thus, followership is not always a rewarding path.

Market-Nicher Strategies

An alternative to being a follower in a large market is to be a leader in a small market, or niche. Smaller firms normally avoid competing with larger firms by targeting small markets of little or no interest to the larger firms. For example, Logitech International expanded worldwide by making every variation of computer mouse imaginable. This niche success enabled the company to expand into other peripherals, such PC headsets and Webcams.[39]

Even large, profitable firms are now setting up business units or brands for specific niches. The key idea in nichemanship is specialization. Table 9.4 shows the specialist roles open to nichers. However, because niches can weaken, the firm must continually create new niches, expand niches, and protect its niches. By developing strength in two or more niches, the company increases its chances for survival.

Balancing Customer and Competitor Orientations

We have stressed the importance of a company's positioning itself competitively as a market leader, challenger, follower, or nicher. However, a company must not spend all

TABLE 9.4   Specialized Niche Roles

Niche Specialty	Description
End-user specialist	The firm specializes in serving one type of end-use customer.
Vertical-level specialist	The firm specializes at some vertical level of the production-distribution value chain.
Customer-size specialist	The firm concentrates on selling to small, medium or large customers.
Specific-customer specialist	The firm limits its selling to one or a few customers.
Geographic specialist	The firm sells only in a certain locality, region, or area of the world.
Product or product-line specialist	The firm carries or produces only one product line or product.
Product-feature specialist	The firm specializes in producing a certain type of product or product feature.
Job-shop specialist	The firm customizes its products for individual customers.
Quality-price specialist	The firm operates at the low- or high-quality ends of the market.
Service specialist	The firm offers one or more services not available from competitors.
Channel specialist	The firm specializes in serving only one channel of distribution.

of its time focusing on competitors. A *competitor-centered company* looks at what competitors are doing (increasing distribution, cutting prices, introducing new services) and then formulates competitive reactions (increasing advertising expenditures, meeting price cuts, increasing the sales-promotion budget). This kind of planning has both pluses and minuses. On the positive side, the company develops a fighter orientation, training its marketers to be alert for weaknesses in its competitors' and its own position. On the negative side, the company is too reactive. Rather than formulating and executing a consistent customer-oriented strategy, it determines its moves based on its competitors' moves rather than its own goals.

A *customer-centered company* focuses more on customer developments in formulating its strategies. Its marketers might learn, for example, that the total market is growing at 4 percent annually, while the quality-sensitive segment is growing at 8 percent annually. They might also find that the deal-prone customer segment is growing fast, but these customers do not stay with any supplier for very long. Additionally, they might find that more customers are asking for a 24-hour hotline, which no one else offers. In response, this company could put more effort into reaching and satisfying the quality segment, avoid cutting prices, and research the possibility of installing a hotline.

Clearly, the customer-centered company is in a better position to identify new opportunities and set a strategy toward long-run profits. By monitoring customer needs, it can decide which customer groups and emerging needs are the most important to serve, given its resources and objectives.

EXECUTIVE SUMMARY

Deciding on positioning requires the determination of a frame of reference—by identifying the target market and the nature of the competition—and the ideal points-of-parity and points-of-difference brand associations. To determine the proper competitive frame of reference, marketers must understand consumer behavior and how consumers make brand choices. Points-of-difference are associations unique to the brand that are also strongly held and favorably evaluated by consumers. Points-of-parity are associations not necessarily unique to the brand but perhaps shared with other brands. Category point-of-parity associations are those viewed by consumers as necessary to a legitimate and credible offering within a certain category. Competitive point-of-parity associations are associations designed to negate competitors' points-of-difference.

A market offering can be differentiated along five dimensions: product (form, features, performance quality, conformance quality, durability, reliability, repairability, style, design); services (order ease, delivery, installation, customer training, customer consulting, maintenance and repair, miscellaneous services); and personnel, channel, or image (symbols, media, atmosphere, and events). A company's closest competitors are those seeking to satisfy the same customers and needs and making similar offers. Firms should also watch for latent competitors who may offer new or other ways to satisfy the same needs. A company should identify competitors by using both industry and market-based analyses.

A market leader has the largest share in the relevant product market. To remain dominant, the leader looks for ways to expand total market demand, tries to protect its current share, and perhaps tries to increase its market share. A challenger attacks the leader and other rivals in an aggressive bid for more share, choosing from five types of general attack and then selecting specific attack strategies. A follower is a runner-up firm willing to maintain its market share and not rock the boat; it can play the role of counterfeiter, cloner, imitator, or adapter. A market nicher serves small segments not being served by larger firms. The key to nichemanship is specialization. Although a competitive orientation is important in today's global markets, companies should maintain a good balance of consumer and competitor monitoring.

NOTES

1. Claudia H. Deutsch, "A Fresh Approach to Marketing for Procter's 'Fresh Approach to Laundry,'" *New York Times*, August 8, 2005, p. C7; Jennifer Reingold, "What P&G Knows About the Power of Design," *Fast Company*, June 2005, pp. 56+; Jack Neff, "P&G Kisses Up to the Boss: Consumers," *Advertising Age*, May 2, 2005, pp. 18+; Jack Neff, "Management: P&G vs. Martha," *Advertising Age*, April 8, 2002, p. 24.
2. Leonard M. Fuld, *The New Competitor Intelligence: The Complete Resource for Finding, Analyzing, and Using Information About Your Competitors* (New York: John Wiley, 1995); John A. Czepiel, *Competitive Marketing Strategy* (Upper Saddle River, NJ: Prentice Hall, 1992).
3. Kevin Lane Keller, Brian Stenthal, and Alice Tybout, "Three Questions You Need to Ask About Your Brand," *Harvard Business Review*, September 2002, pp. 80–89.
4. Gregory S. Carpenter, Rashi Glazer, and Kent Nakamoto, "Meaningful Brands from Meaningless Differentiation: The Dependence on Irrelevant Attributes," *Journal of Marketing Research*, August 1994: 339–50.
5. "Brooks Bros. Has Opened a 3,500-Sq.-Ft. Store in Florence, Italy," *Chain Store Age*, January 2005, p. 18; Naomi Aoki, "An Alteration at Brooks Brothers Derailed by Casual Era Retailer Returns to Its Roots," *Boston Globe*, November 12, 2003, p. E1.
6. Bridget Finn, "Selling Cool in a Bottle—of Dish Soap," *Business 2.0*, December 2003, pp. 72–73.
7. Some of these bases are discussed in David A. Garvin, "Competing on the Eight Dimensions of Quality," *Harvard Business Review* (November–December 1987): 101–109.

8. See Bernd Schmitt and Alex Simonson, *Marketing Aesthetics: The Strategic Management of Brand, Identity, and Image* (New York: Free Press, 1997).

9. See Philip Kotler, "Design: A Powerful but Neglected Strategic Tool," *Journal of Business Strategy*, Fall 1984, pp. 16–21. Also see Christopher Lorenz, *The Design Dimension* (New York: Basil Blackwell, 1986).

10. William C. Copacino and Jonathan L.S. Byrnes, "How to Become a Supply Chain Master," *Supply Chain Management Review*, March–April 2002, pp. S37+.

11. For a comprehensive discussion of Cemex, see Adrian J. Slywotzky and David J. Morrison, *How Digital Is Your Business?* (New York: Crown Business, 2000), ch. 5.

12. Mark Sanchez, "Herman Miller Offers Training to Its Furniture Users," *Grand Rapids Business Journal*, December 2, 2002, p. 23.

13. See "The 25 Best Sales Forces," *Sales & Marketing Management*, July 1998, pp. 32–50.

14. For a similar list, see Leonard L. Berry and A. Parasuraman, *Marketing Services: Competing Through Quality* (New York: Free Press, 1991), p. 16.

15. Michael E. Porter, *Competitive Strategy* (New York: Free Press, 1980) pp. 22–23.

16. Bob Tedeschi, "As Their Core Businesses Prosper, Some Companies Try to Expand Their Horizons with New Product Lines," *New York Times*, September 6, 20004, p. C5; Leslie Kaufman with Saul Hansell, "Holiday Lessons in Online Retailing," *New York Times*, January 2, 2000, sec. 3, pp. 1, 14.

17. Michael Krantz, "Click Till You Drop," *Time*, July 20, 1998, pp. 34–39; Michael Krauss, "The Web Is Taking Your Customers for Itself," *Marketing News*, June 8, 1998, p. 8.

18. Hiawatha Bray, "The Boston Globe Upgrade Column," *Boston Globe*, July 12, 2004, (www.boston.com/globe). Jonathan Gaw, "Britannica Gives In and Gets Online," *Los Angeles Times*, October 19, 2000, p. A1; Jerry Useem, "Withering Britannica Bets It All on the Web," *Fortune*, November 22, 1999, pp. 344, 348.

19. Tom Lowry, Ronald Grover, and Catherine Yang with Steve Rosenbush and Peter Burrows, "Mega Media Mergers: How Dangerous?" *BusinessWeek*, February 23, 2004, pp. 34–42.

20. See Kathryn Rudie Harrigan, "The Effect of Exit Barriers Upon Strategic Flexibility," *Strategic Management Journal* 1 (1980): 165–176.

21. Porter, *Competitive Strategy*, ch. 13.

22. Jeffrey F. Rayport and Bernard J. Jaworski, *E-Commerce* (New York: McGraw-Hill, 2001), p. 53.

23. Porter, *Competitive Strategy*, ch. 7.

24. William E. Rothschild, *How to Gain (and Maintain) the Competitive Advantage* (New York: McGraw-Hill, 1989), ch. 5.

25. Porter, *Competitive Strategy*, ch. 7.

26. "Cadbury Outstrips Rivals After Adams Gum Buy," *Evening Standard*, February 23, 2005, (www.thisislondon.co.uk); "Business Bubbles," *The Economist*, October 12, 2002, p. 68.

27. Janet Adamy, "Nature's Way—Behind a Food Giant's Success," *Wall Street Journal*, February 1, 2005, p. A1.

28. These six defense strategies, as well as the five attack strategies, are taken from Philip Kotler and Ravi Singh, "Marketing Warfare in the 1980s," *Journal of Business Strategy* (Winter 1981): 30–41. For additional reading, see Gerald A. Michaelson, *Winning the Marketing War: A Field Manual for Business Leaders* (Lanham, MD: Abt Books, 1987); Al Ries and Jack Trout, *Marketing Warfare* (New York: McGraw-Hill, 1990); Jay Conrad Levinson, *Guerrilla Marketing* (Boston, MA: Houghton-Mifflin Co., 1984); and Barrie G. James, *Business Wargames* (Harmondsworth, England: Penguin Books, 1984).

29. "Heinz Is Getting Back to Basics," *Food Institute Report*, May 5, 2003, p. 2; "Leader of the Pack," *Pittsburgh Post-Gazette*, April 1, 2000.

30. Porter, *Competitive Strategy*, ch. 4; Jaideep Prabhu and David W. Stewart, "Signaling Strategies in Competitive Interaction: Building Reputations and Hiding the Truth," *Journal of Marketing Research* 38 (February 2001): 62–72.

31. Jehoshua Eliashberg and Thomas S. Robertson, "New Product Preannouncing Behavior: A Market Signaling Study," *Journal of Marketing Research* 25 (August 1988): 282–292; Roger J. Calantone and Kim E. Schatzel, "Strategic Foretelling: Communication-Based Antecedents of a Firm's Propensity to Preannounce," *Journal of Marketing* 64 (January 2000): 17–30.

32. Gerry Kermouch, "Spiking the Booze Business," *BusinessWeek*, May 19, 2003, pp. 77–78.

33. Philip Kotler and Paul N. Bloom, "Strategies for High Market-Share Companies," *Harvard Business Review* (November–December 1975): 63–72. See also Porter, *Competitive Strategy*, pp. 221–226.

34. Robert D. Buzzell and Frederick D. Wiersema, "Successful Share-Building Strategies," *Harvard Business Review* (January–February 1981): 135–144.

35. Linda Hellofs and Robert Jacobson, "Market Share and Customer's Perceptions of Quality: When Can Firms Grow Their Way to Higher Versus Lower Quality?" *Journal of Marketing* 63 (January 1999): pp. 16–25.

36. Cary Hatch, "When Should You Try Guerilla Marketing?" *ABA Bank Marketing*, March 2005, p. 53; Shari Caudron, "Guerrilla Tactics," *IndustryWeek*, July 16, 2001, pp. 53+; "If You Can't Stand the Heat, Stay Out of the Streets," *Brandweek*, November 12, 2001, p. 36.

37. Theodore Levitt, "Innovative Imitation," *Harvard Business Review*, September–October 1966, pp. 63ff. Also see Steven P. Schnaars, *Managing Imitation Strategies: How Later Entrants Seize Markets from Pioneers* (New York: Free Press, 1994).

38. Stuart F. Brown, "The Company that Out-Harleys Harley," *Fortune*, September 28, 1998, pp. 56–57.

39. Allen J. McGrath, "Growth Strategies with a '90s Twist," *Across the Board* (March 1995): 43–46; Antonio Ligi, "The Bottom Line: Logitech Plots Its Escape from Mouse Trap," *Dow Jones Newswire*, February 20, 2001.

CHAPTER 10

Setting Product Strategy and Marketing Through the Life Cycle

In this chapter, we will address the following questions:

1. What are the characteristics of products, and how can they be classified?
2. How can a company build and manage its product mix and product lines?
3. How can companies use packaging, labeling, warranties, and guarantees as marketing tools?
4. What are the main stages in developing and managing new products?
5. What factors affect the rate of diffusion and consumer adoption of new products?
6. What marketing strategies are appropriate at each stage of the product life cycle?

MARKETING MANAGEMENT AT STEINWAY

Perhaps no other high-end product combines the painstaking craftsmanship and long-time market dominance of a Steinway piano. Now more than 150 years old, Steinway & Sons still builds its finest concert pianos by hand in America and Germany, based on 120 proprietary patents and product innovations. Mass-produced pianos take roughly 20 days to build, whereas each concert Steinway takes at least nine months to build and requires 12,000 parts, many made on the premises. In addition, Steinway works with a partner in China to design and manufacture more-affordable pianos under the Boston and Essex brands, competing with Yamaha and Kawai.

One reason Steinway's concert pianos are so highly coveted—and command such a high profit margin—is that the company can produce only a few thousand such models per year. "We have 2 percent of all keyboard unit sales in the U.S.," says Bruce Stevens, Steinway's president. "But we have 25 percent of the sales dollars and about 35 percent of the profits." Because of its legendary quality, graceful design, and technical excellence, Steinway is far and away the market leader in concert pianos (with market share exceeding 95 percent); in addition, it is the most popular piano brand among composers and musicians. Even as electronic keyboards and other nontraditional pianos capture the interest of certain segments, Steinway remains the leader at the top end of the market.[1]

At the heart of a great brand is a great product, which in turn is a key element in the market offering. This holds true whether the product is a Steinway piano, a Starbuck's espresso, or a Sci-Fi Channel television show. In this chapter, we examine the concept of product; basic product decisions; new product development and adoption; and the product life cycle. Chapter 11 looks at how companies design and manage services, and Chapter 12 explores pricing decisions. For marketing success, all three elements must be meshed into a competitively attractive offering.

PRODUCT CHARACTERISTICS AND CLASSIFICATIONS

A **product** is anything that can be offered to a market to satisfy a want or need, including *physical goods, services, experiences, events, persons, places, properties, organizations, information,* and *ideas*. The customer will judge the offering by three basic elements: product features and quality, services mix and quality, and price appropriateness (Figure 10.1). As a result, marketers must think about the level of each product's features, benefits, and quality.

Product Levels

Marketers plan their market offering at five levels, as shown in Figure 10.2.[2] Each level adds more customer value, and together the levels constitute a **customer value hierarchy**. The most fundamental level is the **core benefit:** the fundamental service or benefit that the customer is really buying. A hotel guest is buying "rest and sleep." The purchaser of a drill is buying "holes." Marketers must see themselves as benefit providers.

At the second level, the marketer has to turn the core benefit into a **basic product**. Thus, a hotel room includes a bed, bathroom, and towels. At the third level, the marketer prepares an **expected product**, a set of attributes and conditions that buyers

FIGURE 10.1   Components of the Product Offering

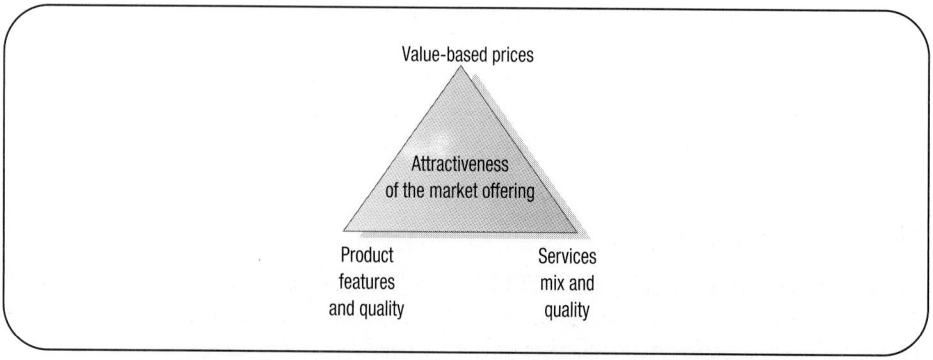

FIGURE 10.2   Five Product Levels

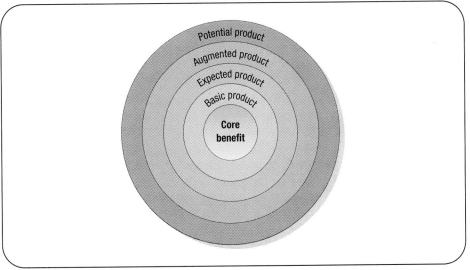

"sell the sizzle not the steak"
Elmore Wheeler

normally expect when they buy this product. Hotel guests expect a clean bed, fresh towels, and so on. Because most hotels can meet this minimum expectation, the traveler normally will settle for whichever hotel is most convenient or least expensive.

At the fourth level, the marketer prepares an **augmented product** that exceeds customer expectations. In developed countries, brand positioning and competition take place at this level. (In less-developed countries, competition takes place mostly at the expected product level.) Product augmentation leads the marketer to look at the user's total **consumption system:** the way the user performs the tasks of getting and using products and related services.[3] As Levitt notes: "The new competition is not between what companies produce in their factories, but between what they add to their factory output in the form of packaging, services, advertising, customer advice, financing, delivery, and other things that people value."[4]

However, product augmentation adds cost, so the marketer must determine whether customers will pay enough to cover the extra cost (of high-speed Internet access in a hotel room, for example). Moreover, augmented benefits soon become expected benefits, which means that competitors have to search for still other features and benefits. Additionally, as companies raise the price of their augmented product, some competitors can offer a "stripped-down" version at a much lower price. Thus, the hotel industry has seen the growth of fine hotels offering augmented products (Ritz-Carlton), as well as lower-cost lodgings offering basic products (Motel 6).

At the fifth level stands the **potential product**, which encompasses all of the possible augmentations and transformations the product might undergo in the future. Here, a company searches for entirely new ways to satisfy its customers and distinguish its offer.

Product Classifications

Marketers have traditionally classified products on the basis of three characteristics: durability, tangibility, and consumer or industrial use. Each product classification is associated with a different marketing-mix strategy.[5]

- *Durability and tangibility. Nondurable goods* are tangible goods normally consumed in one or a few uses (such as beer and soap). Because these goods are consumed quickly and purchased frequently, the appropriate strategy is to make them available in many locations, charge a small markup, and advertise heavily to induce trial and build preference. *Durable goods* are tangible goods that survive many uses (such as refrigerators). These normally require more personal selling and service, command a higher margin, and require more seller guarantees. *Services* are intangible, inseparable, variable, and perishable products (such as haircuts or legal advice), so they usually require more quality control, supplier credibility, and adaptability.

- *Consumer-goods classification.* Classified according to consumer shopping habits, these products include **convenience goods** (such as newspapers) that are usually purchased frequently, immediately, and with little effort; **shopping goods** (such as furniture) that the customer, in the process of selection and purchase, compares on the basis of suitability, quality, price, and style; **specialty goods** (such as cars) with unique characteristics or brand identification for which a sufficient number of buyers are willing to make a special purchasing effort; and **unsought goods** (such as smoke detectors) that consumers do not know about or do not normally think of buying.

- *Industrial-goods classification. Materials and parts* are goods that enter the manufacturer's product completely. Raw materials can be *farm products* (wheat) or *natural products* (lumber). Farm products are sold through intermediaries; natural products are sold through long-term supply contracts, with price and delivery as key purchase factors. *Manufactured materials and parts* are either *component materials* (iron) or *component parts* (small motors); again, price and supplier reliability are important factors. **Capital items** are long-lasting goods that facilitate developing or managing the finished product, including *installations* (factories) and *equipment* (trucks), both sold through personal selling. **Supplies and business services** are short-lasting goods and services that facilitate developing or managing the finished product; these include *maintenance and repair services* and *business advisory services.*

PRODUCT RELATIONSHIPS

A **product system** is a group of diverse but related items that function in a compatible manner. A **product mix** (also called a **product assortment**) is the set of all products and items that a particular marketer offers for sale. To illustrate, NEC's product mix consists of communication products and computer products. A company's product mix can be described in terms of width, length, depth, and consistency. The *width* refers to how many different product lines the company carries. The *length* refers to the total number of items in the mix. The *depth* of a product mix refers to how many variants of each product are offered. The *consistency* refers to how closely related the product lines are in end use, production requirements, distribution channels, or some other way.

These four product-mix dimensions permit the company to expand its business by adding new product lines, thus widening its product mix; lengthening each product line; deepening the product mix by adding more variants; and pursuing more product-line consistency.

Product-Line Analysis

In offering a product line, the company normally develops a basic platform and modules that can be expanded to meet different customer requirements. As one example, many homebuilders show a model home to which additional features can be added, enabling the builders to offer variety while lowering production costs. Product-line managers need to know the sales and profits of each item so they can determine which items to build, maintain, harvest, or divest.[6] The manager must calculate each item's percentage contribution to total sales and profits. A high concentration of sales in a few items means line vulnerability. On the other hand, the firm may consider eliminating items that deliver a low percentage of sales and profits—unless these exhibit strong growth potential.

The manager must also review how the line is positioned against competitors' lines. A useful tool is a product map showing which competitive products compete against the company's products on specific features or benefits. This helps management identify different market segments and determine how well the firm is positioned to serve the needs of each. These analyses set the stage for decisions about product-line length.

Product-Line Length

Companies seeking high market share and market growth will carry longer lines; companies emphasizing high profitability will carry shorter lines of carefully chosen items. **Line stretching** occurs when a firm lengthens its product line. With a down-market stretch, a firm introduces a lower price line. Moving downmarket can be risky. When Kodak introduced Funtime film to counter lower-priced brands, the price was not low enough to match the lower-priced competitive products. After regular customers started buying Funtime—cannibalizing the core brand—Kodak withdrew Funtime.

With an upmarket stretch, a company enters the high end of the market for more growth, higher margins, or to position itself as a full-line manufacturer. All of the leading Japanese automakers have launched an upscale automobile under new brands: Toyota launched Lexus; Nissan launched Infinity; and Honda launched Acura. Companies serving the middle market can stretch their product lines in both directions, as Starwood Hotels has done with the Luxury Collection, St. Regis, and W brands (for the top of the upscale market), and Four Points by Sheraton (moderately priced market).[7] By basing the development of these brands on distinct target markets with unique needs, Starwood ensures against overlap between brands.

Adding more items within the present range also lengthens the product line. There are several motives for *line filling*: seeking incremental profits, satisfying dealers who complain about lost sales because of missing items in the line, trying to utilize excess capacity, seeking to be the leading full-line company, and plugging holes to keep out competitors.

Line Modernization, Featuring, and Pruning

Product lines need to be modernized. This happens continuously in rapidly changing markets, where timing is critical to avoid hurting sales of current products or losing sales to competitors. In *line featuring*, the manager showcases one or a few items in the line to attract customers, lend prestige, or achieve other goals. If one end of the line is selling well and the other end is not, the company may use featuring to boost demand for the slower sellers, especially if those items are produced in a factory that is idled by lack of demand. In addition, managers must periodically review the entire line for pruning, identifying weak items through sales and cost analysis. They may also prune when the company is short of production capacity or demand is slow.

PACKAGING, LABELING, WARRANTIES, AND GUARANTEES

Most physical products have to be packaged and labeled. Some packages—such as the Coke bottle—are world famous. Many marketers have called packaging a fifth P, along with price, product, place, and promotion; however, packaging and labeling are usually treated as an element of product strategy. Warranties and guarantees can also be important to a firm's product strategy.

Packaging

Packaging includes all the activities of designing and producing a product's container. The package might include up to three levels of material. Paco Rabanne cologne comes in a bottle (*primary package*) inside a cardboard box (*secondary package*) that is in a corrugated box (*shipping package*) containing six dozen boxes of Paco Rabanne.

Several factors have contributed to packaging's growing use as a potent marketing tool:

- *Self-service.* The typical supermarket shopper passes by some 300 items per minute. Given that 53 percent of all purchases are made on impulse, an effective package attracts attention, describes features, creates confidence, and makes a favorable impression.
- *Consumer affluence.* Rising consumer affluence means consumers are willing to pay a little more for the convenience, appearance, dependability, and prestige of better packages.
- *Company and brand image.* Packages contribute to instant recognition of the company or brand.
- *Innovation opportunity.* Innovative packaging can bring benefits to consumers and profits to producers. After Dutch Boy developed the easy-to-open, easy-to-carry Twist & Pour paint container, its sales increased, and it was able to add distribution at higher retail prices.[8]

From the perspective of both the firm and consumers, packaging must achieve a number of objectives.[9] It must identify the brand, communicate descriptive and persuasive information, facilitate product transportation and protection, assist at-home storage, and aid product consumption. All packaging elements must be in harmony and must fit with the product's pricing, advertising, and other marketing elements. Next come *engineering tests* to ensure that the package stands up under normal conditions; *visual tests*, to ensure that the script is legible and the colors harmonious; *dealer tests*, to ensure that dealers find the packages attractive and easy to handle; and *consumer tests*, to ensure favorable market response.

Tetra Pak, a major Swedish multinational, provides an example of the power of innovative packaging. Milk and other perishable liquid foods stored in its "aseptic" package can be distributed without refrigeration, allowing dairies to distribute milk in a wider area without investing in refrigerated trucks and facilities. Supermarkets can carry Tetra Pak–packaged products on ordinary shelves, saving on costly refrigerator space. It recently introduced easy-pour resealable containers for wines. The firm's motto is "The package should save more than it costs."[10]

Labeling

Every physical product must carry a label, which may be a simple tag attached to the product or an elaborately designed graphic that is part of the package. Labels perform several functions. First, the label *identifies* the product or brand—for instance, the name Sunkist stamped on oranges. The label might also *grade* the product, the way canned peaches are grade labeled A, B, and C. The label may *describe* the product: who made it, where it was made, when it was made, what it contains, how it is to be used, and how to use it safely. Finally, the label might *promote* the product through attractive graphics.

Labels eventually need freshening up. Ivory soap's label has been redone 18 times since the 1890s, with gradual changes in the lettering. Legal concerns about labels (and packaging) stretch back to the early 1900s and continue today. The Food and Drug Administration (FDA) requires processed foods to carry nutritional labeling that clearly states the amounts of protein, fat, carbohydrates, and calories, plus vitamin and mineral content as a percentage of the recommended daily allowance.[11] Consumerists have lobbied for laws to require *open dating* (to describe product freshness), *unit pricing* (to state the product cost in standard measurement units), *grade labeling* (to rate the quality level), and *percentage labeling* (to show the percentage of each important ingredient).

Warranties and Guarantees

All sellers are legally responsible for fulfilling a buyer's normal or reasonable expectations. Warranties are formal statements of expected product performance by the manufacturer. Products under warranty can be returned to the manufacturer or designated repair center for repair, replacement, or refund. Warranties, whether expressed or implied, are legally enforceable. Mitsubishi Motors North America, for instance, offers a 10-year, 100,000-mile warranty on certain parts to signal its confidence in the quality and reliability of its vehicles.[12]

Many sellers offer either general guarantees or specific guarantees.[13] The purpose is to reduce the buyer's perceived risk and provide assurances that the company and its offerings are dependable. Some firms offer specific guarantees that differentiate their offerings. For instance, Standard Chartered Nakornthon Bank in Thailand attracts small- and medium-sized business customers by guaranteeing that loan officers will say yes or no to a loan application within four days—or the customer will receive 500 baht per day until the bank makes a decision.[14]

MANAGING NEW PRODUCTS

A company can add new products in two ways: through acquisition (buying another company, buying another firm's patent, or buying a license or franchise) or through development (using its own laboratories, hiring independent researchers, or hiring a new-product-development firm). Six categories of new products are:[15]

1. *New-to-the-world products.* New products that create an entirely new market.
2. *New product lines.* New products that allow a company to enter an established market for the first time.
3. *Additions to existing product lines.* New products that supplement established lines (flavors and so on).

4. *Improvements and revisions of existing products.* New products that provide improved performance or greater perceived value and replace existing products.

5. *Repositionings.* Existing products that are targeted to new markets or market segments.

6. *Cost reductions.* New products that provide similar performance at lower cost.

Most established companies focus on *incremental innovation*. Newer companies create *disruptive technologies* that are cheaper and more likely to alter the competitive space. Established companies can be slow to react or invest in these disruptive technologies because they threaten their investment. Then they suddenly find themselves facing formidable new competitors, and many fail.[16] To ensure that they don't fall into this trap, incumbent firms must monitor customers' and prospects' preferences over time and uncover evolving, difficult-to-articulate needs.[17]

Why New Products Fail—and Succeed

New products are failing at a disturbing rate. Recent studies put the rate at 95 percent in the United States and 90 percent in Europe.[18] New products fail for many reasons: ignoring or misinterpreting market research; overestimating market size; high development costs; poor design; incorrect positioning, ineffective advertising, or wrong price; insufficient distribution support; and competitors who fight back hard. On the other hand, Cooper and Kleinschmidt found that unique, superior products succeed 98 percent of the time, compared with products with a moderate advantage (58 percent success) and those with a minimal advantage (18 percent success).[19] The company must carefully define and assess the target market, product requirements, and benefits

FIGURE 10.3 The New-Product Development Decision Process

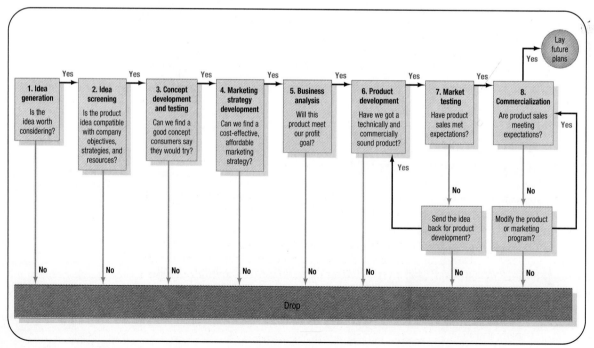

before proceeding with a new product. Other success factors include technological and marketing synergy, quality execution, and market attractiveness.[20]

New Product Development

The stages in the new product development process are shown in Figure 10.3. Many firms have multiple, parallel development projects working through the process, each at a different stage.[21] The process is not always linear, however; some firms recognize the value of returning to earlier stages to make improvements before moving ahead.

Idea Generation   The process starts with the search for ideas (see "Marketing Skills: Finding New Product Ideas" below). Some marketing experts believe that the greatest opportunities and highest leverage with new products are found by uncovering the best possible set of unmet customer needs or technological innovation.[22] New-product ideas can come from interacting with others (customers, scientists, competitors, employees, channel members, top management) and from using creativity-generating techniques (listing attributes; identifying relationships; listing combinations of dimensions related to a problem; reversing normal assumptions; finding new

MARKETING SKILLS: FINDING NEW PRODUCT IDEAS

How do marketers find promising new product ideas? Marketers for the most innovative companies never stop searching for good ideas; in fact, they search consistently and systematically for product possibilities. The first step is to view every contact with customers and prospects as an opportunity to identify unmet or changing needs, spark new thoughts about solving old problems, or turn up ideas for applying old technology and techniques to new problems. In addition to formal research, marketers set up informal meetings to find out what customers like and dislike, what features and benefits they value, and why. It is also necessary to comb through complaints and inquiries, visit trade shows, scan business publications, and surf the Web.

In addition, marketers should strengthen their connections inside the firm. They need to tap into feedback gathered by employees who meet or talk with customers on a regular basis, such as salespeople and technicians. It is important to encourage employees and managers from every organizational function and level to submit ideas and respond to submissions. Marketers also gain insight by learning about market changes observed by colleagues in other locations. They must document ideas and keep them all in an "idea vault" that can be easily accessed, because an idea that seems unfeasible today may turn out to be tomorrow's hot new possibility.

Marketers at the Dutch multinational corporation Philips cast a wide net to find new product ideas. The idea for its HeartStart home heart defibrillator came from Mary Lynn Grizzell, a mother in Washington state whose children have a serious heart condition. She asked Philips to make a purse-size defibrillator so she could respond quickly if one of the children had a heart attack at home. The company got to work, and today the FDA-approved HeartStart is in thousands of U.S. and European homes, ready to be used if the need arises.[23]

contexts; mind-mapping). For instance, Procter & Gamble's brand managers visit consumers at home to watch how they perform household chores and ask about sources of frustration. Toyota says its employees submit 2 million ideas every year for improving products, production, and services.

Idea Screening The second step is to screen out weaker ideas, because product-development costs rise substantially with each successive development stage. Most companies require ideas to be described on a standard form for review by a new-product committee. The description states the product idea, target market, and competition, along with estimates of market size, product price, development time and costs, manufacturing costs, and rate of return. The committee reviews each idea against criteria such as: Does the product meet a need and offer superior value? Will it deliver the expected sales volume, sales growth, and profit? Next, the company estimates each product idea's overall probability of success and determines which are high enough to warrant continued development.

Concept Development A *product idea* is a possible product the company might offer to the market. In contrast, a *product concept* is an elaborated version of the idea expressed in consumer terms. A product idea can be turned into several concepts by asking: Who will use this product? What primary benefit will it provide? When will people consume or use it? By answering such questions, a company can often form several product concepts, select the single most promising concept, and create a *product-positioning map* for it. Figure 10.4a shows the positioning of a product concept, a low-cost instant breakfast drink, compared to other breakfast foods already on the market. These contrasts can be used in communicating and promoting the concept to the market.

Next, the product concept is turned into a *brand concept*. To transform the low-cost instant breakfast drink concept into a brand concept, the company must decide how much to charge and how calorific to make its drink. Figure 10.4b shows the positions of three instant breakfast drink brands. The new brand concept would have to be distinctive in the medium-price, medium-calorie market or the high-price, high-calorie market.

Concept Testing Concept testing involves presenting the product concept to appropriate target consumers and getting their reactions. The concepts can be presented symbolically or physically. The more the tested concepts resemble the final product or experience, the more dependable concept testing is. In the past, creating physical prototypes was costly and time-consuming, but computer-aided design and manufacturing programs have changed that. Today firms use *rapid prototyping* to design products on a computer and create plastic models to obtain feedback from potential consumers.[24] Companies are also using *virtual reality* to test product concepts.

Consumer preferences for alternative product concepts can be measured through **conjoint analysis**, a method for deriving the utility values that consumers attach to varying levels of a product's attributes.[25] Respondents are shown different hypothetical offers formed by combining varying levels of the attributes, then asked to rank the various offers. Management can identify the most appealing offer and the estimated market share and profit the company might realize. Note that the most customer-appealing offer is not always the most profitable for the firm.

Marketing Strategy After a successful concept test, the new-product manager will draft a three-part preliminary marketing strategy for introducing the new product into the market. The first part describes the target market's size, structure, and behavior; the

FIGURE 10.4   Product and Brand Positioning

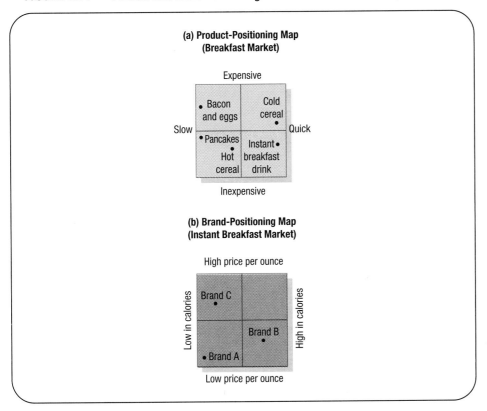

(a) Product-Positioning Map
(Breakfast Market)

(b) Brand-Positioning Map
(Instant Breakfast Market)

planned product positioning; and the sales, market share, and profit goals sought in the first few years. The second part outlines the planned price, distribution strategy, and marketing budget for the first year. The third part describes the long-run sales and profit goals and marketing-mix strategy over time. This plan forms the basis for the business analysis that is conducted before management makes a final decision on the new product.

Business Analysis   The company evaluates the proposed new product's business attractiveness by preparing sales, cost, and profit projections to determine whether these satisfy company objectives. If they do, the concept can move to the development stage. As new information emerges, the business analysis must be revised and expanded accordingly.

Estimated total sales is the sum of estimated first-time sales, replacement sales, and repeat sales. For one-time purchased products such as a retirement home, sales rise at the beginning, peak, and later approach zero as the number of potential buyers is exhausted; if new buyers keep entering the market, the curve will not drop to zero. Infrequently purchased products, such as cars, exhibit replacement cycles dictated by physical wearing out or by obsolescence due to changing styles, features, and performance; therefore, sales forecasting calls for estimating first-time sales and replacement sales separately. For frequently purchased products such as soap, the number of first-time buyers initially increases and then decreases as fewer buyers are left (assuming a fixed population). Repeat purchases occur soon, providing the product satisfies some buyers. The sales curve eventually plateaus, representing a level of steady repeat-purchase volume; by this time, the product is no longer a new product.

Management also analyzes expected costs and profits based on estimates prepared by research and development (R&D), manufacturing, marketing, and finance departments. Companies use other financial measures to evaluate new-product proposals. The simplest is **break-even analysis**, in which management estimates how many units of the product the company will have to sell to break even with the given price and cost structure.

The most complex method of estimating profit is **risk analysis**. Here, three estimates (optimistic, pessimistic, and most likely) are obtained for each uncertain variable affecting profitability under an assumed marketing environment and strategy for the planning period. The computer simulates possible outcomes and computes a rate-of-return probability distribution showing the range of possible rates of returns and their probabilities.[26]

Product Development Up until now, the product has existed only as a word description, a drawing, or a prototype. The next step involves a jump in investment that dwarfs the costs incurred in the earlier stages. At this stage the company will determine whether the product idea can be translated into a technically and commercially feasible product. If it cannot, the accumulated project cost will be lost except for any useful information gained in the process.

The job of translating target customer requirements into a working prototype is helped by a set of methods known as *quality function deployment* (QFD). The methodology takes the list of desired *customer attributes* (CAs) generated by market research and turns them into a list of *engineering attributes* (EAs) that the engineers can use. For example, customers of a proposed truck may want a certain acceleration rate (CA). Engineers can turn this into the required horsepower and other engineering equivalents (EAs). The methodology permits the measuring of the trade-offs and costs of providing the customer requirements. A major contribution of QFD is that it improves communication between marketers, engineers, and the manufacturing people.[27]

The R&D department will develop one or more physical versions of the product concept, looking for one that customers believe embodies the key attributes described in the concept statement, that performs safely under normal use, and that can be produced within the budget. Internet technology has led to more rapid prototyping and more flexible development; prototype-driven firms such as Microsoft cherish quick-and-dirty tests.[28]

When the prototypes are ready, they undergo rigorous functional tests and customer tests. *Alpha testing* means testing the product within the firm to check its performance in different applications. After refining the prototype further, the company moves to *beta testing*, enlisting customers to use the prototype and give feedback. Consumer testing can take a variety of forms, from bringing consumers into a laboratory to giving them samples to use in their homes. In-home placement tests are common with many consumer products. For example, when DuPont developed new synthetic carpeting, it installed free carpeting in several homes in exchange for the homeowners' willingness to report their likes and dislikes about the carpeting.

Market Testing After management is satisfied with functional and psychological performance, the product is ready to be dressed up with a brand name and packaging and put to a market test. The new product is introduced into an authentic setting to learn how large the market is and how consumers and dealers react to handling, using, and repurchasing the product. Not all companies use market testing; the extent of such testing is influenced by the investment cost and risk on the one hand and the time pressure and research cost on the other.

In testing consumer products, the company seeks to estimate four variables: trial, first repeat purchase, adoption, and purchase frequency. The company hopes to find all of these variables at high levels. In some cases, however, it will find many consumers trying the product but few rebuying it. It also might find high permanent adoption but low purchase frequency (as with gourmet frozen foods). Four methods of consumer-goods testing are:

- *Sales-wave research*. Consumers who initially try the product at no cost are reoffered the product or a competitor's product at slightly reduced prices, as many as three to five times (sales waves). The company notes how many customers select its product again and their reported level of satisfaction.

- *Simulated test marketing*. Qualified buyers are asked about brand familiarity and product preferences in a specific category. They look at ads, including one for the new product, then they receive money and go into a store where they can buy any items. The company notes how many people buy the new brand and competing brands as a test of the ad's relative effectiveness in stimulating trial. Consumers are also asked why they bought or did not buy; nonbuyers receive a free sample of the new product and are reinterviewed later to determine product attitudes, usage, satisfaction, and repurchase intention.

- *Controlled test marketing*. A research firm manages a panel of stores that will carry new products for a fee. The company with the new product specifies the number of stores and geographic locations it wants to test. The research firm delivers the product to the stores and controls shelf position; number of facings, displays, and point-of-purchase promotions; and pricing. Sales results can be measured through electronic scanners at the checkout. The company can also evaluate the impact of local advertising and promotions.

- *Test markets*. The company chooses a few representative cities, the sales force sells the trade on carrying the product and giving it good exposure, and the company puts on a complete advertising and promotion campaign in these markets. Marketers must decide on the number and location of test cities, length of the test, what to track, and what action to take. Today, many firms are skipping test marketing and relying instead on faster and more economical methods, such as smaller test areas and shorter test periods.

Business goods also benefit from market testing. Expensive industrial goods and new technologies will normally undergo both alpha and beta testing. New business products are sometimes market-tested at trade shows to see how much interest buyers show, how they react to various features and terms, and how many express purchase intentions or place orders. New industrial products can be tested in distributor and dealer display rooms, where they may be next to the manufacturer's other products and possibly competitors' products. This method yields preference and pricing information in the product's normal selling atmosphere; however, customers will not be able to place early orders and those who come in might not represent the target market.

Commercialization   If the company goes ahead with commercialization, it will face its largest costs to date. The company will have to contract for manufacture or build or rent a full-scale manufacturing facility. Plant size will be a critical decision. When Quaker Oats launched its 100 Percent Natural breakfast cereal, it built a smaller plant than called for by the sales forecast. Demand so exceeded the forecast that for about a year the company could not supply enough of the product to stores. Although Quaker Oats was gratified with the response, the low forecast cost it considerable profit.

In addition to promotion, major decisions during this stage include timing, geographic strategy, target-market prospects, and introductory market strategy. Marketing timing is critical. If a firm learns that a competitor is nearing the end of its development work, it can choose *first entry* (being first to market, locking up key distributors and customers, and gaining reputational leadership; but if the product is not thoroughly debugged, this can backfire); *parallel entry* (launching at the same time as a rival may gain both products more attention); or *late entry* (waiting until a rival has borne the cost of educating the market and revealed problems to avoid).

The company must also decide whether to launch the new product in one locality, one region, several regions, the national market, or the international market. Smaller companies often select one city for a blitz campaign, entering other cities one at a time; in contrast, large companies usually launch within a whole region and then move to the next region, although companies with national distribution generally launch new models nationally. More firms are rolling out new products simultaneously around the globe, a challenge in coordinating activities and obtaining agreement on strategy and tactics.

Within the rollout markets, the company must target its initial distribution and promotion to the best prospect groups. Presumably, the company has already profiled the prime prospects—who would ideally be early adopters, heavy users, and opinion leaders who are able to be reached at a low cost.[29] The company should rate the various prospect groups on these characteristics and target the best group to generate strong sales as soon as possible, motivate the sales force, and attract further prospects.

Finally, the firm needs an action plan for introducing the new product into the rollout markets. To coordinate the many activities involved in launching a new product, management can use network-planning techniques such as *critical path scheduling (CPS)*, which uses a master chart to show the simultaneous and sequential activities that must take place to launch the product. By estimating how much time each activity takes, the planners can estimate the project's completion time. A delay in any activity on the critical path will delay the entire project.[30]

THE CONSUMER ADOPTION PROCESS

Adoption is an individual's decision to become a regular user of a product. How do potential customers learn about new products, try them, and adopt or reject them? In the past, companies used a mass-market approach to introduce new products, on the assumption that most people are potential adopters. Yet consumers have different levels of interest in new products and brands. The theory of innovation diffusion and consumer adoption helps firms identify and target people who adopt products before the majority of consumers in a market.

Stages in the Adoption Process

An **innovation** refers to any good, service, or idea that is *perceived* by someone as new. The idea may have a long history, but it is an innovation to the person who sees it as new. Innovations take time to spread through the social system. Rogers defines the **innovation diffusion process** as "the spread of a new idea from its source of invention or creation to its ultimate users or adopters."[31] The adoption process focuses on the mental process through which a consumer passes from first hearing about an innovation to adoption.

Adopters of new products move through five stages: (1) *awareness* (consumer becomes aware of the innovation but has no information about it); (2) *interest* (consumer is stimulated to seek information); (3) *evaluation* (consumer considers whether to try the innovation); (4) *trial* (consumer tries the innovation to estimate its value); and (5) *adoption* (consumer decides to make full and regular use of the innovation).

Factors Influencing the Adoption Process

Rogers defines a person's innovativeness as "the degree to which an individual is relatively earlier in adopting new ideas than the other members of his social system." As Figure 10.5 shows, innovators are the first to adopt something new, while laggards are the last. Because people differ in their readiness to try new products, there are pioneers and early adopters for each product. After a slow start, an increasing number of people adopt the innovation, the number reaches a peak, and then it diminishes as fewer nonadopters remain.

Another factor affecting adoption is **personal influence**, the effect one person has on another's attitude or purchase probability. Although personal influence is greater in some situations and for some individuals, it is more important in the evaluation stage of the adoption process than in the other stages. It generally has more influence on late adopters and is more important in risky situations, as well.

Five characteristics influence adoption rate. The first is *relative advantage*—the degree to which the innovation appears superior to existing products. The second is

FIGURE 10.5   Adopter Categorization on the Basis of Relative Time of Adoption of Innovations

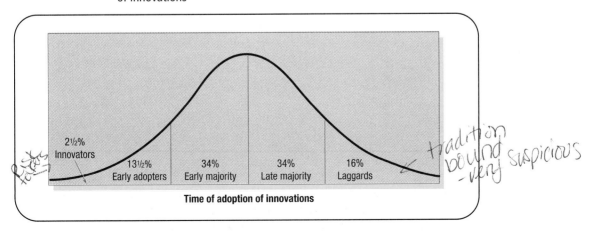

Source: Redrawn from Everett M. Rogers, *Diffusion of Innovations* (New York: The Free Press, 1983).

compatibility, the degree to which the innovation matches consumers' values and expe-riences. Third is *complexity*, the degree to which the innovation is relatively difficult to understand or use. Fourth is *divisibility*—the degree to which consumers can try the innovation on a limited basis. Fifth is *communicability*, the degree to which the benefits are observable or describable to others. Marketers must research and consider these factors in designing a new product and its marketing program.[32]

Finally, organizations vary in their readiness to adopt innovations. Adoption is associated with variables in the organization's environment, the organization itself (size, profits, pressure to change), and its managers. Other forces come into play when trying to get a product adopted into organizations that receive the bulk of their funding from the government. Additionally, negative public opinion can squelch a controversial or innovative product.

MARKETING THROUGH THE PRODUCT LIFE CYCLE

A company's positioning and differentiation strategy must change as the product, market, and competitors change over the *product life cycle* (PLC). To say that a product has a life cycle is to assert four things: (1) Products have a limited life; (2) product sales pass through distinct stages with different challenges, opportunities, and problems for the seller; (3) profits rise and fall at different stages of the product life cycle; and (4) products require different marketing, financial, manufacturing, purchasing, and human resource strategies in each stage.

Product Life Cycles

Most product life-cycle curves are portrayed as a bell-shape (Figure 10.6). This curve is typically divided into four stages.[33] In *introduction*, sales grow slowly as the product is introduced in the market, and profits are nonexistent due to heavy expenses incurred to launch the product. *Growth* is a period of rapid market acceptance and

FIGURE 10.6   Sales and Profit Life Cycles

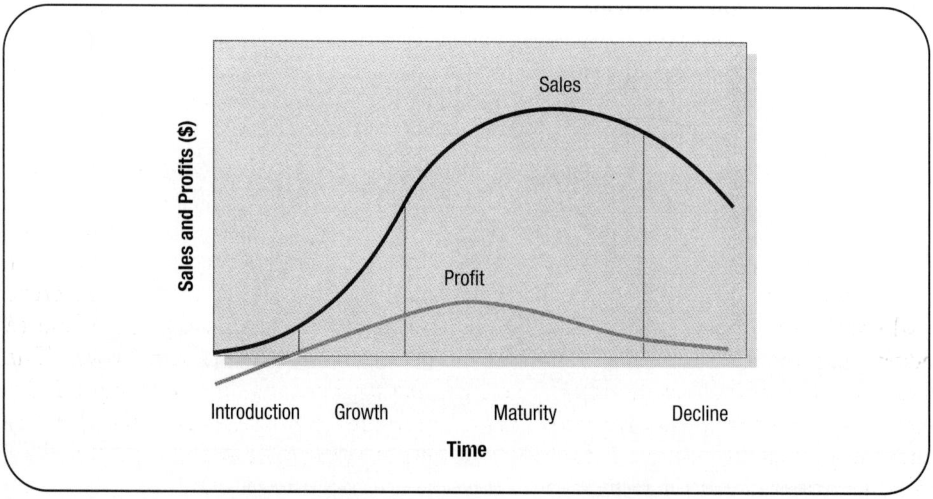

substantial profit improvement. In *maturity*, sales growth slows because the product has achieved acceptance by most potential buyers, and profits stabilize or decline due to higher competition. In *decline*, sales drift downward and profits erode.

Marketing Strategies: Introduction Stage and the Pioneer Advantage

Because it takes time to roll out a new product, work out the technical problems, fill dealer pipelines, and gain consumer acceptance, sales growth tends to be slow at the introductory stage.[34] Additional factors such as product complexity and fewer buyers slow sales of expensive new products. Profits are negative or low in this stage. Promotional expenditures are at their highest ratio to sales because of the need to (1) inform potential consumers, (2) induce product trial, and (3) secure distribution in retail outlets.[35] Firms focus on buyers who are the most ready to buy, usually higher-income groups. Prices tend to be high because costs are high.

Companies must decide when to enter the market with a new product. Being first can be rewarding, but risky and expensive; entering later makes sense if the firm can bring better technology, quality, or brand strength. Yet most studies indicate that the pioneer gains the most advantage. Such pioneers as Amazon.com, Coca-Cola, and Hallmark developed sustained market dominance.

The pioneer advantage is not inevitable. Studying 28 industries in which the imitators surpassed the innovators, Schnaars found several weaknesses among the failing pioneers, including new products that were too crude, were improperly positioned, or that appeared before there was strong demand; product-development costs or that exhausted the innovator's resources; a lack of resources to compete against entering larger firms; and managerial incompetence or complacency. Successful imitators offered lower prices, improved the product more continuously, or used brute market power to overtake the pioneer.[36] Tellis and Golder say the following factors underpin long-term market leadership: vision of a mass market; persistence; relentless innovation; financial commitment; and asset leverage.[37]

Marketing Strategies: Growth Stage

The growth stage is marked by a rapid climb in sales. Early adopters like the product, and additional consumers start buying it. Attracted by the opportunities, new competitors enter with new product features and expanded distribution. Prices remain steady or fall slightly, depending on how quickly demand increases. Companies maintain or increase their promotional expenditures to meet competition and to continue to educate the market, but sales rise much faster than promotional expenditures.

Profits increase as promotion costs are spread over a larger volume, and unit manufacturing costs fall faster than price declines, owing to the producer learning effect. The firm uses several strategies to sustain rapid market growth as long as possible: improving product quality and adding new features and improved styling; adding new models and flanker products; entering new segments; increasing distribution coverage and entering new channels; shifting from product-awareness to product-preference advertising; and lowering prices to attract the next layer of price-sensitive buyers. The growth stage involves a trade-off between high market share and high current profit. By spending money on product improvement, promotion, and distribution, the firm can capture a dominant position. It forgoes maximum current profit in the hope of making even greater profits in the next stage.

Marketing Strategies: Maturity Stage

At some point, the rate of sales growth slows, and the product enters a stage of relative maturity, which normally lasts longer than the previous stages and poses formidable marketing challenges. *Most products are in the maturity stage of the life cycle, and most marketing managers cope with the problem of marketing a mature product.*

Three strategies for the maturity stage are market modification, product modification, and marketing-mix modification. Using market modification, the company might try to expand the market for its mature brand by expanding the number of brand users. This is accomplished by converting nonusers; entering new market segments (as AARP is doing by reaching out to younger, more active seniors); or winning competitors' customers (the way Puffs facial tissues is always wooing Kleenex customers). Convincing current customers to increase their usage of the brand also can increase volume.

With product modification, managers try to stimulate sales by modifying the product's characteristics through quality improvement, feature improvement, or style improvement. *Quality improvement* aims at increasing the product's functional performance—its durability, reliability, and speed. *Feature improvement* adds new features that build the company's image as an innovator and win the loyalty of market segments that value these features. However, feature improvements are easily imitated; unless there is a permanent gain from being first, the improvement might not pay off in the long run.[38] *Style improvement* increases the product's esthetic appeal. This might give the product a unique market identity, but it is difficult to predict whether people—and which people—will like a new style. Also, the company risks losing customers when an old style is discontinued.

Product managers can try to stimulate sales by modifying other marketing-mix elements such as prices, distribution, advertising, sales promotion, personal selling, and services. Sales promotion has more impact at this stage because consumer buying has reached an equilibrium; psychological persuasion (advertising) is not as effective as financial persuasion (sales promotion deals). Although brand managers use sales promotion because its effects are quicker and more visible, too much such activity can hurt brand image and long-run profit performance.

Marketing Strategies: Decline Stage

Sales decline for a number of reasons, including technological advances, shifts in consumer tastes, and increased competition. All lead to overcapacity, increased price-cutting, and profit erosion. As sales and profits decline, some firms withdraw from the market. Those remaining may reduce the number of products they offer. They may withdraw from smaller segments and weaker channels, cut the promotion budget, and further reduce prices.

According to a study of company strategies in declining industries, five possible strategies are:

1. Increasing the firm's investment (to dominate the market or strengthen competitive position).
2. Maintaining the firm's investment level until industry uncertainties are resolved.
3. Decreasing the firm's investment level selectively by dropping unprofitable customer groups, while simultaneously strengthening the firm's investment in lucrative niches.
4. Harvesting ("milking") the firm's investment to recover cash quickly.
5. Divesting the business quickly by disposing of assets as advantageously as possible.[39]

The appropriate decline strategy depends on the industry's relative attractiveness and the company's competitive strength. Consider instant oatmeal, which staged a comeback after the FDA allowed manufacturers to say that eating oatmeal may reduce the risk of heart disease. Quaker Oats, which has a 61 percent share of the hot cereal market, seized the opportunity to tout the benefits of new products such as Take Heart Instant Oatmeal.[40]

If the company were choosing between harvesting and divesting, its strategies would be quite different. *Harvesting* calls for gradually reducing a product's or business's costs while trying to maintain its sales. The first step is to cut R&D costs and plant and equipment investment. The company might also reduce product quality, sales force size, marginal services, and advertising expenditures without letting customers, competitors, and employees know what is happening. Harvesting is difficult to execute, but it can substantially increase the company's current cash flow.[41] If a company wants to divest, it can probably sell the product to another firm if it has

TABLE 10.1   Summary of Product Life-Cycle Characteristics, Objectives, and Strategies

	Introduction	**Growth**	**Maturity**	**Decline**
Characteristics				
Sales	Low sales	Rapidly rising sales	Peak sales	Declining sales
Costs	High cost per customer	Average cost per customer	Low cost per customer	Low cost per customer
Profits	Negative	Rising profits	High profits	Declining profits
Customers	Innovators	Early adopters	Middle majority	Laggards
Competitors	Few	Growing number	Stable number beginning to decline	Declining number
Marketing Objectives				
Strategies	Create product awareness and trial	Maximize market share	Maximize profit while defending market share	Reduce expenditure and milk the brand
Product	Offer a basic product	Offer product extensions, service, warranty	Diversify brands and items	Phase out weak models
Price	Charge cost-plus	Price to penetrate market	Price to match or best competitors	Cut price
Distribution	Build selective distribution	Build intensive distribution	Build more intensive distribution	Go selective: Phase out unprofitable outlets
Advertising	Build product awareness among early adopters and dealers	Build awareness and interest in the mass market	Stress brand differences and benefits	Reduce to level needed to retain hard-core loyals
Sales Promotion	Use heavy sales promotion to entice trial	Reduce to take advantage of heavy consumer demand	Increase to encourage brand switching	Reduce to minimal level

Sources: Chester R. Wasson, *Dynamic Competitive Strategy and Product Life Cycles* (Austin, TX: Austin Press, 1978); John A. Weber, "Planning Corporate Growth with Inverted Product Life Cycles," *Long Range Planning* (October 1976): 12–29; Peter Doyle, "The Realities of the Product Life Cycle," *Quarterly Review of Marketing* (Summer 1976).

strong distribution and residual goodwill; if not, it must decide whether to liquidate quickly or slowly.

Critique of the Product Life-Cycle Concept

The PLC concept helps interpret product and market dynamics. It can be used for planning and control, although it is less useful as a forecasting tool because sales histories exhibit diverse patterns, and the stages vary in duration. Critics claim that life-cycle patterns are too variable in their shape and duration. They also say that marketers can seldom tell what stage the product is in: A product may appear to be mature when it is actually in a plateau prior to another upsurge. One final criticism is that the PLC pattern is the result of marketing strategies rather than an inevitable course that sales must follow. See Table 10.1 for a summary of the characteristics, marketing objectives, and marketing strategies of the PLC stages.

EXECUTIVE SUMMARY

Marketers need to think through five levels of the product, each of which adds value: the core benefit, basic product, expected product, augmented product, and potential product. Products can be classified in terms of durability and reliability. Consumer goods can be convenience goods, shopping goods, specialty goods, or unsought goods. Industrial goods can be materials and parts, capital items, or supplies and business services.

A product mix can be classified in terms of width, length, depth, and consistency. These four dimensions are the tools for developing the firm's marketing strategy and deciding which product lines to grow, maintain, harvest, and divest. Product-line managers look at sales, profits, and market profile when analyzing a product line and deciding how much to invest in it. The product component of the marketing mix can be changed by line stretching, line filling, modernizing its products, featuring certain products, and pruning. Physical products must be packaged and labeled; well-designed packages create convenience value for customers and promotional value for producers. Warranties and guarantees offer further assurance to customers.

The eight stages of the new product development process are idea generation, screening, concept development and testing, marketing-strategy development, business analysis, product development, market testing, and commercialization. The consumer-adoption process—by which customers learn about new products, try them, and adopt or reject them—is influenced by many factors out of the firm's control, including consumers' and organizations' willingness to try new products, personal influences, and the characteristics of the new product.

The general sequence of stages in the product life cycle is introduction, growth, maturity, and decline; most products are in the maturity stage. Each stage calls for different marketing strategies. The introduction stage is marked by slow growth and minimal profits. Next, the product enters a growth stage marked by rapid sales growth and increasing profits, followed by a maturity stage in which sales growth slows and profits stabilize. Finally, the product enters a decline stage, where the challenge is to identify truly weak products; develop a strategy for each; and phase out weak products while minimizing the hardship to company profits, employees, and customers.

NOTES

1. "Steinway Selects Pearl River to Build Essex Piano Line," *Music Trades*, May 2005, pp. 36+; "New Model, Focused Marketing Fuel Steinway Growth," *Music Trades*, March 2005, pp. 128+; Andy Serwer, "Happy Birthday, Steinway," *Fortune*, March 17, 2003, pp. 94–97.

2. This discussion is adapted from Theodore Levitt, "Marketing Success through Differentiation—of Anything," *Harvard Business Review* (January–February 1980): 83–91. The first level, core benefit, has been added to Levitt's discussion.

3. See Harper W. Boyd Jr. and Sidney Levy, "New Dimensions in Consumer Analysis," *Harvard Business Review* (November–December 1963): 129–40.

4. Theodore Levitt, *The Marketing Mode* (New York: McGraw-Hill, 1969) p. 2.

5. For some definitions, see *Dictionary of Marketing Terms*, ed. Peter D. Bennett (Chicago: American Marketing Association, 1995). Also see Patrick E. Murphy and Ben M. Enis, "Classifying Products Strategically," *Journal of Marketing* (July 1986): 24–42.

6. Robert Bordley, "Determining the Appropriate Depth and Breadth of a Firm's Product Portfolio," *Journal of Marketing Research* 40 (February 2003): 39–53; Peter Boatwright and Joseph C. Nunes, "Reducing Assortment: An Attribute-Based Approach," *Journal of Marketing* 65 (July 2001): 50–63.

7. Peter Sanders, "Cool at the Lower End," *Wall Street Journal*, June 6, 2005, p. B1; Michael Martinez, "Hotel Chains Compete in a Bid to Provide the Comfiest Night's Sleep," *San Jose Mercury News*, June 27, 2005 (www.mercurynews.com).

8. Seth Goldin, "In Praise of Purple Cows," *Fast Company*, February 2003, pp. 74–85.

9. Susan B. Bassin, "Value-Added Packaging Cuts Through Store Clutter," *Marketing News*, September 26, 1988, p. 21.

10. "Tetra Pak, a Supplier of Food and Beverage Processing and Packaging Systems," *Machine Design*, May 5, 2005, p. 53.

11. Siva K. Balasubramanian and Catherine Cole, "Consumers' Search and Use of Nutrition Information: The Challenge and Promise of the Nutrition Labeling and Education Act," *Journal of Marketing* 66 (July 2002): 112–127; John C. Kozup, Elizabeth H. Creyer, and Scot Burton, "Making Healthful Food Choices: The Influence of Health Claims and Nutrition Information on Consumers' Evaluations of Packaged Food Products and Restaurant Menu Items," *Journal of Marketing* 67 (April 2003): 19–34.

12. Jason Stein, "10-year Mitsubishi Warranty Is Small Part of a Larger Plan," *Automotive News*, January 12, 2004, p. 16.

13. "More Firms Pledge Guaranteed Service," *Wall Street Journal*, July 17, 1991, pp. B1, B6; Barbara Ettore, "Phenomenal Promises Mean Business," *Management Review* (March 1994): 18–23. Also see Christopher W. L. Hart, *Extraordinary Guarantees* (New York: Amacom, 1993); Sridhar Moorthy and Kannan Srinivasan, "Signaling Quality with a Money-Back Guarantee: The Role of Transaction Costs," *Marketing Science* 14, no. 4 (1995): 442–446.

14. Krissana Parnsoonthorn, "Service Guarantee Offered," *Bangkok Post*, July 8, 2005 (www.bangkokpost.com).

15. *New Products Management for the 1980s* (New York: Booz, Allen & Hamilton, 1982).

16. Clayton M. Christensen, *The Innovator's Dilemma: When New Technologies Cause Great Firms to Fail* (Boston: Harvard University Press, 1997).

17. Ely Dahan and John R. Hauser, "Product Development: Managing a Dispersed Process," in *Handbook of Marketing*, edited by Bart Weitz and Robin Wensley (London: Sage Publications, 2002), pp. 179–222.

18. See Deloitte and Touche, "Vision in Manufacturing Study," Deloitte Consulting and Kenan-Flagler Business School, March 6, 1998; A.C. Nielsen, "New Product Introduction—Successful Innovation/Failure: Fragile Boundary," A.C. Nielsen BASES and Ernst & Young Global Client Consulting, June 24, 1999.

19. Robert G. Cooper and Elko J. Kleinschmidt, *New Products: The Key Factors in Success* (Chicago: American Marketing Association, 1990).

20. Ibid.

21. Ely Dahan and John R. Hauser, "Product Development: Managing a Dispersed Process," in *Handbook of Marketing*, edited by Weitz and Robin Wensley (Thousand Oaks, CA: Sage, 2002) pp. 179–222.

22. John Hauser and Gerard J. Tellis, "Research on Innovation: A Review and Agenda for Marketing," 2004, working paper, M.I.T.

23. Anne Fisher, "Have a Heart," *Fortune*, July 25, 2005, p. 136; Robert Cooper, *Product Leadership: Crating and Launching Superior New Products* (New York: Perseus Books, 1998).

24. "The Ultimate Widget: 3-D 'Printing' May Revolutionize Product Design and Manufacturing," *U.S. News & World Report*, July 20, 1992, p. 55.

25. For additional information, also see Paul E. Green and V. Srinivasan, "Conjoint Analysis in Marketing: New Developments with Implications for Research and Practice," *Journal of Marketing* (October 1990): 3–19; Dick R. Wittnick, Marco Vriens, and Wim Burhenne, "Commercial Uses of Conjoint Analysis in Europe: Results and Critical Reflections," *International Journal of Research in Marketing* (January 1994): 41–52; Jordan J. Louviere, David A. Hensher, and Joffre D. Swait, *Stated Choice Models: Analysis and Applications* (New York: Cambridge University Press, 2000).

26. See David B. Hertz, "Risk Analysis in Capital Investment," *Harvard Business Review* (January–February 1964): 96–106.

27. John Hauser, "House of Quality," *Harvard Business Review* (May–June 1988): 63–73. Customer-driven engineering is also called "quality function deployment." See Lawrence R. Guinta and Nancy C. Praizler, *The QFD Book: The Team Approach to Solving Problems and Satisfying Customers Through Quality Function Deployment* (New York: AMACOM, 1993); V. Srinivasan, William S. Lovejoy, and David Beach, "Integrated Product Design for Marketability and Manufacturing," *Journal of Marketing Research* (February 1997): 154–163.

28. Tom Peters, *The Circle of Innovation* (New York: Alfred A. Knopf, 1997) p. 96; Mark Borden, "Keeping Yahoo Simple—and Fast," *Fortune*, January 10, 2000, pp. 167–168. See also Rajesh Sethi, "New Product Quality and Product Development Teams," *Journal of Marketing* (April 2000): 1–14.

29. Philip Kotler and Gerald Zaltman, "Targeting Prospects for a New Product," *Journal of Advertising Research* (February 1976): 7–20.

30. For details, see Keith G. Lockyer, *Critical Path Analysis and Other Project Network Techniques* (London: Pitman, 1984). Also see Arvind Rangaswamy and Gary L. Lilien, "Software Tools for New Product Development," *Journal of Marketing Research* (February 1997): 177–184.

31. The following discussion leans heavily on Everett M. Rogers, *Diffusion of Innovations* (New York: Free Press, 1962). Also see his third edition, published in 1983.

32. See Hubert Gatignon and Thomas S. Robertson, "A Propositional Inventory for New Diffusion Research," *Journal of Consumer Research* (March 1985): 849–867; Vijay Mahajan, Eitan Muller, and Frank M. Bass, "Diffusion of New Products: Empirical Generalizations and Managerial Uses," *Marketing Science*, 14, no. 3, part 2 (1995): G79–G89; Fareena Sultan, John U. Farley, and Donald R. Lehmann, "Reflection on 'A Meta-Analysis of Applications of Diffusion Models,'" *Journal of Marketing Research* (May 1996): 247–249; Minhi Hahn, Sehoon Park, and Andris A. Zoltners, "Analysis of New Product Diffusion Using a Four-Segment Trial-Repeat Model," *Marketing Science*, 13, no. 3 (1994): 224–247.

33. Some authors distinguished additional stages. Wasson suggested a stage of competitive turbulence between growth and maturity. See Chester R. Wasson, *Dynamic Competitive Strategy and Product Life Cycles* (Austin, TX: Austin Press, 1978). Maturity describes a stage of sales growth slowdown and saturation, a stage of flat sales after sales have peaked.

34. Robert D. Buzzell, "Competitive Behavior and Product Life Cycles," in *New Ideas for Successful Marketing*, edited by John S. Wright and Jack Goldstucker (Chicago: American Marketing Association, 1956), p. 51.

35. Rajesh J. Chandy, Gerard J. Tellis, Deborah J. MacInnis, and Pattana Thaivanich, "What to Say When: Advertising Appeals in Evolving Markets," *Journal of Marketing Research* 38 (November 2001): 399–414.

36. Steven P. Schnaars, *Managing Imitation Strategies* (New York: Free Press, 1994).

37. Gerald Tellis and Peter Golder, *Will & Vision: How Latecomers Can Grow to Dominate Markets* (New York: McGraw-Hill, 2001).

38. Stephen M. Nowlis and Itamar Simmonson, "The Effect of New Product Features on Brand Choice," *Journal of Marketing Research* (February 1996): 36–46.

39. Kathryn Rudie Harrigan, "Strategies for Declining Industries," *Journal of Business Strategy* (Fall 1980): 27.

40. "Quaker Take Heart Instant Oatmeal," *Nutraceuticals World*, March 2005, p. 130; "Hot Cereal is One Hot Commodity," *Prepared Foods*, January 2000.

41. See Philip Kotler, "Harvesting Strategies for Weak Products," *Business Horizons*, August 1978, pp. 15–22; and Laurence P. Feldman and Albert L. Page, "Harvesting: The Misunderstood Market Exit Strategy," *Journal of Business Strategy* (Spring 1985): 79–85.

CHAPTER 11

Designing and Managing Services

In this chapter, we will address the following questions:

1. How are services defined and classified?
2. How are services marketed, and how can service quality be improved?
3. How do services marketers create strong brands?
4. How can goods-producing firms improve customer support services?

MARKETING MANAGEMENT AT PROGRESSIVE

Progressive Corp., the third-largest U.S. auto insurance firm, shows how a service company can stand out by constantly asking—and answering—the question, "Is there an even better way?" Although auto insurers have never been known as a customer-friendly bunch, Progressive has used this dismal industry perception to its advantage by differentiating itself on the basis of superior service. The company gained notice for offering prospective customers price quotes from up to three rival insurers, as well as its own, an unusual but convenient service that attracted thousands of new accounts. Once it won new customers' business, Progressive went on to streamline the claims and repair process, saving its customers even more time and trouble.

Customers can call a central toll-free number, at any hour, to report a claim. In some cases, one of Progressive's army of 12,000 claims adjusters will speed right to an accident scene—and many times will cut a check right on the spot. In other cases, customers whose cars are involved in smaller accidents can drop their banged-up vehicles at a Progressive claims center, drive off in a rental car, and return to retrieve the repaired car in just a couple of days. Customers who experience the convenience of this "one-stop" concierge claim service are so satisfied that they become intensely loyal to Progressive. Progressive has also broken new ground by targeting drivers in their teens and early twenties with an advertising campaign it calls "an investment that will pay off in the future" in terms of brand recognition and awareness.

Already, these nontraditional but highly valued services are helping Progressive achieve higher revenue and profits.[1]

———

S ervice businesses increasingly fuel the world economy. Moreover, as companies find it harder and harder to differentiate their physical products, they turn to service differentiation, the way Progressive has. Companies seek to develop a reputation for superior performance in on-time delivery, better and faster answering of inquiries, and quicker resolution of complaints. Because it is critical to understand the special nature of services and what that means to marketers, in this chapter we analyze services and how to market them most effectively.

THE NATURE OF SERVICES

Service industries are quite varied. The *government sector*, with its courts, employment services, hospitals, loan agencies, military services, police and fire departments, post office, regulatory agencies, and schools, is in the service business. The *private nonprofit sector*, with its museums, charities, churches, colleges, foundations, and hospitals, is in the service business. A good part of the *business sector*, with its airlines, banks, hotels, insurance firms, law firms, consulting firms, medical practices, and real estate firms, is in the service business. Many workers in the *manufacturing sector*, such as computer operators, accountants, and legal staff, are really service providers, making up a "service factory" providing services to the "goods factory." Those in the *retail sector*, such as cashiers, clerks, salespeople, and customer service representatives, are also providing a service.

A **service** is any act or performance that one party can offer to another that is essentially intangible and does not result in the ownership of anything. Its production may or may not be tied to a physical product.

Categories of Service Mix

A company's offerings often include some services. Five categories of offerings can be distinguished:

1. *Pure tangible good.* The offering is a tangible good such as soap, not accompanied by services.
2. *Tangible good with accompanying services.* The offering consists of a tangible good accompanied by one or more services. General Motors, for example, offers repairs, warranty fulfillment, and other services along with its cars and trucks.
3. *Hybrid.* The offering consists of equal parts of goods and services. For example, people patronize restaurants for both food and service.
4. *Major service with accompanying minor goods and services.* The offering consists of a major service along with additional services or supporting goods. For example, airline passengers are buying transportation service, but they get soft drinks and an airline magazine as well.
5. *Pure service.* The offering consists primarily of a service; examples include babysitting and psychotherapy.

The nature of the service mix also has implications for how consumers evaluate quality. Customers cannot judge the technical quality of some services even after they have received it, as shown in Figure 11.1.[2] At the left are goods high in *search*

FIGURE 11.1 Continuum of Evaluation for Different Types of Products

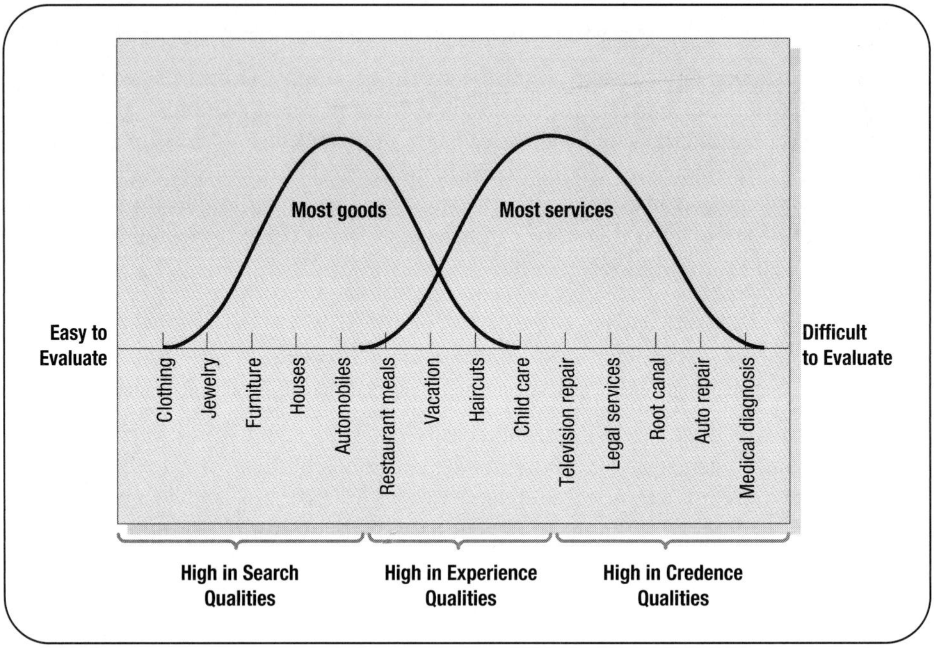

Source: Valarie A. Zeithaml, "How Consumer Evaluation Processes Differ between Goods and Services," in *Marketing of Services,* edited by James H. Donnelly and William R. George. Reprinted with permission of the American Marketing Association (Chicago: American Marketing Association, 1981).

qualities—characteristics the buyer can evaluate before purchase. In the middle are goods and services high in *experience qualities*—characteristics the buyer can evaluate after purchase. At the right are services high in *credence qualities*—characteristics the buyer normally finds hard to evaluate even after consumption.[3]

Because services are generally high in experience and credence qualities, there is more risk in purchase. As a result, service buyers rely on word of mouth rather than on advertising. They also rely heavily on price, personnel, and physical cues to judge quality, and are highly loyal to service providers who satisfy them. And because of the switching costs involved, much consumer inertia can exist.

Distinctive Characteristics of Services

Services have four major characteristics that greatly affect the design of marketing programs: intangibility, inseparability, variability, and perishability.

Intangibility Unlike physical products, services cannot be seen, tasted, felt, heard, or smelled before they are bought. The person getting a face-lift cannot see the exact results before the purchase, just as the patient in the psychiatrist's office cannot know the exact outcome. To reduce uncertainty, buyers will look for signs or evidence of the service quality. They will draw inferences about quality from the place, people, equipment, communication material, symbols, and price that they see. Therefore, the service provider's task is to "manage the evidence," to "tangibilize the intangible."[4] Whereas product marketers are challenged to add abstract ideas, service marketers are challenged to add physical evidence and imagery to abstract offers.

Service companies can try to demonstrate their service quality through *physical evidence* and *presentation*.[5] Carbone and Haeckel propose a set of concepts called *customer experience engineering*.[6] Companies must first develop a clear picture of what they want the customer's perception of an experience to be and then design a consistent set of *performance and context clues* to support that experience. In the case of a bank, whether the teller dispensed the right amount of cash is a performance clue; a context clue is whether the teller was properly dressed. The context clues in a bank are delivered by people (*humanics*) and things (*mechanics*). The company assembles the clues in an *experience blueprint*, a pictorial representation of the various clues. To the extent possible, the clues should address all five senses. The Disney Company is a master at developing *experience blueprints* in its theme parks; so are retailers such as Barnes & Noble.[7]

Inseparability   Services are typically produced and consumed simultaneously, unlike physical goods, which are manufactured, put into inventory, distributed through resellers, and consumed later. If a person renders the service, then the provider is part of the service. Because the client is also present as the service is produced, provider–client interaction is a special feature of services marketing—both provider and client affect the outcome.

Often, buyers of services have strong provider preferences. Several strategies exist for getting around this limitation. One is higher pricing in line with the provider's limited time. Another is having the provider work with larger groups or work faster. A third alternative is to train more service providers and build up client confidence, as H&R Block has done with its national network of trained tax consultants.

Variability   Because services depend on who provides them and when and where they are provided, they are highly variable. Knowing this, service firms can take three steps toward quality control. The first is recruiting the right service employees and providing them with excellent training. This is crucial regardless of whether employees are highly skilled professionals or low-skilled workers.

The second step is standardizing the service-performance process throughout the organization. Companies can do this by preparing a *service blueprint* that depicts every service event and process in a flowchart. This allows management to identify potential fail points and then plan improvements. The third step is monitoring customer satisfaction through suggestion and complaint systems, customer surveys, and comparison shopping. General Electric sends out 700,000 response cards yearly, asking households to rate its service people's performance. Firms can also develop customer information databases and systems to permit more personalized, customized service.[8]

Perishability   Services cannot be stored; once an airplane takes off or a movie starts, any unsold seats cannot be held for future sale. Perishability is not a problem when demand is steady, but fluctuating demand can cause problems. For example, public-transportation companies have to own much more equipment because of higher rush-hour demand. Service providers can deal with perishability in a number of ways. Table 11.1 shows some strategies proposed by Sasser for matching demand and supply in a service business.[9]

For example, Club Med cultivates nonpeak demand at its resorts using e-mails to pitch unsold weekend packages to consumers in its database. Customers learn by mid-week what packages are available that weekend, at discounts of 30 to 40 percent off the standard price.[10] Another example is Disney's Fastpass, which allows visitors to reserve a spot in line and eliminate the wait at its theme parks. A Disney vice president says: "We

TABLE 11.1   Improving the Match Between Service Demand and Supply

Demand-Side Strategies	Supply-Side Strategies
Use differential pricing to shift demand from peak to off-peak periods; movie theaters do this by lowering prices during early evening.	*Hire part-time employees* to meet peak demand; stores hire part-time employees during busy holiday seasons.
Cultivate nonpeak demand to build sales during off-peak periods; hotels do this with their weekend minivacation packages.	*Introduce peak-time efficiency* so employees perform only essential tasks when demand is high; paramedics often assist physicians during busy periods.
Develop complementary services to provide alternatives for waiting customers; banks do this with automatic teller machines.	*Increase consumer participation*; many supermarkets have self-service checkouts where shoppers scan and bag their own groceries.
Install reservation systems to manage demand levels; airlines, hotels, and physicians employ them extensively.	*Plan facilities for future expansion*; an amusement park can buy surrounding land for later development.
	Share services with other providers; hospitals do this by sharing medical-equipment purchases.

Source: Adapted from W. Earl Sasser, "Match Supply and Demand in Service Industries," *Harvard Business Review* (November–December 1976): 133–140.

have been teaching people how to stand in line since 1955, and now we are telling them they don't have to. Of all the things we can do and all the marvels we can create with the attractions, this is something that will have a profound effect on the entire industry."[11]

MARKETING STRATEGIES FOR SERVICE FIRMS

Although service firms once lagged behind manufacturers in their use of marketing, this has certainly changed. Still, not all companies have invested in providing superior service, at least not to all customers. Customer service complaints are on the rise, even though many complaints never actually reach a live human being. Here are some statistics that should give service companies and customer service departments pause:[12]

- *On the phone.* Some 80 percent of U.S. firms haven't figured out how to get customers the help they need.
- *Online.* Forrester Research estimates that 35 percent of all e-mail inquiries to companies don't get a response within 7 days and about 25 percent don't get a response at all.
- *Interactive Voice Response.* While many of America's largest companies have installed Interactive Voice Response Systems, more than 90 percent of financial services consumers say they don't like them.

A Shifting Customer Relationship

Service companies used to offer a welcoming hand to all customers, but they now have so much data on individuals that they can classify their customers into profit tiers. So service is not uniformly bad for all customers. Airlines, hotels, and banks all pamper good customers. Big spenders get special discounts, promotional offers, and lots of special service. The rest of their customers get higher fees, stripped-down service, and at best a voice message to answer inquiries. Financial services giants have software that tells them—in an instant—when a lucrative customer is on the phone and then sends the big spender's call ahead of other callers.[13] Charles Schwab's best customers get their calls answered in 15 seconds; other customers can wait 10 minutes or more.

Companies that provide differentiated levels of service, however, must be careful about claiming superior service—the customers who receive poor treatment will bad-mouth the company and injure its reputation. Delivering services that maximize both customer satisfaction and company profitability can be challenging. There are also shifts that favor the customer in the client relationship. Customers are becoming more sophisticated about buying product support services and are pressing for "services unbundling." They want separate prices for each service element and the right to select the elements they want. Customers also increasingly dislike having to deal with a multitude of service providers handling different types of equipment. Most important, the Internet has empowered customers by letting them vent about bad service or reward good service and, with a mouse click, send their comments around the world.

Holistic Marketing for Services

Because service encounters are complex interactions affected by multiple elements, adopting a holistic marketing perspective is especially important. A host of variables influence the service outcome and whether customers will remain loyal to a service provider. Keaveney identified more than 800 critical behaviors that cause customers to switch services.[14] These behaviors fall into eight categories (see Table 11.2).

TABLE 11.2 Factors Leading to Customer Switching Behavior

Pricing
- High Price
- Price Increases
- Unfair Pricing
- Deceptive Pricing

Inconvenience
- Location/Hours
- Wait for Appointment
- Wait for Service

Core Service Failure
- Service Mistakes
- Billing Errors
- Service Catastrophe

Service Encounter Failures
- Uncaring
- Impolite
- Unresponsive
- Unknowledgeable

Response to Service Failure
- Negative Response
- No Response
- Reluctant Response

Competition
- Found Better Service

Ethical Problems
- Cheat
- Hard Sell
- Unsafe
- Conflict of Interest

Involuntary Switching
- Customer Moved
- Provider Closed

Source: Susan M. Keaveney, "Customer Switching Behavior in Service Industries: An Exploratory Study," *Journal of Marketing* (April 1995): 71–82.

FIGURE 11.2   Three Types of Marketing in Service Industries

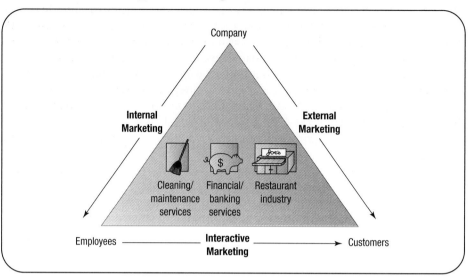

Holistic marketing for services requires external, internal, and interactive marketing (see Figure 11.2).[15] *External marketing* describes the normal work of preparing, pricing, distributing, and promoting the service to customers. *Internal marketing* describes training and motivating employees to serve customers well. Berry has argued that the most important contribution the marketing department can make is to be "exceptionally clever in getting everyone else in the organization to practice marketing."[16]

Interactive marketing describes the employees' skill in serving the client. Clients judge service not only by its *technical quality* (e.g., Was the surgery successful?), but also by its *functional quality* (e.g., Did the surgeon show concern and inspire confidence?).[17] Technology can make service workers much more productive.[18] Respiratory therapists at the University of California at San Diego Medical Center carry handheld computers so they can check patient records and spend more time working directly with patients. Companies must avoid pushing productivity so hard, however, that they reduce perceived quality. Service must be "high-touch" as well as "high-tech."[19]

Differentiating Services

Service marketers frequently complain about the difficulty of differentiating their services. The deregulation of major service industries—communications, transportation, energy, and banking—has resulted in intense price competition. To the extent that customers view a service as fairly homogeneous, they care less about the provider than the price. Thus, service brands must be skillful at differentiation.

One way to differentiate the service offering is by going beyond the *primary service package*, which is what the customer expects, to offer innovative features. Vanguard, the second-largest no-load mutual fund company, has a unique client ownership structure that lowers costs and permits better fund returns. Strongly differentiated from many competitors, the brand grew through word of mouth, public relations, and viral marketing.[20] The firm can add *secondary service features*, the way JetBlue adorns its airplanes with cushy leather seats and seat-back TVs. Its nattily attired flight attendants and a state-of-art Web site also contribute to its consumer-friendly, up-market image.[21]

Other service providers are adding a human element to combat competition from online businesses. For instance, as in-store pharmacies see competition from low-cost online mail-order drugstores, they are playing up the presence of on-site health care professionals. PrairieStone Pharmacy gives its pharmacists more time to speak to customers by investing in machines that handle such tedious tasks as counting pills and filling pill bottles. "We said, 'You're going to focus on patient care, not counting, pouring, licking, and sticking,'" says a cofounder.[22]

Sometimes the firm achieves differentiation through the sheer range of its service offerings and the success of its cross-selling efforts. The major challenge is that most service offerings and innovations are easily copied. Still, the company that regularly introduces innovations will gain a succession of temporary advantages over competitors.

Developing Brand Strategies for Services

Marketers of service offerings must pay special attention to choosing brand elements, establishing image dimensions, and devising the branding strategy.

Choosing Brand Elements The intangibility of services has implications for the choice of brand elements. Because service decisions and arrangements are often made away from the actual service location itself (e.g., at home or at work), brand recall becomes critically important, so an easy-to-remember name is essential. Logos, symbols, characters, and slogans can complement the name to build awareness and image. These other elements often attempt to make the service and some of its key benefits more tangible, concrete, and real, as the "good hands" do for Allstate insurance. In addition, the physical facilities of the service provider—its signage, environmental design and reception area, apparel, collateral material, and so on—are especially important. Note that all aspects of the service delivery process can be branded, which is why UPS has developed such strong equity with its brown trucks.

Establishing Image Dimensions Organizational associations—such as perceptions about the people who make up the organization and who provide the service—are likely to be important brand associations that may affect evaluations of service quality directly or indirectly. One particularly vital association is company credibility and perceived expertise, trustworthiness, and likability. Service firms must therefore design marketing communication and information programs so that consumers learn more about the brand than the information they get from service encounters alone. These programs may involve marketing communications that help the firm to develop the proper brand personality.

Devising Branding Strategy Finally, services also must consider developing a brand hierarchy and brand portfolio that permits positioning and targeting of different market segments. Classes of service can be branded vertically on the basis of price and quality. Vertical extensions often require sub-branding strategies where the corporate name is combined with an individual brand name or modifier. In the hotel and airlines industries, brand lines and portfolios have been created by brand extension and introductions. To illustrate, Hilton Hotels has a portfolio of brands that includes Hilton Garden Inns to target budget-conscious business travelers and compete with the Courtyard by Marriott chain, as well as DoubleTree, Embassy Suites, Homewood Suites, and Hampton Inn.

Cirque du Soleil (French for "circus of the sun") has successfully built its brand by breaking loose from circus convention. It showcases talented trapeze artists, clowns, and other performers in a nontraditional circus setting with lavish costumes, New Age music, and spectacular stage designs. Each production is loosely tied together with a theme such as "mysterious" (*Mystère*). Although most theatrical productions fail, Cirque du Soleil's unique productions bring in an impressive $650 million in total annual revenue. Now the founder wants to brand other services: "We reinvented the circus," he says. "Why not spas, restaurants, and night clubs?"[23]

MANAGING SERVICE QUALITY

The service quality of a firm is tested at each service encounter. If retail clerks are bored, uninformed, or too busy to wait on customers, buyers will think twice about doing business again with that seller.

Customer Expectations

Customers form service expectations from many sources, such as past experiences, word of mouth, and advertising. In general, customers compare the *perceived service* with the *expected service*.[24] If the perceived service falls below the expected service, customers are disappointed. If the perceived service meets or exceeds their expectations, they are apt to use the provider again. Successful companies add benefits that not only satisfy customers but also delight them.

Parasuraman, Zeithaml, and Berry formulated a service-quality model that highlights the main requirements for delivering high service quality.[25] The model shown in Figure 11.3 identifies five gaps that cause unsuccessful service delivery:

1. *Gap between consumer expectation and management perception.* Management does not always correctly perceive what customers want. Hospital administrators may think that patients want better food, but patients may be more concerned with nurse responsiveness.
2. *Gap between management perception and service-quality specification.* Management might correctly perceive the customers' wants but not set a specified performance standard. Hospital administrators may tell the nurses to give "fast" service without specifying it quantitatively.
3. *Gap between service-quality specifications and service delivery.* Personnel might be poorly trained, or incapable or unwilling to meet the standard; or they may be held to conflicting standards, such as taking time to listen to customers and serving them fast.
4. *Gap between service delivery and external communications.* Statements made by company representatives and ads affect customer expectations. If a hospital brochure shows an attractive room, but the patient finds an unappealing room, communications have distorted the customer's expectations.
5. *Gap between perceived service and expected service.* This gap occurs when the consumer misperceives the service quality. The physician may keep visiting the patient to show care, but the patient may interpret this as an indication that something really is wrong.

Based on the service-quality model, these researchers identified five determinants of service quality. In order of importance, they are reliability, responsiveness, assurance, empathy, and tangibles.[26] There is also a *zone of tolerance* or range in which customer perceptions of a service dimension would be deemed satisfactory, anchored by the minimally acceptable level and the level that customers believe can and should be delivered.

FIGURE 11.3   Service-Quality Model

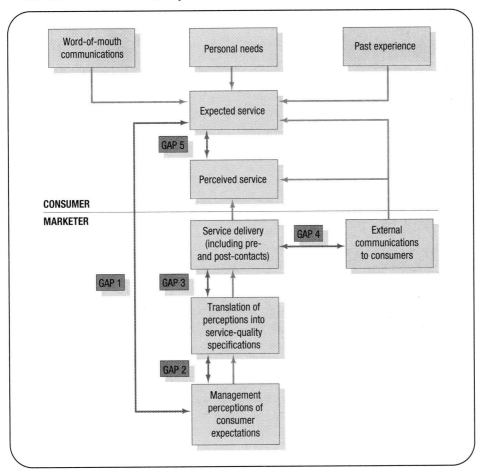

Sources: A. Parasuraman, Valarie A. Zeithaml, and Leonard L. Berry, "A Conceptual Model of Service Quality and its implications for Future Research," *Journal of Marketing* (Fall 1985): 44. Reprinted with permission of the American Marketing Association. The model is more fully discussed or elaborated in Valarie A. Zeithaml and Mary Jo Bitner, *Services Marketing* (New York: McGraw-Hill, 1996), ch. 2.

Best Practices of Service-Quality Management

Well-managed service companies share the following best practices of service-quality management: a strategic concept, a history of top-management commitment to quality, high standards, self-service technologies, systems for monitoring service performance and customer complaints, and an emphasis on employee satisfaction.

Strategic Concept   Top service companies are "customer obsessed." These firms have a clear sense of their target customers and their needs and use a distinctive strategy to satisfy these needs.

Top-Management Commitment   Companies such as Marriott, Disney, and McDonald's are thoroughly committed to service quality. Every month, their management looks not only at financial performance but also at service performance.

Top-management commitment can be demonstrated in various ways. Founder Sam Walton of Wal-Mart required the following employee pledge: "I solemnly swear and declare that every customer that comes within 10 feet of me, I will smile, look them in the eye, and greet them, so help me Sam."

High Standards   The best service providers set high service-quality standards. Citibank aims to answer phone calls within 10 seconds and customer letters within 2 days. Service standards must be set *appropriately* high. A 98 percent accuracy standard may sound good, but it would result in FedEx losing 64,000 packages a day; 10 misspelled words on each page; 400,000 misfilled prescriptions daily; and unsafe drinking water 8 days a year. Companies can be distinguished between those offering "merely good" service and those offering "breakthrough" service aiming at 100 percent defect-free service.[27]

Self-Service Technologies   As is the case with products, consumers value convenience in services.[28] Many person-to-person service interactions are being replaced by self-service technologies.[29] To the traditional vending machines we can add automated teller machines (ATMs), self-checkout at hotels, and self-customization of products online, among others. Not all such technologies improve service quality, but they can make service transactions more accurate, convenient, and faster. In addition, companies should enable customers to call when they need more information than the self-service technology provides, the way many online hotel reservation Web sites include a "Call Me" button. If the customer clicks on it, a service rep will immediately phone the person to answer a question.

Monitoring Systems   Top firms regularly audit service performance, both their own and their competitors'. They use a number of measurement devices: comparison shopping, ghost shopping, customer surveys, suggestion and complaint forms, service-audit teams, and letters to the president. The First Chicago Bank employs a weekly Performance Measurement Program charting its performance on a large number of customer-sensitive issues such as speed in answering customer service phone inquiries. The bank will take action whenever performance falls below the minimum acceptable level. It also raises its performance goal over time. Mystery shopping—the use of undercover shoppers who are paid to report back to the company—is now big business, used by fast-food chains, major retailers, and even large government agencies to pinpoint customer service problems that must be addressed.

Satisfying Customer Complaints   Studies show that although customers are dissatisfied with their purchases about 25 percent of the time, only about 5 percent complain. The other 95 percent either feel that complaining is not worth the effort, or they don't know how to complain or to whom. Of the 5 percent who complain, only about half report a satisfactory resolution. Yet the need to resolve a customer problem in a satisfactory manner is critical. On average, a satisfied customer tells three people about a good product experience, but the average dissatisfied customer gripes to 11 people. If each of them tells still other people, the number of people exposed to bad word of mouth may grow exponentially.

Customers whose complaints are satisfactorily resolved often become more company-loyal than customers who were never dissatisfied. About 34 percent of customers who register major complaints will buy again from the firm if their complaint is resolved; this number rises to 52 percent for minor complaints. If the complaint is resolved quickly, between 52 percent (major complaints) and 95 percent (minor complaints) will buy from the firm again.[30]

Firms that encourage disappointed customers to complain—and empower employees to remedy the situation on the spot—have been shown to achieve higher revenues and profits than firms that do not systematically address service failures.[31] Pizza Hut prints its toll-free number on all pizza boxes. When a customer complains, Pizza Hut sends voice mail to the store manager, who must call the customer within 48 hours and resolve the complaint (see "Marketing Skills: Service Recovery" for more about recovering from service missteps).

Satisfying Both Employees and Customers   Excellent service companies know that positive employee attitudes promote stronger customer loyalty. Sears found a high correlation between customer satisfaction, employee satisfaction, and store profitability. Consider the real estate firm Re/Max, which has made brokers and franchisees the focus of its marketing. One industry observer notes: "Agents perceive that Re/Max is

MARKETING SKILLS: SERVICE RECOVERY

Service missteps can hurt customer relationships and, in severe cases, send formerly loyal customers in search of competitors. By developing good service recovery skills, however, marketers can turn a tense situation into an opportunity for strengthening customer ties. Good service recovery starts with an intense focus on understanding and meeting customers' needs. With this background, marketers can map potential problem areas and identify potential solutions to be implemented if problems arise. In planning for service recovery, consider cross-training and empowerment so employees can solve problems without bouncing customers from one department to another.

The ability to listen carefully and tactfully ask questions (of the customer and the employees involved) will help clarify the problem. Apologize when appropriate and offer a solution that is acceptable to the customer and that fits with the company's objectives. Finally, tell the customer what will happen and when, then follow through to see that the problem was resolved as promised and that the customer is satisfied with the outcome.

Consider how Ocado, an online grocery delivery service, planned for service recovery well in advance of entering the U.K. market. To compete with Sainsbury's and Tesco, two well-established supermarket chains that operate online grocery delivery services, Ocado decided to differentiate itself on the basis of excellent customer service. The company identified key elements that influence customers' perception of customer service quality, such as on-time delivery. Today, its strict standards reinforce its service commitment; in fact, Ocado's advertising urges customers to "be more demanding." Customers can call at any time, before or after delivery, with questions or concerns; call-center employees are trained to resolve any complaints immediately and to the customer's complete satisfaction. For example, if a delivery fails to arrive during the scheduled one-hour slot, employees refund the entire delivery charge. Thanks to this service recovery planning, Ocado was voted "best online grocer" by *Good Housekeeping* magazine's U.K. readers for two consecutive years, and it is gaining market share.[32]

where top agents work. That message is very clear and it's a powerful one to people in the business." Re/Max wants to attract the best agents, who in turn attract the best and most profitable customers—an approach that has led Re/Max agents to the highest average annual commissions in the business.[33]

However, a company must be careful in training employees to be friendly. The Safeway supermarket chain found this out when it instituted an aggressive program to build employee friendliness toward customers, with rules such as: Make eye contact with all customers, smile, and greet each customer. The store employed mystery shoppers to secretly grade workers. Those who were graded "poor" were sent for more training. Although surveys showed that customers liked the program, many employees admitted being stressed out and several quit over the plan.[34]

MANAGING PRODUCT SUPPORT SERVICES

A growing number of product-based industries now offer a service bundle. Manufacturers of equipment such as small appliances, computers, and tractors generally have to provide *product support services*. In fact, product support service is a major battleground for competitive advantage. Some equipment companies, such as John Deere, make over 50 percent of their profits from these services. In the global marketplace, companies that make a good product but provide poor local service support are seriously disadvantaged; those that provide high-quality service outperform their less-service-oriented competitors.

Identifying and Satisfying Customer Needs

To design the best service support program, a manufacturer must identify the services its customers most value. In general, customers worry about three things.[35] First, they worry about reliability and *failure frequency*. A farmer may tolerate a combine that breaks down once a year, but not more often. The second issue is *downtime duration*. The longer the downtime, the higher the cost, which is why customers count on *service dependability*—the seller's ability to fix the product quickly or at least provide a loaner.[36] The third issue is *out-of-pocket costs* of maintenance and repair. How much will regular maintenance and repairs cost?

A buyer considers all of these factors when choosing a vendor, in addition to trying to estimate the **life-cycle cost**, which is the product's purchase cost plus the discounted cost of maintenance and repair less the discounted salvage value. Moreover, buyers may look for additional services from certain vendors. Manufacturers of medical equipment, for example, offer *facilitating services* such as installation, repairs, and financing. They may also add *value-augmenting services*. Herman Miller, a leading office-furniture company, offers quality products coupled with (1) five-year product warranties; (2) quality audits after installation; (3) guaranteed move-in dates; (4) trade-in allowances on furniture systems products; and (5) easy online ordering.

A manufacturer can offer and charge for enhanced product support services in different ways. One specialty organic chemical company provides a standard offering plus a basic level of services. If the customer wants additional services, he or she can pay extra or increase their annual purchases to a higher level, in which case additional services would be included. Many companies offer *service contracts* (also called *extended warranties*) with variable lengths and different deductibles so customers can choose the service level they want beyond the basic package.

Post-Sale Service Strategy

In providing post-sale service, most companies progress through a series of stages. Manufacturers usually start out by running their own parts and service department because they want to stay close to their products and learn about any problems right away. They also find it expensive and time consuming to train others. Often, they discover that they can make good money running the parts-and-service business—and, if they are the only supplier of certain parts, they can charge a premium price. In fact, many equipment manufacturers price their equipment low and compensate by charging high prices for parts and service. This explains why competitors sometimes manufacture the same or similar parts and sell them to customers or intermediaries for less.

Over time, manufacturers—especially those who expand into global markets—switch more maintenance and repair services to authorized distributors and dealers. These intermediaries are closer to customers, operate in more locations, and can offer quicker service. Manufacturers still make a profit on the parts but leave the servicing profit to their intermediaries. Still later, independent service firms emerge. Over 40 percent of auto-service work is now done outside franchised automobile dealerships, by independent garages and chains such as Midas Muffler. Independent service organizations handle computers, telecommunications products, and other items, typically offering lower prices or faster service than offered by the manufacturer or authorized intermediaries.

Customer service choices are increasing rapidly, however, and this is holding down service prices and profits. Equipment manufacturers now have to find new ways of making money on their products, independent of service contracts. Some new car warranties cover 100,000 miles before servicing. On the industrial side, the increase in disposable or never-fail equipment makes business customers less inclined to pay from 2 percent to 10 percent of the purchase price every year for a service. Some business customers handle their own maintenance and repair; as a result, they typically press the manufacturer for lower prices because they are providing their own services.

EXECUTIVE SUMMARY

A service is any act or performance, offered to one party by another, that is essentially intangible and does not result in the ownership of anything. Its production may or may not be tied to a tangible product. Services are intangible, inseparable, variable, and perishable. Each characteristic poses challenges and requires certain strategies. Marketers must find ways to give tangibility to intangibles, to increase the productivity of service providers, to increase and standardize the quality of the service provided, and to match the supply of services during peak and nonpeak periods with market demand. Delivering services that maximize both customer satisfaction and company profitability can be challenging. There are also shifts that favor the customer in the client relationship.

Service marketing must now be done holistically; it calls not only for external marketing, but also for internal marketing to motivate employees, and interactive marketing to emphasize the importance of both "high-tech" and "high-touch." The firm must differentiate the service brand through primary and secondary service features and develop appropriate brand strategies, which may include multiple brand elements. Such strategies also involve brand hierarchies and portfolios, as well as image dimensions to reinforce or complement the offering.

Customers' expectations play a critical role in their service experiences and evaluations. Companies must manage service quality by understanding the effects of each service encounter. Top service companies have a strategic concept, a history of top-management commitment to quality, high standards, self-service technologies, systems for monitoring service performance and customer complaints, and an emphasis on employee and customer satisfaction. Even product-based companies must provide support services for their customers. To provide the best support, a manufacturer must identify the services that customers value most and their relative importance. The service mix includes both presale services (facilitating services and value-augmenting services) and post-sale services (customer service departments, repair and maintenance services).

NOTES

1. Jeff D. Opdyke, "Family Finance: Consumers Increasingly Use Internet to Price Auto Insurance," *Wall Street Journal*, May 25, 2005, p. D2; Lynna Goch, "Gearing Up: Insurers Are Using Driver Safety Programs, Sharply Focused Advertising, and the Internet to Court Teen Drivers," *Best's Review*, October 2003, pp. 20+; Christopher Oster, "Car Insurers Get Into the Repair Business," *Wall Street Journal*, April 8, 2003, p. D1; "In Brief: Progressive Leads Performance List," *American Banker*, March 30, 2004, p. 9 (www.progressive.com).
2. See Valarie A. Zeithaml, "How Consumer Evaluation Processes Differ Between Goods and Services," in Donnelly and George, eds., *Marketing of Services*, edited by J. Donnelly and W.R. George (Chicago: American Marketing Association, 1981), pp. 186–90.
3. Amy Ostrom and Dawn Iacobucci, "Consumer Trade-offs and the Evaluation of Services," *Journal of Marketing* (January 1995): 17–28.
4. See Theodore Levitt, "Marketing Intangible Products and Product Intangibles," *Harvard Business Review* (May–June 1981): 94–102; Leonard L. Berry, "Services Marketing Is Different," *Business*, May–June 1980, pp. 24–30.
5. B. H. Booms and M. J. Bitner, "Marketing Strategies and Organizational Structures for Service Firms," in *Marketing of Services*, edited by J. Donnelly and W. R. George (Chicago: American Marketing Association, 1981), pp. 47–51.
6. Lewis P. Carbone and Stephan H. Haeckel, "Engineering Customer Experiences," *Marketing Management* 3 (Winter 1994): 17.
7. Bernd H. Schmitt, *Customer Experience Management* (New York: John Wiley & Sons, 2003).
8. Debra Zahay and Abbie Griffin, "Are Customer Information Systems Worth It? Results from B2B Services," *Marketing Science Institute Working Paper*, Report No. 02-113, 2002.
9. See W. Earl Sasser, "Match Supply and Demand in Service Industries," *Harvard Business Review* (November–December 1976): 133–140.
10. Carol Krol, "Case Study: Club Med Uses E-mail to Pitch Unsold, Discounted Packages," *Advertising Age*, December 14, 1998, p. 40; www.clubmed.com.
11. Seth Godin, "If It's Broke, Fix It," *Fast Company*, October 2003, p. 131.
12. Bruce Horovitz, "Whatever Happened to Customer Service? Automated Answering, Long Waits Irk Consumers," *USA Today*, September 26, 2003, p. A1.
13. Ibid.
14. Susan M. Keaveney, "Customer Switching Behavior in Service Industries: An Exploratory Study," *Journal of Marketing* (April 1995): 71–82. See also Michael D. Hartline and O. C. Ferrell, "The Management of Customer-Contact Service Employees: An Empirical Investigation," *Journal of Marketing* (October 1996): 52–70; Lois A. Mohr, Mary Jo Bitner, and Bernard H. Booms, "Critical Service Encounters: The Employee's Viewpoint,"

Journal of Marketing (October 1994): 95–106; Linda L. Price, Eric J. Arnould, and Patrick Tierney, "Going to Extremes: Managing Service Encounters and Assessing Provider Performance," *Journal of Marketing* (April 1995): 83–97; Jaishankar Ganesh, Mark J. Arnold, and Kristy E. Reynolds, "Understanding the Customer Base of Service Providers: An Examination of the Differences Between Switchers and Stayers," *Journal of Marketing* 64 (July 2000): 65–87.

15. Christian Gronroos, "A Service Quality Model and Its Marketing Implications," *European Journal of Marketing* 18 , no. 4 (1984): 36–44.

16. Leonard Berry, "Big Ideas in Services Marketing," *Journal of Consumer Marketing* (Spring 1986): 47–51. See also Walter E. Greene, Gary D. Walls, and Larry J. Schrest, "Internal Marketing: The Key to External Marketing Success," *Journal of Services Marketing* 8, no. 4 (1994): 5–13; John R. Hauser, Duncan I. Simester, and Birger Wernerfelt, "Internal Customers and Internal Suppliers," *Journal of Marketing Research* (August 1996): 268–280; Jagdip Singh, "Performance Productivity and Quality of Frontline Employees in Service Organizations," *Journal of Marketing* 64 (April 2000): 15–34.

17. Christian Gronroos, "A Service Quality Model and Its Marketing Implications," pp. 38–39; Michael D. Hartline, James G. Maxham III, and Daryl O. McKee, "Corridors of Influence in the Dissemination of Customer-Oriented Strategy to Customer Contact Service Employees," *Journal of Marketing* (April 2000): 35–50.

18. Nilly Landau, "Are You Being Served?" *International Business* (March 1995): 38–40.

19. Philip Kotler and Paul N. Bloom, *Marketing Professional Services* (Upper Saddle River, NJ: Prentice Hall, 1984).

20. Carolyn Marconi and Donna MacFarland, "Growth by Marketing under the Radar," presentation made at Marketing Science Institute Board of Trustees Meeting: Pathways to Growth, November 7, 2002.

21. Dan McGinn, "BlueSkies," *MBA Jungle* (March/April 2002): 32–34; Melanie Wells, "Lord of the Skies," *Forbes*, October 14, 2002, pp. 130–138; Amy Goldwasser, "Something Stylish, Something Blue," *Business 2.0*, February 1, 2002, pp. 94–95.

22. Jena McGregor, "The Starbucks of Pharmacies?" *Fast Company*, April 2005, pp. 62–63; Christopher Rowland, "The Pharmacists in Chains Promote Personal Touch to Keep Edge Over Mail-Order Firms," *Boston Globe*, December 10, 2003, p. D1.

23. Douglas Hanks III, "Cirque du Soleil Seeks $100M in Funds," *Miami Herald*, September 2, 2005 (www.herald.com); Matthew Miller, "The Acrobat," *Forbes*, March 15, 2004, pp. 100–102.

24. Glenn B. Voss, A. Parasuraman, and Dhruv Grewal, "The Role of Price, Performance, and Expectations in Determining Satisfaction in Service Exchanges," *Journal of Marketing* 62 (October 1998): 46–61.

25. A. Parasuraman, Valarie A. Zeithaml, and Leonard L. Berry, "A Conceptual Model of Service Quality and Its Implications for Future Research," *Journal of Marketing* (Fall 1985): 41–50. See also Susan J. Devlin and H. K. Dong, "Service Quality from the Customers' Perspective," *Marketing Research: A Magazine of Management and Applications*, Winter 1994, pp. 4–13; William Boulding, Ajay Kalra, and Richard Staelin, "A Dynamic Process Model of Service Quality: From Expectations to Behavioral Intentions," *Journal of Marketing Research* (February 1993): 7–27.

26. Leonard L. Berry and A. Parasuraman, *Marketing Services: Competing Through Quality* (New York: The Free Press, 1991), p. 16.

27. See James L. Heskett, W. Earl Sasser, Jr., and Christopher W. L. Hart, *Service Breakthroughs* (New York: Free Press, 1990).

28. Leonard L. Berry, Kathleen Seiders, and Dhruv Grewal, "Understanding Service Convenience," *Journal of Marketing* 66 (July 2002): 1–17.

29. Mary Jo Bitner, "Self-Service Technologies: What Do Customers Expect?" *Marketing Management* (Spring 2001): 10–11; Matthew L. Meuter, Amy L. Ostrom, Robert

J. Roundtree, and Mary Jo Bitner, "Self-Service Technologies: Understanding Customer Satisfaction with Technology-Based Service Encounters," *Journal of Marketing* 64 (July 2000): 50–64.

30. See John Goodman, *Technical Assistance Research Program (TARP)*, U.S. Office of Consumer Affairs Study on Complaint Handling in America, 1986; Albrecht and Zemke, *Service America!*; Berry and Parasuraman, *Marketing Services*; Roland T. Rust, Bala Subramanian, and Mark Wells, "Making Complaints a Management Tool," *Marketing Management* 1, no. 3 (1992): 41–45; Stephen S. Tax, Stephen W. Brown, and Murali Chandrashekaran, "Customer Evaluations of Service Complaint Experiences: Implications for Relationship Marketing," *Journal of Marketing* (April 1998): 60–76.

31. Stephen S. Tax and Stephen W. Brown, "Recovering and Learning from Service Failures," *Sloan Management Review* (Fall 1998): 75–88.

32. Claire Armitt, "Strategic Play—Ocado," *New Media Age*, August 11, 2005, pp. 16+; "Customer Service: Disaffected Nation," *Marketing*, June 8, 2005, p. 32; Julie Demers, "Service Drives a New Program," *CMA Management*, May 2002, pp. 36+; Robert Geier, "How to Create Disaster Recovery Plans for Customer Contact Operations," *Customer Contact Management Report*, January 2002, pp. 1+; Don Merit, "Dealing with Irate Customers," *American Printer*, October 2001, p. 66.

33. Dale Buss, "Success from the Ground Up," *Brandweek*, June 16, 2003, pp. 21–22.

34. Kirstin Downey Grimsley, "Service with a Forced Smile; Safeway's Courtesy Campaign Also Elicits Some Frowns," *Washington Post*, October 18, 1998, p. A1. See also Suzy Fox, "Emotional Value: Creating Strong Bonds with Your Customers," *Personnel Psychology*, April 1, 2001, pp. 230–234.

35. See Milind M. Lele and Uday S. Karmarkar, "Good Product Support Is Smart Marketing," *Harvard Business Review* (November–December 1999): 124–132.

36. Research on the effects of service delays on service evaluations: Shirley Taylor, "Waiting for Service: The Relationship Between Delays and Evaluations of Service," *Journal of Marketing* (April 1994): pp. 56–69; Michael K. Hui and David K. Tse, "What to Tell Customers in Waits of Different Lengths," *Journal of Marketing* (April 1996): 81–90.

Developing Pricing Strategies and Programs

In this chapter, we will address the following questions:

1. How do consumers process and evaluate prices?
2. How should a company set initial prices for its offerings?
3. How should a company adapt prices to meet varying circumstances and opportunities?
4. What should a company do to initiate a price change or respond to a competitor's price change?

MARKETING MANAGEMENT AT UNILEVER

Anglo-Dutch multinational Unilever sees a bright future in India, because the market is large and, with a growing middle class, expanding all the time. However, the market is also highly competitive—and Unilever is feeling the pressure in the form of a price war with Procter & Gamble and others seeking market share and profits in household goods. Unilever has built a $2.2 billion business in India by selling basics such as soap and tea in small, affordable sizes. A single-use sachet of its detergent might cost half a rupee (in U.S. currency, about one cent). Although the profit on each item sold is relatively modest, growth in demand makes the market attractive for Unilever and its rivals.

In addition to competition, another factor keeping prices down is the spread of discount retailing. Despite these pressures, Unilever intends to protect its market share regardless of the profit impact. Meanwhile, local brands such as Nirma are battling to retain their customers by joining the price war. However, the gap between the price of local brands and the prices of Unilever's Surf Excel and P&G's Tide detergents is much narrower than in the past. This, in turn, is encouraging some customers to trade up to the multinational brands. After decades of experience in India, Unilever knows its customers—and it knows that customers pay close attention to prices.[1]

P rice is the one element of the marketing mix that produces revenue; the others produce costs. Price is perhaps one of the most flexible elements; it can be changed quickly, unlike product features, channel commitments, and promotions. Also, price communicates the intended value positioning to the market. However, as Unilever's marketers realize, pricing decisions are complex and difficult. Holistic marketers must therefore consider a number of elements: the company, its marketing strategy, target markets, and brand positionings; the customers; the competition; and the marketing environment.

UNDERSTANDING PRICING

All for-profit organizations and many nonprofit organizations set prices on their offerings. Whether the price is called rent (for an apartment), tuition (for education), fare (for travel), or interest (for borrowed money), the concept is the same. Throughout most of history, prices were set by negotiation between buyers and sellers. Setting one price for all buyers arose with the development of large-scale retailing at the end of the nineteenth century, when many stores followed a "strictly one-price policy" because they carried so many items and had so many employees.

Today, the Internet is partially reversing the fixed pricing trend. Computer technology is making it easier for sellers to use software that monitors customers' movements over the Web and allows them to customize offers and prices. New software applications are also allowing buyers to compare prices instantaneously through online robotic shoppers or "shopbots." As one industry observer noted, "We are moving toward a very sophisticated economy. It's kind of an arms race between merchant technology and consumer technology."[2]

How Companies Price

In small companies, the boss often sets prices. In large companies, division and product-line managers handle pricing. Even here, top management sets general pricing objectives and policies and often approves the prices proposed by lower levels of management. In industries where pricing is a key factor (aerospace, railroads, oil companies), companies will often establish a pricing department to set or assist others in determining appropriate prices. This department reports to the marketing department, finance department, or top management. Others who exert an influence on pricing include sales managers, production managers, finance managers, and accountants.

Effectively designing and implementing pricing strategies requires a thorough understanding of consumer pricing psychology and a systematic approach to setting, adapting, and changing prices.

Consumer Psychology and Pricing

Many economists assume that consumers accept prices as given. Marketers recognize that consumers often actively process price information, interpreting prices in terms of their knowledge from prior purchasing experience, formal communications (advertising, sales calls, and brochures), informal communications (friends, colleagues, or family members), and point-of-purchase or online resources.[3] Purchase decisions are based on how consumers perceive prices and what they consider to be the current actual price—*not* the marketer's stated price. Consumers may have a lower price threshold below which prices signal inferior or unacceptable quality, as well as an upper price threshold above which prices are prohibitive and seen as not worth the money.

- *Reference prices.* Although consumers may have fairly good knowledge of the price range involved, surprisingly few can recall specific product prices accurately.[4] Consumers often employ a **reference price**, comparing a product's price to an internal reference price (pricing information from memory) or an external frame of reference (such as a posted "regular retail price").[5] Sellers may manipulate these reference prices by situating a product among expensive products to imply that it belongs in the same class, stating a high manufacturer's suggested price, or by pointing to a rival's high price.[6]

- *Price–quality inferences.* Many consumers use price as an indicator of quality. Image pricing is especially effective with ego-sensitive products such as perfumes and expensive cars. A $100 bottle of perfume might contain $10 worth of scent, but gift givers pay $100 to communicate their high regard for the receiver. Price and quality perceptions of cars interact.[7] Higher-priced cars are perceived to be high quality. Higher-quality cars are perceived to be higher priced than they actually are. When alternative information about true quality is available, price becomes a less significant indicator of quality.

- *Price cues.* Consumers tend to process prices in a "left-to-right" manner rather than by rounding.[8] Thus, many will see a stereo priced at $299 as in the $200 price range rather than the $300 range. Price encoding in this fashion is important if there is a mental price break at the higher, rounded price. Prices ending in odd numbers also may convey the idea of a discount or bargain, so firms with high-price images should avoid this tactic.[9]

SETTING THE PRICE

In setting a product's price, many factors must be considered.[10] A firm must set a price for the first time when it develops a new product, introduces its regular product into a new distribution channel or geographical area, or enters a bid on new contract work. Moreover, it must decide where to position its product on price and quality; some may have three to five price points or tiers. The following is a six-step procedure for setting pricing policy: (1) selecting the pricing objective; (2) determining demand; (3) estimating costs; (4) analyzing competitors' costs, prices, and offers; (5) selecting a pricing method; and (6) selecting the final price (see Figure 12.1).

FIGURE 12.1   Setting Pricing Policy

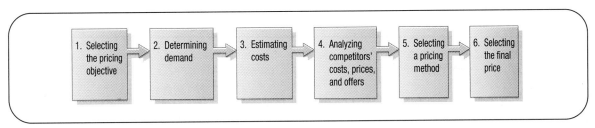

Step 1: Selecting the Pricing Objective

A company can pursue any of five major objectives through pricing: survival, maximum current profit, maximum market share, maximum market skimming, or product-quality leadership. *Survival* is a short-term objective that is appropriate for companies plagued with overcapacity, intense competition, or changing consumer wants. As long as prices cover variable costs and some fixed costs, the company can stay in business.

To gain the *maximum current profit*, companies estimate the demand and costs associated with alternative prices and then choose the price that produces maximum current profit, cash flow, or return on investment. However, by emphasizing current profits, the company may sacrifice long-run performance by ignoring the effects of other marketing-mix variables, competitors' reactions, and legal restraints on price.

Firms choosing the objective of *maximum market share* believe that higher sales volume will lead to lower unit costs and higher long-run profit. With **market-penetration pricing**, the firm sets the lowest price, assuming the market is price sensitive. This is appropriate when the market is highly price sensitive and a low price stimulates market growth; when production and distribution costs fall with accumulated production experience; and when a low price discourages competition.

Many companies favor setting high prices to "skim" the market. **Market-skimming pricing** makes sense when enough buyers have high current demand; when the unit costs of producing a small volume are not so high that they cancel the advantage of charging what the traffic will bear; when the high initial price does not attract more competitors; and when the high price communicates the image of a superior product.

Companies that aim to be *product-quality leaders* can either offer affordable luxuries at prices just high enough not to be out of reach (such as Starbucks coffee) or products combining quality, luxury, and premium prices (such as Absolut superpremium vodka). Nonprofit and public organizations may adopt other pricing objectives. A university aims for *partial cost recovery*, knowing that it must rely on private gifts and public grants to cover the remaining costs, while a nonprofit theater company sets prices to fill the maximum number of seats. As another example, a social services agency may set prices geared to the varying incomes of clients.

Step 2: Determining Demand

Each price will lead to a different level of demand and therefore will have a different impact on a company's marketing objectives. A demand curve shows the relationship between alternative prices and the resulting current demand. Normally, demand and price are inversely related: The higher the price, the lower the demand. For prestige goods, the demand curve sometimes slopes upward because some consumers take the higher price to signify a better product. Still, if the price is too high, the level of demand may fall.

Price Sensitivity   The demand curve shows the market's probable purchase quantity at alternative prices, summing the reactions of many individuals who have different price sensitivities. The first step in estimating demand is to understand what affects price sensitivity. Generally speaking, customers are most price sensitive to products that cost a lot or are bought frequently. They are less price sensitive when price is only a small part of the total cost of obtaining, operating, and servicing the product over its

TABLE 12.1   Factors Leading to Less Price Sensitivity

- The product is more distinctive.
- Buyers are less aware of substitutes.
- Buyers cannot easily compare the quality of substitutes.
- The expenditure is a smaller part of the buyer's total income.
- The expenditure is small compared to the total cost of the end product.
- Part of the cost is borne by another party.
- The product is used in conjuction with assets previously bought.
- The product is assumed to have more quality, prestige, or exclusiveness.
- Buyers cannot store the product.

Source: Adapted from Thomas T. Nagle and Reed K. Holden, *The Strategy and Tactics of Pricing,* 3rd ed. (Upper Saddle River, NJ: Prentice Hall, 2001), ch. 4.

lifetime. A seller can charge a higher price than competitors and still get the business if the customer perceives that it offers the lowest *total cost of ownership* (TCO).

Companies, of course, prefer customers who are less price sensitive. Table 12.1 shows some factors associated with decreased price sensitivity. Companies need to understand the price sensitivity of their customers and prospects and the trade-offs people are willing to make between price and product characteristics. Targeting only price-sensitive consumers may in fact be "leaving money on the table."

Estimating Demand Curves   Companies can use one of three basic methods to estimate their demand curves. The first involves statistically analyzing past prices, quantities sold, and other factors to estimate their relationships. However, building a model and fitting the data with the proper techniques calls for considerable skill. The second approach is to conduct price experiments, as when Bennett and Wilkinson systematically varied the prices of several products sold in a discount store and observed the results.[11] Firms might set different prices in similar territories to see how sales are affected or test prices online, being careful not to alienate customers.[12]

The third approach is to survey consumers about how many units they would buy at different proposed prices.[13] However, buyers might understate their purchase intentions at higher prices to discourage the company from setting higher prices. In measuring the price–demand relationship, the marketer must control for various factors that will influence demand, such as competitive response. Also, if the company changes other marketing-mix factors besides price, the effect of the price change itself will be hard to isolate.[14]

Price Elasticity of Demand   Marketers need to know how responsive, or elastic, demand would be to a change in price. If demand hardly changes with a small change in price, we say the demand is *inelastic.* If demand changes considerably, it is *elastic.* Demand is likely to be less elastic when (1) there are few or no substitutes or competitors; (2) buyers do not readily notice the higher price; (3) buyers are slow to change their buying habits and search for lower prices; and (4) buyers think the higher prices are justified. If demand is elastic, sellers will consider lowering the price to produce more total revenue. This makes sense when production and sales costs for more units do not increase disproportionately.[15]

Price elasticity depends on the magnitude and direction of the contemplated price change. It may be negligible with a small price change and substantial with a large price change; it may differ for a price cut versus a price increase. Finally, long-run price elasticity may differ from short-run elasticity. Buyers may continue to buy from their current supplier after a price increase but they may eventually switch suppliers. The distinction between short-run and long-run elasticity means that sellers will not know the total effect of a price change until time passes.

Step 3: Estimating Costs

Whereas demand sets a ceiling on the price the company can charge for its product, costs set the floor. The company wants to charge a price that covers its cost of producing, distributing, and selling the product, including a fair return for its effort and risk.

Types of Costs and Levels of Production A company's costs take two forms—fixed and variable. **Fixed costs** (also known as **overhead**) are costs that do not vary with production or sales revenue, such as payments for rent, heat, interest, salaries, and other bills that must be paid regardless of output. **Variable costs** vary directly with the level of production. For example, each calculator produced by Texas Instruments (TI) involves a cost of plastic, microprocessing chips, packaging, and the like. These costs tend to be constant per unit produced, but they are called variable because their total varies with the number of units produced. **Total costs** are the sum of the fixed and variable costs for any given level of production. **Average cost** is the cost per unit at that level of production; it is equal to total costs divided by production. Management wants to charge a price that will at least cover the total production costs at a given level of production.

To price intelligently, management needs to know how its costs vary with different levels of production. A firm's cost per unit is high if only a few units are produced every day, but as production increases, fixed costs are spread over a higher level of production results in each unit, bringing the average cost down. At some point, however, higher production will lead to higher average cost because the plant becomes inefficient (due to problems such as machines breaking down more often). By calculating costs for different-sized plants, a company can identify the optimal plant size and production level to achieve economies of scale and bring down the average cost.

Accumulated Production Suppose TI runs a plant that produces 3,000 hand calculators per day. As TI gains experience producing calculators, its methods improve. Workers learn shortcuts, materials flow more smoothly, and procurement costs fall. Then the average cost falls with accumulated production experience. Thus, the average cost of producing the first 100,000 hand calculators is $10 per calculator. When the company has produced the first 200,000 calculators, the average cost has fallen to $9. After its accumulated production experience doubles again to 400,000, the average cost is $8. This decline in the average cost with accumulated production experience is called the **experience curve** or **learning curve**.

Now suppose TI competes against firms A and B in this industry, as shown in Figure 12.2. TI is the lowest-cost producer at $8, having produced 400,000 units in the past. If all three firms sell the calculator for $10, TI makes $2 profit per unit, A makes $1 per unit, and B breaks even. The smart move for TI would be to lower its price to $9 to drive B out of the market; even A will consider leaving. Then TI will pick up the business that would have gone to B (and possibly A). Furthermore, price-sensitive customers will enter the market at the lower price. As production increases beyond 400,000 units, TI's costs will drop even more, restoring its profits

FIGURE 12.2   The Experience Curve

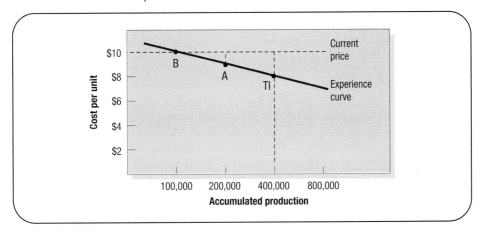

even at a price of $9. TI has used this aggressive pricing strategy repeatedly to gain market share and drive others out of the industry.

Experience-curve pricing is risky because aggressive pricing may give the product a cheap image. This strategy also assumes that competitors are weak followers and may lead the firm into building more plants to meet demand. Meanwhile, a competitor innovates a lower-cost technology, leaving the leader stuck with old technology.

Activity-Based Cost Accounting   Today's companies try to adapt their offers and terms to different buyers. Thus, a manufacturer will negotiate different terms with different retail chains, meaning the costs and profits will differ with each chain. To estimate the real profitability of dealing with different retailers, the manufacturer needs to use **activity-based cost (ABC) accounting** instead of standard cost accounting.[16] ABC accounting tries to identify the real costs (both variable and overhead) associated with serving each customer. Companies that fail to measure their costs correctly are not measuring their profit correctly, and they are likely to misallocate their marketing effort.

Target Costing   Costs change with production scale and experience. They can also change as a result of a concentrated effort by the company's designers, engineers, and purchasing agents to reduce them through **target costing**.[17] Market research is used to establish a new product's desired functions and the price at which it will sell, given its appeal and competitors' prices. Deducting the desired profit margin from this price leaves the target cost that be must achieved. Each cost element—design, engineering, manufacturing, sales—must be examined and different ways considered to bring the final cost projections into the target cost range. If this is not possible, the firm may decide against developing the product because it could not sell for the target price and make the target profit.

Step 4: Analyzing Competitors' Costs, Prices, and Offers

Within the range of possible prices determined by market demand and company costs, the firm must take into account its competitors' costs, prices, and possible price reactions. If the firm's offer contains features not offered by the nearest competitor, their worth to the customer should be evaluated and added to the competitor's price. If the competitor's offer contains some features not offered by the firm, their worth to the customer should be evaluated and subtracted from the firm's price. Now the firm can decide whether it can charge more, the same, or less than the competitor, remembering that competitors can change their prices at any time.

Step 5: Selecting a Pricing Method

The three Cs—the customers' demand schedule, the cost function, and competitors' prices—are major considerations in setting price (see Figure 12.3) . First, costs set a floor to the price. Second, competitors' prices and the price of substitutes provide an orienting point. Third, customers' assessment of unique product features establishes the ceiling price. Companies therefore must select a pricing method that includes one or more of these considerations. We will examine six price-setting methods: markup pricing, target-return pricing, perceived-value pricing, value pricing, going-rate pricing, and auction-type pricing.

Markup Pricing   The most elementary pricing method is to add a standard **markup** to the product's cost. Construction companies do this when they submit job bids by estimating the total project cost and adding a standard markup for profit. Similarly, lawyers and accountants typically price by adding a standard markup on their time and costs.

FIGURE 12.3   The Three Cs Model for Price Setting

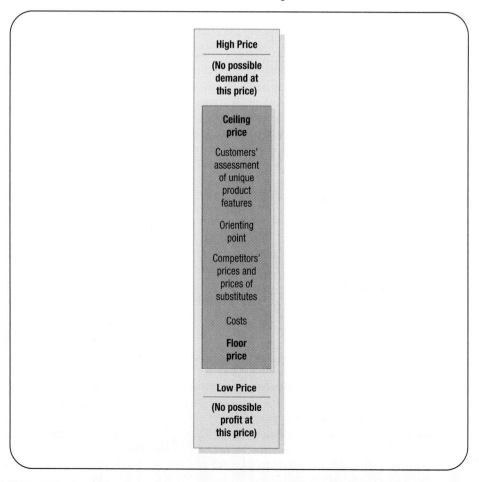

Suppose a toaster manufacturer has the following costs and sales expectations:

Variable cost per unit	$10
Fixed cost	$300,000
Expected unit sales	50,000

The manufacturer's unit cost is given by:

$$\text{Unit cost} = \text{variable cost} + \frac{\text{fixed costs}}{\text{unit sales}} = \$10 + \frac{\$300,000}{50,000} = \$16$$

If the manufacturer wants to earn a 20 percent markup on sales, its markup price is given by:

$$\text{Markup price} = \frac{\text{unit cost}}{(1 - \text{desired return on sales})} = \frac{\$16}{1 - 0.2} = \$20$$

The manufacturer charges dealers $20 per toaster and makes a profit of $4 per unit. If the dealers want to earn 50 percent on their selling price, they mark up the toaster to $40. This is equivalent to a cost markup of 100 percent.

Do standard markups make logical sense? Generally, no. Any pricing method that ignores current demand, perceived value, and competition is not likely to lead to the optimal price. Markup pricing works only if the marked-up price actually brings in the expected level of sales.

Companies introducing a new product often price it high, hoping to recover their costs as rapidly as possible. However, a high-markup strategy could be fatal if a competitor is pricing low. This happened to Philips, the Dutch electronics manufacturer. In pricing its videodisc players, Philips wanted to make a profit on each videodisc player. Yet Japanese rivals priced low and built market share rapidly, which pushed down their costs substantially.

Markup pricing remains popular for a number of reasons. First, sellers can determine costs much more easily than they can estimate demand. By tying the price to cost, sellers simplify the pricing task. Second, when all firms in the industry use this pricing method, prices tend to be similar, which minimizes price competition. Third, many people feel that markup pricing is fairer to both buyers and sellers: Sellers do not take advantage of buyers when demand becomes acute, and sellers earn a fair return on investment.

Target-Return Pricing   In **target-return pricing**, the firm determines the price that would yield its target rate of return on investment (ROI). Target pricing is used by General Motors, which prices its vehicles to achieve a 15–20 percent ROI.

Suppose the toaster manufacturer in the previous example has invested $1 million and wants to earn a 20 percent return on its invested capital. The target-return price is given by the following formula:

$$\text{Target-return price} = \frac{\text{unit cost} + \text{desired return} \times \text{invested capital}}{\text{unit sales}}$$

$$= \$16 + \frac{.20 \times \$1,000,000}{50,000} = \$20$$

FIGURE 12.4 Break-Even Chart

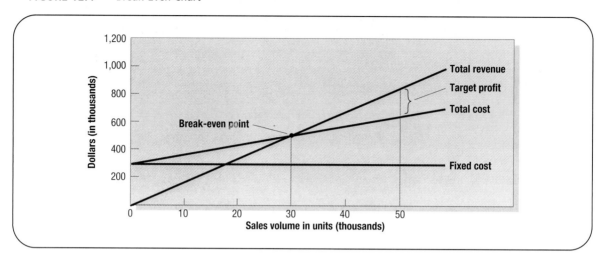

The manufacturer will realize this 20 percent ROI provided its costs and esti-mated sales turn out to be accurate, but what if sales do not reach 50,000 units? The manufacturer can prepare a break-even chart to learn what would happen at other sales levels (Figure 12.4). Fixed costs remain the same regardless of sales vol-ume, while variable costs, not shown in the figure, rise with volume. Total costs equal the sum of fixed costs and variable costs; the total revenue curve rises with each unit sold.

According to this chart, the total revenue and total cost curves cross at 30,000 units. This is the break-even volume. It can be verified by the following formula:

$$\text{Break-even volume} = \frac{\text{fixed cost}}{(\text{price} - \text{variable cost})} = \frac{\$300,000}{\$20 - \$10} = 30,000$$

If the manufacturer sells 50,000 units at $20, it earns a $200,000 profit on its $1 million investment. However, much depends on price elasticity and competitors' prices, two elements ignored by target-return pricing. In practice, the manufacturer needs to con-sider different prices and estimate their probable impacts on sales volume and profits. The firm should also find ways to lower fixed or variable costs, because lower costs will decrease the required break-even volume.

Perceived-Value Pricing An increasing number of companies base price on customers' *perceived value*. They must deliver the value promised by their value proposition, and the customer must perceive this value. They use the other marketing-mix elements, such as advertising, to communicate and enhance perceived value in buyers' minds.[18]

Perceived value is made up of several elements: the buyer's image of the product performance, the channel deliverables, warranty quality, customer support, and softer attributes such as the supplier's reputation and trustworthiness. Furthermore, each potential customer places different weights on these different elements, with the result that some will be *price buyers*, others will be *value buyers*, and still others will be *loyal buyers*. Companies need different strategies for these three groups. For price buyers, companies need to offer stripped-down products and reduced services. For value buyers, companies must keep innovating new value and aggressively reaffirming their value. For loyal buyers, companies must invest in relationship building and customer intimacy.

The key to perceived-value pricing is to deliver more value than the competitor and to demonstrate this to prospective buyers. Basically, a company needs to understand the customer's decision-making process and determine the value of its offering, which it can do through managerial judgments, assessing similar products' value, focus groups, surveys, experimentation, analysis of historical data, and conjoint analysis.[19]

For example, DuPont educated its customers about the true value of its higher-grade polyethylene resin. Instead of claiming only that pipes made from it were 5 percent more durable, DuPont produced a detailed analysis of the comparative costs of installing and maintaining in-ground irrigation pipe. The real savings came from the diminished need to pay the labor and crop-damage costs associated with digging up and replacing the underground pipe. DuPont was able to charge 7 percent more and still double its sales the following year.

Value Pricing   **Value pricing** is a method in which the company charges a fairly low price for a high-quality offering. IKEA, Southwest Airlines, and Wal-Mart practice value pricing. This is not a matter of simply setting lower prices on one's products compared to those of competitors. It is a matter of reengineering operations to become a low-cost producer without sacrificing quality, and reducing prices significantly to attract a large number of value-conscious customers.

An important type of value pricing is **everyday low pricing (EDLP)** , which takes place at the retail level. Retailers using EDLP pricing charge a constant, everyday low price with few or no price promotions and special sales. These constant prices eliminate week-to-week price uncertainty and can be contrasted to the "high-low" pricing of promotion-oriented competitors. In **high-low pricing**, the retailer charges higher prices on an everyday basis but then runs frequent promotions in which prices are temporarily lowered below the EDLP level.[20]

Wal-Mart is the king of EDLP, offering only a few sale items every month. Some retailers, such as Dollar General, even base their entire marketing strategy around *extreme* everyday low pricing. The most important reason retailers adopt EDLP is that constant sales and promotions are costly and erode consumer confidence in the credibility of everyday prices. Consumers also have less time and patience for such time-honored traditions as watching for specials and clipping coupons. Yet promotions are an excellent way to create excitement and draw shoppers. For this reason, EDLP is not a guarantee of success. As supermarkets face heightened competition from store rivals and alternative channels, many are drawing shoppers using a combination of high-low and EDLP strategies, with increased advertising and promotions.[21]

Going-Rate Pricing   In **going-rate pricing**, the firm bases its price largely on competitors' prices. The firm might charge the same, more, or less than major competitor(s). In oligopolistic industries that sell a commodity such as steel, paper, or fertilizer, firms normally charge the same price. The smaller firms "follow the leader," changing their prices when the leader's prices change rather than when their own demand or costs change. Some firms may charge a slight premium or discount, but they preserve the amount of difference. When costs are difficult to measure or competitive response is uncertain, firms adopt the going price because it seems to reflect the industry's collective wisdom.

Auction-Type Pricing   Auction-type pricing is growing more popular, especially with the growth of the Internet. One major use is to dispose of excess inventories or used goods; another is to obtain goods and services at lower prices (see "Marketing Skills: Planning Online Auctions"). Firms should understand the types of auctions and their pricing procedures.

In *English auctions* (*ascending bids*), one seller puts up an item and bidders raise the offer price until the top price is reached. English auctions are often used to sell antiques, cattle, real estate, used equipment, and vehicles. In *Dutch auctions* (*descending bids*), one seller may propose pricing to many buyers or one buyer may solicit bids from many sellers. In the first kind, an auctioneer announces a high price for a product and then slowly decreases the price until a bidder accepts the price. In the other, the buyer announces something that he wants to buy and potential sellers compete by offering the lowest price. Each seller sees the last bid and decides whether to go lower.

In *sealed-bid auctions*, each would-be supplier submits only one bid and cannot know the other bids. The U.S. government often uses this method to procure supplies.

MARKETING SKILLS: PLANNING ONLINE AUCTIONS

Businesses around the world are embracing online auctions to keep costs down and expand their roster of suppliers and customers. Thus, marketers need to know how to plan and manage an online auction, especially one in which the company solicits bids from suppliers to supply certain components, materials, equipment, or services. Companies sometimes start by experimenting with a few auctions to buy low-risk products that are available from more than a handful of suppliers. The first step is to define what the company wants to buy, including detailed specifications of quality and other attributes, and determine the approximate buying budget.

Next, the marketer alerts suppliers that are known as qualified to provide such products, allowing several weeks' lead time so the suppliers can prepare documentation or bids in advance. New suppliers may be required to show that they can meet the quality level, delivery dates, and other specifications in order to bid. When soliciting bids for multiple items, a firm must decide whether suppliers can bid only on selected items. Once the auction begins, marketers will be busy reviewing bids and proposals and posting bids to keep the auction running smoothly. At the close, marketers should notify all participants of the buying decision and thank everyone for participating.

Sainsbury's Supermarkets, a large U.K. chain, uses online auctions to obtain bids for making private label products such as frozen foods, meat, cosmetics, and beverages. In planning these auctions, quality is as important as price. "In most cases, product samples are evaluated before the auction to ensure all are competing on a 'level playing field,'" says a Sainsbury's executive. "Any products which fall short on quality attributes are simply not included in the auction. At the same time, we want to source at the best price for that quality." Not every auction saves money, but the company has enjoyed an overall financial benefit and will use online auctions in the future.[22]

A supplier will not bid below its cost but cannot bid too high for fear of losing the job. The net effect of these two pulls can be described in terms of the bid's *expected profit.* Using expected profit for setting price makes sense for the seller that makes many bids. The seller who bids only occasionally or who needs a particular contract badly will not find it advantageous to use expected profit. This criterion does not distinguish between a $1,000 profit with a 0.10 probability and a $125 profit with a 0.80 probability. Yet the firm that wants to keep production going would prefer the second contract to the first.

Step 6: Selecting the Final Price

Pricing methods narrow the range from which the company selects its final price. In selecting that price, the company must consider additional factors, including the impact of other marketing activities, company pricing policies, gain-and-risk-sharing pricing, and the impact of price on other parties.

The Influence of Other Marketing Activities   The final price must take into account the brand's quality and advertising relative to competition. When Farris and Reibstein examined the relationships among relative price, relative quality, and relative advertising for 227 consumer businesses, they found that brands with average relative quality but high relative advertising budgets were able to charge premium prices. Consumers seemed willing to pay higher prices for known products than for unknown products. Also, brands with high relative quality and high relative advertising obtained the highest prices, while brands with low quality and advertising had the lowest prices. Finally, the positive relationship between high prices and high advertising held most strongly late in the product life cycle for market leaders.[23]

Company Pricing Policies   The price must be consistent with company pricing policies. To accomplish this, many firms set up a pricing department to develop policies and establish or approve decisions. The aim is to ensure that the salespeople quote prices that are reasonable to customers and profitable to the company.

Gain-and-Risk-Sharing Pricing   Buyers may resist a seller's proposal because of a high perceived level of risk. The seller has the option of offering to absorb part or all of the risk if it fails to deliver the promised value. This happened when Baxter, a medical products firm, proposed an information management system that would save Columbia/ HCA, a health-care provider, millions of dollars over eight years. After Columbia balked, Baxter offered to write a check for the difference if the full savings were not realized—and Baxter got the order.

Baxter could have further proposed that if its system saved Columbia more than the targeted amount, Baxter would share in some of the additional savings—essentially sharing in the gain as well as the risk. An increasing number of firms, especially business marketers who promise great savings, may have to stand ready to guarantee promised savings, and possibly participate if the gains are much greater than expected.

Impact of Price on Other Parties   Management must also consider the reactions of other parties to the contemplated price, including distributors, dealers, and the sales force. How will competitors react? Will suppliers raise their prices when they see the company's price? Will the government intervene and prevent this price from being charged? Moreover, marketers need to know the laws regulating pricing. Sellers are not allowed to talk to competitors about pricing and not allowed to use deceptive pricing practices. For example, it is illegal to set artificially high "regular" prices, then announce a "sale" at prices close to previous everyday prices.

ADAPTING THE PRICE

Companies usually do not set a single price but, rather, a pricing structure that reflects variations in geographical demand and costs, market-segment requirements, purchase timing, order levels, delivery frequency, guarantees, service contracts, and other factors. As a result of discounts, allowances, and promotions, a firm rarely realizes the same profit from each unit sold. Here we will examine the price-adaptation strategies of geographical pricing, price discounts and allowances, promotional pricing, differentiated pricing, and product-mix pricing.

Geographical Pricing

In geographical pricing, the company decides how to price its products to different customers in different locations and countries. For example, should the company charge distant customers more to cover higher shipping costs or set a lower price to win additional business? Another issue is how to get paid. This is particularly critical when foreign buyers lack sufficient hard currency to pay for their purchases. Many buyers want to offer other items in payment; this is **countertrade**, which accounts for 15–25 percent of world trade and takes several forms:[24]

- *Barter.* The direct exchange of goods, with no money and no third party involved. Eminence S.A., a clothing maker in France, bartered $25 million worth of U.S.-produced underwear and sportswear to customers in Eastern Europe in exchange for transportation, magazine advertising space, and other goods and services.
- *Compensation deal.* The seller is paid partly in cash and partly in products. A British aircraft manufacturer used this approach to sell planes to Brazil for 70 percent cash and the rest in coffee.
- *Buyback arrangement.* The seller sells a plant or equipment and accepts products manufactured with the supplied equipment as partial payment. A U.S. chemical firm built a plant for an Indian company and accepted partial payment in cash and the remainder in chemicals manufactured at the plant.
- *Offset.* The seller receives full cash payment but agrees to spend much of the cash in that country within a stated period. For example, PepsiCo sells its cola syrup to Russia for rubles and buys Russian vodka at a certain rate for sale in the United States.

Price Discounts and Allowances

Most companies will adjust their list price and give discounts and allowances for early payment, volume purchases, and off-season buying, as shown in Table 12.2.[25] However, companies must do this carefully or their profits will be much less than planned.[26] Sales management needs to monitor the proportion of customers who are receiving discounts, the average discount, and the particular salespeople who are overrelying on discounting. Higher levels of management should conduct a *net price analysis* to arrive at the "real price" of their offering. The real price is affected not only by discounts, but also by many other expenses that reduce the realized price.

TABLE 12.2   Price Discounts and Allowances

Cash Discount:	A price reduction to buyers who pay bills promptly. A typical example is "2/10, net 30," which means that payment is due within 30 days and that the buyer can deduct 2 percent by paying the bill within 10 days.
Quantity Discount:	A price reduction to those who buy large volumes. A typical example is "$10 per unit for less than 100 units; $9 per unit for 100 or more units." Quantity discounts must be offered equally to all customers and must not exceed the cost savings to the seller. They can be offered on each order placed or on the number of units ordered over a given period.
Functional Discount:	Discount (also called *trade discount*) offered by a manufacturer to trade-channel members if they will perform certain functions, such as selling, storing, and recordkeeping. Manufacturers must offer the same functional discounts within each channel.
Seasonal Discount:	A price reduction to those who buy merchandise or services out of season. Hotels, motels, and airlines offer seasonal discounts in slow selling periods.
Allowance:	An extra payment designed to gain reseller participation in special programs. *Trade-in allowances* are granted for turning in an old item when buying a new one. *Promotional allowances* reward dealers for participating in advertising and sales support programs.

Promotional Pricing

Companies can use several pricing techniques to stimulate early purchase:

- *Loss-leader pricing*. Stores often drop the price on well-known brands to stimulate additional store traffic. This pays if the revenue on the additional sales compensates for the lower margins on the loss-leader items.
- *Special-event pricing*. Sellers will establish special prices in certain seasons to draw in more customers; an example is the back-to-school sale.
- *Cash rebates*. Auto companies and others offer cash rebates to encourage purchase of the manufacturers' products within a specified time period, clearing inventories without cutting the stated list price.
- *Low-interest financing*. Instead of cutting price, the firm can offer customers low- or no-interest financing.
- *Longer payment terms*. Sellers, especially mortgage banks and auto companies, stretch loans over longer periods and thus lower the monthly payments. Consumers often worry less about the cost (i.e., the interest rate) and more about whether they can afford the monthly payment.
- *Warranties and service contracts*. Companies promote sales with free or low-cost warranty or service contracts.
- *Psychological discounting*. Here, the firm sets an artificially high price and then offers the product at substantial savings; for example, "Was $359, now $299." The Federal Trade Commission and Better Business Bureaus fight illegitimate discount tactics.

Promotional-pricing strategies are often a zero-sum game. If they work, competitors copy them and they lose their effectiveness. If they do not work, they waste money that could have been put into other marketing tools, such as building up product quality and service or strengthening product image through advertising.

Differentiated Pricing

Companies often adjust their basic price to accommodate differences in customers, products, locations, and so on. **Price discrimination** occurs when a company sells a product or service at two or more prices that do not reflect a proportional difference in costs. Sellers may set different prices for different classes of buyers, as in these cases:

- *Customer-segment pricing.* Different customer groups pay different prices for the same offering. For example, museums often charge a lower admission fee to students and senior citizens.
- *Product-form pricing.* Different versions of the product are priced differently but not proportionately to their respective costs. Evian may price a 48-ounce bottle of water at $2 and its 1.7-ounce moisturizer spray at $6.
- *Image pricing.* Some companies price the same product at two different levels based on image differences. A perfume manufacturer can put its perfume in one bottle with a certain brand and image, priced at $10 an ounce; the same perfume in another bottle with a different name and image could be priced at $30 an ounce.
- *Channel pricing.* Coca-Cola carries a different price depending on whether it is purchased in a fine restaurant, a fast-food restaurant, or a vending machine.
- *Location pricing.* The same product is priced differently at different locations even though the costs are the same; for example, theaters often vary seat prices according to audience preferences for different locations.
- *Time pricing.* Prices are varied by season, day, or hour. Public utilities use time pricing, varying energy rates to commercial users by time of day and weekend versus weekday. Airlines use **yield pricing** to offer lower prices on unsold inventory before it expires.[27]

The phenomenon of offering different pricing schedules to different consumers and dynamically adjusting prices is exploding.[28] Price discrimination works when (1) the market is segmentable and the segments show different intensities of demand; (2) members in the lower-price segment cannot resell the product to the higher-price segment; (3) competitors cannot undersell the firm in the higher-price segment; (4) the cost of segmenting and policing the market does not exceed the extra revenue derived from price discrimination; (5) the practice does not breed customer resentment and ill will; and (6) the particular form of price discrimination is not illegal.[29]

Product-Mix Pricing

Price-setting logic must be modified when marketing a product mix. In this case, the firm searches for a set of prices that maximizes profits on the total mix. Pricing is difficult because the demand and cost of the various products are interrelated and are subject to different degrees of competition. Six product-mix pricing situations are:

- *Product-line pricing.* Many sellers use well-established price points (such as $200, $400, and $600 for suits) to distinguish the products in their line. The seller's task is to create perceived-quality differences that justify the price differences.
- *Optional-feature pricing.* Automakers and other firms offer optional products, features, and services along with their main product. Pricing these options is a sticky problem

because companies must decide which items to include in the standard price and which to offer as options.

- *Captive-product pricing.* Some products require the use of ancillary, or **captive**, products. In the razor industry, manufacturers often price their razors low and set high markups on blades. However, there is a danger in pricing the captive product too high in the aftermarket (the market for ancillary supplies to the main product). Caterpillar, for example, makes high aftermarket profits by pricing parts and service high. This has given rise to "pirates" who counterfeit the parts and sell them to "shady tree" mechanics to install, sometimes without passing on the cost savings to customers. Meanwhile, Caterpillar loses sales.[30]

- *Two-part pricing.* Many service firms use **two-part pricing**, which consists of a fixed fee plus a variable usage fee. Telephone customers pay a minimum monthly fee plus charges for calls beyond a certain area. The challenge is how much to charge for the basic service and how much for the variable usage. The fixed fee should be low enough to induce purchase; the profit can then be made on the usage fees.

- *By-product pricing.* The production of certain goods—meats, chemicals, and so on—often results in by-products, which can be priced according to their value to customers. Any income earned on the by-products will make it easier for the company to charge less for the main product if competition forces it to do so.

- *Product-bundling pricing. Pure bundling* occurs when a firm only offers its products as a bundle. With *mixed bundling,* a seller offers bundles (at a lower price than if items were purchased separately) and individual products. A theater company will price a season subscription lower than the cost of buying tickets to all performances separately. Because customers may not have planned to buy all of the components, the savings on the price bundle must be substantial enough to induce them to buy the bundle.[31]

INITIATING AND RESPONDING TO PRICE CHANGES

Firms often face the need to cut or raise prices in certain situations.

Initiating Price Cuts

Several circumstances might lead a firm to cut prices. One is excess plant capacity: The firm needs additional business but cannot generate it through increased sales effort or other efforts. In initiating a price cut, however, the company risks triggering a price war. Companies sometimes cut prices in a drive to dominate the market through lower costs. Either the company starts with lower costs than those of its competitors or it initiates price cuts in the hope of gaining market share and lower costs. Three possible traps include (1) customers may assume that lower-priced products have lower quality; (2) a low price buys market share but not market loyalty because the same customers will shift to any lower-price firm; and (3) higher-priced competitors may cut their prices but have longer staying power because of deeper cash reserves.

Initiating Price Increases

A successful price increase can raise profits considerably: if the company's profit margin is 3 percent of sales, a 1 percent price increase will increase profits by 33 percent if sales volume does not drop. In many cases, firms increase prices to maintain profits in the face of *cost inflation* when rising costs—unmatched by productivity gains—squeeze profit margins. In fact, companies often raise their prices by more than the cost increase in anticipation of further inflation or government price controls, a practice called *anticipatory pricing.*

Another factor leading to price increases is *overdemand.* When a company cannot supply all of its customers, it can use one of the following pricing techniques:

- *Delayed quotation pricing.* The firm does not set a final price until the product is finished or delivered. This is prevalent in industries with long production lead times.

- *Escalator clauses.* The firm requires the customer to pay today's price and all or part of any inflation increase that occurs before delivery, based on some specified price index. Such clauses are found in contracts involving major industrial projects.

- *Unbundling.* The firm maintains its price but removes or prices separately one or more elements that were part of the former offer, such as free delivery or installation.

- *Reduction of discounts.* The firm no longer offers its usual cash and quantity discounts.

Marketers should decide whether to raise the price sharply one time or raise it by small amounts several times (consumers prefer the latter). In passing along price increases, the firm must avoid looking like a price gouger.[32]

Reactions to Price Changes

Any price change can provoke a response from the firm's stakeholders; often, customers question the motivation behind price changes.[33] A price cut can be interpreted in different ways: The item is about to be replaced by a new model; the item is faulty and not selling well; the firm is in trouble; the price will drop even further; or the quality has been cut. A price increase, which would normally deter sales, may suggest that an item is "hot" and is a good value.

Competitors are most likely to react to a price change when few firms offer the product, the product is homogeneous, and buyers are highly informed. Anticipating reaction is complicated because each rival may have different interpretations of a price cut: One may think the company is trying to steal the market; another may believe that the company wants lower prices industrywide to stimulate total demand. To understand possible competitive reactions, companies must continuously monitor and analyze rivals' activities.

Responding to Competitors' Price Changes

How should a firm respond to a price cut initiated by a competitor? In markets characterized by high product homogeneity, the firm should find ways to enhance its augmented product; if it cannot find any, it must meet the price reduction. If the competitor raises its price in a homogeneous product market, the other firms might not match it, unless the price increase will benefit the industry as a whole. Then the leader will have to rescind the increase.

In nonhomogeneous product markets, a firm has more latitude to consider: Why did the competitor change the price? Was it to steal the market, to utilize excess capacity, to meet changing cost conditions, or to lead an industrywide price change? Does the competitor plan to make the price change temporary or permanent? What will happen to the company's market share and profits if it does not respond? Are other companies going to respond? What are the competitor's and other firms' likely responses to each possible reaction?

Market leaders often face aggressive price cutting by smaller competitors trying to build market share, the way AMD attacks Intel. The brand leader can respond in several ways:

- *Maintain price and profit margin.* The leader might believe that (1) it would lose too much profit if it reduced its price, (2) it would not lose much market share, and (3) it could regain market share when necessary. However, the attacker may gain more confidence, the leader's sales force may feel demoralized, and the leader may lose more share than expected. Then the leader may panic, lower the price to regain share, and find that regaining market share is more difficult than expected.
- *Maintain price and add value.* The leader could improve its product, services, and communications, which may be less expensive than cutting price and operating at a lower margin.
- *Reduce price.* The firm might match the competitor's price because its costs fall with volume, it would lose market share in a price-sensitive market, and it would be hard to rebuild market share once it is lost, even though this will cut short-term profits.
- *Increase price and improve quality.* The leader could raise its price and launch new brands to bracket the attacking brand.
- *Launch a low-price fighter line.* It might create a separate lower-price brand to combat competition.

The best response varies with the situation. Figure 12.5 portrays a price-reaction program for meeting a rival's price cut. Management should consider the product's stage in the life cycle, its importance in the company's portfolio, the competitor's intentions and resources, the market's price and quality sensitivity, the behavior of costs with volume, and the company's alternative opportunities.

FIGURE 12.5 Price-Reaction Program for Meeting a Competitor's Price Cut

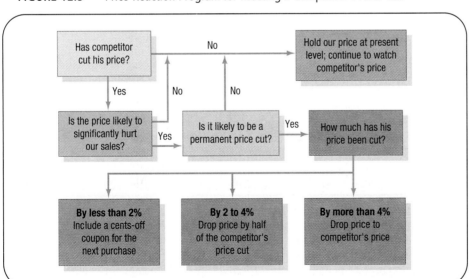

EXECUTIVE SUMMARY

Price is the only marketing element that produces revenue; the others produce costs. Marketers need to recognize that consumers make purchase decisions based on what they consider to be the current actual price. Consumers process and evaluate prices using reference prices, price–quality inferences, and price cues. In setting pricing policy, a firm follows six steps: (1) select the pricing objective, (2) determine demand, (3) estimate costs, (4) analyze competitors' costs, prices, and offers; (5) select a pricing method, and (6) select the final price. The customers' demand schedule, the cost function, and competitors' prices are major considerations in setting price. Six price-setting methods are: markup pricing, target-return pricing, perceived-value pricing, value pricing, going-rate pricing, and auction-type pricing. To adapt prices, firms use geographical pricing, discounts and allowances, promotional pricing, differentiated pricing, and product-mix pricing.

After developing pricing strategies, firms often need to change prices by initiating price cuts or price increases. In raising prices, firms must carefully manage customer perceptions. In addition, firms need to anticipate competitor price changes and prepare contingent response. The strategy here depends on whether the products are homogeneous or nonhomogeneous. Market leaders attacked by lower-priced competitors can maintain price, maintain price and add value, reduce price, increase price and improve quality, or launch a low-price fighter line.

NOTES

1. Jack Neff, "It Worked: Ad Boost Pays Off for Colgate; Unilever Also Sees Sales and Share Uptick, But Both Still Lag Behind P&G," *Advertising Age*, August 8, 2005, pp. 3+; Susanna Howard, "P&G, Unilever Court the World's Poor," *Wall Street Journal*, June 1, 2005, pp. 1+; "Procter & Gamble Poses Competitive Threat to India Detergent Nirma," *The Economic Times*, December 20, 2004, n.p.; Eric Bellman and Deborah Ball, "Unilever, P&G Wage Price War for Edge in India," *Wall Street Journal*, August 11, 2004, p. B1.
2. Michael Menduno, "Priced to Perfection," *Business 2.0*, March 6, 2001, pp. 40–42.
3. For a thorough review of pricing research, see Chezy Ofir and Russell S. Winer, "Pricing: Economic and Behavioral Models," in *Handbook of Marketing*, edited by Bart Weitz and Robin Wensley, (New York, NY: Sage Publications; 2002), 5–86; .
4. Peter R. Dickson and Alan G. Sawyer, "The Price Knowledge and Search of Supermarket Shoppers," *Journal of Marketing* (July 1990): 42–53. For a methodological qualification, however, see Hooman Estalami, Alfred Holden, and Donald R. Lehmann, "Macro-Economic Determinants of Consumer Price Knowledge: A Meta-Analysis of Four Decades of Research," *International Journal of Research in Marketing* 18 (December 2001): 341–355.
5. For a different point of view, see Chris Janiszewski and Donald R. Lichtenstein, "A Range Theory Account of Price Perception," *Journal of Consumer Research* (March 1999): 353–368.
6. K. N. Rajendran and Gerard J. Tellis, "Contextual and Temporal Components of Reference Price," *Journal of Marketing* (January 1994): 22–34.
7. Gary M. Erickson and Johny K. Johansson, "The Role of Price in Multi-Attribute Product-Evaluations," *Journal of Consumer Research* (September 1985): 195–199.
8. Mark Stiving and Russell S. Winer, "An Empirical Analysis of Price Endings with Scanner Data," *Journal of Consumer Research* (June 1997): 57–68.
9. Eric Anderson and Duncan Simester, "Effects of $19 Price Endings on Retail Sales: Evidence from Field Experiments," *Quantitative Marketing and Economics*, 1(1), 2003, pp. 93–110.

10. Shantanu Dutta, Mark J. Zbaracki, and Mark Bergen, "Pricing Process as a Capability: A Resource-Based Perspective," *Strategic Management Journal* 24, no. 7 (2000): 615–630.

11. See Sidney Bennett and J. B. Wilkinson, "Price–Quantity Relationships and Price Elasticity Under In-Store Experimentation," *Journal of Business Research* (January 1974): 30–34.

12. Walter Baker, Mike Marn, and Craig Zawada, "Price Smarter on the Net," *Harvard Business Review* (February 2001): 122–127.

13. John R. Nevin, "Laboratory Experiments for Estimating Consumer Demand—A Validation Study," *Journal of Marketing Research* (August 1974): 261–68; and Jonathan Weiner, "Forecasting Demand: Consumer Electronics Marketer Uses a Conjoint Approach to Configure Its New Product and Set the Right Price," *Marketing Research: A Magazine of Management & Applications,* Summer 1994, pp. 6–11.

14. For an excellent summary of the various methods for estimating price sensitivity and demand, see Thomas T. Nagle and Reed K. Holden, *The Strategy and Tactics of Pricing,* 3d ed. (Upper Saddle River: Prentice Hall, NJ, 2002).

15. For summary of elasticity studies, see Dominique M. Hanssens, Leonard J. Parsons, and Randall L. Schultz, *Market Response Models: Econometric and Time Series Analysis* (Boston: Kluwer Academic Publishers, 1990) pp. 187–191.

16. See Robin Cooper and Robert S. Kaplan, "Profit Priorities from Activity-Based Costing," *Harvard Business Review* (May–June 1991): 130–135.

17. See "Japan's Smart Secret Weapon," *Fortune,* August 12, 1991, p. 75.

18. Tung-Zong Chang and Albert R. Wildt, "Price, Product Information, and Purchase Intention: An Empirical Study," *Journal of the Academy of Marketing Science* (Winter 1994): 16–27. See also G. Dean Kortge and Patrick A. Okonkwo, "Perceived Value Approach to Pricing," *Industrial Marketing Management,* May 1993, pp. 133–140.

19. James C. Anderson, Dipak C. Jain, and Pradeep K. Chintagunta, "Customer Value Assessment in Business Markets: A State-of-Practice Study," *Journal of Business-to-Business Marketing* 1, no. 1 (1993): 3–29.

20. Stephen J. Hoch, Xavier Dreze, and Mary J. Purk, "EDLP, Hi-Lo, and Margin Arithmetic," *Journal of Marketing* (October 1994): 16–27; Rajiv Lal and R. Rao, "Supermarket Competition: The Case of Everyday Low Pricing," *Marketing Science* 16, no. 1 (1997): 60–80.

21. Becky Bull, "No Consensus on Pricing," *Progressive Grocer,* November 1998, pp. 87–90.

22. Amy F. Fischbach, "Bidders Beware," *EC&M Electrical Construction & Maintenance,* February 1, 2005, n.p.; Joel Oberman, "Auction Advice from Europe's eFoodmanager," *Private Label Buyer,* March 2002, p. 17; "Sainsbury's Will Increase Auction Use," *Private Label Buyer,* March 2002, p. 16; Richard Karpinski, "Manufacturer Takes Auctions In-House," *InternetWeek,* November 12, 2001, p. 27; Chris Clark, "Five Auction Steps," *Purchasing,* June 21, 2001, p. S24.

23. Paul W. Farris and David J. Reibstein, "How Prices, Expenditures, and Profits Are Linked," *Harvard Business Review* (November–December 1979): 173–184. See also Makoto Abe, "Price and Advertising Strategy of a National Brand Against Its Private-Label Clone: A Signaling Game Approach," *Journal of Business Research* (July 1995): 241–250.

24. See Michael Rowe, *Countertrade* (London: Euromoney Books, 1989); P. N. Agarwala, *Countertrade: A Global Perspective* (New Delhi: Vikas Publishing House, 1991); and Christopher M. Korth, ed., *International Countertrade* (New York: Quorum Books, 1987).

25. For an interesting discussion of a quantity surcharge, see David E. Sprott, Kenneth C. Manning, and Anthony Miyazaki, "Grocery Price Settings and Quantity Surcharges," *Journal of Marketing* 67 (July 2003): 34–46.

26. See Michael V. Marn and Robert L. Rosiello, "Managing Price, Gaining Profit," *Harvard Business Review* (September–October 1992): 84–94. See also Gerard J. Tellis, "Tackling the Retailer Decision Maze: Which Brands to Discount, How Much, When, and Why?" *Marketing Science* 14, no. 3, pt. 2 (1995): 271–299; Kusum L. Ailawadi, Scott A. Neslin,

and Karen Gedenk, "Pursuing the Value-Conscious Consumer: Store Brands Versus National Brand Promotions," *Journal of Marketing* 65 (January 2001): 71–89.

27. Robert E. Weigand, "Yield Management: Filling Buckets, Papering the House," *Business Horizons*, September–October 1999, pp. 55–64.

28. Charles Fishman, "Which Price Is Right?" *Fast Company*, March 2003, pp. 92–102; John Sviokla, "Value Poaching," *Across the Board* (March/April 2003): 11–12.

29. For more information on specific types of price discrimination that are illegal, see Henry R. Cheeseman, *Business Law* (Upper Saddle River, NJ: Prentice Hall, 2001).

30. See Robert E. Weigand, "Buy In–Follow On Strategies for Profit," *Sloan Management Review*, Spring 1991, pp. 29–37.

31. See Gerald J. Tellis, "Beyond the Many Faces of Price: An Integration of Pricing Strategies," *Journal of Marketing* (October 1986): 155. This article also analyzes and illustrates other pricing strategies.

32. Margaret C. Campbell, "Perceptions of Pricing Unfairness: Antecedents and Consequences," *Journal of Marketing Research* 36 (May 1999): 187–199.

33. For an excellent review, see Kent B. Monroe, "Buyers' Subjective Perceptions of Price," *Journal of Marketing Research* (February 1973): 70–80.

CHAPTER   13

Designing and Managing Value Networks and Channels

MARKETING MANAGEMENT AT BANK OF AMERICA

In the early twentieth century, when Bank of America (BofA) pioneered the idea of nationwide banking, opening a branch was the only way to deliver banking services. Today the bank operates 5,880 branches and 16,7000 automated teller machines in 29 states and Washington, D.C. In addition to serving customers in 150 nations, BofA offers Internet banking to U.S. customers and maintains branches inside other retail outlets, including several Starbucks locations. The purpose of offering so many choices is to allow fast, easy, and convenient access whenever and wherever BofA's customers want to do their banking, whether from home or office, at a branch, at a drive-through ATM, or holding a hot cup of coffee.

BofA recognizes that some customers will always want "high-touch" service, so it opens as many as 200 new branches every year. At the same time, management regularly evaluates the performance of the channel system and closes the lowest-performing branches. Meanwhile, "high-tech" services are gaining in popularity: More than 13 million customers use BofA's online banking services. Branding online ventures can be tricky, however, as competitor Bank One learned after spending millions of dollars to launch WingspanBank as a stand-alone online bank. Because WingspanBank was a separate unit, its customers could not bank at Bank One branches. In the end, WingspanBank attracted only 255,000 customers and closed after only two years. Clearly, physical branches remain an important channel for banking services, even as online banking grows more popular.[1]

Successful value creation needs successful value delivery, as Bank of America is well aware. Holistic marketers are increasingly taking a value network view of their businesses, examining the whole supply chain that links raw materials, components, and manufactured goods and shows how they move toward the final consumers. Not only are marketers looking at their suppliers' suppliers and at their distributors' customers, they are also looking at how to organize company resources to best meet the needs of targeted segments. This chapter discusses the strategic and tactical issues of marketing channels and value networks; Chapter 14 will examine marketing channel issues from the perspective of retailers, wholesalers, and physical-distribution agencies.

MARKETING CHANNELS AND VALUE NETWORKS

Most producers do not sell their goods directly to the final users; between them stands a set of intermediaries performing a variety of functions. These intermediaries constitute **marketing channels** (also called trade channels or distribution channels), sets of interdependent organizations involved in the process of making a product or service available for use or consumption. They are the set of pathways a product or service follows after production, culminating in purchase and use by the final end user.[2]

The Importance of Channels

A **marketing channel system** is the particular set of marketing channels employed by a firm. Decisions about the marketing channel system are among the most critical facing management. In the United States, channel members collectively earn margins that account for 30 to 50 percent of the ultimate selling price, whereas advertising typically accounts for less than 7 percent of the final price.[3] Marketing channels also represent a substantial opportunity cost because they do not just *serve* markets, they must also *make* markets.[4]

The channels chosen affect all other marketing decisions. The company's pricing depends on whether it uses mass merchandisers or high-quality boutiques. The firm's sales force and advertising decisions depend on how much training and motivation dealers need. In addition, channel decisions involve relatively long-term commitments to other firms. When an automaker signs up independent dealers to sell its automobiles, the automaker cannot buy them out the next day and replace them with company-owned outlets.[5]

The firm must decide how much effort to devote to push versus pull marketing. A **push strategy** involves the manufacturer using its sales force and trade promotion money to induce intermediaries to carry, promote, and sell the product to end users.

This is appropriate where there is low brand loyalty in a category, brand choice is made in the store, the product is an impulse item, and product benefits are well understood. A **pull strategy** involves the manufacturer using advertising and promotion to persuade consumers to ask intermediaries for the product, thus inducing the intermediaries to order it. This is appropriate when there is high brand loyalty and high involvement in the category, when people perceive differences between brands, and when people choose the brand before they go to the store. Top marketing companies such as Nike and Intel skillfully employ both push and pull strategies.

Value Networks

The company should first think of the target market and then design the supply chain backward from that point, a view called **demand-chain planning**. Northwestern's Don Schultz says: "A demand chain management approach doesn't just push things through the system. It emphasizes what solutions consumers are looking for, not what products we are trying to sell them."[6] The concept of a **value network**—a system of partnerships and alliances that a firm creates to source, augment, and deliver its offerings—takes an even broader view. A value network includes a firm's suppliers and its suppliers' suppliers, and its immediate customers and their end customers. The value network includes valued relations with others such as university researchers and regulatory agencies.

Demand-chain planning yields several insights. First, the firm can estimate whether more money is made upstream or downstream, in case it might want to integrate backward or forward. Second, the company is more aware of disturbances anywhere in the supply chain that might cause costs, prices, or supplies to change suddenly. Third, companies can go online with business partners for faster, more accurate, and less costly communications, transactions, and payments. With the advent of the Internet, companies are forming more numerous and complex relationships with other firms.

THE ROLE OF MARKETING CHANNELS

Why would a producer delegate some of the selling job to intermediaries? Delegation means relinquishing some control over how and to whom the products are sold. Producers do gain several advantages by using intermediaries:

- *Many producers lack the financial resources to carry out direct marketing.* For example, General Motors sells its cars through more than 8,000 dealer outlets in North America alone. Even General Motors would be hard-pressed to raise the cash to buy out its dealers.
- *Producers who do establish their own channels often can earn a greater return by increasing investment in their main business.* If a company earns a 20-percent rate of return on manufacturing and a 10-percent return on retailing, it does not make sense to do its own retailing.
- *In some cases, direct marketing simply is not feasible.* The William Wrigley Jr. Company would not find it practical to establish small retail gum shops throughout the world or to sell gum by mail order. It would have to sell gum along with many other small products and would end up in the drugstore and grocery store business. Wrigley finds it easier to work through the extensive network of privately owned distribution organizations.

FIGURE 13.1   How a Distributor Increases Efficiency

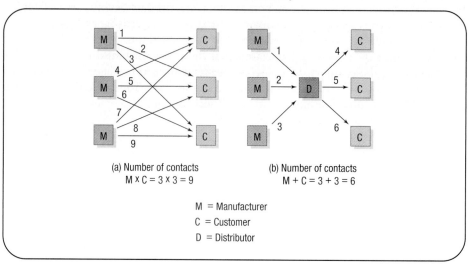

(a) Number of contacts
M × C = 3 × 3 = 9

(b) Number of contacts
M + C = 3 + 3 = 6

M = Manufacturer
C = Customer
D = Distributor

Intermediaries normally achieve superior efficiency in making goods widely available and accessible to target markets. Through their contacts, experience, specialization, and scale of operation, these specialists usually offer the firm more than it can achieve on its own. According to Stern and his colleagues: "Intermediaries smooth the flow of goods and services . . . . This procedure is necessary in order to bridge the discrepancy between the assortment of goods and services generated by the producer and the assortment demanded by the consumer. The discrepancy results from the fact that manufacturers typically produce a large quantity of a limited variety of goods, whereas consumers usually desire only a limited quantity of a wide variety of goods."[7]

Figure 13.1 shows how working through intermediaries can cut costs. Part (a) shows three producers, each using direct marketing to reach three customers, for a total of nine contacts. Part (b) shows the three producers working through one distributor, who contacts the three customers for a total of only six contacts. Clearly, intermediaries reduce the number of contacts and the work.

Channel Functions and Flows

A marketing channel performs the work of moving products from producers to consumers, overcoming the time, place, and possession gaps that separate goods and services from those who need or want them. Members of the marketing channel perform a number of key functions, as shown in Table 13.1. Some functions (physical, title, and promotion) constitute a *forward flow* of activity from the company to the customer; other functions (ordering and payment) constitute a *backward flow* from customers to the company. Still others (information, negotiation, finance, and risk taking) occur in both directions. Five flows are illustrated in Figure 13.2 for the marketing of forklift trucks. If these flows were superimposed in one diagram, the complexity of even simple marketing channels would be apparent.

The question is not *whether* these channel functions need to be performed—they must be—but rather *who* is to perform them. All channel functions have three

TABLE 13.1   Channel Member Functions

- Gather information about potential and current customers, competitors, and other actors and forces in the marketing environment.
- Develop and disseminate persuasive communications to stimulate purchasing.
- Reach agreements on price and other terms so that transfer of ownership or possession can be effected.
- Place orders with manufacturers.
- Acquire the funds to finance inventories at different levels in the marketing channel.
- Assume risks connected with carrying out channel work.
- Provide for the successive storage and movement of physical products.
- Provide for buyers' payment of their bills through banks and other financial institutions.
- Oversee actual transfer of ownership from one organization or person to another.

things in common: They use up scarce resources; they can often be performed better through specialization; and they can be shifted among channel members. If a manufacturer shifts some functions to intermediaries, its costs and prices go down, but the intermediaries must add a charge to cover their work. Still, if the intermediaries are more efficient than the manufacturer, prices to consumers should be lower. If consumers perform some functions themselves, they should enjoy still lower prices. In general, changes in channel institutions reflect the discovery of more efficient ways to combine or separate the economic functions that provide assortments of products to target customers.

FIGURE 13.2   Five Marketing Flows in the Marketing Channel for Forklift Trucks

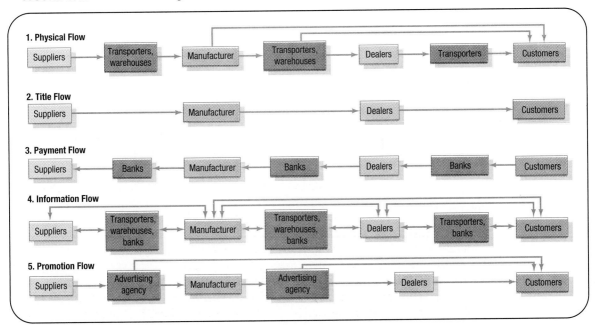

Channel Levels

The producer and the final customer are part of every channel. We will use the number of intermediary levels to designate the length of a channel. Figure 13.3a illustrates several consumer-goods marketing channels of different lengths, while Figure 13.3b illustrates industrial marketing channels.

A **zero-level channel** (also called a *direct-marketing channel*) consists of a producer selling directly to final customers through door-to-door sales, Internet selling, mail order, telemarketing, TV selling, and other methods. A **one-level channel** contains one intermediary, such as a retailer. A **two-level channel** contains two intermediaries; a **three-level channel** contains three intermediaries. From the producer's perspective, obtaining information about end users and exercising control becomes more difficult as the number of channel levels increases.

Channels normally describe a forward movement of products. One can also talk about *reverse-flow channels*, which bring products back for reuse (such as refillable bottles), refurbishing items for resale, recycling products, or disposal of products and packaging. Several intermediaries play a role in these channels, including manufacturers' redemption centers, community groups, traditional intermediaries such as soft-drink intermediaries, trash-collection specialists, recycling centers, trash-recycling brokers, and central-processing warehousing.[8] Noranda is a recycling partner for Hewlett-Packard, which encourages consumers and small businesses to recycle their old computers through a low-cost recycle-by-mail program. Using this reverse-flow channel, nearly 2 million tons of computer equipment arrive every month at the company's recycling center in California.[9]

FIGURE 13.3 Consumer and Industrial Marketing Channels

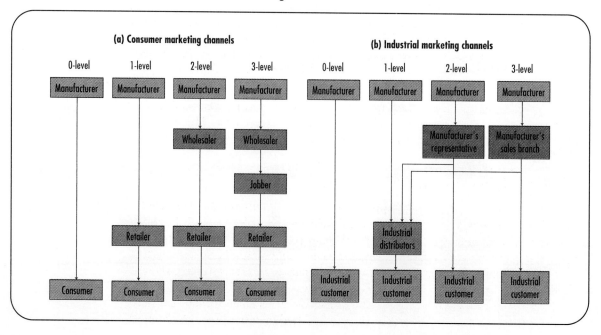

Service Sector Channels

Producers of services and ideas also face the problem of making their output available and accessible to target populations. For instance, schools develop "educational-dissemination systems" and hospitals develop "health-delivery systems." These institutions must determine agencies and locations for reaching a population that is spread out over an area. As Internet technology advances, service industries such as retailing, banking, travel, and insurance are operating through new channels. Kodak offers its customers four ways to print their digital photos—minilabs in retail outlets, home printers, the online Kodak EasyShare Gallery, and self-service kiosks.[10]

CHANNEL-DESIGN DECISIONS

Designing a marketing channel system involves analyzing customer needs, establishing channel objectives, identifying major channel alternatives, and evaluating major channel alternatives.

Analyzing Customers' Desired Service Output Levels

Because the point of a marketing channel is to make a product available to customers, the marketer must understand what its target customers actually want. Channels produce five service outputs:

1. *Lot size.* The number of units the channel permits a typical customer to purchase on one occasion. In buying for its fleet, Hertz wants a channel from which it can buy a large lot size; a household wants a channel that permits buying a lot size of one.
2. *Waiting time.* The average time customers of that channel wait for receipt of the goods. Customers normally prefer fast delivery channels.
3. *Spatial convenience.* The degree to which the marketing channel makes it easy for customers to purchase the product.
4. *Product variety.* The assortment breadth provided by the channel. Normally, customers prefer a greater assortment, which increases the chance of finding what they need.
5. *Service backup.* The add-on services (credit, delivery, installation, repairs) provided by the channel. The greater the service backup, the greater the work provided by the channel.[11]

Providing greater service outputs means increased channel costs and higher prices for customers, just as a lower level means lower costs and prices. The success of discount resellers (online and offline) indicates that many consumers will accept lower outputs if they can save money.

Establishing Objectives and Constraints

Channel objectives should be stated in terms of targeted service output levels. Under competitive conditions, channel institutions should arrange their functional tasks to minimize total channel costs and still provide desired levels of service outputs.[12] Usually, planners can identify several market segments that want different service levels. Effective planning requires determining which market segments to serve and the best channels for each.

Channel objectives vary with product characteristics. Perishable products require more direct marketing. Bulky products, such as building materials, require channels that minimize the shipping distance and the amount of handling. Nonstandard products, such as custom-built machinery, are sold directly by company sales representatives. Products requiring installation or maintenance services, such as heating systems, are usually sold and maintained by the company or franchised dealers. High-unit-value products such as turbines are often sold through a company sales force rather than intermediaries.

Channel design must also take into account the strengths and constraints of different types of intermediaries. For example, manufacturers' reps can contact customers at a low cost per customer because several clients share the total cost; however, the selling effort per customer will be less intense than if company reps were selling. In addition, channel design is influenced by such factors as competitors' channels, economic conditions, and legal regulations and restrictions. U.S. law looks unfavorably on channel arrangements that may tend to substantially lessen competition or create a monopoly.

Identifying Major Channel Alternatives

The next step is to identify channel alternatives. Most companies now use a mix of channels to reach different segments at the least cost. These are described by (1) the types of available intermediaries, (2) the number of intermediaries needed, and (3) the terms and responsibilities of each channel member.

Types of Intermediaries   A firm needs to identify the types of intermediaries available to carry on its channel work. Some intermediaries—*merchants* such as wholesalers and retailers—buy, take title to, and resell the merchandise. *Agents* such as brokers, manufacturers' representatives, and sales agents search for customers and may negotiate on the producer's behalf but do not take title to the goods. *Facilitators*, including transportation companies, independent warehouses, banks, and advertising agencies, assist in the distribution process but neither take title to goods nor negotiate purchases or sales. Increasingly, companies are searching for innovative marketing channels to reach new or existing customers. Medion sold 600,000 PCs in Europe, mostly via one- or two-week "burst promotions" at Aldi supermarkets.[13]

Number of Intermediaries   In deciding how many intermediaries to use, companies can use one of three strategies: exclusive, selective, or intensive distribution. **Exclusive distribution** means severely limiting the number of intermediaries. Firms such as automakers use this approach to maintain control over the service level and service outputs offered by the resellers. Often it involves *exclusive dealing* arrangements, in which resellers agree not to carry competing brands.

Selective distribution involves the use of more than a few but less than all of the intermediaries who are willing to carry a particular product. In this way, the producer avoids dissipating its efforts over too many outlets, and it gains adequate market coverage with more control and less cost than intensive distribution. Disney uses selective distribution for its videos and DVDs, selling through movie rental chains, company stores, other retailers, online retailers, and Disney's catalog and online site.[14]

Intensive distribution consists of the manufacturer placing the goods or services in as many outlets as possible. This strategy is generally used for items such as tobacco products, soap, snack foods, and gum, products for which the consumer requires a great deal of location convenience.

Terms and Responsibilities of Channel Members   The firm must determine the rights and responsibilities of participating channel members. Each channel member must be treated respectfully and be given the opportunity to be profitable.[15] The main elements in the "trade-relations mix" are price policies, conditions of sale, territorial rights, and specific services to be performed by each party.

Price policy calls for the producer to establish a price list and schedule of discounts and allowances that intermediaries see as equitable and sufficient. *Conditions of sale* refers to payment terms and producer guarantees. Most producers grant cash discounts to distributors for early payment. Producers might also provide distributors a guarantee against defective merchandise or price declines. A guarantee against price declines gives distributors an incentive to buy larger quantities.

Distributors' territorial rights define the distributors' territories and the terms under which the producer will enfranchise other distributors. Distributors normally expect to receive full credit for all sales in their territory, whether or not they did the selling. *Mutual services and responsibilities* must be carefully spelled out, especially in franchised and exclusive-agency channels. McDonald's provides franchisees with a building, promotional support, a recordkeeping system, training, and general administrative and technical assistance. In turn, franchisees are expected to satisfy company standards regarding physical facilities, cooperate with new promotional programs, furnish requested information, and buy supplies from specified vendors.

Evaluating the Major Alternatives

Once the company has identified its major channel alternatives, it must evaluate each alternative against appropriate economic, control, and adaptive criteria. From an economic perspective, each channel alternative will produce a different level of sales and costs. Figure 13.4 shows the value added per sale and cost per transaction of six different sales channels. The firm should determine whether its own sales force or a sales agency will produce more sales; next, it estimates the costs of selling different volumes through each channel. Companies that can switch their customers to lower-cost channels without losing sales or service quality will gain a **channel advantage**.[16]

In addition, using a sales agency poses a control problem because the agency is an independent firm seeking to maximize its profits. Agents may concentrate on customers who buy the most, but not necessarily of the producer's goods. Furthermore, agents might not master the details of every product they carry or handle all promotion materials effectively. To develop a channel, the members must make some mutual commitments for a specified period; this reduces the producer's ability to respond to a changing marketplace. In dynamic, volatile, or uncertain environments, producers need channels and policies that provide high adaptability.

FIGURE 13.4   The Value-Adds Versus Costs of Different Channels

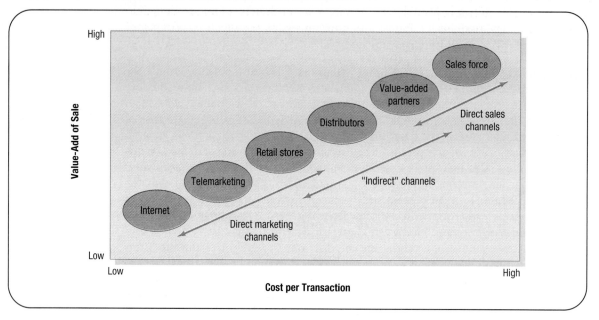

Source: Oxford Associates, adapted from Dr. Rowland T. Moriarty, Cubex Corp.

CHANNEL-MANAGEMENT DECISIONS

After a firm has chosen a channel alternative, individual intermediaries must be selected, trained, motivated, and evaluated. Marketers must also be ready to modify channel arrangements over time.

Selecting Channel Members

Companies need to select their channel members carefully because to customers, the channels are the company. Producers should determine what characteristics distinguish the better intermediaries and examine the number of years in business, other lines carried, growth and profit record, financial strength, cooperativeness, and service reputation of potential channel members. If the intermediaries are sales agents, producers should evaluate the number and character of other lines carried and the size and quality of the sales force. If the intermediaries want exclusive distribution, the producer should evaluate locations, future growth potential, and type of clientele.

Training Channel Members

Companies need to plan and implement careful training programs for their intermediaries. The fast-growing Culver's restaurant chain requires its Midwestern franchisees to work 60 hours in one of the 5 restaurants Culver owns and then work 12-hour days, 6 days a week for 4 months at headquarters, learning every facet of how the company operates logistically and financially.[17] Channel training is also a good competitive tool. Kyocera Mita arranged for J.D. Power and Associates to survey its customers and certify dealers that meet or exceed benchmarks for sales and service satisfaction. This certification "recognizes Kyocera Mita Total Solution Provider dealers for outstanding customer experience and allows them to differentiate within the dealer marketplace, helping to contribute to increased customer traffic and higher sales," said Michael Pietrunti, vice president of marketing at Kyocera Mita America. "This certification positions dealers as industry-wide leaders in customer satisfaction."[18]

Motivating Channel Members

Companies should look at their channel members in the same way they look at their end users. This means determining intermediaries' needs and tailoring the channel positioning to provide superior value to these intermediaries. To improve intermediaries' performance, the company should provide training, market research, and other capability-building programs. The company must also constantly reinforce that its intermediaries are partners in the joint effort to satisfy customers.

Producers vary greatly in **channel power,** the ability to alter channel members' behavior so that the members take actions they would not have taken otherwise.[19] Often, gaining intermediaries' cooperation can be a huge challenge.[20] More sophisticated producers go beyond merely gaining cooperation and instead try to forge a long-term partnership with channel members. The manufacturer communicates clearly what it expects from its distributors in the way of market coverage and other channel issues and may establish a compensation plan for adhering to these policies.

Evaluating Channel Members

Producers must periodically evaluate intermediaries' performance against such standards as sales-quota attainment, average inventory levels, customer delivery time, treatment of damaged and lost goods, and cooperation in promotional and training programs (see "Marketing Skills: Evaluating Intermediaries"). A producer will occasionally discover that it is paying too much to particular intermediaries for what they are actually doing. For example, a manufacturer that was compensating a distributor for holding inventories found that the stock was actually held in a public warehouse at the manufacturer's expense. Producers should therefore set up functional discounts in which they pay specified amounts for the intermediary's performance of each agreed-upon service. Underperformers need to be counseled, retrained, remotivated, or terminated.

Modifying Channel Arrangements

Channel arrangements must be reviewed periodically and modified when distribution is not working as planned, consumer buying patterns change, the market expands, new competition arises, innovative distribution channels emerge, or the product moves into later stages in the product life cycle. No marketing channel remains effective over the entire product life cycle. Early buyers might be willing to pay for high-cost value-added channels, but later buyers will switch to lower-cost channels. In competitive markets with low entry barriers, the optimal channel structure will inevitably change over time. The change could involve adding or dropping individual channel members, adding or dropping particular market channels, or developing a totally new way to sell goods.

MARKETING SKILLS: EVALUATING INTERMEDIARIES

How important is it for marketers to evaluate and manage suppliers, wholesalers, retailers, and other intermediaries? One company found, through rigorous analysis, that unpredictable supplier deliveries were causing it to hold $200 million in excess inventory to guard against out-of-stock conditions. By evaluating its suppliers on the basis of standards such as on-time delivery, this company slashed its costs—and began to manage intermediaries through charge-backs based on performance problems.

Start by determining how suppliers (and their suppliers) as well as distributors can influence the company's performance. Sometimes a tiny widget supplied by one minor supplier can be a pivotal ingredient in the production process, which makes that supplier's on-time delivery and product quality particularly critical. Another important step is to translate companywide strategic goals and measurements into specific targets and measures for value-network members. At Cisco, corporate targets for customer satisfaction are translated into detailed intermediary measures of on-time deliveries, defect rates, and similar elements. Good communication will help intermediaries understand the company's expectations and encourage information sharing for mutual benefit. Finally, measure and reward performance on an ongoing basis to keep the network efficient, reactive, and reliable.

A key criterion for toymaker Cranium is how well an intermediary can support the company's drive for growth. To get an edge in its highly competitive industry, the company often works with channel members that typically do not carry toys. Early on, it arranged to sell its Cranium game in Starbucks outlets, an innovative deal that built Cranium's brand and boosted demand. Once the game caught on, Cranium went after even more rapid revenue growth by selling games for children through discount stores. Although Cranium continues to test new games at Starbucks, its products are also in Whole Foods Market and other nontraditional intermediaries. By constantly analyzing how channels and intermediaries contribute to growth, Cranium makes the most of profit opportunities while putting its products in front of the target audience in new and unusual ways.[21]

Adding or dropping an individual channel member requires an incremental analysis to determine what the firm's profits would look like with and without this intermediary. Sometimes a producer considers dropping all intermediaries whose sales are below a certain amount. For example, Navistar once noticed that 5 percent of its dealers sold fewer than four trucks a year. It cost the company more to service these dealers than their sales were worth, but dropping the dealers could have system-wide repercussions. The unit costs of producing trucks would be higher because the overhead would be spread over fewer trucks, some employees and equipment would be idled, some customers would go to competitors, and other dealers might become insecure. All of these factors have to be taken into account before modifying channel arrangements.

The most difficult decision involves revising the overall channel strategy.[22] Distribution channels can become outmoded over time, as a gap arises between the existing distribution system and the ideal system that would satisfy target customers' (and producers') requirements. This is why Avon's door-to-door system for selling cosmetics had to be modified as more women entered the workforce, and, as noted in the chapter opener, Bank of America both opens and closes bank branches even as it offers online banking.

CHANNEL DYNAMICS

Distribution channels do not stand still. New wholesaling and retailing institutions emerge, and new channel systems evolve. We look next at the recent growth of vertical, horizontal, and multichannel marketing systems and see how these systems cooperate, conflict, and compete.

Vertical Marketing Systems

One of the most significant recent channel developments is the rise of vertical marketing systems. A **conventional marketing channel** comprises an independent producer, wholesaler(s), and retailer(s). Each is a separate business seeking to maximize its own profits, even if this goal reduces profit for the system as a whole. No channel member has complete or substantial control over other members.

A **vertical marketing system (VMS)**, by contrast, comprises the producer, wholesaler(s), and retailer(s) acting as a unified system. One channel member, the *channel captain*, owns the others, franchises them, or has so much power that they all cooperate. The channel captain can be the producer, the wholesaler, or the retailer. VMSs arose as a result of strong channel members' attempts to control channel behavior and eliminate conflict from independent channel members pursuing their own objectives. They achieve economies through size, bargaining power, and elimination of duplicated services. VMSs have become the dominant mode of distribution in the U.S. consumer marketplace, serving between 70 percent and 80 percent of the total market. There are three types of VMSs: corporate, administered, and contractual.

A *corporate VMS* combines successive stages of production and distribution under single ownership. Companies that desire a high level of control over their channels favor vertical integration. For example, Sears obtains over 50 percent of the goods it sells from companies that it partly or wholly owns.

An *administered VMS* coordinates successive stages of production and distribution through one member's size and power. Manufacturers of a dominant brand are able to secure strong trade cooperation and support from resellers. Thus Procter & Gamble and Campbell Soup can command cooperation from their resellers in connection with displays, shelf space, promotions, and price policies.

A *contractual VMS* consists of independent firms at different levels of production and distribution integrating their programs on a contractual basis to obtain more economies or sales impact than they could achieve alone. Johnston and Lawrence call them "value-adding partnerships" (VAPs).[23] Contractual VMSs are of three types:

1. *Wholesaler-sponsored voluntary chains* organize groups of independent retailers to better compete with large chains. These wholesalers work with participating retailers to standardize selling practices and achieve buying economies so the group can compete with chains.

2. *Retailer cooperatives* arise when the stores take the initiative and organize a new business entity to carry on wholesaling and possibly some production. Members of retail cooperatives concentrate their purchases through the co-op and jointly plan their advertising; members share in profits in proportion to their purchases.

3. *Franchise organizations* are created when a channel member called a *franchisor* links several successive stages in the production–distribution process. Franchises include manufacturer-sponsored retailer franchises (Ford and its dealers); manufacturer-sponsored wholesaler franchises (Coca-Cola and its bottlers); and service-firm-sponsored retailer franchises (Ramada Inn and its motel franchisees).

Horizontal Marketing Systems

Another channel development is the **horizontal marketing system**, in which two or more unrelated companies put together resources or programs to exploit an emerging marketing opportunity. Many supermarket chains have arrangements with local banks to offer in-store banking. Citizen Bank has 256 branches inside New England supermarkets. Each company lacks the capital, know-how, production, or marketing resources to venture alone, or it is afraid of the risk. The companies might work with each other on a temporary or permanent basis or create a joint venture company. H&R Block, Inc., for example, arranged to provide customers with information about car insurance through GEICO.

Multichannel Marketing Systems

Once, many companies sold to a single market through a single channel. Today, with the proliferation of customer segments and channel possibilities, more companies have adopted multichannel marketing. **Multichannel marketing** occurs when a single firm uses two or more marketing channels to reach one or more customer segments. As one example, the Parker-Hannifin Corporation (PHC) sells pneumatic drills to the lumber, fishing, and aircraft industries. Instead of selling through one distributor, PHC established three separate channels: forestry equipment distributors, marine distributors, and industrial distributors. There appears to be little conflict because each type of distributor sells to a separate target segment.

By adding more channels, companies can gain three important benefits. The first is increased market coverage. The second is lower channel cost—companies may add a new channel to lower the cost of selling to an existing customer group (selling by phone rather than personally visiting small customers). The third is more customized selling—such as adding sales force to sell more complex equipment. However, new channels typically introduce conflict and control problems. Different channels may end up competing for the same customers, and, as the new channels become more independent, the company may have difficulty maintaining cooperation among all members.

Conflict, Cooperation, and Competition

No matter how well channels are designed and managed, there will be some conflict, if for no other reason than that the interests of independent business entities do not always coincide. **Channel conflict** is generated when one channel member's actions prevent the channel from achieving its goal. **Channel coordination** occurs when channel members are brought together to advance the goals of the channel, as opposed to their own potentially incompatible goals.[24] Here we examine three questions: What types of conflict arise in channels? What causes channel conflict? What can be done to resolve conflict situations?

Types of Conflict and Competition   *Vertical channel conflict* means conflict between different levels within the same channel. As one example, General Motors came into conflict with its dealers in trying to enforce policies on service, pricing, and advertising. *Horizontal channel conflict* involves conflict between members at the same level within the channel. Horizontal channel conflict erupted, for instance, when some Pizza Inn franchisees complained that other Pizza Inn franchisees were cheating on ingredients, maintaining poor service, and hurting the brand image.

Multichannel conflict exists when the manufacturer has established two or more channels that sell to the same market. Multichannel conflict is likely to be especially intense when the members of one channel get a lower price (based on larger volume purchases) or work with a lower margin. For instance, when Pacific Cycles purchased Schwinn, it decided to supplement the brand's higher-end 2,700-dealer network with some of its own channels where it sold its own mid-tier bikes through large retail chains such as Target. Even though Pacific Cycles offered exclusive models to the existing Schwinn network, over 1,700 dealers pedaled away. A key question was whether the sales gains from the big retail chains would offset the loss from the dealer defections.[25]

Causes of Channel Conflict   Why does channel conflict erupt? One major cause is *goal incompatibility*. For example, the manufacturer may want to achieve rapid market penetration through a low-price policy. The dealers, in contrast, may prefer to work with high margins for short-run profitability. Sometimes conflict arises from *unclear roles and rights*. HP may sell PCs to large accounts through its own sales force, but its licensed dealers may also be trying to sell to large accounts. Territory boundaries and credit for sales often produce conflict.

Conflict can also stem from *differences in perception*, as when the producer is optimistic about the short-term economic outlook and wants dealers to carry more inventory, while its dealers are more pessimistic about future prospects. At times, conflict can arise because of the intermediaries' *dependence* on the manufacturer. The fortunes of exclusive dealers, such as auto dealers, are greatly affected by the manufacturer's product and pricing decisions, creating high potential for conflict.

Managing Channel Conflict   Some channel conflict can be constructive and lead to more dynamic adaptation in a changing environment. Too much conflict can be dysfunctional, however, so the challenge is not to eliminate conflict but to manage it better. There are several mechanisms for effective conflict management.[26] One is the adoption of superordinate goals. Channel members come to an agreement on the fundamental goal they are jointly seeking, whether it is survival, market share, high quality, or customer satisfaction. They usually do this when the channel faces an outside threat, such as a more efficient competing channel, an adverse piece of legislation, or a shift in consumer desires.

A useful step is to exchange persons between two or more channel levels. General Motors executives might work briefly in some dealerships, and some dealership owners might work in GM's dealer policy department, to help participants appreciate the other's viewpoint. *Cooptation* is an effort by one organization to win the support of the leaders of another organization by including them in advisory councils, boards of directors, trade associations, and the like. As long as the initiating organization treats the leaders seriously and listens to their opinions, cooptation can reduce conflict.

With chronic or acute conflict, diplomacy, mediation, or arbitration may be needed. *Diplomacy* takes place when each side sends a person or group to meet with its counterpart to resolve the conflict. *Mediation* means having a skilled, neutral third party reconcile the two parties' interests. *Arbitration* occurs when the two parties agree to present their arguments to an arbitrator and accept the arbitration decision.

Legal and Ethical Issues in Channel Relations

For the most part, companies are legally free to develop whatever channel arrangements suit them. In fact, the law seeks to prevent companies from using exclusionary tactics that might keep competitors from using a channel. Here we briefly consider the legality of exclusive dealing, exclusive territories, tying agreements, and dealers' rights.

With exclusive dealing, the seller allows only certain outlets to carry its products and requires that these dealers not handle competitors' products. Both parties benefit from exclusive arrangements: The seller obtains more loyal and dependable outlets, and the dealers obtain a steady source of supply of special products and stronger seller support. Exclusive arrangements are legal as long as they do not substantially lessen competition or tend to create a monopoly, and both parties have voluntarily entered into the agreement.

Exclusive dealing often includes exclusive territorial agreements. The producer may agree not to sell to other dealers in a given area, or the dealer may agree to sell only in its own territory. The first practice increases dealer enthusiasm and commitment and is perfectly legal—a seller has no legal obligation to sell through more outlets than it wishes. The second practice, whereby the producer tries to keep a dealer from selling outside its territory, is a major legal issue.

The producer of a strong brand sometimes sells it to dealers only if they will take some or all of the rest of the line. This practice is called full-line forcing. Such **tying agreements** are not necessarily illegal, but they do violate U.S. law if they tend to lessen competition substantially. Note that a producer's right to terminate dealers is somewhat restricted. In general, sellers can drop dealers "for cause," but not if, for instance, the dealers refuse to cooperate in a doubtful legal arrangement, such as exclusive dealing or tying agreements.

E-COMMERCE MARKETING PRACTICES

E-business describes the use of electronic means and platforms to conduct a company's business. **E-commerce** means that the company or site transacts or facilitates the selling of products and services online. E-commerce has given rise to e-purchasing and e-marketing. **E-purchasing** means companies decide to buy goods, services, and information from various online suppliers. **E-marketing** describes company efforts to inform buyers, communicate, promote, and sell its offerings online. The *e* term will eventually be dropped when most business practice is online.

We can distinguish between **pure-click** companies, those that have launched a Web site without any previous existence as a firm, and **brick-and-click** companies, existing companies that have added an online site for information and/or e-commerce.

Pure-Click Companies

There are several kinds of pure-click companies: search engines, Internet service providers (ISPs), commerce sites, transaction sites, content sites, and enabler sites. Commerce sites sell all types of products and services, notably books, music, toys, insurance, clothes, and so on. Among the most prominent commerce sites are Amazon, eBay, and Expedia. Commerce sites use various strategies to compete: Hotels, the information leader in hotel reservations; Buy.com, the low-price leader; and Winespectator, the single category specialist.

The Internet is most useful when the shopper seeks greater ordering convenience (e.g., books and music) or lower cost (e.g., stock trading or news reading). It is also useful when buyers need information about product features and prices (e.g., automobiles or computers). The Internet is less useful for products that must be touched or examined in advance. However, even this has exceptions. People can order furniture from EthanAllen.com, major appliances from Sears.com, and expensive computers from Dell.com without trying them in advance.

Although the popular press has given the most attention to business-to-consumer (B2C) Web sites, even more activity is being conducted on business-to-business (B2B) sites, which make markets more efficient. In the past, buyers had to exert a lot of effort to gather information on worldwide suppliers. With the Internet, buyers have easy access to a great deal of information from (1) supplier Web sites; (2) *infomediaries*, third parties that add value by aggregating information about alternatives; (3) *market makers*, third parties that create markets linking buyers and sellers; and (4) *customer communities*, Web sites where buyers can swap stories about suppliers' offerings.

The net impact of these mechanisms is to make prices more transparent. In the case of undifferentiated products, price pressure will increase. In the case of highly differentiated products, buyers will gain a better picture of their true value. Suppliers of superior products will be able to offset price transparency with value transparency; suppliers of undifferentiated products will have to drive down their costs in order to compete.

Brick-and-Click Companies

Many brick-and-mortar companies have agonized over whether to embrace e-commerce. Some opened Web sites describing their businesses but resisted adding e-commerce because they feared that channel conflict would arise from competing with their offline retailers, agents, or their own stores.[27] The question is how to sell both through intermediaries and online. There are at least three strategies for trying to gain acceptance from intermediaries: (1) offer different brands or products on the Internet; (2) offer the offline partners higher commissions to cushion the negative impact on sales; and (3) take orders on the Web site but have retailers deliver and collect payment. Harley-Davidson asks customers who want to order accessories online to select a participating dealer. The dealer, in turn, fulfills the order, adhering to Harley's standards for prompt shipping.[28]

Some pure or predominantly online companies have invested in brick-and-mortar sites. Most companies brand their online ventures under their existing brand names. It is difficult to launch a new brand successfully, as Bank One's experience with WingspanBank shows. Thus, companies may need to decide whether to drop some or all of their retailers and go direct. Banks, however, have found that some customers prefer to conduct certain transactions in person: 80 percent of new checking and savings accounts are still opened in physical bank branches.[29]

EXECUTIVE SUMMARY

Most producers do not sell their goods directly to final users. Between producers and final users stands one or more marketing channels, a host of marketing intermediaries performing a variety of functions. Companies use intermediaries when they lack the financial resources to carry out direct marketing, when direct marketing is not feasible, and when they can earn more by doing so. The most important functions performed by intermediaries are information, promotion, negotiation, ordering, financing, risk taking, physical possession, payment, and title.

Manufacturers have many alternatives for reaching a market. They can sell direct or use one-, two-, or three-level channels, depending on their analysis of customer needs, channel objectives, and identification and evaluation of major channel alternatives, including the types and numbers of intermediaries. Effective channel management calls for selecting intermediaries, then training and motivating them. The goal is to build a long-term, mutually profitable partnership. Individual members must be periodically evaluated and channel arrangements may need to be modified over time. Three of the most important channel trends are the growth of vertical marketing systems, horizontal marketing systems, and multichannel marketing systems.

All channels have the potential for conflict and competition resulting from goal incompatibility, poorly defined roles and rights, perceptual differences, or interdependent relationships. Companies can manage conflict by striving for superordinate goals, exchanging people among channel levels, coopting the support of leaders in different parts of the channel, and through diplomacy, mediation, or arbitration. Management must consider legal and ethical issues relating to practices such as exclusive dealing or territories, tying agreements, and dealers' rights. E-commerce has grown in importance as firms have adopted "brick-and-click" channel systems. Channel integration must recognize the distinctive strengths of online and offline selling and maximize their joint contributions.

NOTES

1. Paul Davis, "B of A to Close 100 Branches," *American Banker*, July 7, 2005, p. 20; Eve Tahmincioglu, "Small Banking in a Big Bank World," *New York Times*, June 30, 2005, p. C10; Jennifer Saranow, "New Bean Counters: Banks Share Space with Coffee Shops," *Wall Street Journal*, March 22, 2005, p. D3; Janny Scott, "More Banks Than a Roll of Dimes Stake Their Claim," *New York Times*, February 7, 2004, p. B1; Patricia A. Murphy, "Why WingspanBank Couldn't Stay Aloft," *Banking Wire*, September 17, 2001, p. 7.
2. Anne T. Coughlan, Erin Anderson, Louis W. Stern, and Adel I. El-Ansary, *Marketing Channels*, 6th ed. (Upper Saddle River, NJ: Prentice Hall, 2001).

3. Louis W. Stern and Barton A. Weitz, "The Revolution in Distribution: Challenges and Opportunities," *Long Range Planning* 30, no. 6 (1997): 823–829.

4. For an insightful summary of academic research, see Erin Anderson and Anne T. Coughlan, "Channel Management: Structure, Governance, and Relationship Management," in *Handbook of Marketing*, edited by Bart Weitz and Robin Wensley (London: Sage Publications, 2001), pp. 223–247. See also Gary L. Frazier, "Organizing and Managing Channels of Distribution," *Journal of the Academy of Marketing Sciences* 27, no. 2 (1999): 226–240.

5. E. Raymond Corey, *Industrial Marketing: Cases and Concepts*, 4th ed. (Upper Saddle River, NJ: Prentice Hall, 1991), ch. 5.

6. Mike Troy, "From Supply Chain to Demand Chain, a New View of the Marketplace," *DSN Retailing Today*, October 13, 2003, pp. 8–9.

7. Coughlan, Anderson, Stern, and El-Ansary, *Marketing Channels*, pp. 5–6.

8. For additional information on reverse-flow channels, see Marianne Jahre, "Household Waste Collection as a Reverse Channel—A Theoretical Perspective," *International Journal of Physical Distribution and Logistics* 25, no. 2 (1995): 39–55; and Terrance L. Pohlen and M. Theodore Farris II, "Reverse Logistics in Plastics Recycling," *International Journal of Physical Distribution and Logistics* 22, no. 7 (1992): 35–37.

9. Chris Gaither, "Giving PCs the Boot," *Boston Globe*, April 22, 2003, p. F1.

10. "Ofoto Takes on a New Identity," *Chain Drug Review*, February 28, 2005, p. 13; Faith Keenan, "Big Yellow's Digital Dilemma," *BusinessWeek*, March 24, 2003, pp. 80–81.

11. Louis O. Bucklin, *Competition and Evolution in the Distributive Trades* (Upper Saddle River, NJ: Prentice Hall, 1972). Also see Stern, et al., *Marketing Channels*.

12. Louis P. Bucklin, *A Theory of Distribution Channel Structure* (Berkeley: Institute of Business and Economic Research, University of California, 1966).

13. Bridget Finn, "A Quart of Milk, a Dozen Eggs, and a 2.6-GHz Laptop," *Business 2.0*, October 2003, p. 58.

14. Edward Helmore, "Media: Why House of Mouse Is Haunted by Failures," *The Observer*, February 11, 2001, p. 10 (www.disney.com).

15. For more on relationship marketing and the governance of marketing channels, see Jan B. Heide, "Interorganizational Governance in Marketing Channels," *Journal of Marketing* (January 1994): 71–85.

16. See Lawrence G. Friedman and Timothy R. Furey, *The Channel Advantage*: *Going to Marketing with Multiple Sales Channels* (Boston: Butterworth-Heinemann, 1999). They suggest measuring a channel's profitability by the expense-to-revenue ratio (E/R), the average transaction cost divided by the average order size. The average transaction cost is found by dividing the total expense in operating the channel by the total number of transactions. The lower the E/R, the more profitable the channel.

17. Erin Killian, "Butter 'Em Up," *Forbes*, June 9, 2003, pp. 175–176.

18. americas.kyocera.com/news/.

19. Anderson and Coughlan, "Channel Management: Structure, Governance, and Relationship Management," pp. 223–247.

20. Bert Rosenbloom, *Marketing Channels: A Management View*, 5th ed. (Hinsdale, IL: Dryden, 1995).

21. "America West Announces Partnership with Cranium," *Airline Industry Information*, June 2, 2005, n.p.; Christopher Palmeri, "March of the Toys—Out of the Toy Section," *BusinessWeek*, November 29, 2004, p. 37; Miles Cook and Rob Tyndall, "Lessons from the Leaders," *Supply Chain Management Review*, November–December 2001, pp. 22+; Jennifer Baljko Shah, "Staying Efficient Despite Tough Marketing Dynamics," *EBN*, August 27, 2001, p. 33.

22. For an excellent report on this issue, see Howard Sutton, *Rethinking the Company's Selling and Distribution Channels*, research report no. 885, Conference Board, 1986, p. 26.

23. Russell Johnston and Paul R. Lawrence, "Beyond Vertical Integration—The Rise of the Value-Adding Partnership," *Harvard Business Review* (July–August 1988): 94–101. See also Judy A. Siguaw, Penny M. Simpson, and Thomas L. Baker, "Effects of Supplier Market Orientation on Distributor Market Orientation and the Channel Relationship: The Distribution Perspective," *Journal of Marketing* (July 1998): 99–111; Narakesari Narayandas and Manohar U. Kalwani, "Long-Term Manufacturer–Supplier Relationships: Do They Pay Off for Supplier Firms?" *Journal of Marketing* (January 1995): 1–16.

24. Anne T. Coughlan and Louis W. Stern, "Marketing Channel Design and Management," in *Kellogg on Marketing*, edited by Dawn Iacobucci (New York: John Wiley, 2001), pp. 247–269.

25. Rob Wheery, "Pedal Pushers," *Forbes*, October 14, 2002, pp. 205–206.

26. This section draws on Stern and El-Ansary, *Marketing Channels*, ch. 6. See also Jonathan D. Hibbard, Nirmalya Kumar, and Louis W. Stern, "Examining the Impact of Destructive Acts in Marketing Channel Relationships," *Journal of Marketing Research* 38 (February 2001): 45–61; Kersi D. Antia and Gary L. Frazier, "The Severity of Contract Enforcement in Interfirm Channel Relationships," *Journal of Marketing* 65 (October 2001): 67–81; James R. Brown, Chekitan S. Dev, and Dong-Jin Lee, "Managing Marketing Channel Opportunism: The Efficiency of Alternative Governance Mechanisms," *Journal of Marketing* 64 (April 2001), pp. 51–65.

27. Described in *Inside 1-to-1*, Peppers and Rogers Group newsletter, May 14, 2001.

28. Bob Tedeshi, "How Harley Revved Online Sales," *Business 2.0*, December 2002/January 2003, p. 44.

29. Pallavi Gogoi, "The Hot News in Banking: Bricks and Mortar," *BusinessWeek*, April 21, 2003, pp. 83–84.

Managing Retailing, Wholesaling, and Logistics

In this chapter, we will address the following questions:

1. What are the major types of marketing intermediaries?
2. What marketing decisions do these marketing intermediaries make?
3. What are the major trends in the resaling, wholesaling, and logistics sector?

MARKETING MANAGEMENT AT TRADER JOE'S

Los Angeles–based Trader Joe's began 45 years ago as a convenience store and has carved out a special niche as a "gourmet food outlet discount warehouse hybrid" for selling a constantly rotating assortment of upscale specialty foods and wines at lower-than-average prices. Each of its 235 stores carries about 2,500 products, whereas a typical supermarket stocks about 25,000 items; roughly 80 percent of the merchandise is sold under one of Trader Joe's private label brands (compared to only 16 percent at most supermarkets). The chain carries only those products it can buy and sell at a good price, even if that policy means changing stock weekly.

To get the best possible prices on products, Trader Joe's 18 buyers bypass wholesalers and deal directly with hundreds of suppliers, about 20 to 25 percent of which are overseas. The company will stock a product only after approval by one of its two tasting panels. Even if a product makes it onto the shelf, there is no guarantee it will be popular. Trader Joe's aims to keep its merchandise assortment fresh and to stock what customers really want, which is why it introduces 20 or more new products each week in place of unpopular items. The chain expands by 15 stores each year, making its final site decisions after an exhaustive study of many potential sites. Inside the stores, the atmosphere is utilitarian, but the employees are *friendly and knowledgeable, and customers who are dissatisfied can get their money back without a hassle. This formula for retailing success, which has helped Trader Joe's push annual sales over $1 billion, is a difficult one to copy—making the grocery chain a formidable competitor in any market.*[1]

In the previous chapter, we examined intermediaries from the viewpoint of manufacturers and service providers who want to build and manage value networks and marketing channels. In this chapter, we view these intermediaries—retailers like Trader Joe's, wholesalers, and logistical organizations—as requiring and forging their own marketing strategies. The best-performing intermediaries use strategic planning, advanced information systems, and sophisticated marketing tools, measuring performance more on a return-on-investment basis than on a profit-margin basis. They segment their markets, hone their market targeting and positioning, and aggressively pursue market expansion and diversification.

RETAILING

Retailing includes all of the activities involved in selling goods or services directly to final consumers for personal, nonbusiness use. A **retailer** or **retail store** is any business enterprise whose sales volume comes primarily from retailing. Any organization that sells to final consumers—whether a manufacturer, wholesaler, or retailer—is engaged in retailing. It does not matter *how* the goods or services are sold (by person, mail, telephone, vending machine, or Internet) or *where* they are sold (in a store, on the street, or in the consumer's home).

Types of Retailers

Retailers exhibit great variety, and new forms keep emerging. Table 14.1 shows the most important types.

Like products, retail-store types pass through stages of growth and decline that can be described as the *retail life cycle*.[2] A type emerges, enjoys a period of accelerated growth, reaches maturity, and then declines. Department stores took 80 years to reach maturity, whereas warehouse retail outlets reached maturity in 10 years. New store types emerge, according to the *wheel-of-retailing hypothesis*, after conventional retail stores increase their services and raise their prices to cover the cost. These higher costs provide an opportunity for new retail forms to emerge with lower prices and less service.[3] Retailers can position themselves as offering one of four levels of service:

1. *Self-service:* The cornerstone of all discount stores, self-service allows customers to save money by carrying out their own locate-compare-select process.
2. *Self-selection:* Customers find their own goods, although they can ask for help.
3. *Limited service:* These retailers carry more shopping goods, and customers need more information and assistance. The stores also offer services (such as credit and merchandise-return privileges).
4. *Full service:* Salespeople are ready to assist in the locate-compare-select process. The high staffing cost, the higher proportion of specialty goods, slower-moving items, and more services, add up to high-cost retailing.

TABLE 14.1 Major Retailer Types

Specialty store: Narrow product line: Athlete's Foot, Tall Men, The Limited, The Body Shop.

Department store: Several product lines: Sears, JCPenney, Nordstrom, Bloomingdale's.

Supermarket: Large, low-cost, low-margin, high-volume, self-service store designed to meet total needs for food and household products: Kroger, Jewel, Food Emporium.

Convenience store: Small store in residential area, often open 24-7, limited line of high-turnover convenience products plus takeout: 7-Eleven, Circle K.

Discount store: Standard or specialty merchandise; low-price, low-margin, high-volume stores: Wal-Mart, Kmart, Circuit City, Crown Bookstores.

Off-price retailer: Leftover goods, overruns, irregular merchandise sold at less than retail. Factory outlets, independent off-price retailers: Filene's Basement, T.J. Maxx; warehouse clubs: Sam's Clubs, Costco, BJ's Wholesale.

Superstore: Huge selling space, routinely purchased food and household items, plus services (laundry, shoe repair, dry cleaning, check cashing). Category killer (deep assortment in one category): Petsmart, Staples, Home Depot; combination store: Jewel–Osco; hypermarket (huge stores that combine supermarket, discount, and warehouse retailing): Carrefour in France, Pyrca in Spain, Meijer's in the Netherlands.

Catalog showroom: Broad selection of high-markup, fast-moving, brand-name goods sold by catalog at discount. Customers pick up merchandise at the store: Inside Edge Ski and Bike.

By combining these different service levels with different assortment breadths, we can distinguish four broad retail positioning strategies:

1. *Bloomingdale's:* Stores with a broad product assortment and high value added; they pay close attention to store design, product quality, service, and image, and they enjoy a high profit margin.
2. *Tiffany:* Stores with a narrow product assortment and high value added; they cultivate an exclusive image and tend to operate on high margin and low volume.
3. *Sunglass Hut:* With a narrow line and low value added, these stores keep costs and prices low by centralizing buying, merchandising, advertising, and distribution.
4. *Wal-Mart:* With a broad line and low value added, these stores keep prices low to create an image of being a place for bargains, and they make up for low margin with high volume.

Although the overwhelming majority of goods and services is sold through stores, *nonstore retailing* has been growing much faster than store retailing. Nonstore retailing falls into four major categories: (1) *direct selling*, a $9-billion industry with over 600 companies (such as Avon) selling door-to-door or at home; (2) *direct marketing*, with roots in direct-mail and catalog marketing (L.L. Bean) and encompassing telemarketing (1-800-FLOWERS), television direct-response marketing (QVC), and electronic shopping (Amazon.com); (3) *automatic vending*, used for items such as cigarettes, candy, and newspapers; and (4) *buying service*, a storeless retailer serving a specific clientele—usually employees of large organizations—who are entitled to buy from retailers that have agreed to give discounts in return for membership.

Many stores remain independently owned, but an increasing number are part of some form of **corporate retailing** (see Table 14.2). Such organizations achieve economies of scale and have greater purchasing power, wider brand recognition, and better-trained employees.

TABLE 14.2   Major Types of Corporate Retail Organizations

Corporate chain store: Two or more outlets owned and controlled, employing central buying and merchandising, and selling similar lines of merchandise. GAP, Pottery Barn, Hold Everything.

Voluntary chain: A wholesaler-sponsored group of independent retailers engaged in bulk buying and common merchandising. Independent Grocers Alliance (IGA).

Retailer cooperative: Independent retailers using a central buying organization and joint promotion efforts. Associated Grocers, ACE Hardware.

Consumer cooperative: A retail firm owned by its customers. Members contribute money to open their own store, vote on its policies, elect a group to manage it, and receive dividends.

Franchise organization: Contractual association between a franchiser and franchisees, popular in a number of product and service areas. McDonald's, Subway, Pizza Hut, Jiffy Lube, 7-Eleven.

Merchandising conglomerate: A corporation that combines several diversified retailing lines and forms under central ownership, with some integration of distribution and management.

Retailer Marketing Decisions

In the past, retailers held customers by offering convenient location, special or unique assortments of goods, greater or better services, and store credit cards. All of this has changed. Today, national brands such as Calvin Klein and Levi Strauss are found in most department stores, in their own shops, in merchandise outlets, and in off-price discount stores; the result is that store assortments have grown more alike.

Service differentiation also has eroded. Many department stores have trimmed services while many discounters have increased services. Customers have become smarter shoppers. They do not want to pay more for identical brands, especially when service differences have diminished. Nor do they need credit from a particular store, because bank credit cards are almost universally accepted. Effective differentiation therefore requires savvy marketing decisions about target market, product assortment and procurement, services and store atmosphere, price, communication, and location.

Target Market   A retailer's most important decision concerns the target market. Until the target market is defined and profiled, the retailer cannot make consistent decisions on product assortment, store decor, advertising messages and media, price, and service levels. Some retailers have defined their target markets quite well. Consider Christopher & Bond, which appeals to 40-something moms—a traditionally overlooked market segment—who prefer classic clothing. By compiling a rich profile of the target, right down to her physical measurements, the store's marketers could then design and make clothes to fill her closet.[4]

Product Assortment and Procurement   The retailer's product assortment—*breadth* and *depth*—must match the target market's shopping expectations. Thus, a restaurant can offer a narrow and shallow assortment (small lunch counters), a narrow and deep assortment (delicatessen), a broad and shallow assortment (cafeteria), or a broad and deep assortment (large restaurant). Next, the retailer must develop a product-differentiation strategy. Some possibilities are to feature national brands not available at competing retailers (Saks uses this strategy); feature mostly private branded merchandise (GAP uses this strategy); feature the latest or newest merchandise first (Hot Topic does this[5]); feature surprise or ever-changing merchandise (like T.J. Maxx), offer customizing services (Harrod's of London uses this strategy); or offer a highly targeted assortment (Brookstone does this).

Some stores use **direct product profitability (DPP)** to measure a product's handling costs (receiving, moving to storage, paperwork, selecting, checking, loading, and space cost) from the time it reaches the warehouse until a customer buys it in the store. Resellers who have adopted DPP learn to their surprise that the gross margin on a product often has little relation to the direct product profit. Some high-volume products may have such high handling costs that they are less profitable and deserve less shelf space than some low-volume products.

Services and Store Atmosphere   The *services mix* is a key tool for differentiating a particular store. For example, a store may offer prepurchase services such as telephone and mail orders, advertising, window and interior display, fitting rooms, shopping hours, fashion shows, and trade-ins. Another option is to offer postpurchase services such as shipping and delivery, gift wrapping, adjustments and returns, alterations and tailoring, installations, and engraving. Finally, some stores emphasize ancillary services such as check cashing, parking, restaurants, repairs, interior decorating, credit, rest rooms, and baby-attendant service.

Atmosphere is another differentiation tool in the store's arsenal. Every store has a physical layout that makes it hard or easy to move around, as well as a "look." The store must embody a planned atmosphere that suits the target market and draws consumers toward purchase. The Kohl's department store chain uses a racetrack model to convey customers past all the merchandise in the store, along with a middle aisle for shoppers in a hurry. This loop yields much higher per-square-foot revenues than other retailers.[6]

Store Activities and Experiences   The growth of e-commerce has forced traditional brick-and-mortar retailers to respond. Now retailers also provide a shopping experience as a strong differentiator, in addition to natural advantages such as products that shoppers can actually see, touch, and test; real-life customer service; and no delivery lag time for many purchases.[7]

To entice Internet-savvy consumers to visit, store retailers are developing new services and promotions. The change in strategy can be noticed in practices as simple as calling each shopper a "guest" (as many stores are beginning to do) or as grandiose as building an indoor amusement park. For instance, retailers such as Bass Pro Shops are providing a place to congregate and in-store entertainment for customers who want fun and excitement.[8] See "Marketing Skills: Experience Marketing" for more on this vital skill.

Price Decision   Price is a key positioning factor and must be decided in relation to the target market, the mix of products and services, and the competition. All retailers would like to achieve both high volumes and high gross margins, but the two usually do not go together. Most retailers fall into the *high-markup, lower-volume group* (fine specialty stores) or the *low-markup, higher-volume group* (mass merchandisers and discount retailers).

Many retailers periodically put low prices on some items to serve as traffic builders or loss leaders, run occasional storewide sales, and plan markdowns on slower-moving merchandise. For example, shoe retailers expect to sell 50 percent of their shoes at the normal markup, 25 percent at a 40 percent markup, and the remaining 25 percent at cost. Still, some retailers have abandoned high-low "sales pricing" in

MARKETING SKILLS: EXPERIENCE MARKETING

Now that most national brands are available through multiple channels and shoppers perceive few real differences between retailers, experience marketing has emerged as a way for a store to set itself apart. Experts advise starting with a thorough understanding of what customers in the targeted segment value and expect. Think about how to build customer relationships by enhancing the store's atmosphere through a sensory experience (feel, look, sound, smell, or taste). Not only must the experience be unique, it must also be brand appropriate and memorable.

A very basic experience might be built around a particular sense; for example, the scent of fresh coffee or baked goods in a food store. The Starbucks store experience includes a rich coffee aroma (smell), soft jazz music (sound), comfortable seating (feel), and hip appointments (look). Ideally, the goal is to create a positive in-store experience that will be "entertaining, educational, aesthetic, and escapist all at once," says one marketer.

The REI retail chain is well known for applying experience marketing in selling outdoor gear and clothing products. Novices and experts alike can rely on salespeople in any of the 79 stores for informed advice about the most appropriate products and services for their needs. Then customers are invited to try before they buy: test climbing equipment on 25-foot walls, feel the protection of a Gore-Tex raincoat under a simulated rain shower, climb into a tent on the selling floor to see exactly how much room it has. From top to bottom, REI stores are a haven for consumers who love the outdoors, with exciting displays, huge product selection, special events, and even a division that sells adventure vacations and one-day sports outings. Thanks to its experience in experience marketing, REI sells nearly $900 million worth of goods and services every year.[9]

favor of everyday low pricing (see Chapter 12). Research shows that supermarket chains practicing everyday low pricing are often more profitable than those practicing high-low sales pricing, but only in certain circumstances.[10]

Communication Decision   Retailers can use a wide range of communication tools to generate traffic and purchases: advertising, special sales, money-saving coupons, frequent shopper rewards, in-store sampling, and in-store couponing. Each retailer must use communications that support and reinforce its image positioning. Fine stores place tasteful ads in high-fashion magazines and carefully train salespeople to greet customers, interpret their needs, and handle complaints. Off-price retailers promote the idea of bargains and large savings, while conserving on service and sales assistance.

Location Decision   Retailers say that the three keys to success are "location, location, and location." Stores have five major location choices, as shown in Table 14.3. Given the relationship between high traffic and high rents, retailers need to support location decisions with assessment methods such as traffic counts, surveys of shoppers' habits, and analysis of competitive locations.[11] Several software models for site location have also been formulated.[12] Retailers can assess a particular location's sales effectiveness by checking the number of people who pass by on an average day; the

TABLE 14.3   Location Options for Retailers

Location	Description
General business district	"Downtown," the oldest and most heavily trafficked city area; rents are normally high but a renaissance is bringing shoppers back to many cities.
Regional shopping center	Large suburban mall containing 40 to 200 stores and, generally, one or more anchor stores such as JCPenney; draws customers from 5–20 mile radius; offers generous parking, one-stop shopping and other facilities; the most successful malls charge high rents and may get a share of stores' sales.
Community shopping center	Smaller mall with one anchor store and 20 to 40 smaller stores.
Strip mall (shopping strip)	A cluster of stores, usually housed in one long building.
Location within a larger store or operation	Concession space rented by McDonald's and other retailers inside the unit of a larger retailer or an operation such as an airport.

percentage who enter the store; the percentage of those entering who buy; and the average amount spent per sale.

Trends in Retailing

Key developments that retailers and manufacturers should take into account in planning competitive strategies are:

- *New retail forms and combinations.* Bank branches are in supermarkets; gas stations include food stores; bookstores feature coffee shops; peddler's carts are in shopping malls, airports, and train stations. Retailers are also experimenting with limited-time-only stores called "pop-ups" that promote specific brands, reach seasonal shoppers for a few weeks in busy areas, and create buzz. To launch its Isaac Mizrahi clothing line, Target set up a temporary store at Rockefeller Center in Manhattan—selling only the Mizrahi line. The publicity prompted shoppers to visit the Target store in Queens, an outer borough of New York City.[13]

- *Growth of intertype competition.* Different types of retailers—discount stores, department stores, Web sites—all compete for the same consumers by carrying the same type of merchandise. The biggest winners are supercenters, dollar stores, warehouse clubs, and the Internet.[14]

- *Competition between store-based and non-store-based retailing.* Consumers now receive sales offers through direct-mail letters and catalogs, television, computers, and telephones. These non-store-based retailers are taking business away from store-based retailers. Major stores have developed their own Web sites, and some online retailers are finding it advantageous to own or manage physical outlets.

- *Growth of giant retailers.* Huge retail organizations have the information technology, logistical systems, and buying power to provide immense volumes of products at appealing prices to masses of consumers. They are crowding out small manufacturers who cannot deliver enough quantity and they often dictate to manufacturers what to make, how to price and promote, and other important decisions.

- *Decline of middle market retailers.* Growth seems to be centered at the top (with luxury offerings) or at the bottom (with discount pricing). Opportunities are scarcer in the middle where retailers such as Sears and JCPenney have struggled. Since 2000, fewer consumers have shopped in supermarkets, department stores, and drugstores every week as newer, more relevant places have come to serve their needs.[15]
- *Growing investment in technology.* Computers help retailers generate better forecasts, control inventory costs, order from suppliers electronically, communicate with outlets, and sell to customers. Technology is also raising productivity through checkout scanning systems, electronic funds transfer, and sophisticated merchandise-handling systems.
- *Global presence of major retailers.* Retailers with unique formats and strong brand positioning are increasingly expanding in other countries.[16] U.S. retailers such as Wal-Mart have gone global to boost profits, as have Italy's Benetton chain, France's Carrefour hypermarkets, and Sweden's IKEA chain.[17]

PRIVATE LABELS

A growing trend and major marketing decision for retailers concerns private labels. A **private label brand** (also called reseller, store, house, or distributor brand) is one retailers and wholesalers develop. Retailers such as Benetton, The Body Shop, and Marks and Spencer carry mostly own-brand merchandise. In Britain, the largest food chains, Sainsbury and Tesco, sell 50 and 45 percent store-label goods, respectively. In the United States, store brands now account for one of every five items sold, a $51.6 billion business last year, according to the Private Label Manufacturers' Association.

Some experts believe that 50 percent is the natural limit for carrying private brands, because consumers prefer certain national brands, and many product categories are not feasible or attractive on a private-brand basis. If that's the case, then Target has reached the "limit." An estimated 50 percent of Target's products are private brands, including the hugely popular housewares designed by Michael Graves and Todd Oldham.

House Brands

Why do intermediaries bother to sponsor their own brands? First, they are more profitable. Intermediaries search for manufacturers with excess capacity who will produce the private label at a low cost. Other costs, such as research and development, advertising, sales promotion, and physical distribution, are also much lower; thus, the private brander can charge less and make a higher profit margin. Second, retailers develop exclusive store brands to differentiate themselves from competitors.

In some cases, there has even been a return to "no branding" of certain staple consumer goods and pharmaceuticals. **Generics** are unbranded, plainly packaged, less expensive versions of common products such as spaghetti, paper towels, and canned peaches. They offer standard or lower quality at a price that may be as much as 20 percent to 40 percent lower than nationally advertised brands and 10 percent to 20 percent lower than retailer private label brands. The lower price of generics is made possible by lower-quality ingredients, lower-cost labeling and packaging, and minimal advertising.

The Private Label Threat

In the confrontation between manufacturers' and private brands, retailers have many advantages and increasing market power. Because shelf space is scarce, many super-markets now charge a *slotting fee* for accepting a new brand; often, retailers also charge for special display space and in-store advertising space. They typically display their own brands more prominently and make sure these are well stocked.

The growing power of store brands is not the only factor weakening national brands. Consumers are more price sensitive, trained in part by the continuous barrage of coupons and price specials; also, they note the better quality as competing manufac-turers and national retailers copy and duplicate the best brands' qualities. The fact that companies have reduced advertising to 30 percent of their total promotion budget has weakened their brand equity. The endless stream of brand extensions and line exten-sions has blurred brand identity and led to a confusing amount of product proliferation.

One way manufacturers have reacted to the private label threat is by spending heavily on consumer-directed advertising and promotion to maintain strong brand pref-erence. The prices have to be somewhat higher to cover the higher promotion cost. At the same time, mass distributors pressure manufacturers to increase trade allowances and deals if they want adequate shelf space. Once manufacturers do this, they have less to spend on advertising and consumer promotion, and their brand leadership spirals down. What national brands should do is invest in R&D, maintain high brand recogni-tion and preference, partner with major mass distributors to build economies of scale, and price their offerings in line with consumers' value perceptions.[18]

WHOLESALING

Wholesaling includes all of the activities involved in selling goods or services to those who buy for resale or business use. Wholesaling excludes manufacturers and farmers (because they are engaged primarily in production) and retailers. Wholesalers (also called *distributors*) differ from retailers in several ways. First, wholesalers pay less atten-tion to promotion, atmosphere, and location because they are dealing with business cus-tomers rather than final consumers. Second, wholesale transactions are usually larger than retail transactions, and wholesalers usually cover a larger trade area than retailers. Third, wholesalers and retailers comply with different legal regulations and taxes.

Why don't manufacturers sell directly to retailers or final consumers rather than through wholesalers? The main reason is efficiency: Wholesalers are often better at handling one or more of these functions:

- *Selling and promoting*. Wholesalers provide a sales force that helps manufacturers reach many small business customers at a relatively low cost.
- *Buying and assortment building*. Wholesalers can select items and build the assort-ments their customers need, saving customers considerable work.
- *Bulk breaking*. Wholesalers achieve savings for their customers through buying in large lots and breaking the bulk into smaller units.
- *Warehousing*. Wholesalers generally hold inventories, reducing the inventory costs and risks to suppliers and customers.
- *Transportation*. Wholesalers can often provide quicker delivery because they are closer to buyers.

- *Financing.* Many wholesalers finance customers by granting credit, and they finance suppliers by ordering early and paying bills on time.
- *Risk bearing.* Some wholesalers absorb part of the risk by taking title and bearing the cost of theft, damage, spoilage, and obsolescence.
- *Market information.* Wholesalers provide information to suppliers and customers regarding competitors' activities, new products, price developments, and so on.
- *Management services and counseling.* Wholesalers often help retailers train staff, plan store layouts and displays, and set up accounting and inventory-control systems. They may also help industrial customers with training and technical services.

The Growth and Types of Wholesaling

Wholesaling has grown in the United States in recent years.[19] A number of factors explain this: the growth of larger factories located some distance from the principal buyers; production in advance of orders rather than in response to specific orders; an increase in the number of levels of intermediate producers and users; and the increasing need for adapting products to the needs of intermediate and final users in terms of quantities, packages, and forms. The major types of wholesalers are described in Table 14.4.

TABLE 14.4   Major Wholesaler Types

Merchant Wholesalers: Independently owned businesses that take title to the merchandise they handle. They are full-service and limited-service jobbers, distributors, mill supply houses.

Full-service Wholesalers: Carry stock, maintain a sales force, offer credit, make deliveries, provide management assistance. Wholesale merchants sell primarily to retailers: Some carry several merchandise lines, some carry one or two lines, others carry only part of a line. Industrial distributors sell to manufacturers and also provide services like credit and delivery.

Limited-service Wholesalers: Cash-and-carry wholesalers sell a limited line of fast-moving goods to small retailers for cash. *Truck wholesalers* sell and deliver a limited line of semiperishable goods to supermarkets, grocery stores, hospitals, restaurants, and hotels. *Drop shippers* serve bulk industries such as coal, lumber, heavy equipment. They assume title and risk from the time an order is accepted to its delivery. *Rack jobbers* serve grocery retailers in nonfood items. Delivery people set up displays, price goods, and keep inventory records; they retain title to goods and bill retailers only for goods sold to end of year. *Producers' cooperatives* assemble farm produce to sell in local markets. *Mail-order wholesalers* send catalogs to retail, industrial, and institutional customers; orders are filled and sent by mail, rail, plane, or truck.

Brokers and agents: Facilitate buying and selling, on commission of 2 to 6 percent of the selling price; limited functions; generally specialize by product line or customer type. *Brokers* bring buyers and sellers together and assist in negotiation; paid by the party hiring them. Food brokers, real estate brokers, insurance brokers. *Agents* represent buyers or sellers on a more permanent basis. Most manufacturers' agents are small businesses with a few skilled salespeople: Selling agents have contractual authority to sell a manufacturer's entire output; purchasing agents make purchases for buyers and often receive, inspect, warehouse, and ship merchandise; commission merchants take physical possession of products and negotiate sales.

Manufacturers' and retailers' branches and offices: Wholesaling operations conducted by sellers or buyers themselves rather than through independent wholesalers. Separate branches and offices are dedicated to sales or purchasing. Many retailers set up purchasing offices in major market centers.

Specialized wholesalers: Agricultural assemblers buy the agricultural output of many farms, petroleum bulk plants and terminals consolidate the output of many wells, and auction companies auction cars, equipment, etc., to dealers and other businesses.

Wholesaler Marketing Decisions

Wholesaler-distributors have faced mounting pressures in recent years from new sources of competition, demanding customers, new technologies, and more direct-buying programs by large buyers. In response, the industry has been working to increase asset productivity by better managing inventories and receivables. Wholesalers have also had to revisit their strategic decisions on target markets, product assortment and services, price, promotion, and place.

Target Market   In defining their target markets, wholesalers can choose a target group of customers by size (only large retailers), type of customer (convenience stores only), need for service (customers needing credit), or other criteria. Within the target group, they can identify the most profitable customers and build relationships through value-added offers such as automatic replenishment systems or training. They can also discourage less-profitable customers by requiring larger orders or adding surcharges to smaller ones.

Product Assortment and Services   The wholesalers' "product" is their assortment. They are under great pressure to carry a full line and maintain sufficient stock for immediate delivery, yet the costs of carrying huge inventories can kill profits. This is why wholesalers are constantly reexamining how many lines to offer and carrying only the more profitable ones. They are also identifying services that help strengthen customer relationships and determining which should be dropped or charged for. The key is to find a distinct mix of services valued by customers.

Price Decision   Wholesalers usually mark up the cost of goods by a conventional percentage, say 20 percent, to cover expenses. Expenses may run 17 percent of the gross margin, leaving a profit margin of approximately 3 percent. In grocery wholesaling, the average profit margin is often less than 2 percent. Wholesalers are now experimenting with new pricing approaches: Some are trying to cut margin on selected lines in order to win important new customers; others are asking suppliers for a special price break that can be turned into an opportunity to increase the supplier's sales.

Promotion Decision   In general, wholesalers rely on their sales force to achieve promotional objectives. Yet most wholesalers see selling as a single salesperson talking to a single customer instead of a team effort to sell and service major accounts. Wholesalers would benefit from adopting some of the image-building techniques used by retailers. They need to develop an overall promotion strategy involving trade advertising, sales promotion, and publicity and make greater use of supplier promotion materials and programs.

Place Decision   Progressive wholesalers have been improving materials-handling procedures and costs by developing automated warehouses and improving their supply capabilities through advanced information systems. For example, W. W. Grainger, Inc. is one of the largest U.S. distributors of equipment, components, and supplies, offering more than 500,000 products through 582 sales offices, a catalog, call centers, and a comprehensive Web site. It maintains national, regional, and zone distribution centers for better product availability, faster order fulfillment, and convenient customer-delivery service.[20]

Trends in Wholesaling

Manufacturers always have the option of bypassing wholesalers or replacing inefficient wholesalers with better ones. Manufacturers complain that wholesalers do not aggressively promote their products; act more like order takers; carry insufficient inventory and, therefore, fail to fill customers' orders quickly; fail to supply up-to-date market, customer, and competitive information; fail to bring down their own costs; and charge too much. Savvy wholesalers have rallied to the challenge, adapting their services to meet their suppliers' and target customers' changing needs as a way of adding value to the channel. They have also reduced operating costs by investing in advanced materials-handling technology, information systems, and the Internet.

Interviewing leading industrial distributors, Narus and Anderson identified four ways that wholesalers can strengthen relationships with manufacturers: (1) seek a clear agreement with their manufacturers about their expected functions in the channel; (2) gain insight into manufacturers' requirements by visiting plants and attending conventions and trade shows; (3) fulfill commitments by meeting volume targets, paying promptly, and providing feedback of customer information to manufacturers; and (4) offer value-added services to help suppliers.[21]

Wholesaling still faces considerable challenges. The industry remains vulnerable to fierce resistance to price increases and the winnowing out of suppliers based on cost and quality. Also, the trend toward vertical integration, in which manufacturers try to control or own their intermediaries, is still strong.

MARKET LOGISTICS

Physical distribution starts at the factory, where managers choose warehouses and transportation carriers that will deliver products to final destinations in the desired time or at the lowest cost. Physical distribution has been expanded into the broader concept of **supply chain management (SCM)**. Supply chain management starts before physical distribution, covering procurement of inputs (raw materials, components, and equipment); conversion into finished products; and product movement to final destinations. An even broader perspective calls for studying the suppliers' suppliers. The supply chain perspective can help a company identify superior suppliers and distributors and help them improve productivity, which ultimately brings down the company's costs.

Market logistics means planning the infrastructure to meet demand, then implementing and controlling the physical flows of materials and final goods from points of origin to points of use to meet customer needs at a profit. Market logistics planning has four steps, as shown in Figure 14.1, which lead to examining the most efficient way to deliver value.

Integrated Logistics Systems

The market logistics task calls for **integrated logistics systems (ILS)**, involving materials management, material flow systems, and physical distribution, abetted by information technology. Third-party suppliers, such as FedEx Logistics Services or Ryder Integrated Logistics, often participate in designing or managing these systems.

FIGURE 14.1   Steps in Market Logistics Planning

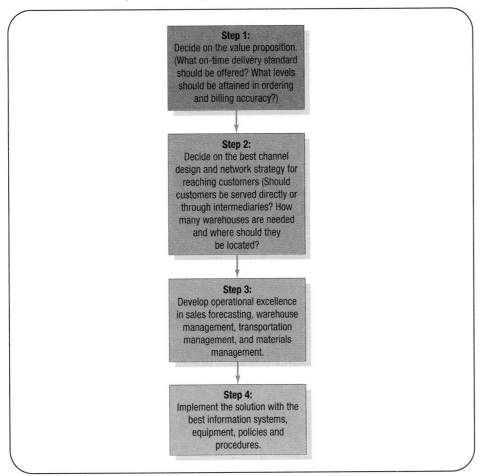

For example, Volvo, working with FedEx, set up a warehouse in Memphis with a complete stock of truck parts. A dealer who needs a part in an emergency calls a toll-free number; FedEx ships the part for same-day delivery to the airport, dealership, or repair site.

Market logistics link several activities, starting with sales forecasting, which helps the company schedule distribution, production, and inventory levels. In turn, production plans indicate the materials that the purchasing department must order. These materials arrive through inbound transportation, enter the receiving area, are stored in raw-material inventory, and later are converted into finished goods. Finished-goods inventory is the link between customer orders and manufacturing activity. Customers' orders draw down the finished-goods inventory level, and manufacturing activity builds it up. Finished goods flow off the assembly line and pass through packaging, in-plant warehousing, shipping-room processing, outbound transportation, field warehousing, and customer delivery and servicing.

Management has become concerned about the total cost of market logistics, which can amount to 30–40 percent of the product's cost. The grocery industry alone thinks it can decrease its annual operating costs by 10 percent, or $30 billion, by revamping market logistics. A typical box of breakfast cereal spends 104 days chugging through a labyrinth of intermediaries to reach the supermarket.[22] No wonder experts call market logistics "the last frontier for cost economies." Lower logistics costs permit lower prices, higher profit margins, or both. Although market logistics can be costly, a well-planned program can be a potent marketing tool, bringing in additional customers and boosting profits through better service, faster cycle time, or lower prices.

Market-Logistics Objectives

Many companies state their market-logistics objective as "getting the right goods to the right places at the right time for the least cost." Unfortunately, no market-logistics system can simultaneously maximize customer service and minimize distribution cost. Maximum customer service implies large inventories, premium transportation, and multiple warehouses, all of which raise market-logistics costs.

Given that market-logistics activities involve strong trade-offs, decisions must be made on a total system basis. The starting point is to study what customers require and what competitors offer. Customers are interested in on-time delivery, supplier willingness to meet emergency needs, careful handling of merchandise, and supplier willingness to take back defective goods and resupply them quickly.

The company must then research the relative importance of these service outputs. For example, service-repair time is very important to buyers of copying equipment. Xerox developed a service-delivery standard that "can put a disabled machine anywhere in the continental United States back into operation within 3 hours after receiving the service request." It then designed a service division of personnel, parts, and locations to deliver on this promise.

The company must also consider competitors' service standards, seeking to match or exceed those levels. Still, the objective is to maximize profits, not sales, which means looking at the costs of providing higher service levels. Some companies offer less service and charge a lower price; others offer more service and charge a premium price. In the end, the company must establish some service promise to the market. One appliance manufacturer set these service standards: to deliver at least 95 percent of the dealer's orders within 7 days of order receipt, to fill the dealer's orders with 99 percent accuracy, to answer dealer inquiries on order status within 3 hours, and to ensure that damage to merchandise in transit does not exceed 1 percent.

The company must design a system that will minimize the cost of achieving its logistical objectives. Each possible market-logistics system will lead to the following cost:

$$M = T + FW + VW + S$$

where

M = total market-logistics cost of proposed system;
T = total freight cost of proposed system;
FW = total fixed warehouse cost of proposed system;
VW = total variable warehouse costs (including inventory) of proposed system; and
S = total cost of lost sales due to average delivery delay under proposed system.

Choosing a market-logistics system calls for examining the total cost (M) associated with different systems and selecting the system that minimizes it. If S is hard to measure, the company should aim to minimize T + FW + VW for a target level of customer service.

Market-Logistics Decisions

Companies make four major decisions with regard to market logistics: How should orders be handled? Where should stocks be located? How much stock should be held? How should goods be shipped?

Order Processing Most companies want to shorten the *order-to-payment cycle*—the elapsed time between an order's receipt, delivery, and payment. This cycle involves many steps, including order transmission by the salesperson, order entry and customer credit check, inventory and production scheduling, order shipment, and receipt of payment. The longer this cycle, the lower the customer's satisfaction and the lower the company's profits.

Still, companies are making great progress. General Electric, for example, operates an information system that checks the customer's credit standing and determines whether and where the ordered items are in stock. The system then issues an order to ship, bills the customer, updates the inventory records, orders new stock, and notifies the sales representative that the order is on the way—in less than 15 seconds.

Warehousing Every manufacturer has to store finished goods until they are sold because production and consumption cycles rarely match. The storage function helps to smooth discrepancies between production and quantities desired by the market. Two warehousing options are *storage warehouses*, which hold goods for moderate-to-long periods, and *distribution warehouses*, which receive goods from company plants and suppliers and move them out as soon as possible. Having more stocking locations means that goods can be delivered to customers more quickly, but it also means higher warehousing costs, which is why many firms are reassessing their warehousing arrangements. When National Semiconductor closed six storage warehouses and set up a central distribution warehouse in Singapore, it cut its standard delivery time by 47 percent, cut distribution costs by 2.5 percent, and boosted sales by 34 percent.[23]

Automated warehouses are equipped with advanced materials-handling systems under the control of a central computer. The computer reads store orders, directs lift trucks and electric hoists to gather goods according to bar codes and move them to loading docks, and issues invoices. Automated warehouses save money by reducing worker injuries, labor costs, pilferage, and breakage while improving inventory control. For instance, when Helene Curtis replaced six older warehouses with a new $32 million facility, its distribution costs dropped by 40 percent.[24]

Inventory Inventory levels represent a major cost. Salespeople would like companies to carry enough stock to fill all customer orders immediately, but this is not cost-effective. *Inventory cost increases at an accelerating rate as the customer service level approaches 100 percent.* Management needs to know how much sales and profits would increase as a result of carrying larger inventories and promising faster order fulfillment times, and then make a decision.

Crafting an inventory strategy means knowing when to order and how much to order. As inventory draws down, management must know at what stock level to place a new order. This stock level is called the *order (reorder) point*. An order point of 20 means reordering when the stock falls to 20 units. The order point should balance the risks of stockout against the costs of overstock. The other decision is how much to order. The larger the quantity ordered, the less frequently an order has to be placed. Here, the company is balancing order-processing costs against inventory-carrying costs. *Order-processing costs* for a manufacturer consist of *setup costs* and *running costs* (operating costs when production is running). If setup costs are low, the manufacturer can produce the item often, and the average cost per item is stable and equal to the running costs. If setup costs are high, however, the manufacturer can cut the average cost per unit by producing a long run and carrying more inventory.

Order-processing costs must be compared with *inventory-carrying costs*. The larger the average stock carried, the higher the inventory-carrying costs, including storage charges, cost of capital, taxes and insurance, depreciation, and obsolescence. This means that marketing managers who want their companies to carry larger inventories must show that the larger inventories would produce incremental gross profit that exceeds the incremental carrying costs.

The optimal order quantity can be determined by analyzing the sum of order-processing costs and inventory-carrying costs at different order levels. As in Figure 14.2, the order-processing cost per unit decreases with the number of units ordered because the costs are spread over more units. Inventory-carrying charges per unit increase with the number of units ordered because each unit remains longer in inventory. The two cost curves are summed vertically into a total-cost curve. The lowest point on the total-cost curve is projected down on the horizontal axis to find the optimal order quantity, Q^*.[25]

Companies are reducing their inventory costs by treating inventory items differently. They are positioning inventory items according to risk and opportunity. They distinguish between bottleneck items (high risk, low opportunity), critical items (high risk, high opportunity), commodities (low risk, high opportunity), and nuisance items (low risk, low opportunity).[26] They are also keeping slow-moving items in a central location while carrying fast-moving items in warehouses closer to customers. The ultimate answer to carrying *near-zero inventory* is to build for order, not for stock.

FIGURE 14.2   Determining Optimal Order Quantity

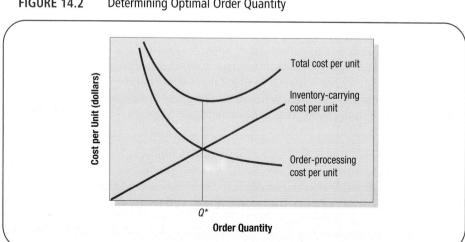

Transportation   Transportation choices affect product pricing, on-time delivery performance, and the condition of the goods on arrival, all of which influence customer satisfaction. In shipping goods to its warehouses, dealers, and customers, the company can choose among rail, air, truck, waterway, and pipeline, using such criteria as speed, frequency, dependability, capability, availability, traceability, and cost. For speed, air and truck are the prime contenders; for low cost, waterway and pipeline are appropriate.

Shippers are increasingly combining two or more transportation modes, thanks to containerization. **Containerization** consists of putting the goods in boxes or trailers that are easy to transfer between two transportation modes. *Piggyback* describes the use of rail and trucks; *fishyback*, water and trucks; *trainship*, water and rail; and *airtruck*, air and trucks. Each coordinated mode offers specific advantages. For example, piggyback is cheaper than trucking alone, yet provides flexibility and convenience.

In deciding on transportation modes, shippers have three broad choices. If the shipper owns its own truck or air fleet, the shipper becomes a *private carrier*. A *contract carrier* is an independent organization that sells transportation services to others on a contract basis. A *common carrier* provides services between predetermined points on a schedule and is available to all shippers at standard rates.

Market Logistics Lessons

Companies have learned several major lessons in handling market logistics. First, they need a senior vice president as the single point of contact for all logistical elements and for accountability for both cost and customer satisfaction. Second, this executive should meet frequently with sales and operations people to review inventory, costs, and service and satisfaction issues and achievements, as well as to discuss any needed changes. Third, software and systems are increasingly critical for competitively superior logistics performance. In the end, market-logistics strategies must be derived from business strategies, rather than solely from cost considerations.

EXECUTIVE SUMMARY

Retailing includes all of the activities involved in selling goods or services directly to final consumers for personal, nonbusiness use. Retailers include store retailing, nonstore retailing, and retail organizations. Like products, retail-store types pass through stages of growth and decline. Major types of retail stores are specialty stores, department stores, supermarkets, convenience stores, discount stores, off-price retailers, superstores, and catalog showrooms. Although most goods and services are sold through stores, nonstore retailing has been growing. The major types of nonstore retailing are direct selling, direct marketing, automatic vending, and buying services. An increasing number of retailers are part of corporate retailing and achieve economies of scale such as greater purchasing power, wider brand recognition, and better-trained employees. Retailers must consider major trends when making decisions about target markets, product assortment and procurement, services and store atmosphere, price, promotion, and location.

Wholesaling includes all of the activities involved in selling goods or services to those who buy for resale or business use. Wholesalers can perform certain functions better and more cost effectively than the manufacturer can, such as selling and promoting, buying and assortment building, bulk breaking, warehousing, transportation, financing, risk bearing, dissemination of market information, and training and consulting. Types of wholesalers include merchant wholesalers; full-service and limited-service wholesalers; brokers; agents; manufacturers' and retailers' sales branches, sales offices, and purchasing offices; and miscellaneous wholesalers such as agricultural assemblers. The most successful wholesalers adapt their services to meet suppliers' and target customers' needs, adding value to the channel. Like retailers, wholesalers must decide on target markets, product assortment and services, price, promotion, and place.

Producers of physical products and services must decide on market logistics—the best way to store and move offerings to market destinations—to coordinate the activities of suppliers, purchasing agents, manufacturers, marketers, channel members, and customers. Major gains in logistical efficiency have come from advances in information technology.

NOTES

1. Steve Powers, "Retail: Tricks of the Trader," *Business 2.0*, September 2005, p. 36; Amy Wu, "A Specialty Food Store with a Discount Attitude," *New York Times*, July 27, 2003, pp. 3–4.
2. William R. Davidson, Albert D. Bates, and Stephen J. Bass, "Retail Life Cycle," *Harvard Business Review* (November–December 1976): 89–96.
3. Stanley C. Hollander, "The Wheel of Retailing," *Journal of Marketing* (July 1960): 37–42.
4. Amy Merrick, "How Gingham and Polyester Rescued a Retailer," *Wall Street Journal*, May 9, 2003, pp. A1, A6.
5. Kimberly L. Allers, "Retail's Rebel Yell," *Fortune*, November 10, 2003, pp. 137–142.
6. Cametta Coleman, "Kohl's Retail Racetrack," *Wall Street Journal*, March 1, 2000, pp. B1+.
7. Kenneth T. Rosen and Amanda L. Howard, "E-tail: Gold Rush or Fool's Gold?" *California Management Review* (April 1, 2000): 72–100; Moira Cotlier, "Census Releases First E-commerce Report," *Catalog Age*, May 1, 2001; Associated Press, "Online Sales Boomed at End of 2000," *Star-Tribune of Twin Cities*, February 17, 2001; "Reinventing the Store," *The Economist*, November 22, 2003, pp. 65–68.
8. For more discussion, see Philip Kotler, "Atmospherics as a Marketing Tool," *Journal of Retailing* (Winter 1973–1974): 48–64; Mary Jo Bitner, "Servicescapes: The Impact of Physical Surroundings on Customers and Employees," *Journal of Marketing* (April 1992): 57–71. Also see B. Joseph Pine II and James H. Gilmore, *The Experience Economy* (Boston: Harvard Business School Press, 1999).
9. Bethany Clough, "REI Considers Fresno, Calif., for New Store," *Fresno Bee*, August 23, 2005 (www.fresnobee.com); Stephane Fitch, "Uphill Battle," *Forbes*, April 25, 2005, p. 62; Tim Palmer, "Sensing a Winner," *Grocer*, January 26, 2002, pp. 40+; "Go Live with a Big Brand Experience," *Marketing*, October 26, 2000, pp. 45+.
10. Frank Feather, *The Future Consumer* (Toronto: Warwick Publishing, 1994), p. 171. Also see Stephen J. Hoch, Xavier Dreze, and Mary E. Purk, "EDLP, Hi-Lo, and Margin Arithmetic," *Journal of Marketing* (October 1994): 1–15; David R. Bell and James M. Lattin, "Shopping Behavior and Consumer Preference for Retail Price Format," *Marketing Science* 17 (Spring 1998): 66–68.
11. R. L. Davies and D. S. Rogers, eds., *Store Location and Store Assessment Research* (New York: John Wiley, 1984).
12. See Sara L. McLafferty, *Location Strategies for Retail and Service Firms* (Lexington, MA: Lexington Books, 1987).

13. Theresa Howard, "Retail Stores Pop Up for Limited Time Only," *USA Today*, May 28, 2004, p. 1B.
14. Wendy Liebmann, "Consumers Push Back," *Brandweek*, February 23, 2004, pp. 19–20.
15. Ibid.
16. For further discussion of retail trends, see Anne T. Coughlan, Erin Anderson, Louis W. Stern, and Adel I. El-Ansary, *Marketing Channels*, 6th ed. (Upper Saddle River, NJ: Prentice Hall, 2001).
17. Shelley Donald Coolidge, "Facing Saturated Home Markets, Retailers Look to Rest of World," *Christian Science Monitor*, February 14, 1994, p. 7; Carla Rapoport with Justin Martin, "Retailers Go Global," *Fortune*, February 20, 1995, pp. 102–108; Amy Feldman, "Wal-Mart: How Big Can It Get?" *Money*, December 1999, pp. 158–164; Kerry Capell and Heidi Dawley, "Wal-Mart's Not-So-Secret British Weapon," *BusinessWeek*, January 24, 2000, p. 132.
18. James A. Narus and James C. Anderson, "Contributing as a Distributor to Partnerships with Manufacturers, " *Business Horizons* (September–October 1987). Also see James D. Hlavecek and Tommy J. McCuistion, "Industrial Distributors—When, Who, and How," *Harvard Business Review* (March–April 1983): 96–101.
19. Bert McCammon, Robert F. Lusch, Deborah S. Coykendall, and James M. Kenderdine, *Wholesaling in Transition* (Norman: University of Oklahoma, College of Business Administration, 1989).
20. Kate Maddox, Sean Callahan, and Carol Krol, "Top Trends," *B to B*, June 13, 2005, pp. 22+; "Annual Meetings: Grainger Out to Build Distribution Efficiency," *Crain's Chicago Business*, May 6, 2002, p. 12.
21. Narus and Anderson, "Contributing as a Distributor to Partnerships with Manufacturers." Also see Hlavecek and McCuistion, "Industrial Distributors—When, Who, and How."
22. Ronald Henkoff, "Delivering the Goods," *Fortune*, November 28, 1994, pp. 64–78.
23. Ibid.
24. Rita Koselka, "Distribution Revolution," *Forbes*, May 25, 1992, pp. 54–62.
25. The optimal order quantity is given by the formula $Q^* = 2DS/IC$, where D = annual demand, S = cost to place one order, and I = annual carrying cost per unit. Known as the economic-order quantity formula, it assumes a constant ordering cost, a constant cost of carrying an additional unit in inventory, a known demand, and no quantity discounts. For more, see Richard J. Tersine, *Principles of Inventory and Materials Management*, 4th ed. (Upper Saddle River, NJ: Prentice Hall, 1994).
26. William C. Copacino, *Supply Chain Management* (Boca Raton, FL: St. Lucie Press, 1997), pp. 122–123.

CHAPTER 15

Designing and Managing Integrated Marketing Communications

In this chapter, we will address the following questions:

1. What is the role of marketing communications?
2. What are the major steps in developing effective communications?
3. What is the communications mix, and how should it be set?
4. What is an integrated marketing communications program?

MARKETING MANAGEMENT AT BMW

Although television advertising is a staple of most car introductions, it was not part of the plan BMW used to bring its new Mini Cooper car to the United States. The original Mini was sold for only seven years in the U.S. market, during the 1960s, before it was withdrawn due to stiff emission regulations. When BMW launched the new Mini, it targeted hip city dwellers in their 20s who wanted a cool, fun, small car for under $20,000. With only $20 million to spend on the introduction, the Mini's marketers planned a guerrilla communications campaign featuring nontraditional uses of billboards, posters, print ads, and grassroots efforts. No television.

To attract attention, the Mini was stacked on top of three Ford Excursion SUVs and driven around national auto shows and 21 major cities. The car showed up in other unusual places such as inside a sports stadium as seats and inside Playboy as a centerfold. Text-only billboards proclaimed: "THE SUV BACKLASH OFFICIALLY STARTS NOW" and "XXL-XL-L-M-S-MINI." Many communications were linked to a cleverly designed Web site that featured product details and a rotating series of online ads, such as the tongue-in-cheek notice warning of the dangers of "counterfeit." Now U.S. sales of Minis have accelerated past 36,000 per year—and BMW's strategy to double that number within five years will be fueled by innovative communications. "You can't just push things into enough eyeballs anymore," says an official at the firm's ad agency. "It has to be so much fun that it's worth their time" and teaches something about the product at the same time.[1]

Modern marketing calls for more than developing a good product, pricing it attractively, and making it accessible. Companies must also communicate with present and potential stakeholders and the general public. The question is not whether to communicate but rather what to say, how to say it, to whom, and how often—difficult decisions as more companies clamor for the consumer's increasingly divided attention. This chapter describes how communications work and what they can do for a company. It also addresses how holistic marketers combine and integrate marketing communications. Chapter 16 examines mass forms of communications (advertising, sales promotion, events and experiences, and public relations); Chapter 17 examines personal forms of communications (direct marketing, including e-commerce, and personal selling).

THE ROLE OF MARKETING COMMUNICATIONS

Marketing communications are the means by which firms attempt to inform, persuade, and remind consumers—directly or indirectly—about the products and brands that they sell. Marketing communications represent the "voice" of the brand and are one way to establish a dialogue and build relationships with consumers.

Marketing communications tell or show consumers how and why a product is used, by what kind of person, and where and when; explain what the company and brand stand for; and offer an incentive for trial or usage. For companies, marketing communications are a way to link brands to other people, places, events, brands, experiences, feelings, and things. As Figure 15.1 shows, communications contribute to brand equity by creating brand awareness, crafting a brand image, eliciting brand responses, and/or facilitating a stronger consumer-brand connection.

Marketing Communications and Brand Equity

Although advertising is often a central element of a marketing communications program, it is usually not the only one—or even the most important one—in terms of building brand equity. The **marketing communications mix** consists of six major modes of communication (see Table 15.1):[2]

1. *Advertising*. Any paid form of nonpersonal presentation and promotion of ideas, goods, or services by an identified sponsor.
2. *Sales promotion*. Short-term incentives to encourage trial or purchase of a product or service.
3. *Events and experiences*. Company-sponsored activities and programs designed to create brand-related interactions.
4. *Public relations and publicity*. Programs promoting or protecting company or product image.

FIGURE 15.1   Integrating Marketing Communications to Build Brand Equity

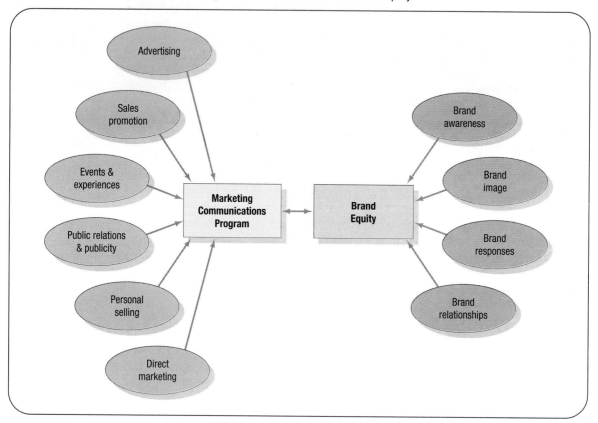

5. *Direct marketing.* Use of mail, telephone, fax, e-mail, or Internet to communicate directly with or solicit response or dialogue from specific customers and prospects.

6. *Personal selling.* Face-to-face interaction with prospective purchasers for the purpose of making presentations, answering questions, and procuring orders.

Company communication actually goes beyond these specific platforms. The product's styling and price, the shape and color of the package, the salesperson's manner and dress, the store or dealership decor, and the company's stationery all communicate something to buyers. Every *brand contact* delivers an impression that can strengthen or weaken a customer's view of the company. From the perspective of building brand equity, marketers should evaluate *all* the different possible communication options according to effectiveness criteria (how well does it work) as well as efficiency considerations (how much does it cost).

Communications Process Models

Marketers should understand the fundamental elements of effective communications. Two models are useful: a macromodel and a micromodel.

Macromodel of the Communications Process   Figure 15.2 shows a communications macromodel with nine elements. Two represent the major parties in a communication—*sender* and *receiver*. Two represent the major communication tools—*message* and

TABLE 15.1   Common Communication Platforms

Advertising	Sales Promotion	Events/ Experiences	Public Relations	Personal Selling	Direct Marketing
Print and broadcast ads	Contests, games, sweepstakes, lotteries	Sports	Press kits	Sales presentations	Catalogs
Packaging—outer		Entertainment	Speeches	Sales meetings	Mailings
Packaging—inserts	Premiums and gifts	Festivals	Seminars	Incentive programs	Telemarketing
Motion pictures	Sampling	Arts	Annual reports	Samples	Electronic shopping
Brochures and booklets	Fairs and trade shows	Causes	Charitable donations	Fairs and trade shows	TV shopping
Posters and leaflets	Exhibits	Factory tours	Publications		Fax mail
Directories	Demonstrations	Company museums	Community relations		E-mail
Reprints of ads	Coupons	Street activities	Lobbying		Voice mail
Billboards	Rebates		Identity media		
Display signs	Low-interest financing		Company magazine		
Point-of-purchase displays	Entertainment				
Audiovisual material	Trade-in allowances				
Symbols and logos	Continuity programs				
Videotapes	Tie-ins				

media. Four represent major communication functions—*encoding, decoding, response,* and *feedback.* The last element in the system is *noise* (random and competing messages that may interfere with the intended communication).[3]

Micromodel of Consumer Responses   Micromodels of marketing communications concentrate on consumers' specific responses to communications. Figure 15.3 summarizes four classic *response hierarchy models.*

FIGURE 15.2   Elements in the Communications Process

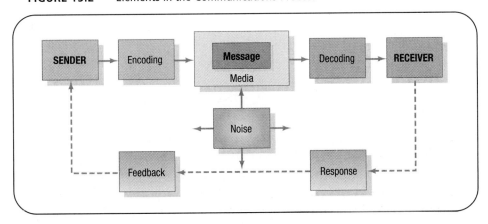

FIGURE 15.3 Response Hierarchy Models

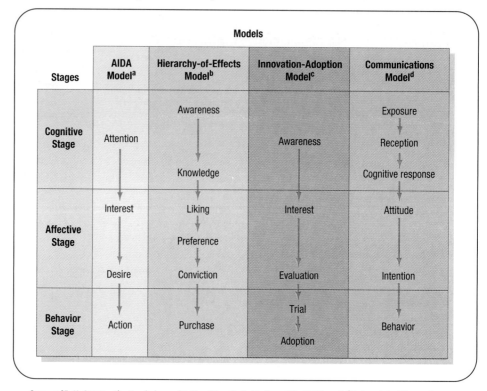

Sources: [a]E. K. Strong. *The Psychology of Selling* (New York: McGraw-Hill, 1925), p. 9; [b]Robert J. Lavidge and Gary A. Steiner, "A Model for Predictive Measurements of Advertising Effectiveness," *Journal of Marketing* (October 1961): 61; [c]Everett M. Rogers, *Diffusion of Innovation* (New York: The Free Press, 1962), pp. 79–86; [d]various sources.

All the models in Figure 15.3 assume that the buyer passes through a cognitive, affective, and behavioral stage, in that order. This "learn-feel-do" sequence is appropriate when the audience has high involvement with a product category perceived to have high differentiation, as in purchasing an automobile. An alternative sequence, "do-feel-learn," is relevant when the audience has high involvement but perceives little or no differentiation within the product category, as in purchasing an airline ticket. A third sequence, "learn-do-feel," is relevant when the audience has low involvement and perceives little differentiation within the product category, as in purchasing salt or batteries. By choosing the right sequence, the marketer can do a better job of planning communications.[4]

DEVELOPING EFFECTIVE COMMUNICATIONS

To develop effective communications requires eight steps. The first five steps are (1) identifying the target audience, (2) determining the objectives, (3) designing the communications, (4) selecting the channels, and (5) establishing the budget. The final three steps will be examined later in this chapter: (6) decide on the media mix, (7) measure the results, and (8) manage integrated marketing communications.

Identify the Target Audience

The first step is to identify a clear target audience: potential buyers of the company's products, current users, deciders, or influencers; individuals, groups, particular publics, or the general public. The target audience is a critical influence on decisions about what to say, how to say it, when to say it, where to say it, and to whom to say it.

A major part of audience analysis is assessing the audience's current image of the company, its products, and its competitors. **Image** is the set of beliefs, ideas, and impressions that a person holds regarding an object. People's attitudes and actions toward an object such as a product or service are highly conditioned by that object's image. In assessing image, marketers research the audience's familiarity with the product, then they ask respondents who know the product how they feel about it. If most respondents have unfavorable feelings toward the product, the organization needs to overcome a negative image problem, which requires great patience because images persist long after the organization has changed. Once people have a certain image, they perceive what is consistent with that image. It will take highly disconfirming information to raise doubts and open their minds—but it can be done.

Determine the Communications Objectives

Rossiter and Percy identify four possible objectives for marketing communications, as follows:[5]

1. *Category need.* Establishing a product or service category as necessary to remove or satisfy a perceived discrepancy between a current motivational state and a desired emotional state.

2. *Brand awareness.* Ability to recognize or recall the brand within the category in sufficient detail to make a purchase. Recognition is easier to achieve than recall, but recall is important outside the store, whereas brand recognition is important inside the store. Brand awareness provides a foundation for brand equity.

3. *Brand attitude.* Evaluation of the brand's perceived ability to meet a currently relevant need. Relevant brand needs may be negatively oriented (problem removal, problem avoidance, incomplete satisfaction, normal depletion) or positively oriented (sensory gratification, intellectual stimulation, or social approval).

4. *Brand purchase intention.* Self-instructions to purchase the brand or to take purchase-related action.

The most effective communications often can achieve multiple objectives.

Design the Communications

Defining the communications to achieve the response will require solving three problems: what to say (message strategy), how to say it (creative strategy), and who should say it (message source).

Message Strategy   In determining message strategy, management searches for appeals, themes, or ideas that tie into the brand positioning and help establish points-of-parity or points-of-difference. Some of these may relate directly to product or service performance (the quality, economy, or value of the brand), whereas others may relate to more extrinsic considerations (the brand as being contemporary, popular, or traditional). It is widely believed that industrial buyers are most responsive to performance messages. They are knowledgeable about the product, trained to recognize value, and accountable to others for their choices. Consumers, when they buy certain big-ticket items, also tend to gather information and estimate benefits.

Creative Strategy   *Creative strategies*, how marketers translate their messages into a specific communication, can be classified as either informational appeal or transformational appeal.[6] An *informational appeal* elaborates on attributes or benefits. Examples in advertising are problem-solution ads (Excedrin stops headache pain quickly), product demonstration ads (Thompson Water Seal can withstand intense rain, snow, and heat), product comparison ads (Verizon offers better Internet access than Comcast), and testimonials from unknown or celebrity endorsers (basketball star LeBron James pitching Coca-Cola and Nike). Such appeals assume the consumer is processing the communication very rationally.

The best ads with informational appeals ask questions and allow consumers to form their own conclusions.[7] If Honda had hammered away that the Element was for young people, this strong definition might have blocked older age groups from buying it. Some stimulus ambiguity can lead to a broader market definition and more spontaneous purchases. A one-sided presentation praising a product might seem to be more effective than two-sided arguments that also mention shortcomings. Yet two-sided messages may be more appropriate, especially when some negative association must be overcome. In this spirit, Heinz ran the message "Heinz ketchup is slow good."[8] Two-sided messages are more effective with more educated audiences and those who are initially opposed.[9]

The order in which arguments are presented is also important.[10] In a one-sided message, presenting the strongest argument first establishes audience attention and interest. This is important in newspapers and other media where the audience often does not attend to the whole message. With a captive audience, however, a climactic presentation might be more effective. In a two-sided message, if the audience is initially opposed, the communicator might start with the other side's argument and conclude with the strongest argument in favor of the product.[11]

A *transformational appeal* elaborates on a non-product-related benefit or image. It might depict what kind of person uses a brand (as when VW advertised to active, youthful people with its "Drivers Wanted" campaign) or what kind of experience results from using the brand (Coast soap has been advertised as "The Eye Opener!"). Transformational appeals often attempt to stir up emotions that will motivate purchase. Many communicators use negative appeals such as fear, guilt, and shame to prompt action (get people to brush their teeth or stop smoking). Also, communicators can use positive emotional appeals such as humor, love, pride, and joy, sometimes employing "borrowed interest" devices such as frisky puppies or sex appeal to attract interest and raise involvement in the ad. The challenge here is to avoid detracting from comprehension and overshadowing the product.[12]

Message Source   Messages delivered by attractive or popular sources can potentially achieve higher attention and recall, which is why advertisers often use celebrities as spokespeople. Celebrities are likely to be effective when they personify a key product attribute, as Catherine Deneuve's beauty did for Chanel No. 5 perfume. Three factors underlying source credibility are expertise, trustworthiness, and likability.[13] *Expertise* is the specialized knowledge the communicator possesses to back the claim. *Trustworthiness* is related to how objective and honest the source is perceived to be.

Friends are trusted more than strangers or salespeople, and people who are not paid to endorse a product are seen as more trustworthy than people who are paid.[14] *Likability* describes the source's attractiveness; qualities like candor, humor, and naturalness make a source more likable. The most credible source would score high on all three factors.

Multinational companies wrestle with several challenges in developing message content for global campaigns. First, they must decide whether the product is appropriate for a country. Second, they must make sure the targeted market segment is both legal and customary. Third, they must decide if the style of the ad is acceptable. Fourth, they must decide whether ads should be created at headquarters or locally.[15]

Select the Communications Channels

Selecting efficient channels to carry the message becomes more difficult as channels of communication become more fragmented and cluttered. For example, pharmaceutical salespeople can rarely wrest more than five minutes' time from a busy physician. Because personal selling is expensive, the industry has added multiple communications channels, including ads in medical journals, direct mail, sampling, telemarketing, Web sites, and conferences.[16]

There are two kinds of communication channels: personal and nonpersonal.

Personal Communications Channels   **Personal communications channels** involve two or more persons communicating directly face-to-face, person-to-audience, over the telephone, or through e-mail. Instant messaging and independent sites to collect consumer reviews are another means of growing importance in recent years. These channels derive their effectiveness through individualized presentation and feedback. Kiehl's, which makes skin-care products, does not advertise or create exciting packaging; instead, it gives away free samples to anyone entering its stores, encouraging widespread word-of-mouth and positive publicity.[17] In many cases, world of mouth ("buzz") is managed.[18]

Companies can stimulate personal influence channels to work on their behalf in several ways:

- *Identify influential individuals and companies and devote extra effort to them.* In technology, influencers might include some large corporations, industry analysts, journalists, policy makers, and early adopters.[19]
- *Create opinion leaders by supplying certain people with the product on attractive terms.* Pepsi liberally sampled its Mountain Dew Code Red and encouraged the core 13- to 19-year-old target audience to stumble on the new flavor in such places as vending machines at malls. As one executive noted, "We allowed these teen influencers to be advocates for the brand."[20]
- *Work through community influentials such as local disk jockeys, class presidents, and presidents of women's organizations.* When Ford introduced the Focus, it gave cars to DJs and trendy people so they would be seen around town in them. Ford also identified 100 influential young consumers in five states and gave them cars to drive around.[21]
- *Use influential or believable people in testimonial advertising.* Accenture, American Express, Nike, and Buick use golf megastar Tiger Woods as an endorser to talk up their respective companies and products.

- *Develop advertising that has high "conversation value."* Incorporate buzz-worthy features into product design. Some ad slogans become part of the cultural vernacular, such as "Whassup?!" for Budweiser.

- *Develop word-of-mouth referral channels to build business.* Professionals often encourage clients to recommend their services. Weight Watchers found that word-of-mouth referrals from people in the program had a huge impact on its business.[22]

- *Establish an electronic forum.* Toyota owners who use an online service such as America Online can hold online discussions to share experiences.

- *Use viral marketing.* Internet marketers can use **viral marketing,** a form of word of mouth (or word of mouse) to draw attention to their sites.[23] Viral marketing involves passing on company-developed products, services, or information from user to user.

Marketers must be careful in reaching out to consumers. Consumers also can resent personal communications if unsolicited: One survey found that roughly 80 percent of the sample of consumers was very annoyed by pop-up ads, spam, and telemarketing.[24] This is why the skill of *permission marketing* is especially important today (see "Marketing Skills: Permission Marketing").

MARKETING SKILLS: PERMISSION MARKETING

Permission marketing has become popular because it is extremely targeted, can be used to build relationships, and is cost-effective. How do marketers develop this skill? According to Seth Godin, the first step is to calculate a customer's worth over the duration of a typical relationship. This determines what the company can afford to spend on acquiring a new customer. Then the marketer creates a series of communications to engage customers in a dialogue. Each message must educate the customer about the value of the company's offers, be customizable as the company learns more about the customer, and provide an incentive (such as more information or a discount) for the customer to respond and continue the relationship. Always ask for a response so results can be measured and to determine which customers should be dropped from the program because they're not interested.

As the interchange continues, the marketer may change or add incentives (customized where appropriate) to encourage the customer to keep granting permission. Over time, the marketer gains the customer's trust and can ask for permission to send additional offers. In this way, the marketer builds a valuable, profitable core of customers who respond at ever-higher levels of permission marketing.

For instance, Cleveland's WXTM and WNCX radio stations are using permission marketing to maintain a dialogue with listeners through e-mail newsletters. The sister stations reach distinctly different audiences (WXTM plays alternative rock and WNCX plays classic rock). Listeners are invited to visit each station's Web site and sign up to receive news about upcoming concerts, music promotions, and more. On WXTM, subscribers become a Radio XPhile and have access to additional content and personalized offers. "It really is a win–win situation for everyone," explains the stations' promotions director. Not only do listeners get the latest information about upcoming contests and promotions, "it helps our advertisers because we can offer special discounts for events."[25]

Nonpersonal Communications Channels   Nonpersonal channels are communications directed to more than one person and include media, sales promotions, events, and publicity.

- *Media* consist of print media (newspapers, magazines); broadcast media (radio, television); network media (telephone, cable, satellite, wireless); electronic media (audiotape, videotape, videodisk, CD-ROM, Web page); and display media (billboards, signs, posters). Most nonpersonal messages come through paid media.

- *Sales promotions* consist of consumer promotions (such as samples, coupons, and premiums); trade promotion (such as advertising and display allowances); and business and sales-force promotion (contests for sales reps).

- *Events and experiences* include sports, arts, entertainment, and cause events as well as less formal activities that create novel brand interactions with consumers.

- *Public relations* include communications directed internally to employees of the company or externally to consumers, other firms, the government, and media.

Much of the recent growth of nonpersonal channels has been with events and experiences. A company can build its brand image through creating or sponsoring events. Events marketers who once favored sports events are now using other venues such as museums and zoos to entertain clients and employees. IBM sponsors symphony performances and art exhibits, Visa is a sponsor of the Olympics, and Harley-Davidson sponsors annual motorcycle rallies.

Integration of Communications Channels   Although personal communication is often more effective than mass communication, mass media might be the major means of stimulating personal communication. Mass communications affect personal attitudes and behavior through a two-step process. Ideas often flow from media sources to opinion leaders and from these to the less media-involved population groups. This two-step flow has several implications. First, the influence of mass media on public opinion is mediated by opinion leaders, people whose opinions are sought or who carry their opinions to others. Second, the two-step flow shows that people interact primarily within their own social groups and acquire ideas from their group's opinion leaders. Third, two-step communication suggests that mass communicators should direct messages specifically to opinion leaders and let them carry the message to others.

Establish the Total Marketing Communications Budget

Industries and companies vary considerably in how much they spend on promotion. Expenditures might amount to 30–50 percent of sales in the cosmetics industry but only 5–10 percent in the industrial-equipment industry, with company-to-company variations. Four common methods for deciding on a budget include:

- *Affordable method.* Many companies set the promotion budget at what management thinks the firm can afford. However, this method ignores the role of promotion as an investment and the immediate impact of promotion on sales volume; it also leads to an uncertain annual budget, making long-range planning difficult.

- *Percentage-of-sales method.* Many firms set promotion expenditures at a specified percentage of sales (either current or anticipated) or of the sales price. Supporters say this method links promotion expenditures to the movement of corporate sales over the business cycle; focuses attention on the interrelationship of promotion cost, selling price, and unit profit; and encourages stability when competing firms spend approximately the same percentage. On the other hand, this method views sales as the determiner of promotion rather than as the result; it provides no logical basis for choosing the specific percentage; nor does it allow for determining the promotion budget each product and territory deserves.

- *Competitive-parity method.* Some companies set their promotion budget to achieve share-of-voice parity with competitors. Although proponents say that competitors' expenditures represent the collective wisdom of the industry and that maintaining competitive parity prevents promotion wars, neither argument is valid. Company reputations, resources, opportunities, and objectives differ so much that promotion budgets are hardly a guide. Furthermore, there is no evidence that competitive parity discourages promotional wars.

- *Objective-and-task method.* Here, marketers develop promotion budgets by defining specific objectives, determining the tasks that must be performed to achieve these objectives, and estimating the costs of performing these tasks. The sum of these costs is the proposed promotion budget. This method has the advantage of requiring management to spell out assumptions about the relationship among dollars spent, exposure levels, trial rates, and regular usage.

DECIDING ON THE MARKETING COMMUNICATIONS MIX

Companies must allocate the marketing communications budget over the six major modes of communication—advertising, sales promotion, public relations and publicity, events and experiences, sales force, and direct marketing. Within the same industry, companies can differ considerably in their media and channel choices. Avon concentrates its promotional funds on personal selling, whereas Revlon spends heavily on advertising.

Characteristics of the Marketing Communications Mix

Each communication tool has its own unique characteristics and costs.

- *Advertising.* Advertising can be used to forge a long-term image for a product (Coca-Cola ads) or trigger quick sales (a Sears ad for a weekend sale). It offers opportunities for amplified expressiveness and is also pervasive, able to reach geographically dispersed buyers efficiently. Certain forms of advertising, such as TV advertising, require a large budget; other forms, such as newspaper advertising, do not.

- *Sales promotion.* Sales-promotion tools—coupons, contests, premiums, and the like—offer three key benefits: (1) communication (gaining attention that may lead the consumer to the product); (2) incentive (offering a concession or an inducement that gives value to the consumer); and (3) invitation (including a distinct invitation to engage in the transaction now). Sales promotion can be used for short-run effects such as dramatizing product offers and boosting sales.

- *Public relations and publicity.* The appeal of public relations and publicity is based on three qualities: (1) high credibility (news stories and features are more authentic and credible than ads); (2) ability to catch buyers off guard (reaching prospects who prefer to avoid salespeople and advertisements); and (3) dramatization (the potential for dramatizing a company or product).

- *Events and experiences.* A well-chosen event or experience seen as highly relevant can get the consumer personally involved. Because events and experiences are live, consumers find them more actively engaging. Also, events are more of an indirect "soft sell."

- *Direct marketing.* All forms of direct marketing—direct mail, telemarketing, Internet marketing—share three characteristics: They are (1) customized (to appeal to the addressed individual); (2) up-to-date (can be prepared very quickly); and (3) interactive (can be changed depending on the person's response).

- *Personal selling.* Personal selling is the most effective tool at later stages of the buying process, particularly in building up buyer preference, conviction, and action. Qualities of personal selling are (1) personal interaction (an immediate and interactive relationship between two or more persons); (2) cultivation (all kinds of relationships can spring up, from a matter-of-fact selling relationship to a deep personal friendship); and (3) response (the buyer feels under some obligation for having listened to the sales talk).

Factors in Setting the Marketing Communications Mix

In developing their promotion mix, companies must consider the type of product market, customer readiness to make a purchase, and product life-cycle stage; market rank is also a factor. First, consumer and business markets tend to require different promotional allocations. Although advertising is used less than sales calls in business markets, it can play a significant role in introducing the firm and its products, explaining product features, generating sales leads, legitimizing the firm and its products, and reassuring customers about purchases. Personal selling can also be effective in consumer markets, by helping to persuade dealers to take more stock and display more of the product, build dealer enthusiasm, sign up more dealers, and grow sales at existing accounts.

FIGURE 15.4   Cost-Effectiveness of Different Communication Tools at Different Buyer-Readiness Stages

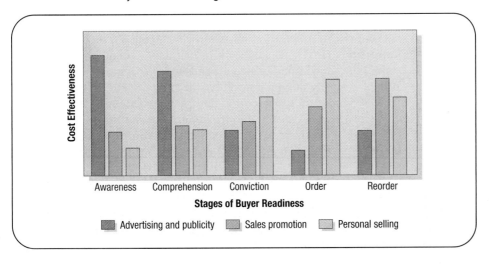

Second, promotional tools vary in cost effectiveness at different stages of buyer readiness, as shown in Figure 15.4. Advertising and publicity are most important in the awareness-building stage. Customer comprehension is affected primarily by advertising, while customer conviction is influenced mostly by personal selling. Closing the sale is influenced mostly by personal selling and sales promotion. Reordering is also affected mostly by personal selling and sales promotion, and somewhat by reminder advertising.

Third, promotional tools vary in cost effectiveness at different stages of the product life cycle. Advertising and publicity are most cost effective in the introduction stage; then all the tools can be toned down in the growth stage because demand is building word of mouth. Sales promotion, advertising, and personal selling grow more important in the maturity stage. In the decline stage, sales promotion continues strong, advertising and publicity are reduced, and salespeople give the product minimal attention.

Measuring Communication Results

After implementing the communications plan, the company must measure its impact. Members of the target audience are asked whether they recognize or recall the message, how many times they saw it, what points they recall, how they felt about the message, and their previous and current attitudes toward the product and company. The communicator should also collect behavioral measures of audience response, such as how many people bought the product, liked it, and talked to others about it.

Suppose 80 percent of the targeted customers are aware of the brand, 60 percent have tried it, and only 20 percent who tried it are satisfied. The communications program has effectively created awareness, but the product failed to meet consumer expectations. However, if 40 percent of the targeted customers are aware of the brand and only 30 percent have tried it—but 80 percent of those who tried it are satisfied—communications should be strengthened to take advantage of the brand's power.

MANAGING THE INTEGRATED MARKETING COMMUNICATIONS PROCESS

As defined by the American Association of Advertising Agencies, **integrated marketing communications (IMC)** is a concept of marketing communications planning that recognizes the added value of a comprehensive plan. Such a plan evaluates the strategic roles of a variety of communications disciplines—for example, general advertising, direct response, sales promotion and public relations—and combines these disciplines for clarity, consistency, and maximum impact through the seamless integration of messages. The wide range of communication tools, messages, and audiences makes it imperative that companies move toward integrated marketing communications.

Coordinating Media

Media coordination can occur across and within media types. Personal and nonpersonal communications channels should be combined for maximum impact. Instead of using a single tool in a "one-shot" effort, a more powerful approach is the *multiple-vehicle, multiple-stage campaign* such as the following sequence:

News campaign about a new product → Paid ad with a response mechanism →
Direct mail → Outbound telemarketing → Face-to-face sales call →
Ongoing communication

Multiple media deployed within a tightly defined time frame can increase message reach and impact. Research has also shown that promotions can be more effective when combined with advertising.[26] The awareness and attitudes created by advertising campaigns can improve the success of more direct sales pitches. Many companies are coordinating their online and offline communications activities. Listing Web addresses in ads (especially print) and on packages allows people to explore a company's offerings, find store locations, and get more info. Dannon uses communications to drive traffic to its Dannon Yogurt homepage so it can forge relationships directly with customers and strengthen customer loyalty with targeted coupon and direct-mail promotional efforts.[27]

Implementing IMC

Integrated marketing communications can produce stronger message consistency and greater sales impact. It also gives someone responsibility to unify the various brand images and messages, and it improves the firm's ability to reach the right customers with the right messages at the right time and in the right place.[28] In addition, it provides a way of looking at the whole marketing process instead of focusing on individual parts of it. Companies such as Motorola and Hewlett-Packard are bringing together advertising, direct marketing, public relations, and employee communications experts into "supercouncils" that meet a few times each year for training and improved communications. Procter & Gamble recently revised its communications planning by requiring that each new program be formulated jointly, with its ad agency sitting together with P&G's public relations agencies, direct-marketing units, promotion-merchandising firms, and Internet operations.

EXECUTIVE SUMMARY

The marketing communications mix includes advertising, sales promotion, public relations and publicity, events and experiences, direct marketing, and personal selling. The communications process includes sender, receiver, message, media, encoding, decoding, response, feedback, and noise. Consumer response to a communication often can be modeled in terms of a response hierarchy and "learn-feel-do" sequence.

Developing effective communications involves eight steps: (1) identify the target audience, (2) determine communications objectives, (3) design the communications, (4) select communications channels, (5) establish the total communications budget, (6) decide on the communications mix, (7) measure the results, and (8) manage the integrated marketing communications process. Communications objectives may involve category need and brand awareness, attitude, or purchase intention. Formulating the communication requires determining what to say (message strategy), how to say it (creative strategy), and who should say it (message source). Communications channels may be personal or nonpersonal. The objective-and-task method of setting the promotion budget, in which budgets are developed by defining specific objectives, is the most desirable.

To determine the marketing communications mix, firms must examine each communication tool's advantages and costs, the company's market rank, the type of market, buyer readiness, and product life-cycle stage. Measuring the mix's effectiveness involves asking members of the target audience whether they recognize or recall the communication, how many times they saw it, what they recall, how they felt about the communication, and their previous and current attitudes. Integrated marketing communications (IMC) recognizes the added value of a comprehensive plan that evaluates the strategic roles of a variety of communications disciplines and combines these disciplines to provide clarity, consistency, and maximum impact through the seamless integration of discrete messages.

NOTES

1. Diana T. Kurylko, "Taking Mini to the Max," *Automotive News Europe*, August 22, 2005, p. 24; Jim Lovel, "CP+B Spot Sells Mini DVD on Web," *Adweek Online*, March 16, 2005, http://www.adweek.com/aw/creative/article_display.jsp?vnu_content_id=1000845006; Margo Suydam, "Let's Motor," *Shoot*, December 5, 2003, pp. 19+; Karen Lundegaard, "BMW 'Mini' Campaign: Odd to the Max," *Wall Street Journal*, February 28, 2002; John Gaffney, "Most Innovative Campaign," *Business 2.0*, May 2002, pp. 98–99; Warren Berger, "Dare-Devils," *Business 2.0*, April 2004, pp. 111–116.
2. Some of these definitions are adapted from Peter D. Bennett, ed., *Dictionary of Marketing Terms* (Chicago: American Marketing Association, 1995).
3. For an alternate communications model developed specifically for advertising communications, see Barbara B. Stern, "A Revised Communication Model for Advertising: Multiple Dimensions of the Source, the Message, and the Recipient," *Journal of Advertising* (June 1994): 5–15. For some additional perspectives, see Tom Duncan and Sandra E. Moriarity, "A Communication-Based Marketing Model for Managing Relationships," *Journal of Marketing* (April 1998): 1–13.
4. Demetrios Vakratsas and Tim Ambler, "How Advertising Works: What Do We Really Know?" *Journal of Marketing* 63, no. 1 (January 1999): 26–43.
5. This section is based on the excellent text John R. Rossiter and Larry Percy, *Advertising and Promotion Management*, 2d ed. (New York: McGraw-Hill, 1997).
6. Ibid.
7. James F. Engel, Roger D. Blackwell, and Paul W. Minard, *Consumer Behavior*, 9th ed. (Fort Worth, TX: Dryden, 2001).
8. See Ayn E. Crowley and Wayne D. Hoyer, "An Integrative Framework for Understanding Two-Sided Persuasion," *Journal of Consumer Research* (March 1994): 561–574.
9. See C. I. Hovland, A. A. Lumsdaine, and F. D. Sheffield, *Experiments on Mass Communication*, vol. 3 (Princeton, NJ: Princeton University Press, 1948), ch. 8; and Crowley and Hoyer, "An Integrative Framework." For an alternative viewpoint, see George E. Belch, "The Effects of Message Modality on One- and Two-Sided Advertising Messages," in *Advances in Consumer Research*, eds. Richard P. Bagozzi and Alice M. Tybout (Ann Arbor, MI: Association for Consumer Research, 1983), pp. 21–26.
10. Curtis P. Haugtvedt and Duane T. Wegener, "Message Order Effects in Persuasion: An Attitude Strength Perspective," *Journal of Consumer Research* (June 1994): 205–218; H. Rao Unnava, Robert E. Burnkrant, and Sunil Erevelles, "Effects of Presentation Order and Communication Modality on Recall and Attitude," *Journal of Consumer Research* (December 1994): 481–490.

11. See Brian Sternthal and C. Samuel Craig, *Consumer Behavior: An Information Processing Perspective* (Upper Saddle River, NJ: Prentice Hall, 1982), pp. 282–284.

12. Kevin Goldman, "Advertising: Knock, Knock. Who's There? The Same Old Funny Ad Again," *Wall Street Journal*, November 2, 1993, p. B10. See also Marc G. Weinberger, Harlan Spotts, Leland Campbell, and Amy L. Parsons, "The Use and Effect of Humor in Different Advertising Media," *Journal of Advertising Research* (May–June 1995): 44–55.

13. Herbert C. Kelman and Carl I. Hovland, "Reinstatement of the Communication in Delayed Measurement of Opinion Change," *Journal of Abnormal and Social Psychology* 48 (1953): 327–335.

14. David J. Moore, John C. Mowen, and Richard Reardon, "Multiple Sources in Advertising Appeals: When Product Endorsers Are Paid by the Advertising Sponsor," *Journal of the Academy of Marketing Science* (Summer 1994): 234–243.

15. Richard C. Morais, "Mobile Mayhem," *Forbes*, July, 6 1998, p. 138; "Working in Harmony," *Soap Perfumery & Cosmetics*, July 1, 1998, p. 27; Rodger Harrabin, "A Commercial Break for Parents," *Independent*, September 8, 1998, p. 19; Naveen Donthu, "A Cross-Country Investigation of Recall of and Attitude Toward Comparative Advertising," *Journal of Advertising* 27 (June 1998): 111; "EU to Try Again on Tobacco Advertising Ban," Associated Press, May 9, 2001.

16. "Rebirth of a Salesman," *The Economist*, April 14, 2001.

17. Rob Eder, "Chain Drug Can Learn a Thing or Two from Kiehl's," *Drug Store News*, August 6, 2001, p. 12; Stephanie Thompson, "Minimal Hype Nets Max Buzz at Kiehl's," *Advertising Age*, April 5, 2004, pp. 4, 33.

18. Renée Dye, "The Buzz on Buzz," *Harvard Business Review* (November–December 2000): 139–146.

19. John Batelle, "The Net of Influence," *Business 2.0*, March 2004, p. 70.

20. Kenneth Hein, "Run Red Run," *Brandweek*, February 25, 2002, pp. 14–15.

21. Malcolm Macalister Hall, "Selling by Stealth," *Business Life*, November 2001, pp. 51–55.

22. Ann Meyer, "Word-of-Mouth Marketing Speaks Well for Small Business," *Chicago Tribune*, July 28, 2003.

23. Emanuel Rosen, *The Anatomy of Buzz* (New York: Currency, 2000), ch. 12; "Viral Marketing," *Sales & Marketing Automation* (November 1999): 12–14; George Silverman, *The Secrets of Word-of-Mouth Marketing* (New York: AMACOM, 2001).

24. Jack Neff, "Spam Research Reveals Disgust with Pop-Up Ads," *Advertising Age*, August 25, 2003, pp. 1, 21.

25. John Lehmann, "Permission Marketing Personalizes the Sales Pitch," *Crain's Cleveland Business*, September 13, 2004, p. 23; Karin Connelly, "Effective Emailing," *Inside Business*, June 2003, pp. 59+; Gina Bernacchi, "Permission Marketing: A New Path for Your Appeals," *Non-Profit Times*, March 15, 2002, p. 23; L. Erwin, "The Secret Behind Permission-Based Marketing," *Point of Purchase*, February 2001, p. 41; Seth Godin, "Permission Marketing," *Credit Union Executive*, January 2001, pp. 42+.

26. William T. Moran, "Insights from Pricing Research," in E. B. Bailey, ed., *Pricing Practices and Strategies* (New York: The Conference Board, 1978), pp. 7–13.

27. Gerry Khermouch, "The Top 5 Rules of the Ad Game," *BusinessWeek*, January 20, 2003, pp. 72–73.

28. Don E. Schultz, Stanley I. Tannenbaum, and Robert F. Lauterborn, *Integrated Marketing Communications: Putting It Together and Making It Work* (Lincolnwood, IL: NTC Business Books, 1992); Don E. Schultz and Heidi Schultz, *IMC, The Next Generation: Five Steps For Delivering Value and Measuring Financial Returns* (New York: McGraw-Hill, 2003).

CHAPTER 16

Managing Mass Communications

In this chapter, we will address the following questions:

1. What steps are involved in developing an advertising program?
2. How should sales promotion decisions be made?
3. What are the guidelines for effective brand-building events and experiences?
4. How can companies exploit the potential of public relations?

MARKETING MANAGEMENT AT VIRGIN GROUP

Flamboyant iconoclast Richard Branson roared onto the British stage in the 1970s with his innovative Virgin Records, signing unknown artists and launching a public-relations marathon that continues to this day. He has since sold Virgin Records, but he has created over 200 Virgin companies worldwide with combined revenues exceeding $8 billion. The Virgin name—the third most respected brand in Britain—and the Branson personality are on a diverse set of offerings such as planes, trains, finance, soft drinks, music, mobile phones, cars, wines, print media, even bridal wear. Despite the diversity, all connote value for money, quality, innovation, fun, and a sense of competitive challenge. The Virgin Group looks for new opportunities in markets with underserved, overcharged customers and complacent competition. "Wherever we find them, there is a clear opportunity area for Virgin to do a much better job than the competition," Branson says. "We introduce trust, innovation, and customer friendliness where they don't exist."

When Branson launched Virgin Cola in the United States, he steered an army tank down Fifth Avenue in New York, garnering interviews on each of the network morning TV shows as a result. A few years later, he plunged into Times Square connected to a crane to announce his mobile phone business. When introducing a line of hip techie gadgets called Virgin Pulse, Branson took center stage at a New York City nightclub. He arrived wearing a pair of flesh-colored tights and a portable CD player to cover the family jewels. Recently,

*Virgin teamed with Volvo in a contest offering the grand prize of a space flight on Branson's
new Virgin Galactic spacecraft. All this public relations activity has made the Virgin brand a
grand jewel in its own right.*[1]

Richard Branson and the Virgin Group are not alone in seeking unusual ways to
bring attention to products and services. Marketers of all kinds are trying to come
to grips with how to best use mass media in the new communication environment. In
this chapter, we examine the nature and use of four mass communication tools: advertising, sales promotion, events and experiences, and public relations.

DEVELOPING AND MANAGING
AN ADVERTISING PROGRAM

Advertising is any paid form of nonpersonal presentation and promotion of ideas,
goods, or services by an identified sponsor. Ads can be a cost-effective way to disseminate messages, whether to build a brand preference or to educate people. In developing an advertising program, marketing managers must always start by identifying the
target market and buyer motives. Then they can make the five major decisions, known
as the five Ms: *Mission:* What are the advertising objectives? *Money:* How much can be
spent? *Message:* What message should be sent? *Media:* What media should be used?
Measurement: How should the results be evaluated? These decisions are summarized
in Figure 16.1 and described in the following sections.

Setting the Objectives

An **advertising goal** (or **objective**) is a specific communication task and achievement
level to be accomplished with a specific audience in a specific period. Advertising

FIGURE 16.1   The Five Ms of Advertising

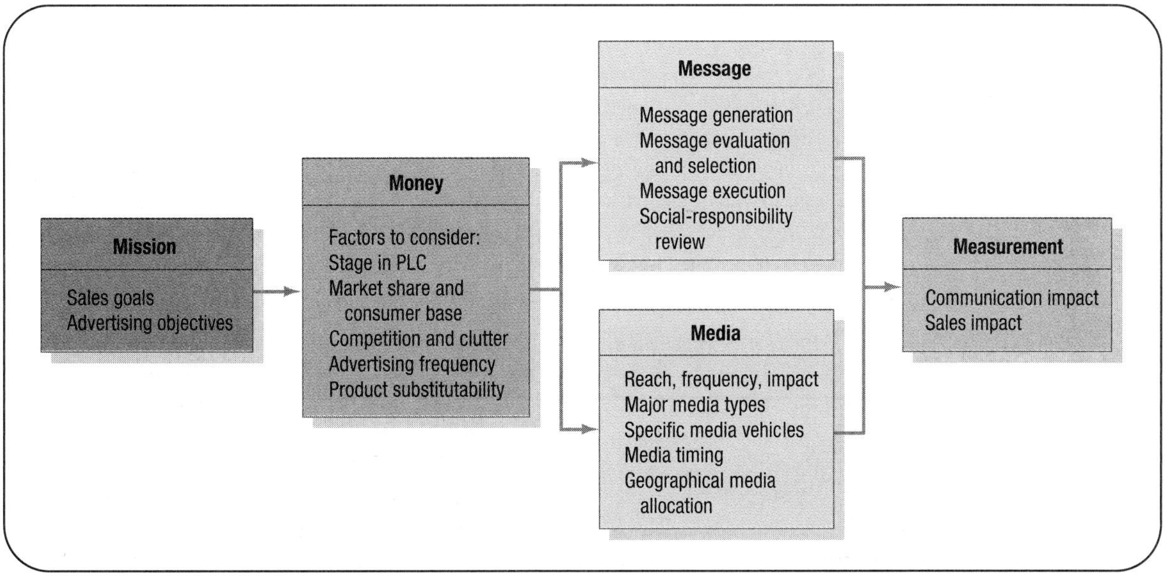

objectives can be classified according to their aim: to inform, persuade, remind, or reinforce. They aim at different stages in the hierarchy of effects discussed in Chapter 15.

Informative advertising aims to create awareness and knowledge of new products or new features of existing products. *Persuasive advertising* aims to create liking, preference, conviction, and purchase of a good or service. Chivas Regal attempts to persuade consumers that it delivers more taste and status than other Scotch whiskey brands. Some persuasive advertising is comparative advertising, which explicitly compares two or more brands.[2]

Reminder advertising aims to stimulate repeat purchase of products. Thus, Coca-Cola ads primarily remind people to purchase Coca-Cola. *Reinforcement advertising* seeks to convince current purchasers that they made the right choice. Car ads often depict satisfied customers enjoying special features of their new vehicle.

The advertising objective should emerge from a thorough analysis of the current marketing situation. If the product class is mature, the company is the market leader, and brand usage is low, the proper objective should be to stimulate more usage. If the product class is new and the company is not the market leader, but the brand is superior to the leader, the proper objective is to convince the market of the brand's superiority.

Deciding on the Advertising Budget

Management should consider these five factors when setting the advertising budget:[3]

1. *Product life cycle stage.* New products typically receive large budgets to build awareness and to gain consumer trial. Established brands usually are supported with lower budgets as a ratio to sales.
2. *Market share and consumer base.* High-market-share brands usually require less advertising expenditure as a percentage of sales to maintain their share. To build share by increasing market size requires larger advertising expenditures. On a cost-per-impression basis, it is less expensive to reach consumers of a widely used brand than to reach consumers of low-share brands.
3. *Competition and clutter.* In a market with many competitors and high advertising spending, a brand must advertise more heavily to be heard. Even ad clutter from non-competitors creates a need for heavier advertising.
4. *Advertising frequency.* The number of repetitions needed to convey the brand's message to customers has an important impact on the advertising budget.
5. *Product substitutability.* Brands in a commodity class (cigarettes, beer, soft drinks) require heavy advertising to establish a differential image. Advertising is also important when a brand offers unique benefits or features.

Developing the Advertising Campaign

In designing and evaluating an ad campaign, it is important to distinguish the message strategy or positioning of an ad (what will be conveyed about the brand) from its creative strategy (how the ad expresses the brand claims). To develop an effective message strategy, advertisers go through three steps: message generation and evaluation, creative development and execution, and social-responsibility review.

Message Generation and Evaluation   A good ad normally focuses on one or two core selling propositions. In refining the brand positioning, the advertiser should conduct market research to determine which appeal works best with its target audience. Once they find an effective appeal, advertisers should prepare a creative brief, typically covering one or two pages. It is an elaboration of the positioning statement and includes key message, target audience, communications objectives (to do, to know, to believe), key brand benefits, supports for the brand promise, and media. All team members working on the campaign must agree on the creative brief before moving ahead. Further, advertisers should make a choice only after considering a number of ad themes; the more that are created, the higher the probability of finding an excellent one.

Creative Development and Execution   The ad's impact depends not only on what is said, but often more importantly, on how it is said. Message execution can be decisive. In preparing an ad campaign, the advertiser can prepare a *copy strategy statement* describing the objective, content, support, and tone of the desired ad. Advertisers must also consider the specific advantages and disadvantages of each medium as they develop the creative strategy. Television, for example, reaches a broad spectrum of consumers, but it can be expensive; print ads can provide detailed product information, yet print media are fairly passive. Radio reaches 96 percent of all Americans ages 12 and older, and it is an inexpensive medium; however, the lack of visual images and the relatively passive nature of the consumer processing are disadvantages.[4]

Social-Responsibility Review   Advertisers and their agencies must be sure advertising does not overstep social and legal norms. Public policy makers have developed a substantial body of laws and regulations to govern advertising. Under U.S. law, for example, companies must avoid false or deceptive advertising and cannot use bait-and-switch advertising to attract buyers under false pretenses. To be socially responsible, advertisers try not to offend the general public, as well as any ethnic groups, racial minorities, or special-interest groups.[5] Every year, the nonprofit trade group Advertising Women of New York singles out ads it feels portray particularly good or bad images of women. In 2004, Sirius Satellite Radio won the TV Grand Ugly award for its "Car Wash" ad, which featured Pamela Anderson in a wet tank top using her entire body to clean a young man's car.[6]

Deciding on Media and Measuring Effectiveness

The advertiser's next task is to choose media to carry the message. The steps here are (1) deciding on reach, frequency, and impact; (2) choosing among media types; (3) selecting specific media vehicles; (4) deciding on media timing; and (5) deciding on geographical media allocation. Then the results of these decisions need to be evaluated.

Deciding on Reach, Frequency, and Impact   **Media selection** is finding the most cost-effective media to deliver the desired number and type of exposures to the target audience. What do we mean by the desired number of exposures? Presumably, the advertiser is seeking a specified advertising objective and response from the target audience—for example, a target level of product trial. The rate of product trial will depend, among other things, on level of brand awareness. The effect of exposures on audience awareness depends on the exposures' reach, frequency, and impact:

- *Reach (R)*. The number of different persons or households that are exposed to a particular media schedule at least once during a specified period.

- *Frequency (F)*. The number of times within the specified time period that an average person or household is exposed to the message.
- *Impact (I)*. The qualitative value of an exposure through a given medium (thus a food ad in *Good Housekeeping* would have a higher impact than in the *Fortune* magazine).

Although audience awareness will be greater with higher reach, frequency, and impact, there are important trade-offs among these elements. The media planner must figure out the most cost-effective combination of reach, frequency, and impact. Reach is most important when launching new products, flanker brands, extensions of well-known brands, or infrequently purchased brands; or when going after an undefined target market. Frequency is most important where there are strong competitors, a complex story to tell, high consumer resistance, or a frequent-purchase cycle.[7]

Many advertisers believe a target audience needs a large number of exposures for the advertising to work. Others doubt the value of high frequency. They believe that after people see the same ad a few times, they either act on it, get irritated by it, or stop noticing it.[8] Another factor arguing for repetition is that of forgetting. The higher the forgetting rate associated with a brand, product category, or message, the higher the warranted level of repetition. However, repetition is not enough. Ads wear out and viewers tune out, so advertisers need fresh executions of the message.

Choosing Among Major Media Types   The media planner has to know the capacity of the major media types to deliver reach, frequency, and impact. The costs, advantages, and limitations of the major media are profiled in Table 16.1.

TABLE 16.1   Profiles of Major Media Types

Medium	Advantages	Limitations
Newspapers	Flexibility; timeliness; good local market coverage; broad acceptance; high believability	Short life; poor reproduction quality; small pass-along audience
Television	Combines sight, sound, and motion; appealing to the senses; high attention; high reach	High absolute cost; high clutter; fleeting exposure; less audience selectivity
Direct mail	Audience selectivity; flexibility; no ad competition within the same medium; personalization	Relatively high cost; "junk mail" image
Radio	Mass use; high geographic and demographic selectivity; low cost	Audio presentation only; lower attention than television; nonstandardized rate structures; fleeting exposure
Magazines	High geographic and demographic selectivity; credibility and prestige; high-quality reproduction; long life; good pass-along readership	Long ad purchase lead time; some waste circulation; no guarantee of position
Outdoor	Flexibility; high repeat exposure; low cost; low competition	Limited audience selectivity; creative limitations
Yellow Pages	Excellent local coverage; high believability; wide reach; low cost	High competition; long ad purchase lead time; creative limitations
Newsletters	Very high selectivity; full control; interactive opportunities; relative low costs	Costs could run away
Brochures	Flexibility; full control; can dramatize messages	Overproduction could lead to runaway costs
Telephone	Many users; opportunity to give a personal touch	Relatively high cost unless volunteers are used
Internet	High selectivity; interactive possibilities; relatively low cost	Relatively new media with a low number of users in some countries

Media planners choose among these media categories by considering four main variables. First is the target audience's media habits. For example, radio, television, and the Internet are effective media for reaching teenagers. Second is the product. Media types have different potentials for demonstration, visualization, explanation, believability, and color. Third is the message. A message announcing a major sale tomorrow will require radio, TV, or newspaper; a message containing technical data might require specialized magazines or mailings. Fourth is cost. Television is more expensive than newspaper and radio advertising. What counts is the cost per thousand exposures.

Given the abundance of media choices, the planner first must decide on how to allocate the budget to the major media types, with the awareness that people are increasingly time-starved and assaulted by media. Attention is becoming a scarce currency, and advertisers need strong devices to capture people's attention.[9] In deciding on the ad budget, marketers must also recognize that consumer response can be S-shaped: An ad threshold effect exists where some positive amount of advertising is necessary before any sales impact can be detected, but sales increases eventually flatten out.[10]

Alternative Advertising Options   For a long time, television was the dominant medium. In recent years, researchers have noticed reduced effectiveness due to increased commercial clutter, increased "zipping and zapping" of commercials, and lower viewing owing to the growth in cable and satellite TV and DVD/VCRs.[11] Furthermore, television advertising costs have risen faster than other media costs. Many marketers are looking for alternative advertising media.[12]

Place advertising, also called out-of-home advertising, is a broadly defined category that captures many different alternative advertising forms. Marketers are using creative and unexpected ad placements to grab consumers' attention, trying to reach people in other environments, such as where they work, play, and, of course, shop. Some of the options include billboards, public spaces (such as sports arenas, parking meters, and bus shelters), product placement (in movies and on TV), and **point-of-purchase**, the location where consumers make purchases (typically a retail setting).

Alternative media present some interesting options for marketers. Ads now can appear virtually anywhere consumers have a few spare minutes or even seconds and thus enough time to notice them. The main advantage is that a very precise and—because of the nature of the setting—captive audience often can be reached in a cost-effective manner with a simple and direct message. The challenge with nontraditional media is demonstrating its reach and effectiveness through credible, independent research. These new marketing strategies and tactics must be ultimately judged on how they contribute, directly or indirectly, to brand equity. On the other hand, consumers may perceive as invasive and obtrusive the unique ad placements that successfully break through clutter. For more on alternative media and imaginative messages, see "Marketing Skills: Advertising in Hard Times."

Selecting Specific Vehicles   The media planner searches for the most cost-effective media vehicles within each chosen media type, relying on media measurement services for estimates of audience size, composition, and media cost. Audience size can be measured according to *circulation*, the number of physical units carrying the advertising; *audience*, the number of people exposed to the vehicle (with pass-on readership, a print vehicle's audience will be larger than circulation figures suggest); *effective audience*, the number of people with target audience characteristics exposed to the vehicle; and

MARKETING SKILLS: ADVERTISING IN HARD TIMES

With all the clutter and competition surrounding most product categories, getting through to the target audience can be difficult even in the best of times. That's why marketers who can plan effective advertising for hard times will be better prepared to handle communications in all kinds of economic climates. First, says Weiden & Kennedy, the ad agency responsible for Nike's memorable "Just Do It" campaign, learn to "make noise." When other companies are cutting back on advertising, advertisers who make their messages stand out will gain an important advantage. Be sure the messages offer insight into what the brand stands for, because customers are especially interested in brands they can trust. Don't make decisions solely based on marketing research: Weiden & Kennedy doesn't show Nike ads to focus groups because people often will reject original or unconventional ideas simply for being different.

Although television is pervasive, it's also costly and may not be necessary. One option is street-level guerilla advertising, such as advertising on sandwich boards and toys, to capture consumer attention. Another is to target carefully to reach influential customer groups with communications at live events, for example, and plan intriguing creative approaches that will bring customers to the brand's Web site for more information. Weiden & Kennedy does this by airing cliff-hanger television commercials whose endings can be seen only on the Nike Web site; it also uses billboard and print ad teasers to capture the audience's imagination and drive people to the Web.

With attendance at movie theaters dwindling, marketers for 20th Century Fox recently began posting scenes from major films online. The idea was to let movie buffs download and view the clips when and where they want, as often as they want. People who wanted to preview Angelina Jolie and Brad Pitt as husband-and-wife assassins could download *Mr. and Mrs. Smith* clips and subscribe for e-mail updates. By building an audience before the movie opened in theaters—and then before it appeared on DVD—the studio sparked positive word-of-mouth, followed by solid sales. "TV is still obviously strong, but there are so many different audiences these days that TV is not their primary way of finding out about movies or anything," says a studio executive.[13]

---

effective ad-exposed audience, the number of people with target audience characteristics who actually saw the ad.

Knowing the audience size, media planners can calculate the cost-per-thousand persons a vehicle reaches. If a full-page ad in *Newsweek* costs $200,000, and the estimated readership is 3.1 million people, the cost of exposing the ad to 1,000 persons is approximately $65. The same ad in *BusinessWeek* may cost $70,000 but reach only 970,000 persons—at a cost per thousand of about $72. The media planner then ranks each magazine by cost per thousand and favors magazines with the lowest cost per thousand for reaching target consumers. The magazines themselves often put together a "reader profile" for their advertisers, summarizing the characteristics of the magazine's readers with respect to age, income, residence, marital status, and leisure activities.

Deciding on Media Timing and Allocation In choosing media, the advertiser faces both a macroscheduling and a microscheduling problem. The *macroscheduling* *problem* involves scheduling advertising in relation to seasons and the business cycle. Suppose 70 percent of a product's sales occur between June and September. The firm can vary its advertising expenditures to follow the seasonal pattern, to oppose the seasonal pattern, or to be constant throughout the year.

The *microscheduling problem* calls for allocating advertising expenditures within a short period to obtain maximum impact. Over a given period, advertising messages can be concentrated ("burst" advertising), dispersed continuously, or dispersed intermittently. The advertiser must also decide whether to leave ad message frequency level, increase it, decrease it, or alternate messages in the schedule.

In launching a new product, the advertiser can choose among ad continuity, concentration, flighting, and pulsing. **Continuity** means scheduling exposures evenly throughout a given period. Generally, advertisers use this method when markets are expanding, with frequently purchased items, and in narrowly defined buyer categories. **Concentration** calls for spending all of the advertising dollars in a single period, which makes sense for products with one selling season or holiday. **Flighting** calls for advertising for a period, followed by a hiatus with no advertising, followed by a second period of advertising activity. It is used when funding is limited, the purchase cycle is relatively infrequent, and with seasonal items. **Pulsing** is continuous advertising at low-weight levels reinforced periodically by waves of heavier activity.[14] Those who favor pulsing say the audience will learn the message more thoroughly, and money can be saved.

A company has to decide how to allocate its advertising budget over space as well as over time. The company makes "national buys" when it places ads on national TV networks or in nationally circulated magazines. It makes "spot buys" when it buys TV time in just a few markets or in regional editions of magazines. The company makes "local buys" when it advertises in local newspapers, radio, or outdoor sites.

Evaluating Advertising Effectiveness Good planning and control of advertising depend on measures of advertising effectiveness. Yet the amount of fundamental research on advertising effectiveness is appallingly small. Most advertisers try to measure an ad's communication effect—its potential effect on awareness, knowledge, or preference—as well as its sales effect.

Communication-effect research seeks to determine whether an ad is communicating effectively. Called *copy testing*, it can be done before an ad is placed (pretesting) and after it is placed (posttesting). Advertisers also need to posttest the overall impact of a completed campaign.

Sales-effect research is complex because sales are influenced by many factors beyond advertising, such as product features, price, and availability, as well as competitors' actions. The sales impact is easiest to measure in direct-marketing situations and hardest to measure in brand or corporate image-building advertising. One approach is shown in Figure 16.2: A company's *share of advertising expenditures* produces a *share of voice* that earns a *share of consumers' minds and hearts* and ultimately a *share of market*.

Researchers try to measure the sales impact through analyzing historical or experimental data. The *historical approach* involves correlating past sales to past advertising expenditures using advanced statistical techniques.[15] Other researchers use an *experimental design* to measure advertising's sales impact. A growing number of researchers are striving to measure the sales effect of advertising expenditures instead of settling for communication-effect measures.[16]

FIGURE 16.2 Formula for Measuring Sales Impact of Advertising

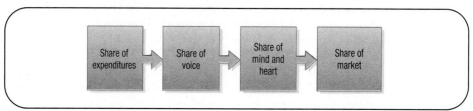

SALES PROMOTION

Sales promotion, a key ingredient in many marketing campaigns, consists of a diverse collection of incentive tools, mostly short term, designed to stimulate trial, or quicker or greater purchase, of particular products or services by consumers or the trade.[17] Whereas advertising offers a *reason* to buy, sales promotion offers an *incentive* to buy. Sales promotion includes tools for *consumer promotion* (samples, coupons, cash refund offers, prices off, premiums, prizes, patronage rewards, free trials, warranties, tie-in promotions, cross-promotions, point-of-purchase displays, and demonstrations); *trade promotion* (prices off, advertising and display allowances, and free goods); and *business* and *sales-force promotion* (trade shows, contests for sales reps, and specialty advertising).

In years past, the advertising-to-sales-promotion ratio was about 60:40. Today, in many consumer-packaged-goods companies, sales promotion accounts for 75 percent of the promotion budget (roughly 50 percent is trade promotion and 25 percent is consumer promotion). Several factors have contributed to this trend, particularly in consumer markets.[18] Promotion is now more accepted by top management as an effective sales tool, more product managers are qualified to use sales-promotion tools, and product managers are under greater pressure to increase current sales. In addition, the number of brands has increased, competitors use promotions frequently, many brands are seen as similar, consumers are more price-oriented, the trade demands more deals from manufacturers, and advertising efficiency has declined because of rising costs, media clutter, and legal restraints.

Purpose of Sales Promotion

Sales-promotion tools can be used to achieve a variety of objectives. Sellers use incentive-type promotions to attract new triers, to reward loyal customers, and to increase the repurchase rates of occasional users. Sales promotions often attract the brand switchers, who are primarily looking for low price, good value, or premiums, so sales promotions are unlikely to turn them into loyal users, although they may make subsequent purchases.[19] Sales promotions used in markets of high brand similarity produce a high sales response in the short run but little permanent gain in market share. In markets of high brand dissimilarity, however, sales promotions can alter market shares permanently. Consumers may engage in stockpiling—buying earlier than usual or buying extra quantities—but sales may then hit a postpromotion dip.[20]

A number of sales promotion benefits flow to manufacturers and consumers.[21] Sales promotions enable manufacturers to adjust to short-term variations in supply and demand; to adapt programs to different consumer segments; to test how high a list price they can charge (because they can always discount); and to sell more than they would normally at the list price. They induce consumers to try new products and promote greater consumer awareness of prices. Also, promotions lead to more varied retail formats, such as the everyday-low-price store and the promotional-pricing store. For retailers, promotions may increase sales of complementary categories (cake mix promotions may help to drive frosting sales), as well as induce some consumers to switch stores.

One challenge is to balance short- and long-term objectives when combining advertising and sales promotion. Advertising typically acts to build long-term brand loyalty, but the question of whether or not sales promotion weakens brand loyalty over time is subject to different interpretations.[22] Sales promotion, with its incessant coupons, deals, premiums, and percentages off, may devalue the product offering in the buyers' minds. Therefore, companies need to distinguish between price promotions (which focus only on price) and added-value promotions (intended to enhance brand image). When a brand is price promoted too often, the consumer begins to buy it mainly when it goes on sale. Therefore, there is risk in putting a well-known brand leader on promotion over 30 percent of the time.[23]

Loyal brand buyers tend not to change their buying patterns as a result of competitive promotion. There is also evidence that price promotions do not build permanent total-category volume. One study of more than 1,000 promotions concluded that only 16 percent paid off.[24] Small-share competitors find it advantageous to use sales promotion because they cannot match the market leaders' large advertising budgets; nor can they obtain shelf space without offering trade allowances or stimulate consumer trial without offering incentives. Price competition is often used by a small brand seeking to enlarge its share, but it is less effective for a category leader whose growth lies in expanding the entire category.[25] The upshot is that many consumer-packaged-goods companies feel forced to use more sales promotion than they wish.

Major Decisions

In using sales promotion, a company establishes its objectives, selects the tools, develops the program, pretests the program, implements and controls it, and evaluates the results.

Establishing Objectives Sales-promotion objectives are derived from broader promotion objectives, which are derived from more basic marketing objectives for the product. For consumers, objectives include encouraging purchase of larger-size units, building trial among nonusers, and attracting switchers away from competitors' brands. For retailers, objectives include persuading retailers to carry new items and higher levels of inventory, encouraging off-season buying, offsetting competitive promotions, building brand loyalty, and gaining entry into new retail outlets. For the sales force, objectives include encouraging support of a new product or model, encouraging more prospecting, and stimulating off-season sales.[26]

Selecting Consumer Promotion Tools Table 16.2 shows the main consumer-promotion tools. We can distinguish between *manufacturer promotions* and *retailer promotions*. The former are illustrated by the auto industry's frequent use of rebates and gifts to motivate test-drives and purchases; the latter include price cuts, retailer coupons, and retailer contests or premiums.

We can also distinguish between sales-promotion tools that are *consumer-franchise building*, reinforcing the consumer's brand understanding, and those that are not. The former imparts a selling message along with the deal, as in the case of coupons that

TABLE 16.2 Major Consumer Promotion Tools

Samples: Offer of a free amount of a product or service.

Coupons: Certificates offering a stated saving on the purchase of a specific product.

Cash Refund Offers (rebates): Provide a price reduction after purchase—consumer sends a specified proof of purchase to the manufacturer who refunds part of the purchase price by mail.

Price Packs (cents-off deals): Promoted on the package or label, these offer savings off the product's regular price.

Premiums (gifts): Merchandise offered at low or no cost as an incentive to buy a particular product.

Frequency Programs: Provide rewards for the consumer's frequency and intensity in buying company products or services.

Prizes (contests, sweepstakes, games): Prizes offer consumers the chance to win cash, trips, or merchandise as a result of purchasing something. A *contest* calls for consumers to submit an entry to be examined by judges who will select the best entries. A *sweepstakes* asks consumers to submit their names for a drawing. A *game* presents consumers with something every time they buy—bingo numbers, missing letters—that might help them win a prize.

Patronage Awards: Values in cash or other forms given to reward patronage of a certain vendor or group of vendors.

Free Trials: Inviting prospects to try the product free in the hope that they will buy the product.

Product Warranties: Explicit or implicit promises by sellers that if the product does not perform as specified, the seller will fix it or will refund the customer's money during a specified period.

Tie-In Promotions: Two or more brands or companies team up on coupons, refunds, and contests to increase pulling power.

Cross-Promotions: Using one brand to advertise another noncompeting brand.

Point-of-Purchase (POP) Displays and Demonstrations: Displays and demonstrations that take place at the point of purchase or sale.

include a selling message. Sales-promotion tools that typically are not brand-building include price-off packs, consumer premiums not related to a product, contests and sweepstakes, consumer refund offers, and trade allowances. Sales promotion used together with advertising seems most effective: In one study, a price promotion combined with feature advertising boosted sales volume by 19 percent; when point-of-purchase display was added, sales volume increased by 24 percent.[27]

Selecting Trade Promotion Tools Manufacturers use a number of trade-promotion tools (see Table 16.3) to (1) persuade an intermediary to carry the product; (2) persuade an intermediary to carry more units; (3) induce retailers to promote the brand by featuring, display, and price reduction; and (4) stimulate retailers and their salespeople to push the product. Today, giant retailers have more power to demand trade promotion at the expense of consumer promotion and advertising.[28] Trade promotions are often complex to administer, difficult to manage, and may even lead to lost revenues.

Selecting Business-Promotion and Sales-Force-Promotion Tools Companies spend billions of dollars on business-promotion and sales-force-promotion tools (see Table 16.4) to gather business leads, impress and reward customers, and motivate the sales force to greater effort. Companies typically develop budgets that remain fairly constant from year to year for each business-promotion tool.

TABLE 16.3   Major Trade Promotion Tools

Price-Off (off-invoice or off-list): A straight discount off the list price on each case purchased during a stated time period.

Allowance: An amount offered in return for the retailer's agreeing to feature the manufacturer's products in some way. An *advertising allowance* compensates retailers for advertising the manufacturer's product. A *display allowance* compensates them for carrying a special product display.

Free Goods: Offers of extra cases of merchandise to intermediaries who buy a certain quantity or who feature a certain flavor or size.

Source: For more information, see Betsy Spethman, "Trade Promotion Redefined," *Brandweek,* March 13, 1995, pp. 25–32.

Developing the Program   In deciding to use a particular incentive, marketers must consider (1) the *size* of the incentive (a certain minimum is necessary if the promotion is to succeed; a higher level will produce more sales response but at a diminishing rate); (2) the *conditions* for participation (whether to offer the incentive to everyone or to select groups); (3) the *duration*; (4) the *distribution vehicle* (each will have a different level of reach, cost, and impact); (5) the *timing;* and (6) the *total sales-promotion budget* (including administrative costs and incentive costs). Increasingly, marketers are blending several media into a total campaign concept.

Pretesting, Implementing, and Controlling the Program   Although most sales-promotion programs are designed on the basis of experience, marketers should pretest to see if the tools are appropriate, if the incentive size is optimal, and if the presentation method is efficient. Marketers can ask consumers to rate or rank various possible deals or they can run trial tests in limited geographic areas. Implementation planning must cover *lead time* (to prepare the program before the launch) and *sell-in time* (beginning with the launch and ending when approximately 95 percent of the deal merchandise is in the hands of consumers).

Evaluating the Program   In general, sales promotions work best when they attract competitors' customers, who then switch. If the company's product is not superior, the brand's share is likely to return to its pre-promotion level. In evaluating sales-promotion

TABLE 16.4   Major Business-Promotion and Sales-Force-Promotion Tools

Trade Shows and Conventions: Industry associations organize annual trade shows and conventions where firms selling products and services to this industry set up booths and display their products. Participating vendors expect several benefits, including generating new sales leads, maintaining customer contacts, introducing new products, meeting new customers, selling more to present customers, and educating customers with publications, videos, and other audiovisual materials.

Sales Contests: A sales contest aims at inducing the sales force or dealers to increase their sales results over a stated period, with prizes (money, trips, gifts, or points) going to those who succeed.

Specialty Advertising: Specialty advertising consists of useful, low-cost items bearing the company's name and address, and sometimes an advertising message, that salespeople give to prospects and customers. Common items are ballpoint pens, calendars, key chains, flashlights, tote bags, and memo pads.

effectiveness and determining who is being attracted, manufacturers can use sales data, consumer surveys, and experiments. Scanner sales data can show who took advantage of the promotion, what they used to buy, and how they behaved toward the brand and other brands. Surveys can help determine recall, attitude, behavior, and subsequent brand-choice behavior among the target audience.[29] Manufacturers who use experiments to vary attributes such as incentive value, duration, and distribution media can use scanner data to learn whether more people bought the product and when.

EVENTS AND EXPERIENCES

By becoming part of a special and more personally relevant moment in consumers' lives, involvement with events can broaden and deepen a company's relationship with the target market. At the same time, daily encounters with brands may also affect consumers' brand attitudes and beliefs. *Atmospheres* are "packaged environments" that create or reinforce leanings toward product purchase. Law offices decorated with oriental rugs and oak furniture communicate "stability" and "success."[30] A five-star hotel will use elegant chandeliers, marble columns, and other tangible signs of luxury.

Recognizing that it can now reach only 15 percent of the population with a prime-time ad, as compared to 40 percent as recently as the mid-1980s, Coca-Cola has diverted money into new initiatives that allow it to embed itself into the favorite activities of its target audience. The company has created "teen lounges" in Chicago and Los Angeles where kids can hang out and buy Cokes from see-through vending machines; it has placed downloadable songs on its myCokeMusic.com Web site in Britain; and it has blended its brand into the content of TV shows from the United States to Venezuela.[31] Like Coca-Cola, more firms are creating product and brand experiences.

Events Objectives

Marketers report a number of reasons why they sponsor events:

1. *To identify with a particular target market or life style.* Customers can be targeted geographically, demographically, psychographically, or behaviorally according to events. Events can be chosen based on attendees' attitudes toward and usage of certain products or brands. Advertisers such as Sony and Pepsi have advertised during ESPN's twice-yearly X Games to reach the elusive 12- to 19-year-old audience.[32]

2. *To increase awareness of company or product name.* Sponsorship often offers sustained exposure to a brand, a necessary condition to build brand recognition. By skillfully choosing sponsorship events or activities, identification with a product, and thus brand recall, can also be enhanced.

3. *To create or reinforce consumer perceptions of key brand image associations.* Events themselves have associations that help to create or reinforce brand associations. Anheuser-Busch chose to have Bud Light become a sponsor of the Ironman and other triathlons because it wanted a "healthy" image for the beer.

4. *To enhance corporate image dimensions.* Sponsorship is used to improve perceptions that the company is likable, prestigious, and so on, so that consumers will favor it in later product choices.

5. *To create experiences and evoke feelings.* The feelings engendered by an exciting or rewarding event may also indirectly link to the brand.

6. *To express commitment to the community or on social issues.* Cause-related marketing consists of sponsorships that involve corporate tie-ins with nonprofit organizations

and charities. Firms such as Stoneyfield Farm, Starbucks, American Express, and Tom's of Maine have made cause-related marketing an important cornerstone of their marketing programs.

7. *To entertain key clients or reward key employees.* Many events include lavish hospitality tents and other special services or activities, which are only available for sponsors and their guests, to engender goodwill and establish valuable business contacts.

8. *To permit merchandising or promotional opportunities.* Many marketers tie in contests or sweepstakes, in-store merchandising, direct response, or other marketing activities with an event, the way Ford and Nokia have done with the hit TV show *American Idol.*

Sponsorship has a number of potential disadvantages. An event's success can be unpredictable and beyond the control of the sponsor. Although many consumers will credit sponsors for providing the financial assistance to make an event possible, some consumers may still resent the commercialization of events.

Major Decisions

Developing successful sponsored events involves choosing the appropriate events; designing the optimal sponsorship program for the event; and measuring the effects of sponsorship.[33]

- *Choosing event opportunities.* An "ideal event" might be one (1) whose audience closely matches the desired target market, (2) that generates much favorable attention, (3) that is unique but not encumbered with many sponsors, (4) that lends itself to ancillary marketing activities, and (5) that reflects or enhances the brand or corporate image of the sponsor. For example, more firms are also using their names to sponsor the arenas, stadiums, and other venues that actually hold the events.[34]

- *Designing sponsorship programs.* Many marketers believe that it is the marketing program accompanying an event sponsorship that ultimately determines its success. A sponsor can identify itself at an event in a number of ways, including banners, signs, and programs. For more significant impact, sponsors typically supplement such activities with samples, prizes, advertising, retail promotions, and publicity. At least two to three times the amount of the sponsorship expenditure should be spent on related marketing activities.

- *Event creation.* This is a key skill in publicizing fund-raising drives for nonprofit organizations. Fund-raisers have developed a large repertoire of special events, including anniversary celebrations, art exhibits, auctions, benefit evenings, bingo games, book sales, cake sales, contests, dances, dinners, fairs, fashion shows, parties in unusual places, rummage sales, tours, and walkathons. No sooner is one type of event created, such as a walkathon, than competitors spawn new versions, such as readathons, bikeathons, and jogathons.[35]

- *Measuring sponsorship activities.* There are two basic approaches to measuring the effects of sponsorship activities: The *supply-side* method focuses on potential exposure to the brand by assessing the extent of media coverage; the *demand-side* method focuses on reported exposure from consumers. On the supply side, some experts maintain that positive editorial coverage can be worth five to ten times the advertising equivalency value; however, sponsorship rarely gets such favorable treatment.[36] On the demand side, surveys of spectators can show how the sponsorship affects awareness, attitudes, intentions, or even sales.

PUBLIC RELATIONS

Not only must the company relate constructively to customers, suppliers, and dealers, it must also relate to a large number of interested publics. A **public** is any group that has an actual or potential interest in or impact on a company's ability to achieve its objectives. **Public relations (PR)** involves a variety of programs that are designed to promote or protect a company's image or its individual products.

The wise company takes concrete steps to manage successful relations with its key publics. PR departments typically perform five functions: (1) *press relations* (presenting news and information about the organization in the most positive light); (2) *product publicity* (publicizing specific products); (3) *corporate communication* (promoting understanding of the organization through internal and external communications); (4) *lobbying* (dealing with legislators and government officials to promote or defeat legislation and regulation); and (5) *counseling* (advising management about public issues and company positions and image during both good times and crises).

Marketing Public Relations

Many companies are turning to **marketing public relations (MPR)** to directly support corporate or product promotion and image making. MPR, like financial PR and community PR, serves a special constituency, namely the marketing department.[37] MPR plays an important role in:

- *Assisting in the launch of new products.* The success of toys such as Pokémon owes a great deal to clever publicity.
- *Assisting in repositioning a mature product.* New York City had bad press in the 1970s until the "I Love New York" campaign began.
- *Building interest in a product category.* Companies and industry groups use MPR to expand consumption of products such as pork and milk.
- *Influencing specific target groups.* McDonald's sponsors special neighborhood events in Latino and African American communities to build goodwill.
- *Defending products that have encountered public problems.* PR professionals must be adept at managing crises, such as the Coca-Cola incident in Belgium over allegedly contaminated soda.
- *Building the corporate image in a way that reflects favorably on its products.* Richard Branson's publicity stunts have created a bold, upstart image for his U.K.-based Virgin Group.

As the power of mass advertising weakens, marketing managers are turning to MPR to build awareness and brand knowledge in a cost-effective manner and to reach local communities and specific audiences. The company does not pay for the space or time obtained in the media; it pays only for a staff to develop and circulate the stories and manage certain events. Nevertheless, it must be planned jointly with advertising.[38]

Major Decisions in Marketing PR

In considering when and how to use MPR, management must establish the marketing objectives, choose the messages and vehicles, implement the plan carefully, and evaluate the results. The main tools of MPR are described in Table 16.5.[39]

TABLE 16.5   Major Tools in Marketing PR

Publications: Companies rely extensively on published materials to reach and influence their target markets. These include annual reports, brochures, articles, company newsletters and magazines, and audiovisual materials.

Events: Companies can draw attention to new products or other company activities by arranging special events like news conferences, seminars, outings, trade shows, exhibits, contests and competitions, and anniversaries that will reach the target publics.

Sponsorships: Companies can promote their brands and corporate name by sponsoring sports and cultural events and highly regarded causes.

News: One of the major tasks of PR professionals is to find or create favorable news about the company, its products, and its people and get the media to accept press releases and attend press conferences.

Speeches: Increasingly, company executives must field questions from the media or give talks at trade associations or sales meetings, and these appearances can build the company's image.

Public-Service Activities: Companies can build goodwill by contributing money and time to good causes.

Identity Media: Companies need a visual identity that the public immediately recognizes. The visual identity is carried by company logos, stationery, brochures, signs, business forms, business cards, buildings, uniforms, and dress codes.

- *Establishing the marketing objectives.* MPR can build *awareness* of a product, a service, a person, an organization, or an idea; add *credibility* by communicating a message in an editorial context; boost sales force and dealer *enthusiasm*; and hold down *promotion costs* because it costs less than media advertising. Whereas PR reaches target publics through the mass media, MPR is increasingly borrowing direct-response marketing techniques and technology to reach target audience members one-on-one.

- *Choosing messages and vehicles.* The MPR manager must identify or develop interesting stories about the product. If there are few stories, the expert should propose newsworthy events to sponsor as a way of stimulating media coverage. For example, PBS wanted to dispel the perception that the musical genre of the "blues" was dying. Its Blues Project included special events, a special Web site, a radio and television series, a teacher's guide, a concert, and more. The campaign received nearly a billion positive media impressions and led to a surge in CD sales of blues music.[40]

- *Implementing and evaluating the plan.* MPR's contribution to the bottom line is difficult to measure because it is used along with other promotional tools. The easiest measure is the number of *exposures* obtained in the media. A better measure would be changes in product awareness, comprehension, or attitude resulting from the MPR campaign (after allowing for the effect of other promotional tools). The most satisfactory measure is sales-and-profit impact, allowing the company to determine its return on MPR investment.

EXECUTIVE SUMMARY

Advertising is any paid form of nonpersonal presentation and promotion of ideas, goods, or services by an identified sponsor. Developing an advertising program is a five-step process: (1) set advertising objectives; (2) establish a budget; (3) choose the advertising message and creative strategy; (4) decide on the media; and (5) evaluate communication and sales effects.

Sales promotion consists of a diverse collection of incentive tools, mostly short term, designed to stimulate quicker or greater purchase of particular products or services by consumers or the trade. Sales promotion includes tools for consumer promotion, trade promotion, and business promotion and sales-force promotion (trade shows and conventions, sales contests, and specialty advertising). In using sales promotion, a company must establish its objectives, select the tools, develop and pretest the program, implement and control it, and evaluate the results.

Events and experiences are a means to become part of special and more personally relevant moments in consumers' lives. Involvement with properly managed events can broaden and deepen the relationship of the sponsor with its target market. Public relations (PR) involves a variety of programs designed to promote or protect a company's image or its individual products. Today marketing public relations (MPR) is used to support the marketing department in corporate or product promotion and image making. MPR can affect public awareness at a fraction of the cost of advertising and is often much more credible. The main tools of MPR are publications, events, news, speeches, public service activities, and identity media.

NOTES

1. Stacy Perman, "Branson: 'I Love to Try Everything,'" *BusinessWeek Online*, August 31, 2005, (www.businessweek.com); "Denver Man Will Boldly Go on Virgin Space Flight," *Wireless News*, March 24, 2005; Sean Hargrave, "Making Waves," *New Media Age*, January 15, 2004, pp. 24–27; Adam Lashinsky, "Shootout in Gadget Land," *Fortune*, November 10, 2003, p. 74; Sam Hill and Glenn Rifkin, *Radical Marketing* (New York: Harper Business, 1999); "Virgin Holiday Store Hires HHM for Major Push," *Precision Marketing*, January 23, 2004, pp. 3–4.

2. See William L. Wilkie and Paul W. Farris, "Comparison Advertising: Problem and Potential," *Journal of Marketing* (October 1975): 7–15.

3. See Donald E. Schultz, Dennis Martin, and William P. Brown, *Strategic Advertising Campaigns* (Chicago: Crain Books, 1984), pp. 192–197.

4. David Ogilvy, *Ogilvy on Advertising* (New York: Vintage Books, 1983).

5. Kim Bartel Sheehan, *Controversies in Contemporary Advertising* (Thousand Oaks, CA: Sage Publications, 2003).

6. Suzanne Vranica, "Sirius Ad is Best for Most Sexist," *Wall Street Journal*, April 1, 2004, p. B6.

7. Schultz, et al., *Strategic Advertising Campaigns*, p. 340.

8. Herbert E. Krugman, "What Makes Advertising Effective?" *Harvard Business Review* (March–April 1975): 98.

9. Thomas H. Davenport and John C. Beck, *The Attention Economy: Understanding the New Currency of Business* (Boston: Harvard Business School Press, 2000).

10. Demetrios Vakratsas, Fred M. Feinberg, Frank M. Bass, and Gurumurthy Kalyanaram, "The Shape of Advertising Response Functions Revisited: A Model of Dynamic Probabilistic Thresholds," *Marketing Science* 23, no. 1 (Winter 2004): 109–119.

11. Susan Thea Posnock, "It Can Control Madison Avenue," *American Demographics* (February 2004): 29–33.

12. James Betzold, "Jaded Riders Are Ever-Tougher Sell," *Advertising Age*, July 9, 2001, p. S2; Michael McCarthy, "Ads Are Here, There, Everywhere," *USA Today*, June 19, 2001, www.usatoday.com Kipp Cheng, "Captivating Audiences," *Brandweek*, November 29,

1999, p. 64; Michael McCarthy, "Critics Target 'Omnipresent' Ads," *USA Today*, April 16, 2001, www.usatoday.com.

13. Warren Berger, "Just Do It Again," *Business 2.0*, September 2002, p. 81; Brian Steinberg, "Marketing Folks' New Medium May Be Your PC's Hard Drive," *Wall Street Journal*, May 2, 2005, p. B8; R. Kinsey Lowe, "MPAA: Movie Attendance Dips, But So Do Costs," *Los Angeles Times*, March 16, 2005, p. E2.

14. See also Hani I. Mesak, "An Aggregate Advertising Pulsing Model with Wearout Effects," *Marketing Science*, Summer 1992, pp. 310–326; and Fred M. Feinberg, "Pulsing Policies for Aggregate Advertising Models," *Marketing Science*, Summer 1992, pp. 221–234.

15. Kristian S. Palda, *The Measurement of Cumulative Advertising Effect* (Upper Saddle River, NJ: Prentice Hall, 1964), p. 87; David B. Montgomery and Alvin J. Silk, "Estimating Dynamic Effects of Market Communications Expenditures," *Management Science* (June 1972): 485–501.

16. In addition to the sources cited below, see David Walker and Tony M. Dubitsky, "Why Liking Matters," *Journal of Advertising Research* (May–June 1994): 9–18; Abhilasha Mehta, "How Advertising Response Modeling (ARM) Can Increase Ad Effectiveness," *Journal of Advertising Research* (May–June 1994): 62–74; Karin Holstius, "Sales Response to Advertising," *International Journal of Advertising* 9, no. 1 (1990): 38–56; John Deighton, Caroline Henderson, and Scott Neslin, "The Effects of Advertising on Brand Switching and Repeat Purchasing," *Journal of Marketing Research* (February 1994): 28–43; Anil Kaul and Dick R. Wittink, "Empirical Generalizations About the Impact of Advertising on Price Sensitivity and Price," *Marketing Science* 14, no. 3, pt. 1 (1995): G151–160; Ajay Kalra and Ronald C. Goodstein, "The Impact of Advertising Positioning Strategies on Consumer Price Sensitivity," *Journal of Marketing Research* (May 1998): 210–224; Gerard J. Tellis, Rajesh K. Chandy, and Pattana Thaivanich, "Which Ad Works, When, Where, and How Often? Modeling the Effects of Direct Television Advertising," *Journal of Marketing Research* 37 (February 2000): 32–46.

17. From Robert C. Blattberg and Scott A. Neslin, *Sales Promotion: Concepts, Methods, and Strategies* (Upper Saddle River, NJ: Prentice Hall, 1990). An up-to-date and comprehensive review of academic work on sales promotions can be found in Scott Neslin, "Sales Promotion," in *Handbook of Marketing*, edited by Bart Weitz and Robin Wensley (London: Sage Publications, 2002), pp. 310–338.

18. Roger A. Strang, "Sales Promotion—Fast Growth, Faulty Management," *Harvard Business Review* (July–August 1976): 116–119.

19. Kusum Ailawadi, Karen Gedenk, and Scott A. Neslin, "Heterogeneity and Purchase Event Feedback in Choice Models: An Empirical Analysis with Implications for Model Building," *International Journal of Research in Marketing* 16 (1999): 177–198. See also Eric T. Anderson and Duncan Simester, "The Long-Run Effects of Promotion Depth on New Versus Established Customers: Three Field Studies," *Marketing Science* 23, no. 1 (Winter 2004): 4–20.

20. Carl Mela, Kamel Jedidi, and Douglas Bowman, "The Long Term Impact of Promotions on Consumer Stockpiling," *Journal of Marketing Research* 35, no. 2 (May 1998): 250–262; Harald J. Van Heerde, Peter S. H. Leeflang, and Dick Wittink, "The Estimation of Pre- and Postpromotion Dips with Store-Level Scanner Data," *Journal of Marketing Research* 37, no. 3 (August 2000): 383–395.

21. Paul W. Farris and John A. Quelch, "In Defense of Price Promotion," *Sloan Management Review* (Fall 1987): 63–69.

22. Robert George Brown, "Sales Response to Promotions and Advertising," *Journal of Advertising Research* (August 1974): 36–37. Also see Carl F. Mela, Sunil Gupta, and Donald R. Lehmann, "The Long-Term Impact of Promotion and Advertising on Consumer Brand Choice," *Journal of Marketing Research* (May 1997): 248–261; Purushottam Papatla and Lakshman Krishnamurti, "Measuring the Dynamic Effects of Promotions on Brand

Choice," *Journal of Marketing Research* (February 1996): 20–35; Kamel Jedidi, Carl F. Mela, and Sunil Gupta, "Managing Advertising and Promotion for Long-Run Profitability," *Marketing Science* 18, no. 1 (1999): 1–22.

23. For a summary of the research on whether promotion erodes the consumer franchise of leading brands, see Blattberg and Neslin, *Sales Promotion: Concepts, Methods, and Strategies.*

24. Magid M. Abraham and Leonard M. Lodish, "Getting the Most Out of Advertising and Promotion," *Harvard Business Review* (May–June 1990): 50–60. See also Shuba Srinivasan, Koen Pauwels, Dominique Hanssens, and Marnik Dekimpe, "Do Promotions Benefit Manufacturers, Retailers, or Both?" *Management Science*, vol. 50, no. 5 (May), pp. 617–629.

25. F. Kent Mitchel, "Advertising/Promotion Budgets: How Did We Get Here, and What Do We Do Now?" *Journal of Consumer Marketing* (Fall 1985): 405–447.

26. For a model for setting sales promotions objectives, see David B. Jones, "Setting Promotional Goals: A Communications Relationship Model," *Journal of Consumer Marketing* 11, no. 1 (1994): 38–49.

27. See John C. Totten and Martin P. Block, *Analyzing Sales Promotion: Text and Cases*, 2d ed. (Chicago: Dartnell, 1994), pp. 69–70.

28. See Paul W. Farris and Kusum L. Ailawadi, "Retail Power: Monster or Mouse?" *Journal of Retailing* (Winter 1992): 351–369.

29. Joe A. Dodson, Alice M. Tybout, and Brian Sternthal, "Impact of Deals and Deal Retraction on Brand Switching," *Journal of Marketing Research* (February 1978): 72–81.

30. Philip Kotler, "Atmospherics as a Marketing Tool," *Journal of Retailing* (Winter 1973–1974): 48–64.

31. Dean Foust, "Coke: Wooing the TiVo Generation," *BusinessWeek*, March 1, 2004, pp. 77–78.

32. Monte Burke, "X-treme Economics," *Forbes*, February 2, 2004, pp. 42–44.

33. The Association of National Advertisers has a useful source: *Event Marketing: A Management Guide*, which is available at www.ana.net/bookstore.

34. Ian Mount, "Exploding the Myths of Stadium Naming," *Business 2.0*, April 2004, p. 82.

35. Dwight W. Catherwood and Richard L. Van Kirk, *The Complete Guide to Special Event Management* (New York: John Wiley, 1992).

36. William L. Shankin and John Kuzma, "Buying That Sporting Image," *Marketing Management* (Spring 1992): 65.

37. For an excellent account, see Thomas L. Harris, *The Marketer's Guide to Public Relations* (New York: John Wiley, 1991). Also see Thomas L. Harris, *Value-Added Public Relations* (Chicago: NTC Business Books, 1998).

38. Tom Duncan, *A Study of How Manufacturers and Service Companies Perceive and Use Marketing Public Relations* (Muncie, IN: Ball State University, 1985). For more on how to contrast the effectiveness of advertising with the effectiveness of PR, see Kenneth R. Lord and Sanjay Putrevu, "Advertising and Publicity: An Information Processing Perspective," *Journal of Economic Psychology* (March 1993): 57–84.

39. For more on cause-related marketing, see P. Rajan Varadarajan and Anil Menon, "Cause-Related Marketing: A Co-Alignment of Marketing Strategy and Corporate Philanthropy," *Journal of Marketing* (July 1988): 58–74.

40. "Arts, Entertainment & Media Campaign of the Year 2004," *PRWeek*, n.d. (www.prweek.com/us/events/index.cfm?fuseaction=awardDetail&id=20432).

CHAPTER 17

Managing Personal Communications

In this chapter, we will address the following questions:

1. How can companies use integrated direct marketing for competitive advantage?
2. How can companies do effective interactive marketing?
3. What decisions do companies face in designing and managing a sales force?
4. How can salespeople improve their selling, negotiating, and relationship marketing skills?

MARKETING MANAGEMENT AT CANON USA

Personal communications are the key to Canon USA's success in marketing copiers and other imaging equipment to businesses throughout the country. Canon uses direct mail and e-mail to establish and build relationships with business buyers well in advance of any purchase decision. "[Customers] may get messages from us six months to a year before the purchase," says David Hughes, manager of database marketing. Through focus groups, surveys, and other research techniques, Canon has found that one-third of customers prefer to receive information by mail, one-third prefer to get information via e-mail, and one-third will accept either. Despite the interactivity of e-mail messages, Hughes notes that Canon's response rate for direct mail is "almost always higher—and many times, up to five times higher."

This stream of communications sets the stage for personal attention from one of the 11,000 internal and external salespeople who sell Canon products. With imaging technology changing so rapidly, Canon has created its own "Learning Zone" training Web site to keep salespeople updated on the latest product developments. Representatives can go online at the office or in the field and review lessons at their own pace; later they have the opportunity to hone their expertise with classroom training. Thanks to the Learning Zone, more reps are completing more courses more quickly. Because it is easy and cost-efficient to post materials on the Web site, Canon is constantly adding new training courses. As a result, its sales professionals are better prepared to meet the challenges of forging long-term customer relationships in the highly dynamic, highly competitive imaging market.[1]

Today, marketing communications are increasingly seen as an interactive dialogue between the company and its customers. To make the sale to customers, marketers like Canon USA work both hard and smart. Companies must ask not only "How can we reach our customers?" but also "How can our customers reach us?" Personalizing communications—and saying and doing the right thing to the right person at the right time—is critical. This chapter examines how companies personalize their marketing communications for more impact. We begin by evaluating direct marketing and e-marketing; then we consider personal selling and the sales force.

DIRECT MARKETING

Direct marketing is the use of consumer-direct channels to reach and deliver goods and services to customers without marketing middlemen. These channels include direct mail, catalogs, telemarketing, interactive TV, kiosks, Web sites, and mobile devices. Direct marketers seek a measurable response, typically a customer order. This is sometimes called **direct-order marketing**. Today, many direct marketers use direct marketing to build long-term customer relationships by sending birthday cards, information, or small premiums to strengthen bonds over time.[2]

More and more business marketers have turned to direct mail and telemarketing in response to the high and increasing costs of reaching business markets through a sales force. In total, sales from direct marketing generate almost 9 percent of the U.S. economy.[3] Direct sales include sales to the consumer market (53 percent), B2B (27 percent), and fund-raising by charitable institutions (20 percent).[4]

The Benefits of Direct Marketing

Consumers find home shopping fun, convenient, and hassle-free; it saves time; introduces a larger selection of merchandise; and allows comparative shopping. Business customers also benefit by learning about offerings without meeting salespeople. Direct marketers benefit as well: They can buy mailing lists for almost any segment (left-handed people, millionaires); customize and personalize messages; build relationships; reach the most interested prospects at the right moment; easily test alternative media and messages; and easily measure campaign results.

Direct Mail

Direct-mail marketing involves sending an offer, announcement, reminder, or other item to a person. Using highly selective mailing lists, direct marketers send out millions of mail pieces each year—letters, flyers, and other "salespeople with wings." Direct mail is popular because it permits target market selectivity, can be personalized, is flexible, and allows early testing and response measurement. Although the cost per thousand people reached is higher than with mass media, the people reached are better prospects for purchases and charitable contributions.

Direct marketers must decide on their objectives, target markets, and prospects; offer elements, means of testing the campaign, and measures of campaign success.

- *Objectives.* A campaign's success is judged by the response rate. An order-response rate of 2 percent is normally considered good (this number varies with product category and price). Direct mail can achieve other objectives as well, such as producing leads, strengthening customer relationships, informing and educating customers, reminding customers of offers, and reinforcing customer purchase decisions.

- *Target markets and prospects.* Direct marketers need to identify the characteristics and specific names of prospects and customers who are most able, willing, and ready to buy. Direct marketers usually apply the R-F-M formula (recency, frequency, monetary amount), selecting customers according to how much time has passed since their last purchase, how many times they have purchased, and how long they have been a customer. Prospects can also be identified on the basis of such variables as age, sex, income, education, and previous mail-order purchases; occasions; and consumer lifestyle. In B2B direct marketing, the prospect is often a group of people that includes decision makers and influencers.

- *Offer elements.* Nash sees the offer strategy as consisting of five elements—the *product,* the *offer,* the *medium,* the *distribution method,* and the *creative strategy.*[5] All of these elements can be tested. In addition, the marketer has to decide on five components of the mailing itself: the outside envelope, sales letter, circular, reply form, and reply envelope. Direct mail can be followed up by e-mail, which is less expensive and less intrusive than telemarketing.

- *Testing elements.* One of the great advantages of direct marketing is the ability to test, under real marketplace conditions, elements such as products and features, copy platform, mailer type, envelope, prices, and mailing lists. Response rates typically understate a campaign's long-term impact; this is why some firms measure the impact of direct marketing on awareness, intention to buy, and word of mouth.

- *Measuring success: lifetime value.* By adding up the planned costs, the direct marketer can figure out in advance the needed break-even response rate (net of returned merchandise and bad debts). Even when a campaign fails to break even in the short run, it can be worthwhile if the expected profit on all future purchases is considered. For an average customer, one would calculate the average customer longevity, average customer annual expenditure, and average gross margin, minus the average cost of customer acquisition and maintenance (discounted for the opportunity cost of money).[6]

Catalog Marketing

In catalog marketing, companies may send full-line merchandise catalogs, specialty consumer catalogs, and business catalogs, usually in print form but also sometimes as CDs, videos, or online. JCPenney sends general merchandise catalogs; IKEA sends furniture catalogs; Grainger sends industrial and office supply catalogs to businesses. Many direct marketers have found that combining catalogs and Web sites can be an effective way to sell.

Catalogs are a huge business—about 71 percent of Americans shop from home using catalogs by phone, mail, and Internet, spending an average of $149 per catalog order.[7] Successful catalog marketing depends on the ability to manage customer lists carefully so that there is little duplication or bad debts, to control inventory, to offer quality goods so that returns are low, and to project a distinctive image. Some companies distinguish their catalogs by adding literary or information features, sending swatches of materials, operating a special hot line to answer questions, sending gifts to their best customers, and donating some of the profits to good causes.

Catalogs are catching on in Asia and Europe. In just a few years foreign catalogs—mainly from the United States and Europe—have won 5 percent of the $20-billion Japanese mail-order market. A full 90 percent of L.L. Bean's international sales come from Japan. By putting their catalogs online, firms have better access to global customers than ever before, while cutting printing and mailing costs.

Telemarketing

Telemarketing is the use of the telephone and call centers to attract prospects, sell to existing customers, and provide service by taking orders and answering questions. Companies use call centers for *inbound telemarketing* (receiving calls from customers) and *outbound telemarketing* (initiating calls to prospects and customers). Telemarketing includes (1) *telesales*, taking orders from catalogs or ads and calling to cross-sell products, upgrade orders, introduce new products, open new accounts, and reactivate former accounts; (2) *telecoverage*, calling customers to maintain and nurture key account relationships and give more attention to neglected accounts; (3) *teleprospecting*, generating and qualifying new leads for closure by another sales channel; and (4) *customer service and technical support*, answering customers' service and technical questions.

Effective telemarketing depends on choosing the right telemarketers, training them well, and providing performance incentives. Although telemarketing is a major direct-marketing tool and helps to replace more expensive field sales calls, consumers sometimes find it intrusive. As a result, the Federal Trade Commission established a National Do Not Call Registry in October 2003, and more than 105 million Americans have already signed up to prevent telemarketers from calling them at home. Only political organizations, charities, telephone surveyors, or firms with existing relationships with consumers are exempt.[8]

Other Media for Direct-Response Marketing

Direct marketers use all the major media to make offers to potential buyers. Newspapers and magazines carry abundant print ads offering books, clothing, vacations, and other goods and services that individuals can order by dialing a toll-free number. Radio ads present offers to listeners 24 hours a day.

In recent years, *direct-response TV advertising* through 30- and 60-minute infomercials has become more prominent. These often resemble documentaries and include testimonials plus a toll-free number for ordering or getting further information about complex or expensive goods and services, which is why Pfizer, General Motors, and many other firms have used infomercials.[9] Some television channels are dedicated to selling goods and services. The Home Shopping Network (HSN) broadcasts 24 hours a day, offering bargain prices on clothing, jewelry, power tools, and other products. Viewers call in orders on a toll-free number and receive delivery within 48 hours.

Some firms are using kiosk marketing. A *kiosk* is a small building or structure that houses a selling or information unit. Kiosks include newsstands, refreshment stands, and free-standing carts whose vendors sell watches, costume jewelry, and other items, often in transit stations or malls. Kiosks can also be computer-linked vending machines and "customer-order-placing machines" in stores, airports, and other locations. McDonald's found that customers who used its kiosks to order spent 30 percent more per order.[10]

INTERACTIVE MARKETING

The newest channels for direct marketing are electronic.[11] The Internet provides marketers and consumers with opportunities for much greater *interaction* and *individualization*. Companies used to send standard media—magazines, newsletters, ads—to everyone. Today they can send individualized content and consumers themselves can further individualize the content, resulting in interaction and dialogue with much larger groups. Broadband connections are becoming more common, allowing marketers to market through rich media ads combining animation, video, and sound with interactive features.

For example, when Unilever launched Axe Deodorant body spray, its agency created commercials purporting to be home videos and posted them on Axe's Web site, supported by banner ads on the Web sites of men's magazines. Within four months, 1.7 million people had visited the site; by year-end, Axe had almost 4 percent of the $2 billion U.S. male deodorant market.[12]

The exchange process in the age of information has become increasingly customer initiated and customer-controlled. Even after marketers enter the exchange process, customers define the rules of engagement and insulate themselves with the help of agents and intermediaries if they so choose. Customers define what information they need, what offerings they are interested in, and what prices they are willing to pay.[13]

The Benefits of Interactive Marketing

Interactive marketing offers many unique benefits.[14] It is highly accountable and its effects can be easily traced. Eddie Bauer cut its marketing cost per sale by 74 percent by concentrating on higher-performing ads.[15] Marketers can buy ads from sites that are related to their offerings as well as place advertising based on contextual keywords from online search outfits like Google. In that way, the Web can reach people who have actually started the buying process. The Web is especially effective at reaching people during the day. Young, high-income, high-education customers' total online media consumption exceeds that of TV.[16]

Designing an Attractive Web Site

A key challenge is designing a site that is attractive on first viewing and interesting enough to encourage repeat visits. As shown in Table 17.1, Rayport and Jaworski have proposed that effective Web sites feature the 7Cs design elements.[17] To bring visitors back again and again, marketers must embrace an eighth C—constant change.[18]

Visitors will judge a site's performance on its ease of use and its physical attractiveness. Ease-of-use breaks down into three attributes: (1) the site downloads quickly, (2) the first page is easy to understand, and (3) the visitor can easily navigate to other pages that open quickly. Physical attractiveness is determined by these factors: (1) the

TABLE 17.1   Elements of Effective Web Design

Design Element	Description
Context	Layout and design.
Content	Text, pictures, sound, and video on the site.
Community	How the site enables user-to-user communication.
Customization	Site's ability to tailor itself to different users or allow users to personalize the site.
Communication	How the site enables site-to-user, user-to-site, or two-way communication.
Connection	Degree to which the site is linked to other sites.
Commerce	Site's capabilities to enable commercial transactions.

Source: Jeffrey F. Rayport and Bernard J. Jaworski, *E-Commerce* (New York: McGraw-Hill, 2001), p. 116.

individual pages are clean looking and not overly crammed with content, (2) the type-faces and font sizes are very readable, and (3) the site makes good use of color (and sound). Certain types of content function well to attract first-time visitors and to bring them back again: (1) deep information with links to related sites, (2) changing news of interest, (3) changing free offers to visitors, (4) contests and sweepstakes, (5) humor and jokes, and (6) games.

Placing Ads and Promotion Online

A company has to decide which forms of Internet advertising will be most cost-effective in achieving advertising objectives. **Banner ads** are small, rectangular boxes containing text and perhaps a picture. Companies pay to place banner ads on relevant Web sites (although some ads are placed on a barter basis). The larger the audience reached, the more the placement will cost.

Many companies get their name on the Internet by sponsoring special content on Web sites that carry news, financial information, and so on. *Sponsorships* are best placed in well-targeted sites where they can offer relevant information or service in exchange for being acknowledged as the sponsor of that particular service on the Web site. A **microsite** is a limited area on the Web managed and paid for by an external advertiser/company. Microsites are particularly useful for companies selling low-interest products such as insurance. People rarely visit an insurance company's Web site. However, the insurance company can create a microsite on used-car sites that offers advice for buyers of used cars and at the same time a good insurance deal.

The hottest growth area has been **search-related ads**.[19] Thirty-five percent of all searches are reportedly for products or services. Search terms are used as a proxy for the consumer's consumption interests and relevant links to product or service offerings are listed along side the search results. Advertisers pay only if people click on the links; the cost per click depends on how high the link is ranked and the popularity of the keyword searched. Average click-through is about 2 percent, much more than comparable online ads.[20] One Samsung executive estimated that it was 50 times cheaper to reach 1,000 people online than on TV, so the firm now spends 10 percent of its advertising budget online.[21] A newer trend, **content-target advertising**, links ads to the content of Web pages, not to keywords.

E-Marketing Guidelines

Here are some important guidelines followed by pioneering e-mail marketers:[22]

- *Give the customer a reason to respond.* Companies should offer powerful incentives for reading e-mail pitches and online ads, like e-mail trivia games, scavenger hunts, and instant-win sweepstakes.
- *Personalize the e-mail content.* IBM's iSource is distributed directly to customers' office e-mail each week, delivering only "the news they choose" (announcements and updates). Customers who agree to receive the newsletter select from topics listed on an interest profile.
- *Offer something the customer could not get via direct mail.* Because e-mail campaigns can be carried out quickly, they can offer time-sensitive information. For instance, Travelocity sends frequent e-mails pitching last-minute cheap airfares.
- *Make it easy to "unsubscribe."* Online customers should have a positive exit experience. According to one study, the top 10 percent of Web users who communicate much more often online typically share their views by e-mail with 11 friends when satisfied but contact 17 friends when they are dissatisfied.[23]

Online merchants face many challenges in expanding the public's use of e-commerce. Customers will have to feel that the information they supply is secure and confidential, not to be sold to others. Companies must encourage communication by inviting questions, suggestions, and even complaints via e-mail. Some sites include a call-me button—when the customer clicks, the phone rings and a customer representative is on the line, ready to answer a question. Smart online marketers respond quickly to inquiries by sending out newsletters, special product or promotion offers based on purchase histories, service reminders, or announcements of special events.

Direct marketing must be integrated with other communications and channel activities.[24] Citigroup, AT&T, IBM, Ford, and American Airlines have used integrated direct marketing to build profitable relationships with customers over the years. Retailers such as Nordstrom regularly send catalogs to supplement in-store sales. Companies such as L.L. Bean and The Sharper Image established strong brand names and made fortunes in the direct-marketing mail-order and phone-order business, then opened retail stores.

DESIGNING THE SALES FORCE

The original and oldest form of direct marketing is the field sales call. Today most industrial firms rely heavily on a professional sales force to locate prospects, develop them into customers, and grow the business; or they hire manufacturers' representatives and agents to carry out the direct-selling task. In addition, consumer companies such as Avon, Tupperware, insurance agents, and stockbrokers use a direct-selling force. U.S. firms spend over a trillion dollars annually on sales forces and sales force materials—more than they spend on any other promotional method. Nearly 12 percent of the total workforce works full-time in sales occupations, in nonprofit as well as for-profit organizations. Hospitals and museums, for example, use fund-raisers to solicit donations.

Although personal selling is an important marketing tool, companies are sensitive to the high and rising costs (salaries, commissions, bonuses, travel expenses, and benefits) of maintaining a sales force. Because the average cost of a personal sales call ranges from $200 to $300, and closing a sale typically requires four calls, the total cost can range from $800 to $1,200.[25] Not surprisingly, companies are trying to increase the productivity of the sales force through better selection, training, supervision, motivation, and compensation.

Six types of sales representatives can be distinguished, ranging from the least to the most creative types of selling:[26]

1. *Deliverer.* A salesperson whose major task is the delivery of a product (water, fuel).
2. *Order taker.* A salesperson who acts predominantly as an inside order taker (behind a counter) or outside order taker (calling on supermarket managers).
3. *Missionary.* A salesperson whose major task is to build goodwill or to educate the actual or potential user, rather than to sell (the medical "detailer" representing a pharmaceutical firm).
4. *Technician.* A salesperson with a high level of technical knowledge (the engineering salesperson who is primarily a consultant to client companies).
5. *Demand creator.* A salesperson who relies on creative methods for selling tangible products (vacuum cleaners or siding) or intangibles (insurance or education).
6. *Solution vendor.* A salesperson whose expertise lies in solving a customer's problem, often with a system of the firm's goods and services (such as computer systems).

Figure 17.1 shows the basic steps in designing a sales force.

Sales Force Objectives and Strategy

Companies need to define the specific objectives they want their sales force to achieve. For example, a company might want its sales representatives to spend 80 percent of their time with current customers and 20 percent with prospects, and 85 percent of their time on established products and 15 percent on new products.

The specific allocation scheme depends on the offerings and customers, but regardless of the selling context, salespeople will have one or more of the following tasks to perform: prospecting (searching for prospects or leads); targeting (deciding how to allocate their time among prospects and customers); communicating (conveying information about the company's products); selling (approaching, presenting, answering objections, and closing sales); servicing (consulting on problems, rendering technical assistance, arranging financing, expediting delivery); information gathering (conducting market research and doing intelligence work); and allocating (deciding which customers will get scarce products during shortages).

To implement the firm's sales objectives, a common strategy is for sales representatives to act as "account managers," arranging fruitful contact among people in

FIGURE 17.1   Designing a Sales Force

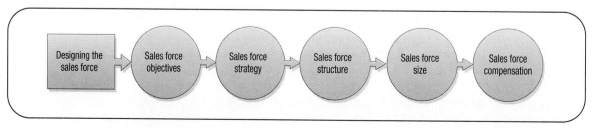

the buying and selling organizations. Increasingly, effective sales requires teamwork and the support of other personnel, such as top management, especially when national accounts or major sales are at stake; technical people, who supply technical information and service to the customer; customer service representatives, who provide installation, maintenance, and other services; and an office staff, consisting of sales analysts, order expediters, and administrative personnel.

Once the company decides on an approach, it can use either a direct or contractual sales force. A **direct (company) sales force** consists of full- or part-time paid employees who work exclusively for the firm. This sales force includes inside sales personnel who conduct business from the office (using the telephone, fax, and e-mail) and receive visits from prospective buyers; and field sales personnel who travel and visit customers. A **contractual sales force** consists of manufacturers' reps, sales agents, and brokers, who are paid a commission based on sales.

Sales Force Structure

The sales force strategy has implications for the sales force structure. If the company sells one product line to one end-using industry with customers in many locations, it would use a territorial sales force structure. If the company sells many products to many types of customers, it might need a product or market sales force structure. Some companies need a more complex structure. Motorola, for example, manages four types of sales forces: (1) a strategic market sales force composed of technical, applications, and quality engineers and service personnel assigned to major accounts; (2) a geographic sales force calling on customers in different territories; (3) a distributor sales force calling on and coaching Motorola distributors; and (4) an inside sales force doing telemarketing and taking orders.

Companies typically single out major accounts (also called key accounts, national accounts, global accounts, or house accounts) for special attention. The largest accounts may have a strategic account management team, consisting of cross-functional personnel who are permanently assigned to one customer and may even maintain offices at the customer's facility. For example, Procter & Gamble has a strategic account team working with Wal-Mart in Bentonville, Arkansas, an arrangement that has saved the firms $30 billion jointly through supply chain improvements.[27] See "Marketing Skills: Major Account Management" for more on this important skill.

Sales Force Size

After the company determines the sales force strategy and structure, it is ready to consider sales force size, based on the number of customers it wants to reach. One widely used method for determining sales force size is the five-step *workload approach*: (1) group customers into size classes by annual sales volume; (2) establish call frequencies, the number of calls to be made per year on each account in a size class; (3) multiply the number of accounts in each size class by the call frequency to arrive at the total yearly sales-call workload; (4) determine the average number of calls a sales rep can make per year; and (5) divide the total annual calls (calculated in step 3) required by the average annual calls made by a rep (in step 4) to see how many reps are needed.

Suppose the company has 1,000 A accounts and 2,000 B accounts; A accounts require 36 calls a year (36,000 calls yearly), and B accounts require 12 calls a year (24,000

MARKETING SKILLS: MAJOR ACCOUNT MANAGEMENT

Major accounts represent considerable sales and profit potential, which is why companies often assign major account managers to work with these important customers. On average, each major account manager works with nine accounts, reporting to the national sales manager (who reports to the vice president of marketing and sales). Major accounts normally receive more favorable pricing based on purchasing volume. However, they look more for added value than a price advantage and appreciate the personal attention and advice from a major account manager.

What do major account managers do? They act as the single point of contact between buyer and seller; understand and respond to customer needs and decision processes; look for ways to add value through appropriate solutions to customer problems; negotiate contracts with their customers; and provide tailored, responsive customer service. To be effective, they need communication, marketing, management, and financial expertise. One major account manager says, "My position must not be as a salesman, but as a 'marketing consultant' to our customers and a salesman of my company's capabilities as opposed to my company's products."

California Eastern Laboratories (CEL), which sells semiconductor components through 13 sales offices, piloted a major account management program with one key client, Motorola. Within four years, its sales to Motorola had increased 566 percent. CEL then added three more major account managers to work with other large customers. Rather than simply shift top salespeople into these positions, the company chose employees with both sales and marketing experience, paving the way for closer, more productive relationships with the customers.[28]

calls). This company needs a sales force that can make 60,000 sales calls a year. If the average rep can make 1,000 calls a year, the company would need 60 representatives.

Sales Force Compensation

To attract top-quality sales reps, the company needs an attractive compensation package. The four components of sales force compensation are a fixed amount, a variable amount, expense allowances, and benefits. The *fixed amount*, a salary, is intended to satisfy the sales reps' need for income stability. The *variable amount*, which might be commissions, a bonus, or profit sharing, is intended to stimulate and reward greater effort. *Expense allowances* enable sales reps to meet the expenses involved in travel, lodging, dining, and entertaining. *Benefits*, such as paid vacations and life insurance, provide security and job satisfaction.

Fixed compensation receives more emphasis in jobs with a high ratio of non-selling to selling duties and when the selling task is technically complex and involves teamwork. Variable compensation receives more emphasis in jobs where sales are cyclical or depend on individual initiative. Fixed and variable compensation give rise to three basic types of compensation plans—straight salary, straight commission, and combination salary and commission. Three-quarters of firms use a combination of salary and commission, though the relative proportion varies widely.[29]

Straight-salary plans provide sales reps with a secure income, make them more willing to perform nonselling activities, and give them less incentive to overstock customers. These plans are easy to administer, and they lower turnover. Straight-commission plans attract higher sales performers, provide more motivation, require less supervision, and control selling costs. Combination plans offer the benefits of both plans while reducing their disadvantages. Such plans allow companies to link the variable portion of a salesperson's pay to a wide variety of strategic goals. Some see a trend toward deemphasizing volume measures in favor of factors such as gross profitability, customer satisfaction, and customer retention. For example, IBM partly rewards salespeople on the basis of customer satisfaction as measured by customer surveys.[30]

MANAGING THE SALES FORCE

Effective management of the sales force is needed to implement the company's chosen sales force design and achieve its sales objectives. Sales force management covers the steps in recruiting and selecting, training, supervising, motivating, and evaluating representatives (see Figure 17.2).

Recruiting and Selecting Sales Representatives

At the heart of a successful sales force is the selection of effective representatives. One survey revealed that the top 27 percent of the sales force brought in over 52 percent of the sales. Beyond differences in productivity is the waste in hiring the wrong people. The average annual turnover rate for all industries is almost 20 percent. Turnover leads to lost sales, costs of finding and training replacements, and a strain on existing salespeople to pick up the slack.

In selecting sales reps, the company can start by asking customers what traits they prefer in salespeople. Most customers want honest, reliable, knowledgeable, and helpful reps. Determining what traits will actually lead to sales success, however, is a challenge. Numerous studies have shown little relationship between sales performance on one hand, and background and experience variables, current status, lifestyle, attitude, personality, and skills on the other. More effective predictors have been composite tests and assessment centers where the working environment is simulated and applicants are assessed in an environment similar to the one in which they would work.[31]

After management develops selection criteria, the next step is to recruit applicants by various means, including soliciting names from current sales reps, using employment agencies, placing print and online job ads, and contacting graduating college students. Selection procedures can vary from an informal interview to prolonged

FIGURE 17.2   Managing the Sales Force

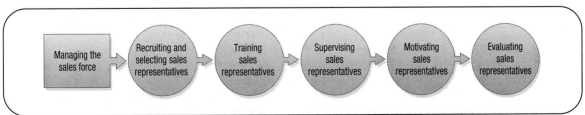

testing and interviewing. Although test scores are only one information element in a set that includes personal characteristics, references, past employment history, and interviewer reactions, they are weighted quite heavily by some companies. Gillette, for example, claims that tests have reduced turnover by 42 percent and have correlated well with the subsequent progress of new reps.

Training and Supervising Sales Representatives

Today's customers expect salespeople to have deep product knowledge, add ideas to improve the customer's operations, and be efficient and reliable. This requires companies to make a much higher investment in sales training. New reps may spend a few weeks to several months in training. The median training period is 28 weeks in industrial-products companies, 12 in service companies, and 4 in consumer-products companies. Training time and method varies with the complexity of the selling task and the type of person recruited for sales. Training often involves a variety of methods, including role-playing, audio- and videotapes, CD-ROMs, and Web-based distance learning. For instance, IBM uses a computerized self-study system in which trainees practice sales calls with an on-screen actor portraying a buying executive.

Companies vary in how closely they supervise sales reps. Reps paid mostly on commission generally receive less supervision. Those who are salaried and must cover definite accounts are likely to receive substantial supervision. With multilevel selling, used by Avon and others, independent distributors are also in charge of their own sales force selling company products. These independent contractors or reps are paid a commission not only on their own sales, but also on the sales of people they recruit and train.[32]

Sales Rep Productivity

How many calls should a company make on a particular account each year? Some research has suggested that sales reps spend too much time selling to smaller, less profitable accounts when they should focus on larger, more profitable accounts.[33] Therefore, companies often specify how much time reps should spend prospecting for new accounts. Spector Freight, for instance, wants sales representatives to spend 25 percent of their time prospecting and stop calling on a prospect after three unsuccessful calls. Prospecting standards are used because many reps, left to their own devices, will spend most of their time with current customers, who are known quantities, rather than with prospects, who might never buy. Some firms rely on a missionary sales force to open new accounts.

Studies have shown that the best sales reps are those who manage their time efficiently.[34] One planning tool is *time-and-duty analysis*, which helps reps understand how they spend their time and how they might increase their productivity. In general, sales reps spend time planning, traveling, waiting, selling, and in administrative tasks (report writing and billing, attending sales meetings, and talking to others in the company about production, delivery, billing, sales performance, and other matters). With so many duties, it is no wonder that actual face-to-face selling time amounts to as little as 29 percent of total working time![35]

Companies are constantly seeking ways to improve sales force productivity. These may include training sales representatives in the use of "phone power"; simplifying record keeping and administrative time; and using the computer and the

Internet to develop call and routing plans, supply customer and competitive information, and automate order preparation. In addition, company Web sites can help define the firm's relationships with individual accounts, identify those whose business warrants a sales call, and allow sales reps to focus on issues best addressed in person.

To reduce the time demands on their outside sales force, many firms have increased the size and responsibilities of the inside sales force. Inside salespeople are of three types. *Technical support people* provide technical information and answer customers' questions. *Sales assistants* provide clerical backup for outside reps by confirming appointments, checking credit, following up on deliveries, and answering customers' questions. *Telemarketers* find new leads, qualify and sell to them, reactivate old accounts, and attend to neglected accounts.

Motivating Sales Representatives

The majority of sales representatives require encouragement and special incentives. This is especially true of field selling: Reps usually work alone, their hours are irregular, and they are often away from home. They confront aggressive, competing sales reps; they often lack the authority to do what is necessary to win an account; and they may lose large orders that they have worked hard to obtain.[36] Most marketers believe that the higher the salesperson's motivation, the greater the effort and the resulting performance, rewards, and satisfaction—and thus further motivation. This thinking implies that sales managers must be able to convince salespeople that they can sell more by working harder or by being trained to work smarter and that the rewards for better performance are worth the extra effort.

To increase motivation, marketers reinforce intrinsic and extrinsic rewards of all types. One study measuring the importance of different rewards found that the reward with the highest value was pay, followed by promotion, personal growth, and sense of accomplishment.[37] The least-valued rewards were liking and respect, security, and recognition. In other words, salespeople are highly motivated by pay and the chance to get ahead and satisfy their intrinsic needs, and they are less motivated by compliments and security. However, the researchers also found that the importance of motivators varied with demographic characteristics: Financial rewards were mostly valued by older, longer-tenured people and those who had large families. Rewards such as recognition were more valued by young reps who were unmarried or who had small families and usually more formal education.

Many firms set annual sales quotas based on dollar sales, unit volume, margin, selling effort or activity, and product type. Management often ties salesperson compensation to degree of quota fulfillment. Sales quotas are developed from the annual marketing plan. Management first prepares a sales forecast, which becomes the basis for planning production, workforce size, and financial requirements. Then the firm can establish sales quotas for regions and territories, often setting the total higher than the sales forecast to encourage managers and salespeople to perform at their best levels. If they fail to make their quotas, the firm might still make its sales forecast.

Each area sales manager divides the area's quota to arrive at an individual quota for each sales rep. A common approach to individual quotas is to set the individual rep's quota at least equal to the person's last year's sales plus some fraction of the difference between area sales potential and last year's sales. The more the rep reacts favorably to pressure, the higher the fraction should be.

Evaluating Sales Representatives

We have been describing the *feed-forward* aspects of sales supervision—how management communicates what sales reps should be doing and motivates them to do it. However, good feed-forward requires good *feedback*, which means getting regular information from reps to evaluate their performance. Information about reps can come from sales reports, personal observation, customer letters and complaints, customer surveys, and conversations with other sales reps. Many firms require their reps to develop an annual territory marketing plan for developing new accounts and increasing business from existing accounts. This report casts sales reps into the role of market managers and profit centers. Sales managers study these plans, make suggestions, and use them to develop sales quotas.

Sales reps write up completed activities on *call reports* and, in addition, submit expense reports, new-business reports, lost-business reports, and reports on local business and economic conditions. These reports provide raw data from which sales managers can monitor sales performance by (1) average number of sales calls per rep per day, (2) average sales call time per contact, (3) average revenue per sales call, (4) average cost per sales call, (5) entertainment cost per sales call, (6) percentage of orders per hundred sales calls, (7) number of new customers per period, (8) number of lost customers per period, and (9) sales force cost as a percentage of total sales.

Sales reports, along with other observations, supply the raw materials for evaluation. There are several approaches to conducting evaluations. One type of evaluation compares current performance to past performance and to overall company averages on key indicators. These comparisons help management pinpoint specific areas for improvement. For example, if a rep's average gross profit per customer is lower than the company's average, that rep could be concentrating on the wrong customers or not spending enough time with each customer. Evaluations can also assess the rep's knowledge of the firm, products, customers, competitors, territory, and responsibilities; relevant personality characteristics; and any problems in motivation or compliance.[38]

PRINCIPLES OF PERSONAL SELLING

Personal selling is an ancient art that has spawned many principles. The major steps involved in any effective sales process are shown in Table 17.2.[39] Also important for personal selling are negotiation and relationship marketing.

Negotiation

Marketing is concerned with exchange activities and the manner in which the terms of exchange are established. In *routinized exchange*, the terms are set by administered programs of pricing and distribution. In *negotiated exchange*, price and other terms are set through bargaining, in which two or more parties negotiate long-term binding agreements. In addition to price, other issues to be negotiated are contract completion time; quality of goods and services offered; purchase volume; responsibility for financing, risk taking, promotion, and title; and product safety. Sales reps who must bargain need preparation and planning skills, knowledge of subject matter being negotiated, the ability to think clearly and rapidly under pressure and uncertainty, the ability to express thoughts verbally, good listening skills, judgment and general intelligence, integrity, the ability to persuade others, and patience.[40]

TABLE 17.2   Major Steps in Effective Selling

Sales Step	Application in Industrial Selling
Prospecting and qualifying	Firms generate leads and then qualify them by mail or phone to assess level of interest and financial capacity. Hot prospects are turned over to the field sales force; warm prospects receive telemarketing follow-up.
Preapproach	The sales rep researches what the prospect needs, who is involved in buying decisions, and the buyers' personal characteristics and buying styles. The rep also sets call objectives to qualify the prospect, gather information, or make an immediate sale; decides whether to visit, call, or write; plans the timing of the approach; and sets an overall sales strategy.
Approach	To get the relationship off to a good start, the salesperson needs a positive opening line, followed by key questions and active listening to understand the buyer's needs.
Presentation and demonstration	The rep tells the product "story" to the buyer, using a *features, advantages, benefits,* and *value* approach. Reps should guard against spending too much time on product features (product orientation) and not enough on benefits and value (customer orientation).
Overcoming objections	Salespeople must handle objections posed by customers during the presentation or when asked for the order. Here, the rep must maintain a positive approach, ask for clarification, ask questions that lead the buyer to answer his or her own objection, deny the validity of the objection, or turn the objection into a reason for buying.
Closing	Attempting to close the sale, the rep can ask for the order, recapitulate points of agreement, offer to help write up the order, ask whether the buyer wants A or B, get the buyer to make minor choices such as color or size, or show what the buyer will lose by not ordering now. The rep might offer the buyer an inducement to close, such as a special price or a token gift.
Follow-up and maintenance	To ensure customer satisfaction and repeat business, the rep should cement details such as delivery time and purchase terms immediately after closing. Also, the rep should schedule a follow-up call to check on proper installation and training after delivery. This helps detect problems, shows interest, and reduces any cognitive dissonance. Further, each account needs a maintenance and growth plan.

Relationship Marketing

The principles of personal selling and negotiation we have described are largely transaction oriented, intended to close a specific sale. However, in many cases the company wants to build a long-term supplier–customer relationship by demonstrating that it has the capabilities to serve the account's needs in a superior way. Because today's customers are large and often global, they prefer suppliers who can sell and deliver a coordinated set of products and services to many locations, solve problems in different locations quickly, and work closely with customer teams to improve products and processes. With a properly implemented relationship management program, the firm begins to focus as much on managing its customers as on managing its products. However, relationship marketing is not effective in all situations. Ultimately, companies must judge which segments and which specific customers will respond profitably to relationship management.

EXECUTIVE SUMMARY

Direct marketing is the use of consumer-direct channels to reach and deliver goods and services to customers without intermediaries. Direct marketers plan campaigns by deciding on objectives, target markets and prospects, offers, and prices; then they test and establish measures to determine success. Major channels for direct marketing include face-to-face selling, direct mail, catalog marketing, telemarketing, television, and kiosks, plus interactive channels such as Web sites. Interactive marketing provides marketers with more opportunities for dialogue and individualization through well-designed Web sites, as well as online ads and promotions.

Sales personnel serve as a company's link to its customers. Designing the sales force requires decisions regarding objectives, strategy, structure, size, and compensation. Determining strategy requires choosing the most effective mix of selling approaches. Choosing the sales force structure entails dividing territories by geography, product, or market (or some combination of these). To determine how large the sales force should be, management estimates the total workload and calculates how many sales hours (and hence salespeople) will be needed. Compensating the sales force entails determining what types of salaries, commissions, bonuses, expense accounts, and benefits to give and how much weight customer satisfaction should have in determining total compensation.

There are five steps to managing the sales force: (1) recruiting and selecting representatives; (2) training representatives in sales techniques and in the company's products, policies, and customer-satisfaction orientation; (3) supervising the sales force and helping reps use their time efficiently; (4) motivating the sales force and balancing quotas, monetary rewards, and supplementary motivators; and (5) evaluating individual and group sales performance. The personal selling process involves prospecting and qualifying customers, preapproach, approach, presentation and demonstration, overcoming objections, closing, and follow-up and maintenance. Negotiation and relationship marketing are important principles for personal selling today.

NOTES

1. Brandon Hall, "Sales Training Makeovers," *Training*, May 2005, pp. 14+; Carol Krol, "Canon Develops Sales Through Traditional Mail," *B to B*, October 11, 2004, p. 30; "Canon Tops for Copiers," *Office Products International*, May 2003, p. 18.
2. The terms *direct-order marketing* and *direct-relationship marketing* were suggested as subsets of direct marketing by Stan Rapp and Tom Collins in *The Great Marketing Turnaround* (Upper Saddle River, NJ: Prentice Hall, 1990).
3. Michael McCarthy, "Direct Marketing Gets Cannes Do Spirit," *USA Today*, June 17, 2002, p. 4B.
4. Figures supplied by Direct Marketing Magazine, phone 516-716-6700.
5. Edward L. Nash, *Direct Marketing: Strategy, Planning, Execution*, 3d ed. (New York: McGraw-Hill, 1995).
6. The *average customer longevity* (N) is related to the *customer retention rate* (CR). Suppose the company retains 80 percent of its customers each year. Then the average customer longevity is given by: $N = 1/(1 - CR) = 1/.2 = 5$.
7. Lorie Grant, "Niche Catalogs' Unique Gifts Make Money Less of an Object," *USA Today*, November 20, 2003, p. 3B; Olivia Barker, "Catalogs Are Complementary with Online Sales, Purchases," *USA Today*, December 4, 2002, p. 4E.
8. Steve Ivey, "After 2 Years, Do Not Call Registry 'An Incredible Success,'" *Chicago Tribune*, September 30, 2005, (www.chicagotribune.com); Meghann Cuniff, "Decline in Telemarketing Means Boom for Direct Mail Businesses," *The Bulletin (Bend, OR)*, July 11, 2005, (www.ftc.gov/donotcall).

9. Jim Edwards, "The Art of the Infomercial," *Brandweek*, September 3, 2001, pp. 14+.

10. Charles Fishman, "The Tool of a New Machine," *Fast Company*, May 2004, pp. 92–95.

11. Tony Case, "Growing Up," *Interactive Quarterly*, April 19, 2004, pp. 32–34.

12. Thomas Mucha, "Spray Here. Get Girl," *Business 2.0*, June 1, 2003.

13. Asim Ansari and Carl F. Mela, "E-Customization," *Journal of Marketing Research* 40, no. 2 (May 2003): 131–145.

14. David L. Smith and Karen McFee, "Media Mix 101: Online Media for Traditional Marketers," September 2003 (advantage.msn.com/articles/MediaMix101_2.asp).

15. Paul C. Judge, "Will Online Ads Ever Click?" *Fast Company*, March 2001, pp. 181–192.

16. Online Publisher's Association, "OPA Media Consumption Study," January 2002.

17. Jeffrey F. Rayport and Bernard J. Jaworski, *E-Commerce* (New York: McGraw-Hill, 2001), p. 116.

18. Bob Tedeschi, "E-Commerce Report," *New York Times*, June 24, 2002, p. C8.

19. "Prime Clicking Time," *The Economist*, May 31, 2003, p. 65; Ben Elgin, "Search Engines Are Picking Up Steam," *BusinessWeek*, March 24, 2003, pp. 86–87.

20. "Global Click-Through Rates Level Off in 2004 After Year of Decline," *New Media Age*, November 25, 2004, p. 10; Ned Desmond, "Google's Next Runaway Success," *Business 2.0*, November 2002, p. 73.

21. Heather Green, "Online Ads Take Off Again," *BusinessWeek*, May 5, 2003, p. 75.

22. Seth Godin, *Permission Marketing: Turning Strangers into Friends and Friends into Customers* (New York: Simon & Schuster, 1999).

23. Chana R. Schoenberger, "Web? What Web?" *Forbes*, June 10, 2002, p. 132.

24. Stan Rapp and Thomas L. Collins, *Maximarketing* (New York: McGraw-Hill, 1987).

25. Bill Keenan, "Cost-per-call Data Deserve Scrutiny," *Industry Week*, January 10, 2000.

26. Adapted from Robert N. McMurry, "The Mystique of Super-Salesmanship," *Harvard Business Review* (March–April 1961): 114. Also see William C. Moncrief III, "Selling Activity and Sales Position Taxonomies for Industrial Salesforces," *Journal of Marketing Research* (August 1986): 261–270.

27. See John F. Martin and Gary S. Tubridy, "Major Account Management," in *AMA Management Handbook*, edited by John J. Hampton (New York: Amacom, 1994) pp. 3-25–3-27; Sanjit Sengupta, Robert E. Krapfel, and Michael A. Pusateri, "The Strategic Sales Force," *Marketing Management*, Summer 1997, pp. 29–34; Robert S. Duboff and Lori Underhill Sherer, "Customized Customer Loyalty," *Marketing Management*, Summer 1997, pp. 21–27; Tricia Campbell, "Getting Top Executives to Sell," *Sales & Marketing Management*, October 1998, p. 39.

28. Steven Miranda, "Beyond BI," *Financial Executive*, March–April 2004, pp. 58+; Noel Capon, *Key Account Management and Planning: The Comprehensive Handbook for Managing Your Company's Most Important Strategic Asset* (New York: Free Press, 2001); Sallie Sherman, Joseph Sperry, and Samuel Reese, *The Seven Keys to Managing Strategic Accounts* (New York: McGraw-Hill Trade, 2003); Michele Marchetti, "A Hiring Decision You Can't Afford to Screw Up," *Sales & Marketing Management*, June 1999, pp. 13+; Martin and Tubridy, "Major Account Management", in *AMA Management Handbook*; Sengupta, Krapfel, and Pusateri, "The Strategic Sales Force"; Duboff and Sherer, "Customized Customer Loyalty."

29. Luis R. Gomez-Mejia, David B. Balkin, and Robert L. Cardy, *Managing Human Resources* (Upper Saddle River, NJ: Prentice Hall, 1995), pp. 416–418.

30. "What Salespeople Are Paid," *Sales & Marketing Management*, February 1995, pp. 30–31; Christopher Power, "Smart Selling: How Companies Are Winning Over Today's Tougher Customer," *BusinessWeek*, August 3, 1992, pp. 46–48; William Keenan Jr., ed., *The Sales & Marketing Management Guide to Sales Compensation Planning: Commissions, Bonuses & Beyond* (Chicago: Probus Publishing, 1994).

31. Sonke Albers, "Salesforce Management—Compensation, Motivation, Selection, and Training," in *Handbook of Marketing*, edited by Bart Weitz and Robin Wensley (London: Sage Publications, 2002), pp. 248–266.

32. Nanette Byrnes, "Avon Calling—Lots of New Reps," *BusinessWeek*, June 2, 2003, pp. 53–54.

33. Michael R. W. Bommer, Brian F. O'Neil, and Beheruz N. Sethna, "A Methodology for Optimizing Selling Time of Salespersons," *Journal of Marketing Theory and Practice* (Spring 1994): 61–75. See also Lissan Joseph, "On the Optimality of Delegating Pricing Authority to the Sales Force," *Journal of Marketing* 65 (January 2001): 62–70.

34. Thomas Blackshear and Richard E. Plank, "The Impact of Adaptive Selling on Sales Effectiveness Within the Pharmaceutical Industry," *Journal of Marketing Theory and Practice* (Summer 1994): 106–125.

35. Dartnell Corporation, 30th Sales Force Compensation Survey. Other breakdowns show that 12.7 percent is spent in service calls, 16 percent in administrative tasks, 25.1 percent in telephone selling, and 17.4 percent in waiting/traveling.

36. Willem Verbeke and Richard P. Bagozzi, "Sales Call Anxiety: Exploring What It Means When Fear Rules a Sales Encounter," *Journal of Marketing* 64 (July 2000): 88–101.

37. Gilbert A. Churchill, Jr., Neil M. Ford, and Orville C. Walker, Jr., *Sales Force Management: Planning, Implementation and Control*, 4th ed. (Homewood, IL: Irwin, 1993). Also see Jhinuk Chowdhury, "The Motivational Impact of Sales Quotas on Effort," *Journal of Marketing Research* (February 1993): 28–41; Murali K. Mantrala, Prabhakant Sinha, and Andris A. Zoltners, "Structuring a Multiproduct Sales Quota-Bonus Plan for a Heterogeneous Sales Force: A Practical Model-Based Approach," *Marketing Science* 13, no. 2 (1994): 121–144; Wujin Chu, Eitan Gerstner, and James D. Hess, "Costs and Benefits of Hard-Sell," *Journal of Marketing Research* (February 1995): 97–102; Manfred Krafft, "An Empirical Investigation of the Antecedents of Sales Force Control Systems," *Journal of Marketing* 63 (July 1999): 120–134.

38. See Philip M. Posdakoff and Scott B. MacKenzie, "Organizational Citizenship Behaviors and Sales Unit Effectiveness," *Journal of Marketing Research* (August 1994): 351–363.

39. Some of the following discussion is based on W. J. E. Crissy, William H. Cunningham, and Isabella C. M. Cunningham, *Selling: The Personal Force in Marketing* (New York: John Wiley, 1977), pp. 119–129.

40. For additional reading, see Howard Raiffa, *The Art and Science of Negotiation* (Cambridge, MA: Harvard University Press, 1982); Max H. Bazerman and Margaret A. Neale, *Negotiating Rationally* (New York: The Free Press, 1992); James C. Freund, *Smart Negotiating* (New York: Simon & Schuster, 1992); Frank L. Acuff, *How to Negotiate Anything with Anyone Anywhere Around the World* (New York: American Management Association, 1993); Jehoshua Eliashberg, Gary L. Lilien, and Nam Kim, "Searching for Generalizations in Business Marketing Negotiations," *Marketing Science* 14, no. 3, pt. 1 (1995): G47–G60.

C H A P T E R   1 8

Managing Marketing in the Global Economy

In this chapter, we will address the following questions:

1. What major decisions does a firm face in planning for international marketing?
2. What are the keys to effective internal marketing?
3. How can a company improve its marketing implementation skills?
4. What tools can a company use to monitor and improve its marketing activities?

MARKETING MANAGEMENT AT AVON PRODUCTS

From Birmingham to Bosnia to Beijing, Avon is known for its personal care products—and for its support of good causes. Founded in 1886, the New York–based firm was selling cosmetics in Canada by 1914 and was operating in parts of Europe and South America by 1960. More recently, Avon has pursued growth by entering Russian, Chinese, and Eastern European markets. Today, with 5 million representatives selling in more than 120 countries, Avon's annual sales are approaching $8 billion. Although each country has a local marketing team, a brand president— reporting to Avon's president—has overall responsibility for managing global branding strategy.

As it goes about the business of marketing beauty products, jewelry, and gifts, the company also sponsors fundraising events and sells merchandise to raise money for charity. Avon's Breast Cancer Research Crusade, launched in 1992, has raised more than $350 million through annual Walk for Breast Cancer events in major U.S. cities, as well as star-studded fundraising dinners. In addition, Avon sells Crusade-branded products and gives 100 percent of the proceeds to cancer education, screening, treatment, and research. Not only do these efforts bring together executives, employees, sales representatives, customers, and suppliers for a good cause, they also bring to life the principles in Avon's Code of Business Conduct and Ethics. As the CEO recently observed, "Avon's impeccable reputation is built upon a proud heritage of doing well by doing right."[1]

Although the opportunities for companies to enter and compete in foreign markets are significant, the risks can also be high. Companies selling in global industries, however, really have no choice but to internationalize their operations. Avon, for example, competes with such global rivals as the French cosmetics giant L'Oréal and the Anglo-Dutch multinational Unilever. In this chapter, we review the major decisions in expanding into global markets, examine how companies organize marketing, and explore how marketing implementation is managed and controlled. We also look at how firms can evaluate their weaknesses and strengths in marketing, including their use of ethical and socially responsible marketing.

MANAGING GLOBAL MARKETING

Many firms have marketed internationally for decades—Nestlé, Shell, Bayer, and Toshiba are familiar to consumers around the world. However, as global competition intensifies, domestic companies that never thought about foreign rivals suddenly find them in their backyards. A **global industry** is one in which the strategic positions of competitors in major geographic or national markets are fundamentally affected by their overall global positions.[2] A **global firm** operates in two or more countries and captures advantages (in R&D, production, logistics, marketing, and finance) in its costs and reputation that are not available to purely domestic competitors.

Global firms plan, operate, and coordinate their activities on a worldwide basis. Ford's "world truck" has a European-made cab and a North American-built chassis, is assembled in Brazil, and is imported into the United States for sale. Otis Elevator gets its door systems from France, small geared parts from Spain, electronics from Germany, and special motor drives from Japan; it uses the United States for systems integration. Small- and medium-sized firms can practice global nichemanship. The Poilane Bakery sells 15,000 loaves of old-style bread each day in Paris—2.5 percent of all bread sold in that city—via company-owned delivery trucks. The company also ships its breads via FedEx to loyal customers in 20 countries.[3]

For a company of any size to go global, it must make a series of decisions (see Figure 18.1).

Deciding Whether to Go Abroad

Several factors are drawing companies into the international arena. A firm may discover that some foreign markets offer higher profit opportunities than the domestic market. It may need a larger customer base to achieve economies of scale or may need international service for current customers going abroad or may want to reduce dependence on any one market. Moreover, the company's domestic market may be under attack from global firms offering better products or lower prices. The company might then want to counterattack these competitors in their home markets.

Before making a decision to go abroad, the company must weigh several risks. First, the company might not understand foreign customer preferences and fail to offer a competitively attractive product. Second, it might not understand the other country's business culture or know how to deal effectively with foreign nationals. Third, it might underestimate foreign regulations and incur unexpected costs. Fourth, it may lack managers with international experience. Finally, the other country might

FIGURE 18.1   Major Decisions in International Marketing

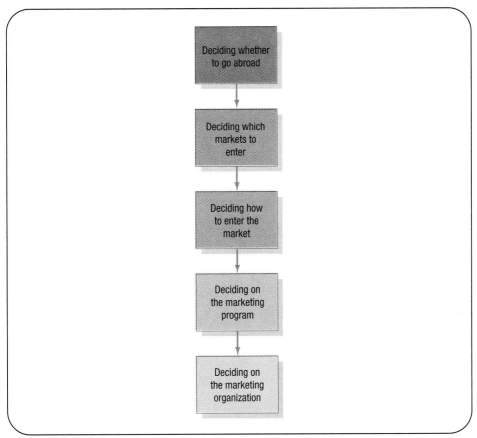

change its commercial laws, devalue its currency, or undergo a political revolution and expropriate foreign property.

Deciding Which Markets to Enter

In deciding to go abroad, the company needs to define its marketing objectives and policies. What proportion of foreign to total sales will it seek? Most companies start small when they venture abroad, but others have bigger plans. Ayal and Zif have argued that a company should enter fewer countries when (1) market entry and market control costs are high; (2) product and communication adaptation costs are high; (3) population and income size, and growth are high in the initial countries chosen; and (4) dominant foreign firms can establish high barriers to entry.[4]

The company must also decide on the types of countries to consider. The product, geography, income and population, political climate, and other factors influence attractiveness. The developed nations and the prosperous parts of developing nations account for less than 15 percent of the world's population. Is there a way for marketers to serve the other 85 percent, which has much less purchasing power? Some marketers capitalize on the potential of developing markets by changing their conventional marketing practices to sell their products and services more effectively.[5] Smaller packaging and lower prices are often critical in markets where incomes are limited. For example, Unilever's 4-cent sachets of detergent and shampoo have been a big hit in rural India, where 70 percent of the country's population still lives.[6]

Deciding How to Enter the Market

Next, the firm must determine the best strategy for entering a foreign market. As shown in Figure 18.2, each successive strategy involves more commitment, risk, control, and profit potential.

- *Indirect and direct exporting.* Companies typically start with indirect exporting, working through independent intermediaries that will sell their products. This involves less investment and less risk, because the intermediaries bring know-how and services to the relationship. Eventually companies may decide to handle their own exports; this entails higher investment and risk but also offers higher potential return.[7] Companies may exhibit at overseas trade shows or set up country-specific Web sites for key markets.

- *Licensing.* Here, the licensor issues a license to a foreign firm to use a manufacturing process, trademark, patent, trade secret, or other item of value for a fee or royalty. The licensor gains entry at little risk; the licensee gains production expertise or a

FIGURE 18.2 Five Modes of Entry into Foreign Markets

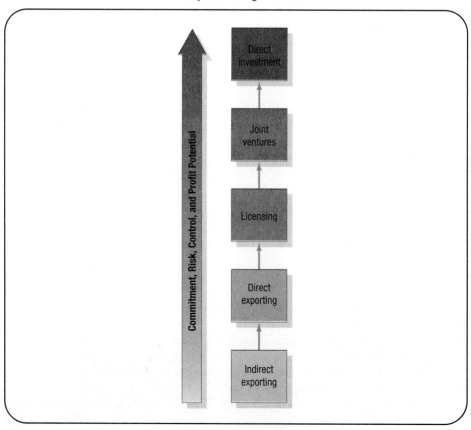

well-known product or brand name. However, the licensor has less control than it does over its own production and marketing; if the licensee is very profitable, the firm has given up profits. If and when the contract ends, the company might find it has created a competitor.

- *Joint ventures.* Foreign investors may join with local investors to create a **joint venture** company in which they share ownership and control. One drawback is that the partners might disagree over investment, marketing, or other policies. Another is that one partner might want to reinvest earnings for growth, but the other partner might want to declare more dividends. Joint ownership can also prevent a multinational company from carrying out specific manufacturing and marketing policies on a worldwide basis.

- *Direct investment.* The ultimate form of foreign involvement is direct investment, when a firm buys all or part of a foreign-based assembly or manufacturing facility or builds its own facilities. General Motors has invested billions of dollars in auto manufacturers around the world, such as Fiat Auto Holdings, Isuzu, Daewoo, Suzuki, Saab, and AvtoVAZ.[8] This strategy leads to cost economies, like cheaper labor or raw materials, government investment incentives, and freight savings. It helps the company strengthen its image in the host country by creating jobs. Also, it leads to deeper relationships with government, customers, local suppliers, and distributors, enabling the firm to adapt its products better to the local environment. However, it entails currency risks and expropriation risks; in addition, reducing or eliminating operations may be expensive because of government-required severance pay to employees.

Deciding on the Marketing Program

International companies must decide how much to adapt their marketing strategy to local conditions.[9] At one extreme are companies that use a globally *standardized marketing mix* worldwide, which keeps costs low, allows for brand image consistency, and enables the firm to leverage ideas quickly and efficiently. At the other extreme is an *adapted marketing mix*, where the marketing program is adjusted to each target market. This allows for differences in consumer needs, wants, usage patterns, and response, as well as differences in the legal environment and in marketing institutions. Between the two extremes, many possibilities exist. Keegan has distinguished five strategies for adapting product and communications to a foreign market (see Figure 18.3).[10]

FIGURE 18.3 Five International Product and Communication Strategies

	Product		
	Do Not Change Product	Adapt Product	Develop New Product
Do Not Change Communications	Straight extension	Product adaptation	Product invention
Adapt Communications	Communication adaptation	Dual adaptation	

Product   Some types of products travel better across borders than others—food and beverage marketers have to contend with widely varying tastes.[11] **Straight extension** means introducing the product in the foreign market without any change. Straight extension has been successful with cameras, consumer electronics, and many machine tools. Before assuming that its domestic product can be introduced "as is" in another country, the company should determine which of the following elements would add more revenue than cost: features; brand; labeling and packaging; colors; advertising themes, media, and execution; prices; sales promotion.

   Product adaptation involves altering the product to meet local conditions or preferences. The company might develop a *regional version* of its product, a *country version*, a *city version*, or different *retailer versions*. **Product invention** consists of creating something new, in one of two forms. *Backward invention* is reintroducing earlier product forms that are well adapted to a foreign country's needs. *Forward invention* is creating a new product to meet a need in another country. Product invention is costly, but the payoffs can be great, particularly if the innovation can be launched elsewhere. Many U.S. companies not only invent new products for overseas markets, they lift products and ideas from their international operations and bring them home. Häagen-Dazs originally developed the dulce de leche flavor, named for the locally popular caramelized milk, for sale in Argentina. Then the company launched it internationally; very quickly, dulce de leche became one of the top 10 flavors in America.[12]

Communications   Companies can run the same marketing communications programs as used in the home market or change them for each local market, a process called **communication adaptation.** If it adapts both the product and the communications, the company engages in **dual adaptation.**

   Consider the message. One approach is to use the same message everywhere, varying the language, name, and colors.[13] Another is to use one theme globally and adapt the copy to each local market. For example, a Camay soap commercial showed a beautiful woman bathing. In Venezuela, a man was seen in the bathroom; in Japan, the man waited outside. The positioning stays the same, but the creative execution reflects local sensibilities. The third approach is to develop a global pool of ads, from which each country selects the most appropriate one. Finally, some companies allow their country managers to create country-specific ads—within guidelines, of course.

   The use of media also requires international adaptation because media availability varies from country to country, as does regulation of media advertising featuring products such as tobacco and alcohol. Marketers also must adapt sales promotion techniques to different markets, taking into account laws that prevent or limit tools such as discounts, rebates, and coupons. Personal selling tactics may have to change too. The direct, no-nonsense approach favored by Americans may not work as well in Europe, Asia, and other places where a more indirect, subtle approach can be more effective.[14]

Price   When a company sells abroad, it faces a *price escalation* problem because it must add the cost of transportation, tariffs, importer margin, wholesaler margin, and retailer margin to the product's factory price. Depending on these added costs, as well as the currency-fluctuation risk, the product might have to sell for two to five times as much in another country to make the same profit for the manufacturer. Thus, the company can set a uniform price in all markets, set a market-based price in each market, or set a cost-based price in each market.

Many multinationals are dealing with the problem of the **gray market,** in which branded products are diverted from normal or authorized distribution channels in the country of product origin or across international borders. Dealers in the low-price country find ways to sell some of their products in higher-price countries, thus earning more. Multinationals try to prevent gray markets by policing the distributors, by raising their prices to lower-cost distributors, or by altering the product characteristics or service warranties for different countries. The Internet is helping reduce price differentiation among countries, because when companies sell online, customers can easily find out how much products sell for in different countries.

Distribution Channels   Distribution channels within countries vary considerably. Thus, companies should examine how products move within each country and take a whole-channel view of distributing products to final users. To sell soap in Japan, Procter & Gamble has to sell to a general wholesaler, who sells to a product wholesaler, who sells to a product-specialty wholesaler, who sells to a regional wholesaler, who sells to a local wholesaler, who finally sells to retailers. All these distribution levels can mean that the consumer's price ends up double or triple the importer's price. If P&G takes the soap to tropical Africa, the company might sell to an import wholesaler, who sells to several jobbers, who sell to petty traders (mostly women) working in local markets.

Another difference lies in the size and character of retail units abroad. Large-scale retail chains dominate the U.S. scene, but much foreign retailing is in the hands of small, independent retailers. Their markups are high, but the real price is brought down through haggling. Incomes are low, and people must shop daily for small amounts; they are limited to whatever quantity can be carried home on foot or on a bicycle. Breaking bulk remains an important function of intermediaries and helps perpetuate the long channels of distribution, which are a major obstacle to the expansion of large-scale retailing in developing countries. When entering any country, the multinational must choose the right distributors, invest in them, and set up performance goals to which they can agree.[15]

INTERNAL MARKETING

Internal marketing requires that everyone in the organization buy into the concepts and goals of marketing and engage in choosing, providing, and communicating customer value. Over the years, marketing has evolved as it has grown from work done by the sales department into a complex group of activities spread through the organization.[16] Many companies are now focusing on key processes because departmental organization is viewed as a barrier to the smooth performance of fundamental business processes. Let's look at how marketing departments are being organized and how they can work effectively with other departments.

Organizing the Marketing Department

Modern marketing departments may be organized in a number of different, sometimes overlapping ways:[17] functionally, geographically, by product or brand, by market, in a matrix, by corporate/division.

Functional Organization The most common form of marketing organization consists of functional specialists (such as the sales manager and marketing research manager) who report to a marketing vice president, who coordinates their activities. The main advantage of a functional marketing organization is its administrative simplicity. However, this form loses effectiveness as products and markets increase. First, a functional organization often leads to inadequate planning for specific products and markets because products not favored by anyone are neglected. Second, each functional group competes with the others for budget and status. The marketing vice president constantly has to weigh the claims of competing functional specialists and faces a difficult coordination problem.

Geographic Organization A company selling in a national market often organizes its sales force (and sometimes other functions, including marketing) along geographic lines. The national sales manager may supervise four regional sales managers, who each supervise six zone managers, who in turn supervise eight district sales managers, who supervise 10 salespeople. Several companies are now adding *area market specialists* (regional or local marketing managers) to support the sales efforts in high-volume, distinctive markets. For example, McDonald's spends about 50 percent of its advertising budget regionally.

Product- or Brand-Management Organization Companies producing a variety of products and brands often establish a product- (or brand-) management organization, not to replace the functional organization but as another layer of management. A product manager supervises product category managers, who in turn supervise specific product and brand managers. A product-management organization makes sense if the company's products are quite different or if the sheer number of products is beyond the ability of a functional organization to handle.

The product-management organization has several advantages. The product manager can concentrate on developing a cost-effective marketing mix for the product; react more quickly to marketplace changes; and watch over smaller brands. On the other hand, this organization can lead to conflict and frustration when product managers have insufficient authority to carry out their responsibilities. In addition, product managers become experts in their product but rarely achieve functional expertise, and appointing product managers and associate product managers for even minor products can bloat payroll costs. Also, brand managers normally move up in a few years to another brand or transfer to another company, leading to short-term thinking that plays havoc with long-term brand building. Fragmentation of markets means brand managers must increasingly please regional and local sales groups. Finally, product and brand managers tend to focus on building market share rather than on building customer relationships—the primary lever for value creation.

To counter these disadvantages, more companies are switching from product managers to *product teams.* Some firms believe that each major brand should be run by a *brand-asset management team* (*BAMT*) consisting of key representatives from major functions affecting the brand's performance. These BAMTs report to a BAMT Directors Committee, which itself reports to a Chief Branding Officer. Another approach to the product-management organization is to eliminate product manager positions for minor products and assign two or more products to each remaining manager. This is feasible where two or more products appeal to a similar set of needs.

A fourth alternative for product-management organization is to introduce *category management,* in which a company focuses on product categories to manage its brands. Procter & Gamble, which pioneered the brand management system, and several other top firms have shifted to category management.[18] P&G wanted to ensure that all categories received adequate resources. Further, because retailers have tended to think in terms of product categories and the profitability derived from different departments and sections, P&G wanted to deal with the trade along similar lines. Yet category management is not a panacea, because it is still product-driven. Thus, Colgate moved from brand management (Colgate toothpaste) to category management (toothpaste category) to customer-need management (mouth care), finally focusing the organization on a basic customer need.[19]

Market-Management Organization Many companies sell their products to a diverse set of markets; Canon, for instance, sells fax machines to consumer, business, and government markets. When customers fall into different user groups with distinct buying preferences and practices, a *market management organization* is desirable. A markets manager supervises several market managers (also called market-development managers, market specialists, or industry specialists). The market managers draw upon functional services as needed or may even have functional specialists reporting to them.

Market managers are staff (not line) people, with duties similar to those of product managers. This system has many of the same advantages and disadvantages of the product manager system. Its strongest advantage is that the marketing activity is organized to meet the needs of distinct customer groups. In a *customer management organization*, companies organize to understand and deal with individual customers rather than with the mass market or even market segments.

Matrix-Management Organization Companies that produce many products flowing into many markets may adopt a matrix organization. DuPont was a pioneer in developing the matrix structure. Before being spun off, its textile fibers department had separate product managers for rayon and other fibers plus separate market managers for menswear and other markets. The product managers each sought to expand the sales and profits of his or her fiber; the market managers sought to meet their market's needs rather than push a certain fiber. Ultimately, the sales forecasts from the market managers and the product managers should have added up to the same grand total. Companies like DuPont can go one step further and view the market managers as the main marketers and their product managers as suppliers.

A matrix organization would seem desirable in a multiproduct, multimarket company. However, this system is costly and often creates conflicts, as well as questions about authority and responsibility. Still, matrix management gained advocates because companies provide the context in which a matrix can thrive—flat, lean team organizations focused around business processes that cut horizontally across functions.[20]

Corporate-Divisional Organization As multiproduct-multimarket companies grow, they often convert their larger product or market groups into separate divisions with their own departments and services. This raises the question of what marketing services and activities should be retained at corporate headquarters. Some corporations leave marketing to each division, some have a small corporate marketing staff, and some prefer to maintain a strong corporate marketing staff. Still, certain activities must occur within the organization in a top-down fashion. Webster sees the role of marketing at the corporate level as (1) promoting a culture of customer orientation, (2) assessing market attractiveness in terms of customer needs and competitive offerings;

and (3) developing the overall value proposition and vision in terms of delivering superior value to customers.[21]

Global Organization   Companies that market internationally can organize in three ways. Those just going global may start by establishing an export department with a sales manager and a few assistants (and limited marketing services). As they go after global business more aggressively, they can create an international division with functional specialists (including marketing) and operating units structured geographically, according to product, or as international subsidiaries. Finally, companies that become truly global have top corporate management and staff who plan worldwide operations, marketing policies, financial flows, and logistical systems. In these organizations, the global operating units report to top management, not to the head of an international division.

Relations with Other Departments

In the typical organization, each business function has a potential impact on customer satisfaction. Under the marketing concept, all departments need to "think customer" and work together to satisfy customer needs and expectations. The marketing department must drive this point home. The marketing vice president, or CMO, has two tasks: (1) to coordinate the company's internal marketing activities and (2) to coordinate marketing with finance, operations, and other company functions to serve the customer.

Recognizing the potential for internal conflict and for breakdowns in internal communication, management needs a balanced orientation in which marketing and other functions jointly determine what is in the company's best interests. Solutions include joint seminars to understand each others' viewpoints, joint committees and liaison personnel, personnel exchange programs, and analytical methods to determine the most profitable course of action.[22] Marketing should periodically propose a function-to-function meeting to facilitate greater understanding and collaboration among other departments. Working together toward common goals makes marketing more effective.

MANAGING THE MARKETING PROCESS

Marketing implementation is the process that turns marketing plans into action assignments and ensures that such assignments are executed in a manner that accomplishes the plan's stated objectives.[23] A brilliant strategic marketing plan counts for little if it is not implemented properly. Whereas strategy addresses the *what* and *why* of marketing activities, implementation addresses the *who*, *where*, *when*, and *how*. Strategy and implementation are closely related, in that one layer of strategy implies certain tactical implementation assignments at a lower level. For example, top management's strategy to "harvest" a product must be translated into specific actions and assignments.

Bonoma has identified four sets of skills for implementing marketing programs: (1) diagnostic skills (the ability to determine what went wrong); (2) identification of company level (the ability to discern whether problems occurred in the marketing function, the marketing program, or the marketing policy); (3) implementation skills (the ability to budget resources, organize effectively, motivate others); and (4) evaluation skills (the ability to evaluate results).[24] For efficient implementation and better

TABLE 18.1   Types of Marketing Control

Type of Control	Prime Responsibility	Purpose of Control	Approaches
I. Annual-plan control	Top management Middle management	To examine whether the planned results are being achieved	■ Sales analysis ■ Market share analysis ■ Sales-to-expense ratios ■ Financial analysis ■ Market-based scorecard analysis
II. Profitability control	Marketing controller	To examine where the company is making and losing money	Profitability by: ■ product ■ territory ■ customer ■ segment ■ trade channel ■ order size
III. Efficiency control	Line and staff management Marketing controller	To evaluate and improve the spending efficiency and impact of marketing expenditures	Efficiency of: ■ sales force ■ advertising ■ sales promotion ■ distribution
IV. Strategic control	Top management Marketing auditor	To examine whether the company is pursuing its best opportunities with respect to markets, products, and channels	■ Marketing-effectiveness rating instrument ■ Marketing audit ■ Marketing excellence review ■ Company ethical and social responsibility review

return on marketing investments, organizations can use specialized software specifically designed to manage marketing processes, assets, and resources.

Evaluation and Control

To deal with the many surprises that occur during the implementation of marketing plans, the marketing department has to monitor and control marketing activities continuously. Table 18.1 lists four types of marketing control needed by companies: annual-plan control, profitability control, efficiency control, and strategic control.

Chapter 2 described how companies use marketing metrics to analyze marketing plans and their profitability. Annual-plan control shows whether the company achieved the sales, profits, and other goals established in its annual plan. The heart of annual-plan control is management by objectives (see Figure 18.4). First, management sets monthly or quarterly goals. Second, management monitors its performance in the marketplace. Third, management determines the cause of any serious performance deviations. Fourth, management takes corrective action to close the gaps between goals and performance.

This control model applies to all levels of the organization. Top management sets annual sales and profit goals that become specific goals for lower levels of management. Each product manager is committed to attaining specified levels of sales and costs; each regional district and sales manager and each sales representative is also committed to specific goals. Each period, top management reviews and interprets the results.

FIGURE 18.4   The Control Process

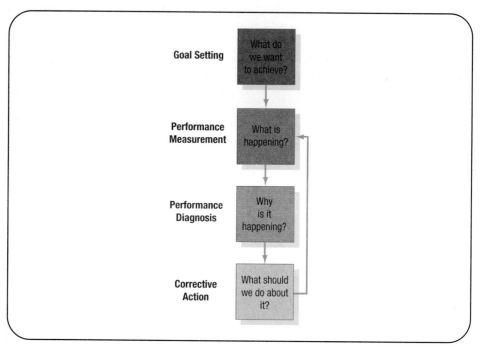

Efficiency Control

If a profitability analysis reveals poor profits for certain products, territories, or markets, management must ask whether there are more efficient ways to manage the sales force, advertising, sales promotion, and distribution in connection with these marketing entities.

Some companies have established a *marketing controller* position to improve marketing efficiency. Marketing controllers work out of the controller's office but specialize in the marketing side of the business. At companies such as General Foods and Johnson & Johnson, they perform a sophisticated financial analysis of marketing expenditures and results, analyzing adherence to profit plans, helping prepare brand managers' budgets, measuring the efficiency of promotions, analyzing media production costs, evaluating customer and geographic profitability, and educating marketing personnel on the financial implications of marketing decisions.[25]

Strategic Control

From time to time, companies need to undertake a critical review of overall marketing goals and effectiveness. One way to do this is with a marketing effectiveness review, which examines the degree to which a company or division exhibits the five major attributes of a marketing orientation: customer philosophy (serving customers' needs and wants), integrated marketing organization (integrating marketing with other key departments), adequate marketing information (conducting timely, appropriate marketing research), strategic orientation (developing formal marketing plans and strategies), and operational efficiency (using marketing resources effectively and flexibly). Most companies and divisions score in the fair-to-good range.[26]

Companies that discover marketing weaknesses should undertake a **marketing audit,** a comprehensive, systematic, independent, and periodic examination of a company's (or business unit's) marketing environment, objectives, strategies, and activities to identify problem areas and opportunities and recommend a plan for improving marketing performance.[27] The marketing audit examines six major marketing components: (1) the macroenvironment and task environment, (2) marketing strategy, (3) marketing organization, (4) marketing systems, (5) marketing productivity, and (6) marketing function (the 4 Ps).

Successful companies also perform marketing excellence reviews to gauge their performance in relation to the best practices of high-performing businesses. The resulting profile exposes weaknesses and strengths and highlights where the company might change to become a truly outstanding player in the marketplace. Finally, firms need to evaluate whether they are truly practicing ethical and socially responsible

MARKETING SKILLS: CAUSE-RELATED MARKETING

Many firms blend social responsibility with marketing through *cause-related marketing*, linking their contributions to a designated cause to customers' engaging (directly or indirectly) in revenue-producing transactions with the firm. Cause-related marketing can produce a number of benefits: improving social welfare; creating differentiated brand positioning; building strong consumer bonds; enhancing the company's public image; creating goodwill; boosting internal morale and galvanizing employees; and driving sales. Marketers start by choosing which cause(s) to support. Focusing on one or a few main causes will simplify execution and maximize impact. Often, marketers choose causes that fit their company's or brand's image and that matter to their employees and shareholders.

The next step is to brand the program. One approach is to develop a new self-branded organization associated with the cause, such as the Ronald McDonald House Charities. This helps augment existing consumer associations via emotional and imagery appeals. Another approach is to co-brand as a cause's sponsor or supporter, the way Sealy donates beds as a sponsor of NASCAR's Victory Junction Gang Camp for seriously ill children. Co-branding complements the brand's image with specific associations "borrowed" or "transferred" from the cause. A third option is to partner with a cause and brand the program linked to the cause. As an example, retailer Colorado Cyclist sponsors the Rocky Mountain Challenge bike ride to benefit the Tyler Hamilton Foundation for MS.

Haircare marketer Wella U.K. chose to cobrand as a sponsor of Comic Relief's biennial Red Nose Day, which raises money to reduce poverty and help the elderly and youth in crisis in the United Kingdom and Africa. Wella created the Official Red Nose Day Red Hairspray, with 25 percent of the product's revenue donated to the charity. It also mounted a campaign to involve hair salons in the one-day event. Wella's public relations manager says the cobranding has been beneficial in several ways: "We are trying to tap into the consumer market of 18-to-25-year-old women but are also targeting salons. It allows us to position ourselves as the supplier of choice," she says. "The red spray is opening up business leads and delivering massive exposure and awareness. It also lets us contemporize the Wella brand, which has been around for 175 years."[28]

marketing (for more about marketing and social responsibility, see "Marketing Skills: Cause-Related Marketing").

Business success and continually satisfying customers and other stakeholders are closely tied to high standards of business and marketing conduct. The most admired companies abide by a code of serving people's interests, not only their own. Raising the level of socially responsible marketing calls for proper legal, ethical, and socially responsible behavior. Management must adopt and disseminate a written code of ethics, build a company tradition of ethical behavior, and hold employees responsible for knowing and observing ethical and legal guidelines.[29] Individual marketers also must practice a "social conscience" in dealing with customers and stakeholders.[30]

EXECUTIVE SUMMARY

In deciding to go abroad, a company needs to define its international marketing objectives and policies and determine how many and which countries it will enter, based on market attractiveness, risk, and competitive advantage. Once a company decides on a particular country, it must determine the best mode of entry: indirect exporting, direct exporting, licensing, joint ventures, or direct investment. Each succeeding strategy involves more commitment, risk, control, and profit potential. Firms going global can pursue a product strategy of straight extension, product adaptation, or product invention and a communication strategy of either communication adaptation or dual adaptation. At the price level, firms may encounter price escalation and gray markets. At the distribution level, firms need to take a whole-channel view of distributing products to the final users.

Companies can organize the marketing department by function, geography, product and brand, market segment, or a matrix organization of both product and market managers. Some have strong corporate marketing, some have limited corporate marketing, and others place marketing only in the divisions. Companies that market in other countries can create an export department, an international division, or a global organization. Effective marketing requires the company's departments to cooperate and exhibit a customer focus.

Marketing implementation turns marketing plans into action assignments and ensures that execution accomplishes the plan's stated objectives. Companies can apply four types of control: annual-plan control, profitability control, efficiency control, and strategic control. Efficiency control focuses on ways to increase the efficiency of the sales force, advertising, sales promotion, and distribution. Strategic control entails a periodic reassessment of the company and its strategic approach to the marketplace using marketing effectiveness and marketing excellence reviews, as well as the marketing audit. In addition, companies need to evaluate whether they are practicing ethical and socially responsible marketing.

NOTES

1. Mike Esterl, "Avon Works Out the Wrinkles," *Wall Street Journal*, August 31, 2005, p. B3; "Careers: What's It Really Like Inside Avon," *Marketing*, March 23, 2005, p. 79; Ramin Setoodeh, "Calling Avon's Lady," *Newsweek*, December 27, 2004, pp. 98+; Emily Farris, Faye Brookman, and Julie Naughton, "Beauty Firms Think Pink," *WWD*, October 31, 2003, pp. 10+; (www.avon.com).

2. Michael E. Porter, *Competitive Strategy* (New York: The Free Press, 1980), p. 275.
3. Ron Lieber, "Give Us This Day Our Global Bread," *Fast Company*, March 2001, p. 158.
4. Igal Ayal and Jehiel Zif, "Market Expansion Strategies in Multinational Marketing," *Journal of Marketing* (Spring 1979): 84–94.
5. Niraj Dawar and Amitava Chattopadhyay, "Rethinking Marketing Programs for Emerging Markets," *Long Range Planning* 35, no. 5 (October 2002): 457–474.
6. Manjeet Kripalani, "Battling for Pennies in India's Villages," *BusinessWeek*, June 10, 2002, p. 22E7.
7. For an academic review, see Leonidas C. Leonidou, Constantine S. Katsikeas, and Nigel F. Piercy, "Identifying Managerial Influences on Exporting: Past Research and Future Directions," *Journal of International Marketing* 6, no. 2 (1998): 74–102.
8. Joann Muller, "Global Motors," *Forbes*, January 12, 2004, pp. 62–68.
9. Shaoming Zou and S. Tamer Cavusgil, "The GMS: A Broad Conceptualization of Global Marketing Strategy and Its Effect on Firm Performance," *Journal of Marketing* 66 (October 2002): 40–56.
10. Warren J. Keegan, *Multinational Marketing Management*, 5th ed. (Upper Saddle River, NJ: Prentice Hall, 1995), pp. 378–381.
11. Arundhati Parmar, "Dependent Variables: Sound Global Strategies Rely on Certain Factors," *Marketing News*, September 16, 2002, p. 4.
12. David Leonhardt, "It Was a Hit in Buenos Aires—So Why Not Boise?" *BusinessWeek*, September 7, 1998, pp. 56–58; Marlene Parrish, "Taste Buds Tango at New Squirrel Hill Café," *Pittsburgh Post-Gazette*, February 6, 2003, (www.post-gazette.com/food/20030206tango0206fnp4.asp).
13. For an interesting distinction based on the concept of global consumer culture positioning, see Dana L. Alden, Jan-Benedict E.M. Steenkamp, and Rajeev Batra, "Brand Positioning through Advertising in Asia, North America, and Europe: The Role of Global Consumer Culture," *Journal of Marketing* 63 (January 1999): 75–87.
14. John L. Graham, Alma T. Mintu, and Waymond Rogers, "Explorations of Negotiations Behaviors in Ten Foreign Cultures Using a Model Developed in the United States," *Management Science* 40 (January 1994): 72–95.
15. David Arnold, "Seven Rules of International Distribution," *Harvard Business Review*, (November–December 2000): 131–137.
16. For a broad historical treatment of marketing thought, see D. G. Brian Jones and Eric H. Shaw, "A History of Marketing Thought," in *Handbook of Marketing*, edited by Barton A. Weitz and Robin Wensley (London: Sage Publications, 2002).
17. Frederick E. Webster Jr., "The Role of Marketing and the Firm," in *Handbook of Marketing*, edited by Barton A. Weitz and Robin Wensley (London: Sage Publications, 2002), pp. 39–65.
18. Zachary Schiller, "The Marketing Revolution at Procter & Gamble," *BusinessWeek*, July 25, 1988, pp. 72–76; Laurie Freeman, "P&G Widens Power Base: Adds Category Managers," *Advertising Age*, October 12, 1987, pp. 1+.
19. For further reading, see Robert Dewar and Don Schultz, "The Product Manager, an Idea Whose Time Has Gone," *Marketing Communications* (May 1998): 28–35; "The Marketing Revolution at Proctor & Gamble," *BusinessWeek*, July 25, 1988, pp. 72–76; Kevin T. Higgins, "Category Management: New Tools Changing Life for Manufacturers, Retailers," *Marketing News*, September 25, 1989, pp. 2, 19; George S. Low and Ronald A. Fullerton, "Brands, Brand Management, and the Brand Manager System: A Critical Historical Evaluation," *Journal of Marketing Research* (May 1994): 173–190; Michael J. Zanor, "The Profit Benefits of Category Management," *Journal of Marketing Research* (May 1994): 202–213.
20. Richard E. Anderson, "Matrix Redux," *Business Horizons*, November–December 1994, pp. 6–10.
21. Frederick E. Webster Jr., "The Role of Marketing and the Firm," in *Handbook of Marketing*, edited by Barton A. Weitz and Robin Wensley (London: Sage Publications, 2002), pp. 39–65.

22. Benson P. Shapiro, "Can Marketing and Manufacturing Coexist?" *Harvard Business Review* (September–October 1977): 104–114. Also see Robert W. Ruekert and Orville C. Walker Jr., "Marketing's Interaction with Other Functional Units: A Conceptual Framework with Other Empirical Evidence," *Journal of Marketing* (January 1987): 1–19.

23. For more on developing and implementing marketing plans, see Marian Burk Wood, *The Marketing Plan: A Handbook* (Upper Saddle River, NJ: Prentice Hall, 2003); and H. W. Goetsch, *Developing, Implementing, and Managing an Effective Marketing Plan* (Chicago: American Marketing Association; Lincolnwood, IL: NTC Business Books, 1993).

24. Thomas V. Bonoma, *The Marketing Edge: Making Strategies Work* (New York: Free Press, 1985). Much of this section is based on Bonoma's work.

25. Sam R. Goodman, *Increasing Corporate Profitability* (New York: Ronald Press, 1982), ch. 1. Also see Bernard J. Jaworski, Vlasis Stathakopoulos, and H. Shanker Krishnan, "Control Combinations in Marketing: Conceptual Framework and Empirical Evidence," *Journal of Marketing* (January 1993): pp. 57–69.

26. For further discussion of this instrument, see Philip Kotler, "From Sales Obsession to Marketing Effectiveness," *Harvard Business Review* (November–December 1977): 67–75.

27. See Philip Kotler, William Gregor, and William Rodgers, "The Marketing Audit Comes of Age," *Sloan Management Review* (Winter 1989): 49–62.

28. Robert Gray, "Cause-Related Marketing: Red Nose Returns," *Marketing*, March 9, 2005, p. 28; Pat Auger, Paul Burke, Timothy Devinney, and Jordan J. Loviere, "What Will Consumers Pay for Social Product Features?" *Journal of Business Ethics* 42 (2003): 281–304; Hamish Pringle and Marjorie Thompson, *How Cause-Related Marketing Builds Brands* (New York: John Wiley & Sons, 1999); Christine Bittar, "Seeking Cause and Effect," *Brandweek*, November 11, 2002, pp. 19–24; "Marketing, Corporate Social Initiatives, and the Bottom Line," Marketing Science Institute Conference Summary, *MSI Report No. 01-106*, 2001; Rajan Varadarajan and Anil Menon, "Cause-Related Marketing: A Co-Alignment of Marketing Strategy and Corporate Philanthropy," *Journal of Marketing* 52 (1988): 58–74.

29. Shelby D. Hunt and Scott Vitell, "The General Theory of Marketing Ethics: A Retrospective and Revision," in *Ethics in Marketing*, edited by John Quelch and Craig Smith (Chicago: Irwin, 1992).

30. Marc Gunther, "Tree Huggers, Soy Lovers, and Profits," *Fortune*, June 23, 2003, pp. 98–104.

Glossary

Activity-Based Cost (ABC) Accounting procedures that can quantify the true profitability of different activities by identifying their actual costs, 37, 223.

Adoption an individual's decision to become a regular user of a product, 190.

Advertising any paid form of nonpersonal presentation and promotion of ideas, goods, or services, by an identified sponsor, 295.

Advertising Goal or Objective a specific communication task and achievement level to be accomplished with a specific audience in a specific period of time, 295.

Advertising Objective see *Advertising Goal*, 295.

Aspirational Groups groups a person hopes to join, 85.

Associative Network Memory Model a conceptual representation that views memory as consisting of a set of nodes and interconnecting links where nodes represent stored information or concepts and links represent the strength of association between this information or concepts, 90.

Attitude person's enduring favorable or unfavorable evaluation, emotional feeling, and action tendencies toward some object or idea, 93, 125.

Augmented Product a product that includes features that go beyond consumer expectations and differentiate the product from competitors, 179.

Available Market the set of consumers who have interest, income, and access to a particular offer, 48.

Average Cost the cost per unit at a given level of production; it is equal to total costs divided by production, 222.

Banner Ads on the Internet, small, rectangular boxes containing text and perhaps a picture, 318.

Basic Product what specifically the actual product is, 178.

Belief descriptive thought that a person holds about something, 93.

Brand name, term, sign, symbol, or design, or a combination of these, intended to identify the goods or services of one seller or group of sellers and to differentiate them from those of the competitors, 136.

Brand Associations all brand-related thoughts, feelings, perceptions, images, experiences, beliefs, attitudes, and so on that become linked to the brand node, 90.

Brand Audit a consumer-focused exercise that involves a series of procedures to assess the health of the brand, uncover its sources of brand equity, and suggest ways to improve and leverage its equity, 143.

Brand Awareness consumers' ability to identify the brand under different conditions, as reflected by their brand recognition or recall performance, 140.

Brand Contact any information-bearing experience a customer or prospect has with the brand, the product category, or the market that relates to the offering, 140.

Brand Dilution when consumers no longer associate a brand with a specific product or highly similar products or start thinking less favorably about the brand, 148.

Brand Elements those trademarkable devices that serve to identify and differentiate the brand such as a brand name, logo, or character, 139, 207.

Brand Equity the added value endowed to products and services, 71, 137, 279.

Brand Extension a company's use of an established brand to introduce a new product, 148.

Brand Image the perceptions and beliefs held by consumers, as reflected in the associations held in consumer memory, 140.

Brand Knowledge all the thoughts, feelings, images, experiences, beliefs, and so on that become associated with the brand, 137.

Brand Personality the specific mix of human traits that may be attributed to a particular brand, 87.

Brand Portfolio the set of all brands and brand lines a particular firm offers for sale to buyers in a particular category, 149.

Brand Promise the marketer's vision of what the brand must be and do for consumers, 138.

Branding endowing products and services with the power of a brand, 136.

Branding Strategy the number and nature of common and distinctive brand elements applied to the different products sold by the firm, 146.

Break-Even Analysis a means by which management estimates how many units of the product the company would have to sell to break even with the given price and cost structure, 188.

Brick-and-Click existing companies that have added an online site for information and/or e-commerce, 255.

Business Database complete information about business customers' past purchases; past volumes, prices, and profits; and related data, 77.

Business Market all the organizations that acquire goods and services used in the production of other products or services that are sold, rented, or supplied to others, 102.

Buying Center several participants with differing interests, authority, status, and persuasiveness who are the decision-making unit of a buying organization, 106.

Captive Products products that are necessary to the use of other products, such as razor blades or film, 233.

Category Extension using the parent brand to brand a new product outside the product category currently served by the parent brand, 148.

Category Membership the products or sets of products with which a brand competes and which function as close substitutes, 156.

Channel Conflict when one channel member's actions prevent the channel from achieving its goal, 252.

Channel Coordination when channel members are brought together to advance the goals of the channel, as opposed to their own potentially incompatible goals, 252.

Channel Power the ability to alter channel members' behavior so that they take actions they would not have taken otherwise, 249.

Co-Branding when two or more existing brands are combined into a product or are marketed together, 147.

Communication Adaptation changing marketing communications programs for each local market, 336.

Communication-Effect Research determining whether an ad is communicating effectively, 301.

Company Demand company's estimated share of market demand at alternative levels of company marketing effort in a given time period, 50.

Company Sales Forecast expected level of company sales based on a chosen marketing plan and an assumed marketing environment, 50.

Competitive Advantage a company's ability to perform in one or more ways that competitors cannot or will not match, 70.

Conformance Quality the degree to which all the produced units are identical and meet the promised specifications, 159.

Conjoint Analysis a method for deriving the utility values that consumers attach to varying levels of a product's attributes, 186.

Consumer Behavior the behavior consumers display in searching for, purchasing, using, evaluating, and disposing of goods, services, and ideas, 84.

Consumer Involvement the level of engagement and active processing undertaken by the consumer in responding to a marketing stimulus, 94.

Consumerist Movement an organized movement of citizens and government to strengthen the rights and powers of buyers in relation to sellers, 60.

Containerization putting the goods in boxes or trailers that are easy to transfer between two transportation modes, 275.

Content-Target Advertising links ads not to keywords but to the contents of Web pages, 318.

Contractual Sales Force manufacturers' reps, sales agents, and brokers, who are paid a commission based on sales, 321.

Convenience Goods products purchased frequently, immediately, and with a minimum of effort, 180.

Conventional Marketing Channel an independent producer, wholesaler(s), and retailer(s), 251.

Core Benefit the service or benefit the customer is really buying, 178.

Core Competency attribute that (1) is a source of competitive advantage by contributing significantly to perceived customer benefits, (2) has applications in a wide variety of markets, (3) is difficult for competitors to imitate, 24.

Core Values the belief systems that underlie consumer attitudes and behavior, and that determine people's choices and desires over the long term, 88.

Corporate Culture the shared experiences, stories, beliefs, and norms that characterize an organization, 29.

Corporate Retailing corporately owned retailing outlets that achieve economies of scale, greater purchasing power, wider brand recognition, and better-trained employees, 261.

Countertrade when buyers offer other items as payment because they lack sufficient hard currency to pay for their purchases, 230.

Cues stimuli that determine when, where, and how a person responds, 89.

Culture the fundamental determinant of a person's wants and behavior, 84.

Customer Churn high rate of customer defection, 73.

Customer Database organized collection of comprehensive data about individual customers, prospects, or suspects that is current, accessible, and actionable for marketing purposes, 77.

Customer Equity total of the discounted lifetime values of all of a firm's customers, 71.

Customer Lifetime Value the net present value of the stream of future profits expected over the customer's lifetime purchases, 76.

Customer Perceived Value (CPV) difference between total customer's evaluation of all the benefits and the total customer cost, 64.

Customer Performance Scorecard how well the company is doing year after year on particular customer-based measures, 35.

Customer Profitability Analysis a means of assessing and ranking customer profitability through accounting techniques such as Activity-Based Costing (ABC), 69.

Customer Relationship Management (CRM) process of managing detailed information about individual customers and managing all customer encounters to maximize customer loyalty, 72.

Customer Value Hierarchy five product levels that must be addressed by marketers in planning a market offering, 178.

Customer-Based Brand Equity the differential effect that brand knowledge has on consumer response to the marketing of that brand, 137.

Customerization combination of operationally driven mass customization with customized marketing in a way that empowers consumers to design the offering of their choice, 118.

Data Mining use of statistical and mathematical techniques to extract information about individuals, trends, and segments, 39, 78.

Data Warehouse a collection of current data captured, organized, and stored in a company's contact center, 77.

Database Marketing process of building, maintaining, and using customer databases and other databases (products, suppliers, resellers) for marketing purposes, 77.

Demand-Chain Planning designing the supply chain based on adopting a target market perspective and working backward, 241.

Direct (Company) Sales Force number of full- or part-time paid sales employees who work exclusively for the company, 321.

Direct Marketing the use of consumer-direct (CD) channels to reach and deliver goods and services to customers without using marketing middlemen, 314.

Direct-Order Marketing marketing in which direct marketers seek a measurable response, typically a customer order, 314.

Direct Product Profitability (DPP) a way of measuring a product's handling costs from the time it reaches the warehouse until a customer buys it in the retail store, 263.

Dissociative Groups those groups whose values or behavior an individual rejects, 85.

Drive a strong internal stimulus impelling action, 89.

Dual Adaptation adapting both the product and the communications to the local market, 336.

Durability a measure of a product's expected operating life under natural or stressful conditions, 160.

E-Business the use of electronic means and platforms to conduct a company's business, 254.

E-Commerce a company or site offers to transact or facilitate the selling of products and services online, 254.

E-Marketing company efforts to inform buyers, communicate, promote, and sell its offerings online, 254.

Environmental Threat challenge posed by an unfavorable external trend or development that would lead, in the absence of defensive marketing action, to deterioration in sales or profit, 30.

E-Purchasing purchase of goods, services, and information from online suppliers, 254.

Everyday Low Pricing (EDLP) in retailing, a constant low price with few or no price promotions and special sales, 227.

Exchange the process of obtaining a desired product from someone by offering something in return, 3.

Exclusive Distribution severely limiting the number of intermediaries to maintain control over the service level and outputs offered by resellers, 246.

Expected Product a set of attributes and conditions buyers normally expect when they purchase a particular product, 178.

Experience Curve (learning curve) a decline in the average cost that occurs with accumulated production experience, 222.

Fad a craze that is unpredictable, short-lived, and without social, economic and political significance, 52.

Family of Orientation parents and siblings, 86.

Family of Procreation spouse and children, 86.

Features characteristics that enhance the basic function of a product, 159.

Fixed Costs costs that do not vary with production or sales revenue, 222.

Flexible Market Offering the product and service elements that all segment members value, plus discretionary options that some segment members value, 117.

Focus Group a gathering of six to ten people who are carefully selected based on certain demographic, psychographic, or other considerations and brought together to discuss various topics of interest, 45.

Forecasting the art of anticipating what buyers are likely to do under a given set of conditions, 51.

Form the size, shape, or physical structure of a product, 159.

Frequency Programs (FPs) programs to reward customers who buy frequently and/or in substantial amounts, 76.

Generics unbranded, plainly packaged, less expensive versions of common products, 266.

Global Firm a firm that operates in more than one country and captures R&D, production, logistical, marketing, and financial advantages in its costs and reputation that are not available to purely domestic competitors, 332.

Global Industry an industry in which the strategic positions of competitors in major geographic or national markets are fundamentally affected by their overall global positions, 332.

Goal Formulation the process of developing specific goals for the planning period, 31.

Going-Rate Pricing price based largely on competitors' prices, 227.

Gray Market branded products diverted from normal or authorized distribution channels in the country of product origin or across international borders, 337.

High-Low Pricing charging higher prices on an everyday basis but then running frequent promotions and special sales, 227.

Holistic Marketing a concept based on the development, design, and implementation of marketing programs, processes, and activities that recognizes their breadth and interdependencies, 8.

Horizontal Marketing System two or more unrelated companies put together resources or programs to exploit an emerging market opportunity, 252.

Image set of beliefs, ideas, and impressions that a person holds regarding an object, 283.

Industry a group of firms that offer a product or class of products that are close substitutes for one another, 163.

Ingredient Branding a special case of co-branding that involves creating brand equity for materials, components, or parts that are necessarily contained within other branded products, 147.

Innovation any good, service, or idea that is perceived by someone as new, 191.

Innovation Diffusion Process the spread of a new idea from its source of invention or creation to its ultimate users or adopters, 191.

Institutional Market schools, hospitals, nursing homes, prisons, and other institutions that must provide goods and services to people in their care, 102.

Integrated Logistics Systems (ILS) materials management, material flow systems, and physical distribution, abetted by information technology (IT), 270.

Integrated Marketing mixing and matching marketing activities to maximize their individual and collective efforts, 9.

Integrated Marketing Communications (IMC) a concept of marketing communications planning that recognizes the added value of a comprehensive plan, 290.

Intensive Distribution the manufacturer placing the goods or services in as many outlets as possibile, 247.

Internal Branding activities and processes that help to inform and inspire employees, 141.

Joint Venture a company in which multiple investors share ownership and control, 335.

Learning changes in an individual's behavior that arise from experience, 89.

Learning Curve the decline in the average cost with accumulated production experience, 222.

Life Stage defines a person's major concern within his or her life cycle, such as deciding to buy a new home, 122.

Life-Cycle Cost the product's purchase cost plus the discounted cost of maintenance and repair less the discounted salvage value, 111, 212.

Lifestyle person's pattern of living in the world as expressed in activities, interests, and opinions, 88.

Line Extension using the parent brand to brand a new product that targets a new market segment within a category currently served by the parent brand, 148.

Line Stretching lengthening the product line beyond its current range, 181.

Loyalty a customer's commitment to re-buy or re-patronize a preferred product or service, 65.

Market-Buildup Method identifying all the potential buyers in each market and estimating their potential purchases, 51.

Market Demand total volume that would be bought by a defined customer group in a defined geographical area, within a given period, in a defined marketing environment under a defined marketing program, 49.

Market Logistics planning the infrastructure to meet demand, then implementing and controlling the physical flows or materials and final goods from points of origin to points of use, to meet customer requirements at a profit, 270.

Market Opportunity Analysis (MOA) system used to determine the attractiveness and probability of success in each market opportunity, 30.

Market Partitioning investigating the hierarchy of attributes consumers examine in choosing a brand if they use phased decision strategies, 132.

Market Potential limit approached by market demand as industry marketing expenditures approach infinity for a given marketing environment, 48.

Market Share level of selective demand for the company's product, 35, 49.

Market-Penetration Pricing   pricing strategy where prices start low to drive higher sales volume from price-sensitive customers and produce productivity gains, 220.

Market-Skimming Pricing   pricing strategy where prices start high and are slowly lowered over time to maximize profits from less price-sensitive customers, 220.

Marketer   someone who seeks a response (attention, a purchase, a vote, a donation) from another party, called the prospect, 5.

Marketing   process of planning and executing the conception, pricing, promotion, and distribution of ideas, goods, and services to create exchanges that satisfy individual and organizational goals, 3.

Marketing Audit   comprehensive, systematic, independent, and periodic examination of a company's (or SBUs) marketing environment, objectives, strategies, and activities, 343.

Marketing Channel System   the particular set of marketing channels employed by a firm, 240.

Marketing Channels   sets of interdependent organizations involved in the process of making a product or service available for use or consumption, 240.

Marketing Communications   the means by which firms attempt to inform, persuade, and remind consumers—directly or indirectly—about products and brands that they sell, 14, 279.

Marketing Communications Mix   advertising, sales promotion, events and experiences, public relations and publicity, direct marketing, and personal selling, 279, 288.

Marketing Forecast   the expected market demand corresponding to the level of industry marketing expenditure, 49.

Marketing Information System (MIS)   people, equipment, and procedures that gather, sort, analyze, evaluate, and distribute information to marketing decision makers, 41.

Marketing Intelligence System   set of procedures and sources used by managers to obtain everyday information about developments in the marketing environment, 42.

Marketing Management   the art and science of choosing target markets and getting, keeping, and growing customers through creating, delivering, and communicating superior customer value, 3, 10.

Marketing Metrics   the set of measures that helps firms to quantify, compare, and interpret their marketing performance, 34.

Marketing Network   the company and its supporting stakeholders, with whom it has built mutually profitable business relationships, 9.

Marketing Opportunity   area of buyer need in which a company can perform profitably, 30.

Marketing Plan   written document that summarizes what the marketer has learned about the marketplace, indicates how the firm plans to reach its marketing objectives, and helps direct and coordinate the marketing effort, 33.

Marketing Public Relations (MPR)   publicity and other activities that build corporate or product image to facilitate achievement of marketing goals, 308.

Marketing Research   systematic design, collection, analysis, and reporting of data and findings that are relevant to a specific marketing situation facing the company, 42.

Markup   pricing an item by adding a standard increase to the product's cost, 224.

Mass Marketing   the mass production, distribution and promotion of one product for all buyers, 117.

Media Selection   finding the most cost-effective media to deliver the desired number and type of exposures to the target audience, 297.

Megamarketing   the strategic coordination of economic, psychological, political, and public relations skills, to gain the cooperation of a number of parties in order to enter or operate in a given market, 131.

Membership Groups   groups having a direct influence on a person, 85.

Microsales Analysis   examination of specific products and territories that failed to produce expected sales, 35.

Microsite   a limited area on the Web managed and paid for by an external advertiser/company, 318.

Mission Statement   statement of why the organization exists, which is shared with managers, employees, and (in many cases) customers, 27.

Motive   a need that is sufficiently pressing to drive a person to act, 88.

Multichannel Marketing   a single firm uses two or more marketing channels to reach one or more customer segments, 252.

Opinion Leader   the person in informal, product-related communications who offers advice or information about a specific product or category, 85.

Organization   a company's structures, policies, and corporate culture, 29.

Organizational Buying   decision-making process by which formal organizations establish the need for purchased products and services and identify, evaluate, and choose among alternative brands and suppliers, 102.

Overall Market Share   the company's sales expressed as a percentage of total market sales, 35.

Overhead   costs that do not vary with production or sales revenue, 222.

Packaging   designing and producing the container for a product, 182.

Partner Relationship Management (PRM)   activities to build mutually satisfying long-term relations with key partners such as suppliers, distributors, ad agencies, and marketing research suppliers, 32.

Penetrated Market   the set of consumers who are buying a company's product, 48.

Perception   process by which an individual selects, organizes, and interprets information inputs to create a meaningful picture of the world, 89.

Performance Quality   the level at which the product's primary characteristics operate, 159.

Personal Communications Channels   two or more persons communicating directly face-to-face, person-to-audience, over the telephone, or through e-mail, 285.

Personal Influence   the effect one person has on another's attitude or purchase probability, 285.

Personality   distinguishing psychological characteristics that lead to relatively consistent and enduring responses to environmental stimuli, 87.

Place Advertising   ads that appear outside of home and where consumers work and play, 299.

Point-of-Purchase   the location where a purchase is made, typically in a retail setting, 304.

Positioning   act of designing the company's offering and image to occupy a distinctive place in the target market's mind, 155.

Potential Market   the set of consumers who profess a sufficient level of interest in a market offer, 48.

Potential Product   all the possible augmentations and transformations the product or offering might undergo in the future, 179.

Price Discrimination a company sells a product or service at two or more prices that do not reflect a proportional difference in costs, 232.

Private Label Brand brands developed and marketed by retailers and wholesalers, 266.

Product anything that can be offered to a market to satisfy a want or need, 178.

Product Adaptation altering the product to meet local conditions or preferences, 336.

Product Invention creating something new via product development or other means, 336.

Product Mix (Assortment) set of all products and items that a particular marketer offers for sale, 180.

Product System group of diverse but related items that function in a compatible manner, 180.

Profitable Customer a person, household, or company that over time yields a revenue stream that exceeds by an acceptable amount the company's cost stream of attracting, selling, and servicing that customer, 69.

Prospect an individual or group from whom a marketer seeks to get a response such as a purchase, a vote, or donation, 5.

Psychographics the science of using psychology and demographics to better understand consumers, 123.

Public any group that has an actual or potential interest in or impact on a company's ability to achieve its objectives, 308.

Public Relations (PR) variety of programs that are designed to promote or protect a company's image or its individual products, 308.

Pull Strategy when the manufacturer uses advertising and promotion to persuade consumers to ask intermediaries for the product, thus inducing the intermediaries to order it, 241.

Pure-Click companies that have launched a Web site without any previous existence as a firm, 255.

Push Strategy when the manufacturer uses its sales force and trade promotion money to induce intermediaries to carry, promote, and sell the product to end users, 240.

Quality the totality of features and characteristics of a product or service that bear on its ability to satisfy stated or an implied needs, 68.

Reference Groups all the groups that have a direct or indirect influence on a person's attitudes or behavior, 85.

Reference Price pricing information a consumer retains in memory which is used to interpret and evaluate a new price, 219.

Relationship Marketing building mutually satisfying long-term relationships with key parties, in order to earn and retain their business, 8, 327.

Relative Market Share market share in relation to a company's largest competitor, 35.

Reliability a measure of the probability that a product will not malfunction or fail within a specified time period, 160.

Repairability a measure of the ease of fixing a product when it malfunctions or fails, 160.

Retailer (Retail Store) any business enterprise whose sales volume comes primarily from retailing, 260.

Retailing all activities involved in selling goods or services directly to final consumers for personal, nonbusiness use, 260.

Role the activities a person is expected to perform, 86.

Sales Analysis measuring and evaluating actual sales in relation to goals, 35.

Sales Budget conservative estimate of the expected sales volume; used primarily for making current purchasing, production, and cash-flow decisions, 50.

Sales Promotion collection of incentive tools, mostly short term, designed to stimulate quicker or greater purchase of particular products or services by consumers or the trade, 302.

Sales Quota sales goal set for a product line, company division, or sales representative, 50.

Sales-Variance Analysis a measure of the relative contribution of different factors to a gap in sales performance, 35.

Satisfaction a person's feelings of pleasure or disappointment resulting from comparing a product's perceived performance (or outcome) in relation to his or her expectations, 66.

Scenario Analysis developing plausible representations of a firm's possible future that make different assumptions about forces driving the market and include different uncertainties, 29.

Search-Related Ads online ads in which search terms are used as a proxy for the consumer's consumption interests and relevant links to offerings are listed along side the search results, 318.

Selective Distribution the use of more than a few but less than all of the intermediaries who are willing to carry a particular product, 246.

Served Market all the buyers who are able and willing to buy a company's product, 35.

Served Market Share a company's sales expressed as a percentage of the total sales to its served market, 35.

Service any act or performance that one party can offer to another that is essentially intangible and does not result in the ownership of anything, 201.

Shopping Goods products that the customer, in the process of selection and purchase, characteristically compares on the basis of suitability, quality, price, and style, 180.

Social Classes homogeneous and enduring divisions in a society, which are hierarchically ordered and whose members share similar values, interests, and behavior, 85.

Specialty Goods products with unique characteristics or brand identification for which a sufficient number of buyers are willing to make a special purchasing effort, 180.

Stakeholder-Performance Scorecard a measure to track the satisfaction of various constituencies who have a critical interest in and impact on the company' s performance, 35.

Status one's position within his or her own hierarchy or culture, 86.

Straight Extension introducing a product in a foreign market without any change in the product, 336.

Strategic Business Unit (SBU) a business that can be planned separately from the rest of the company, with its own set of competitors and a manager who is responsible for strategic planning and profit performance, 27.

Strategic Group firms pursuing the same strategy directed to the same target market, 31.

Strategy a company's game plan for achieving its goals, 31.

Style a product's look and feel to the buyer, 160.

Subculture subdivisions of a culture that provide more specific identification and socialization, such as nationalities, religions, racial groups, and geographical regions, 57.

Supersegment a set of segments sharing some exploitable similarity, 130.

Supply Chain the partnerships a firm forges with suppliers and distributors to deliver value to customers; also known as a value delivery network, 14, 24.

Supply Chain Management (SCM) procuring the right inputs (raw materials, components, and capital equipment); converting them efficiently into finished products; and dispatching them to the final destinations, 270.

Target Costing   determining the cost that must be achieved to sell a new product, with the desired functions, at the price consumers are willing to pay, given the offering's appeal and competitors' prices, 223.

Target Market   the part of the qualified available market the company decides to pursue, 13, 48, 262.

Target-Return Pricing   determining the price that would yield the firm's target rate of return on investment (ROI), 225.

Telemarketing   the use of telephone and call centers to attract prospects, sell to existing customers, and provide service by taking orders and answering questions, 316.

Total Costs   the sum of the fixed and variable costs for any given level of production, 222.

Total Customer Cost   perceived monetary value of the bundle of costs that customers expect to incur in evaluating, obtaining, using, and disposing of the product or service, 64.

Total Customer Value   bundle of benefits that customers expect from a given product or service, 64.

Total Quality Management (TQM)   an organization-wide approach to continuously improving the quality of all the organization's processes, products, and services, 68.

Transaction   a trade of values between two or more parties: A gives X to B and receives Y in return, 3.

Transfer   in the case of gifts, subsidies, and charitable contributions: A gives X to B but does not receive anything tangible in return, 3.

Trend   direction or sequence of events that has some momentum and durability, 52, 270.

Two-Part Pricing   pricing that consists of a fixed fee plus a variable usage fee, 233.

Tying Agreement   agreement in which producers of strong brands sell their products to dealers only if dealers purchase related offerings, 254.

Unsought Goods   products that consumers do not know about or do not normally think of buying, 180.

Value Chain   a group of strategically relevant activities that create value and cost in a specific business, 23.

Value-Delivery Network   *see* supply chain, 24.

Value-Delivery System   all the experiences the customer will have on the way to obtaining and using the offering, 63.

Value Network   a system of partnerships and alliances that a firm creates to source, augment, and deliver its offerings, 241.

Value Pricing   winning loyal customers by charging a fairly low price for a high-quality offering, 227.

Value Proposition   the whole cluster of benefits the company promises to deliver, 66.

Variable Costs   costs that vary directly with the level of production, 222.

Vertical Integration   situation in which manufacturers try to control or own their suppliers, distributors, or other intermediaries, 164.

Vertical Marketing System (VMS)   producer, wholesaler(s), and retailer(s) acting as a unified system, 251.

Viral Marketing   drawing attention to an Internet site by passing company-developed products, services, or information from user to user, 286.

Wholesaling   all of the activities involved in selling goods or services to those who buy for resale or business use, 267.

Yield Pricing   situation in which companies offer (1) discounted but limited early purchases, (2) higher-priced late purchases, and (3) the lowest rates on unsold inventory just before it expires, 232.

Zero-Level Channel   a manufacturer selling directly to the final customer (also known as direct marketing channel), 244.

Index

A

Account managers, 320
Accountable marketing, 75
Accumulated production, 222
Activities and experiences, 263
Activity-based cost (ABC) accounting, 37, 223, 347
Activity-based costing, 69
Adapted marketing mix, 335
Adding
    financial benefits, 76
    social benefits, 76
Administered VMS, 251
Adoption
    of products, 190, 347
Advertising, 295, 347
    banner, 318, 347
    budget, 296
    campaign, 296
    content-target, 318, 348
    decision, 295
    frequency, 296
    goal or objective, 295, 347
    higher-performing, 317
    informative, 296
    persuasive, 296
    place, 299, 351
    reinforcement, 296
    reminder, 296
    search-related, 318, 352
Affordable budget method, 287
Age and life-cycle stage, 87, 122
Agents, 246
Alpha testing, 188
Amazon.com, 163
American Marketing Association, 136
American Society for Quality Control, 68
Analysis, 30
    audience, 283
    break-even, 188, 347
    business, 187
    conjoint, 186, 348
    customer profitability, 69, 348
    customer value, 167
    marketing expense-to-sales, 35
    microsales, 35, 351
    product value, 110
    product-line, 180
    profitability, 36
    risk, 188
    sales, 35, 352
    sales-variance, 35, 352
    scenario, 29, 352
    SWOT, 30
    time-and-duty, 324
Annual plan control, 341
Annual sales quotas, 325
Anti-pollution pressures, 58

Appeal
    informational, 284
    transformational, 284
Apple computer, 1, 172
Area market potential, 51
"Aseptic" package, 182
Aspirational groups, 85, 347
Assessing growth opportunities, 28
Associative network memory model, 90, 347
Attitude, 93, 125, 347
Auction-type pricing, 228
Audience analysis, 283
Audit, marketing, 343, 350
Augmented product, 179, 347
Available market, 48, 347
Average cost, 222, 347
Avon, 331
Awareness-building stage, 290
Axe, 317
Ayal and Zif, 333

B

B2B (business to business), 126
Baby boomers, 54
Backward invention, 336
Bank of America (BofA), 239
Banner ads, 318, 347
Barnes & Noble, 163
Bases for segmenting
    business markets, 125
    consumer markets, 120
Basic
    marketing, 75
    product, 178, 347
Bass Pro Shops, 263
Bauer Eddie, 317
BB&T Corporation, 126
Behavior(s), 84
    consumer, 84, 348
    customer switching, 205
    postpurchase, 95
Behavioral
    data, 45
    segmentation, 123
Belief, 93, 347
Ben & Jerry's, 12
Benefit segments, 124
Beta testing, 188
"Billboard" effect, 148
Blanket contract, 111
BMW, 278
Bonoma, 340
Boston Beer Company, 2
Brand, 136, 347
    associations, 90, 347
    audits, 143, 347
    awareness, 140, 347
    bonding, 141
    category membership, 157

    contact, 140, 347
    crisis, 145
    dilution, 148, 347
    element choice criteria, 139
    elements, 139, 207, 347, See also Table 8.2
    equity, 71, 137, 279, 347
    equity drivers, 138
    equity management, 144
    extensions, 148, 347
    identity, 267
    image, 140, 347
    knowledge, 137, 347
    leader, 235
    loyalty, 136
    personality, 87, 347
    portfolios, 149, 347
    promise, 138, 347
    reinforcement, 144
    sponsor, 267
    strategies, 207
    tracking, 143
    valuation, 144
Brand-asset management team (BAMT), 338
Branding, 136, 347
    decision, 146
    ingredient, 147, 350
    internal, 141, 350
    strategy, 146, 207, 347
Break-even
    analysis, 188, 347
    chart, 226
Brick-and-click, 255, 347
    companies, 255
Budget(s)
    advertising, 296
    affordable, 287
    competitive-parity, 288
    objective-and-task, 288
    percentage-of-sales, 287
Building loyalty, 75
Burst promotions, 246
Business
    analysis, 187
    buying process, 109
    customers, 108, See also Table 6.2
    database, 77, 347
    market, 102, 347
    market segmentation, 125
    mission, 30
    promotion, 304
    regulation, 101
    relationships, 112
    unit strategic planning, 29
Buyer-readiness stage, 125
Buyers' bargaining, 162
Buygrid framework, 109
Buying center, 106, 348
Buying situation, 104
Buyphases, 109
By-product pricing, 233

C

California Eastern Laboratories
(CEL), 322
Call centers, 316
Calvin Klein, 262
Camay, 336
Campaign
developing the advertising, 296
multiple-stage, 291
Canon, 313
Capital items, 180
Captive products, 233, 348
Captive-product pricing, 233
Cardinal Health, 104
Cash cows, 150
Catalog marketing, 315
Category
extension, 148, 348
management, 338
membership, 156, 348
Caterpillar, 64, 116
Cause-related marketing, 12
Challenger strategies, 170
Changing role of governments, 58
Channel-design decisions, 245
Channel-management decisions, 248
Channels
advantage, 16, 247
alternatives, 246
arrangements, 249
communications, 285
consumer marketing, 244
conventional market, 251, 348
coordination, 252, 348
design, 246
differentiation, 161
distribution, 337
dynamics, 251
evaluating members, 249
functions and flows, 242
industrial marketing, 244
integration of communications, 287
levels, 244
marketing, 240, 350
member functions, 243
nonpersonal communications, 287
objectives, 245
personal communications, 285, 351
personal influence, 285
power, 249, 348
selecting and training members, 248
zero-level, 244, 353
Christopher & Bond, 262
Claritas Inc., 120
Cleveland's, 286
Clustered preferences, 120
Co-branding, 147, 348
Coca-Cola, 117
Commercialization, 190
Communication(s)
adaptation, 336, 348
channels, 14, 285
decision, 264
integrated marketing, 290
marketing, 14, 279, 350
mass, 287
objectives, 283
personal, 285
platforms, 281
postpurchase, 95

process models, 280
research, 301
strategies, 335
Company
customer base, 73
demand, 50, 348
pricing policies, 229
sales forecast, 50, 348
sales potential, 50
Competition, 15
and clutter, 296
conflict and, 252
entry barriers, 164
exit barriers, 164
Competitive
advantage, 70, 348
forces and competitors, 161
frame of reference, 156
spheres, 27
strategies, 167
Competitive-parity budget method, 288
Competitor
cost and offers, 223
identification of, 162
map, 165
myopia, 163
objectives, 166
price changes, 234
strengths and weaknesses, 166
Competitor-centered company, 173
Concentrated marketing, 120
Concept
holistic marketing, 8
marketing, 7
product, 7
product development, 186
production, 6
selling, 7
societal marketing, 12
testing in new products, 186
Conflict and competition in channel, 252
Conformance quality, 159, 348
Conjoint analysis, 186, 348
Consumer, *See also* Customer
adoption process, 190
attitudes and belief, 93
behavior, 84, 348
buying process, 92
cultural factors, 84
evaluation process, 93
involvement, 94, 348
promotion tools, 303
psychology and pricing, 218
savings, 56
Consumer marketing channels, 244
Consumer-goods testing, 189
Consumerist movement, 60, 348
Containerization, 275, 348
Content-target advertising, 318, 348
Continuity, 301
Contract carrier, 275
Contraction defense, 169
Contractual sales force, 321, 348
Contractual VMS, 251
Control
types of marketing, 341
Convenience goods, 180, 348
Conventional marketing channel,
251, 348
Conversion model, 125
Cooperation, 252

Cooptation, 253
Copy strategy statement, 297
Core
benefit, 178, 348
business processes, 23
competencies, 24, 348
Core values, 88, 348
high persistence of, 57
Corporate
credibility, 112
culture, 29, 348
mission, 26
retail organizations, 262
retailing, 261, 348
strategic planning, 26
VMS, 251
Corporate-divisional organization, 339
Cost
average, 222
estimating, 222
fixed, 222, 349
inventory-carrying, 274
life-cycle, 111, 212
order-processing, 274
structure, 164
total customer, 64
types, 222
variable, 222
Counteroffensive defense, 169
Countertrade, 230, 348
Creative
development and execution, 297
implementation, 33
strategy, 284
Credit availability, 56
Critical path scheduling (CPS), 190
Cues, 89, 348
Cultural factors and behavior, 84
Culture, 84, 348
corporate, 29, 348
organization, 29
Customer
churn, 73, 348
complaints, 210
database, 77, 348
equity, 71, 348
expectations, 208
lifetime value, 76, 348
loyalty, 65
management organization, 339
performance scorecard, 35, 348
profitable, 69, 351
satisfaction, 67
switching behavior, 205
touch point, 72
value analysis, 167
value delivery process, 22
value triad, 14
winning back, 96
Customer lifetime value (CLV), 70
Customer perceived value (CPV), 64, 348
Customer profitability analysis (CPA),
69, 348
Customer relationship management
(CRM), 72, 78, 348
Customer value assessment (CVA), 111
Customer value hierarchy, 178, 348
Customer-based brand equity, 137, 349
Customer-development process, 74
Customer-focused value proposition, 155
Customer-oriented strategy, 173

Customerization, 118, 349
Customers' desired service output
  levels, 245
Customized marketing, 118

D

Dannon, 291
Data
  behavioral, 45
  collection phase, 47
  mining, 39, 78, 349
  sources, 45
  warehouse, 77, 349
Databases, 42
  downside of, 78
  marketing, 77, 349
Debt, 56
Decisions, 273
  international marketing, 333
  marketing PR, 308
  research and, 41
Decline stage of product life cycle, 194
Defending market share, 168
Defense strategies
  contraction, 169
  counteroffensive, 169
  flank, 168
  mobile, 169
  position, 168
  preemptive, 169
Delayed quotation pricing, 234
Dell, 3, 89
Demand
  and supply strategies, 204, See also
    Table 11.1
  company, 50, 348
  determining, 220
  estimating future, 51
  market, 49, 350
  measurement, 49
  price elasticity of, 221
  total market, 168
Demand-chain planning, 241, 349
Demographic
  business segmentation, 126
  consumer segmentation, 122
  environment, 53
Differentiated
  marketing, 130
  oligopoly, 163
  pricing, 232
Differentiating services, 206
Differentiation strategies, 159
Diffusion and adoption, 190
Direct (company) sales force, 321, 349
Direct
  investment, 335
  mail marketing, 314
  marketing, 314, 349
  marketing channel, 244
  order marketing, 314, 349
  product profitability, 263, 349
Disney, 203
Dissociative groups, 85, 349
Distribution channels, 337, See also Channels
Distributors' territorial rights, 247
Do Not Call Registry, 316
Drive, 89, 349
Drucker, Peter, 27

Dual adaptation, 336, 349
DuPont, 227, 339
Durability, 160, 349
Durable goods, 180

E

Eastman Kodak, 165
E-business, 254, 349
E-commerce, 254, 349
  marketing practices, 254
Economic environment, 55
Efficiency control, 342
E-marketing, 254, 349
  guidelines, 319
Employees and internal marketing, 206
Encoding and communications, 90
Entry barriers in competition, 164
Entry into foreign markets, 334
Environment
  broad, 15
  demographic, 53
  economic, 55
  external, 30
  internal, 30
  marketing, 15
  natural, 58
  political-legal, 59
  social-cultural, 56
  task, 15
  technological, 58
Environmental threat, 30, 349
E-purchasing, 254, 349
Equity
  brand, 136, 279
  customer, 137
Estimating
  costs, 222
  demand curves, 221
  future demand, 51
Ethics
  business, 344
  channel, 254
  targeting, 131
Ethnic markets, 54
Evaluating
  advertising effectiveness, 301
  channel members, 249
  major alternatives, 247
  market segments, 128
Event(s)
  creation, 307
  experiences, 306
  marketers, 287
  objectives, 306
  opportunities, 307
  sponsored, 307
Everyday low pricing (EDLP), 227, 349
Exchange, 3, 349
  distribution, 246
  negotiated, 326
  routinized, 326
  transaction, 3
  transfer, 3
Exclusive distribution, 246, 349
Exit barriers in competition, 164
Expanding market share, 170
Expectancy-value model, 94
Expected product, 178, 349
Experience curve (learning curve), 222, 349

Experiential marketing, 118
Experimental research, 45
Expertise, 284
External marketing, 206

F

Factors influencing the adoption process, 191
Fad, 52, 349
Family and buying behavior, 86
Features, 159, 349
FedEx Logistics Services, 270
Feedback and control, 32
Financial
  model, 36
  success, 2
Five product levels, 179
Five-stage model of buying, 91
Fixed compensation, 322
Fixed costs, 222, 349
Flank defense, 168
Flanker brands, 150
Flexible market offering, 117, 349
Flighting, 301
Focus group, 45, 349
Focus-group research, 45
Food and Drug Administration (FDA), 183
Forecasting, 51, 349
Ford, 11
Form, 159, 349
Forward invention, 336
Four Cs, 9
Four Ps, 9
Franchise organizations, 252
Frequency programs (FPs), 76, 349
Freud, Sigmund, 88
Full market coverage, 130
Functional
  hubs, 110
  organization, 338

G

Gain-and-risk-sharing pricing, 229
GAP, 262
Gender
  description and product specification,
    109
  segmentation, 122
General Electric, 273
General Foods, 342
General Motors, 335
Generation, 122
Generation X, 54
Generation Y, 54
Generics, 266, 349
Geographic
  organization, 338
  segmentation, 120
  shifts in population, 55
Geographical pricing, 230
Geographical-expansion strategy, 168
Global
  firm, 332, 349
  industry, 332, 349
  marketing, 332
  organization, 340
Globalization, 8
  degree of, 164

Goal formulation, 31, 349
Godin, Seth, 286
Going-rate pricing, 227, 349
Goods
    convenience, 180, 348
    durable, 180
    nondurable, 180
    shopping, 180
    specialty, 180, 352
    unsought, 180, 353
Google, 135
Government market, 104
Grassroots marketing, 118
Gray market, 337, 349
Growth
    diversification, 28
    integrative, 28
    intensive, 28
    special-interest groups, 60
    stage of product life cycle, 193
    worldwide population, 54

H

Hallmark, 116
Heinz, 168
Herzberg, Frederick, 88
Hewlett-Packard, 8, 157
Higher-performing ads, 317
High-low pricing, 227, 349
Holdout customers, 170
Holistic marketing, 8, 349
    concept, 8
    designing brand-building programme, 140
    for services, 205
    framework, 25
    orientation, 25, 84
Home shopping, 314
Home Shopping Network (HSN), 316
Homogeneous preferences, 119
Honda, 284
Horizontal
    channel conflict, 253
    marketing systems, 252, 350
Household patterns, 55
Hughes, 313

I

IBM, 118
IBM's iSource, 319
Idea(s)
    generation, 185
    new product, 185
    screening, 186
Image, 283, 350
    brand, 140, 347
    differentiation, 161
Implementation
    evaluating, 309
    marketing plan, 341
    programs, 32
Income
    distribution, 56
    segmentation, 122
Income-distribution patterns, 56
Incremental analysis, 250
Indirect and direct exporting, 334
Industrial marketing channels, 244
Industry competition, 163, 350

Informational appeal, 284
Informative advertising, 296
Ingredient branding, 147, 350
Initiating price increases, 233
Innovation, 191, 350
    diffusion process, 191, 350
Inseparability of services, 203
Institutional market, 102, 350
Intangibility of services, 202
Integrated logistics systems (ILS), 270, 350
Integrated marketing, 9, 350
Integrated marketing communications (IMC),
    290, 350
    advertising, 295
    implementation, 291
    interaction, 317
    mass communication, 294
    objectives, 283
    personal communication, 313
    public relation, 308
    sales force, 319
    sales promotion, 302
Integration of communications channels, 287
Intel, 147
Intensive distribution, 247, 350
Interactive marketing, 206, 317
Intermediaries, 242, See also Channels
Intermediary levels, 244
Internal
    branding, 141, 350
    environment, 30
    marketing, 118, 206, 337
    records, 41
Internet
    e-bussiness, 254
    e-commerce, 254
    marketing, 118
    service provider, 255
Introduction stage, 193
Inventory, 273

J

Joint ventures, 335, 350
John Deere, 4
Johnson & Johnson, 342

K

Kiehl's, 285
Kiosk, 316
Komatsu, 65

L

Labeling, 183
Laddering, 88
"Learn-feel-do sequence", 282
Learning, 89, 350
Learning and behavior, 89
Learning curve, 222, 350
Legal and ethical issues, 254, See also Ethics
Legal and political environment, 59
Lenovo, 6
Levels
    channel, 244
    customers' desired service output, 245
    five product, 179
    intermediary, 244

    product, 178
    production, 222
Levi Strauss, 262
Licensing, 334
Life cycle
    age and stage, 87, 122
    cost, 111, 212, 350
    product, 192
    retail, 260
Life stage, 122, 350
Lifestyle, 88, 350
Lifestyle and values, 88
Line extension, 148, 350
Line modernization, featuring, and
    pruning, 181
Line stretching, 181, 350
"Line-extension trap", 148
Local marketing, 118
Location
    decision, 264
    options for retailers, 265
Lotus Development Corporation, 32
Loyalty, 65, 350
    building, 75
    customer, 65

M

Macroenvironment, 52
Macroscheduling, 300
Management
    brand equity, 144
    category, 338
    marketing, 3, 10, 351, See also Table 1.1
    sales force, 323
    service-quality, 209
    strategic brand, 135
Managing
    channel conflict, 253
    multiple segments, 131
    new products, 183
    service quality, 208
Market(s), See also Marketing
    available, 48, 347
    bases for segmenting business, 125
    bases for segmenting consumer, 120
    business, 102, 347
    coverage, 130
    demand, 49, 350
    entry into foreign, 334
    ethnic, 54
    forecast, 49, 350
    government, 104
    gray, 337, 349
    institutional, 102, 350
    logistics, 270, 350
    offering, 13
    partitioning, 132, 350
    penetrated, 48, 351
    planning, 270
    potential, 48, 350
    served, 35, 352
    share, 35, 49, 350
    share and consumer base, 296
    small business, 131
    specialization, 130
    targeting, 127
    testing, 188
    to measure, 48
Market opportunity analysis (MOA),
    30, 350

Market segmentation
    business markets, 125
    consumer markets, 120
    criteria, 120
    ethical issues, 131
    levels, 117
Market targets, 13, 48, 262, 353
    ethical choice of, 132
Market-buildup method, 51, 350
Market-challenger attack, 170
Market-follower strategies, 172
Market-leader strategies, 167
Market-management organization, 339
Market-nicher strategies, 172
Market-penetration pricing, 220, 350
Market-penetration strategy, 168
Market-skimming pricing, 220, 350
Marketer, 5, 350
Marketing. *See also* Market, Sales
    accountable, 75
    audit, 343, 350
    basic, 75
    catalog, 315
    cause-related, 12
    channel system, 240, 350
    communications, 14, 279, 288, 350
    concentrated, 120
    concepts, 7
    controller, 342
    core concepts, 12
    CRM, 72
    customized, 118
    dashboard, 35
    database, 77, 349
    department, 337
    differentiated, 130
    direct, 314, 349
    distribution, 14
    environment, 15
    expense-to-sales analysis, 35
    expense-to-sales ratio, 35
    experiential, 118
    external, 206
    global, 332
    grassroots, 118
    holistic, 8, 349
    implementation, 340
    implementation management, 33
    integrated, 9, 350
    integrating, 140
    intelligence system, 42, 350
    interactive, 206, 317
    internal, 11, 206, 337
    Internet, 118
    local, 118
    logistics, 270, 350
    mass, 117, 351
    metrics, 34, 351
    mix, 10, 37, 170
    multichannel, 252, 351
    multicultural, 85
    network, 9, 351
    niche, 117
    objectives, 309
    offerings and brand, 14
    opportunities, 30, 351
    permission, 286
    personalizing, 140
    plan, 33, 351
    planning, 15
    proactive, 75
    reactive, 75

    relationship, 8, 327, 352
    research, 42, 351
    research process, 44
    segment, 117
    social responsibility, 12
    strategies, 186, 193
    undifferentiated, 130
    viral, 286, 353
Marketing information system (MIS), 41, 350
Marketing public relations (MPR), 308, 351
    tools, 309, *See also* Table 16.5
Marketing research
    contact methods, 46
Markup, 224, 351
    pricing, 224
Maslow, Abraham, 88
Mass
    communications, 287
    marketing, 117, 351
Matrix-management organization, 339
Maturity stage, 194
Maximizing customer lifetime value, 68
McDonald's, 12
McKinsey & Company, 32
Measuring
    brand equity, 143
    communication results, 290
    marketing performance, 34
    satisfaction, 66
    sponsorship activities, 307
Media
    coordination, 290
    for direct-response marketing, 316
    selection, 297, 351
    types, 298
Mediamark, 47
Megamarketing, 131, 351
Members
    evaluating channel, 249
    selecting channel, 248
    terms and responsibilities of channel, 247
    training channel, 248
Membership groups, 85, 351
Memory
    encoding, 90
    retrieval, 90
Message
    source, 284
    strategy, 283, 296
    vehicles, 309
Metamarket, 6
Metric, 34
Micromodel of consumer responses, 281
Microsales analysis, 35, 351
Microscheduling problem, 301
Microsite, 318, 351
Microsoft, 27
Mission statement, 27, 351
Mix
    adapted marketing, 335
    marketing, 10, 37, 170
    population age, 54
    product, 180, 351
    service, 201, 263
    standardized marketing, 335
    trade-relations, 247
Mobile defense, 169
Mobility barriers, 164
Model(s)
    associative network memory, 90, 347
    communications process, 280
    conversion, 125

    expectancy-value, 94
    financial, 36
    five-stage, 91
    marketing-mix, 37
    market-share-maximization, 166
    response hierarchy, 281
Modified rebuy, 104
Monitoring systems, 210
Monopolistic competition, 163
Motivation, 88
    channel members, 249
    cues, 90
    sales representatives, 325
Motive, 88, 351
Motorola, 321
Multichannel
    conflict, 253
    marketing, 252, 351
    marketing systems, 252
Multicultural marketing, 85
Multinational companies, 285

N

Narus and Anderson, 270
National Semiconductor, 273
Natural
    environment, 58
    market segments, 120
Negotiated exchange, 326
New-market segment strategy, 168
New-product development decision
    process, 184
New-task buying, 105
Niche marketing, 117
Nielsen Media Research, 43
Nike, 24, 83, 139
"Noncontrollables", 53
"Nondurable goods", 180
Nonpersonal communications channels, 287
Nonstore retailing, 261
Non-store-based retailers, 265
North American Industry Classification
    System (NAICS), 51

O

Objective-and-task budget, 288
Objectives, 272, 303
Observational research, 45
Occupation and economic circumstances, 87
Oligopoly, 163
One-level channel, 244
"One-to-one marketing", 118
Opinion leader, 85, 351
Opportunism, 113
Order (reorder) point, 274
Order processing, 273
    costs, 274
Order-routine specification, 111
Organization, 29, 351
    buying process, 109
    corporate-divisional, 339
    culture, 29
    customer management, 339
    franchise, 252
    functional, 338
    geographic, 338
    global, 340
    market-management, 339
    matrix-management, 339

Organization (*Continued*)
  product-management, 338
  retail, 262
Organizational buying, 102, 351
Outsourcing and free trade, 56
Overall market share, 35, 351
Overdemand, 234
Overhead, 222, 351

P

Packaging, 182, 351
Partner relationship management (PRM), 32, 351
Partnership marketing, 75
Penetrated market, 48, 351
PepsiCo, 162
Perceived risk, 95
Perceived-value pricing, 226
Percentage-of-sales budget, 287
Perception and consumer behavior, 89, 351
Performance
  marketing plan, 35
  quality, 159, 351
  review, 112
Permission marketing, 286
Personal
  communications channels, 285, 351
  influence, 285, 351
  influence channels, 285
  selling and representatives, 326
  selling principles, 326
Personality, 87, 351
Personality and self-concept, 87
Personalizing marketing, 140
Personnel differentiation, 161
Persuasive advertising, 296
Pioneer advantage, 193
Place advertising, 299, 351
Poilane Bakery, 332
Point-of-purchase (POP), 304, 351
Points-of-difference (PODs), 156
Points-of-parity, 156
Political-legal environment, 59
Population age mix, 54
Porter, Michael, 23
Position defense, 168
Positioning, 155, 351
  strategy, 155
Postpurchase
  behavior, 95
  communications, 95
Post-sale service strategy, 213
Potential
  market, 48, 351
  product, 179, 351
Preemptive
  cannibalization, 149
  defense, 169
Preference segments, 119
Price, 218
  adaptation, 230
  buyers, 226
  changes, 234
  cues, 219
  cuts, 233
  decision, 263
  discounts and allowances, 230
  discrimination, 232, 351
  elasticity of demand, 221
  escalation, 336
  impact of, 229
  policy, 247

reference, 219, 352
  sensitivity, 220
  value, 227
Price–quality inferences, 219
Pricing
  auction-type, 228
  by-product, 233
  captive-product, 233
  delayed quotation, 234
  differentiated, 232
  everyday low, 227
  gain-and-risk-sharing, 229
  geographical, 230
  going-rate, 227, 349
  high-low, 227, 349
  market-penetration, 220, 350
  market-skimming, 220, 350
  markup, 224
  objective, 220
  perceived-value, 226
  product-bundling, 233
  product-mix, 232
  promotional, 231
  sales pricing, 263
  target-return, 225, 353
  two-part, 233, 353
  yield, 232, 353
Pringle, 12
Private label brand, 266, 351
PRIZM clusters, 15, 120
Proactive marketing, 75
Problem recognition in buying, 109
Process
  business buying, 109
  buying decision, 91
  communications, 280
  consumer adoption, 190
  consumer buying, 92
  consumer evaluation, 93
  factors influencing the adoption, 191
  innovation diffusion, 191, 350
  new-product development decision, 184
Procter & Gamble, 154, 338
Product, 178, 351
  adaptation, 336, 351
  assortment and procurement, 262
  augmented, 179, 347
  basic, 178, 347
  captive, 233, 348
  characteristics, 178
  classifications, 179
  concept, 7
  development, 188
  differentiation, 159
  expected, 178, 349
  invention, 336, 351
  levels, 178
  life cycle, 192
  life cycle stage, 296
  mix (assortment), 180, 351
  potential, 179, 351
  relationships, 180
  service quality, 68
  specialization, 130
  substitutability, 296
  support services, 212
  system, 180, 351
  value analysis, 110
  variety, 245
Product-bundling pricing, 233
Product-line analysis, 180
Product-line length, 181

Product-management organization, 338
Product-mix pricing, 232
Production concept, 6
Profitability
  analysis, 36
  control, 341
  customer, 69, 351
  pricing, 220
Progressive Corp., 200
Promotion techniques, 9
Promotional
  pricing, 231
  tools, 290
Proposal solicitation, 110
Prospect, 5, 352
Psychographics, 123, 352
  segmentation, 123
Public, 308, 352
Public relations (PR), 308, 352
Pull strategy, 241, 352
Pulsing, 301
Purchase decisions, 94, 219
Pure monopoly, 163
Pure-click, 255, 352
  companies, 255
Push strategy, 240, 352

Q

Qualitative research techniques, 46
Quality, 68, 352
  conformance, 159, 348
  performance, 159, 351
  product and service, 68
Quality function deployment (QFD), 188
Questionnaire
  research, 46

R

R&D budgets, 59
Raw materials
  shortage of, 58
Rayport and Jaworski, 317
Reach, 297
Reactive marketing, 75
Reducing customer defection, 75
Reduction of discounts, 234
Reference
  groups, 85, 352
  prices, 219, 352
REI retail chain, 264
Reinforcement advertising, 296
Relationship
  equity, 71
  marketing, 8, 327, 352
  strengthen, 270
Relative market share, 35, 352
Reliability, 160, 352
Reminder advertising, 296
Repairability, 160, 352
Research, *See also* Marketing research
  approaches, 45
  effective marketing, 43
  experimental, 45
  focus-group, 45
  instruments, 46
  marketing, 42, 351
  objectives, 44
  observational, 45

plan development, 45
survey, 45
Response hierarchy models, 281
Retail, 260, *See also* Table 14.1
    cooperatives, 252
    house brands, 266
    life cycle, 260
    location options for, 265
    marketing decisions, 262
    retailing, 261
    store atmosphere, 262
    store types, 260
Reverse-flow channels, 244
Risk analysis, 188
Risk-and-gain sharing, 108
Robinson, Patrick, 104
Rolex, 172
Ronald McDonald House Charities, 343
Routinized exchange, 326
Royal Dutch/Shell Group, 29
Ryder Integrated Logistics, 270

S

Sales
    analysis, 35, 352
    assistants, 325
    budget, 50, 352
    conditions of, 247
    force compensation, 322
    force management, 323
    force objectives and strategy, 320
    force size, 321
    force structure, 321
    forced design, 319
    forecast methods, 52
    forecasting, 271
    forecasts, 48
    pricing, 263
    promotions, 302, 352
    quota, 50, 352
    reports, 326
    representatives evaluation, 326
    representatives motivation, 325
    training, 324
Sales-force-promotion tools, 304
Sales-promotion programs, 305
Sales-variance analysis, 35, 352
Sampling plan, 46
SAP, 101
Satisfaction, 66, 352
    gauging customer, 67
    measuring, 66
    total customer, 66
    value, 14
Satisfying customer complaints, 210
Search-related ads, 318, 352
Scenario analysis, 29, 352
Schultz, Howard, 21
Scorecard
    customer performance, 35, 348
    stakeholder-performance, 35, 352
Secondary brand associations, 142
Segment
    benefit, 124
    evaluating and selecting market, 128
    marketing, 117
    service-motivated, 127
Segment-by-segment invasions, 131
Segmentation
    criteria, 127
    gender, 122

sequential, 126
variables business markets, 126, *See also*
    Table 7.2
variables consumer markets, 121, *See also*
    Table 7.1
Segmentation process
    steps, 128, *See also* Table 7.3
Segmentation, targeting, positioning
    (STP), 22
Selective
    attention, 89
    distortion, 89
    distribution, 246, 352
    retention, 89
    specialization, 130
Selecting
    channel members, 248
    market segments, 128
    trade promotion tools, 304
Self-service, 260
Self-service technologies, 210
Selling concept, 7
Served market, 35, 352
Served market share, 35, 352
Service(s), 201, 352
    backup, 245
    blueprint, 203
    characteristics of, 202
    contracts, 212
    differentiation, 160
    mix, 201, 263
    quality, 209
    recovery, 211
    sector channels, 245
Service-motivated segment, 127
Shifting customer relationship, 204
Shifts of secondary cultural values, 57
Shopping goods, 180, 352
Siemens Medical Systems, 5
Single-segment concentration, 128
Slotting fee, 267
Small office/home office market, 131
Social classes, 85, 352
Social responsibility
    cause-related marketing, 343
    marketing, 12
    review, 297
Social-cultural environment, 56
Societal marketing concept, 12
Solution selling, 108
Sony, 163
Southwest Airlines, 25
Spatial convenience, 245
Specialty goods, 180, 352
Sponsored events, 307
Stage
    age and life-cycle, 122
    buyer-readiness, 125
    decline, 194
    growth, 193
    life, 122
    maturity, 194
Stakeholder
    and holistic marketing, 25
    and marketing network, 9
    and performance, 35
Stakeholder-performance scorecard, 35, 352
Standard markup, 224
Starbucks, 21
Status, 86, 352
Steinway, 177
Stockless purchase plans, 111

Straight extension, 336, 352
Straight rebuy, 104
Strategic
    brand management, 135
    control, 342
    group, 31, 352
    planning, 26
Strategic business units (SBUs), 27, 352
Strategies
    brand, 207
    challenger, 170
    communication, 335
    competitive, 167
    defense, 168
    differentiation, 159
    generic, 31
    market-follower, 172
    market-leader, 167
    market-nicher, 172, *See also* Table 9.4
    service firms, 204
Strategy, 31, 352
    branding, 146, 347
    company's customer base, 73, *See also*
        Table 4.1
    creative, 284
    customer-oriented, 173
    formulation, 31
    geographical-expansion, 168
    market-penetration, 168
    marketing-mix, 10, 170
    message, 283, 296
    new-market segment, 168
    positioning, 155
    post-sale service, 213
    pull, 241, 352
    push, 240, 352
    service, 207
Structural ties, 77
Style, 160, 352
Subcultures, 57, 352
Supersegment, 130, 352
Supplier selection, 111
Supply chain, 14, 24, 352
Supply chain management (SCM), 270, 353
Survey research, 45
SWOT analysis, 30
System(s)
    buying, 105
    channel, 240
    contracting, 105
    horizontal marketing, 252, 350
    integrated logistics, 270
    marketing channel, 240, 350
    marketing information, 41
    marketing intelligence, 42, 350
    monitoring, 210
    multichannel marketing, 252
    product, 180, 351

T

Target
    audience, 283
    costing, 223, 353
    market, 13, 48, 262, 353
Target-return pricing, 225, 353
Task environment, 15
Technology
    change, 59
    environment, 58
    marketing decisions and, 41

Telemarketing, 316, 325, 353
Tesco, 5
Testing
    alpha, 188
    beta, 188
    concept, 186
    consumer-goods, 189
    market, 188
Tetra Pak, 183
Thompson, 12
Three-level channel, 244
Time-constrained consumers, 88
Tools
    consumer promotion, 303
    major consumer promotion, 304
    promotional, 290
    sales-force-promotion, 304
    selecting trade promotion, 304
Total costs, 222, 353
Total customer
    cost, 64, 353
    satisfaction, 66
    value, 64, 353
Total market
    demand, 168
    marketing communications budget, 287
    potential, 50
Total quality management (TQM), 68, 353
Trade-relations mix, 247
Trader Joe's, 259
Training channel members, 248
Transaction, 3, 353
Transfer, 3, 353
Transformational appeal, 284
Trend, 52, 270, 353
    retailing, 265
Two-level channel, 244
Two-part pricing, 233, 353
Tying agreements, 254, 353

U

Unbundling, 234
Undifferentiated marketing, 130
Unsought goods, 180, 353
Unsuccessful service delivery, 208
Updating segmentation schemes, 131
U.S. Steel, 15

V

VALS, 123
Value
    buyers, 226
    chain, 23, 353
    core, 88, 348
    customer lifetime, 76, 348
    equity, 71
    networks, 241, 353
    perceive, 226
    pricing, 227, 353
    proposition, 66, 155, 353, *See also*
        Table 9.1
    satisfaction, 14
    total customer, 64, 353
Value-adding partnerships (VAPs), 251
Value-delivery network, *See* Supply chain
Value-delivery system, 65, 353
Variability of services, 203
Variable
    costs, 222, 353
Vertical
    channel conflict, 253
    hubs, 110
    integration, 164, 353
    marketing channel, 251, 353
    marketing system, 251, 353
Viral marketing, 286, 353

W

Waiting time, 245
Wal-Mart, 42
Walt Disney, 4
Warehouse, data, 77
Warehousing, 273
Warranties and guarantees, 183
Website
    design, 317
    e-commerce, 254
Webster, 102
Wells Fargo, 42
Wheel-of-retailing hypothesis, 260
Wholesaling, 267, 353
    brick-and-click companies, 255
    distributors, 269
    pure-click companies, 255
    trends, 270
    types, 268
Wind, 102
Workload approach to compensation, 321
W.W. Grainger, Inc., 269

X

Xerox, 11, 67, 110

Y

Yield pricing, 232, 353

Z

Zero-level channel, 244, 353